Agribusiness Management

Today's food and agribusiness managers operate in a rapidly changing, highly volatile, international, high technology, consumer-focused world. This new edition of *Agribusiness Management* was written to help prepare students and managers for a successful career in this new world of food and fiber production and marketing.

Agribusiness Management uses four specific approaches to help readers develop and enhance their capabilities as agribusiness managers. First, this edition of the book offers a contemporary focus that reflects the issues that agribusiness managers face both today and are likely to face tomorrow. Specifically, food sector firms and larger agribusiness firms receive more attention in this edition, reflecting their increasing importance as employers of food and agribusiness program graduates. Second, the book presents conceptual material in a pragmatic way with illustrations and examples that will help the reader understand how a specific concept works in practice. Third, the book has a decision-making emphasis, providing contemporary tools that readers will find useful when making decisions in the contemporary business environment. Finally, *Agribusiness Management* offers a pertinent set of discussion questions and case studies that will allow the reader to apply the material covered in real-world situations.

The bottom-line on this fourth edition of *Agribusiness Management*: this book is contemporary, solid on the fundamentals, practical and applicable. It provides students and adult learners with an essential understanding of what it takes to be a successful agribusiness manager in today's rapidly evolving, highly unpredictable marketplace.

Freddie Barnard is Professor in the Department of Agricultural Economics at Purdue University, USA.

Jay Akridge is Glenn W. Sample Dean of Agriculture at Purdue University, USA.

Frank Dooley is Professor in the Department of Agricultural Economics at Purdue University, USA.

John Foltz is Associate Dean and Director of Academic Programs for the College of Agricultural and Life Sciences at the University of Idaho, USA.

Routledge Textbooks in Environmental and Agricultural Economics

Agribusiness Management

Fourth edition

Freddie Barnard, Jay Akridge, Frank Dooley and John Foltz

LONDON AND NEW YORK

First published 2012
by Routledge
2 Park Square, Milton Park, Abingdon, Oxon OX14 4RN

Simultaneously published in the USA and Canada
by Routledge
711 Third Avenue, New York, NY 10017

Routledge is an imprint of the Taylor & Francis Group, an informa business

British Library Cataloguing in Publication Data
A catalogue record for this book is available from the British Library

Library of Congress Cataloging in Publication Data
Agribusiness management / Freddie Barnard...[et al.]. – 4th ed.
    p. cm.
    1. Agricultural industries – Management. I. Barnard, Freddie L.
    HD9000.5.A339 2012
    630.68 – dc23   2011038607

ISBN: 978-0-415-59695-4 (hbk)
ISBN: 978-0-415-59696-1 (pbk)
ISBN: 978-0-203-12418-5 (ebk)

Typeset in Times New Roman
by Cenveo Publisher Services

Printed and bound in the United States of America by
Edwards Brothers Malloy

Contents

List of plates

List of figures

List of tables

About the authors

Dr. Freddie Barnard is Professor in the Department of Agricultural Economics at Purdue University. He works in the area of agricultural finance and focuses on two major groups: agricultural lenders and producers. In addition, he teaches the undergraduate course in agribusiness management. He is involved in educational projects across the country that educate lenders on how to improve the quality of decision-making. Examples include his work with the industry-wide Farm Financial Standards Council that provides uniformity in financial reporting and analysis for the agriculture industry. He also prepares instructional materials for agricultural lenders and producers, and teaches at several agricultural credit schools across the country.

Dr. Jay Akridge is the Glenn W. Sample Dean of Agriculture at Purdue University. He is responsible for administering the academic programs in the College of Agriculture, the Indiana Agricultural Experiment Station, and the Purdue Cooperative Extension Service. Before being named Dean he was the James and Lois Ackerman Professor of Agricultural Economics and served as director of the Purdue Center for Food and Agricultural Business and the MS-MBA in food and agribusiness management. He has received several awards for teaching, including the Charles Murphy Award for Distinguished Undergraduate Teaching—Purdue's highest teaching award—and the USDA Food and Agricultural Sciences Excellence in Teaching Award. He was added to the Purdue University Book of Great Teachers in 2003. His research has examined the buying behavior of commercial agricultural producers, innovations in marketing strategies by agribusiness firms, and adoption of new technology by agribusiness. He has worked with agribusiness managers in the areas of strategy and marketing in many countries including Lithuania, Australia, Argentina, Cameroon, and China. A native Kentuckian, his family owns and operates a fourth-generation farm supply business in Fredonia, KY.

Dr. Frank Dooley is a Professor at Purdue University in the Department of Agricultural Economics. He has won many awards for outstanding teaching and advising, including the Agricultural and Applied Economics Association Outstanding Undergraduate Teacher and the Charles B. Murphy Outstanding Undergraduate Teaching Award from Purdue University. He is also an active presenter in programs at the Center for Food and Agricultural Business. His research program in agribusiness focuses upon transportation and supply chain management. His work has studied issues in the food manufacturing and retailing, ethanol, transportation, and country grain elevator industries.

Dr. John Foltz is Associate Dean and Director of Academic Programs for the College of Agricultural and Life Sciences at the University of Idaho. He works with student academic issues and student organizations as well as student recruitment and retention efforts for the College. Previously, he served as a Professor in the Department of Agricultural Economics and Rural Sociology. He is an award-winning teacher and advisor, having received his College's Outstanding Advising award, and the University of Idaho award for teaching excellence. He is a seven-time recipient of the University of Idaho's Faculty Excellence Award, chosen by students as their most influential faculty member. His research has looked at country-of-origin labeling (COOL) in the beef industry; exploring the feasibility of carbon credit marketing by Idaho dairies; investigating the demand for consultants by Idaho dairy and potato farmers; researching consumer perceptions of trout as a food item; and teaching research involving class attendance and student performance, building the industry–institution interface and the use of case studies in the classroom. He co-writes a bi-monthly management column for *Feed and Grain* magazine. He received his Bachelor's and Master's degrees from Ohio State University. Upon graduation, he worked as a district manager for Ralston Purina in Ohio and Pennsylvania marketing livestock feed and animal health products. Subsequently, he received his Ph.D. in agricultural economics from Purdue.

Preface

This is an exciting time to be involved in the food and agribusiness industries. International markets are an inseparable reality for agribusiness managers. Information technology and the Internet make entirely new models for conducting business both possible and practical. Biotechnological developments raise exciting and challenging business and policy issues. Relationships among players in this system have continued to evolve and, as a result, the food production and marketing system is far more complex and interrelated today than it was a mere decade ago. Add to this the challenge of feeding an estimated nine billion people on earth by 2050—and agriculture and agribusiness will continue to be the nexus of attention!

This rapidly changing, highly volatile, international, high-technology, consumer-focused world is the one in which today's food and agribusiness managers operate. This fourth edition of *Agribusiness Management* was written to help prepare students and managers for a successful career in this new world of food and fiber production and marketing.

What's new

The basic objective of this text has not changed through four editions: to give students and managers a fundamental understanding of the key concepts needed to successfully manage businesses, adding value to farm products and/or providing inputs to production agriculture. While there are many concepts in this book that will apply to the farm or production agriculture business, the text is focused on the food and input supply sectors of the food production and marketing system.

This new edition of *Agribusiness Management* uses four specific approaches to help readers develop and enhance their capabilities as agribusiness managers. First, it offers a contemporary focus that reflects the issues that food and agribusiness managers face both today and likely will face tomorrow. Specifically, food sector firms and larger agribusiness firms receive more attention in this edition, reflecting their increasing importance as employers of food and agribusiness program graduates. Second, the book presents conceptual material in a pragmatic way with illustrations and examples that will help the reader understand how a specific concept works in practice. Third, it has a decision-making emphasis, providing managerial tools that readers will find useful when making decisions in the contemporary business environment. Finally, it offers a pertinent set of discussion questions and case studies that will allow the reader to apply the material covered in real-world situations.

More specifically, the opening section of the text has been completely re-organized to help students better understand the food and agribusiness marketplace, as well as management and basic economic principles. The second section includes chapters on forms of business organization and international agribusiness management, which is an area no contemporary book on agribusiness can ignore. In the third section, we start our discussion on the four functional areas of management—marketing, finance, supply chain, and human resources. Ultimately, all business activity revolves around the customer, and the text reflects this customer-oriented philosophy. The marketing management section has been substantially revised to reflect the current thinking in this area. The finance section also received a complete overhaul, and includes chapters on financial reporting and analysis, with increased emphasis on credit analysis and management. The fifth section, supply chain management, was completely rewritten to reflect the current thinking in this area. Finally, the human resource section was re-written, again to reflect what we now know about managing people.

Preparing for a new food and agribusiness market requires the application of concepts and tools to current situations. This edition of *Agribusiness Management* ends every chapter with discussion questions that are either new or have been revised for this text. Also included are cases that cover a variety of situations and types of firm. We feel you will find this mix of cases to be a distinguishing feature of the book.

The bottom-line on this fourth edition of *Agribusiness Management*: this book is contemporary, solid on the fundamentals, practical and applicable. It provides students and adult learners with an essential understanding of what it takes to be a successful agribusiness manager in today's rapidly evolving, highly unpredictable marketplace.

The readership

Agribusiness Management was written for students. There are tremendous career opportunities in the food and agribusiness industries. In this book, you will be exposed first to the breadth of these opportunities, from research and development manager for a biotech company, to a logistics manager for a major food retail organization. You need to understand the marketplace and some of the unique institutional features of the food production and marketing system before embarking on a career as an agribusiness manager. Preparing for a career in agribusiness management also requires that you understand the fundamentals of management—the basic tasks of planning, organizing, directing, and controlling and the basic functions of marketing, finance, operations and logistics, and human resource management. In this book you will find all of these topics covered in a straightforward way. And, we hope the many food and agribusiness examples and case studies bring these concepts to life for you. This is a book you will continue to use as a reference as your managerial career unfolds.

Agribusiness Management was written for managers and soon to be managers who are already in the workforce. We have had the opportunity over the past 25 years to work with literally thousands of managers through the activities of the Center for Food and Agricultural Business at Purdue University. Most of the case studies and examples in this book come from these industry relationships and interactions. As the business environment changes, and as people assume new responsibilities, we see a need to retool in areas that an individual has not recently been applying in his/her job. For example, the production manager in a food processing firm who has been asked to serve on a task force focused on helping the firm become more customer oriented may need a "refresher" in marketing management. These individuals (and corporate learning and development directors and training managers) will find this book useful in sharpening their skill set.

Agribusiness Management was written for instructors. Over time, we have found that every instructor has his or her own take on what an agribusiness management course should look like. Some are introductory courses, other have more of a capstone orientation. Some of these courses are part of an entire curriculum in agribusiness management. In other cases, a program may offer only a course or two in the agribusiness area. The organization of this book is structured in a way that instructors will find convenient when developing their course, wherever that course fits in the program's overall curriculum.

An instructor could easily use the material in this edition over a single semester, or over a two semester or three-quarter course, covering each topic in more detail. Some instructors will find that moving through the book from start to finish sequentially as part of a one-semester course makes the most sense. Others may drop chapters on specialized topics like international business or human resource management, because these topics are covered in other courses. For an advanced course, the book has plenty of rigor. Supplemented with outside case studies, this is an excellent text for a capstone-type course where the material here would be covered more quickly, and more time spent on some of the more advanced ideas. The new and updated cases and the discussion questions will be of value to all instructors as they serve the needs of students hungry for applications and illustrations of the concepts and tools covered in the book.

Outline of book

In Part I, "Agribusiness Management: Scope, Functions, and Tasks," we focus on the food and agribusiness industries and the role of the agribusiness manager. In addition, a set of economic concepts of fundamental importance to agribusiness managers is covered. Part I exposes readers to the tremendous variety of firms that comprise the food production and marketing system. The core focus of this book is the four functional areas of management—marketing, finance, supply chain, and human resources. Readers will better understand the role that managers of food and agribusiness firms play as they execute the four tasks of management—planning, organizing, directing, and controlling.

Part II, "Agribusiness Management: Organization and Context," leads readers toward better understanding the context or environment in which agribusiness managers operate by taking them inside the different forms of business organization, including cooperatives given their prominence in the food and agribusiness markets. This section also provides a glimpse into the issues an agribusiness manager must face when doing business outside of the United States. The challenges of serving international markets, of sourcing raw materials from international locations, and from competing with international firms have all emerged as key issues in the past decade. Looking to the future, this area promises to be even more important.

We begin our look at the four functional areas of management in Part III with "Marketing Management for Agribusiness." This section covers the fundamental concepts and tools an agribusiness manager uses in identifying its target market, and taking its product-service-information offering to the market. The marketing mix—product, price, promotion, and place—is covered in some detail. In addition, important tools for making marketing decisions are discussed. All of this material is presented in the context of the strategic marketing planning framework.

Part IV, "Financial Management for Agribusiness," starts with basic financial statements, and moves through financial ratios and financing the agribusiness on to tools for making operating and capital investment decisions. This section addresses the fundamental elements of finance that any agribusiness manager should understand. A series of integrated examples, and clear explanations of key terms, will help you better understand the language and concepts of finance. More importantly, you will better understand how to use financial information when making managerial decisions.

Part V, "Operations Management for Agribusiness," looks at supply chain management. This section takes you into areas such as production planning, total quality management, and logistics management. Production/operations and supply chain management in agribusiness firms have undergone a profound change over the past two decades. And, these two chapters will provide a fundamental understanding of the key elements in this important area.

Finally, in Part VI, "Human Resource Management for Agribusiness," we look at key issues involved in managing a firm's people resources. First, we explore issues around organizational structure and leadership. Then, we turn our attention to the personnel functions of hiring, training, evaluation, and compensation of employees. The final section—the issues surrounding the human resource area—are likely the most pressing of all to an agribusiness firm facing a rapidly changing operating environment.

This is an exciting time to be preparing for or retooling for a career in the food and agribusiness industries. We have tried to capture some of that excitement in *Agribusiness Management*. We hope that you find this book readable and interesting, challenging, and pragmatic, and most of all helpful as you better prepare yourself or your students for successful careers in the food production and marketing system.

Web-based supplements

Agribusiness Management is supported by a set of supplementary materials, which are available at the text's support Web site: http://www.routledge.com/books/details/9780415596961/

Acknowledgments

Any large project involves an equally large number of individuals, and this book is no exception. Our most important acknowledgment is to Research Development Editor Kathleen Erickson, who served a variety of roles while working on both the third and fourth editions, ranging from conducting background research to discussing content and focus as both editions of this manuscript moved from idea to reality.

Also, we want to acknowledge the work done on previous editions of this textbook by Drs. Steven P. Erickson and W. David Downey. Their work provided the foundation for the fourth edition. Dr. Erickson passed away before the third edition of this book was published. He was a brilliant, award-winning educator, who received numerous teaching awards, including the American Agricultural Economics Association's Distinguished Undergraduate Teaching Award and the Charles B. Murphy Award for Outstanding Undergraduate Teaching (Purdue's highest teaching award). Dr. W. David Downey is Professor Emeritus of Purdue University. As a professor of agricultural sales and marketing at Purdue, Dr. Downey taught courses in agri-selling and agri-marketing strategy to undergraduate students from several disciplines. He was instrumental in the development of a curriculum in which students could earn a four-year B.S. degree in agri-sales and marketing—the first such program in the U.S. He received much recognition for professional excellence, including four major teaching awards from Purdue University and two national awards from the American Agricultural Economics Association.

Also, we need to acknowledge the role of both students and managers we have worked with for the past 30 years. Their input, comments, and suggestions have played an important part in shaping the ideas and presentation of this text. In addition, we sincerely appreciate the students enrolled in the undergraduate agribusiness course at Purdue University during the fall semester of 2011, who took the time to review and comment on the chapters, discussion questions, and cases studies contained in this textbook.

Finally, we sincerely appreciate the sacrifices made by our families, since the time spent revising this textbook was time that would have otherwise been spent at home and with family members. Their understanding enabled the authors to invest the time required for this textbook to become a reality.

Part I

Agribusiness management

Scope, functions, and tasks

Plate Part I Retail Food Shot
Productive, diverse, efficient: Part I explores today's food, production agriculture, and agribusiness sectors. Photo courtesy of USDA.

1   The business of agribusiness

Objectives

- Describe management's role in agribusiness
- Provide an overview of the functional responsibilities of management
- Describe the unique characteristics of the food and agribusiness industries
- Describe the size, scope, and importance of the food production and marketing system
- Understand the farm-food marketing bill and what it means to producers and consumers
- Provide an overview of the food sector, the production agriculture sector, and the input supply sector
- Outline trends in home and away-from-home food consumption, and trends among the types of firms that serve these markets
- Explore the production agriculture sector, and some of the key changes occurring on U.S. farms
- Outline the major inputs used by the production agriculture sector and key trends in input use
- Understand the types of firms involved in producing and distributing inputs to production agriculture

Introduction

It is exciting and diverse. It is changing quickly. It relies on the weather, uses an incredible array of technology, is tied in every way to our natural resources, and embraces the world. If you eat, you are involved in it as a consumer of its final products. If you farm, you are involved in it as a producer of the raw materials that ultimately make their way to the end consumer. It is the extremely efficient, very complex, global, food and fiber production and marketing system.

This system is vast and it is fascinating: the next time you walk through your local grocery store, think about the number and type of diverse activities involved in growing, harvesting, transporting, processing, and distributing food throughout the 50 states in the United States, and, more broadly, our world. The process by which a 260-pound hog moves from Carroll County, Indiana to a suburban superstore in Los Angeles (now in the form of a hot dog in a pre-packaged children's meal) is very complex, yet it occurs every day in the food production and marketing system.

This food production and marketing system is made up of thousands of businesses, ranging from the small cow-calf producer in western Kentucky, to some of the largest corporations in the world. And, it is **management** that drives and directs the firms, farms, and food companies that come together in the food production and marketing system. A retail supermarket, a major corn processor, the local farm supply store, and a family farmer: each have a person or a group of people responsible for making sure that things get done. These are the **managers**. Their titles range from chief executive officer to president to foreman to son or daughter or spouse. However, wherever they are found within an organization, managers are responsible for assuring successful completion of the functions, tasks, and activities that will determine an organization's success.

This book focuses on the management of food, fiber, and agribusiness firms. We will take a careful look at food and agricultural business management and our definition of food and agricultural businesses is quite broad. So, when we use the term **agribusiness management** in the text, we are talking about the management of any firm involved in the food and fiber production and marketing system. Our discussion of agribusiness management in this book provides information, concepts, processes, ideas, and experiences that can contribute to your effectiveness in performing the functions and tasks of agribusiness management.

This chapter will first introduce you to the key functions of agribusiness management. Then, we will explore some the characteristics that make the food and agribusiness markets unique places to practice the art and science of management. The ever-changing food and agribusiness industries are then discussed. We will look at firms that (1) move final products through the food and fiber system to the ultimate consumer, (2) transform raw agricultural products into the final products desired by consumers, (3) produce raw food and fiber products, and (4) supply inputs to the farm or production sector.

The key functions of management in agribusiness

As you can imagine, the responsibilities of managers in agribusiness are highly varied and can range from ordering **inputs** for the year ahead, to hiring and firing individuals, to making the decision to sell a multi-billion dollar international subsidiary. A chief executive officer, for instance, is responsible for the overall activities of a large, diversified food or agribusiness firm. In such firms, teams of managers are likely responsible for specialized areas within the firm. On a smaller farm business, one individual may assume roles ranging from chief executive officer, to manager, to laborer, managing multiple projects at different levels simultaneously.

To better understand the form and process by which managers perform the tasks that are required to create and sustain a viable business, the practice of management can be broken down into four key functions:

- Marketing management
- Financial management
- Supply chain management
- Human resource management

Ultimately, no matter how large or small the firm, managers have responsibilities in each of these areas. These four functions of management are explored in some detail in this book. However, it is important to have a basic understanding of each area as we develop our understanding of agribusiness management.

Marketing management

Marketing, in a broad sense, is focused on the process by which products flow through the U.S. food system from producer to final consumer. It involves the physical and economic activities performed in moving products from the initial producer through intermediaries to the final consumer. **Marketing management** involves understanding customer needs and effectively positioning and selling products and services in the marketplace. In agribusiness, marketing management is a key function within each of the sectors of agribusiness: the food sector, the production agriculture sector, and the input supply sector. Marketing management represents an integration of several different activities: selling, advertising, web page design, promotions, marketing research, new-product development, customer service, and pricing—all focused on customer needs, wants, and, ultimately, the quest for customer satisfaction.

It is this function of management that is most closely focused on the end-user, or the consumer/customer of the product or service produced. It is often argued that without satisfied customers effectively reached through marketing and sales, no business could successfully operate. Thus, marketing management plays a fundamentally important role in most food and agribusiness firms. Marketing management is focused on careful and planned execution of how, why, where, when and who sells a product or service and to whom it is sold. Decisions here include what products to produce, what services to offer, what information to provide, what price to charge, how to promote the product, and how to distribute the product.

This management function is closely tied to the customer's decision processes, and buyers differ widely in the food production marketing system—from teenagers for a food manufacturing firm, to a soybean processor for a farmer, to a large integrated swine business for an animal health firm. The ways in which agribusiness buyers—all of the buyers just mentioned and many more—make a purchase decision continues to evolve and change.

Financial management

Profit is the driver for agribusinesses as they work to generate the greatest possible returns from their resources. Successful achievement of this objective means making good decisions, and it means carefully managing the financial resources of the firm. **Financial management** is involved in these areas and includes generating the data needed to make good decisions, using the tools of finance to make effective decisions, and managing the assets, liabilities, and owner's investment in the firm.

Financial information allows managers to understand the current "health" of the firm as well as to determine what actions the business might take to improve or grow. **Balance sheets** and **income statements** can provide a wealth of information useful in making decisions. Financial analysis provides agribusiness managers with insights by which to better base decisions. The tools of finance such as budgeting, ratio analysis, financial forecasting, and breakeven analysis can be used by agribusiness managers to develop long-range plans and make short-run operating decisions.

Another way in which the financial agribusiness scene continues to change is in the sourcing of funds. Agribusiness firms are increasingly accessing larger amounts of funds or money from national and international capital and financial markets. To be competitive in those markets, firms must generate rates of return comparable to other industries. In the past, small agribusiness companies may have been allowed by local lenders to exhibit only modest financial performance. Today, the national and international financial markets expect performance in agriculture comparable to that in other industries if they are going to provide the agribusiness sector with the funding needed for expansion, growth, consolidation, technological advancement, and modernization.

The sheer amounts of funds needed to finance the future operations of a company will continue to increase dramatically. So will the need for managers who understand the tools and techniques used to source and manage those funds. For most agribusinesses, financial management will be a critical component of agribusiness management.

Supply chain management

New technologies and concepts are rapidly hitting the workplace. This, in turn, changes the way agribusinesses do what they do. The push for quality, the drive for lower costs, changes in the supply chain, and general pressures to be more efficient in meeting consumer demands are swiftly altering the production and distribution activities of agribusiness. **Supply chain management** focuses on these areas and provides the tools managers need to meet these operations and logistical challenges. As a result, supply chain management has come to the forefront as a key management function for the agribusiness manager.

Operations management focuses on the direction and the control of the processes used to produce the goods and services that we buy and use each day. It involves several interrelated, interacting systems. Operations management involves the strategic use and movement of resources. For instance, a snack food factory begins its process with corn from a food-grade corn producer and ends with tortilla chips, corn chips, crackers, etc. Managers must worry about issues of scheduling, controlling, storing, and shipping as the corn moves from the producer's truck to the supermarket.

Logistics management involves the set of activities around storing and transporting goods and services. Shipping and inventory costs are huge costs of doing business for many food and agribusiness firms. The logistics management function is focused on new ways to lower these costs, by finding better ways to ship and store product. Given advances in information technology, the analytical tools of supply chain management, and improved shipping technologies, this has been a dynamic area for food and agribusiness firms. In addition, the growth of global markets depends upon the performance of well managed supply chains.

Successful agribusinesses are those who consistently produce faster, better, and cheaper. The management of logistics in food and agricultural supply chains will become increasingly focused on building such time-based advantage. Quicker response to consumer needs, faster delivery times, shorter product development cycles and more rapid recovery after service problems are all components of time-based advantage in supply chain management. At the same time, there is an incredible push for quality, safety, and integrity in food system production processes. Effective supply chain management will continue to be crucial in the successful execution of any strategic plan for agribusiness firms.

Human resources management

In the end, management is about people. Without the ability to manage the human element—the resources each business has in its employees—businesses do not succeed. When combining efficient management of the marketing/finance/supply chain functions of the business, with the thoughtful management of the human side of the business, managers are on the road to successful implementation of their strategy.

Agribusiness managers who can manage people well can significantly impact both productivity and financial success. **Human resources management** encompasses managing two areas: the mechanics of the personnel administration, and the finer points of motivating people to offer and contribute their maximum potential. Decisions here include how to organize the firm, where to find people, how to hire them, how to compensate them and how to evaluate them.

Today's lean agribusiness firms continue to demand more performance from their managers, sales force, and service and support personnel. For instance, in addition to superb selling skills, sales representatives will be expected to have intimate knowledge of technology and a fundamental understanding of the general management problems of their producer customers. Service personnel must be able to maintain increasingly complex equipment. Technical support staff will need to be experts at assimilating and using the massive amount of production data that a large dairy farm or crop farm using site-specific management practices will generate.

These types of demands will require agribusinesses to hire individuals with greater initial skills as well as with the ability to grow into different jobs throughout the course of their careers. Agribusinesses will need to be flexible while providing continuing education and development of key skills. Some examples of such skills are general business, negotiation, problem-solving, technical, information management, and communication. Recognition of raw ability, and then development and fine-tuning these skills and abilities will be the human resource challenge. Managed well, that challenge will profitably produce for the company. And, this is the role of human resource management in the food and agribusiness firm.

Unique dimensions of the food and agribusiness markets

It may be easy to argue that management theory and principles are the same for any type of business enterprise. The largest businesses in the country such as General Electric and Wal-Mart and the smallest one-person agribusiness are guided by many of the same general principles. And, in many cases, good management is good management, regardless of the type of firm, or the market it is operating in.

Yet key differences between large and small businesses or between agribusinesses and other types of firms arise in the specific business environment facing the organization. While there are similarities, the markets facing General Electric's wide range of businesses differ substantially. The automotive industry is different from the retail industry. Likewise the unique characteristics of the food production and marketing system cause management practices to differ for agribusiness firms. Our job is to better understand the similarities and differences in the functions and tasks of a food and agribusiness manager compared to other managers.

As a professional, the manager might be compared to a physician. The knowledge and principles of medicine are the same, but patients differ in such vital details as age, gender, body mass index, and general health. The physician's skill is to apply general medical principles to the specific individual to create the optimal outcome for the patient given the unique set of circumstances at hand. The manager, utilizing specific tools of marketing, financial, supply chain management, and human resource management, must attempt to solve the problem at hand and create the best outcome for the firms long-term profitability.

Food and agribusiness markets differ from other markets in at least eight key ways, influencing the business situation that food and agribusiness managers must practice. While one can find examples of other industries where each point is important (for example, seasonality is important to toy companies), combined these factors form the distinguishing features of the food and agribusiness marketplace.

Food as a product. Food is vital to the survival and health of every individual. Food is one of the most fundamental needs of humans, and provides the foundation for economic development—nations first worry about feeding their people before turning their attention to higher order needs. For these reasons, food is considered a critical component of national security. And, as a result, the food system attracts attention from governments in ways other industries do not.

Biological nature of production agriculture. Both crops and livestock are biological organisms—living things. The biological nature of crops and livestock makes them particularly susceptible to forces beyond human control. The variances and extremes of weather, pests, disease, and weeds exemplify factors that greatly impact production. These factors affecting crop and livestock production require careful management. Yet in many cases, little can be done to affect them outright. The gestation cycle of a sow or the climate requirements of wine grapes provide examples.

Seasonal nature of business. Partly as a result of the biological nature of food production, firms in the food and agribusiness markets can face highly seasonal business situations. Sometimes this seasonality is supply driven—massive amounts of corn and soybeans are harvested in the fall. Sometimes this seasonality is demand driven—the market for ice cream has a series of seasonal peaks and valleys, as do the markets for turkey and cranberries. Such ebbs and flows in supply and demand create special problems for food and agribusiness managers.

Uncertainty of the weather. Food and agribusiness firms must deal with the vagaries of nature. Drought, flood, insects, and disease are a constant threat for most agribusinesses. All market participants, from the banker to the crop production chemical manufacturer are concerned with the weather. A late spring can create massive logistical problems for firms supplying inputs to the crop sector. Bad weather around a key holiday period can ruin a food retailer's well-planned promotional event.

Types of firms. There is tremendous variety across the types of businesses in the food and agribusiness sectors. From farmers to transportation firms, brokers, wholesalers, processors, manufacturers, storage firms, mining firms, financial institutions, retailers, food chains, and restaurants—the list is almost endless. Following a loaf of bread from the time it is seed wheat prepared for shipment to the farmer until its placement on the retail grocer's shelf involves numerous types of business enterprises. The variety in size and type of agribusinesses, ranging from giants like ConAgra to family farms, shapes the food and agribusiness environment.

Variety of market conditions. The wide range of firm types and the risk characteristics of the food and agribusiness markets have led to an equally wide range of market structures. Cotton farmers find themselves in an almost textbook case of the perfectly competitive market where individual sellers have almost no influence over price. At the same time, Coca-Cola and PepsiCo have a literal duopoly in the soft drink market. Some markets are global, others local. Some markets are characterized by near equal bargaining power between buyer and seller, while others may be dramatically out of balance in one direction or the other.

Rural ties. Many agribusiness firms are located in small towns and rural areas. As such, food and agribusiness are likely the backbone of the rural economy and have a very important role in rural economic development.

Government involvement. Due to almost every other factor raised above, the government has a fundamental role in food and agribusiness. Some government programs influence commodity prices and farm income. Others are intended to protect the health of the consumer through safe food and better nutrition information. Still other policies regulate the use of crop protection chemicals, and affect how livestock producers handle animal waste. Tariffs and quotas impact international trade. School lunch programs and food stamps help shape food demand. The government, through policies and regulations, has a pervasive impact on the job of the food and agribusiness manager.

Each of these special features of the food production and marketing system affects the environment where an agribusiness manager practices their craft. Agribusiness is unique and thus, requires unique abilities and skills of those involved with this sector of the U.S. economy.

The food production and marketing system

The highly efficient and effective **food production and marketing system** in the U.S. is a result of a favorable climate and geography; abundant and specialized production and logistics capabilities; intense use of mechanical, chemical, biological, and information technologies; and the creative and productive individuals who lead and manage the firms which make up the food and agribusiness industries. This U.S. food production and marketing system produces enormous supplies of food and fiber products. These products not only feed and clothe U.S. consumers, but are also exported to the international marketplace to fulfill needs of consumers around the world.

The food production and marketing system encompasses all the economic activities that support farm production and the conversion of raw farm products to consumable goods. This broad definition includes a farm machinery manufacturer, a fertilizer mine, a baby food factory, the paper firm that supplies cardboard boxes, rail and trucking firms, wholesalers, distributors, and retailers of food, restaurateurs, and many, many others.

The U.S. food production and marketing system is extremely large, directly employing over ten million workers, generating $646 billion worth of value-added products and services in 2009 (Table 1.1). The output of this system represents 4.6 percent of the total value added production to the gross domestic product (GDP) of the U.S. economy.

Note that the U.S. economic activity also includes the contributions of firms providing inputs to the farm, forestry, and fisheries sectors. In 2009, $207.6 billion of energy, materials, and purchased inputs were used by farming and related ventures, representing 1.5 percent of GDP (Table 1.1). In addition, the food and agribusiness sectors are key contributors to the economic activity of transportation, wholesaling, and retailing in the U.S. Prior estimates put this effort at 5.4 percent of U.S. GDP (Edmonson 2000).

Food and agricultural systems vary widely across the globe. Countries with higher per capita GDP (over $25,000) typically have a lower proportion of their population (under 3 percent) involved in production agriculture (Table 1.2). In contrast, the characteristics of the less developed countries find a lower GDP per capita and a higher proportion of the population involved in production agriculture. In China, 40 percent of the population is involved in farming, while in India the figure is 52 percent. The continued economic growth of these countries is fueling a tremendous demand for additional inputs, as well as branded food products. As a result, many U.S. firms are attempting to establish joint ventures with firms in these countries to aid in this development process, and build future markets in the process.

Table 1.1 Contribution of the food and agricultural industries to the U.S. economy, 2009

	Value Added to GDP (billion $)	% Share of U.S. GDP	Number of FTE Workers (000)	% Share of Total U.S. Employment
U.S. GDP	14,119.0		121,805	
Farms	104.0	0.74	634	0.52
Forestry, fishing, and related activities	29.2	0.21	425	0.35
Food and beverage and tobacco products	206.1	1.46	1,578	1.30
Textile mills and textile product mills	17.6	0.12	240	0.20
Apparel and leather and allied products	11.7	0.08	189	0.16
Food services and drinking places	277.1	1.96	7,366	6.05
Total for Food and Agricultural Industries	645.70	4.57	10,432	8.56
Total Inputs for Farms, Forestry and Fisheries	207.6	1.47		
Energy inputs	21.6	0.15		
Materials inputs	127.5	0.90		
Purchased inputs	58.5	0.41		

Source: U.S. Department of Commerce.

Table 1.2. Indicators of U.S. agriculture sector efficiency

Country	GDP per Capita[a] 2010 (U.S. $)	% Labor Force in Agriculture[a]	% of GDP in Agriculture[a]	Average Farm Size in 2000[b]Acres	% Personal Consumption Expenditures Spent on Food Consumed at Home 2007[c]
United States	47,400	0.7	1.2	440.7	5.7
Argentina	14,700	5.0	8.5	1,439.2	20.2
Australia	41,300	3.6	4.0	8,014.0	10.7
Brazil	10,900	20.0	6.1	179.8	24.6
Canada	39,600	2.0	2.0	675.5	9.2
China	7,400	39.5	9.6	1.7	34.9
Egypt	6,200	32.0	13.5	2.0	38.8
Germany	35,900	2.4	0.8	100.0	11.4
India	3,400	52.0	16.1	3.3	32.4
Japan	34,200	3.9	1.1	3.0	14.6
Mexico	13,800	13.7	4.2	60.7	24.2
South Korea	30,200	7.3	3.0	2.6	15.4
Spain	29,500	4.2	2.9	59.1	13.6
United Kingdom	35,100	1.4	0.9	175.1	8.6

Source: [a] Central Intelligence Agency.
[b] Food and Agriculture Organization.
[c] Meade 2008.

Farm size varies dramatically, even among developed countries (Table 1.2). Geography or limited farmland, climate, crop, or livestock focus, or simply the area needed to maintain a viable production unit helps explain this variation. This has important implications for the types of agricultural inputs needed in different parts of the globe. An 8,000 acre wheat farmer in Australia has much different expectations and needs from equipment and technology than a Chinese farmer on his or her two-acre plot.

The overall efficiency of the U.S. food and fiber sector is illustrated by the proportion of personal consumption expenditures allocated to food consumed at home. For the average U.S. consumer, only about 6 percent of their total personal consumption expenditures are for food consumed at home (Table 1.2). In Japan this figure is about 15 percent, while food accounts for almost one-third of an Indian consumer's personal consumption expenditures. The efficiency of the U.S. food production and marketing system is really quite remarkable. Consider this: with 8.4 percent of the world's agricultural land and 4.5 percent of the world's population, the U.S. food system produces 13 percent of the world's livestock and 14 percent of the world's crops (FAO). In 2009, the U.S. produced 41 percent of the world's soybeans, 41 percent of the corn, 16 percent of the grain sorghum, and 9 percent of the wheat.

A primary requirement for being a successful agribusiness manager is a solid understanding of this food production and marketing system. Regardless of what specific part of the food system you work in, it is important to understand what happens to food and fiber products both before they reach your firm, and after they leave your firm and head to the consumer.

Plate 1.1 Traditional Agriculture
Income spent on food by a country's people is heavily influenced by the agricultural production technologies in use. Photo courtesy of USDA Natural Resources Conservation Service

The farm-food marketing bill—a perspective on the system

An important part of understanding agribusiness comes from understanding just how and what consumers spend on food. In 2009, Americans consumers spent $1.2 trillion on food for at home and away from home consumption—up 95 percent from the $607 billion spent in 1993 (Figure 1.1). A better understanding of just what that spending is all about comes from looking at the farm-food marketing bill.

The **farm-food marketing bill** breaks down the proportion of the consumer's food dollar that goes to the farmer for raw products and that goes to the food industry for "marketing" those raw farm products to end consumers (Canning 2011). Marketing includes the value added from processing, packaging, transportation, retail trade, food services, energy, financial and insurance, and other to make agricultural products ready for the consumer. In 2008, for every dollar spent on food, $0.84 was spent on marketing the product, while $0.16 went to the farmer (Figure 1.2).

From 1993 to 2009, the farm share of the marketing bill rose from $112 to $187 billion, while the marketing share has increased by $500 billion to $996 billion (Figure 1.1). This long-term trend reflects continuing increases in farm productivity (which keeps farm prices relatively low), the increase in consumer demand for convenient, highly processed food products, increases in food consumed away from home, and increases in prices for many components of the marketing bill including labor, transportation, and energy. In turn, this fuels the steady widening of the food marketing bill as compared to the farm value of consumer food expenditures.

Figure 1.3 identifies the value added to the consumer food dollar in 2008 by ten different industry sectors. The farm and agribusiness share represents 11.6 cents of each consumer food dollar, net of farm costs (Canning 2011). The retail trade and food services sectors contribute almost half of the value added to the consumer food dollar, at 13.6 and 33.7 cents, respectively. The food processing sector is 18.6 cents of each food dollar. The 22.5 cents for

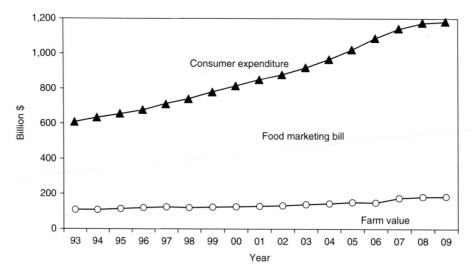

Figure 1.1 Farm value and the marketing bill for consumer food expenditures, 1993–2009
Source: Canning 2011.

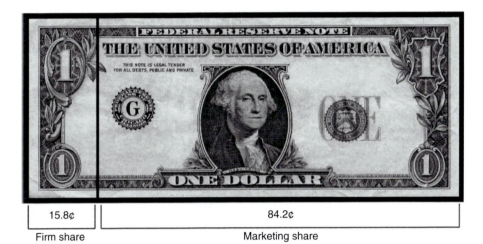

Figure 1.2 2008 farm-food marketing bill
　　　　　Source: Canning 2011.

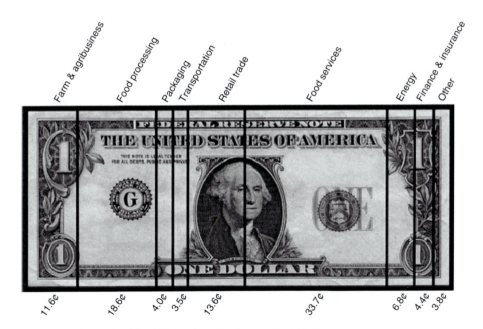

"Other" comprises advertising (2.0¢) and legal and accounting (1.8¢)

Figure 1.3 Industry sector value-added for the 2008 food marketing bill
　　　　　Source: Canning 2011.

all other sectors suggests that the impact of the food and agribusiness sector as defined in Table 1.1 is undervalued. Yet without the contribution of transportation, energy, or packaging, the product would not reach the end consumer.

In the food dollar accounts, the ten industry sectors that transform agricultural commodities to food products use four main factors of production to add value. The four are salary and benefits, property income, output taxes, and imports. At 50.8 cents per food dollar, salary and benefits comprise half of the food dollar (Figure 1.4). The 33.0 cents of property income represents payments for machinery, equipment, structures, natural resources, product inventory, or other assets that compensate the various owners for services provided (Canning 2011). The remainder of the 2008 food dollar is split between the U.S. government for taxes and imports or international assets.

The three primary sectors of the food system

The U.S. food production and marketing system, for purposes of discussion in this text, is divided into three sectors: the food sector, the production agriculture sector, and the input supply sector (Figure 1.5).

We start with the **food sector**. This is the sector in which food processing, marketing, and distribution occurs (Figure 1.5). Here we have firms such as Kraft, Hormel, Kroger, and McDonald's, as well as thousands of other firms, large and small. This group closely tracks consumer tastes and preferences, adapting to meet changing needs.

Next in line is the **production agriculture sector**. Purchased inputs, natural resources, and managerial talent are combined to produce crop and livestock products. Agribusinesses in this sector vary in size, number, and focus—from the local grower selling strawberries to neighbors to the 100,000 head cattle feedlot; from the rice farmer in Louisiana to the canola grower in North Dakota; from the pork producer in North Carolina to the mega-dairy in Arizona.

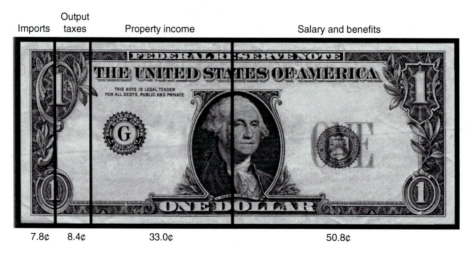

Figure 1.4 Factor payments for the 2008 food marketing bill
Source: Canning 2011.

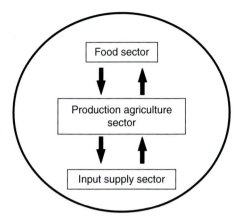

Figure 1.5 The food production and marketing system

The food production and marketing system ends (or begins) with the many, varied activities that take place in the **input supply sector**. This sector is responsible for providing the thousands of different inputs—both products and services—to production agriculture. Firms here include DuPont, Syngenta, John Deere, DeLaval, or your local cooperative, as well as hundreds of other firms that manufacture and distribute the inputs that farmers and ranchers need in their businesses. Let's take a closer look at each of these sectors.

The food sector

At some point, it all comes down to getting raw farm commodities processed, packaged, distributed, and sold to the consumer. A very wide variety of processing and marketing firms are responsible for adding value or utility to commodities as they leave the farm gate. We will start our look at the food sector with food retailers and away from home food firms. Then, we will look at wholesaling firms, food manufacturers and processors, and assembly and transportation firms. We will end this section with a focus on the linkages across firms in the food sector, and between the food sector and the other sectors in the food production and marketing system.

Food retailing

The food retailing sector accounts for 13.6 percent of the value-added to the consumer food dollar (Figure 1.3). No longer is food moved just through the typical supermarket, as the food retailing sector has fragmented since the late 1980s. Food store formats are classified into three general categories: grocery stores, supercenters, or other food stores.

The grocery category includes traditional supermarkets, as well as convenience stores, superettes, and small grocery stores, and specialty food stores (such as meat markets, fish markets, or bakeries). The category of warehouse clubs and supercenters was first dominated by warehouse stores such as BJ's Wholesale Club or Costco. More recently, growth in this sector has been driven primarily by Wal-Mart and Target. Other food stores include food retailed via mass merchandisers, drug store/combination stores, mail-order, home-delivered

Plate 1.2 Man shopping
There are a variety of retail store formats competing for the business of U.S. food consumers.
Photo courtesy of USDA

food, and farmers markets. Key attributes for some of the most common store formats are briefly described (Kaufman 2007):

- *Supermarket*: the conventional prototype typically carries about 15,000 items in a 10,000 to 25,000 square foot store.
- *Superstore*: has at least 40,000 square feet, which leads to a greater variety (25,000 items) of products, especially non-food items. The strategy is to promote the convenience of one-stop shopping, by providing additional service and selection.
- *Convenience store (without gasoline)*: a small grocery store, selling a limited variety of basic foods, snack foods, and non-food products, typically with extended hours. Grocery products account for 45 percent of sales. Ready-to-eat and fountain beverages represent about 10 percent of sales. Packaged liquor, beer, and wine, and tobacco products account for another 35 percent of sales.
- *Warehouse Club Stores*: no-frills, membership-based, wholesale-retail hybrid outlets. These "box stores" serve both small businesses and individual consumers in a large warehouse-style environment. Grocery products (in large and multi-pack sizes) account for about 30 percent of sales. General merchandise (clothing, electronics, small appliances, and automotive products) accounts for 70 percent of sales. Following a low-price strategy, these stores typically stock fast moving, non-perishable products, carrying 6,000 to 12,000 items in stores from 10,000 to 15,000 square feet.

- *Supercenter*: a large combination supermarket and discount general merchandise store, averaging 170,000 square feet of floor space. Grocery products account for up to 40 percent of floor space.

Total food store sales have climbed from $242 billion in 1986 to $600 billion in 2009 (Figure 1.6). In 1986, grocery stores accounted for 89 percent of food sales, while warehouse club and supercenter sales were inconsequential. Since then sales at warehouse clubs and supercenters have steadily increased, accounting for 19 percent of food sales in 2009. This growth has largely come from an erosion of sales at supermarkets, whose market share of the food dollar for at home consumption has fallen to 66 percent. Other food stores have accounted for roughly 15 percent of the market over time. They may be poised for growth as the local foods movement gains traction (Martinez 2010).

Since 1997, the total number of grocery stores has fallen by almost 9 percent, to 63,384 stores in 2009 (Figure 1.7). The number of convenience stores and specialty stores has been relatively stable at around 25,000 stores each over this time frame. In contrast, the number of warehouse and supercenters has almost tripled, from 1,530 to 4,411 stores, as consumers are drawn by the convenience of one-stop shopping and competitive prices.

The 1990s saw widespread consolidation in the grocery industry, as small "mom and pop" chains were acquired or merged by larger grocers, who adapted to compete with the entry into food retailing by Wal-Mart. This has resulted in fewer, but larger food retailing firms. Table 1.3 identifies the ten largest chain stores in terms of total annual sales. Wal-Mart has become the number one food retailer, followed by Kroger and Costco. This consolidation has led to a steady increase in industry concentration. From 1992 to 2009, the market share for the top four grocery firms more than doubled, from 17 to 37 percent, while the

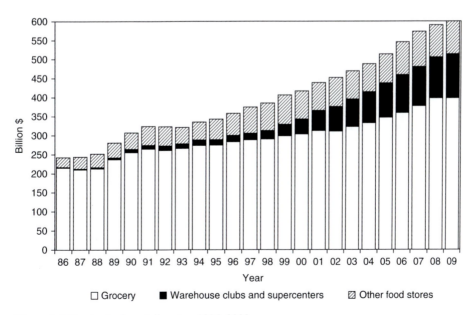

Figure 1.6 Food sales by retail sector, 1986–2009
Source: Clauson 2010.

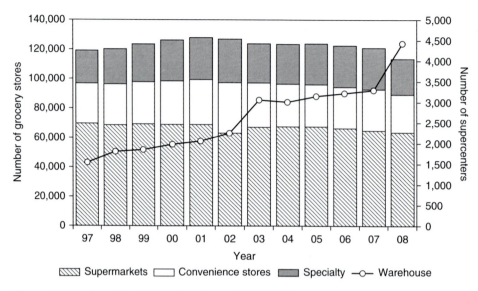

Figure 1.7 Number of food stores, by category, 1997–2008
Source: County Business Patterns.

Table 1.3 Sales of the ten largest U.S. food retailers in 2009

Rank/Retailer	Number of Food Stores Owned	U.S. Food Store Sales (billion dollars)
1. Wal-Mart Stores	4,624	262.0
2. Kroger Co.	3,634	76.0
3. Costco Wholesale Corp.	527	71.4
4. Supervalu	2,450	41.3
5. Safeway	1,730	40.8
6. Loblaw Cos.	1,036	29.9
7. Publix Super Markets	1,018	24.3
8. Ahold USA	707	22.3
9. Delhaize America	1,608	19.0
10. 7-Eleven	6,123	17.5

Source: *Supermarket News* 2010.

share for the top 20 firms climbed from 39 to 64 percent (Table 1.4). Concerns over increasing concentration led to a series of five hearings conducted by the Department of Justice and Agriculture in 2010 about antitrust enforcement (U.S. Department of Justice).

Food retailing remains an extremely competitive industry with little margin for error. Warehouse and supercenters compete in part because of their supply chain management expertise. For example, Wal-Mart is a leader in the adoption of information technologies such as radio frequency identification (RFID) or centralized checkout stands. All types of food retailers are increasingly looking to store or private label offerings. While some

Table 1.4 Concentration ratios for top four, eight, and twenty firms' share of U.S. grocery store sales, 1992–2009

Year	Top 4 Firms %	Top 8 Firms %	Top 20 Firms %
1992	17	26	39
1997	19	31	46
2002	30	44	56
2003	33	47	59
2004	34	47	59
2005	36	49	62
2006	35	48	60
2007	38	50	64
2008	38	51	65
2009	37	50	64

Source: Kaufman and Kumcu 2010.

argue that fewer and larger retail food outlets will mean a more general selection offered by retailers, others insist that larger retailers can offer a broader assortment of more competitively priced products to customers. The industry is mature, and performance will be driven by disposable income, consumer tastes and preferences, and female participation in the workforce.

Food service

The food services sector comprises the largest share of the 2008 food dollar, at 33.7 percent (Figure 1.3). The food service industry, which employs 9.2 million people, consists of three major types of firms—traditional restaurants, fast food/quick service restaurants, and institutional food service firms. The nation's 528,000 restaurants hit $533 billion in sales in 2009, up from $248 billion in 1990 (Figure 1.8).

The food service industry saw steady growth, especially since 1990 as busy people, dual career families, and a more affluent, mobile society chose the luxury, or some would say the necessity, of eating more meals away from home. In 1960, only 26 percent of the food dollar was spent on food away from home (Figure 1.9). Since 2000, the proportion of the food dollar spent eating out and at home has been almost equal. The USDA predicts that by 2020, 52 percent of the food dollar will be spent on food away from home.

TRADITIONAL RESTAURANTS

Traditional restaurants, also called full-service restaurants, saw sales of roughly $213 billion in 2009 (Clauson and Leibtag 2011). Despite a slowdown in the general economy, affluent baby boomers are the most frequent customers at full-service restaurants. Reflecting a cultural change among Americans, eating out at full-service restaurants plays an important social function for today's customers. Whereas 30 years ago socializing and entertaining were done at one's home, today's consumer meets family, friends, and co-workers at the local restaurant for leisure, conversation, and convenience. There is a growing disparity among restaurant types. Substantial growth is expected for casual dining restaurants with per person checks in the range of $15–$20. These full-service restaurants may cater to families

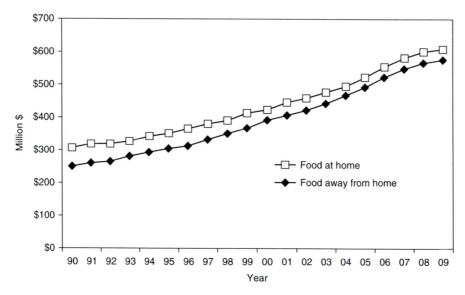

Figure 1.8 Sales of food at home and away from home, 1990–2009
Source: Clauson 2010.

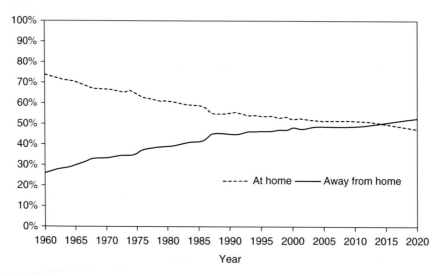

Figure 1.9 Percentage of sales of food-at-home and away-from-home, 1960–2020
Source: Westcott 2011.

or those looking for a more relaxed dining experience. Cuisines at full-service restaurants have shifted towards Italian, Mexican, Japanese, Thai, Caribbean, and Middle Eastern foods, as U.S. tastes broaden.

FAST FOOD/QUICK SERVICE

The words "fast" and "quick" not only describe the service provided by these restaurants, they also describe the rate at which this industry changes. Since 1990, fast service food firms such as McDonald's, Taco Bell, and Wendy's have more than doubled their sales, from $87 to $195 billion. Established as part of American culture, fast food restaurants have stepped into the next dimension of customer service by experimenting with the offerings and specials on their menus, and faster, better means of providing customers with both fast and nutritious foods. Rising concerns about obesity are leading to new menus. Today's fast food/quick service restaurants often have central wholesale warehouses and buying offices, and many have expanded internationally as U.S. markets have become saturated.

INSTITUTIONAL FOOD SERVICE

In 2009, over 38,000 firms were involved in institutional food marketing, with sales of $128 billion. This category includes food offered at hotels, schools and colleges, government offices, corporate eating establishments, airlines, hospitals, etc. Institutional food services account for an important portion of the food people consume daily. Some types of institutional food service firms expanded rapidly during the 1990s (recreation and entertainment facilities, and retail hosts such as gas stations and bookstores), while sales through other firms in this category were stable or declining (hospitals, vending machines, and the military). Trends and changes in the institutional food service industry will continue to reflect consumer demands for convenience and nutrition. For instance, 30 years ago, it would have been unusual to see ethnic foods, a food now considered common, on the menu of a major university's dorm cafeteria.

Food wholesaling

In 2009, food wholesaling represented a $678 billion dollar business conducted by 26,745 wholesalers employing almost 800,000 employees (County Business Patterns). While there are several ways to categorize the work done by **wholesalers**, three basic categories capture most firms in this industry. **Merchant wholesalers** represent the largest percentage of food wholesale sales accounting for 70 percent of the total. Merchant wholesalers primarily buy groceries and grocery products from processors or manufacturers, and then resell those to retailers, institutions, or other businesses. **Manufacturers' sales offices and sales branches (MSBOs)** are wholesale outfits typically run by large grocery manufacturers or processors to market their own products. **Wholesale agents and brokers** are wholesale operators who buy and/or sell as representatives of others for a commission. Wholesale brokers and agents typically do not physically handle the products, nor do they actually take title to the goods.

Most wholesale operations focus on sales to retailers, other wholesalers, industrial users, and, in some cases, the final consumer. A wholesaler may buy directly from the producer and sell to another wholesaler or food processor. More typically, however, the wholesaler buys from the food processor or manufacturer and sells to a retailer. The make-up of the wholesale trade sector involves a large group of varied organizations—some quite small and some very large. Chain stores own their warehousing facilities, but typically break this out into a separate operating unit with the objective of generating a profit.

Wholesalers perform a variety of functions for their retail customers. It is important to note that wholesalers are facilitators and that they may take market risk if they take title to the goods they handle. These firms are responsible for distributing the product in appropriate quantities across a geographic region. Often wholesalers will finance inventory purchases for the retailer. In this case, the retailer does not have to borrow money from the bank, but uses the wholesaler as a source of operating funds. Many wholesalers offer services like automatic ordering, customer traffic surveys, and a suggested shelf-stocking arrangement, among others. The idea is for the wholesaler to forge a profitable working relationship with their retail clients.

Merchant grocery wholesalers are classified into three groups by the types of products they distribute: (1) general line distributors, (2) specialty distributors, and (3) miscellaneous distributors. First, general line distributors operate 8 percent of the total number of food wholesalers, but employ 17 percent of the wholesaler workforce (Wholesale Trade 2011). Also known as broad line or full line distributors, these companies handle a complete line of groceries, health and beauty products, and household products. Supervalu, Nash Finch, and Sysco are examples of general line distributors. Second, specialty distributors are typically smaller than general line distributors, and focus on specific items such as packaged frozen food, dairy products, meat or fish products, confectionery, or fresh fruit and vegetables. Specialty wholesales account for 54 percent of the food wholesaling establishments, employing 46 percent of the workforce. Finally, miscellaneous distributors carry narrow lines of dry groceries (coffee, snack foods, bread, or soft drinks), which are distributed directly to retail food stores. Accounting for 12,000 food wholesalers, miscellaneous food wholesalers employ 37 percent of the wholesale industries' workers.

Food processing and manufacturing

In 2007, U.S. food processors accounted for 11 percent of the value of shipments from all U.S. manufacturing plants, or $590 billion (2007 Economic Census). The Census of Manufacturers from the U.S. Census Bureau counted 25,616 food processing plants across the nation. An additional $139 billion of processing was performed by 3,717 beverage manufacturers, 102 tobacco manufacturers, 423 fiber, yarn and thread mills, and 239 tanneries. While the number of manufacturers has remained constant since 1997, the value of shipments has risen 10 percent, from $535 billion in 1997.

The food processing and manufacturing industry turns raw agricultural commodities either into ingredients for further processing or final consumer products. Meat packers, bakers, flour millers, wet corn mills, breakfast cereal companies, brewers, snack firms, and tanneries are examples of food and fiber processors and manufacturers. These complex firms serve highly varied markets. For example, soybean processors in central Illinois break down soybeans into two major components: soybean oil and soybean meal, each with its own unique market conditions. Literally hundreds of products utilize soybean oil as an ingredient, ranging from margarine to cosmetics. The primary market for soybean meal is as a high protein livestock feed supplement.

Processors of meat products account for about 22 percent of the total value added by food processors and manufacturers (Figure 1.10). Processors of bakery, fruits, and vegetables and dairies all account for more than 10 percent of total processing activity. While over 21,000

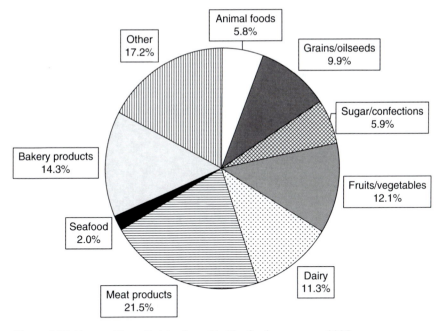

Figure 1.10 Composition of total value-added by food processors, 2007
Source: 2007 Economic Census.

firms are engaged in food processing activities, most own but a single processing plant (McDonald 2000). On the other end of the continuum, the 50 largest processing firms account for 52 percent of the total value added in the processing industries (2007 Economic Census).

The sharp increase in concentration among food processing industry firms in the last 30 years has led to a few large companies marketing a wide variety of commodity and branded products. Major commodity processing industries, such as animal feed, grain milling, and meat packing, are dominated by giants such as Smithfield Foods, Cargill, ADM, and ConAgra. Among well-known food processing and manufacturing firms are Nestlé, Kraft, General Mills, Mars, and Coca-Cola.

Our final group of food sector firms includes those that acquire or assemble commodities from agricultural producers, and store and transport these products for food manufacturing and processing firms. Transportation and logistics firms facilitate the marketing and processing phases of the food sector. Firms ranging in size from the grain handling giant Cargill, to local cooperatives that handle grain, are involved in the collection, storage, and transportation of agricultural commodities. A similar process then ensues as products are shipped to food retailers.

Transportation output is measured in ton-miles, a metric which tracks the interrelationship between weight and distance. For example, if a 25 ton truckload of wheat moves 200 miles to market, that trip generated 5,000 ton-miles. Agricultural and food products are important users of the U.S. transportation system. Agricultural commodities shipped from growers to processors accounted for 13 percent of the ton-miles in 2007 (Commodity Flow Survey 2009). Shipments from food processors to retailers account for another 8 percent of the total ton-miles.

A good example is provided by the way that grain moves from farm to processor. Grain typically moves from the farm either to local elevators or to sub-terminal elevators located near transportation centers. These firms make money on grain movement, not on speculating that the grain they hold will go up in price. Small local grain elevators may sell to a larger sub-terminal or terminal elevator, or directly to a processor. Terminal elevators assemble grain from smaller country elevators to amass a quantity of grain that will fill unit trains or barges. Unit trains might move corn to the southeast to feed poultry. Or a group of barges might be transported down the Mississippi River and the delivered grain shipped to the international market.

Managing transportation and storage firms brings a unique set of challenges. A grain buyer for a terminal elevator located close to rail lines and a navigable river must be knowledgeable of rail rates, the availability of rail cars, and barge rates. Often these rates can change significantly overnight. Risk management is paramount, as commodity prices change quickly. Margins for these firms are typically razor thin, hence cost management is a priority.

Linkages in the food sector

Many of the organizations involved in the food sector have successfully integrated forward or backward in the food system. Goals for such a strategy include increased operating efficiency and reduced market risk. For example, many firms are involved in both processing and marketing activities and have at least partially integrated back to the production sector by entering partnering or contracting arrangements with producers. Smithfield Foods is a good example of a firm with such a position in the market. The link helps reduce market risk by reducing material quality problems and supply problems.

This arrangement is common in the poultry, fruit, and vegetable production sectors. In the Midwest, for example, the Redenbacher Popcorn Company has producer agreements that guarantee supply before the crop is planted in the spring. Redenbacher contracts with producers by guaranteeing a specific price for popcorn grown on a specific number of acres. The firm provides seed and purchases all popcorn grown on the acreage under contract. Producers deliver production to a local processing facility.

Kroger, one of the top food retailers, owns 40 food processing plants that are used to manufacturer store label products, including dairy, snack foods, and bakery items. Anheuser-Busch owns malting plans and can-manufacturing operations. Firms like ConAgra have a presence at almost every level of the food system. As mentioned earlier, such linkages are common and make the lines between industries very blurry, and the resulting firms quite complex.

The production agriculture sector

At the hub of our food production and marketing system is the production agriculture sector. **Production agriculture** includes the farms and ranches that produce the crop and livestock products that provide inputs to the food and fiber sector. And, these farms and ranches are the customers of the firms that make up the input supply sector. As mentioned earlier, relatively few individuals are responsible for a staggering quantity of output in the U.S. production agriculture sector. Today's U.S. farmer produces enough food and fiber in a year to feed and clothe 155 people. More than 40 percent of the corn grown in the world is produced in the United States.

Every industry in the food system is impacted in some way by production agriculture. And like the food and input supply sectors, the production agriculture sector has been undergoing profound change in response to a variety of market forces. In this section, we will explore the dynamic production agriculture sector of our food production and marketing system.

Farm demographics

So what is a farm? The United States Department of Agriculture (USDA) defines a **farm** as "any establishment from which $1,000 or more of agricultural products were sold or would normally be sold during the year" (Ahearn and Weber 2010). This definition includes many part-time farmers with limited acreage and very modest production. The USDA definition of a farm includes the small hobby farmer that sells one horse or ten lambs per year as well as the commercial operator that farms 8,000 acres or produces 700,000 head of hogs annually. The definition includes those who farm part-time and those who have farmed full-time for generations. The Economic Research Service (ERS) of the USDA classifies farms into three groups: rural residence farms, intermediate farms, and commercial farms. **Rural residence farms** include limited resource, retirement, and residential/lifestyle farms. **Intermediate farms** include operators reporting farming as the major occupation and gross sales under $250,000, while **commercial farms** are family farms with income over $250,000 or non-family farms (Ahearn and Weber 2010).

The makeup of the farms varies widely, depending upon the farm typology. Most farms (71 percent) are classified as rural residence farms, yet they produce only 6.7 percent of the market value of farm products (Table 1.5). The rural residence farms are roughly a quarter section of land, with operators 58 years old. Intermediate farms make up 16 percent of all farms, producing 8 percent of farm production, while commercial farms produce 86 percent

Table 1.5 Farm characteristics, by type of farm, 2007

Type of Farm	Number of farms	% of Farms	Average Acres	% Market Value of Farm Products	% of Government Payments	Average Age
Rural residence	1,566,774	71.1	162	6.7	25.3	58.2
Intermediate	359,025	16.3	533	7.8	18.2	54.3
Commercial	278,993	12.7	1,712	85.5	56.6	54.5
Total	2,204,792	100.0	418	100.0	100.0	57.1

Source: 2007 Census of Agriculture.

of all farm products with only 13 percent of the farms. At 1,712 acres, commercial farms are more than triple the size of intermediate farms. Operators reporting farming as their major occupation are slightly younger, around 54 years old.

The past century was a period of huge change for production agriculture in this country. Changes in farm numbers and farm size are reflective of this change. Historically, individual families or extended families have owned and operated the nation's farms. The family provided the land, labor, and other capital necessary to run the business. As market prices fluctuated, farm families adapted by doing without or diversifying in some way. As mechanization or finances allowed, more land was acquired—ideally to send a child to college, or to provide a living for additional family members coming into the business.

As time moved on, farm expansion required additional inputs such as seed, fertilizer, chemicals, credit, animal health products, or farm machinery be purchased. Technology-fueled expansion made it possible for farmers to operate and productively manage ever larger farm businesses, and farm size grew. However, when fluctuations in price or crop losses caused lean years, farmers still had obligations to pay suppliers. Financing became a necessary and critical component of the family farm business. As we will see later in this book, such debt financing also carries a risk.

Average land values over time reflect the economic health of the farm sector (Table 1.6). Land values grew from $196 to $737 per acre during the 1970s, as America planted from fence row to fence row to meet a surge in worldwide demand. In turn, farm expansion financed by debt and secured through inflated land values of the 1970s created severe financial problems for some producers, as well as their suppliers. Some of these farms were not able to survive the farm crisis of the 1980s and farm foreclosures contributed to an overall decline in farm numbers. Thus, the 1980s saw a retreat in farm land values. Farm land values have steadily increased since 1990, as production agriculture has seen a resurgence driven by strong growth in biofuels and export markets.

Total land in farms in the U.S. continues to decline slowly, due in part to conservation programs, as well as continued development of housing tracts, malls, and factories

Table 1.6 Number of farms, land in farms, average size of farm, 1970–2009

Year	Farms	Land in Farms (1,000 acres)	Average Size (acres)	Average Farm Land Value ($/acre)
1970	2,949,140	1,102,371	373.8	196
1975	2,521,420	1,059,420	420.2	340
1980	2,439,510	1,038,885	425.9	737
1985	2,292,530	1,012,073	441.5	713
1990	2,145,820	986,850	459.9	683
1995	2,196,400	962,515	438.2	844
2000	2,166,780	945,080	436.2	1,090
2005	2,098,690	927,940	442.2	1,610
2006	2,088,790	925,790	443.2	1,830
2007	2,204,950	921,460	417.9	2,010
2008	2,200,100	919,910	418.1	2,170
2009	2,200,010	919,800	418.1	2,100

Source: McGath 2011.

(Table 1.6). In 2009, a total of 920 million acres was farmed, down from its peak of 1.2 billion acres in 1954. The 2.2 million farms and ranches in the U.S. in 2009 has been relatively stable since 1985. Texas reports the most farms in the U.S. with 247,500; Missouri is in second with some 108,000 farms.

Larger and more specialized farming operations have evolved since the 1930s. As a result, a much smaller group of producers accounts for the majority of agricultural production. The 2007 Census of Agriculture showed that about 93 percent of all agricultural production came from 16 percent of U.S. farms, and 74 percent of the total came from only 5 percent of the farms—about 116,000 farmers (Figure 1.11).

Despite all of the changes, today families or family businesses still own nearly 96 percent of the nation's farms. However, it is important to note that many of these family-run farming operations are very large and sophisticated businesses. At the same time, non-family owned corporate farms, particularly in the livestock and poultry industries, are increasing in number. In 2007, such operations accounted for 22.3 percent of total farm sales.

Farm income

Net farm income in the U.S. is determined by prices of farm products, production yields, and farm production expenses. Farm prices can be highly volatile, moving upward quickly in response to low tomato yields, or plunging if the market doesn't need all of the pork produced by U.S. producers. Note that the commodity nature of most agricultural markets means that individual farmers have little control over the price of their production. They can take steps to manage their price risk, but cannot do much about the actual price they receive. Production expenses can also be volatile. Fuel costs can soar when general market supplies are short. The price of nitrogen fertilizer, which is made from natural gas, can increase very quickly if natural gas is in short supply.

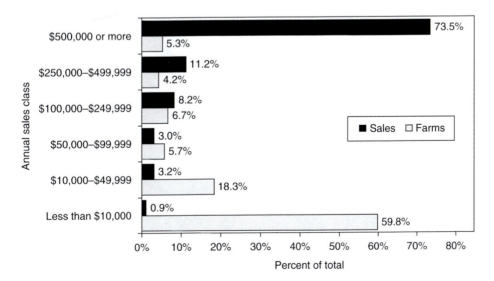

Figure 1.11 Distribution of farms by sales class, 2007
Source: 2007 Census of Agriculture.

Given the importance of the production agriculture sector, it has been the policy of the U.S. government since the 1930s to support the income of farmers when market conditions are not favorable. There are a wide variety of such programs that assist farmers, and these vary by commodity. Some crop and livestock products, such as peanuts, wheat, and dairy products, have substantial government involvement. Other crop and livestock products such as soybeans, pork, and lettuce have much lower levels of government involvement. When combined across all crops, total payments from the government have been an important, but declining, component of net farm income in the U.S. (Table 1.7). The government payments are especially important for rural residence farms (Table 1.5).

Future issues

The production agriculture sector continues to evolve. Consolidation in the sector has been rapid to date, and farms are getting larger every year—especially in the livestock sector. International competition, volatile input prices, environmental and food safety regulations, and rapid deployment of new technology have all placed substantial pressure on the owner/manager of a production agriculture business. Agricultural producers have responded to these pressures with an increased emphasis on financial and risk management; a focus on control of assets like land and machinery as opposed to ownership; and the general application of many of the management ideas we will address in this book. For many years people talked about farming as "a way of life." While the "way of life" aspect remains important to many producers, successful commercial agricultural producers in today's business environment are astute, sophisticated business managers running large and complex organizations.

The input supply sector

The **input supply sector** of the food production and marketing system comprises the firms that manufacture and distribute myriad inputs used by the production agriculture sector. The agricultural input industry umbrella is a broad one and includes a wide range of firms that

Table 1.7 Net income from farming, 1970–2009

Year	Net Income (millions $)	Government Payments (millions $)	Payments as % of Farm Income
1970	14,365.9	3,717.4	25.9
1975	25,510.2	807.1	3.2
1980	16,141.4	1,285.7	8.0
1985	28,509.3	7,704.2	27.0
1990	46,260.7	9,298.0	20.1
1995	39,770.8	7,279.5	18.3
2000	50,684.9	23,221.6	45.8
2005	78,763.0	24,395.9	31.0
2006	57,436.4	15,788.8	27.5
2007	70,323.0	11,903.4	16.9
2008	86,597.6	12,241.7	14.1
2009	62,187.1	12,262.6	19.7

Source: McGath 2011.

provide products and services to agricultural producers. Animal nutrition, seed, machinery and equipment, fertilizer, crop protection, and credit and banking firms would be among the enterprises which fall under the general category of input suppliers.

A description of just what these industries look like today only vaguely resembles their appearance just a few years ago. During the last 40 years, these industries, like the food and production agriculture sectors, have experienced vast and dynamic change. Taking a quick look at the history books helps define today's agricultural input business. A rapidly growing agriculture fueled a prosperous input supply sector in the 1970s. The massive adjustments of the production sector in the 1980s brought an equally huge reorganization of the input supply industries. Since the 1990s, continued consolidation in the livestock sector has reshaped the input supply industries serving animal agriculture. Consolidation in the agronomic industries via mergers and acquisitions has led to fewer, larger players at both the manufacturing and the distribution levels.

The productivity of the agricultural production sector continues to increase, in no small part, due to the products and services provided by the input supply sector. Improved varieties of seed may be attributed to advances in biotechnology among other more conventional developments, which allow improved and lower-cost production methods. Animal nutrition, farm machinery and equipment, agricultural pesticides and herbicides, and the many facilitating services offered to producers help increase the productivity of the production agriculture sector. Information technologies such as global positioning and monitoring systems have seen widespread adoption. For purpose of this text, we have categorized the farm input supply sector into three areas:

- Manufacturing
- Distribution
- Services

We will explore each of these three areas in the remainder of this section.

Manufacturing

Manufacturers in the input supply sector include many company names you may well recognize. John Deere, Syngenta, Pfizer Animal Health, and Monsanto are just a handful of examples of large organizations that spend millions of dollars annually in research and development to bring improved products to the producer. Virtually everything it takes to run the farm or ranch must be purchased from an input supplier of some sort. Farmers purchase over 72 percent of all inputs used for production. In 2010, farm production expenditures were $287.3 billion (Table 1.8). On average, a U.S. farmer spends about $100,000 dollars per year to run the farm business and these expenses for farmers represent the sales of the input supply sector. Input manufacturers are responsible to the research, development, production, and manufacturing that makes these products possible.

Livestock and poultry products include feed, feed supplements, and health products which are required in the production of meat, milk, and fiber products such as wool. Providing producers with products such as these requires access to and use of high technology, often large manufacturing plants, and a sizable research and development budget to support efforts of this scale. In addition to products that feed animals and keep them healthy, other input firms manufacture products for housing livestock, storing and managing livestock waste, and moving livestock from farm to market.

Table 1.8 Farm production expenses (billion $).

Item	2008	2009	2010	2011
Farm Origin Inputs	79.8	77.0	79.9	85.1
Purchased Feed	46.9	45.0	45.2	49.7
Livestock Purchased	17.7	16.5	19.5	19.3
Seed	15.1	15.5	15.3	16.1
Manufactured Inputs	55.0	49.0	49.5	55.6
Fertilizer and Lime	22.5	20.1	18.2	20.9
Pesticides	11.7	11.5	11.1	11.9
Fuels & Oils	16.2	12.7	15.6	18.1
Electricity	4.5	4.6	4.6	4.7
Total Interest Charges	15.4	15.2	15.0	15.4
Other Operating Expenses	93.7	89.5	91.8	98.2
Repair and Maintenance	14.8	14.7	15.5	16.6
Contract and Hired Labor	29.7	28.7	28.8	30.1
Machine Hire and Custom Work	4.1	3.9	4.0	4.3
Marketing, Storage and Transportation	10.1	10.3	10.4	11.3
Miscellaneous Operating Expenses	35.0	31.9	33.2	35.9
Overhead Expenses	49.0	50.4	51.1	53.3
Depreciation	28.7	30.1	30.6	31.4
Property Taxes	10.7	10.4	10.6	10.9
Rent	9.6	9.8	9.9	11.1
Total Production Expenses	293.0	281.0	287.3	307.5

Source: McGath 2011.

Trucks, tractors, and combines are all examples of manufactured products supplied to farmers through the input supply sector. Deere & Company is one of the oldest firms in the U.S. and is a Fortune 500 company. Deere invests 17 percent of sales in research and development, focused on bringing new and better products to the world's farmers.

At first glance, the seed industry may not seem like it is an input manufacturing industry. However, seed firms annually invest millions of dollars in developing and producing or "manufacturing" hundreds of new hybrids and varieties of seed. Chemical companies such as Syngenta and DuPont produce crop protectants that reduce weed and insect pressure, or protect the crop from disease. Recent developments in biotechnology have led to many products that bring these two industries together. Some crops have been modified to resist certain pests. Other crops have been modified to resist a particular herbicide, making weed control much easier. These crops have not been without controversy, and broader market acceptance of these **genetically modified organisms (GMOs)** has evolved slowly outside the U.S.

Distribution

Farm production inputs move from the manufacturer to the farm through a very wide variety of sales, marketing, and distribution channels. Using the technology developed by manufacturers also requires accurate and timely technical information, as well as timely access to the products. This is the job of **input distributors**—individuals, companies, outlets of national organizations, cooperatives, e-businesses, etc.—responsible for getting the products from

Plate 1.3 Input application
Advancements in technology by input suppliers contribute to productivity gains in the production agriculture sector. Photo courtesy of USDA Natural Resources Conservation Service

the manufacturer to the farm, and providing a set of services that insure productive use of the inputs.

These distribution firms represent a very wide range of organizations. Sometimes, a major national manufacturer owns the distribution firm. Memphis-based Helena Chemical Company is an international company producing fertilizers, spray adjuvants, and specialty products. Helena reaches farmers through its retail and wholesale locations throughout the U.S. In other cases, the distributor is a franchise of a manufacturer. The local dealer network of John Deere provides a good example. In still other cases, the distribution network is independent of the manufacturing sector.

Local agricultural cooperatives are heavily involved in the distribution of inputs. A **cooperative** is a member-owned, democratically controlled business from which the benefits are received in proportion to use. Local farmers who are cooperative members buy and sell products through the cooperative and thus, the cooperative is a distributor or agricultural products and/or services.

Stores or chains that offer everything from pet food to tractor parts operate as a retail business from which producers make purchases. Tractor supply provides a good example. Given the very wide range of inputs that farmers use in their businesses, and given the equally wide range of farmers involved in production agriculture, it comes as little surprise that the distribution system involves such a wide range of organizations.

Services and financing

The **agricultural services and financing** area includes farm management services, veterinary care, consulting businesses, and farm lending just to name a few of the types of businesses involved in this area. Larger farms and fewer farmers, combined with increases in absentee land ownership, have greatly contributed to an increase in the number of farm management firms and services offered in the last decade. Frequently, farm management services are hired to oversee land rental, crop production, financial and tax management for the absentee landlord.

Financing the production agriculture sector is big business. In 2009, the farm production sector controlled about $2.1 trillion of total assets—all those resources of value involved in farming. At the same time, total farm debt amounted to $245.4 billion. This debt includes debt on farmland and machinery, equipment, buildings, as well as production loans. Countless banks offer agricultural loans and related services to farmers.

The Farm Credit System serves as a lender to the farm sector providing production and farm real estate loans. In 2009, the Farm Credit System had loaned a total of $98 billion with roughly 60 percent being in long-term real estate loans. The Farm Credit System has provided approximately 35 to 40 percent of the total debt capital needed by the farm production system for farmland and operating funds in recent years. Other agricultural lenders include commercial banks and non-traditional lenders such as the captive finance companies of other input organizations.

Looking ahead

Managing in this diverse, multi-faceted field of agribusiness requires a wide range of skills and talents. In addition to a strong background in management, agribusiness managers need a deep understanding of the biological and institutional factors surrounding the production of food and fiber. In the first part of this book, we will look more closely at the tasks of management and some key economic concepts that are important to managers. Then we will turn our attention to the types of organizations we find in the food and agribusiness markets, and explore some elements of the context within which agribusiness managers make decisions.

With this broader perspective in hand, we turn our attention to a deeper look at the four functional areas of management. First, we explore the area of marketing and sales. Then, we will consider the management of the financial resources of the agribusiness. The final two parts deal with the important areas of supply chain management and human resource management. It is our goal that this book will provide you with a solid foundation for your further study—and practice—of agribusiness management.

Summary

The food production and marketing system is a complex, dynamic, and extremely productive part of the total U.S. economy. The study of agribusiness includes understanding basic management principles and practices. Four key functions of management are marketing, finance, supply chain management, and human resources management. An understanding of these functional areas is critical to the successful agribusiness manager.

There are a number of factors that combine to create a unique business environment for firms and managers in the food production and marketing system. This system is a highly efficient one. Over time, consumers have demanded more and more services with their food products. As a result, the proportion of the food dollar that goes to production agriculture has declined, and the marketing bill has expanded.

The definition of agribusiness used in this book includes three important sectors: the food sector, the production agriculture sector, and the input supply sector. In their combined activities, these three areas provide a tremendous variety of food and fiber products to consumers both in the U.S. and around the world. In this food system, each sector is tied to the next in the task of developing, producing, and delivering food products to the consumer. The food sector includes a wide range of firms including processors, manufacturers, wholesalers, and retailers. Many of these firms are global firms offering brands we are all familiar with. Others are focused on manufacturing ingredients that are inputs for other food companies. The production agriculture sector is undergoing dramatic change as the number of farms declines, and their size increases. Finally, the input supply sector provides the product and service inputs required by the farm production sector. Tractors, seed, crop protection products, capital, and advice are examples of products/services provided by input supply firms.

Discussion questions

1   List and define the four functions of agribusiness management.
2   What are five reasons the agribusiness sector may be considered unique? How or why could agribusiness and firms outside the agribusiness sectors make different decisions in similar situations?
3   The food marketing bill continues to grow each year—the proportion of the total farm-food marketing bill going to the food sector continues to increase. Interpret this trend. What are the reasons for this increase? How does this marketing bill affect farmers? Explain.
4   What are three significant trends facing food retailers? How have these impacted the food retailing industry?
5   Why have away from home eating establishments become so popular? Do you expect these trends to continue? Why or why not?
6   The size of U.S. farms has continued to increase. What are the positive dimensions of this trend? What are the negative dimensions of this trend? How does this trend impact the food sector and the input supply sector?
7   Environmental regulations and public acceptance of biotechnology were mentioned as important issues facing production agriculture, and hence input supply firms. Take one of these two issues, or the broader social issue of your choice, and outline some of the key implications of the issue for firms manufacturing and distributing inputs to farmers.

Case study

In this chapter, we look at three key sectors of the food production and marketing system—the food sector, the production agriculture sector, and the input supply sector. For this case study, pick a specific food or fiber product. The product could be cotton jeans, watermelon, frozen dinners, snack chips, beef steak, pizza—pick something you have an interest in. Then, using the library or the Internet, locate the name of one firm for each of the three sectors of agribusiness that is involved in some way in the production and distribution of your product. For pizza, this might be Pizza Hut (food sector), a family-owned tomato grower/shipper (production agriculture), and DowAgro Sciences (input supply sector). After you have identified your three companies, answer each of the questions below:

1　Briefly describe each of your firms. What markets do they serve? How large are the firms? What products do they produce?
2　How are these firms linked to the product you chose to research?
3　What is similar about the firms you chose? What is different about the firms you chose?
4　How are these firms related in the production and distribution of your product? Is this an explicit link (do they share the same parent company, for instance), or are they loosely related through open markets?

References and additional reading

2007 Census of Agriculture. "United States Summary and State Data." U.S. Department of Agriculture. AC-07-A-51. 2009. www.agcensus.usda.gov/Publications/2007/Full_Report/usv1.pdf

2007 Economic Census, Manufacturing. "U.S. Census Bureau". 2009. www.census.gov/econ/census07/

Ahearn, Mary and Jeremy Weber. "Briefing Room: Farm Household Economics and Well-Being: Glossary." U.S. Department of Agriculture, Economic Research Service. 2010. www.ers.usda.gov/briefing/wellbeing/glossary.htm

Canning, Patrick. "A Revised and Expanded Food Dollar Series: A Better Understanding of Our Food Costs." U.S. Department of Agriculture, Economic Research Service. ERR-114. 2011. www.ers.usda.gov/Publications/ERR114/

Central Intelligence Agency. "The World Factbook." 2011. www.cia.gov/library/publications/the-world-factbook/index.html

Clauson, Annette. "Briefing Room: Food CPI and Expenditures: Table 14. U.S. Department of Agriculture, Economic Research Service." 2010. www.ers.usda.gov/Briefing/CPIFoodAndExpenditures/Data/Expenditures_tables/table14.htm

Clauson, Annette and Ephraim Leibtag. "Briefing Room: Food CPI and Expenditures." U.S. Department of Agriculture, Economic Research Service. 2011. www.ers.usda.gov/Briefing/CPIFoodAndExpenditures/

Commodity Flow Survey. "U.S. Census Bureau, Business and Industry," Sector 00: CF0700A07: Geographic Area Series: Shipment Characteristics by Origin Geography by Commodity by Mode: 2007, 2009. factfinder.census.gov/servlet/DatasetMainPageServlet?_lang = en&_ts = 326114744380 &_ds_name = EC0700A1&_program = ECN

County Business Patterns. Various years. "U.S. Census Bureau." censtats.census.gov/cgi-bin/cbpnaic/cbpsel.pl

Edmonson, William. "Briefing Room: Food Market Structures—The U.S. Food and Fiber System." U.S. Department of Agriculture, Economic Research Service. 2000. www.ers.usda.gov/briefing/foodmarketstructures/foodandfiber.htm

Food and Agriculture Organization. "2000 World Census of Agriculture: Main Results and Metadata by Country (1996–2005)." United Nations, Rome, Italy. 2010. www.fao.org/docrep/013/i1595e/i1595e.pdf

Kaufman, Phil. "Food Marketing System in the U.S.: Retail Food Glossary." U.S. Department of Agriculture, Economic Research Service. 2007. www.ers.usda.gov/Briefing/FoodMarketingSystem/foodretailingglossary.htm

Kaufman, Phil and Aylin Kumcu. "Briefing Room: Food Marketing System in the U.S.: Food Retailing." U.S. Department of Agriculture, Economic Research Service. 2010. www.ers.usda.gov/Briefing/FoodMarketingSystem/foodretailing.htm

Martinez, Steve W. "Varied Interests Drive Growing Popularity of Local Foods." Amber Waves. U.S. Department of Agriculture, Economic Research Service. 2010. www.ers.usda.gov/AmberWaves/december10/Features/LocalFoods.htm

McDonald, James. "Briefing Room: Food Market Structures—Food Processing" U.S. Department of Agriculture, Economic Research Service. 2000. www.ers.usda.gov/briefing/foodmarketstructures/processing.htm

McGath, Chris. "Farm Income: Data Files." U.S. Department of Agriculture. Economic Research Service. 2011. www.ers.usda.gov/data/farmincome/finfidmuxls.htm

Meade, Birgit. "Briefing Room: Food CPI and Expenditures: 2007 Table 97." United States Department of Agriculture. U.S. Department of Agriculture, Economic Research Service. 2008. www.ers.usda.gov/briefing/cpifoodandexpenditures/data/Table_97/2007table97.htm

Supermarket News. "SN's Top 75 for 2010." 2010. supermarketnews.com/profiles/downloads-2010

U.S. Department of Commerce. "Gross-Domestic-Product-(GDP)-by-Industry Data." Bureau of Economic Analysis, Washington, DC. 2011. www.bea.gov/industry/gdpbyind_data.htm

U.S. Department of Justice. "Agriculture and Antitrust Enforcement Issues in Our 21st Century Economy". 2011. www.justice.gov/atr/public/workshops/ag2010/index.html#overview

Westcott, Paul. "USDA Agricultural Projections to 2020." U.S. Department of Agriculture, Economic Research Service. OCE-2011-1. 2011. www.usda.gov/oce/commodity/archive_projections/USDAAgriculturalProjections2020.pdf

Wholesale Trade. "U.S. Census Bureau". 2011. www.census.gov/econ/wholesale.html

2 Managing the agribusiness

Objectives

- Define management and explain the role of a manager
- Understand the decision-making environment for agribusiness managers
- Describe the tasks of planning, organizing, directing, and controlling in agribusiness management
- Understand the steps in the planning process
- Define leadership and compare it to management
- Explain the differences among policies, procedures, and practices
- Describe management by exception, and understand how this idea is used by agribusiness managers

Introduction

Success or failure? Stellar performer or also-ran? For an agribusiness firm, success or failure is sometimes driven by the broader marketplace—a boom in export demand, a rapid price hike for fuel. Other times winning and losing comes down to chance—a lucky break in the market, a competitor's mistake. The broader marketplace and chance are clearly beyond the agribusiness firm's direct control. Although these external factors are certainly important, the agribusiness firm also has influence on whether performance is stellar or mediocre. Decisions made by the firm's managers—the allocation of investment funds, the people hired, the products introduced, the plants constructed, the deals entered, and many more—all determine whether the firm will be able to capitalize on a favorable market or how well prepared the firm is for challenges.

While any firm will take a favorable trend or a lucky break, relying on factors outside the firm to determine performance simply leaves too much to chance. So, we will assert that firm performance hinges in large part on how effectively a manager uses the organization's resources. Managers are hired to utilize firm resources in the best possible manner to achieve the performance objectives of the firm's owners. They use resources to capitalize on market trends and to manage downside risk. Managers deploy resources to take advantage of fortunate circumstances or to minimize the fallout from unlucky ones. Managers drive performance in agribusiness firms.

Who are these managers leading today's agribusinesses? They are each unique individuals who vary in age, gender, background, education, ethnicity, geographic location, and so on. Each faces a different management situation—unique because of their industry, commodity, location, employees, competitors, etc. Given that people and situations differ, a specific recipe for what it takes to be a successful manager is challenging to define. While there are certain management skills and principles that can be learned, these skills must be adapted by each individual to fit the unique situation they face.

Given this responsibility, how do agribusiness managers actually accomplish their task? Perhaps a few individuals are "born managers," but managing is not innate to most people. For most of us, managing is a learned skill, and this book is about helping you move down the path toward being an effective manager. Business education has come of age, and the reasons why some organizations succeed while others fail are understood. Today's successful agribusiness managers are guided by a set of principles that constitute sound management. In this chapter, we will take a closer look at this business of management. We will explore the key tasks of any manager to provide a foundation for our further exploration of agribusiness management.

Today's agribusiness managers

Management is both an art and a science. Managers must efficiently combine available human, financial, and physical assets to maximize the long-run profits of an operation by profitably satisfying its customer's demands. Management requires individuals be technically knowledgeable about the organization's product and/or function. They must be good and effective communicators. The ability to motivate people is also essential. They must be proficient in the technical skills of management such as accounting, finance, forecasting, and so on.

In addition to a strong background in management, agribusiness managers need a strong understanding of the biological and institutional factors surrounding the production of food and fiber. In other words, not only must they excel at the normal concerns of business management, agribusiness managers must also factor in the uncertainty of the weather, the perishable nature of many of agriculture's products, government policies, and the rapidly changing technology employed in agriculture. They must possess the ability to quickly adapt to changes in market conditions that result from changes in these uncertain factors of weather, product perishability, government policies, technology, etc. Managers must be able to mix each of these skills and perspectives in the right proportion to deliver the greatest long-run net benefit for the firm.

Defining management in agribusiness

Successful managers feel like managers, see themselves as managers, and are both ready and willing to play the managerial role. When successful managers look in the mirror, they see a leader, a person who is willing to accept the responsibility for change and become the catalyst for action. The success-minded manager is comfortable with this managerial role, and accepts responsibility and authority as a challenge rather than as a curse. Nicholas Murray Butler, the longtime president of Columbia University, once placed managers in three classes: "the few who make things happen, the many who watch things happen, and the majority who have no idea what has happened!"

We define **management** in this text as the art and science of *successfully* pursuing desired results with the *resources available* to the organization. Several key words in this definition are italicized to stress the elements of successful management.

Art and *science* are the first two key words, and as mentioned above, management is both an art and a science. Because management deals largely with people, management principles must be viewed as imperfect, at best. Yet many management principles and tools can help us make better decisions in an imperfect world. Everyone cannot become the top manager for a firm, but everyone can use management principles to foster continual growth and progress toward their personal managerial potential. The third key word is *successful*. Whatever else good management is, it must be successful in meeting desired and predetermined goals or results. Managers must know where they are headed in order to achieve such success.

Finally, consider the *resources available*. Each organization possesses or has at its command a variety of resources—financial, human, facilities, equipment, patents, and so on. Successful managers coax the highest potential returns from the resources available. They recognize the difference between what should be and what is. At the same time, they know how to expand the firm's resource base when resource constraints hamper potential. They use what they have to get what they want and need, and deal in the realm of the possible.

A **manager** can be defined as that person who provides the organization with leadership and who acts as a catalyst for change. He or she is responsible for the management of the organization. Good managers are most effective in an environment that permits creative change. Such managers live to make things happen. Success as a manager, then, necessitates the ability to understand and be comfortable with the managerial role, to accept responsibility, and to provide leadership for change.

Distinctive features of agribusiness management

In many ways, management principles and concepts are the same for any business. Both the largest business in the country and the smallest one-person agribusiness are guided by the same general principles. The differences between managing large and small businesses, between agribusinesses and other kinds of businesses, rests in the art of applying fundamental management principles to the specific situation facing the business. In this chapter many general management principles will be applied to the unique context of agribusiness and agribusiness management.

Recall from Chapter 1 the eight points that distinguish the agribusiness management environment:

1. Food as a product
2. Biological nature of production agriculture
3. Seasonal nature of business
4. Uncertainty of the weather
5. Types of firms
6. Variety of market conditions
7. Rural ties
8. Government involvement

Thus, agribusiness is unique, and requires that the agribusiness manager use the principles of management in a distinct way.

The four key tasks of agribusiness managers

Management has been described using as many concepts as there are authors in the field. Some describe management as a division of four areas of functional responsibility, such as finance, marketing, supply chain management, and personnel. Others view it as coordinating resources, such as money, markets, materials, machinery, methods, and manpower.

Still others view management in terms of approaches or processes—i.e., industrial engineering, organizational, and behavioral concepts. Finally, some consider management as a series of four tasks, the perspective we will take in this book.

The functions of management discussed in Chapter 1 address four key areas (marketing, finance, supply chain management, and human resources) of the firm. Any food or agribusiness firm must make decisions in all four areas. While these management functions are important to understand, they don't tell the whole story of what management is all about. We use the term manager to describe a wide swath of individuals, from chief executive officer to district sales manager. What does a manager who runs a small, independent crop consulting firm have in common with a senior executive in a multi-billion dollar food company? The answer is simple. In each of these agribusinesses, it's what these managers do that makes their jobs similar. All effective agribusiness mangers execute four principle tasks in their work:

- Planning
- Organizing
- Directing
- Controlling

Each of these tasks plays a part of the agribusiness manager's overall role in managing the people and events within his/her power to generate the best possible outcome for the organization. Each task deals with a specific aspect of what agribusiness managers actually do as they manage.

Figure 2.1 illustrates this task-oriented concept of management as a wheel. The four tasks of management are the spokes that connect the manager with the goals, objectives, and results desired by the organization. It is only through planning, organizing, directing, and controlling that the firm's (and manager's) goals are achieved. Overall, management can be no stronger than the weakest spoke in this wheel. Now add **motivation** as the torque, or speed, or effectiveness, with which the tasks are accomplished. Motivation provides the motion by which the wheel either moves forward or reverses, but it is not another task. Strong motivation results in speedy, efficient, successful and forward-moving management. On the other hand, a lack of motivation can result in a discouraging reversal. The axle on which the entire wheel of management turns is **communication**. Again, this is not another task, but without effective and timely communication, the wheel of management soon begins to wobble and squeak.

A manager in one situation may be heavily involved in planning activities and have little or nothing to do with controlling or directing. Another manager's job might be heavily involved in the directing task, while still others are involved in all four tasks. Regardless of which tasks are prevalent in one's job, it is critical for agribusiness managers to understand what goes on in each of the four areas—planning, organizing, directing, and controlling—since someone, somewhere in the organization must undertake these tasks to get a product or service to market. The manager that fully grasps the total picture and where they fit in will have greater success at carrying out their tasks effectively.

Planning

Planning can be defined as forward thinking about courses of action based on a full understanding of all factors involved and directed at specific goals and performance objectives.

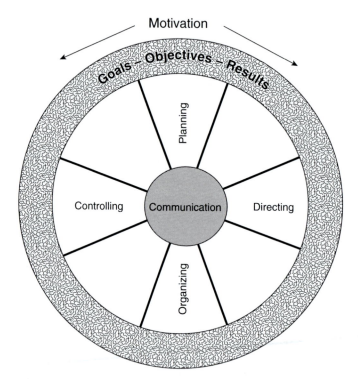

Figure 2.1 The wheel of management

Let's examine this definition in more detail. The first segment focuses on forward thinking, which means just that, looking ahead. This is not a forecast but an action-oriented statement—thinking about the future. To look forward, it is vital to be well aware of the events of world and key trends. The second element concerns courses of action, which implies developing alternatives or methods of accomplishing specific goals and objectives, based on a full understanding of all factors involved. Here is where the facts and consequences of the various factors affecting the alternative courses of action are weighed. Finally, there is the most important part of all, as well as the most neglected: directed at specific goals and objectives, or, in other words, focusing on some end-point, some target.

Types of planning

The planning task represents the preparation of the agribusiness firm for future business conditions. Since the future can be defined to include various time periods and it is uncertain, the planning task can take a number of forms. The three types of planning discussed in this chapter are strategic, tactical, and contingency.

Strategic planning is focused on developing courses of action for the longer term. Long term may be two or three years for a very small agribusiness, while a major corporate organization may be looking at a 20-year (or longer) time horizon. Strategic plans tackle the broadest elements of an agribusiness firm's strategy: what countries will we operate in; what businesses will we be in; what plants will we build, what technologies will be developed?

Plate 2.1 Man and woman planning
Planning efforts should be forward thinking and directed toward specific goals. Photo courtesy of
USDA Natural Resources Conservation Service.

While strategic plans are found at all large agribusiness companies, they are also important for the small food processor or the sales manager for a swine genetics company. It is the long-term time horizon that characterizes the strategic planning activity.

Any planning activity is focused on achieving some goal, on moving the firm in some direction. Therefore, in many strategic planning situations, one of the first steps is the development of a mission statement or a statement of vision. A **mission statement** helps to spell out this direction for a firm and describes the destination. When developing a mission for a company or even for a department, management must think strategically about the firm's business in a future time period. Briefly stated in between one and three sentences, a mission statement usually describes who the company is, what they do, and where they are headed. In many cases, it has three parts:

- Key markets (who we serve)
- Contribution (what we do)
- Distinction (how we do it differently)

Some examples of firm mission statements are shown below:

As a leading branded food company with a focus on profitable growth and inspired by our founder's charge to "Originate, don't imitate," we market a balanced portfolio of highly differentiated quality products. We engage our employees by creating an environment where careers are fostered, people make a difference and integrity is absolute.

By doing things Our Way, the principles that have helped us grow and succeed for more than 100 years can guide our daily actions to support four key areas—our people, our processes, our products and our performance.

(Hormel Foods)

Because the need for food and energy is both vital and growing, we must look ahead, plan and grow. Our vision is to be the most admired global agribusiness. Creating value. Growing responsibly. Serving vital needs.

(Archer Daniels Midland)

The challenge: meeting the needs of today while preserving the planet for tomorrow.

The solution: Producing more—We are working to double yields in our core crops by 2030. These yield gains will come from a combination of advanced plant breeding, biotechnology, and improved farm-management practices.

The solution: Conserving more—We've strengthened our goal of doubling crop yields by committing to doing it with one-third fewer resources such as land, water, and energy per unit produced.

The solution: Improving lives—We're working to help farmers achieve big increases in yield and productivity. And for all of the world's farmers who raise themselves from poverty to prosperity, many more people will also prosper.

(Monsanto)

A mission statement should be specific to the firm. Generically worded statements that apply to any firm are not useful. Such generic statements do not paint a mental picture of where the firm is destined, and offer no guidance on which activities to pursue and what strategies to follow. In contrast, a good strategic mission statement must be pointed. It must have specific relevance to the company in both its direction and destination. Many agribusiness companies have found that in addition to company stated missions, teams and working groups supervised by various levels of managers also benefit by developing a "team" mission. Team members benefit from being involved in developing their own working group's mission. To inspire those involved, this type of mission statement should be expressed in language that attracts the attention of people, creates a vivid image, and provokes emotion and excitement. If managers are maintaining the big picture perspective, they can help employees understand where we need to go. Thus, by keeping the focus on a company's mission, all can better achieve their goals more effectively.

Tactical planning involves short-term plans consistent with the strategic plan. As such, tactical plans are a crucial part of implementing the agribusiness firm's strategic plan. While strategic planning is focused on what we do in three years (or five years, or 20 years), tactical planning is focused on what we do tomorrow (or next month, or next year). For example, a chemical company's strategic plan could include a goal of increasing its market share by 20 percent in three years by using a strategy of expanding its geographic market. The firm's tactical plan may focus on how to increase sales in the next quarter in specific geographic regions that have less competition, and will likely include specific action steps for getting this done.

Contingency planning is the development of alternative plans for various possible business conditions. It is part of the strategic and tactical planning process for a firm. A contingency plan provides guidance when something unexpected happens. Some contingency planning is conducted to prepare for potential crises that may occur. For example, a seed company markets varieties specific to the growing conditions of a particular geographic region of the country. However, a prolonged wet period during the planting season would cause the seed company to implement a contingency plan based on delayed planting, which may result in providing an additional supply of short-season varieties. On the other hand, a food company may need a contingency plan for the best-case scenario. What do they do if demand for their new organic frozen entrée grows at ten times the initial forecast? How will they handle the extra production and distribution? Thus, both bad and good outcomes can create the need for a contingency plan.

Levels of planning

Table 2.1 illustrates the three levels of planning. As the level of planning moves from the chief executive to the line worker, several changes occur. At top management levels, plans are strategic and have a tendency toward flexibility, are longer range, are usually written, are more complex, and are broader in nature. At the lower levels, plans are specific in nature, are for immediate action, are usually unwritten, and tend toward simplicity. Although plans tend to be unwritten at the lower levels, almost all managers benefit from having written plans. Upon writing down a plan, the plan becomes more focused and any inconsistencies or gaps are likely to be made visible. Written plans tend to organize and consolidate thoughts, are easier to communicate, and provide a source for further reference.

Depending on the structure of the firm, another reason the nature of planning changes from the top management level to lower levels is the allocation of resources. Top executives develop strategic plans that generally add or subtract resources from the agribusiness, while those plans made at the lower levels are operational and generally relate to using the existing resources in the most efficient manner. Table 2.1 illustrates the need for all these plans to mesh in a consistent manner so that the long-range goals of the organization can be achieved. The challenge is to help those at all levels of the organization understand the long-range goals and how the short-range performance objectives are intermediate steps for accomplishing those goals.

Table 2.1 Levels and nature of planning in the agribusiness

Strategic Level	*Tactical Level*	*Operational Level*
Top Management	*Middle Management*	*Line Employees*
Very Flexible	Somewhat Flexible	Inflexible
Long-term	Intermediate-term	Immediate
Written Analyses	Written Reports	Unwritten
Complex, Detailed	Less Detail, Outlined	Simple
Broad	General	Very Specific

The planning process

Six steps in the planning process provide structure to the process and are designed to provide management with as much information as is available when developing the strategic or tactical plan. These six steps follow:

1. Gather facts and information that have a bearing on the situation.
2. Analyze what the situation is and what problems are involved.
3. Forecast future developments.
4. Set performance objectives, the benchmarks for achieving strategic goals.
5. Develop alternative courses of action and select those that are most suitable.
6. Develop a means of evaluating progress, and readjust the plan as the process unfolds.

Step 1: gather facts

Gathering facts and information is the first step of the planning process. Although it should be noted that information gathering is a recurring part of the process. Its place as a first step is easily justified, since adequate information must be available to formulate or synthesize a problem or opportunity. Fact gathering is subdivided into two parts: gathering sufficient information to identify the need for a plan in the first place and systematic gathering of specific facts needed to make the plan work once it has been developed. Two challenges can limit fact gathering. First, some managers tend to skip or minimize this step because of the difficulty of gathering data. Instead of planning, they resort to a "seat of the pants" or "gut-feel" philosophy, which reduces the likelihood of success. Second, a manager should not become so engrossed in fact gathering that inaction results.

Step 2: analyze the facts

The groundwork for developing a sound plan is provided during the process of **analyzing facts**. This process answers such questions as "Where are we?" and "How did we get here?" It helps pinpoint existing problems and opportunities, and provides the framework upon which to base successful decisions. An analysis of facts will prevent mistakes and allow for the most efficient use of the organization's resources.

Step 3: forecast change

Forecasting change is the third key element of good planning. The ability to determine what the future holds may be the highest form of management skill. As managers ascend the organizational ladder, the demands on their abilities in this area steadily increase. Forecasting becomes more difficult as the situation becomes broader, more complex, or for a longer time horizon. Forecasting is interrelated with the other five steps and it is a logical extension of analysis into a future time setting. Some say, "No one can predict the future in our business." While no one can be expected to predict accurately all future developments, this is hardly a good reason for not attempting to anticipate what the future might entail. Many failures that occur in forecasting result from sloppy, ambiguous, and generalized thinking. Other failures arise from a poor job of collecting facts. Forecasting change is not a guessing game; it is part of a disciplined approach to planning.

Step 4: set goals/performance objectives

The development of goals and/or performance objectives is the next step in the planning process. **Goals** are the specific quantitative or qualitative aims of the company or business group that provide direction and standards one can use to measure performance. Top management, boards of directors, and/or chief executives often develop these goals to help bring focus and specificity to the organization's mission (see above). The mission statement is the target toward which goals are aimed. In turn, goals are the targets toward which performance objectives are aimed. Well-stated goals should:

1.   Provide guides for the performance objectives and results of each unit or person
2.   Allow appraisal of the results contributed by each unit or person
3.   Contribute to successful overall organizational performance

Performance objectives are then set for specific units and/or individuals. They provide the performance targets at the unit and/or individual levels that are needed to accomplish the broader, longer-range strategic goals. Performance objectives are usually set for shorter time periods than strategic goals and usually are defined by measurable results. Note that all these processes are going on continuously during the planning process. Performance objectives cannot be set in a vacuum, but must be attainable. Therefore, performance objectives must be a consequence of the gathering and analyzing of relevant information and facts.

Some management specialists consider setting goals or performance objectives to be the first step in the planning process. In our discussion of strategic planning above, we started the strategic planning process by developing vision and mission statements. In a way these individuals are correct, but our approach to planning, accumulating, and evaluating information occurs before goal setting is part of the process of setting performance objectives. In practice, many of these steps occur simultaneously—data may be used to develop an initial set of goals which leads to a need for more data, which requires refining the goals and so on. The Wheel of Management in Figure 2.1 suggests that the planning process is a continual loop.

Step 5: develop alternatives

After the performance objectives have been set, agribusiness managers must explore different ways of getting wherever they want to go by **developing alternative** courses of action. Here again the relationship between performance objectives and results can be seen. The results achieved depend upon the alternative activities selected to meet the objectives. Alternatives must be weighed, evaluated, and tested in the light of the agribusiness' resources.

Imagination is crucial since new ways and/or new paths may be the key to success. It is important in this step to be creative, yet practical, in generating alternatives. The conditions surrounding each decision must be carefully considered. For example, a firm might believe that equipping its sales representatives with smart phones and training them in the use of a new database management package might be the best alternative to improve the productivity of the sales force. However, the firm's budget situation may mean that only one-third of the sales representatives can get new phones, or there may be poor wireless coverage in parts of the sales territory. So, the firm may need to look for other (low cost) options to boost sales performance to complement the use of smart phones and new software.

Step 6: evaluate results

Management specialists have found monitoring progress to be a high priority in planning. Carefully reviewing, assessing, or **evaluating results** shows whether the plan is on course and allows both the analysis of new information and the discovery of new opportunities. Evaluation cannot be left to chance. It must be incorporated into the planning process, since a plan is only good so long as the situation remains unchanged. An evaluation also reveals whether results met performance objectives or where the results fell short or overshot objectives. Evaluation also points out weaknesses in plans and programs so that those portions that are ineffective can be changed. In a fast-changing world, continuous evaluation is essential to planning success. Evaluation also triggers the next round of planning.

Organizing

People working effectively towards accomplishing the company's goals; these are objectives of every manager—no matter what industry, function, or organization. There must be a structure in place to make it possible for people to work effectively toward accomplishing goals. The management task of organizing provides that structure or framework in which to operate. **Organizing** represents the systematic classification and grouping of human and other resources in a manner consistent with the firm's goals. The organizing process is important at each level of a company or firm. And, it is the manager's challenge to design an organizational structure that allow employees both to accomplish their own work, while simultaneously reaching the goals and objectives of the organization.

The organizing task occurs continuously throughout the life of the firm. Done effectively, this task helps management establish accountability for the results achieved; prevents "buck-passing" and confusion as to who is responsible; and details the nature and degree of authority given to each person as the activities of the firm are accomplished. This task is especially important in today's business environment in which many firms frequently restructure their operations. This restructuring may be the result of efforts to improve efficiency, reduce costs, or as the result of a merger or acquisition. The manager must develop an effective organizational structure before he or she can implement the strategies needed to achieve the goals developed in the planning task. Organizing involves:

- Setting up the organizational structure
- Determining the jobs to be done
- Defining lines of authority and responsibility
- Establishing relationships within the organization

Until all employees understand their relationships to other employees and to the agribusiness as a whole, cooperation, teamwork, and coordinated action remain impossible to achieve. If members of a band fail to understand their connection to the whole, discord rather than harmony will result. Thus, as part of the organizing task, the agribusiness manager must see to it that each employee has a clearly defined role, and that when the employee accomplishes his or her goal, the goals for the organization are furthered.

For example, the overall sales goal for a firm can be broken down to performance objectives for regions or divisions and ultimately individual sales representatives. An example is provided in Figure 2.2. The planning process in this seed company is structured as described above, with all levels of the organization involved in planning. However, as indicated

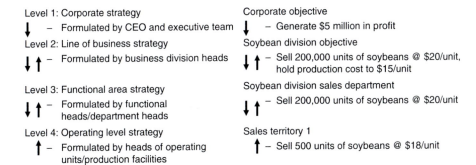

Level 1: Corporate strategy
 ↓   – Formulated by CEO and executive team
Level 2: Line of business strategy
 ↓ ↑ – Formulated by business division heads

Level 3: Functional area strategy
 ↓ ↑ – Formulated by functional
       heads/department heads
Level 4: Operating level strategy
 ↑   – Formulated by heads of operating
       units/production facilities

Corporate objective
 ↓   – Generate $5 million in profit
Soybean division objective
 ↓ ↑ – Sell 200,000 units of soybeans @ $20/unit,
       hold production cost to $15/unit
Soybean division sales department
 ↓ ↑ – Sell 200,000 units of soybeans @ $20/unit

Sales territory 1
 ↑   – Sell 500 units of soybeans @ $18/unit

Figure 2.2 Levels of planning and goals for seed company

earlier, the scope of that planning will become more focused as we move from the CEO to the operating level. Likewise, the scope of the goals will become more focused as we move down the organization. In terms of results, the flow is from bottom to top—if Sales Territory 1 achieves the goal of selling 500 units of soybeans at $18/unit, this helps the Soybean Division Sales Department achieve its goal, which helps the Soybean Division, etc. In the end, accomplishment of each person's sales objective contributes directly to the accomplishment of the firm's strategic goal.

Organizational structure

An **organizational structure** is the framework of a company. It provides the beams, braces, and supports to which the appropriate "building materials" are attached. Different jobs are connected to different parts of the whole framework. It is the formal framework by which jobs are grouped, coordinated, and further defined. Whether they are called groups, departments, or teams, coordinated communication and cooperation among work groups is essential. Consider the Carlson Seed Company. The family run seed business has a research group headed by Michael, a plant breeder. Michael's research group is deeply involved in developing a particular early season, stacked-trait soybean variety.

Paul heads the production group of this small company. While Paul and his staff may not necessarily be interested in the specifics of what the research group is coming up with on the genetic level, it is essential they understand what development of this particular early season soybean variety means to their production efforts. Paul realizes the importance of knowing what else is going on in their business. As a savvy production manager, he realizes that getting this variety ready for sale may mean juggling their current people resources—what time of year to have extra workers available, which projects people work on. It may mean that production juggles mechanical resources, such as changing bagging processes or movement through the dryer system. It may mean devoting more acreage to producing seed—which may displace production of some other product, and on and on it goes.

Even though the production department may not have anything to do with the ongoing genetic research, it does benefit them, other departments, and the company in general to understand the organizational structure, and the goals within that structure. A working knowledge of the organizational structure is essential to managers if they are to put plans into action.

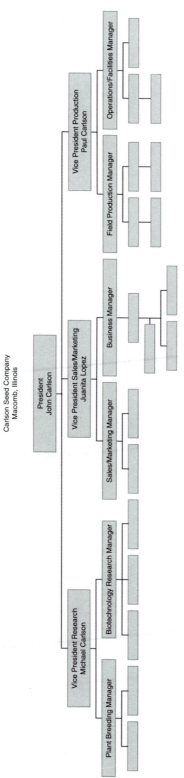

Figure 2.3 Organizational chart for Carlson seed company

An organizational structure exists in all businesses. It might be argued that even a one-person agribusiness has an organizational structure, with one person wearing many organizational hats. Organizing, then, involves formalizing a plan to show the interrelationships of each job and each individual within the organization (Figure 2.3). Such an organizational structure clarifies who reports to whom. It helps clarify who has responsibilities for specific tasks. An organizational structure also helps clarify who has authority for specific decisions. Finally, for new employees, an organizational chart can point to potential career paths within the company.

An **organizational chart** shows the formal organizational structure of a company. It helps capture some important ideas including division of labor, chain of command, bureaucracy, and organizational design.

The **division of labor** is the manner in which jobs are broken into components and then are assigned to members or groups. The objective is to accomplish more by delegating specific tasks to groups or individual who use specialized equipment and training, as well as a learning curve effect to successfully and efficiently accomplish more than can be done by one alone.

Chain of command is illustrated in organizational structure by the authority – responsibility relationships or links between managers and those they supervise. This continuum exists throughout the company. The chain of command should be clear so employees know to whom they report and are accountable.

Bureaucracy is a word with many negative connotations in today's vernacular. However, bureaucracy was developed as a highly specialized organization structure in which work is divided into specific categories and carried out by special departments. A strict set of guidelines determines the course of activities to ensure predictability and reduce risk. A bureaucracy is a tightly run, unyielding organizational structure. This organizational structure does work well for some types of businesses. However, given the variability and unpredictability of the weather and other uncontrollable circumstances, many food and agribusinesses do not operate under this form of organizational structure, and go to lengths to take bureaucracy out of their internal processes.

Directing

Directing is guiding the efforts of others toward achieving a common goal. It is accomplished by:

- Selecting, allocating, and training personnel
- Staffing positions
- Assigning duties and responsibilities
- Establishing the results to be achieved
- Creating the desire for success
- Seeing that the job is done and done properly

Directing involves leading, supervising, motivating, delegating, and evaluating those whom you manage. Managers are directing when they see to it that the efforts of each individual are focused on accomplishing the common goals of the organization. Leading is at the very heart of the management process and is founded on a good organizational plan or structure that provides for responsibility, authority, and evaluation.

The task of direction may be described as the task of making the organization take on life, of creating the conditions that make for interest in the job, vigor of action, imaginative thinking, and continuous teamwork. This goal is one that cannot be reached by magic formulas. Its achievement rests in large measure upon the leadership qualities exhibited by the manager.

The manager as leader

In the past, leadership was treated as simply a part of management, but today firms view management and leadership differently. The manager's duties include efforts to perform the various management tasks and functions. In contrast, a leader influences the attitudes and behavior of followers and motivates them to do their best work. The increasing importance of leadership in today's business environment requires that we explore it in more detail.

Besides providing instructions on how to complete a task and information on the desired results, leadership also provides incentives to complete that task correctly and in a timely manner. So an important aspect of leadership is the motivation of employees. Part of motivation is creating a vision for the organization or the group that inspires the members. Another method used to motivate employees is to delegate authority by assigning employees more responsibility, which encourages employees to take more pride in their jobs and raise their self-esteem. Of course, such assignments should be combined with incentives tied to the organizations' goals and the individuals' performance objectives as determined in the planning task. Leadership is also the process by which the manager attempts to unleash each person's individual potential, once again, as a contribution toward organizational success. Leaders recognize that the results of a person's activities count for more than the activities themselves.

Finally, for managers to be effective leaders they need initiative, which is the willingness to take action. Some managers who recognize the need for changes are unwilling to take action because making changes takes more effort than living with the status quo.

Other directing roles

The manager must also interpret programs, plans, policies, procedures, and practices within the organization. Every department, division, or organization must have a court of last resort. Human nature is such that even those with the best intentions may differ in their interpretations of facts or information. In such cases, it is the manager's task to deliver this interpretation—to become, in effect, the Supreme Court for those who are being supervised. By quickly resolving a difference between two individuals, the manager can help both of them return to their respective task at hand.

Part of the manager's directing task involves the encouragement of employees' growth as individuals. An individual who is developing new skills and expertise becomes more productive for the agribusiness, as well as for himself or herself. Special provisions for growth in responsibility should be built into the opportunities presented by any job, and job challenge must be maintained for the individual. Promotion policies should be clear, and all concerned should understand them. Each employee's performance should be appraised regularly and evaluated for the unique contributions that the employee can make to the organization.

The good manager encourages employees to discover hidden talents by stimulating them through varied assignments that offer continually increasing challenges and opportunities.

A manager should not hesitate to provide encouragement for more formalized training in courses, workshops, seminars, educational meetings, and the like. Formal education can benefit both the organization and the employee. A good manager maintains a regular schedule of interaction with employees. Application of this technique acquaints the manager with the problems and personalities of employees. Such contact also enables the manager to develop an awareness of each employee's strengths and weaknesses. This, in turn, will help the employee to develop a confidence in "the boss." Both the manager and the employee will be sensitive to issues as they unfold, helping to reduce the chance of unpleasant surprises.

Shaping the work climate

Creating a work climate for success helps a manager improve employee efforts to the point where employees approach their potential. Without a healthy work climate, none of the skills and principles of management can flower and bear fruit. Principles used to create the right work climate include:

1. Set a good example.
2. Conscientiously seek participation.
3. Be goals- and results-centered.
4. Give credit and blame as needed: credit in public, blame in private.
5. Be fair, consistent, and honest.
6. Inspire confidence and lend encouragement.

Good managers know how to use these principles to create a productive working climate. One key to a productive work climate is the free flow of communication. The agribusiness manager is responsible for designing and implementing the communications process within a given area of responsibility. Free flow of communication means communications must flow not only downward (from management to subordinates), but also upward (from subordinates to managers) and laterally (at the same level) to be effective. Too often managers depend almost exclusively on downward communications and then wonder why goals, policies, and procedures are misunderstood or not implemented.

Successful communications require feedback. Feedback allows the manager to determine whether understanding has indeed occurred. It also allows the good ideas and potential contributions of each employee to be part of the mix of collective wisdom and knowledge found in the organization. The manager must provide the opportunity for this feedback and involvement through a carefully designed communications process involving committees, meetings, memos, emails, text messages, and individual contacts.

Policies, procedures, practices

As managers complete the directing task, they typically develop guidelines or policies for how tasks should be completed. **Policies** are used to guide the thinking process during planning and decision-making. A policy sets the boundaries within which an agribusiness employee can exert individual creativity. Policies make it unnecessary for subordinates to constantly get approval for plans and decisions with top management. For example, one farm equipment dealer instituted a policy that the general manager must approve all purchases that totaled $500 or more. The purpose of this policy was to protect the business against unexpected large cash outlays. At the same time, it gave the employee the discretion to use their judgment.

Policies are best adapted to recurring problems in areas that are vital to achieving the long-range goals of the agribusiness. Although policies are closely tied to goals, they are not goals. Because they are not goals, policies should never be used to restrict managers as they make decisions about long-range, complex problem situations.

A **procedure** is a step-by-step guide to implement a policy for a specific activity or function. In many cases, there is a definite need to define a precise course of action. A procedure should not, in most cases, be applied to complex tasks of a long-range nature.

When the aforementioned farm equipment dealer sought to implement its new purchasing policy, the procedure involved called for an employee to fill out a requisition form, submit it to the general manager for approval, and then send it to the purchasing director. Procedures work best when they are applied to routine and recurring tasks of a relatively simple nature that require control. Both policies and procedures are of tremendous value to the new or newly promoted employee who is learning on the job. They also ensure uniform performance by all employees and prevent unauthorized actions.

Practices represent what is actually done in the agribusiness, and they may conflict with policies and procedures. Managers have to be sure that policies make sense, are relevant, and are enforced, in order for them to become widespread practices. If employees of the farm equipment dealer routinely ignore the policy and procedure regarding the limits on spending,

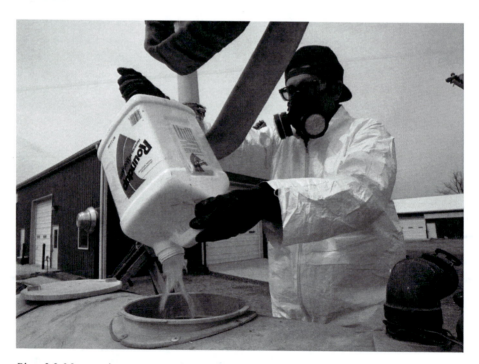

Plate 2.2 Man pouring crop protection products
Controlling involves careful monitoring and evaluation of a firm's business and operating activities. Photo courtesy of USDA Natural Resources Conservation Service.

the store may find itself in a serious cash bind. A course of action established on a recurring basis can become a practice by tradition or habit more than anything else. The status of routine practices can become as important as that of either formal policies or procedures, and even more difficult to change, so the agribusiness manager must ensure that practices coincide with policies and procedures. Conversely, managers should be aware of business practices as they institute new policies and procedures.

Controlling

The **controlling task** represents the monitoring and evaluation of activities. To evaluate activities, managers should measure performance and compare it against the standards and expectations they set. In essence, the controlling task assesses whether the goals and performance objectives developed within the planning task are achieved.

Control in management includes an information system that monitors plans and processes to ensure that they are meeting predetermined goals, and sounds a warning when necessary so that remedial action can be taken. If all people were perfect and their work without flaw, there would be no need for controls. Everything would come out according to plan. But what actually happens may not be what was expected. All people make mistakes; they forget, they fail to take action, they lose their tempers, and they behave, in short, like normal human beings. In addition, even when people do exactly what they are supposed to do, the market, the competition, the weather, the equipment, etc. may not cooperate.

Control is complementary to the other three tasks of management. It compensates for the misjudgments, the unexpected, and the impact of change. Proper controls offer the organization the necessary information and time to correct programs and plans that have gone astray. They should also indicate the means of correcting deficiencies. Control requires meaningful information and knowledge, and not that which is outmoded or not germane to meeting organizational goals. Much valuable time can be squandered or wasted by a control program unless a careful check of its real value is made periodically.

If the need for control information is not real, frustration, disrespect, and inaccuracy are likely to result. Employees cannot respect a control program that is misused by management. Management can consume valuable time reviewing useless control data, or it can fail to separate the relevant from the irrelevant, with poor performance as the consequence.

All business activities produce results. These results should be matched carefully to well-conceived objectives that aim toward organizational goals. One of the most important purposes of control is to evaluate the progress being made toward organizational goals. A good example of this type of control is found in the budget or forecast comparison. Is one over or under the budget? Are forecasts of sales and expenses in line with predictions? The information or control required in all areas must be based on predetermined, written goals. Only then can the agribusiness manager tell whether the reality matches the plans through which success is sought.

Management by exception

An important management technique called **management by exception** holds the basic premise that managers should not spend time on management areas that are progressing according to plan. Rather, they should focus their efforts on areas in which everything is not progressing as it should. If sales are in line with the forecast, the manager can devote the bulk of his or her efforts to other areas, such as production, personnel, costs, and expansion. Consider this example.

The sales forecasts for the Phoenix Fertilizer Company are given in Figure 2.4. Sales are divided into dry and liquid fertilizer. The sales forecast is the anticipated or predetermined course of action, i.e., the objective, of the marketing department. Sales objectives are essential in keeping the sales force focused and in allowing key executives to make remedial decisions related to sales performance, should the agribusiness deviate from its established objectives.

This annual sales forecast for fertilizer was developed by combining all of the individual sales representative's estimates of sales for the coming year. Then the marketing manager met with other key individuals, such as the executive vice president, production vice president, new products manager, and purchasing director, to determine whether anticipated input (costs) matched anticipated output (revenue). The committee determined that the control program for sales would be reported on a component basis—that is, by dry and liquid fertilizer sales—and on a monthly basis, with a quarterly review of other specific sales items to be made as a supplement to the overall sales control program. The committee also decided to report the sales in tons because this was the most meaningful measure for all concerned.

The executive vice president and controller agreed that the information needed could be secured from company records. They began with lasts year's sales forecast, actual sales from last year, and current customer sales invoicing. The office manager would prepare the monthly control information report, and it would be shared with all employees of the company, as well as with the company's banker. The sales manager was given the principal responsibility for accomplishing the objectives of the control program.

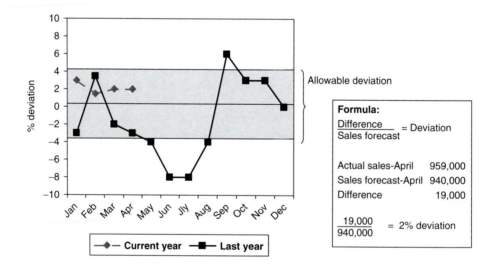

Sales forecast - Current year (1000 tons)

	Jan	Feb	Mar	Apr	May	Jun	Jly	Aug	Sep	Oct	Nov	Dec
Dry fertilizer	575	690	699	690	720	751	610	590	700	700	650	630
Liquid fertilizer	252	250	244	250	220	252	270	277	240	250	255	260
Total	827	940	943	940	940	1003	880	867	940	950	905	890

Figure 2.4 Management by exception graph for Phoenix fertilizer

Joseph Drake, the sales manager of Phoenix Fertilizer Company, decided to use a new approach for the control report: management by exception graphs instead of raw data. He had decided on this reporting technique for the following reasons:

1. It allows one to ignore those management areas where performance is on target, and to concentrate on problem areas instead.
2. It allows one to see at a glance the whole situation, and the comparative data are illustrated clearly as a graph.
3. It is simple and easy to prepare and is easily understood by anyone, even those unskilled in financial management.
4. It allows for a clearer interpretation of the many interrelated factors than raw data can provide.

To construct the management by exception graph, the first thing the committee had to do was to establish an allowable deviation. In terms of the sales forecast, allowable deviation means the amount by which actual sales could fall or rise above the sales forecast before management had to determine whether remedial action was needed. In the Phoenix Fertilizer Company, the team decided that sales could deviate from the forecast by 4 percent in either direction before remedial action would be taken (Figure 2.4). A deviation of more than 4 percent either below or above the sales forecast would affect such areas as inventory of raw and finished product, production scheduling, capital and cash positions, labor needs, advertising and promotion programs, and pricing policy. Each of these areas would have to be reviewed by the management team if sales deviated from the forecast by more than the allowable range. This, of course, is the major purpose of a control program: to sound an alarm for further study and action.

Once the allowable deviation was established, all that remained was designing the management by exception graph (Figure 2.4). At the bottom is Phoenix's sales forecast for the current year. A graph such as the one in Figure 2.4 could also show several different but related factors, such as total sales, last year's sales, dry sales, and liquid sales, through the use of different symbols or lines. For the sake of simplicity in illustrating the principles involved, only the deviation for total current and last year's sales are shown. And, last year's sales are figured as a deviation from last year's sales forecast, not from the current sales forecast. The shaded area is the allowable deviation from the sales forecast or goals. To the right of the graph are the formula and an example of how the deviations are calculated.

Joseph Drake remembered that last year several of Phoenix's competitors had suddenly lowered their prices in April, and that because Phoenix had not been alert enough, it had taken them several months to meet this challenge. As a result, many thousands of dollars of sales and consequent profits had been lost. Joseph was determined that this would not happen again. Phoenix had been forced to lower its prices substantially to recover lost customers and was now operating on a narrowing gross margin as cost increased, largely due to higher natural gas prices. Joseph knew that other manufacturers were feeling the same pinch, but each had to fight for market share to meet overhead costs.

To illustrate the value of the management by exception approach assume that September sales were up by 6 percent, or 2 percent over the allowable deviation. The marketing department would have immediately taken a careful survey of competitors' prices. Perhaps some major competitors were trying to adjust prices upward to meet increased cost. If this were true, Phoenix would have several alternatives. Phoenix could increase its price, thereby widening its gross margin and profits, but maintaining the same relative market share. Or it could hold prices as competitors increased theirs, to increase the volume of sales and market share, thereby causing increased turnover and increased profits. Plant capacity, growth objectives, available funds, and dealer reaction would all play a part in the final decision. Good financial records and proper analysis of them would also be essential to the final decision.

Many of the tools that the agribusiness manager would need in order to obtain the information and knowledge necessary to sound decision-making will be developed in later chapters, but the final decision will still be somewhat subjective in nature. It will be made by an individual or a team of individuals and will involve the ability to weave the facts together into a complex whole using innate knowledge and experience, using analytic tools where possible, making the best educated decision, and being willing to take the responsibility for the decision.

Major areas of management responsibilities

Each of the key tasks of management—planning, organizing, directing, and controlling—is used in managing the four major functions of an agribusiness. The management functions are implemented through the use of the various skills, principles, and tools that have become part of the professional agribusiness manager's knowledge and ability. To be successful, the agribusiness manager must be able to execute the four tasks for each of the four basic functions of the agribusiness; that is, financial management and planning, marketing and selling, supply chain management, and personnel or human resources management. It is important to note that managing the financial function of an agribusiness involves planning, organizing, directing, and controlling. The same holds for the other three functions. The balance of this book is built around the four basic functions of the agribusiness, and is designed to help students acquire the know-how of the professional agribusiness manager.

Summary

Management is the process of achieving desired results with the resources available. A key to successful management is accepting responsibility for leadership and making business decisions through the skillful application of management principles. Management of the agricultural business is unique because of the biological nature of production, the importance of food to people, the seasonality of food and agricultural markets, and the perishablility of agricultural products, among other reasons.

The management process is often divided into four tasks: planning, organizing, directing, and controlling. Planning is determining a course of action to accomplish stated goals; organizing is fitting people and resources together in the most effective way; directing pertains to supervising and motivating people; and the controlling task monitors performance and makes adjustments to stay on purpose. Each of these is a necessary ingredient for accomplishing the established organizational goals.

Discussion questions

1. Define management in your own words. What are the differences in the four tasks of management and the four functions of an agribusiness?
2. Pick any food or agribusiness firm. Compare this firm and the market it serves to the list of distinctive features of the food and agribusiness markets. Which of these features seem to be most important for the firm you have chosen?

3. How and why does planning change as one progresses up the organizational ladder?
4. Describe the steps in the planning process. Using these steps, develop a plan for obtaining a summer internship with a food or agribusiness firm.
5. What are the most important components of the agribusiness manager's role as director?
6. What are the advantages of using the management by exception approach to control programs?
7. Assume that Phoenix Fertilizer reported actual sales of 1,006 and 1,083 thousand tons for May and June of the current year. Using these data, add two months to the Phoenix management by exception graph. Interpret the deviations for these two months. What actions might be suggested by these results?

Case study: Hart Cherry Cooperative

The Hart Cherry Cooperative was organized two years ago to pit and freeze member-farmers' cherries. The cooperative is experiencing difficulty in keeping grower-members' cherries separate. Most of the cherries are harvested mechanically by shaking them from the trees. They are placed in pallet tanks by the grower and brought into the plant for processing. The cooperative owns all the pallet tanks. When the grower unloads the pallet tanks on the concrete pad, the cherries have to be cooled with running cold water until they are ready for processing. There is considerable variation in quality among the loads of cherries brought in

Plate 2.3 Cherries
Accurate identification of each grower's cherry crop is a challenge for Hart Cherry Cooperative.
Photo courtesy of USDA Natural Conservation Service.

by members. Some loads have large quantities of small twigs and leaves in them, some are rotten or soft, and some have other undesirable qualities.

This is the first year that the cooperative has owned all the pallet tanks. The cooperative board decided that it was best for the cooperative to own them, since growers had been continually taking other growers' pallet tanks whenever their own were unavailable. The policy of the cooperative board and management is that each grower's cherries must be identified so that growers can be paid separately, on the basis of the quantity and quality of their product.

The practice as it had developed this year was for the members to unload their pallets onto the pad. Each member was then supposed to put a name card on each pallet. The problem was that sometimes the growers' new, inexperienced, or uncaring truck drivers were failing to put cards on, cards were falling off, or sometimes two or more cards were on the same pallet.

Questions

1. Develop a procedure that will help solve the problem by ensuring that each grower's cherries are properly identified.
2. Develop a plan to ensure the procedure you develop will be carried out in practice. Include in your plan how the procedure will be communicated to both employees and grower-members. Include in your plan steps to receive feedback on the procedure from both employees and grower-members.

3 Economics for agribusiness managers

Objectives

- Explain the differences between accounting and economic profit
- Understand how supply and demand interact to determine market equilibrium
- Learn what causes market equilibrium to shift
- Explain how agribusiness managers use price, income, and cross price elasticity of demand

Introduction

In the first two chapters, we outlined the importance of the agribusiness sector and discussed what it means to be a manager. It is also important to understand that agribusiness firms operate within a broader economic environment. To be effective decision-makers, agribusiness managers must understand the economics of the world in which they operate. Economic principles are useful to predict business trends and serve as the basis for many management decisions. The study of economics includes two different areas: macroeconomics and microeconomics.

Macroeconomics focuses on the "big picture" view of the economic system. If you have taken a course in macroeconomics, you have studied topics like national income, gross domestic product, inflation, unemployment, and interest rates. The Federal Reserve System, or "the Fed," can affect the economy by changing monetary policy, which focuses on interest rates and the supply of money to the economy. Likewise, Congress can impact the economic system through fiscal policy, which includes government spending and taxing programs.

Agribusinesses are greatly affected by macroeconomics because global demand for various food and fiber products is constantly changing. General economic conditions are influenced by such factors as weather, government policies, and international developments. Macroeconomics is concerned with how the different elements of the total economy interact. An individual firm has relatively little impact on the total economy. However, skill at anticipating and interpreting the macroeconomic environment is critical to the success of any agribusiness manager.

For example, the Fed may use monetary policy to raise interest rates to fight inflation. Since interest rates have an important impact on purchases of tractors, combines, and other farm machinery, so farm equipment manufacturers pay close attention to interest rates. Food consumption patterns are also affected by the economy's health. In a boom period, more expensive, luxury food items may sell well. However, during a recession, food purchasing habits may shift as incomes fall. Managers of food companies follow such developments very closely.

Microeconomics is the application of basic economic principles to decisions within the firm. Every agribusiness faces tough questions when it comes to allocating its limited resources. Managers must decide the best way to use physical, human, and financial resources in the production and marketing of goods and services to meet customers' needs and generate a profit. Tools of economic analysis are essential to the manager who must make daily business decisions. In fact, most of the management tools developed in this book are based on fundamental microeconomic concepts.

The successful agribusiness manager must assemble a variety of different types of information, and then use that information effectively to make the best possible decisions for the short- and long-run financial health of the firm. A few years ago, if a firm made less profit, it might mean the firm's management had used poor judgment. In today's extremely competitive marketplace, a poor decision may lead to failure of the firm.

Thus, **economics** studies how individuals, firms, and society choose to combine scarce resources (land, labor, capital, and management) to satisfy unlimited wants and best meet consumer needs. These four scarce resources are often referred to as the **factors of production**, each of which must receive a payment or return. For example, labor is paid a wage, while management typically receives a salary. Likewise, returns to land are often referred to as rent and returns to capital are represented by interest payments. The way market forces work to allocate returns to these factors is at the heart of a capitalistic economy.

Our book assumes that most students have some understanding of economics (although a review of your microeconomics may prove helpful). Yet many students find economic concepts difficult to understand. In part, this is due to examples used in economic classes; just what is a widget? In part, it arises because of confusing terminology and jargon. For example, inputs, factors of production, and resources all refer to the same thing.

As such, the goal of this chapter is not to review a student's knowledge of economics. Rather, in Chapter 2 we highlighted the importance of gathering information and facts when making decisions. A professional manager understands and uses economic concepts to interpret information, both to assess the broader marketplace, and to improve the effectiveness of their decision-making. Thus, in this chapter we will look at three key economic concepts and explain their relevance for agribusiness managers. We consider profit, supply and demand, market equilibrium, price, income, and cross price elasticities.

Profit

Profit is a term used by both accountants and economists. However, accounting profit and economic profit are different. The accountant looks at **accounting profit** as the net income that remains after all actual, measurable costs are subtracted from total revenue. Accounting profit is used as a performance measure about firm success. The economist agrees with the accountant that actual costs must be considered. Economists, however, go further to calculate **economic profit** by also examining the opportunity costs of alternative uses for resources within the firm. As such, economic profit provides insights about the long-run potential for an industry. If economic profits are positive, more firms will enter. If economic profits are negative, some firms will choose to exit the market to find more appealing (i.e., profitable) ventures. Thus, the key to understanding the difference between accounting and economic profit begins by classifying costs as being explicit or implicit.

An explicit cost involves payments made to suppliers of resources, such as land, labor, materials, fuel, and the like. Explicit costs are usually measured by an accountant. But firms do not pay for all resources used in production. For example, a farmer does not write a rent check to himself or herself for land that they own. A new food business may not have to pay property taxes for five years as part of an economic development incentive provided by the county government. Since there was no cash outlay for use of the resource, economists access an implicit cost associated with that use.

Since the accountant cannot precisely measure the expenditure of the opportunity cost, they do consider it in the calculation of accounting profit. Economists force an examination of both explicit and implicit costs. The economist feels in the long run all costs must be considered to analyze alternative courses of action. An example can clarify.

Susan Lambert owns and operates her own landscaping firm. She is a 31-year-old, with a college degree, and she has been quite satisfied with her business. Susan's business operates in a warehouse owned by her parents. She currently has $400,000 of her own money invested in the business. Susan draws an annual salary of $35,000. They are letting her use the building rent free as she gets her business started. Her parents could earn $25,000 if they rented it to someone else.

Last year her business had total revenues of $335,000 (Table 3.1). She gave her accountant various receipts for payments for plants and materials, labor, utilities, taxes and insurance, and her draw for salary. Since the accountant can measure all of these costs, the total explicit costs were calculated to be $260,000. Accounting profit is then the total revenue of $335,000 minus explicit costs of $260,000, equaling $75,000.

Plate 3.1 Landscaping
Determining the optimal use of specific inputs is an important decision for agribusiness managers.
Photo courtesy of USDA Natural Resources Conservation Service.

Table 3.1 Susan Lambert's accounting and economic profit

Item	Typical Year		Bad Year	
	Subtotal ($)	Total ($)	Subtotal ($)	Total ($)
Total revenues		335,000		320,000
Plants and materials	150,000		150,000	
Labor	40,000		40,000	
Utilities	25,000		25,000	
Taxes and insurance	10,000		10,000	
Draw of salary	35,000		35,000	
Total explicit costs		*260,000*		*260,000*
Accounting profit		75,000		60,000
Foregone interest	32,000		32,000	
Unrealized rent	25,000		25,000	
Foregone income	15,000		30,000	
Total implicit costs		*72,000*		*87,000*
Economic profit		3,000		(27,000)

Starting with her accounting profit of $75,000, Susan must now consider the appropriate implicit costs involved in her decision to operate her business. This requires determining what alternative uses or opportunity costs there are for Susan's time, the cost of the building provided by her parents, and her investment in the business.

One essential resource that she contributes to the firm is her own time and talent. Susan figures that she could sell her business and go to work for someone else for a salary of $50,000 annually, given her experience and contacts, or $15,000 more than she paid herself last year. This opportunity cost takes into account Susan's time and management abilities. Of course, some entrepreneurs place a non-monetary value on being their own boss. Second, eventually she will have to pay the rental cost of the building. Either her parents will sell it to someone else (who will expect $25,000 in rent) or she will inherit the property (and be responsible for expenses or she could earn $25,000 by renting it to someone else). Finally, Susan must consider the opportunity costs of her own investment of $400,000 in the business. What are some alternative uses for this investment? Perhaps she could put it into a mutual fund account earning an average of 8 percent or buy government bonds at 5 percent. The opportunity costs would be 8 percent of $400,000 or $32,000 each year, because that is the most profitable alternative use for Susan's money.

Thus, Susan's total implicit costs are $72,000 for foregone interest, unrealized rent, and foregone income (Table 3.1). Her economic profit is $3,000, or the accounting profit of $75,000 less the implicit costs of $72,000. Her economic profit represents the real financial reward that Susan received for risking her own resources in the business. As long as this amount is positive, it suggests that the decision to commit resources to this business is a good one. Given that she has been fully compensated for her time, the $3,000 of economic profit can be viewed as a reward over and above what she needs to receive to be in this business.

But what happens when Susan has a bad year; Table 3.1 now shows an accounting profit of only $60,000 and she is offered a job at Home Depot for $65,000? Economic profit in this situation becomes negative ($60,000 – $25,000 – $32,000 – $30,000 = –$27,000). This indicates that, had it been pursued, the (lost) opportunity to invest her capital in mutual funds

Plate 3.2 Saleslady
Agribusiness managers must determine how to allocate resources such as sales time and effort across competing enterprises. Photo courtesy of USDA.

and to take the new job would have yielded higher returns than the landscaping business. Even though the accounting profit would still be positive, the negative economic profit clearly indicates problems. Should this trend continue for a few years, it would make sense for Susan to sell out, unless she feels that the freedom and psychological rewards from running her own business offset the negative economic profit.

Before investing sums of money in specific alternatives, managers must be able to estimate opportunity costs. This estimate helps managers to decide whether any given use for their resources of time and money is the very best opportunity available. However, some shortcomings of the economic profit concept should be recognized.

First, many of the "imputed" values for implicit costs in reality are hard to estimate. In the case of Susan Lambert, what interest figure will yield the "correct" opportunity cost for the situation? For some people the 8 percent rate will apply, but other investors have the know-how and time to research other possibilities and invest at rates of 12 percent or higher. The same argument applies to the salary figure specified: this may or may not be realistic, depending on the situation.

Second, a potentially faulty assumption is made that employment in industry would be currently available for Susan. Furthermore, a change in employment might cause personal or family problems. Weighing adjustments of this kind, in dollar terms, can be extremely difficult if not impossible. It also explains why accountants do not try to measure them.

Finally, different types of investments may be difficult to directly compare with one another in a way that will satisfy the opportunity cost concept. For example, investment in blue-chip or high-quality stocks cannot be directly compared with speculative ventures such as investing in futures and options funds, since the two types of investments involve two completely different classes of risk. Having raised these limitations of the implicit cost idea, it is also clear that this concept is a powerful one for managers making resource allocation decisions.

In a free market system, economic profits should not exist. The theory goes that other firms will be attracted into markets earning economic profit. Once this happens, production will increase, prices will drop, and economic profits will fall to zero. But in the real world economic profits do exist. And the possibility of earning economic profit is the motivating force behind most business decisions.

There are four explanations for economic profit in our market economy. First, profit is the reward for taking a risk in a business. When a private property owner invests personal resources in a business project, there are no guarantees of a return to this investment. The greater the risk involved, the greater the potential profit for successful ventures, if the venture is to attract any investors. Second, profits result from the control of scarce resources. In the U.S. economic system, most property is owned and controlled by private citizens. If a citizen owns a resource that others want, the others will bid the price up, which generates a profit for its owner. The greater the demand for a resource, the higher its price will be, and the greater the profit reward to its owners. Third, profits exist because some people have access to information that is not widespread. Resource owners who have special knowledge, such as secret processes or formulas, can use this information exclusively and can thereby maintain significant advantages over their competition. The concept of patents and copy-rights evolved as part of a formal attempt to encourage creativity by ensuring that the creator profits from his or her ideas. Fourth, profits exist simply because some businesses are managed more effectively than others. The managers of such businesses are often creative planners and thinkers whose day-to-day organizations are extremely efficient. The reward for doing the job well often results in economic profit.

The profit motive is the "spark plug" of a free market economic system. The prospect of earning and keeping economic profit serves as the incentive for creativity and efficiency among people. It stimulates risky ventures and drives people to develop ways of cutting costs and improving techniques, always in an effort to satisfy consumers' desires.

The economics of markets

Supply and demand, and the resulting market equilibrium price and quantity, are among the most fundamental economic concepts. Supply is defined as the quantities that sellers are willing and able to place on the market at different prices during a particular time period. The law of supply reflects a direct relationship between price and quantity, which means sellers are willing to provide more products for sale in the market as prices increase.

The buyer or consumer side of the market is represented by the demand curve. **Demand** is the quantity that consumers are willing and able to buy in the market at various prices during a particular time period. As with supply, we are concerned with a price–quantity relationship. The law of demand finds an inverse relationship between price and quantity, or buyers are willing to purchase less as price increases.

The supply and demand relationship can be described in three ways. To illustrate, assume that a food manufacturer sells an organic gluten-free breakfast cereal to grocers, with prices ranging from $20 to $40 per case. From market research, they have data on how many cases will be sold per month at the different prices. Supply and demand can be portrayed as a table of prices and quantities called a demand and a supply schedule (Table 3.2). For each price, demand is the total quantity sold, while the total quantity produced represents what a firm will supply.

Second, supply and demand is commonly shown graphically, as in Figure 3.1. Third, the supply and demand curves from Figure 3.1 can also be expressed as an algebraic function of prices and quantities, or

(1) $P = \alpha_s + \beta_s Q_s$

(2) $P = \alpha_D - \beta_D Q_D$

where:

Q_s is quantity supplied,

Q_D is quantity demanded,

P = price, and α and β are parameters that indicate the relationship between

the variables P and Q.

In this case, the upward sloping supply curve for equation (1) is $P = 5 + 1Q_S$, while the downward sloping demand curve for equation (2) is expressed as $P = 92.5 - 2.5Q_D$.

The process of price discovery means that market equilibrium for quantity and price is determined (or discovered) through transactions between producers and consumers. Only one price and quantity will "clear the market" at a given point in time. At equilibrium, everything that producers are willing to sell will equal everything that consumers want to buy. Thus, at market equilibrium the quantity demanded is simply equal to the quantity supplied. For example, the supply and demand curves intersect in Figure 3.1 at the price (P_1) of $30 and the quantity ($Q_1$) of 25,000 cases. Alternatively, simultaneously solving equations (1) and (2) gives the same result.

The textbook version of supply and demand is seldom encountered. Rather than having the theoretical supply and demand curves as in Figure 3.1, firms typically only have a handful of observations of prices and quantities. For example, a firm may have only three points of information (A, B, and C) instead of a complete supply curve, and no formal estimate of a demand curve (Figure 3.2). Yet even with only one point, the concepts of supply and demand are understood and used in decision-making.

Table 3.2 Demand and supply schedules for cereal

Price per case ($)	Total quantity sold (1,000 cases per month)	Total quantity produced (1,000 cases per month)
20.00	29	15
22.50	28	18
25.00	27	20
27.50	26	23
30.00	25	25
32.50	24	28
35.00	23	30
37.50	22	33
40.00	21	35

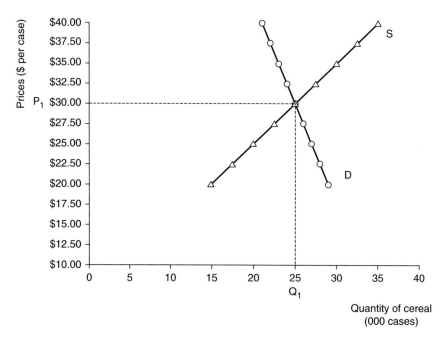

Figure 3.1 Supply and demand of cereal

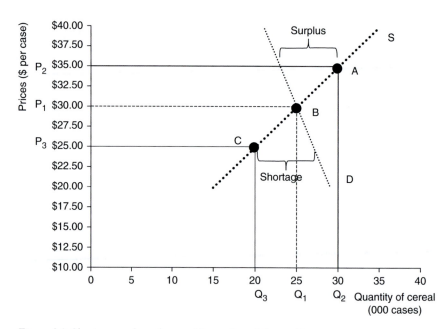

Figure 3.2 Shortages and surpluses with supply and demand

Assume that the firm starts at point A in Figure 3.2, intending to supply 30,000 cases of cereal at $35 per case. However, at that price, realized demand is only 23,000 cases. The result of charging a price that is too high is the firm would soon notice that inventory had started to accumulate. At point C, the firm encounters the opposite problem. If they set the price at $25 per case, they will face a shortage because demand is 27,000 when only 20,000 cases are supplied. Only when the firm operates near point B would one conclude that they must be near market equilibrium because they neither faced shortages nor are they building accumulations of inventory. Thus, inventory build-ups or persistent shortages are signs that markets are out of adjustment. Firms may raise or lower prices, or adjust production levels as they seek to move towards equilibrium. In short, firms clearly understand market equilibrium and constantly make choices with it in mind, even when they don't have complete supply and demand graphs.

The supply and demand curves presented in Figure 3.1 are drawn with the assumption of *ceteris paribus*, which means "with other things the same." However, several factors can act to shift an entire demand or supply curve. The smart agribusiness manager understands that the world is constantly changing. He or she makes it part of their job to read the business and trade press for their industry to stay informed about such changes. Farmers read trade magazines or follow web pages from publications like Farm Journal, Grainnet, or Precision Agriculture, while a grocer would read Supermarket News. Yet that is not enough; they both need to read a general business magazine or newspaper like the *Wall Street Journal* or *Bloomberg-BusinessWeek* to stay apprised of general business and economic trends. The key is to identify factors that might shift supply and demand curves, and then consider what that change means for equilibrium prices and quantities. Therefore, the best agribusiness managers anticipate the future by constantly looking for factors that might shift demand or supply curves in their respective industry.

The amount of product that a company is willing to supply depends heavily on marginal cost. Thus, agribusiness managers watch for changes in factors that affect their cost structure and the location of a supply curve. A change in one of these factors can cause a supply curve to shift to the right or to the left. The position of the supply curve in Figure 3.1 is fixed because of the assumption of *ceteris paribus*, meaning that the supply shifters are stable. When supply increases from S to S2, the entire curve shifts to the right (Figure 3.3). In this case, costs have fallen and the firm is now willing to provide a greater quantity (Q_2) at the same price (P_1). If costs rose, the supply curve would shift to the left to S3, and the firm would only be willing to provide Q_3.

Known as determinants of supply or simply supply shifters, six factors can shift a supply curve. Examples of how these factors cause the supply curve to shift include:

1. *Change in technology*: The development of new seed increases yield (shifts supply to the right).
2. *Change in the price of inputs*: Rising diesel fuel prices raise the cost of production (shifts supply to the left).
3. *Weather*: Poor weather conditions, such as a severe drought, cause crop shortages which shift the supply curve to the left, while favorable weather conditions lead to bumper crops and shifts the supply curve to the right.
4. *Changes in the price of other products that can be produced*: An increase in the price of corn causes farmers to shift acres to corn (shifts to the right) and away from other crops such as soybeans, wheat or cotton (shifts supply to the left).

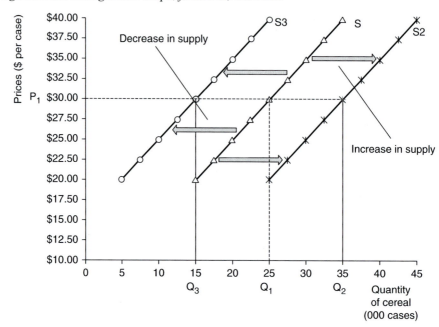

Figure 3.3 Shifts in supply curves

5. *Subsidies or taxes*: New taxes raise costs and shift the supply curve to the left. Subsidies to providers act to lower costs and shift supply curves to the right.
6. *Number of suppliers*: If fewer farms raise hogs, the supply will shift to the left. Conversely, if more farms decide to raise hogs, the supply curve will shift to the right.

A demand curve can also shift or change position over time. Demand increases when buyers are willing and able to buy more at the same price (Figure 3.4). When this occurs, the demand curve shifts to the right. Demand decreases when the opposite occurs: buyers purchase less at any given price. When the entire demand curve shifts, a change in demand has occurred.

There are five factors that can cause a demand curve to shift. The five determinants of demand are:

1. *Income*: As incomes rise, consumers can afford to buy more, and this shifts the demand curve to the right if the good is a normal good. A normal good means that as income increases, buyers desire more of the product.
2. *Tastes and preferences*: Changes in emotional and psychological wants can shift demand in either direction. For example, one set of consumers gets satisfaction from buying local foods, shifting demands for those foods to the right. Conversely, low-carb diets shifted demand to the left for pasta, breads, and potatoes. Tastes and preferences are heavily influenced by consumer psychological and emotional factors, and the media, and can be quite complex.
3. *Expectations*: When buyers expect the price to fall, they may postpone purchases, thereby causing the demand curve to shift to the left. If buyers expect prices to rise in the future, the demand curve can shift to the right.

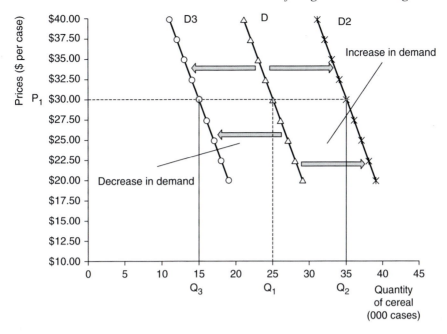

Figure 3.4 Shifts in demand curves

4. *Number of buyers*: Sheer increases in the population or number of buyers can shift the demand to the right. Another way to increase the number of buyers is to identify new markets for an existing product. For example, Roundup© was initially an herbicide for farm use. Today, a wide range of related Roundup© products are also available for home lawncare, while government agencies use it to eradicate illegal drugs or invasive species.
5. *Price of substitutes or complements*: A fall in the price of a close substitute product will shift the demand curve to the left, while a fall in the price of a complementary product will cause demand to shift to the right.

A skilled manager must be able to draw inferences from what he or she reads or hears. In practice, demand and supply are not static, but are in a constant state of fluctuation. At any point in time, "price" represents the market's best guess of the current supply–demand situation. Because conditions are based on buyers' and sellers' judgments of the actual supply and demand, the situation is highly volatile and can change both rapidly and frequently. Market prices for a great many agricultural products and supplies change throughout the day as managers obtain additional information. For example, a USDA crop report might indicate that soybean yields in Argentina are worse than expected because of drought. This weather shift would shift supply to the left, and means that soybean prices are likely to rise.

The supply and demand curves represent a theoretical relationship between price and quantity at a given point in time. The curves here have been illustrated by straight-line functions. This was done to facilitate explanation of the curves; but most supply and demand curves are actually curvilinear over some range of price and quantity, and may be quite complex. Agricultural economists spend considerable time and effort attempting to estimate demand and supply relationships for specific commodities in order to better understand the dynamics of markets.

Derived demand

The demand for most agricultural products is a **derived demand**. Derived demand is not based directly on general consumer demand, but rather on the need for a product that indirectly relates to consumer demand. For example, the agricultural producer's demand for fertilizer is derived from the consumer's demand for corn. When export demand for corn shifts because of economic growth in China, the price of corn increases. In turn, this also increases the demand for fertilizer, since higher corn prices encourage farmers to produce more corn. This is one reason why agribusiness managers and marketing experts are so concerned about general economic trends. Anything that significantly shifts consumer demand for agricultural products will also have an impact on the demand for farm inputs through the process of derived demand.

Elasticities of demand

Besides understanding shifts in supply and demand, agribusiness managers are also concerned with predicting how consumers will respond to changes in price, income or prices of other goods. Economists calculate three different types of **elasticity** as a measure of how quantity demanded responds to a change in price, income, or price of other goods, respectively. Understanding how to interpret the various types of elasticity allows agribusiness managers to make informed decisions. The most common type of elasticity is price elasticity of demand, or a measure of consumer response to price changes. Income elasticity of demand measures the response of quantity demanded to changes in income, while cross price elasticity of demand measures how the quantity demanded for one product responds to a price change in a different product.

Calculating price elasticity of demand

Price elasticity of demand reflects the percentage change in the quantity demanded when the price changes by 1 percent. If the quantity demanded for bluegrass seed increases by 1 percent when its price decreases by 1 percent, the price elasticity of demand for bluegrass seed is 1.0. The formula for price elasticity of demand or ε_d is:

$$\text{Price Elasticity of demand} = \varepsilon_d$$

$$= \frac{\text{\% change in quantity demanded}}{\text{\% change in price}}$$

$$= \left[\frac{\text{new quantity} - \text{old quantity}}{\text{new quantity} + \text{old quantity}}\right] \times \left[\frac{\text{new price} + \text{old price}}{\text{new price} - \text{old price}}\right]$$

As Figure 3.5 shows, if the price of bluegrass seed decreased from $40 to $30 per 100-pound unit, the quantity demanded would increase from 100 to 200 units.

$$\text{Price Elasticity of demand} = \varepsilon_d = \left[\frac{200-100}{200+100}\right] \times \left[\frac{30+40}{30-40}\right] = \frac{100}{300} \times \frac{70}{-10} = -2.33$$

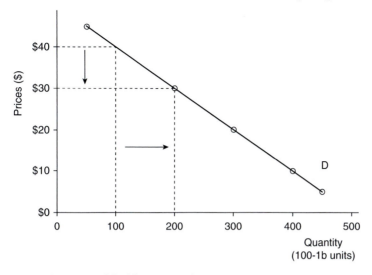

Figure 3.5 Demand for bluegrass seed

This means that when the price drops by 1 percent, the quantity demanded increases by 2.33 percent. Because percentage change in quantity demanded shifted more than price shifted, the demand for bluegrass seed responded to the price change. But if the price fell from $20 to $10 per unit, quantity would increase from 300 to 400 100-pound units. On a percentage basis, demand is less responsive at this level.

$$\text{Price Elasticity of demand} = \varepsilon_d = \left[\frac{400-300}{400+300}\right] \times \left[\frac{10+20}{10-20}\right] = \frac{100}{700} \times \frac{30}{-10} = -0.43$$

These price elasticities of demand use the formula for arc elasticity of demand. This measures the percentage change over a segment of the demand curve rather than evaluating change at a specific point on the curve. The coefficient for price elasticity of demand should always be negative, since change is measured along the demand curve which has a negative slope. As price increases, quantity demanded decreases, or vice versa, as calculated price elasticities of demand will always be negative. Typically, one takes the absolute value of price elasticity of demand, and thus, ignores the negative sign.

Interpreting elasticity of demand

There are three levels of price elasticity of demand or ε_d (Table 3.3). If price elasticity of demand in absolute terms is greater than 1.0, demand is **price elastic**. This means that a small change in price will result in a relatively large change in the quantity demanded. Thus, because quantity demanded responds to a price decrease, total revenue will increase when ε_d is price elastic. Types of products for which demand is price elastic include products for which there are many close substitutes, luxury goods, and products that make up a large portion of the consumer's budget.

Table 3.3 Interpretation of price elasticity of demand

Absolute value of price elasticity of demand coefficient	Demand is	Effect on total revenue of a price increase	Effect on total revenue of a price decrease
Greater than 1.0 ($\|\varepsilon_d\| > 1.0$)	Elastic	Total revenue decreases	Total revenue increases
Equal to 1.0 ($\|\varepsilon_d\| = 1.0$)	Unit elastic	Total revenue is unchanged	Total revenue is unchanged
Less than 1.0 ($\|\varepsilon_d\| < 1.0$)	Inelastic	Total revenue increases	Total revenue decreases

On the other hand, if the absolute value of price elasticity of demand is between 0 and 1.0, demand is said to be **price inelastic**. Here a change in price has a relatively small impact upon the quantity demanded. A price decline for an elastic demand means that consumers do not respond, and total revenue will actually fall. Goods that fit into this category are typically necessities, products that account for a very small part of the consumer's budget, or products that have no close substitutes. The demand for natural gas to run and heat a large production facility is fairly inelastic—it is essential to the efficient production process and, at least in the short run, it has no substitutes. Thus, this production facility may have no option but to pay higher natural gas bills during the winter to maintain production capacity of the facility. However, over the longer term, the firm may switch from natural gas to oil, electricity, or some other alternative fuel source. So, the period of time under consideration also affects the price elasticity of demand.

The other two types of demand elasticity—**income** and **cross price elasticity of demand**—are calculated in a similar manner as for price elasticity of demand. A manager is most interested in the sign for these two elasticities. Thus, we do not take the absolute value.

For most products, **income elasticity of demand** will have a positive sign and these products are classified as **normal goods**. This means that the quantity demanded of these goods will rise as income increases. However, for a few goods, income elasticity will have a negative sign and are classified as inferior goods. In this case, the quantity demanded will fall as income increases. Examples of inferior goods include staples of a college student's diet, like Ramen noodles or tuna. These are the last things a recent graduate will purchase and consume as they start their career because they can now afford better food.

The cross price elasticity of demand is used to classify how demand relates to price changes in other goods. The relationship between two goods can be classified as complements, independent, or substitutes. Grocers, for one, carefully study these relationships as they determine how to adjust orders of different items as they put certain goods on sale each week.

Cross price elasticity of demand < 0.0 Complement goods

Cross price elasticity of demand = 0.0 Independent goods

Cross price elasticity of demand > 0.0 Substitute goods

If the sign for cross price elasticity of demand is negative, the two goods are deemed to be complements, like hamburgers and buns. This means if the price of buns is on sale, consumers will also buy complementary goods that are eaten with the buns, like hamburger meat, ketchup, mustard, etc. In contrast if the sign for cross price elasticity of demand is positive, the goods are substitutes for each other. One classic example is Coke and Pepsi. If the price of Pepsi is higher, the demand for Coke will increase. Finally, if the sign is near zero, it means that the demand for one good does not depend on the price change in another good. For example, the demand for coffee will not change if ketchup is put on sale.

Summary

Agribusiness managers must have a clear understanding of economics to be successful. Economics involves the allocation of scarce resources, that is, land, labor, capital, and management, to meet the needs of society. Macroeconomics focuses on a "big picture" view of our economic system. Microeconomics is the application of basic economic principles to decisions within the firm.

The profit motive is used as an incentive that guides businesses in fulfilling consumer wants as consumers express these wants in the marketplace with their dollars. Several economic concepts provide insights for agribusiness managers. Opportunity cost is the income given up by not choosing the next best alternative for the use of resources. Economic profit is defined as accounting profit less opportunity cost. Economic profit then forces managers to explore alternative uses of resources.

Supply captures the relationship between price and quantity supplied. Demand curves slope downward from left to right, indicating that larger quantities are only purchased at lower prices. Applying supply and demand principles is important in understanding how markets work, and how prices move. Elasticity estimates for demand help agribusiness managers examine the potential impact of changes in price, income, or other prices on quantity demanded.

Discussion questions

1. Why should agribusiness managers be interested in macroeconomics? Give a specific example of one macroeconomic development and describe the impact of this development on the food and agribusiness industries.
2. What is your opportunity cost associated with attending college? Be specific.
3. Consider the supply of milk. What are at least three different developments that might shift the supply curve for milk? Be specific.
4. Consider the demand for frozen yogurt. What are three different developments that might shift the demand curve for frozen yogurt? Be specific.
5. How might the marketing manager of an agribusiness firm use elasticity of demand coefficients? Be specific.

Case study: Armstrong Agribusiness, Inc.

A local agribusiness enterprise has employed a consultant to estimate its supply curve for a specific tractor part and to estimate the demand faced for this part in its local marketplace. The consultant has determined the following:

Demand: $Q = 220 - 4P$

Supply: $Q = 40 + 2P$

1. Given these two estimates, solve for the market equilibrium price and quantity.
2. Now plot the individual supply and demand curves together for price levels from $5 through $50 in increments of $5 (i.e., $5, $10, $15, etc.) Is the market equilibrium the same on your graph as calculated in Question 1?
3. This tractor part is often replaced if producers have extra income. What happens to the supply and demand curves if net farm income is expected to increase by 10 percent?
4. Given the original demand price–quantity relationships, calculate the elasticity of demand when:
    a) Prices increase from $20 to $25
    b) Prices increase from $35 to $40
5. Given the original market equilibrium, what would happen to Armstrong Agribusiness if a market price of $50 were set for this part? Explain. Use a graph if you believe this will facilitate your analysis.

Part II

Agribusiness management

Organization and context

Plate Part II Apples on display
Part II explores the structure and organization of important types of food and agribusiness firms.
Photo courtesy of USDA Natural Resources Conservation Service.

4 The organization of an agribusiness

Objectives

- Identify some of the important factors involved in selecting the best organizational form for an agribusiness
- Understand proprietorships, partnerships, corporations, cooperatives, limited liability companies, and strategic alliances as forms of business organization
- Summarize the advantages and disadvantages of each of these organizational forms
- Outline and discuss some of the special forms of partnerships and their relative advantages and disadvantages, as well as some of the various types of partner
- Discuss the scope and scale of cooperative involvement in the food and agribusiness sector
- Identify the basic principles that ensure that cooperatives serve the needs of member-patrons
- Understand the role and impact of current individual and corporate tax laws on a firm's organizational structure

Introduction

An agribusiness may be a firm with billions of dollars of sales that employs thousands of people, or it may be as small as an individual who is a part-time seed corn salesperson. Agribusinesses may engage in a variety of activities that are related to the production, processing, marketing, and distribution of food and fiber products. Though the one-person or one-family agribusiness is not uncommon, most of the actual business volume in agribusiness is conducted by enterprises that employ hundreds or even thousands of people.

Every agribusiness is owned by someone, and it is the circumstances of ownership that give an organization its specific legal form. There are five basic business forms: the sole proprietorship, the partnership, the corporation, the limited liability company (LLC), and the cooperative. The form of organization is not necessarily dictated by the size or type of agribusiness: nearly every conceivable size and kind of agribusiness may use any of these five business organization forms. In addition to these five forms, strategic alliances are also used by agribusinesses as a form of business organization. Strategic alliances can take a variety of forms, and represent an important way that food and agribusiness firms can work together.

The many advantages and disadvantages of each of the five organizational forms must be weighed carefully when attempting to choose the proper one for a specific firm because each form tends to fit some situations better than others. And, even if an agribusiness is organized one way, customers, suppliers, and partners may be organized in another way. So, it is important to understand these different business forms for a number of reasons. This chapter will discuss the important characteristics of each of the five forms of business organization as well as strategic alliances, and outline the factors that affect their choice for a specific agribusiness situation.

Factors influencing choice of business form

Each form of business organization has its own individual characteristics. Owners and managers must choose the most appropriate form for their unique circumstances. An agribusiness may want to change its legal form of organization as it grows or as economic and other conditions change. When deciding which form of organization is best, an owner or owners must answer several important questions:

1. What type of business is it, where will it be conducted, and what are the owners' objectives and philosophies for the agribusiness?
2. How much capital is available for the firm's start-up?
3. How much capital is needed to support the agribusiness?
4. How easy is it to secure additional capital for the agribusiness?
5. What tax liabilities will be incurred and what tax options are available?
6. How much personal involvement in the management and control of the agribusiness do the owners desire?
7. How important are the factors of stability, continuity, and transfer of ownership to the firm's owners?
8. How desirable is it to keep the affairs of the agribusiness private, and carefully guard any public disclosure?
9. How much risk and liability are the owners willing to assume?
10. How much will this form of organization cost and how easy is this form of agribusiness to organize?

A careful evaluation of these factors will allow the selection of the most appropriate form of business organization in each case.

The sole proprietorship

The oldest and simplest form of business organization is the **sole** or **individual proprietorship**, an organization owned and controlled by one person or family. In the United States, it is the most popular business organization. In 2006, there were 22 million nonfarm sole proprietorships, which together comprised almost 72 percent of the business entities in the United States that year (www.census.gov/compendia/statab/2010/tables/10s0728.pdf). In that same year, it was estimated that this relatively large number of small businesses accounted for only about 4 percent of total U.S. business receipts.

Proprietorships tend to be small businesses, although there are notable exceptions. The fortune amassed by the eccentric billionaire Howard Hughes (1905–76), for example, was largely accumulated from a sole proprietorship. When a business reaches a certain size, other forms of business organizations usually become more attractive for a variety of reasons. Some very large corporations are essentially owned and controlled by a single individual, but the advantages of the corporate business form at some point resulted in the firm changing from a proprietorship to the corporate form of organization.

Advantages of proprietorships

The legal requirements necessary to organize as a sole proprietorship are minimal. About all that is required is an individual's desire to start a business and the purchase of a license, if one is required for that particular kind of business. If the owner wishes to do business under an assumed name, that is, if the business is to be conducted under a name other than that of the owner, most states require that the assumed name be registered (this is where you will see something like "Mike Jones dba Jones Feed and Supply" on legal documents, where dba means "doing business as").

Jessica Alverson is a good example. She decided to start a floral shop, which she wanted to call Fragrant Floral rather than using her own name for the business. Consequently, she registered the new name. Thereafter, those who did business with Fragrant Floral were aware that they were really doing business with Jessica Alverson.

The **proprietorship** gives the individual owner complete control over the business, subject only to government regulations that are applicable to all businesses of that particular type. The owner exerts complete control over plans, programs, policies, and other management decisions. No one else shares in this control unless the owner specifically delegates a portion of the control to someone else. All profits and losses, all liability to creditors and liability from other business activities are vested in the proprietor. The costs of organizing and dissolution are typically low. The business affairs are completely secret from all outsiders, except for select governmental units such as the IRS (Internal Revenue Service) and lending institutions that supply borrowed funds.

Whenever capital is needed it is supplied by the owner from personal funds or is borrowed against either the owner's business or personal assets. Personal and business assets are not strictly separated as they are in some other business forms; therefore, if the owner as an individual is financially sound, lenders will be more likely to extend funds. A proprietor can sell their business to whomever they wish, whenever they wish, and for whatever price they are willing to accept. They can take on as much risk or liability as they wish, but it is important to note that they are personally liable for whatever risk they assume.

A sole proprietor pays no income tax as a separate business entity. All income that the business earns is taxed as personal income even though the IRS requires the filing of a separate form to show business income and expenses. Since a proprietor cannot pay him/herself a salary, the amount left over at the end of the year is treated as personal income or salary. The proprietor may choose to keep this money in the business or use part or all of it for personal expenditures.

The proprietorship can conduct business in any of the 50 states without special permission other than whatever licenses are required for that particular kind of business. This is a right guaranteed by the United States Constitution, which provides that "citizens of each state shall be entitled to the privileges and immunities of citizens of several states." The person who desires the lowest cost (to organize), simplest, most self-directed, most private, and most flexible form of agribusiness will choose the sole proprietorship.

Disadvantages of proprietorships

Perhaps the most important disadvantage of the proprietorship is the owner's personal liability for all debts and liabilities of the business, which can extend even to the owner's personal estate. In a proprietorship, there is no separation between business assets and personal assets. Consequently, this form of business organization is characterized by what is called unlimited liability. The owner's liability does not stop with business assets; it also extends to personal assets. Such assets can be, and often are, used to satisfy financial obligations. Thus, if Fragrant Floral starts losing money, and the bank demands payment on a loan made to the business, Jessica Alverson is personally liable for the payment of the loan. If the business cannot cover the loan, the bank can typically demand payment from Jessica's personal savings and investments, or other assets she owns.

Another important disadvantage relates to the generally limited amount of capital funds that one person can contribute. Lenders are also somewhat reluctant to lend to an individual owner unless the owner's personal equity can guarantee the loan. Proprietorships often find that they are starved for capital, and this serious disadvantage may do more than stunt growth. Thousands of bankruptcies each year can be traced to a serious shortage of capital when a business is started.

While freedom from business taxes is generally an advantage, it may also be a disadvantage. Since business profit in a proprietorship is considered personal income to the owner, a high business profit may throw the owner into a higher tax bracket than would the corporate form of business organization. This is especially disadvantageous if extensive funds are needed for the growth and expansion of the business. Corporate tax rates along with other tax regulations may provide an advantage in such cases.

The concentration of control and profits in one individual may also be a disadvantage. Many highly trained and motivated employees want to participate financially in the business where they work (i.e., they may have a desire to own a portion of the business). They may also be uneasy about the fact that their futures depend on the health and viability of a single person. Thus, proprietorships may experience some difficulty in hiring and keeping good people. Without good, highly motivated employees, the owner may find as the business grows—that he or she is "wearing too many hats"—with the end result that the business suffers.

Finally, the proprietorship lacks stability and continuity because it depends so heavily on one person. The death or disability of that one person, in effect, ends the business. Proprietorships may be difficult to sell or to pass on to heirs. This is particularly true if they become sizeable businesses. Individual shares or parts of the business cannot be parceled out to several individual owners or to heirs in the same way that shares of a corporation can.

For example, Molly's Steakhouse was a regionally noted restaurant in a small Midwest town. Molly established and managed this business profitably for roughly 30 years. However, Molly was always in charge of everything: food ordering and preparation, tabulating the bill, and collecting money. Food servers had few responsibilities, and turnover among employees was high. Molly refused to bring any family members into the business. But, the food was excellent, and Molly had a very good business, though it remained quite small because she "just couldn't work any more hours." Then, Molly was hospitalized and had a lengthy recovery period. As a result, Molly simply closed the doors and her restaurant went out of business. Some planning and forethought on Molly's part could have averted the closing of this small, but profitable proprietorship.

Partnerships

A **partnership** is the association of two or more people as owners of a business. There is no limit to the number of people who may join a partnership. Apart from the fact that a partnership involves more than one person, it is similar to the proprietorship. Partnerships can be based upon written or oral agreements, or on formal contracts between the parties involved.

However, it is strongly urged that if you consider joining a partnership, that the partnership agreement should be in writing to avoid disagreement and misunderstanding among partners at a later date.

Partnerships can be formed by law whenever two or more people act in such a way that reasonable people would be led to believe they are associated for business purposes. In 2006, there were approximately 2.9 million partnerships in the United States, and they accounted for about 10 percent of total business receipts. Partnerships are the simplest form of business organization by which a number of people can pool their resources and talents for mutual benefit.

There are basically two kinds of partnership: general partnerships and limited partnerships. Below we discuss how each of these partnership arrangements works in agribusiness.

General partnerships

By far the most common form of partnership is what is called a general partnership. Continuing with our Fragrant Floral example—after a couple of years in operation, Jessica Alverson has been very impressed with one of her employees, Erika Lewandowski. Erika has expressed an interest in becoming involved in the business, and has some money from an inheritance she is willing to invest in the business. Jessica and Erika decide to enter a partnership, and rename the business Fragrant Floral and Perfect Gifts. The new name reflects the partner's desire to expand the business into a broader line of gift items. So, with Erika's commitment of capital and her desire to be further involved in the business, a new partnership is formed.

In a **general partnership**, each individual partner—regardless of the percentage of capital contributed—has equal rights and liabilities, unless stated otherwise in a partnership agreement. A general partner has the authority to act as an agent for the partnership, and normally participates in the management and operation of the business. Each general partner is liable for all partnership debts, and may share in profits, in equal proportion with all other partners. If the partnership struggles and has financial problems, all liabilities are shared equally among the partners for as long as sufficient personal resources exist.

However, when one partner's resources are exhausted, remaining parties continue to be liable for the remaining debt. General partners may contract among themselves to delegate certain responsibilities to each other, or to divide business revenues or costs in some special manner (e.g., according to funds invested or job responsibility). Each general partner can bind the partnership to fulfill any business deal made. While the partnership is usually treated as a separate business for the purposes of accounting, it is not legally regarded as an entity in itself, but as a group of individuals or entities. Thus, there is no separate business tax paid by the partnership. Like the proprietorship, partners may not pay themselves a salary. Money left at year's end is divided among the partners and this is their profit or "salary" from the partnership. The income is taxed at the individual rate.

Limited partnership

All partnerships are required by law to have at least one general partner who is responsible for the operation and activities of the business, but it is possible for other partners to be involved in the business on a limited basis. A **limited partnership** permits individuals to contribute money or other ownership capital without incurring the full legal liability of a general partner. A limited partner's liability is generally limited to the amount that the individual has personally invested in the business. The state laws regulating limited partnerships must be strictly adhered to and these acts spell out the limited status of partners: first, the limited partner can contribute capital but not services to the partnership, and second, the limited partner's surname cannot appear in the business's name (unless the partnership had previously been carried on under that name, or unless a general partner has the same surname). Limited partnerships are relatively few in number; therefore, the balance of the discussion of partnerships will apply to general partnerships. However, it is important to note that if a limited partner takes an active role in managing the business, their limited liability may cease.

Advantages of partnerships

Partnerships are just about as easy to start as proprietorships. They require very little expense, although an attorney competent in partnership law should be engaged to draw up the partnership agreement. The partnership may operate under an assumed or fictitious name, provided it is registered in accordance with state laws. A partnership can generally bring together many more resources than a proprietorship because of the increase in the number of people involved. These added resources are not only financial in nature; the business also benefits from the variety of unique talents that many different individuals can bring to it. Partners are a team, and because each team member shares in the responsibility and profits, partners are more likely to be motivated than employees of a single proprietorship or corporation. Additional partners can be brought in if more money or talent is needed.

Partners, as individuals, pay taxes only on the income generated from their share of the profits. There is no business tax *per se*, and this can be a considerable advantage, depending on the income of the partners. Control or management of business decisions and policies is concentrated among the partners. Generally, partners divide the responsibilities of the business: that is, one will head sales; another will head operations, input acquisition, etc. This can be done on either a formal or an informal basis. Partners may sell their interest in the business to others if the remaining partners agree. The business affairs of a partnership are confined to the partnership, and this element of privacy is one of the prime reasons why many people choose to do business as partners. Partnerships share the same privileges of doing business in other states as does the proprietorship form of business organization.

Disadvantages of partnerships

By far the biggest disadvantage of the partnership is the unlimited liability of each general partner. There are many known cases where one partner has generated financial obligations for the partnership, and then because that individual has been personally insolvent, the other partners have had to pay the bills. Even limited partners must be very careful that they do not give any appearance of being active in the management of the business. The law has frequently been enforced on the basis of a person's actions rather than on the basis of the written documents. If a person acts as a general partner would act, then that partner may be forced to accept all the liabilities that such status would incur, even if the formal, written agreement says the individual is a limited partner.

The liability of general partners has created a second disadvantage: partnerships usually have only a limited number of members. Imagine a partnership with 100 members, each able to bind the partnership legally to contracts and to other obligations. Of course, the limited partnership was created to alleviate this problem, but it has not been very successful.

A limited partnership often suffers from a lack of available funds and talented people when compared to a corporation.

Another disadvantage is the lack of continuity and stability of a partnership. When a partner leaves the partnership as a result of withdrawal, death, or incapacity, a new partnership must be formed. The old partner's share must be liquidated, and this can often place a severe burden on the partnership's capital position. Another problem is that which occurs if one of the partners becomes incapacitated by accident, ill health, old age, or for some reason fails to pull a full share of the load. Often the only way to remove such a partner is to liquidate the entire business. When a partner leaves, it is often hard to determine what that individual's share is worth. For this reason, a formula and pay-off method should be incorporated in the original partnership agreement. Then the business may more easily be dissolved and a new one can be formed. If the means for establishing the value of the partner's share and the process for transfer and acceptance of new partners has been firmly established in the written partnership agreement, this transition can be reasonably smooth. While being taxed on income as separate individuals can be an advantage in some situations, it can be a disadvantage in others (just as with the sole proprietorship).

Finally, one very important consideration is the need for a carefully drafted, written partnership agreement. Any person entering into a partnership should find the most competent legal assistance possible, an attorney who is familiar with the problems of partnerships, and trust that attorney to prepare an agreement for the agribusiness. When partnerships are

Plate 4.1 Presentation to a group
The right form of business organization is required to cover the varied goals of firm owners, employees, and customers. Photo courtesy of USDA Natural Resources Conservation Service.

formed, the members are all on good terms and cannot imagine feeling any other way about each other, but situations change and people change. Not only will a written contract of partnership provide solutions if problems occur, but it will also serve as a ready reference as important decisions are made in the partnership.

Types of partners

In forming a partnership, the business entity may include a variety of different partners. Some of the more common types of partners are outlined below with a set of characteristics unique to that particular partner:

A **general partner** is one who is active in the management of the partnership, typically has an investment in the business, and is subject to unlimited liability. If nothing is in writing, all partners are assumed to be general partners.

A **limited partner** has taken steps to limit their liability in the partnership. This agreement must be in writing. Also, limited partners may not take an active role in managing the partnership.

A **senior partner** is typically an individual who helped form the partnership or one who has seniority in the business. Senior partners typically run the business, have an investment in the firm, and tend to receive the major portion of partnership profits.

A **junior partner** is typically younger and has not been in the business as long as a senior partner. Junior partners tend to receive a smaller portion of the business profits. Junior partners rarely take an active role in managing the business affairs of the partnership.

A **secret partner** is an individual who desires to take an active role in managing the partnership but is not known to be a partner by the general public. Thus, secret partners do have unlimited liability. An individual may desire to become a secret partner due to involvement in other business ventures. If the partnership fails, the general public will not know of this individual's involvement, thus other businesses controlled by this person would be unaffected by negative public opinion.

A **silent partner** is known by the public and not active in managing the partnership. An individual may seek to be a silent partner to add name recognition to a firm and to continue having the advantage of limiting liability in the enterprise.

A **dormant partner** is not active in managing the partnership and is not known by the general public. Thus, dormant partners retain limited liability. The reason firms may seek dormant partners is to obtain additional investment capital for the business.

A **nominal partner** means "in name only." Nominal partners are not active in the business and have no investment. If Jake Smith owned a horse ranch and named it Jake Smith and Sons, assuming they have no investment in the business, Jake's sons would be nominal partners.

The corporation

A **corporation** is a special legal entity endowed by law with the powers, rights, liabilities, and duties of a person (in fact a corporation is sometimes referred to as an "artificial" person). The corporate form of business organization typically facilitates the accumulation of greater amounts of capital when compared to proprietorships and partnerships. Without the corporate form of organization it is impossible to imagine the creation of today's large business entities, which employ hundreds of thousands of people and are worth billions of dollars.

In 2006, there were only about 5.8 million corporations in the United States, or about 19 percent of all businesses. However, they generated about 83 percent of all business receipts. Many corporations are multinational giants. The 500 largest corporations, as rated by *Fortune* magazine, generate two-thirds of all industrial sales in the United States. However, most corporations are relatively small, and many are really one-person businesses whose owners have chosen the corporate form of organization as the best for their unique business circumstances. As a matter of fact, in 2006, 81 percent of all United States corporations had annual receipts of less than $1 million (www.census.gov/compendia/statab/2010/tables/10s0729.pdf).

Nonprofit corporations

Most corporations are formed for profit-making purposes; however, there are thousands of nonprofit corporations in existence. These **nonprofit corporations** embrace many areas of activity, including those of religious, governmental, labor, and charitable organizations. Federal and state laws specify the numerous forms that these nonprofit corporations may take, along with very specific regulations as to their purpose and operation. A competent attorney can advise whether a nonprofit corporate form of organization is the most appropriate for a particular agribusiness situation. Again, the legal interpretation will be made on the basis of the ways in which the corporation acts, and not on the basis of how it is described in written legal documents.

Examples of nonprofit corporations include some cooperatives, some agricultural trade and research groups, and some farm organizations, such as the National Dairy Herd Improvement Association, Inc. Nonprofit corporations are exempt from certain forms of taxation, and generally they cannot enrich members financially. In many cases, the nonprofit corporation must secure a formal exemption from paying corporate income taxes.

The nature of the corporation

The corporation as we know it today is a rather recent innovation compared to proprietorships and partnerships. The early American colonists were very suspicious of this form of organization, and it was not until the 1860s that most states provided laws allowing for the formation of corporations. A corporation can own property, incur debts, and be sued for damages, among other things. The important distinction to remember is that the owners (stockholders) and managers do not own anything directly. The corporation itself owns the assets of the corporation.

Forming a corporation requires strict adherence to the laws of the state in which the business is being formed. Usually, one or more persons join together to create a corporation. A series of legal documents must be created and examined by the state's designated department for establishing corporations. If the legal formalities are in proper order, and if the proper fee for incorporation has been paid, a charter authorizing the applicants to do business as a corporation is issued. Additionally, a corporation maintains the following legal documents: **articles of incorporation**, which are filed with the state and which set forth the basic purpose of the corporation and the means of financing it; the **bylaws**, which specify such rules of operation as election of directors, duties of officers and directors, voting procedures, and dissolution procedures; and **stock certificates** or shares detailing amounts of the owners' investments.

The laws relating to the formation of proprietorships and partnerships are fairly well established and uniform throughout the nation, but considerable differences in the requirements for forming a corporation exist among the various states. Individual state laws and statutes must be carefully considered by those who wish to form a corporation. Selection of an attorney who is well versed in the corporate law of the specific state of interest is essential to avoid potentially serious organizational problems in the agribusiness corporation.

Stock of the corporation

When corporations are formed, shares of stock are sold to those who are interested in investing and risking their money in the enterprise. A share of **stock** is a piece of paper, in prescribed legal form, which represents each person's amount of ownership in the corporation. **Common stock** normally carries the privilege of voting for the board of directors that oversees the activities of the corporation. **Preferred stock** differs from common stock in that it is usually nonvoting, and has a preferred position in receiving dividends and in redemption in the case of liquidation. Thus, voting rights are exchanged for lower risk on the investment of capital in the corporation.

Each state has what are commonly called **blue-sky laws**, which regulate the way in which corporate stock may be sold and which protect the rights of investors (the origin of the term is a bit obscure—some people attribute it to a former Supreme Court Justice who wrote about companies selling stock which was not worth much more than a "patch of blue sky;" others state that it arose because criminals were willing to sell naïve investors a "piece of the great blue sky," and these laws were enacted to protect against this). Individual state laws must be consulted prior to the sales of stock in a corporation. The most common way of financing corporations is through the sales of stock, but financing through bonds, notes, debentures, and numerous means of borrowing against assets is also practiced.

Thus, there are two specific types of stockholders in a for-profit corporation. Common stockholders are willing to take risk. They invest in the corporation typically because they believe the value of their stock will increase over time (this increase in value comes about as the firm invests in new and additional assets, inventory and technology, combined with a typical increase in brand value—known as "goodwill"). They are also the true owners of the business. At the annual meeting, common stockholders are the ones that vote for the board of directors of the corporation. Each common stockholder has one vote per share of common stock. Some corporations have started issuing nonvoting common stock, but this is not prevalent across most corporations.

Those who desire to control a business may embark on an attempt to acquire the majority of shares of a firm. Also, current stockholders can sign a proxy vote that allows an individual to vote for them at the annual meeting. Many well-publicized attempts to take over corporations are noted as "hostile takeovers." In these sorts of cases, current corporate management does not desire to lose their control of the firm. Proxy fights may ensue, where the takeover candidate attempts to gain control by enlisting stockholder approval or by simply bidding at a higher level than the current market price for outstanding shares.

In contrast, preferred stockholders tend to take less risk on their investment in the corporation. The price of preferred stock typically fluctuates less than common stock in publicly traded corporations. Also, preferred stockholders often invest for the dividends granted by the corporation. Once a firm has established a trend of paying quarterly dividends, management may not wish to break the record. Thus, some firms, even in an economic downturn, may choose to borrow money to pay their quarterly dividends to preferred shareholders.

How the corporation functions

The common stockholders in a corporation elect the **board of directors**, the number of which may vary according to the bylaws of the organization. The responsibility of the board of directors is to supervise the affairs of the corporation. In a large corporation, the thousands of individual stockholders exercise very little actual control. Those they vote for to serve as directors may be unknown to them and are often preselected by a small group of majority stockholders who are allied with top management of the corporation. The board represents the interests of the stockholders, and their major function is to elect officers, hire top management, and evaluate the progress of the business. Also, the board usually has a major role in shaping the vision and mission for the business. In a small corporation there is usually a very close relationship between stockholders and the board of directors; in fact, there could be only one stockholder who, in effect, is in complete control of the corporation.

Advantages of corporations

The primary advantage of the corporate form of business organization is that the **stockholders** (owners) are not personally liable for the debts of the organization, and in most

Plate 4.2 Woman at computer
Stock prices for important markets such as the New York Stock Exchange are widely reported as is other relevant information. Photo courtesy of USDA Natural Resources Conservation Service.

cases are not responsible for the liability that occurs through the corporation's business activities. The assets of the corporation are all that are at risk in settling most claims. The stockholders can, therefore, only lose the amount they have invested in the firm. With the corporate structure it is possible to delegate authority, responsibility, and accountability, and to secure outstanding, highly motivated personnel. Corporations can offer their personnel such benefits as profit sharing and stock-purchase plans, which encourage a high degree of dedication and loyalty to the corporation.

Transfer of ownership is also easier in a corporation than in other business forms. Usually, a stockholder can sell shares of stock to anyone for any price that the buyer is willing to pay. An owner can also transfer individual equity to heirs or to others much more easily than in the proprietorship or partnership. However, sale of stock in a small, unknown corporation may not be easy. Finding someone who is willing to risk investment becomes much easier once a stock is traded. As a corporation becomes larger and begins to develop a ready market for its stock, brokerage houses that specialize in the sale of stock and who are in constant touch with potential investors, may trade the stock. New issues of stock may be purchased by a group of brokerage houses, who, in turn, sell the stock to the general public. Many companies have their stock traded in secondary markets that list daily price movements and facilitate the buying and selling of these stocks. Examples of these markets include the New York Stock Exchange and NASDAQ (originally standing for National Association of Securities Dealers Automated Quotations); NASDAQ merged with the American Stock Exchange in 1988, and bought the Philadelphia Stock Exchange (the oldest stock exchange in America, having been in operation since 1790) in 2007.

Because corporations' ownership rights are traded freely, it is relatively easy for them to raise large amounts of equity capital. The combined investments of hundreds and even thousands of investors have made the huge corporate giants of American business possible. However, these investment funds are not automatic just because the corporation has decided to sell stock. Buyers invest because of the proven performance or anticipated future performance of the firm.

Finally, the corporation is perpetual in nature. Death, withdrawal, or retirement of its shareholders has little effect on the life of the corporation. This is another advantage that makes investment in a corporation more attractive to those with funds to risk.

Disadvantages of corporations

The greatest disadvantages of the corporate form of organization are taxation and regulation. The corporation is taxed on funds it earns as profit; then, after it has paid dividends to its stockholders, the stockholders must again pay income tax on the amount that is received as dividends—in effect a "double taxation" on these profits. (This may not always be a disadvantage, as will be discussed later in this chapter.) In addition, there are many states that impose special levies and taxes on corporations, and there are many more laws and regulations controlling the activities of corporations than there are for other organizational forms.

The corporation must accept a lack of privacy because reports must be made to stockholders and states and because the federal government may require disclosure whenever a stock offering is made to prospective purchasers. A corporation that is chartered to do business in one state may not do business in another state unless it complies with the second state's laws of registration, taxation, and so forth. Finally, individual owners (stockholders) of larger corporations have little, if any, control over management and policies of the corporation. Often their only recourse in the event of dissatisfaction is to sell their stock.

The costs of taxes, records (which must be comprehensive), and operation of the corporate business can be significantly higher than the costs for other forms of organization; for that reason the corporate form should be evaluated carefully before it is adopted by an agribusiness.

Finally, in smaller corporations, the issue of limited liability is not always so clear. Banks and other lenders may insist on personal guarantees from stockholders for loans before lending a small corporation money. Boards of directors may be sued for a variety of reasons, and the board may well be the owners of the corporation. So, while the corporate form clearly offers more legal protection than proprietorship or partnership, specific circumstances may make such protection relatively thin.

Closely held corporations

A special form of corporation has been designed to offset some of the disadvantages of the regular corporation. This form is called the **S-corporation**. Subchapter S of the Internal Revenue Code makes it possible for the owners of a corporation to elect to be taxed as individuals, in the same manner as owners of a partnership or proprietorship. So, the benefits of incorporating as an S-corporation can be significant. This type of corporation can avoid the double taxation paid by a regular corporation.

An S-corporation must meet several qualifications: there cannot be more than 100 stockholders, the stockholders must be individual persons rather than corporations, and they cannot be nonresident aliens. Additionally, the election to be taxed as individuals must occur prior to the start of the corporation's fiscal year. Owners, therefore, cannot simply wait to see which method of taxation would be better once the year is over and the returns prepared. In addition, the S-corporation must be a domestic corporation. It must be a corporation that is organized under state law. The S-corporation can issue only one class of stock if organized after May 27, 1992. Finally, the S-corporation cannot have passive income of more than 25 percent of total receipts in three consecutive years. Examples of passive income would be rent, royalties, interest, and dividends.

The rules to qualify for this status essentially guarantee that the S-corporation is relatively small, and often family-held, and the corporation is production-oriented. While there are a number of benefits, there can be many pitfalls to this form of organization and agribusiness corporations should consult competent legal and accounting professionals before selecting it.

Fragrant Floral and Perfect Gifts, Inc.

Let's revisit Fragrant Floral and Perfect Gifts. Jessica and Erika have been in business together about a year. And, after attending a management course at a local community college, they are introduced to the corporate form of business organization. They decide they like the idea of limiting their personal liability through the use of the corporation. They also like some of the ways that the corporate form of organization eases transitions. What if Erika wanted to move away, but did not want to give up her investment in the business? In addition, they have been talking about expanding the business by establishing another location—so access to investment capital becomes more important. A corporation would help make this possible. After reviewing the advantages and disadvantages, they believe they should become an S-corporation, to help better manage their personal tax situation.

Plate 4.3 Fragrant Floral
If Fragrant Floral is organized as a proprietorship, Jessica Alverson takes on all risks and rewards for her business. Photo courtesy of USDA Natural Resources Conservation Service.

So, working with an attorney, they develop a set of articles of incorporation, and a set of bylaws. They file this paperwork with the state and are granted corporate status. They issue 110 shares of stock, 50 each to Jessica and Erika. In addition, a friend in the landscaping business, Peter Yu, is excited about the possibilities for Fragrant Floral and Perfect Gifts, and he buys ten of the shares. Jessica, Erika and Peter are on the board of directors, and Jessica is chairperson of the board. Fragrant Floral and Perfect Gifts, Inc. is open for business!

Cooperatives

Owned, operated and controlled by members, a **cooperative** is a distinct form of the corporate form of business. Cooperatives are committed to helping members improve the prices they receive for the products they produce and/or reduce the prices paid for the inputs necessary to grow those products. Cooperatives also exist to help members find markets, and/or improve the negotiating position of members. Cooperatives provide economic and/or operational benefits to member-owners, and then return the profit to the member-owners based on each member's use of the cooperative. The user-member is the total emphasis for the cooperative. In contrast, generating profit for the owners of the firm is the purpose of the non-cooperative business enterprise. This is a very important difference.

Cooperatives are a very important part of the agribusiness industry. Approximately one-third of all grain and nearly 80 percent of milk is marketed through cooperatives. From an input supply standpoint, nearly one-half of farmer purchases of petroleum, 40 percent of fertilizer purchases, one-third of farm chemicals and nearly 20 percent of livestock feed is purchased through a cooperative. Cooperatives provide almost one-third of all agricultural credit. Because of the importance of agricultural cooperatives, the discussion below goes into a bit more depth about cooperatives than the other business forms covered in this chapter.

Characteristics of food and agricultural cooperatives

Cooperatives resemble other forms of business in some ways. They must follow sound business practices and may perform similar functions. Cooperatives have facilities to maintain, employees to hire, advertising to develop, and so forth. There are bylaws, policies, and activities that must be performed to carry out the business at hand. Ultimately, cooperatives must generate a return (member benefits plus direct financial returns) on the investment of their members, which justifies continued membership in the cooperative.

But, in some ways, cooperatives are distinctly different from other businesses. The ownership structure, the way they are controlled, their purpose and how benefits are shared or distributed are unique to cooperatives and how they operate. Three specific features delineate cooperatives from non-cooperative businesses:

- Member owned, member controlled
- Operation at cost
- Limited returns on capital

Member owned, member controlled

A fundamental principle undergirding cooperatives is that they must be owned and controlled by the people who conduct business with them. It is imperative that cooperatives maintain their orientation toward servicing those who patronize them. And there is no better way to ensure this than to require that active patron-members—who are also owners of the business—control the cooperative.

Originally, and even today in most cooperatives, this requirement meant one vote for each active patron-member regardless of how much business that member transacts with the cooperative or how much stock the individual member may have accumulated. Democratic control has gained almost universal acceptance as a basic cooperative principle.

Member control of cooperatives is executed through a **board of directors**, which is selected in open elections from the ranks of active members. The board takes on the responsibilities of sensing and representing the best interests of all members, setting overall policy, hiring and directing top management, and monitoring the cooperative's performance in achieving its objectives. However, some highly critical decisions involving such issues as mergers or large investments may be taken directly to the membership for a vote. This contrasts with a non-cooperative business, where the owners, whose number of votes is determined individually by the amount of stock they own, elect the directors. Consequently, most board members are stockholders with relatively large ownership interests.

Operation at cost

In most cases, a cooperative's net income is distributed to individual members in proportion to the volume of business that they have done with the cooperative. A cooperative may choose to retain profits rather than pay them out as patronage returns (see below), but when it does, it normally must pay corporate income tax just as any corporation must (there are some exceptions to this rule, discussed briefly below). The obligation to return profits to members is a primary factor that separates cooperatives from other forms of business. Non-cooperatives are not so obligated and, after paying any tax on profits that may be due, will return profits to the owners of the business in proportion to the owner's investment, or will keep the profits in the business as retained earnings for future growth.

Cooperatives may do some business with individuals who are not members. In the case of such non-patron business, any excess of income over and above the expenses generated specifically by that transaction does not have to be returned to the customer (although it may be in some cases). Instead, many cooperatives elect to treat this additional income as regular profit, to pay taxes on it just as any business would, and to use the profits to fund growth of the cooperative. An agribusiness can maintain its cooperative status as long as not more than half its business is transacted with non-members.

Limited returns on capital

Since the basic purpose of cooperatives is to operate at cost in order to benefit member-patrons directly in their own business, many state cooperative laws require that returns on invested capital be limited. Limiting returns on member equity to a nominal amount helps to ensure that members holding stock in the cooperative are not tempted to view the cooperative as an investment in and of itself, but rather as a service to their own business. Typically, returns on capital cannot be greater than 8 percent, although this rule varies from state to state. In practice, most cooperatives pay no dividends on their stock; therefore limiting returns is often a moot point.

Other issues unique to co-ops

Patronage refunds

Patronage refunds allow cooperatives to distribute net returns or margins to members or patrons:

- On an annual basis
- Consistent with standard accounting procedures
- Without regard to how much was earned on individual transactions

Many cooperatives opt to return net earnings to members; however, this does not happen on a transaction-by-transaction basis. Instead, cooperatives usually charge market prices for supplies and services furnished to their members and patrons. Operating at normal market prices allows many cooperatives to finance growth by special methods, such as retaining a portion of cash savings and making patronage refunds in the form of stock or other obligations. They also offer competitive prices for products delivered for further processing and marketing. This mode of operation generally allows them to generate sufficient income to cover costs and meet the continuing needs for operating capital.

When their fiscal year ends, a cooperative then figures its earnings on business conducted on a cooperative basis. If there are any earnings, they are returned to the cooperative's patrons (as patronage refunds) as cash and/or equity (cooperative stock) allocations on the basis of business volume conducted with the cooperative that year.

Financing of cooperatives

Cooperatives have some unique financing options at their disposal. Revolving fund financing is a highly advantageous option that is unique to cooperatives. Based on the principle that cooperative members should be willing to finance growth of their own organization, this method gives cooperatives the option of issuing patronage refunds in the form of stock or equity allocations, rather than in the form of cash. The idea is that the cooperative is a logical extension of the member's own business, and each member has an obligation to contribute directly to its financing in proportion to that member's use of the cooperative's services. The advantage to the cooperative is that since ownership of stock represents ownership of valuable assets, it satisfies the co-op's obligation to return the excess of income over expenses to patron-members, while at the same time retaining the actual cash earnings for use in financing the business. Theoretically, the cooperative "revolves" the stock periodically, thus allowing older stock to be cashed in.

Non-cooperative businesses argue that this is an unfair advantage, since any excess of income over expenses (profits) that non-cooperatives make is taxed first before it is retained for use by the business or distributed as dividends. Since 1962, legislation has required cooperatives to return a minimum of 20 percent of all patronage refunds in cash rather than in the form of ownership stock if they use this form of financing.

Refunds in the form of stock are considered to be income; so cooperative patron-members are required to pay taxes on that stock. Farmers in tax brackets that are higher than 20 percent will find that this type of financing can cause a net outflow of cash, since they must pay out more in taxes on the stock than they actually receive in cash refunds. Hence, many profitable cooperatives will pay out 40 to 50 percent of their net earnings in cash.

Advantages of agricultural cooperatives

For the farmer-member, a cooperative provides a number of advantages. One of the reasons cooperatives came about was to allow agricultural producers to "level the playing field" when they deal with suppliers of inputs, or with those who purchase their farm products. In essence, farmers are allowed to work together "cooperatively," or collude, and have been provided legal authority under the **Capper–Volstead Act of 1922** to do this. This act exempts them from anti-trust legislation, provided their cooperative meets the criteria discussed previously. This is a powerful advantage not enjoyed by other types of businesses. A cooperative can also provide a needed market where none existed before—again to provide input supplies or to process and market products produced by farmers.

Disadvantages of agricultural cooperatives

Those who are critical of cooperatives say that many of them—even the local ones—have gotten so large that the farmer member is far removed from having any significant voice in the business. Such critics also argue that the board of directors is sometimes elected on the basis of popularity rather than genuine ability to make policy decisions in a multi-million-dollar business. While these charges are serious, and one could probably find evidence of situations in which they are justified, it would be unfair and incorrect to assume that they are the general rule.

Another possible disadvantage of the cooperative form of business arises from the requirement in many states that each member of a cooperative only be allowed one vote on issues for consideration, regardless of how many shares of cooperative stock the individual may own. As farms have consolidated and gotten larger, some feel that those with larger business volume and/or the number of shares of stock should have more say in the operation of the cooperative.

Cooperatives: a brief history

Again, because of the importance of cooperatives to agriculture a bit of background helps to understand their context. Ancient Egypt had traces of cooperative-like organizations as early as 3000 B.C. and there are vestiges of cooperative ideas in Greek, Roman, and Chinese cultures. The first farmers' cooperatives are reported to be those of Swiss dairy farmers, who made cheese cooperatively as early as the thirteenth century.

Early Americans also experimented with cooperatives. Benjamin Franklin organized a mutual insurance company (a cooperative) in 1752. However, many people recognize the first formal cooperative of modern times to be the Rochdale Society of Equitable Pioneers in England in 1844. The original 28 members of this early cooperative joined in an effort to purchase supplies for their businesses. The Rochdale Principles, adopted by the Rochdale Society to guide the operation of their cooperative, included the following points:

1. Capital should be of member's own providing and bear a fixed rate of interest.
2. Only the purest provisions procurable should be supplied to members.
3. Full weight and measure should be given.
4. Market prices should be charged and no credit given or asked.
5. "Profits" should be divided pro rata upon the amount of purchases made by each member.
6. The principle of one member, one vote should govern, and that there should be equality of the sexes in membership.
7. Management should be in the hands of the officers and committees elected periodically.
8. A definite percentage of profits should be allotted to education.
9. Frequent statements and balance sheets should be presented to members.

While some of the principles have been modified over time, this set of Rochdale principles still provides the basic organizing framework for cooperatives today.

Limited liability companies

A **limited liability company (LLC)** is a type of business organization form that closely resembles a partnership, but provides its members with limited liability. Thus, creditors or others who have a claim against an LLC can pursue the assets of the LLC to satisfy debt and other obligations, but they cannot pursue personal or business assets owned by the individual members of the LLC.

Advantages of LLCs

Limited liability companies can include any number of members and ownership is distributed in accordance to the fair market value of the assets contributed. Also, net income generated by an LLC is passed on to its members in proportion to their shares of ownership. The net income is then reported on the members' individual tax returns and taxes are paid by the members and not by the LLC. An LLC is not required to file articles of incorporation as would be true of a corporation. However, it is still a good idea to record contributions and distributions of assets, revenue, and expenses, as well as agreements as to how the LLC will operate. These can be included in an article of organization or an operating agreement.

Disadvantages of LLCs

Although the LLC has the limited liability advantage of a corporation, it does not have some of the other advantages associated with the corporate form of organization. The LLC cannot deduct the cost of employee benefits, such as insurance costs and the use of vehicles by members. Also, it does not automatically continue in the event of the death of a member. Instead, it may be perpetual, end on a set date, or upon an event such as a death of a member, as outlined in the articles of organization or operating agreement.

Limited liability companies are an attractive organizational form for those individuals who desire the simplicity and flexibility provided by a partnership combined with the limited liability offered by a corporation. Competent and experienced legal counsel should be sought when considering this form of organization.

Strategic alliances

Many agribusinesses have formed **strategic alliances** and related cooperative relationships with other firms. Strategic alliances are cooperative agreements between firms that go beyond normal firm-to-firm dealings, but fall short of being a merger or full partnership and ownership. Such alliances can include joint research efforts, technology-sharing agreements, joint use of production facilities, agreements to market each other's products and the like.

Advantages of strategic alliances

There are several advantages to firms that form strategic alliances. First, firms can collaborate on technology or the development of new products. The areas of computer hardware and software and biotechnology are examples. Second, firms can improve supply chain efficiency by working together. An alliance between a feed firm and a large integrated swine business would provide an example. Third, firms can gain economies of scale in production and/or marketing. A food firm might enter into a strategic alliance with a broker to distribute its products into a new region of the country. Here, the focus is market expansion and the scale economies this can bring. Fourth, firms, particularly small firms, can fill voids in their technical and manufacturing expertise. A firm in the precision agriculture arena may have an alliance with a major farm equipment manufacturer to collaborate on the development of a new sensor-based system for harvesting melons. Fifth, firms can acquire or improve market access. A firm selling animal health products and an e-business firm might enter into a strategic alliance. The e-business firm provides the information technology infrastructure, and access to customers. The animal health firm provides products and an existing customer list.

Finally, allies can direct their combined competitive energies into building competitive advantage and defeating a mutual rival.

Disadvantages of strategic alliances

There can also be disadvantages to forming strategic alliances. First, establishing effective coordination between independent companies is both challenging and time consuming. How are responsibilities divided? How will returns be divided? These questions, and a hundred more like them, must be answered in a successful alliance.

Second, there may be language and cultural barriers to overcome, as well as attitudes of suspicion and mistrust. This issue includes the need for mutually shared goals. If two alliance partners have different objectives from the alliance, the seeds for long-run problems have been planted.

Third, the relationship may cool at some point in the future and the desired benefits may never be realized, but information may have already been shared. This commonly occurs when there is management turnover among the alliance partners. The situation and personalities that were part of the original deal change over time, and the new management team may look at the world—and the deal—differently.

Finally, a firm may become too dependent on another firm's expertise and capabilities and fail to develop its own internal capabilities. Firms must be careful with respect to what they do themselves, and what they depend on from a partner. In the animal health example above, the alliance may be a wonderful move for the animal health firm. Or, it could leave them vulnerable in three years if a competitor purchases their alliance partner and they have no internal e-business capabilities.

A strategic alliance is an attractive organizational form for those firms that want to preserve their independence rather than merge with another firm when trying to either remain competitive or enhance their competitive position. This form of organization enables those firms to collaborate with other firms to enhance their own capabilities, develop new products, and compete more effectively. However, as mentioned above, there are also disadvantages that should be seriously considered before forming a strategic alliance.

Taxation

As discussed earlier in this chapter, proprietorships, partnerships, Subchapter S corporations and limited liability companies pay taxes on their business profits at the personal rate. Corporations, however, have a separate tax rate for corporate profits. If the corporation distributes dividends to shareholders, then these individuals also pay personal income tax on this amount. Hence, many corporate profits are subject to double taxation—first, the corporate profits are taxed, and then the dividends (paid from after-tax profits) are taxed again.

A proprietorship completes either Schedule C or Schedule F (farms and ranches) to report business income, expenses, and profit or loss. This amount is then carried forward to the individual's Form 1040 where it would be taxed at the individual rate. Likewise, partners and members of a limited liability company complete Schedule K to tabulate their profit distribution from the business and carry this forward to their Form 1040 to pay personal taxes on their share of profits from the business. The partnership and LLC must complete Form 1065 to show all partnership income and profit distributions. Also, S-corporation shareholders report income from the corporation on their Form 1040.

Corporations report their sales, expenses, and profits on Form 1120 for ordinary corporations and Form 1120S for S-corporations. Taxes on regular corporations are calculated from the tax rates included in the tax table used for corporations. The point here is that tax issues do enter in an important way when selecting a form of business organization, especially for smaller businesses. And, when making these choices small business owners and entrepreneurs need competent legal and tax advice.

Summary

Agribusinesses represent nearly every conceivable kind of business organization. A great many are owned and controlled by one person as a proprietorship, or by two or more people as a partnership. These forms of business are the simplest forms and allow their owners complete flexibility, minimize red tape, and incur no corporate profits tax. But owners are personally liable for any debts or lawsuits against their business. Also, the longevity of the business is limited to the life of their owners. The LLC is a relatively new type of business organization that closely resembles a partnership, but provides its members with limited liability and the opportunity to influence the longevity of the business.

The corporation is an organization created for the purpose of carrying on business. Because it is a legal entity, it can own property in its own right, sue or be sued, and carry on business on its own behalf. Its owners are separate legal entities; thus their liability is limited to the amount of their investment in the firm. Also, the life of a corporation does not depend on how long its owners live. However, corporations must pay a special corporate profits tax and must regularly report their activities to federal and state governmental units. The S-corporation is a special type of corporation for small firms; they gain the benefits of a corporation, but are exempt from corporate profits tax.

Cooperatives are a type of corporation that allows individuals and/or businesses to work together or "cooperate" in marketing products or in buying inputs. They are an important part of the agribusiness landscape and have a focus on the member-user. Limited Liability Companies (LLCs) closely resemble a partnership, but provide their members with limited liability and can include any number of members.

Strategic alliances are agreements to cooperate that stop short of formal legal combinations. These alliances offer a number of benefits and are commonly used in food and agribusiness markets. But, there are clearly some limitations and problems to be managed, so firms must explore both the advantages and disadvantages before forming a strategic alliance. What will work in one situation may not work in another situation.

Selecting the best form of business organization for a particular agribusiness is an infrequent business decision for both management and owners, but an extremely important one. As an agribusiness firm grows, it must often consider moving toward becoming a regular corporation. And the timing of that decision is highly important.

Discussion questions

1. What are some of the questions that business managers/owners should consider when deciding on which form of business organization is best?
2. What are some of the characteristics of the sole proprietorship which make it an attractive form of business?
3. Explain the concept of unlimited liability as it relates to sole proprietorships.
4. Discuss the differences between a general and limited partnership.

5. Outline the reasons why a corporation may be referred to as an "artificial person," and discuss why corporations suffer from "double taxation" on their profits.
6. Discuss some of the advantages and disadvantages of the corporate form of business.
7. How does an agricultural cooperative benefit its member owners (i.e., what is the economic basis of their advantage over other types of businesses)?
8. Cooperatives are "member-owned, member-controlled." How does this unique structure differ from non-cooperative corporations and what advantages and/or disadvantages does this allow?
9. How does a Limited Liability Company (LLC) differ from a partnership and a corporation, and what advantages do these characteristics provide?
10. Why would a firm consider entering into a strategic alliance?

References and additional reading

www.census.gov/compendia/statab/2010/tables/10s0728.pdf
www.census.gov/compendia/statab/2010/tables/10s0729.pdf

5 International agribusiness

Objectives

- Understand why agribusinesses may choose to seek out international markets
- Develop an understanding of the importance of international markets to U.S. food and agribusiness firms
- Describe some of the challenges that agribusinesses face when pursuing international markets
- Understand the elements of a society's culture, and how these elements shape the operating environment for an international firm
- Identify the different methods that food and agribusiness firms might use to enter international markets

Introduction

Why would an already successful domestic agribusiness consider entering the more risky international marketplace? After all, selling into unfamiliar international markets is full of uncertainties. The agribusiness could be conservative and continue with its strategy of expanding into other U.S. markets. But, despite the unknowns, there are many reasons why a U.S.-based firm would want to "go global."

In many U.S. food and agribusiness markets, market growth is leveling off and the market is approaching maturity, or a time of slow growth. At the same time, the markets in many other countries are growing very fast, or have the potential to grow fast, offering new business opportunities. For example, China is one of the fastest-growing markets in the world. In 2010, USDA's Foreign Agricultural Service (FAS) cites China as the fourth largest market for U.S. agricultural exports (www.fas.usda.gov/itp/china/India_Chinamarket022010.pdf). Prior to economic reforms in 1978, nearly four in five Chinese worked in agriculture; by 1994, only one in two did. The British Broadcasting Company (BBC) recently reported that although China's per capita income is only a fraction of that in many industrial countries, it has grown by an average of 10 percent a year for the last two decades (http://news.bbc.co.uk/2/hi/business/520874.stm).

U.S. agribusinesses are also finding that their competition in the domestic market is increasing from foreign-owned and controlled companies. Foreign firms have entered the U.S. market bringing new competition, replacing domestic competitors, and/or have joined forces with domestic agribusinesses. In any case, the competition in U.S. agribusiness markets has become increasingly fierce as each firm, U.S. or foreign, tries to capture a larger piece of the market. Combining the increased competition in the U.S. market from international companies with the opportunities in international markets, the threat is clear: if a U.S. food or agribusiness company doesn't produce and sell it, someone else in the world will!

So, why should an agribusiness manager be interested in better understanding international business? In this chapter, we will explore this question and identify some of the reasons why the international marketplace is of great interest to agribusiness managers. We will also examine some of the reasons why doing business internationally may be challenging, and some of the strategies agribusiness firms use to "go global."

Why does U.S. agribusiness need international markets?

There are many reasons for agribusinesses, and the U.S. economy, to be interested in the international business arena. From an economic standpoint, the exporting of U.S. agricultural products boosts employment within the U.S. economy. In 2008, it was estimated that more than 8,000 jobs were created for every $1 billion in agricultural exports (this is down from the 18,000 jobs estimated to be created by every $1 billion in agricultural exports in 1998) (www.ers.usda.gov/Data/TradeMultiplier/econeffects/2008overview.aspx). This implies that nearly 920,000 jobs in the agricultural sector were the direct result of farm product exports of $115.4 billion in 2008. Agricultural exports help boost rural economies: approximately one-third of those agricultural export jobs were located in rural areas. Although most of these rural jobs are in the production of agricultural products, others are in more labor-intensive industries such as wholesale and retail trade, services, and food processing and feed processing.

Benefits from doing business internationally

From a managerial standpoint, international markets hold appeal for a number of reasons. Some of these reasons are shown in the list below:

- Exports and sales
- Take advantage of scale economies
- Capture benefits of a global brand
- Reduce risk by diversifying across markets
- Lower costs of production
- Access lower-cost raw materials through international sourcing
- Broaden access to credit
- Leverage experiences from operating in international markets into domestic markets

While each reason in the list may not be part of a specific international opportunity for an agribusiness firm, the list does provide a snapshot of several important reasons agribusinesses find international business attractive.

Clearly, one reason to pursue international markets is to expand sales by capitalizing on growth opportunities in other countries. Some newly industrialized countries are experiencing extraordinary growth when compared with established markets such as the United States, Europe and Japan. Entering a newly industrialized country may offer agribusiness companies a piece of this potential for rapidly growing sales and profits. In addition, product life cycles can often be extended by selling products in foreign countries. The potential for expanding international sales is especially important if the domestic market is experiencing

Plate 5.1 Lettuce harvest
Global marketers promote branded food and fiber products in every corner of the world. Photo courtesy of USDA Natural Resources Conservation Service.

slow, or no, sales growth. A related advantage of serving a larger international market is to achieve scale economies because of larger production volumes.

Name or **brand recognition** is another benefit a company works toward in globalization efforts. Global recognition of corporate logos and brands increases both the efficiency and effectiveness of a company's advertising efforts. Brands are very expensive to develop, and if a firm can spread those development costs across a broader market, profits can increase. As a result, many companies competitively vie for sponsorship of world-televised sporting events. Reinforcement of brand or logo recognition can be a powerful tool in these cases of sponsorship. For example, in the 2010 soccer World Cup held in South Africa, sponsor company logos were shown and/or mentioned in more than 97 countries and in numerous languages on both television, radio and over the internet. Firms like Coca-Cola, PepsiCo, and McDonald's have brands that are recognized in virtually every country in the world.

Agribusinesses may be able to reduce their overall risk exposure by broadening the number of markets from which they purchase inputs and sell products because they are not dependent on a single, local market. Organizations with operations in several countries may stand to be less affected by slow periods in their domestic market when actively engaged in business abroad. Sourcing inputs internationally may also significantly lower costs of production. Such cost advantages allow firms to lower prices, giving them an important advantage.

Global firms may also have easier access to credit and gain valuable experience from operating in other markets. Firms serving international markets can move technology around the world, locating new markets for the results of their research and development in the process. For example, firms in the hybrid corn seed business regularly rely on genes from seed obtained from such places as Argentina, Italy, and northeast Iowa to develop a superior hybrid that performs well across the same latitudes worldwide. In other cases, firms may identify a new product opportunity in an international market, and be able to bring this idea home to the domestic market.

Opportunities for smaller firms

It's not only the multinational conglomerates finding opportunities and success in the international marketplace. Small agribusinesses have found niches in serving needs around the world. Their active pursuit of placing and developing products for international markets has in many cases met with great success. While large companies reap the benefits of deep pockets—economies of scale and greater returns on their investment in research and development—smaller agribusiness firms are often more flexible, allowing them to adapt to the changing structure and demands of the international food industry. As with all business in the international marketplace, successful global business endeavors by the small firm require an understanding of the unique characteristics and structures of the customer in each given instance (Connor and Schiek 1997).

Although countless factors influence the global marketplace during any business day, a few key factors have helped increase the number of opportunities for small agribusiness firms in the international arena. First, emerging markets have entered into the world trade picture at a rate unequaled since post-World War II. Those markets are opening up to conduct business with international suppliers, partners, etc. These nations include those in Eastern Europe, other countries of the former USSR, India, Latin America, China, and other Asian countries. Many African countries are moving continually closer to allowing or welcoming business from outside their borders.

The second key factor opening doors of world markets for smaller businesses is technology. Simply put, today's small food and agribusinesses are often "well wired"—connected via the internet by computer, modem, email, telephone, cell phone, and fax—making them very competitive with much larger firms for emerging-market growth potential. Essentially, the world is truly available to creative, innovative businesses. However, unlike the world market of post-World War II when the multinational companies controlled these markets, markets today are often open to the best competitors. Companies that succeed will be flexible enough to adapt to constant change and adjust to an array of challenges. Those companies are often the small, agile companies.

A global market

Up to this point in this chapter we have talked about why agribusinesses may choose to conduct business in an international location. There is, however, a different viewpoint on international business. Instead of thinking about stepping into an international market, many of today's successful firms approach business from the perspective of conducting business in a global market. This distinction is subtle, but significant. A global perspective is a philosophy, an attitude, and or an approach to conducting business abroad. Global agribusiness management is guided by concepts that view the world as one market. And firms with a global perspective run their businesses this way.

Let's take a look at one important area—marketing—and explore the differences in these two perspectives. Global marketing is based on identifying and targeting cross-cultural similarities. International marketing management is based on the premise of cross-cultural differences and is guided by the belief that each foreign market requires its own culturally adapted marketing strategy. Today, a global market has evolved on many levels and for products/services that previously did not exist.

How is it possible to develop a global marketing strategy for some products? Information technology and access to information, goods and services not only in this country, but also across the globe, has changed our world. Truly the business culture of today is more global than at any time in the past. In many ways, our familiarity with the tastes, preferences, attitudes, and cultures of other countries has exploded in the past decade or two. Salsa sales in the United States surpassed the sales of ketchup within the past decade, and ethnic food sales in general are at all-time highs and continuing to increase. Travel is another factor that has led to the globalization of today's marketplace. By exposing a greater number of people from various cultures to one another and to other places, an underlying melding of cultures, or at the very least, the understanding of them occurs.

A more mobile society has changed the landscape of our marketplace at home as well as abroad. Demographics from the state of California offer an example. California, the most populous state in the nation, is also the clear leader in ethnic "mixing" in North America. Consider that in 1970, 80 percent of Californians were non-Latin whites. As of 2010, heavy immigration from Asia and Latin American has changed California's population mix to 42 percent non-Latin whites (http://quickfacts.census.gov/qfd/states/06000. html). California, Texas, New Mexico, and Hawaii are all states where non-Latin whites are not the majority. This type of mobilization of the population is not isolated to the United States alone by any means. It is occurring around the globe. For example, diversity is not limited just to ethnicity, but religion as well. Islam is widely considered Europe's fastest growing religion, with immigration and above average birth rates leading to a rapid increase in the Muslim population. France's Muslim population now makes up 10 percent of the total population of the country (http://news.bbc.co.uk/2/hi/europe/4385768. stm). These changes mean that people bring their cultures, their traditions and religions, their needs, their connections and networks with them from the lands from which they came.

Each of these factors has provided agribusinesses with more opportunity for marketing global products that will not only be accepted, but also preferred by the new, informed, exposed and well-traveled, global consumers. In response, global agribusinesses develop a universal strategy for marketing products to the world rather than producing single strategies for individual countries or markets.

International agribusiness trends

U.S. food and agribusiness industries continue to gain momentum in international markets even though most food is consumed in the country in which it is produced. According to a recent USDA Economic Research Service report, the United States has a 24 percent share of world commercial processed food sales (www.ers.usda.gov/publications/aib794/aib794g. pdf). The United States remains the world leader in exports of agricultural commodities and at the same time is an increasingly important player in the exporting and importing of food and food products.

The growing population in the global market

The Food and Agriculture Organization (FAO) of the United Nations defines food security as the state of affairs where all people at all times have access to safe and nutritious food to maintain a healthy and active life. World population in 2010 was roughly 6.7 billion people. While population is growing more slowly than forecast a few years ago, it is still predicted that it will be a number of years before population growth stabilizes. Predictions of future populations put the global population between 8 and 12 billion by 2050 with nearly all the growth expected in the developing world (Figures 5.1 and 5.2).

Given these population growth estimates, there is little doubt that food demand will increase significantly in the years ahead. Many experts estimate the growing population will mean that a doubling of food production will be necessary during the next 30 years. Of course, food demand is more than just population—income to buy food is also important. So, the realized increase in demand for food will depend on both population growth and income growth. With respect to income, the world continues to grow more polarized. There is a greater disparity among the "haves" and the "have-nots." While the number of people in the low-income bracket grows faster than the total world population, the share of income controlled by the upper-income bracket of the population has also been rising significantly. This phenomenon is measured by the "Gini coefficient." This metric is a number between 0 and 1, where 0 corresponds with perfect equality (where everyone has the same income) and 1 corresponds with perfect inequality (where one person has all the income and everyone else has zero income). Figure 5.3 shows countries scored by Gini coefficient.

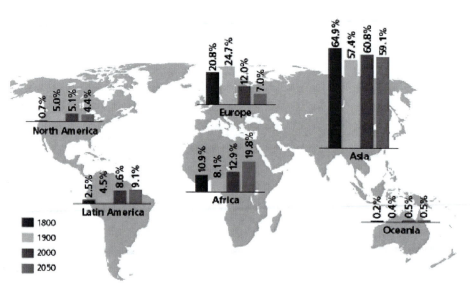

Figure 5.1 World population distribution by region, 1800–2050
Source: United Nations Population Division, *Briefing Packet, 1998 Revision of World Population Prospects.*

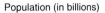

Population (in billions)

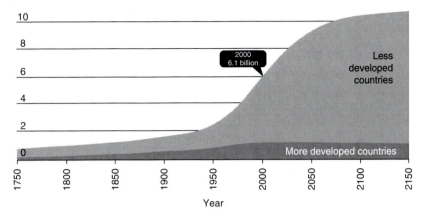

Figure 5.2 World population growth
Source: United Nations, "World Population Prospects," The 1998 Revision.

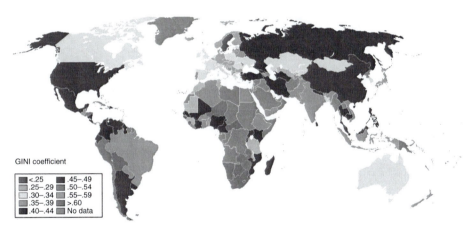

Figure 5.3 Countries of the world by Gini coefficient
Source: CIA - The World Factbook 2009.

The world is becoming more urbanized as well, with more people moving into cities. The attraction of urban areas is due in part to the jobs available at these business hubs. In 2008, for the first time in human history, the world's population was evenly split between urban and rural areas. In 1975, only one-third of the world's population lived in urban areas.

So, not only will the sheer numbers of people on the planet increase, but it is also likely that the numbers of individuals with the ability to pay for products will increase. If current reforms are merely sustained in the countries with food security deficits, it is likely there will be improved food security for an increasing number of people. The translation is thus: opportunities for food and agricultural businesses will continue to grow; and the international marketplace will offer increased possibilities.

U.S. agribusiness trade and investment grows abroad

The U.S. food industry is growing—and it is growing abroad. Two key factors responsible for that growth are trade and investment. International trade, both imports and exports of food and food products, is increasing faster than domestic sales. The United States Department of Agriculture reported that U.S. agricultural exports in fiscal year 2009 were $98.6 billion (USDA ERS). In contrast, agricultural imports into the United States in 2009 were $76.2 billion, leaving a surplus in U.S. agricultural trade of $22.4 billion (www.ers.usda.gov/Data/FATUS).

The U.S. agricultural industry is dependent on the export market. Today, roughly 30 cents of every $1 earned on agricultural products comes from exports. Strong export competition continues to influence the projected trends in the export market. Strengthening global economic growth may provide a foundation for gains in trade and U.S. agricultural exports. These factors point to the possibility of rising market prices, increases in farm income, and stability in the financial condition of the U.S. agricultural sector.

Finally, growth prospects for U.S. agricultural exports, particularly in the consumer food products area, are shifting. As growth in the markets of developed countries such as Canada, Japan, and the European Union slows over time, developing countries and their strong growth economies have become targets for increased food exports. Interestingly, the competitive market and characteristics of consumer food products between developed countries and developing countries differ (Table 5.1). The successful international marketer must address such differences.

Bulk commodities, high-value products

Agricultural exports are composed of two categories: value-added products and bulk commodities (Table 5.2). Value-added or **high-value products (HVPs)** are agricultural products that have received additional processing or require special handling or shipping. HVPs include unprocessed foods such as fresh fruit or eggs, as well as processed and semi-processed grains, oilseeds, animals and animal products, horticultural products, sugar and tropical products. HVPs have been further categorized into intermediate commodities and consumer products (beverages, meats, and frozen dinners). Intermediate commodities are those that have received some processing (soybean meal), are used as inputs on the farm (animal feeds, seed), or are used by food manufacturers (flour). Bulk commodities, such as wheat, corn, soybeans, rice, and tobacco have historically comprised much of U.S. agricultural exports. However, exports of value-added products increasingly comprise a larger portion of total agricultural exports.

Table 5.1 Characteristics of developed and developing markets for food

Developed Countries	Developing Countries
Saturation	Increasing Demand
Food safety	Food security
Buyer's market	Seller's market
Concentration	Fragmentation

Table 5.2 USDA agricultural trade values

	2007	2008	2009	2010	2011[1]
	(Billion Dollars)				
Agricultural Exports:					
Livestock, poultry, and dairy	16.36	21.77	18.63	21.54	23.0
Grains, feeds, and products	24.30	38.33	26.28	27.29	35.4
Oilseeds and products	13.67	22.81	20.87	25.37	28.3
Horticultural products	18.02	20.79	20.63	22.61	24.3
Tobacco, unmanufactured	1.14	1.28	1.20	1.22	1.2
Cotton and linters	4.29	4.75	3.51	4.76	8.0
Other exports	4.44	5.18	5.18	5.87	6.3
Total agricultural exports:	82.22	114.91	96.30	108.66	126.5
Bulk commodities exports	31.57	50.65	36.80	41.02	NA
High-value product exports	50.65	64.26	59.50	67.64	NA
High-value product share	61.6%	55.9%	61.8%	62.2%	NA
Agricultural Imports:					
Livestock, poultry, and dairy	12.03	12.18	10.68	10.84	11.5
Grains, feeds, and products	5.99	7.88	7.37	7.48	8.2
Oilseeds and products	4.03	6.59	5.35	5.27	5.6
Horticultural products	32.39	34.71	33.02	35.55	38.5
Sugar and tropical products	14.14	16.36	15.34	18.32	20.3
Other imports	1.48	1.6	1.64	1.49	1.4
Total agricultural imports:	70.06	79.32	73.40	78.95	85.5
Net agricultural trade balances	12.16	35.59	22.9	29.71	41.0

Note: [1] forecast for fiscal 2011.
Source: http://usda.mannlib.cornell.edu/usda/current/AES/AES-11-30-2010.pdf

In 1970, wheat, corn, and soybeans comprised 68 percent of the total value of all U.S. agricultural exports. Forty years later in 2010, the composition of U.S. agricultural exports had changed dramatically and just 31 percent of total export value consisted of these bulk commodities (www.ers.usda.gov/Data/FATUS). The rapid growth in HVP exports began after 1985 with the devaluation of the U.S. dollar relative to other currencies. Since that time, incomes have continued to increase in countries such as South Korea, Taiwan, Mexico, and China, and this has helped to spur demand for HVPs. Most of these countries are experiencing changes in lifestyle—convenience and western-style foods are increasingly being sought out and preferred by consumers. Import tariffs and other barriers have also declined during this time period providing another reason for the rapid increase in HVP exports (see World Trade Organization discussion below). Also, the U.S. government, recognizing the value of advertising, began to fund promotions of agricultural products abroad. This, along with the success of other U.S. firms abroad, has increased the interest of U.S. firms in exporting agricultural products abroad.

As a result of these factors, exports of HVPs and bulk commodities have continued to increase—with HVPs increasing an average of 11 percent per year during the decade of the 2000s, and bulk commodities increasing an average of 14 percent per year during the same period.

Plate 5.2 Grain harvest equipment
While shipping more high-value products every year, the export of bulk commodities continues to be important to U.S. agriculture. Photo courtesy of USDA Natural Resources Conversation Service.

World Trade Organization

Political, social, and economic changes over the last decade alone have dramatically altered the way business is done in the international marketplace as well as the number of entities ready and willing to conduct international business. That growth and excitement has been building significantly over the course of the last five to six decades.

In 1947, an international organization was established to reduce trade barriers through multilateral trade negotiations. That organization was known as **GATT** (General Agreement on Tariffs and Trade). Beginning in 1988, GATT negotiations intensified with the goal of developing a stronger organization. In 1995, the **World Trade Organization (WTO)** was formed and all GATT agreements at the then current round of negotiations (the Uruguay Round) were incorporated into the WTO. The WTO now has 153 members and WTO rules apply to over 97 percent of international trade.

The WTO's efforts stretch beyond its parent organization's focus of reducing tariffs on manufactured goods. Tariffs tend to distort markets because market signals (supply and demand) are not communicated as efficiently or effectively. The reduction of tariffs (taxes on imported or exported goods) allows products to trade more freely. It is generally recognized by most economists that free trade benefits society because costs and benefits are more evenly distributed. The WTO works to eliminate nontariff barriers as well. It can be used to mediate trade disputes, or to challenge environmental, health, and other regulations that may serve legitimate social goals, but which may be regarded as impediments to international trade.

A reduction in global trade barriers has led to an increase in trade over the past several decades. While the WTO has numerous objectives, one of the primary ones is the reduction of tariffs. The WTO has been successful in cutting worldwide tariffs to 5 percent (Veseth and Uchitelle 2002)—down from 40 percent at the end of World War II. In addition, it has made trade more transparent, as it has negotiated with countries to convert non-tariff trade barriers into tariffs. Such changes clearly support the importance of the international market-place for food and agribusiness firm managers. While some criticize and others praise the WTO, one fact is clear: growth in international trade and investment is developing at a faster pace than before and a lot of that growth can be attributed to the existence of the WTO.

Challenges in international markets

The path to successfully doing business in international agribusiness markets certainly has its challenges. Some of the more dominant issues that firms face entering these markets are discussed in this section. These challenges include: cultural differences, exchange rate fluc-tuations, accounting system differences, uncertainty of the political and economic climate, property rights issues, regulations, sanitary and phytosanitary (SPS) rules, trade specifica-tions, and the challenges of management in an international environment.

Plate 5.3 Woman riding planter
Food and agribusiness managers deal with people across the world who use different technologies and for whom costs of production vary dramatically. Photo courtesy of USDA Natural Resources Conservation Service.

Cultural differences

Culture is the set of socially transmitted behaviors, acts, beliefs, speech, and all other products of human work and thought that characterize a particular population. Culture is transmitted from one generation to the next, not inherited automatically at birth. Instead, culture is learned and it helps to define perceptions, beliefs, practices, communication styles, relationships, and family roles. Cultures vary dramatically around the world, and such differences must be understood by a firm attempting to operate in an international market.

The concept of culture is very broad and thus some system is needed for describing a particular culture. Anthropologists, for example, consider culture in a total systems approach, and look at a culture based on its systems of education, economics, politics, religion, health, recreation, and kinship. A simpler approach to understanding a culture is by looking at ten general characteristics or dimensions. It must be emphasized, however, that this is a simple model, and it is not the only way to analyze a culture. The dimensions are the following:

Sense of self and space. Sense of self, or individualism, concerns how much an individual values personal freedom over responsibility to family or national groups. Sense of space is concerned with the physical space we use in our culture. Americans have a sense of space that requires more distance between individuals than that required in Latin America and Arab cultures. Also, the size and location of an executive's office in the United States conveys a great deal about the status of the executive, but it is a poor indicator of power in some Arab nations.

Communication and language. Communication systems, both verbal and nonverbal, distinguish cultures from one another. More importantly, communication is effective when the receiver ends up with the message the sender intended to send. It has been said that as much as 70 percent of a message is nonverbal. Nonverbal messages include gestures, facial expressions, posture, stance, eye contact, and use of color. For example, Far Eastern cultures tend to value politeness over blunt truth. In Indonesia it is impolite to disagree with someone. Indonesians rarely say "no." You are expected to be able to differentiate a polite "yes" (which really means "no") from an actual "yes." There are several verbal and nonverbal expressions the Indonesians use to signal when "yes" actually means "no." In Japan, a response like "I'll consider it," may actually mean no. In Taiwan, brutal honesty is not appreciated. A direct "no" is usually considered rude. "Yes" could mean "maybe" or "I understand." "Maybe" most often means "no."

Dress and appearance. Garments, adornments, and body decorations distinguish cultures. Subcultures also wear distinguishing clothing—managers may dress differently in different cultures.

Food and eating habits. Food is selected, prepared, presented, and eaten differently in different cultures. Although Europeans and American use the same dining utensils, you can distinguish the two from which hand holds the implement.

Time and time consequences. Different messages may be conveyed by the amount of notice given to or by a meeting, invitations to future commitments, or the time of departure. To be 30 minutes late for an appointment with a business associate may be considered rude in the United States, but it may be early and unexpectedly reliable in Puerto Rico.

Relationships. The value of relationships in a culture is most easily viewed by the importance of the family unit (and the extended family). Age, gender, status, wealth, power, and wisdom are other aspects that may affect the type and degree of relationships within a culture.

Values and norms. Needs and wants may vary between cultures. Acceptable behavior within a culture reflects the values held by that culture. Underdeveloped cultures may value adequate food, clothing, and shelter. A more developed culture may take these items for granted and may place high value on money, status, and civility. Even further, values and norms can have definitive impacts on food and agribusiness firms. For example, as societies become more affluent, they become less concerned about whether there is enough food (hunger and food security concerns) and more interested in how food is produced (issues related to animal welfare, organic production, energy use/food miles and sustainability).

Beliefs and attitudes. All cultures have some interest in a "higher power" or the supernatural as seen in their various religions. Attitudes toward oneself, others, and the world also distinguish cultures. U.S. business philosophy assumes that people can substantially influence and affect the future. Other cultures may believe that events will occur regardless of what they do.

Mental process and learning. Some cultures emphasize abstract thinking and conceptualization while others prefer learning and memory. However, most cultures do recognize and reward reasoning processes.

Work and work habits. Work and success at work may be viewed differently in different cultures. Work habits, attitudes toward work and authority, and how work is rewarded and measured may all vary within a culture. Some cultures view success at work in terms of the status of the position held within the company, while other cultures view success in terms of the total income earned.

The international agribusiness firm must be sensitive to differences in cultures and make the appropriate adjustments in their business approaches. The experienced agribusiness manager will try to accept the values of the local culture and will seek to work within the accepted behaviors. Adjustments, if necessary, by international agribusiness firms are generally made in three categories:

- *Product adaptations*: Products may undergo modifications and/or the way products are marketed may change.
- *Individual*: A manager who is overseas for the first time must learn the local language and make adjustments in dealing with people.
- *Institutional*: Hiring practices and organizational structure often must change when working in a new country. For example, an agribusiness must take into account class distinctions, different religions, or different tribes that may require adjustments in hiring and placing people within an organization.

Exchange rate fluctuations

Exchange rates determine the worth of one country's currency relative to that of another country. An example of an exchange rate is one U.S. dollar may be equivalent to 116 Japanese yen. This exchange rate will change and fluctuate over time. Agricultural trade is very sensitive to changes in the exchange rate relative to some other industries because agricultural goods are more homogeneous (U.S. wheat and Canadian wheat are nearly perfect substitutes). When the value of the dollar rises relative to other competitors' currencies, U.S. agricultural goods become more expensive—and thus less competitive. Therefore, the export performance of U.S. agriculture is closely tied to changes in the value of the dollar relative to other currencies.

Export profits can also be reduced significantly with highly fluctuating exchange rates. For example, a U.S. agribusiness agrees to sell 3,000 tons of corn to a Japanese buyer for 12,500 yen per ton. If the exchange rate increased in terms of foreign currency per U.S. dollar between the time of the contract and the actual time of payment, then the U.S. firm would earn a lower profit because it would receive fewer dollars for the corn.

Agribusinesses can deal with exchange rates in several ways. Sometimes U.S. exporters agree to accept payment in foreign currency because they can more effectively manage the exchange rate risk. This approach can be a bargaining chip as well because foreign firms may be willing to pay a higher price in their home currency. Another method to deal with fluctuating exchange rates between the United States and the importer is to negotiate payment in another country's currency that is relatively stable. Still another method is to agree to divide the gains and losses in the exchange market, or to use the futures markets and manage the risk using currency futures.

Accounting differences

The internationalization of business is also made complex by the different accounting methods that are used in each country. Financial terms are often quite different—"inventory" in the United States is "stocks" in the United Kingdom; "retained earnings" in the United States is "profit and loss reserve" in the United Kingdom. Some financial statements do not even exist in other countries. The "statement of cash flows," an important accounting statement in the U.S. financial market, does not exist in countries like Germany and Japan.

Financial statement format often varies from one country to another. In the United States, assets are presented in order of their liquidity—the most liquid or current assets are listed first followed by less liquid assets. British financial statements are listed exactly in the opposite order. In fact, assets and liabilities are listed together.

The accounting for noncurrent assets can vary substantially between countries. In the United States, large equipment and capital assets are valued on balance sheets at their historical cost. The value of these assets is depreciated as a means of allocating the costs of these assets to their use over time. However, the original asset value on the balance sheet never changes. That is, an asset's value on the balance sheet rarely reflects the replacement cost or market value of that asset. Firms in countries such as Australia, Canada, and the United Kingdom periodically appraise their assets and make adjustments to reflect their current market value. Depreciation is then estimated using these adjusted asset values.

Research and development (R & D) expenditures are also accounted for differently between countries. In the United States, R & D costs are treated as an expense in the period in which they are incurred. In Brazil, R & D expenditures are capitalized to provide an incentive for companies to invest in developing new products.

As noted, exchange rates between countries fluctuate because of many different factors. These fluctuations may make it difficult to combine the financial data of foreign subsidiaries with domestic subsidiaries. Companies that trade stock or debt securities on exchanges located in other countries (such as the Nikkei in Japan) as well as the United States may have to prepare different financial reports that comply with the particular accounting standards for that country. As you might imagine, these differences in accounting standards between countries have added much complexity to issuing financial statements in a timely, accurate manner.

International law and property rights issues

A global agribusiness must understand the many legal systems of the countries in which it operates. Once an international firm enters a country, it automatically becomes subject to all of that country's laws. Some governments may monitor daily business activities very closely while others may regulate only the large-scale activities of an agribusiness.

Probably the most important legal issues arising out of operating in the global economy are the interpretation and enforcement of various regional trade agreements. Examples of such agreements include the North American Free Trade Agreement (NAFTA), the World Trade Organization (WTO), and several other large regional trade groups including the European Union (EU), the Association of Southeast Asian Nations (ASEAN), and the Asia-Pacific Economic Cooperation Group (APEC). Each of these represents a restructuring, reorganizing, and refocusing for companies as they respond to the changing competitive mix of the global marketplace.

These alliances, agreements, and trade initiatives affect the practice of business world-wide. They mean companies will continue to inspect the hows and whys of conducting business efficiently enough and effectively enough to be competitive in the world market. For example, the 1994 North American Free Trade Agreement (NAFTA) spurred U.S. exports to Canada and Mexico. The NAFTA agreement reduced tariffs on agricultural commodities and removed trade barriers.

Most countries protect intellectual property rights (IPR) such as trademarks, patents, and publications. However, because these patents are issued in a particular country, they are valid and legal only within that country's jurisdiction. Some countries, most notably several in the Far East, do not have—or have not enforced—laws that protect these intellectual property rights, though progress is being made on this front.

Since joining the World Trade Organization, China has strengthened its legal framework and amended its IPR laws and regulations to comply with the WTO Agreement on Trade-Related Aspects of Intellectual Property Rights (TRIPS). Despite stronger statutory protection, China continues to be a haven for counterfeiters and pirates. According to one copyright industry association, the piracy rate remains one of the highest in the world (over 90 percent) and U.S. companies lose over one billion dollars in legitimate business each year to piracy. On average, 20 percent of all consumer products in the Chinese market are counterfeit. If a product sells, it is likely to be illegally duplicated. U.S. companies are not alone, as pirates and counterfeiters target both foreign and domestic companies (U.S. Embassy in China).

Private property, and the protection of it, is another important international legal issue. Individual nations, including the United States, reserve the right to take over private property when it is in the best interest of the host country. In the United States, as with other countries, the government may take over private property for a "public purpose" (the United States uses the laws of condemnation or eminent domain to do this). But, the interpretation of what "public purpose" means is often at issue.

Sanitary and phytosanitary regulations

Sanitary and phytosanitary (SPS) regulations (with phytosanitary defined as sanitary with regard to pests and pathogens) are intended to protect human, animal, and plant life or health. SPS regulations have been instituted in many countries because consumers in developed countries demand higher levels of food safety. However, in some cases, these SPS regulations have become a tool to use in protecting domestic agribusinesses and producers from competition (and thus in these cases are termed "nontariff barriers").

The WTO agreement stresses the desirability of common SPS regulations, and the agreement provides a framework for distinguishing legitimate SPS regulations from those that are not. Three international organizations (the FAO/WHO Codex Alimentarius Commission for food; the International Animal Health Organization for animal health; and the FAO's Secretariat of the International Plant Protection Convention for plant health) have been designated as sources of scientific expertise and internationally agreed-upon standards. These organizations work to promote and address SPS-related regulations in areas such as food additives, pesticide residues, animal health, and plant health.

The benefits of standardized SPS regulations are enormous because firms can develop new products that simultaneously meet the requirements of all markets rather than developing and testing configurations of products that meet different regulations. However, the concerns that brought about many of the SPS regulations must be considered in establishing more general standards.

Management challenges

Managing employees, clients, or accounts can be a challenge even when all are operating under the same roof. Throw in several thousand miles, a different language, culture, government, and monetary system and one has a management challenge on hand to say the least. Astute and deft handling of the numerous political and economic uncertainties in an international market can be among a manager's most challenging problems. Managing such issues and events may become heightened or intensified when put in motion in the international arena.

Entering international markets

As the global marketplace becomes reality to an ever-increasing number of agribusinesses, an evolutionary process becomes evident. This evolution may take place by design or by happenstance, immediately or over a course of years. However, many observers point to three phases of evolution as a firm moves from a domestic to a global perspective.

Some companies arrive in the international market via detour—some even by accident. Introduction to the international market for these companies may be the result of an interaction with an international buyer or perhaps an export company. Often, in these cases, the international market is not treated any differently than the domestic market. Changes to the product, the marketing, and so forth are not made to fit the international market—firms simply sell what they have always sold, but to a new, international customer group.

However, over time, many of those same firms shift to purposeful rather than incidental marketing of their products abroad and enter the second phase of the evolution. This means a deeper level of involvement, assigning resources specifically to developing markets in specific countries, looking for opportunities in production and distribution of the products, etc. This phase of the evolution of the global firm is known as the export marketing phase. Here, the business conducted internationally is viewed as a sideline to the normal domestic endeavor, but it is recognized as a separate and unique business.

The third phase emerges when a firm truly develops a global perspective, and manages its business accordingly. Decision-making at all levels is done in a global context. Production and raw material sourcing decisions are optimized around the world, marketing similarities are exploited globally, and the firm may focus on building global brands. Managers move across borders regularly to better understand the nuances of running a global enterprise. For all three phases of evolution, decisions about market entry must be made—how do food and agribusiness firms enter other countries?

Modes of entry

Three general methods are used to enter an international market: exporting, licensing, and foreign production. There are, of course, many variations of these methods including indirect and direct exporting, franchising, and foreign direct investment through acquisition, joint venture, or greenfield investment. The choice of entry method into the global arena depends on a firm's external and internal factors. External forces that influence the method of entry are factors such as the political, economic, and cultural arrangement of the target market. Internal firm factors include the agribusiness's strategic and financial goals, the firm's financial resources, the type of product that is being produced, and the sensitivity of the product or production method to the firm's competitiveness, and the firm's international market experience (Stern, El-Ansary, and Coughlan). Historically, many firms have used a strategy that gradually increases their presence in the global market over time.

Exporting

There are two general means used to export an agribusiness's products: indirect and direct exporting. Most agribusinesses, especially those with little international marketing experience, initially enter the global market via indirect exporting.

Indirect exporting uses a trading company or an export management company to handle the logistics of exporting. These trading experts manage the exporting and importing procedures and regulations, and they use their established relationships with buyers and distributors to distribute the product. Advantages offered through working with a trading company include the expertise, knowledge, experience, and connections in the market. These trading companies' networks within the distribution channels can be extremely useful to first-time exporters. Although overall, using indirect exporting may reduce profitability, many firms perceive this to be a low-risk strategy that entails substantially lower investment.

Direct exporting is where the agribusiness itself handles the details of exporting their product. At this point, the firm conducts research, establishes contacts in the country, and sets up its distribution channels. Firms often open an overseas sales office to manage the operations in that country. Direct exporting involves investments and salaries for the items mentioned previously. In turn, the potential for profits are much higher, and the firm can exert more control over product distribution.

In general, the advantages of exporting (over the other methods) are lower risk, lower fixed costs (compared to investing in a new plant in a country), and increased speed in reaching the global market. Several U.S. government agencies assist exporters as well. The disadvantages of exporting are primarily managing the trade barriers or protectionism that may exist in a country. Regulations, inspections, tariffs, and quotas are just some of the barriers that may be encountered, as well as less control and long distribution channels. Control over pricing, promotion, distribution, and quality are some of the other problems that may be experienced. As a result, agribusinesses wanting more control and lower costs may decide to look at licensing or direct investment as a means of entering a country's market.

Licensing

Licensing involves contracting with a firm (licensee) in the target market to produce and distribute the firm's (licensor) product. In return, the licensor receives a fee or royalty, one that can be profitable given that little capital is required by the licensor. Licensing can be especially attractive with agricultural products that are perishable and bulky or where the receiving country has restrictions on imports.

There are also disadvantages to licensing. The license may entail giving secret product formulas or processing technologies to the licensee, a key source of competitive advantage for the firm, and the licensee, may also become a competitor selling products where they are currently being sold. Also, if sales take off, the licensee could decide to establish and sell competing products, depending on the nature of the agreement that was signed. Finally, the licensor could find its brand image hurt if the licensee has not maintained sufficient control over product quality or promotion.

Direct investment

Agribusinesses use a variety of investment means to enter and serve a foreign market. These can fall broadly into three areas: greenfield investments, joint ventures, and acquisitions.

Greenfield investments are direct investments by a firm into a particular country (so called because they are a project that lacks any constraints imposed by prior work—the analogy being that of construction on a "green field" where there is no need to remodel or demolish an existing structure). An example would be a new plant built by a multinational firm or foreign subsidiary. Greenfield investments are often the only method of investing in a developing country where no other plants exist. High costs and risks are the drawbacks of these types of investments because unexpected market deterioration may prevent the firm from achieving a return on its investment. Another concern of greenfield investments may be the lack of understanding of the regulations and rules in the existing markets as well as the distribution channels that must be established. In fact, the distribution channel may be "closed" in the sense that other firms may have contractual distribution arrangements that prevent the new firm from selling its products through the existing system.

To counter the difficulties, risk, and costs associated with greenfield investments, an agribusiness may choose to establish a joint venture. A **joint venture** is a form of a strategic alliance (discussed in Chapter 4) that involves two or more firms that share resources in research, production, marketing, or financing, as well as costs and risks. Problems may arise with joint ventures in deciding which firm will have controlling interest; in establishing and maintaining working relationships; and in determining how critical decisions will be made. It also must be noted that joint ventures are not permanent partnerships—they do have an end point. In fact, across all industries, the average life of joint ventures has been estimated to be about three and a half years.

Purchasing a firm or a controlling interest in the firm, known as an **acquisition**, is the third method of direct investment. There are several advantages of an acquisition, but the first step requires finding a suitable company that is available (not likely in less-developed countries) at a reasonable price. Compared to greenfield investments, an acquisition may result in a lower investment to gain control of a production facility. Perhaps importantly,

Table 5.3 Comparing exporting and investing in international markets

Choose exporting when...	Choose investment when...
Financial resources are small	Financial resources are large
Little experience in the new market	Experienced in the new market
Barriers of trade for product do not exist	High barriers to trade exist
Target market is small	Target market is large
Growth potential is limited	Growth potential is high
Barriers to investment and ownership exist	Barriers to investment or ownership do not exist
Control of market is unimportant	High desire for market control
Globalization is not a high business priority	Firm's goals include an international presence
Foreign market is unstable	Stable political and economic climate
Foreign market is culturally "distant"	Market is culturally "similar"

employees, access to distribution channels, market knowledge, experience, and reputation may also be obtained in the purchase. An acquisition can allow a firm to gain country and market-specific knowledge without incurring a long and costly learning process.

However, the acquired firm may contain unrelated or undesirable business lines. And, the firm may have to make significant investments in new equipment, and it may need to change the mindset of current employees to the acquiring firm's style of management. In the global food products industry, the number of mergers and acquisitions taking place ranged from about 100 such transactions in 2002, peaked with nearly 300 such transactions in 2007, and numbered around 130 by the end of the decade (Key and Company, LLC 2011).

Table 5.3 compares the factors that distinguish the decision to export or invest. It should be emphasized that choosing to export, license, or invest is not an either/or proposition. Firms that decide to invest in production facilities in a country may export products to the country as well. In the case of U.S. firms, many have invested in foreign markets and used their new base market to export to other markets. In contrast, foreign firms investing in the United States have done so primarily to serve the U.S. market.

Start-up strategy

In general, most firms follow the same series of steps once they have decided to enter the global market. First, markets are evaluated for their overall profit opportunities for that firm's products. Factors that they consider include market size, rate of growth, and adaptability of that agribusiness's product to that country's culture, consumer income levels, and the political and economic climate of that country.

If the agribusiness determines that the market is promising, the next step taken is choosing the strategy to enter that market. In general, initial entry is made through exporting the firm's products. If sales of the product start to grow, then the firm follows with some form of licensing or investment into production facilities in the receiving country. This allows for higher profits, more control, and greater flexibility over the distribution and sales of the product.

Summary

International agribusiness is a field that has seen significant growth over the last several decades. Advantages to conducting business abroad include sales growth, taking advantage of scale economies, risk reduction, lower production costs and access to lower-cost raw materials, access to credit, and experience from operating in other markets. The internationalization of our world, our attitudes, and our abilities to be connected are greatly responsible for the growing trend called globalization. Some companies have done away with their domestic versus international distinctions and instead are competing in global industries with global strategies and approaches.

Exports and international sales have become even more important to the food and agribusiness markets. With population and income increases comes the potential for increased demand for high-value agricultural products. Such trends affect the entire food production and marketing system.

Fueling the internationalization of our business world are the political, economic, and demographic shifts occurring around the world—shifts that in many cases create new business opportunities. The evolutionary steps taken by world leaders and governments to open the doors to international trade include efforts of the North American Free Trade Agreement (NAFTA), and the General Agreement on Tariffs and Trade (GATT), which is now the World Trade Organization (WTO).

Challenges of doing business internationally include exchange rate fluctuations, cultural differences, accounting differences, and regulatory issues. Agribusinesses entering the international market generally do so using one of three general strategies: exporting, licensing, and foreign production. Variations of these methods include indirect and direct exporting, franchising, and foreign direct investment through acquisition, joint venture, or greenfield investment.

Discussion questions

1. Discuss several of the benefits from doing business internationally.
2. Discuss some of the opportunities for smaller agribusinesses in the international marketplace.
3. Developed and developing countries have differing characteristics regarding the demand for food. Discuss these differences and some of their implications for agribusiness firms.
4. Define food security and discuss how and why it affects agribusiness.
5. One of the goals of the World Trade Organization (WTO) is to reduce tariffs. How does this improve world trade and how does increased world trade benefit society?
6. What is "culture," and why is the understanding of culture important?
7. How can cultural differences inhibit trade? Give an example.
8. How can exchange rates affect trade?
9. Exporting is one strategy firms can use to enter foreign markets. Discuss the differences between indirect and direct exporting.
10. Discuss some of the advantages and disadvantages of using a joint venture to enter a foreign market.

References and additional reading

Central Intelligence Agency. *World Factbook*. 2009. www.cia.gov/library/publications/the-world-factbook

Connor, John M. and William A. Schiek. *Food Processing: An Industrial Powerhouse in Transition*. 2nd ed. New York: John Wiley & Sons. 1997.

Key and Company, LLC. "Data from Presentation to Farm Foundation Roundtable," Atlanta, Georgia, citing data from Capital IQ, January 6, 2011.

Krajewski, Lee J. and Larry P. Ritzman. "Operations Management: Strategy and Analysis." Reading, MA: Addison-Wesley Publishing Co., 2000.

Rue, Leslie W. and Lloyd Byars. "Management Theory and Application." 4th ed. Homewood, IL: Irwin Professional Publishing, 1986.

Stern, Louis W., Adel I. El-Ansary, and Anne T. Coughlan. "Marketing Channels." 7th ed. Upper Saddle River, NJ: Prentice Hall, 2006.

United Nations Population Division. *Briefing Packet, 1998 Revision of World Population Prospects,* no date.

United Nations. "World Population Prospects," 1998 Revision, no date.

Veseth, Michael and Louis Uchitelle. "The Rise of the Global Economy", 2002

http://news.bbc.co.uk/2/hi/europe/4385768.stm

http://news.bbc.co.uk/2/hi/business/520874.stm

www.ers.usda.gov/Data/FATUS

www.ers.usda.gov/Data/TradeMultiplier/econeffects/2008overview.aspx

www.ers.usda.gov/publications/aib794/aib794g.pdf

www.fas.usda.gov/itp/china/India_Chinamarket022010.pdf

http://quickfacts.census.gov/qfd/states/06000.html

http://usda.mannlib.cornell.edu/usda/current/AES/AES-11-30-2010.pdf

Part III

Marketing management for agribusiness

Plate Part III Windmills
Marketing and sales activities of food and agribusiness firms, the focus of Part III, must continually shift with the changing direction of customer needs and wants. Photo courtesy of USDA Natural Resources Conservation Service.

6   Strategic market planning

Objectives

- Outline the marketing concept
- Review the evolution of marketing in the food and agribusiness industries
- Present the market planning framework
- Discuss the components of a SWOT analysis
- Examine the market segmentation concept
- Develop the fundamental idea of positioning

Introduction

Ask people what they think of when the term "marketing" is mentioned and most will answer "advertising" or "selling." While advertising and selling may be two of the most visible marketing activities, marketing in food and agribusiness firms involves far more than these two methods of marketing communication. In reality, marketing includes a wide spectrum of decisions and activities that center on effectively reaching your customers, prospects, and public, and providing them with information about your products or services that satisfy their needs and wants. The full marketing process involves identifying customer needs, developing products and services to meet these needs, establishing promotional programs and pricing policies, and designing a system for distributing products and services to customers. **Marketing management** is concerned with managing this total process.

The marketing concept

Marketing can be defined as the process of anticipating the needs of targeted customers and finding ways to meet those needs profitably. There are several key ideas in this definition. Marketing is about anticipation. Good marketers are always working to anticipate what their customers' needs will be in the future. This may mean anticipating the features farmers will be looking for in a new tractor or it might involve anticipating the type of seasonings consumers will want in a new frozen chicken entrée. Good marketing involves having the right products and services available when the customer is ready to buy them. It follows that good agribusiness marketers know a lot about their customers.

A second key idea is the notion of a **target market**. Clearly, "one size does not fit all" in the food and agricultural markets. Good marketers understand this and focus their efforts on the unique needs of specific target markets or market segments. They know that the small livestock farmer in Kentucky needs a very different set of products and services than does the large turf seed operation in the Willamette Valley of Oregon. Good marketers understand that a high-income, dual-career couple with no children has different needs than a young, middle-income family with two children. While agribusiness firms may pursue more than one target market, their approach to any single-market segment involves a set of decisions tailored to the unique needs of the segment.

The final key idea in the definition of marketing is that of profitability. After careful study of a particular target market, the agribusiness marketer will likely generate a long list of products and services that the customer might be interested in. Such a list for the small Kentucky livestock farmer might include extended credit, a 1-800 phone number for questions, a well-trained, professional salesperson that makes on-farm calls, a staff nutritionist who is always available for consultation, a website with links to useful information sources, and so on. A large corn and soybean commercial producer farming several thousand acres in Iowa may be looking for an entirely different experience. They may only want access to superior performance in products, or want those products combined with technical and tactical professional support from their supplier. The challenge for the agribusiness marketer is deciding which of these things the customer will actually pay for. Agribusiness marketers must provide customers with a set of products and services at prices that generate an acceptable rate of return for their firm.

The evolution of marketing

Traditionally, marketing was viewed as "selling what you have" and some agribusinesses still approach marketing in this way. More effective agribusiness marketers, on the other hand, focus on "having what you can sell"—anticipating customer needs. The starting point for any marketing program must be the identification of customer needs—and satisfying customer needs is the primary focus for any market-driven organization. However, marketing has evolved in agribusiness firms over time and most of today's effective agribusiness marketers didn't start with a focus on customers.

Many agribusinesses that achieved early success usually did so because they had a successful and unique product that satisfied a specific customer need. And, some agribusiness firms continue to operate with a central focus on the product. Here, the idea is to create a product that is so good customers will seek it out. This approach to marketing is known as being **product-driven**. The old saying "build a better mousetrap and the world will beat a path to your door" reflects this marketing philosophy.

In a product-driven organization, product development, research, engineering, and operations are the primary focus. These firms produce a product in high demand and sales are good, so customer needs aren't a primary concern—at least in the short run. Given this, what is the problem with this marketing philosophy? Make no mistake—great products and services are a fundamental part of any agribusiness firm's success. But it is not uncommon for a product-driven organization to become so focused on producing its product or service that it becomes insensitive to changes in farmer or consumer needs. The drive for internal operating efficiency may get more attention than new features customers may want. Sales may slow as competitor products that are similar are introduced to the market. Marketers in these firms then begin a search for ideas to help generate increased sales.

Product-driven marketing continues to evolve due to web-based access to products and services. Historically, many agricultural customers were limited to obtaining products within a short drive of their operation. Today, web-based sales make more products more readily available to farm customers. Purchases of parts, animal health products, even seed and barge-loads of fertilizers can be ordered online. Acquiring farm inputs online poses both an opportunity and a challenge for the customer. You order and receive a product, but typically, the support stops there.

When sales growth slows, many firms will adopt a new approach to marketing which centers around intensifying the sales effort. Organizations that focus primarily on communicating the benefits of their products are called **sales-driven**. This approach may involve taking the firm's core product to a new level, and introducing a number of variations or extensions to serve existing customers better or serve an entirely new group of customers. It may involve a search for new geographic markets where the firm has not been before. The sales-driven organization may add more sales people and ask them to work harder selling the features and benefits of the firm's products and services. Or it may spend increasing amounts on promoting the firm's products through a variety of advertising activities.

The idea behind the sales approach to marketing is that customers just don't know enough about the product—if the message is delivered effectively, sales growth will occur. Like good products, effective sales and market communications efforts are important to the success of any agribusiness. But, sales-driven agribusinesses fail to ask one important question—do we have what the customer wants to buy? Failure to carefully consider this question leaves a sales-driven organization highly vulnerable to competitors who are more in tune with changing customer needs.

Frustrated with sales efforts that are ineffective, successful firms ultimately turn their total attention to customer needs. Truly understanding what the customer needs to run their farm or agribusiness more efficiently and profitably or how consumer food tastes and convenience demands are changing becomes central to everything they do. This focus on customer needs drives all decisions in the organization, from product development efforts, to production location decisions, to asset allocation—decisions are made with a clear vision of how the firm intends to satisfy the customer in mind. Ultimately, these firms are looking to establish a deep and lasting relationship with their customer. This type of organization is called **market-driven**.

A market-driven agribusiness is one with a good product and a good sales effort, but also one with a clear understanding of what type of customers it is trying to serve and what these customers want and need from the firm both now, and over the lifetime of the relationship. It is a firm that takes ideas like "the customer is king" and "getting close to the customer"

Table 6.1 Characteristics of product-driven, sales-driven, and market-driven organizations

Characteristics of Product-Driven, Sales-Driven, and Market-Driven Organizations

Product-Driven	Sales-Driven	Market-Driven
Focus on product	Focus on making the sale	Focus on what the customer needs/wants
My product is great—you should want it	Communicates benefits of products/services.	Develop and provide solutions for the customer
	Reach the people and they will buy	Understands what "type" of customer most values their offerings
		Combines good product and good sales effort—plus incorporates customer understanding

very seriously. Market-driven firms invest in **market research** to better understand their customers, then use the information generated to guide decision making. These are agribusiness firms that are focused on building a long-term relationship with their targeted customers and firms that are willing to make some short-run sacrifices to do this. This focus on the right relationship with customers becomes the overarching goal for the market-driven organization. Some other key differences between product/sales-driven firms and market-driven firms are summarized in Table 6.1. The remainder of this chapter focuses on the keys to building a market-driven strategy.

As a sales and marketing professional, you may work for a company which deploys a combination of marketing strategies within its product lineup. Understanding each of these marketing techniques, along with the company's goals, can help you better succeed in achieving your employer's goals.

Components of a strategic marketing plan

The **strategic marketing plan** integrates all business activities and resources logically to meet customers' needs and to generate a profit. It involves five sets of marketing activities and decisions that must fit together in a consistent fashion (Figure 6.1):

1   Conduct a SWOT analysis
2   Choose a target market
3   Choose a position
4   Develop the appropriate marketing mix
5   Evaluate and refine the marketing plan

Building a strategic marketing plan involves a careful assessment of the marketplace. A **SWOT analysis** (strengths, weaknessness, opportunities, threats) is an objective evaluation of the firm's strengths and weaknesses and its opportunities and threats. The focus of this analytic phase is to uncover business opportunities and challenges and to understand what advantages the firm brings to the market and where the firm is at a disadvantage.

Conducting a sound SWOT analysis is critical for both firms and sales and marketing professionals. It is common to want to talk about our strengths and opportunities. Understanding where your company and your products are strongest helps you know, understand, and articulate those benefits to your customers and prospects. At the same time, a good SWOT analysis helps you better understand your weaknesses and threats. Admitting and understanding those weaknesses can best allow alignment of marketing messages, positioning and pricing to minimize their effects. Ultimately, a firm understanding of weaknesses and threats can help you best position your products and services and mitigate risks in presenting to prospects and customers.

Based on an assessment of market opportunities and an evaluation of the firm, an agribusiness will select a target market (or target markets)—a group/s of customers who will respond in similar fashion to a given offer. Consistent with the needs of the target market, the firm will define what **position** it wants to take in the market. Here the focus is deciding what the firm wants to be known for among the target customers.

This position is created by a set of key decisions a marketer must make—the marketing mix. The **marketing mix** is often referred to as the four Ps of marketing—product decisions, price decisions, promotion decisions, and place (or distribution) decisions. Finally, since markets are dynamic with customer needs continually changing and competitors always on

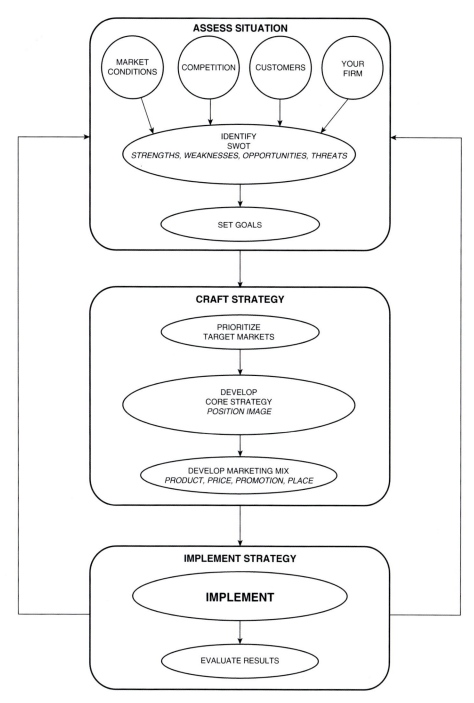

Figure 6.1 The market planning process

the move, good marketing always involves an evaluation and refinement stage. Here actual results are checked against forecast results and appropriate adjustments made. The first three steps will be the focus of the remainder of the chapter. The marketing mix and evaluation of the marketing strategy will be explored in Chapter 7.

Conducting a SWOT analysis

Assessing the competitive environment requires careful study of (1) general trends in the market, (2) strengths and weaknesses of key competitors, (3) current and anticipated customer needs, and (4) the firm's strengths and weaknesses. The results of such study are summarized as a SWOT analysis. Strengths and weaknesses represent a look at what is going on inside the firm while the opportunities and threats capture what is happening outside the firm in the market (Figure 6.2). This analysis phase of the market planning process is done with a single purpose in mind—to identify the business opportunities the competitive environment presents.

General trends in the market

A manager should be informed about the industry and market segment. General trends in the market that may be of interest include key technological trends, the general economic situation, important political developments, and weather patterns. Marketers may rely on government or independent statistics, influential bloggers, the trade press, industry experts, company research staff, and outside consultants to help them frame the general trends in the market. Knowing the industry situation and trends allows marketers to approach the market prepared to address their products' strengths, weaknesses, opportunities, and threats.

Here's an example. Results of a market assessment might tell the livestock feeding equipment manufacturer that:

- Large livestock farmers have aggressively invested in production technology.
- The long-term forecast for interest rates is stable to declining.

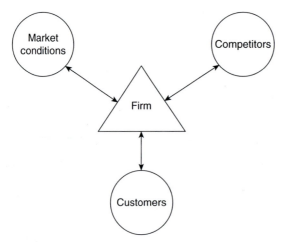

Figure 6.2 SWOT analysis

- Government reductions in farm program outlays will lead to more variability in grain prices.
- Growing conditions in the Corn Belt are likely to be excellent next season.
- World grain stocks are declining.
- Fuel prices are trending lower.

Such an assessment of general trends tells the equipment manufacturer much about how the business environment will greet their next new product introduction. For any sales organization, understanding key market factors influencing their buyers' decision-making process allows a prepared approach to marketing products or services.

Assessment of competitor strengths and weaknesses

A manager should also understand and respect the competition in his/her market segment. Customers will always evaluate an agribusiness firm's products and services relative to competitive products and services. This may involve a comparison of tangible features like horsepower, yield, and price, and/or it may be a comparison of more intangible features like reputation, product knowledge, and convenience. It is important for agribusiness marketers to understand what they are going up against in the marketplace.

Good marketers know how their products and services compare with competitor products and services in those areas that are important to the target customer. Such insights help

Plate 6.1 A customer interview
Evaluating the strengths and weaknesses of competitors is a fundamental part of strategic market planning. One way to obtain information is to interview customers. Photo purchased from © iStickphoto.com/.

marketers understand what they should focus on in their marketing strategy. For example, a hybrid seed corn company might have a group of corn hybrids with average yield characteristics, but exceptional drought tolerance when compared against hybrids from competitors. Here, the seed company may focus on marketing those hybrids in regions of the country more vulnerable to drought, leaving regions with more normal weather to companies with superior yielding, but less drought tolerant hybrids.

A thorough competitor analysis may also turn up business opportunities—a group of customers the competitor doesn't service well, a product feature that customers are interested in, but is not currently offered, or an entire market segment that has been overlooked and which may offer new business to an opportunistic firm. Competitor intelligence may involve market research, use of secondary data like trade press articles, informal data collection by the firm's field sales force, or extensive web-based research. Such data is collected and evaluated with a key question in mind: "How does the competitor stack up against our own efforts in this area?"

Understanding customer needs and wants

Here it is critical to have a fundamental understanding of what the customer will need from the organization, both today and in the future. Food companies study trends in demographics of consumers—older consumers have different needs than younger consumers—and they study cultural changes affecting food choices—trends toward eating lighter, eating away from home, and consuming less fat have important implications for marketing strategies. For agribusiness firms selling to farmers and ranchers, "knowing the customer" typically means thoroughly understanding the customer's business and the role the firm's product plays on the farmer or rancher's operation.

Back to the livestock feed equipment example, if the firm is targeting pork production operations with rapid growth potential, it will be critical to understand the types of changes in feeding systems farmers make as they expand their production capacity. By carefully studying pork operations with growth potential, the firm may find that equipment capacities must be re-engineered, that there is a big demand for engineering expertise to assist in planning equipment needs, and that financing programs are well received given that capital for expansion can be tight. Armed with this information, the agribusiness marketer can incorporate features that will address these issues into the firm's marketing plan.

Firms can gain insights into what their customers want from them through a wide variety of techniques and activities. Some of these techniques are very informal—a breakfast meeting with six key customers, for example. Some are more sophisticated—a virtual shopping exercise where consumers' shopping movement and actions are recorded and analyzed. Data and research can be purchased from firms that track/benchmark such market data. Many larger agribusinesses employ professional marketing researchers or outside consultants to study their customers, their competition, and trends in the marketplace. Even many smaller firms develop their plans only after they have conducted special studies of their customers. Marketing research can be based on complex statistical techniques, focus group insights, or it can simply result from informal interviews and observations, or web-based surveys. Analysis of internal transactions data or market mapping exercises can provide insight. But, in any case, marketing research should provide objective, analytical information on which to base marketing decisions. (More discussion of market analysis techniques is presented in Chapter 8.)

Assessing the firm's strengths and weaknesses

A final key part of the SWOT analysis involves understanding what the firm does well (strengths) and areas the firm could improve (weaknesses). This evaluation plays an important role in the market planning process.

First, the marketer may identify a unique strength that can be cultivated into an advantage. Perhaps the firm has the most extensive distribution system in the market and therefore has an advantage in terms of moving product to customers quickly. Second, the firm may identify an area where improvement is needed if a particular customer group is to be served. An example here might be a retail plant food operation that wants to target larger grain producers, yet finds its key sales personnel lacking in agronomic expertise. To be successful in this market the firm will need to invest in people and training to enhance the expertise of its field sales presence. Finally, the firm may identify a weakness of such magnitude that it becomes a constraint on decision-making. A small feed mill may find that it does not have the scale of operations to serve a very large, integrated pork production operation in its local market area—and investment in such capacity may not be a prudent business decision.

Like assessing the marketplace, such an internal evaluation typically involves a careful review of the firm's entire operation. Some of the key questions to be asked are shown in Table 6.2. Making an objective evaluation can be a challenge. It is easy to be biased when assessing the firm's operation. Securing outside feedback is very important here. Many of

Table 6.2 Assessing internal strengths and weaknesses

Marketing
How effective are our product development activities?
How do our prices compare with the competition?
How much do we spend on advertising and promotion compared to the competition?
Is our social networking strategy driving relationships effectively with our targeted customers?
How satisfied are our customers?
How does our sales force compare to the best sales force in our industry?

Finance
How profitable is our organization?
What is our debt position?
Do we use our investment in current assets such as receivables effectively?
How well do we manage cash flow during the seasonal swings of our business?
Do we do an effective job of investing in new technology and replacing old assets?

Operations/Logistics
Do we deliver to our customers on time and accurately?
How well do we manage our investment in inventory?
How well do we manage quality through our production process?
What are our transportation costs relative to those of our competitors?
Have we effectively managed the risks in our supply chain—both risks to our employees and risks to our customers?

Human Resources
How does our training program compare to those of the best firms in the market?
Do we have an effective compensation program?
What do our turnover rates look like relative to industry standards?
Do we provide advancement opportunities for employees?
Do we have an effective work environment—do employees enjoy working here?

the tools described above for competitor and customer analysis also can be used here to get an outside perspective on firm strengths and weaknesses.

Benchmarking is another technique that can be used to assess internal strengths and weaknesses. Benchmarking involves identifying a non-competitive firm that is known for excellence in a particular area, and then carefully studying that firm to see how they deliver this excellence. The findings of this study are then compared against the agribusiness firm's current practices and key differences explored further. Such a benchmarking study can provide the firm with extremely valuable information that is helpful in identifying strengths and weaknesses as well as suggesting strategies for dealing with each.

Market segmentation

Market segmentation groups customers into segments or categories according to some set of characteristics. Here, the agribusiness manager is interested in developing groups of customers that respond in a similar fashion to a given offer. These groups are called market segments, target markets, or market niches. By recognizing the common characteristics, needs, or buying motives of each unique segment in the total market, an agribusiness can design specialized marketing strategies that may appeal to the particular segments it wants to serve. This idea is illustrated in Figures 6.3 and 6.4. Figure 6.3 shows the "market" for a particular farm input as viewed by a firm using a mass market strategy. Here, the firm takes one offering to the entire market. In Figure 6.4, a firm using market segmentation has identified four distinct groups or segments in the market, and the shading indicates that this firm has chosen to focus their marketing resources on two of the four segments.

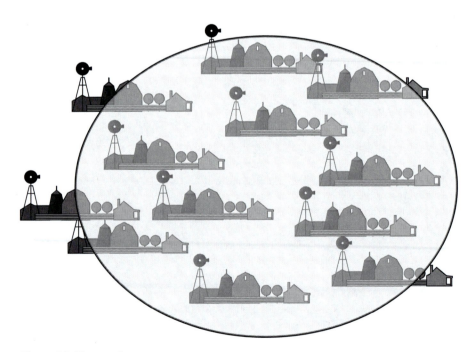

Figure 6.3 Mass market strategy

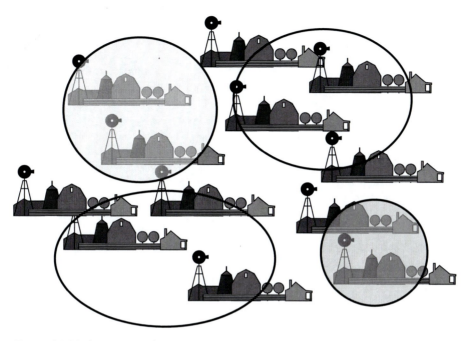

Figure 6.4 Market segmentation strategy

The number of ways that a market can be segmented is limited only by the agribusiness marketer's imagination. (To prove this statement, just think about the variety of restaurants and the market segments they aim to serve that are present in any mid-size city.) A few particular ways to segment a market are discussed here. A **geographic segmentation** may be appropriate for some markets. Food tastes and preferences clearly vary geographically and certain products have much more appeal in some regions than others.

Demographic segmentation is used in many markets. Age, income, size of household, education, number of children, type of employment, and so on can all be important market segmentation variables. Such demographic segments are heavily used in the food industry. The marketing plan developed to promote hot dog consumption among children under the age of 16 might look far different than the marketing activities developed to reach the 22–29-year-old consumer.

For the farm market, segmenting customers by **operating characteristics** is typically useful. This may involve such characteristics as type of operation (crop versus livestock, for example), size of operation, production technology used (no-till versus conventional till; heavy precision technology users versus non-precision technology users, etc.), and form of ownership (owner/operator versus cash rent versus crop share). Demographic variables like those mentioned above can be used in concert with the characteristics of the farm operation to further define the market segments.

In other instances, **psychographic** or **behavioral market segments** may be developed. Here, the focus is on more than physical characteristics. The marketer may be interested in wine buyers who value image and prestige in their purchase. Or, the farm lender may be interested in those buyers who value a relationship with their lender, as compared to those who don't. Such segmentation approaches are relatively sophisticated, and are heavily used by branded food companies to market products aimed at the "healthy lifestyle" segment (Healthy Choice), the "gourmet" segment (Opus One wine), or the "young and rebellious" segment (Red Bull), among many others. Such segmentation approaches require a variety of demographic, behavioral, and psychological data to construct—all tied back to some common set of needs the group is seeking in the product or service.

To illustrate the segmentation concept, consider a feed manufacturer. This firm will recognize dairy, beef, pork, and poultry as clearly different market segments with different needs. Further, dairy farmers' operations may be classified as small, medium, or large, according to herd size. The needs (and therefore the marketing strategy employed) of a small, part-time farmer who owns his property and milks 50 cows will be far different than a large commercial dairy with 10,000 cows using the latest computerized feeding and milking systems. With a thorough understanding of the needs of the target segment in hand, special promotional programs and pricing strategies can be developed. Marketing programs for such targeted market segments are thought to be far more productive than mass marketing efforts aimed at the total market.

A key point here is that there are clearly definable differences between market segments. If such differences do not exist, a mass market strategy works just fine. Typically, designing marketing plans for different segments involves a substantial commitment of firm resources. So, careful thought must go into the market segmentation employed. Well-defined market segments will pass the following test:

1. *Measurable*: Can the market segment be identified and evaluated? In some cases, market segmentation can be developed easily using readily available demographic data. In other cases, it may be very difficult to identify how many and which farmers want to buy based on a relationship with the supplier as opposed to those who simply want to buy on price.
2. *Substantive*: Is the market segment large enough to serve? Some segments may be well defined and measurable, but be simply too small to justify the required resource commitment.
3. *Actionable*: Can the firm effectively serve the segment? In some cases, the firm may identify a large, well-defined segment, but simply not have the people, products, or services needed to effectively serve the segment.

In addition to these questions, agribusiness firms look at several other factors as they make their choice of target market. The level of competition is important. A segment may pass the three-question test posed above, but still not be an appealing segment if every competitor in the marketplace is aggressively pursuing the segment. Growth is another key issue. A segment may be too small to be worth the firms' effort now, but if it has substantial growth potential, it may make sense to stake a claim on the segment early and then grow sales as the segment grows. Finally, the firm has to be focused on the profitability of serving any given segment—in the end, can the firm deliver value to the segment at a profit?

Every agribusiness firm must decide on its optimal level of emphasis on a given segment, since limited resources must be directed to the area where they will be most productive. Decisions about the segments that represent the most efficient use of resources rest on data about the type of product, competitive behavior, size of the company, and other factors.

Plate 6.2 Dairy cows
Market segmentation requires careful assessment of the specific needs of different types of customers. Photo courtesy of USDA Natural Resources Conservation Service.

Some firms may choose a single area of concentration, using the rationale that concentrating all their efforts on a single class of customers allows them to do a better job and may effectively block out new competition. A farm supply store that caters only to larger commercial farmers would be one example. Another farm supply store might develop a "dual segment" concentration by building a special display area for lawn and garden equipment and seasonal nursery stock, so that it appeals to suburban homeowners. In another area of the facility, they may have a special office area to work directly with commercial farmers. Of course, there are a host of factors involved in market strategy decisions, including firm size, location, experience, and competition. But once the market segment or segments have been targeted, the agribusiness must concentrate on the products and services that will succeed there.

Positioning

You know the customers you will target, you understand their needs, and you have a clear picture of the marketplace, your product, and the benefits it offers to your customers. *You* clearly understand the value you are delivering. But how do you communicate that value to your prospects and customers? To answer this question, marketers use a concept called **positioning**. Positioning has been defined as the process of creating the desired image in the customer's mind. Al Ries and Jack Trout, in their marketing classic *Positioning: The Battle for Your Mind* (1982: 2), state: "Positioning starts with a product, a piece of merchandise, a service, a company, an institution or even a person....But positioning is not what you do to the product. It is what you do to the mind of the prospect."

Note that the emphasis is not on the product itself but on customer perceptions. The idea is to secure a place in the customer's mind for your product based on some factor or factors that differentiate your product from the competition. For example, you may want a place in the customer's mind that says that you are the yield leader, that you have the most complete line of products, or that you have best product support.

When an agribusiness brings a product or service to the market, it is important that they be very clear on what image or position they are trying to create. The desired position of the product or service becomes the bridge between the needs and wants of the target market and the specific actions the firm will take to satisfy those needs and wants (the marketing mix).

In many cases, the firm summarizes the desired position with a simple statement that captures the essence of what the firm is trying to accomplish. Some examples include:

'Nothing Runs Like a Deere'—John Deere
'Science with Service'—Pioneer Hi-Bred International
'Beef, it's what's for dinner'—National Cattlemen's Beef Association

Deere is communicating reliability and quality. Pioneer is telling producers their products use the latest science to put bushels in the bin, with the support needed to get it done. The National Cattlemen's Beef Association is urging consumers to choose beef for their next dinner option. In every case, these statements of position communicate a specific message to the customer—hopefully about a trait, characteristic, or feature that is important to the customer.

To better understand the idea of position, it is important to understand the idea of competitive advantage. An agribusiness firm's **competitive advantage** is that set of competencies where the firm has a clear and distinct advantage over the competition. Competitive advantage is the firm's edge in the marketplace, it is the reason customers choose to do business with the firm as opposed to buying from another organization. How you convey that to the customer is key to the sale. Customers want a competitive advantage that benefits them and their operation. Clearly establishing those competitive benefits relative to the customer's needs and wants allows you to earn a place in the mind of the customer—effectively positioning your product/services.

Harvard Business School Professor Michael Porter suggests there are two ways to build a competitive advantage. First, the firm can attempt to provide customers with unique products and services unavailable from other firms. This approach is called a **differential advantage**. Pursuing a differential advantage means that you focus on being a value added firm by providing services that enhance your product and capitalize on what makes your firm unique. Agribusiness firms differentiate themselves in a tremendous variety of ways, including product performance, delivery, product quality, taste, packaging, customer service, technical expertise, image—the list could go on. Any area that customers perceive to be important becomes a potential basis for differentiation. Firms pursuing a differential advantage stress their uniqueness in their positioning.

The other way to claim a competitive advantage is to be a low-cost leader. **Cost leadership** involves meeting the market's product offering with an offering of comparable quality and features, but beating the market on price. Hence, cost leaders work hard at running extremely efficient operations. Cost management is a central focus, and every potential area of efficiency that does not undermine the product/service offering is pursued with a vengeance. Firms positioning themselves as cost leaders will emphasize price in their message, while assuring the market that their quality is acceptable.

If an agribusiness firm's product/service offering is perceived as identical to that of another firm, the sale will go to the firm with the lower price—a commodity transaction. In the end, the challenge is to identify just what things add value for the customer and then to deliver them flawlessly. Such a fundamental understanding of the market combined with superb execution can put distance between an agribusiness firm and its competitors.

Note that the position is generally built on the firm's differential advantage—i.e., things like yield advantage, breadth of inventory, quality of sales force, etc. The challenge here is to take those things that make the firm unique—the competitive advantage—and turn them into the desired image with the target customers—the position.

Positioning/differential advantage in practice

How does this work in practice? Let's take a look at how a seed firm might apply some of the ideas to develop its position. Consider the following scenario. A turfgrass seed company markets seed lines that are primarily proprietary. The firm's research department has finished work on a new variety of dwarf fescue. The variety has fared very well in public evaluations. This variety has a distinctive dark green color, produces a dense, durable turf, and is hardier than other varieties. The firm has decided to try to build on these features and establish a differentiated product that will command a premium price over commodity fescues. How can the concept of positioning be used to accomplish this objective?

The first question to ask is what position does the firm own? That question is followed by what position does it want to own? Ries and Trout call this "thinking in reverse" because when answering the questions you don't focus on the product, but on the target market. How do customers see your firm? To return to the turfgrass example, let's say that after some serious thought and several long focus-group sessions with the potential customers, the firm finds their current position is based on their ability to provide premium varieties of seed which meet the changing needs of customers. This position has been developed through a heavy emphasis on research that has enabled the firm to consistently release high-performing new products.

Here, the current position is consistent with the desired position, given the goals for the new variety. The next question relates to the competition—is this a position the firm occupies by itself? Here, the firm may find that two of their competitor's positions overlap their own. This is important information—the firm will want to make sure their marketing plan strengthens and enhances their position and puts some distance between their firm and the competition.

In the case of the new dwarf fescue, what position should the firm take? For the residential market, two key ideas seem to surface—easy care and environmental awareness—and the position could build on these two benefits. The variety does not grow as fast or as tall as other varieties. The fact that the homeowner spends less time mowing is an important benefit. To complement the easy care benefit, the firm could also position the product as environmentally sensitive. The variety needs less fertilizer and water than other varieties and the slow growth of the product means fewer clippings to dispose of. This new product could be positioned as the grass that delivers more free time to an environmentally conscious consumer.

Having established the positioning, let's take a quick look at how the firm might actually communicate these ideas to the market. (This process—developing the marketing mix—will be considered in more detail in Chapter 7.)

You can communicate tangible attributes—those characteristics that can be identified with some precision—of the product by using university test plot data, public evaluations, the firm's test plots, on-farm weigh tests, etc. For the easy to care for and environmentally sensitive turfgrass, data on number of mowings required, the amount of fertilizer and water needed, and the number of bags of clippings removed could help communicate in a tangible fashion the two ideas in the position. These two notions can't be fully supported with facts and figures however, and an agribusiness marketer must think about communicating the more intangible side of these concepts.

Communicating the intangible takes a little more creativity. However, in the long run, effective communication of these points can become your greatest differential advantage. Going back to our dwarf fescue example, the firm might pursue a number of activities to demonstrate the intangible benefits and support distributor marketing of the product. The firm could develop point-of-purchase materials for the dealer that showed the homeowner resting over a dwarf fescue lawn in a hammock while a neighbor was busy mowing. Or, a direct mail piece targeted at new homeowners could show piles of clippings and fertilizers that compared the dwarf variety and regular varieties. A website application might allow the homeowner to calculate lawn care-time saved, or compute the environmental footprint of the new variety. The firm could arrange to get one of its researchers interviewed on regional television or radio about the environmental features of the new variety. Or, an email campaign targeted at individuals who are in the firm's target market could be conducted. Finally, the seed could be packaged in a bag made of recycled paper. (Note also that the product's name should be consistent with its position.)

After deciding on the market position the firm will seek, they must then develop a marketing mix that will support the position. Claims ring hollow if the firm can't deliver the promised product/service bundle at an acceptable price. And, the market communications effort is fundamental to communicate and support the desired message. Finally, the product/service bundle must be made available in a way that supports the position as well.

In the end, nothing is more critical to communicating value than delivery. There is a significant difference between saying you are doing something for your customers and actually getting the job done. If you ask a manager or a sales representative if they add value to their product, they'll tell you "yes" every time. Adding value is equated with meeting customer needs—and what firm does not think that they are striving to meet their customers' needs? Given the similarity of value adding activities among firms, the bottom line is that delivery of the bundle you communicate may well be the way your firm is able to differentiate itself in the marketplace.

Summary

Marketing is the process of anticipating the needs of targeted customers and finding ways to meet those needs profitably. The strategic market planning process begins with a careful assessment of the business environment and a critical evaluation of the firm's strengths and weaknesses. The results of this assessment are summarized in a SWOT analysis. The focus here is identifying key business opportunities in the market—those areas where the agribusiness should focus its marketing resources.

The market assessment provides data for a fundamental choice the agrimarketer must make: What target market(s) should the firm pursue? A target market is a group of customers and prospects that will respond in similar fashion to a given offer. Agribusiness marketers can segment a market on a wide range of characteristics—demographic, geographic, business, psychographic, etc. The key for the marketer is to identify a target group with unique needs that the firm can serve profitability.

An important part of the strategic market planning process is determining the position the firm wants to take with its target market. The position serves as a focal point for the firm's marketing mix—it captures the essence of the message the firm is trying to send the market. An agribusiness firm's position is typically drawn from its competitive advantage—the firm's unique edge over rival firms.

The set of decisions agribusiness managers make as part of the strategic market planning process may be among the most fundamental choices facing an agribusiness firm. Decisions about what markets to pursue and what position to take in these markets drive much of the rest of the firm's business activities.

Discussion questions

1. Explain the difference between a product- or sales-oriented firm and a market-oriented firm. Why is this difference important to an agribusiness manager?
2. A key part of the SWOT analysis is evaluating the impact of broad market factors such as government policies, international trade developments, new technologies, and so on. For the agribusiness industry of your choice, identify five key trends in the industry marketplace and describe the opportunities and threats each trend represents for agribusiness firms in that industry.
3. How can an agribusiness manager evaluate the strengths and weaknesses of their organization? Why is it important to understand what an agribusiness does well, and to understand those areas where performance is not as strong?
4. What is meant by a market segment? U-pick fruit and vegetable farms (farms where customers harvest their own fruit and vegetables) probably appeal more to some market segments than to others. Identify and describe two market segments that you believe might be important to this type of agribusiness. What are the key needs of these two segments that a marketing manager for the U-pick farm would need to focus on?
5. Select three different products—one marketed online, one in a newspaper, one from a farm magazine. Describe the market segment targeted for each product.
6. Focusing on one of the target markets you identified for the U-pick farm described in Question 4, what position should the firm take in the market? Based on the key needs you identified for one of the market segments, write a positioning statement for the firm. What key themes will you stress in your statement?
7. Two types of competitive advantage are described in the chapter. Identify a food or agribusiness firm pursuing a differential advantage. Also, identify a food or agribusiness firm pursuing a cost advantage. Compare and contrast these two strategies. What is similar about the two firms? What is different? Explain why you think each company took that position.
8. Using the food and agricultural trade press, or an online source, identify a firm communicating tangible value in its message and one communicating intangible value. Compare and contrast these messages and how the firms are actually communicating these two different messages.

Case study: Richmond Supply and Elevator, Inc.

Richmond Supply and Elevator (RS&E) is a family-owned feed, fertilizer, and grain company located in Central Iowa. The firm is owned and managed by Lance and Paul Taylor, the sons of the original owner, Joe Taylor.

RS&E handles the Rapid Gain line of animal feeds. The firm currently employs eight full-time personnel, in addition to Lance and Paul. In 2011, roughly 15 percent of their total $12 million in sales was feed, 60 percent was grain, and 25 percent was fertilizer. Richmond sold about 4,000 tons of feed in 2010. Over time the firm has been profitable, but not exceptionally so. In 2010, the firm reported a loss of $50,000 on sales of $12 million while in 2011 the net income after taxes was $65,000 on about the same level of sales.

The Market. Consolidation has been the keyword in the central Iowa market and a smaller number of larger farm customers have been the result. RS&E had more than 180 feed accounts in 1999. In 2010, RS&E was serving fewer than 50 farmers (because farm size had increased), but was selling twice as much feed (through some good management decisions and some competitors going out of business). The average customer farms about 1,500 acres, typically one-half in corn and one-half in soybeans. Hogs are essentially the only livestock in Richmond's market area and swine feed makes up 90 percent of Richmond's feed tonnage.

Competition. Richmond has a number of other firms handling feed in its market area. RS&E's toughest competition comes from a Lake Feeds dealer, Princeton Elevator, Inc. Lake Feeds entered the market ten years ago and has pursued expansion aggressively. They market a quality product and sell aggressively on the farm. The Lake Feeds dealer has held its price up over the period, taking some of the price pressure off Richmond. Lance feels that Lake Feeds' growth has primarily come by taking business away from companies selling cheap, low-quality feed. In fact, RS&E's tonnage has increased over the past five years, despite the presence of Lake Feeds. Lance believes that Lake Feeds' aggressive quality push has actually helped Richmond increase sales.

The Firm. Lance (38) is the older of the brothers and handles the "inside" jobs—waiting on customers, writing orders, ordering, monitoring the books, and so on. Paul (36) handles the firm's operations—overseeing the fertilizer plant, feed mill, and grain elevator. Paul also handles RS&E's outside selling effort. The firm takes a very low-pressure approach to selling on the farm. Paul's customer visits are viewed as problem solving and public relations—not really sales calls. Paul makes few calls on farmers to whom RS&E doesn't currently sell. Lance and Paul considered hiring an outside salesperson, but feel they just "can't make it pay" at this point. They are also looking into more email communications with their customers but have not made this move yet. Of the other 16 employees, two drive feed trucks, two run the feed mill, one is a bookkeeper, and the rest are general warehouse employees/drivers. With the exception of one warehouse employee who has been with Richmond four years, all employees have been with the firm at least five years. Lance and Paul also hire seasonal labor to help them through the Spring and Fall peak selling seasons.

The firm owns two bulk feed delivery trucks. Their feedmill was constructed in 1990 and is in excellent condition. Paul figures the mill runs at about 80 percent of capacity. The firm is located about 60 miles from the nearest Rapid Grow feed plant. RS&E sells little pelleted complete feed, choosing instead to push concentrate feeds and keep their feedmill in use, reducing hauling costs in the process.

The brothers are looking into the construction of overhead feed holding bins to reduce truck waiting time. They would also like to get more bulk bins on the farms of their customers to reduce unloading time. "We must take steps to increase efficiency over the longer run," said Lance. The brothers are considering remodeling the office/showroom and acquiring a new computer system to handle accounting tasks and keep customer records more efficiently.

Marketing. Quality and service are key components of RS&E's business philosophy. They focus their sales effort on Rapid Grow's premium products and feel they get a good gross margin on what they sell (13 percent in 2011). The brothers are very conservative about growth—about 5 percent a year is all they want. "We cannot let our current level of customer support slip," said Lance. "And, we are willing to let some opportunities go by to make sure that we can keep our current customers happy," he added.

Customer service is delivered in several ways, according to Lance. Quality feed products are the cornerstone and the brothers have been very pleased with the Rapid Grow line over time. Nutritional support is another component of customer service. This is done by drawing on Lance's excellent knowledge of swine nutrition and by making heavy use of a talented local veterinarian who doesn't sell feed or animal health products. In addition, they draw on Rapid Grow's nutritional experts whenever necessary. They have a good, but not great, company website. And, they have been thinking about how more extensive use of the Internet might help them build even better relationships with their farmer customers.

Richmond has worked hard to maintain margins, attempting to increase gross margins on feed over time. For the most part they have been successful at increasing per-ton margins on feed. RS&E is not the cheapest feed company in the market, nor do they intend to be. "We will make money on what we sell," said Lance. They offer a 2 percent discount for cash. In addition, they have a volume discount program that Lance admits is a bit "informal." Richmond rarely advertises and holds farmer meetings only occasionally. "Unless there is a new product to push, I'm just not a great believer in meetings," said Lance.

Summary. Lance and Paul have built a good business over time. However, their market is changing rapidly and the competition is getting tougher. The brothers wonder just what position they should take in the market. What will they need to do to support this position? What steps are necessary for a thorough evaluation of their challenges/opportunities? How will they communicate the value their products and services provide to their customers? Clearly, Lance and Paul have many tough decisions to make.

Questions

1. What are the key opportunities and threats facing Richmond Supply and Elevator in the marketplace?
2. What are the key strengths and weaknesses of RS&E?
3. Based on the limited information in the case, describe the firm's target market. In your opinion, does the firm have a good grasp of who their target market is and what this market wants from the firm?
4. What position should the firm take with their target market? What key themes should they emphasize in their positioning statement?
5. Is RS&E a product-driven firm, a sales-driven firm, or a market-driven firm? Explain your answer.

References and additional reading

Anderson, Dave. *How to Deal with Difficult Customers: 10 Simple Strategies for Selling to the Stubborn, Obnoxious, and Belligerent.* Hoboken, NJ: J. Wiley & Sons, 2007.

Lent, Robin, Geneviève Tour, and Alain-Dominique Perrin. *Selling Luxury: Connect with Affluent Customers, Create Unique Experiences Through Impeccable Service, and Close the Sale.* Hoboken, NJ: Wiley, 2009.

Levinson, Jay Conrad, Jeannie Levinson, and Amy Levinson. *Guerrilla Marketing: Easy and Inexpensive Strategies for Making Big Profits from Your Small Business.* 4th ed. Boston, MA: Houghton Mifflin, 2007.

Peters, Tom. *Thriving on Chaos.* Excel/A California Limited Partnership, 1987.

Porter, Michael E. *Competitive Strategy: Techniques for Analyzing Industries and Competition.* New York: The Free Press, 1980.

——, *Competitive Advantage: Creating and Sustaining Superior Performance.* New York: The Free Press, 1985.

Ries, Al and Jack Trout. *Positioning: The Battle for Your Mind.* New York: Warner Books, 1982.

Walker, Orville C. and John W. Mullins. *Marketing Strategy: A Decision-focused Approach.* New York: McGraw-Hill/Irwin, 2011.

7 The marketing mix

Objectives

- Discuss the elements of the marketing mix
- Explore how agribusinesses create value for their customers
- Review product adoption and product life cycles in agribusiness markets
- Identify key features of agribusiness pricing strategies
- Summarize various methods of product promotion and market communications
- Explore the role of personal sales in the marketing strategy of an agribusiness
- Examine channels of distribution in agribusiness

Introduction

When an agribusiness marketer thoroughly understands the needs of the target market and has identified the appropriate position for their product or organization, the truly creative work begins. At this point, the agribusiness marketer must take a general idea such as "Nothing Runs Like a Deere," turn that idea into a tangible product/service/information offering, and then communicate the desired position to the target market.

In this chapter, we'll examine how agribusiness marketers must translate the position they want to create for the target market into a product/service/information bundle that serves customer needs and communicates the desired image. This set of decisions involved in accomplishing this task is called the marketing mix.

The marketing mix

Countless decisions face today's agribusiness marketer—particularly once the target markets are identified and a company position is chosen. As an example, let's use large commercial vegetable growers in the San Joaquin Valley of California as a potential target market for John Deere. What specific products, services, and information will be provided to these growers? How will this bundle be priced? How will the value provided by these products and services be communicated to the target market? What is the best distribution channel to use to effectively service this group of large California growers? This set of critical decisions—the four Ps of marketing: product, price, promotion, and place—is called the **marketing mix** (Figure 7.1). The marketing mix is that combination of price, product, promotion, and place strategies implemented by a firm to support a specific position in the market. The ultimate job of the agribusiness marketer is to craft a marketing mix consistent with the firm's desired position that creates good value for the customer.

Figure 7.1 The marketing mix

Each of these four elements of the marketing mix, the four Ps, are explored individually in this chapter. But, keep in mind that each of these elements must complement one another in order to create the intended position in the market. For example, how would the California vegetable growers respond if they were called on by a John Deere salesperson that did not understand the technical features of the high quality tractor the growers were interested in? Or how would the growers react if the salesperson was very knowledgeable, but the tractor failed three times during the first week of operation? What would these growers think about John Deere if the promotional literature they received on the tractor was sketchy and unprofessional? For an agribusiness marketing program to be successful, all elements of the marketing mix must communicate a clear and consistent story—the position—to the target market.

Product/service/information decisions

Product/service/information decisions form the heart of the marketing strategy and are among the most fundamental decisions an agribusiness makes. (We will use the term product instead of product/service/information in this section, but don't forget that service and information are critical to the firm's strategy in this area.) Decisions that must be made here include:

The mix of different products and services offered,
The extent of each product line,
The specific characteristics of each product sold, and
The level and type of information provided in the bundle.

Plate 7.1 Marketing mix
Successful marketing requires the right marketing mix: the correct combination of product, price, place, and promotion strategies. Photo courtesy of Purdue University Centre for Food and Agricultural Business.

In the end, it is this bundle of products, services, and information that creates value for the buyer.

The value bundle

When developing a product strategy, the agribusiness marketer begins with the needs of the target market clearly in mind. What set of products, services, and information can the firm deliver to meet the needs of the target market? One especially useful concept that can help answer this question and guide development of a product strategy is the idea of the **value bundle**. The value bundle is the set of tangible and intangible benefits customers receive from the products and services an agribusiness provides. The fundamental challenge when developing a product strategy is determining what to include and what not to include in the value bundle for the target market.

What is value? And, more importantly, how do customers define value? Value to the customer is defined as the ratio of what they receive (perceived benefits) relative to what they give up (perceived costs) (Figure 7.2). As customers make purchasing decisions, they compare the perceived benefits of the purchase against the perceived costs. If the value equation is tipped in favor of the benefits, i.e., the benefits exceed the costs, the customer has found a good value and will make the purchase, provided another supplier isn't providing more value/lower cost on the same bundle.

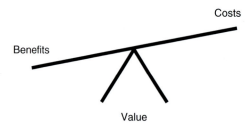

Figure 7.2 The value equation

In the definition of value, note the importance of the word "perceived." Some benefits and costs will be tangible and easily measurable—the horsepower of a tractor or the per unit cost of fruit juice, for example. But intangible benefits and costs can be just as important (or more important) in the purchase decision—the prestige or the peace of mind that comes with owning the "best" farm equipment, or the convenience that comes with a special type of juice package.

There is no easy way to measure benefits like prestige or convenience, but customers will form highly unique opinions—perceptions—about the value of such benefits. Because many benefits are intangible, the agribusiness marketer must not only know how the customer defines value, they must make sure the value their bundle provides is clearly communicated to the customer. In the end, no matter what the agribusiness marketer thinks about their products and services, it is the customer's perception of benefits and costs that will determine whether or not a purchase is made.

Many firms dedicate significant dollar investments to more clearly measuring and categorizing the value customers place on intangible benefits. Such market research efforts may include focus groups, wherein groups of targeted customers are brought together to explain their feelings associated with using a product or service. Other market research tools include surveys, and online response tools to name a couple. A salesperson working with a customer one-on-one can also provide unique insights into the value of these intangible product or service benefits. Intangible benefits are important enough for companies to invest in market research to more clearly understand the customers' perceptions. More information on these tactics is included in Chapter 8.

To relate the customer's definition of value to the agribusiness firm's product strategy, it is helpful to visualize the firm's product offering as consisting of four distinct, but highly interrelated, parts. This way of looking at the value bundle has been called the **total product concept** by some authors (Manning and Reece 1990). The total product concept is a means to relate the customers' definition of value to the agribusiness firm's product strategy by visualizing the four parts of the firm's product offering: the generic product, the expected product, the value added product, and the potential product (Figure 7.3). Understanding these different levels can help an agribusiness marketer better understand how value is added, and ultimately, can guide development of the product strategy.

The foundation for a firm's product offering is the **generic product**. This is the standard product with no special services or features attached. For DEKALB Genetics, this is a unit of hybrid seed corn, while for Ocean Spray, it might be cranberry juice. There is little or no differentiation at the generic product level—at this level customers see all agribusiness firms

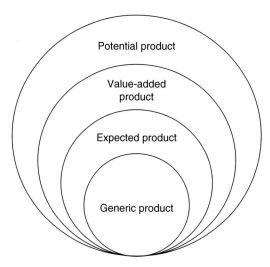

Figure 7.3 The total product concept
Source: Manning and Reece 1990.

as alike in the market. A firm stopping here in developing a product strategy will compete solely on price, since the firm is not providing customers with any value above and beyond what any other firm is doing.

Let's use a retailer of fertilizer to illustrate the total product concept. The generic product for this firm might be bulk fertilizer and crop protection products. There are no services attached and the set of products carried by the firm can be purchased from any other firm in the market. The generic product is a true commodity in the mind of the customer.

Most agribusinesses don't stop with the generic product. The **expected product** builds on the generic product by surrounding it with the bare minimum set of features/services that the customer expects when they make a purchase. Like the generic product, the firm doesn't get much credit by providing the expected product—at this level the firm has simply met customer expectations. On the other hand, firms not providing the expected product are discounted heavily in the mind of customers because even the bare minimum is not being provided.

The expected product for the fertilizer retailer might include a standard custom application service, standard agronomic recommendations, grid soil sampling, a 30-day credit policy, some minimum set of equipment available for rent, standard complaint-handling service, a web site with basic information, and a clean and neat facility. Again, the focus is on the minimum set of product-related services the customer expects to receive. While the firm has added value to the generic product at this level, the customer still sees a commodity since only their minimum expectations have been met.

To this point, most of the focus has been on tangible products and service. For the value added and potential products, value is driven almost totally by customers' perceptions about the more intangible attributes surrounding the products and services. The **value added product** is the first opportunity for the agribusiness firm to truly exceed the customer's expectations. The focus at the value added product level is satisfying customer needs in a way that isn't expected and providing services or a level of service that isn't being provided by competitors. Here, the firm goes beyond the tangible, physical properties of the product and the minimum services that are typically provided with the product. Higher levels of customer service, unique information, and the intangible benefits that go along with features such as reputation, trust, integrity, and safety may all be part of the value added product.

Following our retail fertilizer example, retail customers may expect the standard custom application service as part of the expected product. However, the custom application service provided by the most highly trained drivers in the market and a guarantee that the driver will be in the field within 60 minutes of the promised time is likely to exceed customer expectations. A comprehensive agronomic plan developed by a trained agronomist and updated annually with a personal visit from the agronomist may send signals that this firm is adding more value than competitors. Or weekly text messages to key accounts giving updates of changes in growing conditions and pest and disease problems may clearly communicate that this firm goes above and beyond for their customers. It is this level of attention to customer needs that drives the value added product and starts to more clearly delineate firms in the market.

One last dimension of the product exists, the **potential product**. Here, the focus is on the future—what is the next benefit that customers will seek from the firm? How will the product bundle be managed to add even more value for customers? Once the value added product is successful, the firm must actively look for other possibilities in the marketplace because competitors will seek to emulate any success the firm may enjoy.

The potential product for the retail fertilizer firm might include investing in a new information management system to allow the firm to track comprehensive yield, fertility, and weed and pest data by field for customers. Or, it might mean acquiring a multiple-nutrient variable rate applicator guided by a global positioning system (GPS) which will allow the firm to apply precise levels of fertilizer on an as-needed basis as the rig moves across a field. It could be an interactive website that allows producers online access to a databank of key agronomic information. The potential product may mean bundling up these types of services with even more professional advice to deliver a precision agronomic package far superior to any other offering in the market. The focus here is innovation and making sure the firm stays ahead of competitor attempts to deliver the value added product and the expected product.

Note that the ability to meet and exceed customer expectations is heavily influenced by what competitors offer. Unfortunately, if any of the value added attributes provided by a firm are also provided by competitors, in the customer's mind these benefits may become expected, taken for granted, and will not be as effective in differentiating the product offering. In this case, which is probably the typical one, actual delivery of the benefit becomes the deciding factor: if the firm does the same thing as a competitor, but can do it better in a way customers truly perceive to be unique, and beneficial to their operation, then there is still an opportunity for differentiation.

Value is a matter of customer perception—it is based on what the customer believes to be true. As managers, it is sometimes easy to lose sight of what customers value. Marketing games of one-upmanship can lead to a "bell-and-whistle war" with little regard for whether the customer actually wants the new feature provided. Just because a major competitor has added another service does not mean that it is time to add the same service. Failing to carefully consider the new feature from the customer's perspective may add cost to the product for something that is not valued by the customer. Letting customer needs—current and anticipated—guide construction of the value bundle is a fundamentally important marketing concept.

Product adoption and diffusion

The manner in which customers adopt a new technology, a product, or a service is another important part of a firm's product strategy. The adoption process is tied closely to a product's life cycle and suggests how new products should be introduced into the market. E. M. Rogers, using hybrid seed corn as the focus, did the classic research into the adoption–diffusion of new products. Rogers (1995) suggested that ideas are diffused through the market in systematic stages:

1. *Awareness*: at this stage, people have heard about the product but lack sufficient information to make a purchasing decision
2. *Interest*: a potential customer becomes interested enough to learn more about the product
3. *Evaluation*: the customer decides whether or not to try the product
4. *Trial*: the customer samples the product
5. *Adoption*: the customer integrates the product into a regular-use pattern

Some individuals who adopt products more quickly than others tend to be **opinion leaders.** These people are watched carefully and followed by other customers in the market. Some opinion leaders actively attempt to influence others within their sphere. This group of opinion leaders is an extremely important one to agrimarketers. And, many agribusinesses spend considerable time and money identifying opinion leaders and working closely with them to build favorable relationships.

As a new idea or technology is introduced into the market, Rogers found it will be adopted in a systematic way as more and more users adopt the idea. He classified users into five distinct categories according to how quickly they adopt a new idea.

Rogers's research (Figure 7.4) suggests that the total number of individuals willing to try a totally new idea is very small, perhaps about 2.5 percent of a given market. **Innovators** are these venturesome people who like to try new ideas. They are not necessarily opinion leaders; since they try so many new things, their peers may regard them as a bit unconventional.

The second wave of individuals who try a new technology are called early adopters. **Early adopters** (about 13.5 percent of a market) are respected individuals who adopt new ideas quickly but with caution, usually after observing the experience of the innovators. They are usually key opinion leaders in the community and are therefore highly important to the agribusiness marketer.

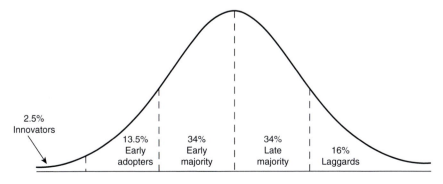

Figure 7.4 Categories of new technology adopters

The **early majority** (about 34 percent of a market) form the third group of adopters. Individuals in the early majority are deliberate people who see themselves as progressive, but not generally as leaders. They form a large and important market for any product or service. Following the early majority in the adoption process are the late majority. The **late majority** (another 34 percent) tends to be skeptical in their view of new ideas, and adopt them only after considerable evidence of performance and/or satisfaction has been shown. This group follows the majority opinion. Finally, **laggards** (16 percent) are tradition-bound individuals who take so long to adopt new ideas that by the time the ideas are adopted, they are no longer new.

This pattern of new technology adoption holds for most new ideas, both within the food and agricultural markets and outside these markets. Agrimarketers who introduce new products can initially focus their total marketing program toward the innovators and early adopters, gradually changing their marketing strategy as the product is accepted by the other adopter categories over time.

Product life cycles

A final concept that is important when developing a product strategy is the product life cycle idea. **Product life cycles** relate to the sales and profits of a product or service over a period of time. Product life cycles are the predictable way in which sales and profits of a product unfold as a product is introduced, sales grow rapidly, the market matures, and the product ultimately declines in the marketplace. There are several distinct phases in the life of a product, from its development and initial introduction to its eventual removal from the market (Figure 7.5).

The **development stage** is that period in which the market is analyzed, and both the product and the broader marketing strategy are developed. During this time there is no revenue, but there are significant expenditures for product and market development. For example, this is the period when a new rabbit feed is researched, formulated, and tested, while plans are developed for its introduction into the market.

The **introductory stage** is that period in which the new product first appears on the market. Usually, there are high costs associated with introducing a new product. The new rabbit feed may require a heavy promotional effort and special offers to dealers to stock the product, both of which reduce the probability of early profits. At some time during the introduction period, the product should begin to show a profit, depending on the degree of its success. A number of introductory strategies are possible. The firm might choose to make heavy introductory expenditures to reduce the time for consumer acceptance. Or it might introduce the product without fanfare, simply adding it to the product line at perhaps a low initial price, in the hope of minimizing introductory costs.

The **growth stage** is a period of rapid expansion, during which sales gain momentum and prices tend to hold steady or increase slightly, as firms try to develop customer loyalty. The distribution system is expanded, which makes the product available to a larger market. Profits expand rapidly because fixed costs are spread over a larger sales base. However, at some point during the growth stage, it is common for costs to begin to increase as the firm attempts to reach increasingly difficult new markets. In addition, the visibility of increasing profits often attracts new competitors to the market. As the firm attempts to reach new, less familiar markets and the effects of competition begin to be felt, growth slows, and profits, while still increasing, begin to increase at a decreasing rate.

261250

Plate 7.2 New product development
Even in the earliest stages of development, the product life cycle is an important consideration
for agribusiness marketers. Purdue Agricultural Communications photo/Tom Campbell. Used by
permission.

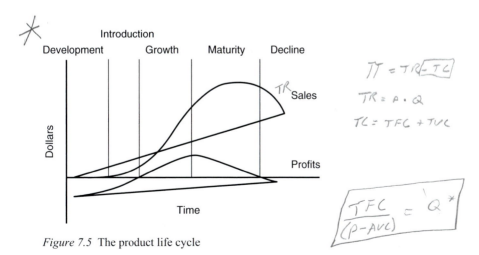

Figure 7.5 The product life cycle

The **maturity stage** is characterized by slow growth or even some decline of sales as the market becomes saturated. Sales lag because most of the potential customers have been tapped and because competitors have entered the market, leaving only new sales to the late majority and laggards and replacement sales to established customers. This stage usually lasts longer than the others, so most products in the market at any point in time are in this stage.

Much marketing activity is designed to prolong the maturity stage by propping up sales and protecting profits. Competition often becomes intense in the maturity stage as competitors battle for market share, often using price as a weapon. Firms struggle to refine their product by changing design, adding features, making new advertising claims, and developing promotional campaigns and incentives to protect or enhance market share. Strategically, firms hope to differentiate their product sufficiently to push it back into the growth stage. But all this additional marketing activity drives costs up, and profits begin to decline. How rapidly profits decline in the maturity stage depends on a host of factors, but this decline is always of major concern to management.

The **decline stage** finds sales declining more rapidly. Changes in consumer preferences or new substitute products may hasten the death of the product. As the product dies, profits slip to zero or become losses, and some firms withdraw from the market. The remaining firms may reduce marketing expenditures, until eventually the product may disappear totally from the market.

Many firms find the decline stage very difficult to manage. Managers who have built their professional careers around the growth of a product are sometimes emotionally involved with the product and are thus reluctant to admit its decline. Marketing managers may legitimately expect sales growth to resume as economic conditions change. In any case, to drop a product from the line and to decide on the best timing for this action is a difficult decision. Yet attempting to prolong the life of a product may drain the firm financially and preclude the development of new products.

The evolution of a product through its life cycle presents the essence of product decisions for the marketing manager in the agribusiness firm. Although each product has a life cycle, the life cycle can look very different from one product to another. Some products have short life cycles lasting only a year or two, while others may have life cycles that span decades. One of the marketing manager's jobs is to use the marketing tools at their disposal to prolong the profitable life stages. In an age of social media with information available everywhere, all the time, product life cycles and the adoption process can become incredibly compressed. Such compression puts pressure on agribusiness marketers as the window for success can be very small before a competing product/service is introduced by a competitor.

Price decisions

Pricing is a critical marketing decision because it so greatly influences the revenue generated by an agribusiness. Pricing decisions do this in two ways:

1. Price impacts revenue as a component of the revenue equation:

    $$(revenue = price \times quantity\ sold)$$

2. The price level itself greatly affects the quantity sold, through its effect on demand relationships for the product or service.

Complications arise because these two price effects work in opposite directions. Lower prices produce less revenue per unit, but usually generate an increase in quantity sold, while the opposite is true when price is increased. Of course, increased sales mean that fixed costs are spread over more units; therefore, per unit costs may be reduced, at least to a point. The net result is that pricing decisions are a real challenge to marketers.

Some price decisions involve highly complex mathematical methods, while others depend on simple rules of thumb or intuitive judgments. The type of product, customer demand, competitive environment, product life-cycle stage, and **product mix** are some of the factors considered in price determination. A successful pricing strategy is made after giving careful consideration given to the value delivered, the cost of the product/service bundle, the goals of the pricing strategy, and the pricing strategies of competitors.

The perceived value of the product bundle becomes a ceiling on the price charged (Figure 7.6). If the firm sets the price higher than the perceived value, the customer's benefit/cost calculation moves in the wrong direction and the customer won't buy the product. Obviously, firms must understand the value they provide to customers when developing a pricing strategy.

The firm's total cost of providing the product bundle provides a floor on price. At least over the longer run, the firm must cover full costs through the sale of the product if it is to remain in business. However, the firm can never focus entirely on costs when making a pricing decision. In the end, customers do not care what it cost the firm to provide a product bundle; they only care about the value it creates for them.

The firm's pricing goals are important considerations in any pricing decision—what does the firm want to accomplish with the pricing strategy? Is the goal to maximize market-penetration, getting as much market share as possible, as quickly as possible? Or is the agribusiness less concerned about market share and more intent on skimming profits in the short-run, knowing that a premium price and strong margins will attract competitors over time? A variety of other goals are possible, each with a unique impact on the firm's pricing strategy.

Finally, the firm must evaluate the competition as it makes pricing decisions. In the end, the agrimarketer wants to know what value competitors add and what pricing goals they have for their bundle of products and services. This is important since the value the

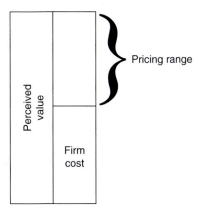

Figure 7.6 Upper and lower limits on pricing decisions

competitor provides sets a standard the agribusiness will be measured against. As mentioned earlier, remember that value is a relative idea and any value bundle provided by an agribusiness is judged relative to that of their competition.

In the end, if a profit cannot be made by pricing the product based on the value it delivers, at least one of three conditions exists. First, costs may simply be too high—the firm needs to become more efficient. Second, the product may not deliver enough value compared to the (efficient) production and marketing cost of the product and continued production should be questioned. Third, the product may support other products in some way and the firm may want to continue production at a loss.

Pricing strategies

Armed with a thorough understanding of the value provided, the costs of producing and delivering the product bundle, the firm's pricing goals, and the competitor's strategies, an agribusiness marketer is ready to make a sound pricing decision. Let's take a look at some ways to put all of this information together by exploring several commonly used pricing strategies.

Cost pricing

Cost-based pricing or **cost-plus pricing** is a pricing method based on adding a constant margin to the basic cost of the individual product or service. This margin is intended to cover overhead and handling costs, and leave a profit. In retail businesses, such as farm supply or food stores, it is a simple matter to "mark up" merchandise by some percentage.

$$\text{Cost}(\$1.00) \times 1.30(\text{markup of 30\%}) = \$1.30(\text{selling price})$$

Farm construction firms sometimes operate on the basis of the cost of materials plus a percentage. The markup theoretically represents the cost of handling the product or performing the service; it therefore varies with different product lines and among different industries. In reality, the markup may not reflect costs accurately and markups may be more likely to be based on tradition rather than logic.

A problem with cost-plus pricing is the difficulty of allocating fixed or overhead costs to a specific product or service. Many accounting systems simply are not adequate to determine how much of the overhead cost should be allocated to each product. And, even if a method for this kind of determination existed, the cost of keeping track of time spent on such related product-specific expenditures is prohibitive in many cases.

Yet, because of its simplicity, the cost-based pricing method is popular, especially for the retailing of large numbers of products. In addition, computerized management information systems allow cost data to be measured and allocated more precisely which facilitates the use of this strategy.

Competitive pricing

Competitive pricing lies at the other end of the spectrum. While cost-based pricing methods tend to ignore market conditions, competitive-pricing methods essentially base price on competitors' prices. This method involves setting price at the "going rate," according to some general market average. An agribusiness employing this strategy may simply follow the price lead of a competitor.

Competitive pricing does not always involve matching the competitors' price; a price may strategically be held above or below that of competitors. A local lawn and garden store might choose to hold its price consistently above that of a large chain discount store. Or a small, independent grain elevator with very low overhead costs may choose to regularly offer two cents per bushel more than a large cooperative competitor who dominates the local market.

Because competitive pricing is the norm in commodity-based markets, the strategy is widespread in agribusiness, and is used many times by smaller firms whose markets are dominated by larger firms. This works well as long as the smaller firm has a favorable cost structure relative to other firms or is small enough not to be a major threat to the larger firm.

When one firm's value bundle is quite similar to another firm in the market, price usually becomes a major factor in the buying decision. When firms struggle to differentiate their products and services, it is difficult to price above the market level. Consequently, most agribusinesses keep a close eye on the market price and vary from it only in subtle ways. Of course, this causes major problems for any agribusiness that does not have an efficient cost structure. Less efficient businesses are forced into financial difficulty because of the necessity of keeping prices competitive. And it is not uncommon for agribusinesses that are in a low-cost position to intentionally exert pressure on their higher-cost competition in order to increase market share. While there is nothing clandestine or illegal about this, the effects can be devastating for the less efficient agribusiness and beneficial for the customers.

CTO (contribution-to-overhead) pricing

CTO (contribution-to-overhead) pricing is a method of encouraging extra sales by selling additional product above and beyond some base sales projection, at a price slightly greater than the additional out-of-pocket costs of handling the product. In other words, CTO pricing, which is also called marginal-cost pricing, ignores the full cost of producing and selling a product, and focuses on the incremental cost of making the sale. This strategy assumes the overhead costs will be covered by normal sales as projected, so that if additional products are sold at any price whatsoever that is above their variable cost, they will make a contribution to overhead and profit that would not otherwise exist. (See Chapter 12 for a detailed description of volume–cost relationships.)

The logic of this pricing method is quite compelling when viewed in terms of the marginal or extra sales opportunity. Since many agribusiness sales are made on a negotiated basis, there is ample opportunity for using CTO pricing methods to increase sales. Whenever fixed costs are a major component of total costs, as they are in many agribusiness industries, there is great temptation to utilize this method of increasing sales, making additional contributions to overhead, and increasing total profits.

The big problem with this strategy is limiting CTO pricing to only marginal or extra sales. In reality, there is a great tendency for competitors to react to the lower "spot" price, which causes the average market price to tumble, leaving the market unstable at best or in a shambles at worst. The key is holding CTO pricing to marginal sales.

Value-based pricing

Value-based pricing is a strategy that prices at a level at or slightly below the estimated perceived value of the product/service bundle. This idea makes sense—if the product is brought to the market at a price at or just lower than the perceived value, it should receive a favorable response from customers. The challenge is determining just what the perceived value of the bundle is to the customer. **Economic value analysis** is one way to formulate a price that reflects the economic value in a product. Here, the price that should be charged for a product is determined by dividing the product's economic value into two parts: the reference value and the differentiation value.

The **reference value** of a product is the price of a competing product or the closest substitute. This reference value forms a starting point for the price calculation. The **differentiation value** is the perceived value of the new product's unique attributes. To determine the price, positive perceived values of attributes are added to the price of the closest substitute (the reference value). Any negative perceived values of attributes are then subtracted from the reference value to find the total economic value of the product. The marketer may use this value-based price directly in the marketing strategy, or the marketer may use this price as a starting point from which to initiate some of the other pricing strategies presented.

Penetration pricing

In a **penetration pricing** strategy, a product is offered at a low price in order to gain broad market acceptance quickly. These strategies are used primarily to introduce new products into a market, particularly price-responsive products that must sell in large volume to reduce per-unit costs. Penetration pricing can quickly cut into the sales of established competitors, even in cases where brand loyalty may be a factor. This strategy is also used in situations when a competitive product is expected to follow quickly, with the logic that the firm in the market first may be able to stake an initial claim on customer loyalty. After a new product has gained customer acceptance, the price may be gradually increased to a more profitable level.

Skimming the market

A **skimming the market** strategy is virtually the opposite of penetration pricing. Skimming involves introducing a product at a high price and making excellent profits on the sales that are made initially. Then, as this relatively limited market becomes saturated, the price is gradually lowered, bringing the price into a range affordable to more customers. The appeal of this strategy is it affords the opportunity to maximize profits on new products as quickly as possible. Skimming the market works best with products that are new, unique, fairly expensive, hard to duplicate quickly, and sold by firms that are well known and respected in the industry.

Discount pricing

Discount pricing offers customers a reduction from the published or list price for some specified reason. Volume discounts are common among agribusinesses. The purpose of a volume discount is to encourage larger purchases, which reduce per unit costs and promote more sales. Volume discounts can be on a per order basis, but they more commonly accumulate throughout the season or year, and may take the form of a rebate at the end of the season. This kind of discount is frequently associated with customer loyalty programs.

Cash discounts are designed to encourage prompt payment for products and services. There are an infinite variety of cash discount programs. Many use terminology such as "5/10, net 30," which means that the customer will receive a 5 percent discount if the invoice is paid within ten days, but the full amount is due in 30 days, regardless. Because of the tremendous seasonality in most agribusiness industries, cash discount programs are widely used.

Early-order discounts are often given by manufacturers of agribusiness products as an incentive to order and/or take possession of products in the off-season. Because of storage and shipping problems in peak season, many manufacturers aggressively promote early shipment with very significant price reductions. Crop protection chemical and seed firms make wide use of early-order programs, sometimes offering a host of non-price incentives to accompany price discounts, such as "one free with each pallet ordered." Sometimes price protection programs are included to protect the early buyer against late-season price reductions by guaranteeing customers that if the price falls later during the heavy-use season, the buyer will receive a rebate, effectively giving them the lower price.

Loss-leader pricing

Loss-leader pricing involves offering one or more products in a product mix at a specially reduced price for a limited time. The idea is to encourage long-term adoption of that particular product. In a retail store setting, the featured item is also expected to draw customers to the store and increase sales in all other product lines. Featured items are sometimes even sold at cost in order to boost store traffic. Loss leader pricing is common in consumer retail settings, such as farm-home stores, nurseries, and food stores.

Psychological pricing

Psychological pricing involves establishing prices that are emotionally satisfying because they sound lower than some virtually equivalent price. Odd prices, such as 99 cents, sound a great deal less to customers than $1. "Two for $1.99," instead of "$1 each," gives the illusion of a special deal, and appeals to the customer's instinctive attraction to a bargain.

Prestige pricing

Prestige pricing, on the other hand, appeals to a high-quality, elite image. Many people have a strong belief that "you get what you pay for" and tend to equate price and quality on an emotional basis. Here, even prices—$50 or $100, for instance—are often used to communicate a prestige image. Prestige pricing is used in agribusiness, especially by any firm that is pursuing a high income, discriminating consumer. Premium dog food, unique food items, and quality wines would all be products likely to carry a prestige price.

An example

To illustrate some of the concepts involved in developing a pricing strategy, let's consider an example. The focus is a manufacturer of agricultural chemicals that is bringing a new nitrification product, Ni-Tri, to the market. Nitrification products are used with anhydrous ammonia to enhance yield and improve dry-down in corn. Farmers look for four attributes in nitrification products: (1) increased yield; (2) drier corn; (3) easier harvest;

and (4) environmental safety. This manufacturing firm is looking to employ perceived value pricing, and needs to estimate the perceived value of their new product.

Ni-Tri's closest competitor is a product called Enforce, which is currently priced at $36.00 per gallon. This $36.00/gallon becomes the reference value for the new product. Based on an economic assessment of Ni-Tri's benefits relative to those of Enforce, the following information is obtained:

Selling Price of Enforce $36.00/gallon
Perceived positive value of drier corn Ni-Tri attribute $2.50/gallon
Perceived positive value of easier harvest Ni-Tri attribute $2.50/gallon
Perceived positive value of environmental safety Ni-Tri attribute   Unknown
Perceived negative value of yield Ni-Tri attribute   −$3.00/gallon
Total economic value $38.00/gallon

Here, the makers of Ni-Tri could price the product somewhere around $38.00 per gallon— $36.00/gallon reference value and $2.00/gallon differentiation value—to reflect the economic value the producer would receive from using the product. Note that it proved impossible to put an economic value on the environmental benefit in the example above. The product manager for Ni-Tri will need to make a judgment call as to just what this benefit will mean to the target market. Accordingly, the final selling price may be a little higher than $38.00 per gallon.

At this point, the firm's pricing goals haven't been considered and the strategy doesn't really address the competition to any degree. Let's consider some other ways of looking at the problem that incorporate pricing goals and competitors in the decision-making process.

One strategic alternative would be to build market share. To increase market share through pricing, it is important to price at a level where the ratio of perceived value to selling price is higher than that of the closest competitor—a form of penetration pricing. If Ni-Tri has a perceived value that is 5 percent higher than Enforce, then Ni-Tri justifies a higher price than the competitive product. As long as the actual price premium is less than 5 percent, then Ni-Tri will be in a position to gain share on Enforce:

$$\frac{\text{Perceived value Ni-Tri}}{\text{Price Ni-Tri}} > \frac{\text{Perceived value enforce}}{\text{Price Enforce}}$$

$$\text{for example}: \quad \frac{\$42 / \text{gallon}}{\$37.40 / \text{gallon}} > \frac{\$40 / \text{gallon}}{\$36 / \text{gallon}}$$

Here, Ni-Tri will take market share away from Enforce since customers will find they get more value from every dollar they spend on Ni-Tri relative to Enforce. As the price of Ni-Tri is reduced, Ni-Tri should pick-up more market share on Enforce.

The same idea could be applied to a situation where Ni-Tri's makers were more concerned with skimming the market and less concerned about market share. Here they would price the product so that the selling price of Ni-Tri was more than 5 percent higher than that of Enforce. Ni-Tri will show a higher margin on each sale, but customers will find Enforce to be the better value over time and Ni-Tri will eventually lose market share.

The firm could combine the above pricing approaches with volume and cash discount programs, and an early order discount program to complete its pricing strategy. One final dimension that should also be mentioned is the issue of competitive response. The above examples have intentionally been over-simplified to illustrate the key concepts involved. But in reality, anticipating and managing the price response of the competition is a crucial part of a successful pricing strategy.

Legal aspects

Pricing is a delicate issue, from both marketing and legal standpoints. There is a great deal of federal legislation that clearly prohibits any form of collusion among firms in establishing prices or discrimination against particular customers. The Sherman Act (1890), the Federal Trade Commission Act (1914), and the Clayton Act (1914) provide the foundation for U.S. antitrust law and prohibit acts (including pricing) that substantially reduce competition among firms.

The Robinson–Patman Act (1936) strengthened the Clayton Act and strongly forbids pricing acts that discriminate among buyers without a cost justification. Any product of like kind and quality that crosses state lines must be offered to all purchasers at the same price, unless it can be clearly demonstrated that the price differences are based on differences in the cost of serving various customers. Similarly, any discounts or allowances made to one customer must be available to all customers. Local businesses that are not involved in interstate commerce and that are the final seller may sell at any price they choose to any customer, so long as they are not in collusion with other sellers. These laws are enforced by the Federal Government through the Department of Justice and the Federal Trade Commission. In addition, competitors and/or customers can sue firms violating these rules. The financial penalties for violations of these pricing laws can run into the hundreds of millions of dollars.

Promotional decisions

Promotional activities in the agribusiness are designed to do one thing—effectively communicate the value of the firm's products and services. Any marketing strategy incorporates a variety of methods for informing customers of the value of the firm's products and services and convincing them the firm provides the best product to suit their needs. This part of the marketing strategy is basically a communications process intended to educate the customer and encourage a positive buying decision.

The **promotion** mix chosen by the agribusiness firm is typically a combination of advertising, personal selling efforts, general public relations activities, and sales support programs. The mix must consider the life-cycle stage of the product, the stage of product adoption in the marketplace, competitors' actions, and available budget. The promotion mix is designed to support and complement the total marketing program (Figure 7.7).

Figure 7.7 The promotion strategy process

Developing a promotion strategy typically involves the following steps:

1. *Identify the target audience*: In general, the target audience falls within the target market. But, the target audience for a specific promotional effort could be any number of different groups, including specific groups of prospects, a group of **key influencers** (people who have some influence on the purchase decision, but don't actually make the decision), or a group of former customers the firm wants back. The target audience determines what the promotional strategy will say, and how, when and where to say it to most effectively reach that specific segment.
2. *Determine the communications objective*: Here the firm decides the action they want to encourage as a result of the communication. This desired action may be an immediate purchase, it may be to remind the customers of something, or it could be to change a non-customer's attitude. This step is clearly related to the product adoption model described earlier. The firm would have a different objective for customers in the awareness stage as compared to customers in the adoption stage.
3. *Design the message*: Here, the marketer creates a message consistent with the communications objective. Ideally, the message will get the audience's attention and elicit the desired action. This is a truly creative phase of the market communications process.
4. *Select the communication channel*: There are a variety of channels available to the agribusiness marketer and these are discussed below. In this step of the process, the marketer decides which of these channels to use. In most cases, a variety of channels are employed. For example, a promotional campaign for a new breakfast cereal might involve television advertising, coupons in the print media and online, a dynamic and informative website, personal sales calls to food retailers, and in-store merchandising support such as signs and display racks.
5. *Manage the implementation of the program*: This step involves allocating the promotional budget to the various activities, coordinating the market communications process, and measuring the results of the process. While heavily centered on management activities, this is a fundamentally important part of any successful market communications effort.

Virtually any marketing communications strategy, no matter how large or small, will go through these steps either formally or informally. Now, the key market communications channels will be discussed.

Advertising

Advertising is mass communication with potential customers, usually through public communications media such as television, radio, newspapers, magazines, or the Internet. Some advertising is **institutional** or **generic advertising**, or intended not to promote a particular product but rather to build goodwill for the total company or industry. Most advertising is **product advertising**, designed to promote a specific product, service, or idea.

Advertising performs several important functions. First, it creates awareness about the product, which facilitates personal selling efforts. In some cases, public exposure through communications media lends a degree of credibility to the product. Psychologically, a potential customer comes to feel that a nationally advertised product must be worth considering.

An advertisement can motivate a customer to seek out the product, or can at least serve as a reminder of the product's existence. Advertising also performs an educational function, helping customers to learn more about the company, the product and its use. Finally, advertising can reinforce the value of a purchase that has already been made. Research suggests that recent purchasers of a product are among those most likely to read an advertisement for that product.

Much advertising is initiated and sponsored by manufacturers of agribusiness products. Some of this advertising is oriented toward the dealer or distributor to influence ordering and selling decisions. But much manufacturer-sponsored advertising is aimed toward the product's end-user; in this case, the farmer or the consumer. The idea is to encourage ultimate demand to "pull the product through the pipeline," hence the term pull strategy.

Geographically broad advertising is usually the sole responsibility of the manufacturer. But local advertising, cooperatively sponsored by the manufacturer and the local dealer or distributor and called **cooperative advertising**, is also very common in agribusiness. The manufacturer, with the name of the local agribusiness inserted and the cost jointly shared, usually prepares local advertisements. The manufacturer may also supply the local agribusiness with flyers, posters, or product brochures, and may even send direct-mail advertisements, with the local business name imprinted on the advertisement, to local customers. Helping dealers develop web sites that ultimately promote the manufacturer's products and services is also an important strategy.

There are a wide variety of communication media ready to carry the agribusiness's message. Television is used heavily by national food manufacturers, but much less used by manufacturers of farm inputs. Radio is used more commonly by local agribusinesses, since it is less expensive and can target the farm audience by tying into agricultural programs such as market news and farm broadcasts.

Magazines are an important media for both food companies and agricultural input companies. A variety of local, regional, and national magazines provide an important method of communication with customers. An enormous number of specialty magazines appealing to tightly defined groups enable marketers to focus on publications of specific interest to their target market. Likewise, agricultural input firms can purchase advertisements in general farm publications serving all of agriculture or very specific publications serving only particular types of producers. Trade magazines geared to specific types of agribusinesses are also widely used to communicate with dealers and distributors. Many of these publications are supported by an aggressive web presence with engaging websites, daily or weekly webletters, blogs or other feedback mechanisms that provide a vehicle for dialogue about a story or issue, and video and audio presentation of news.

Newspapers are an especially important medium for both food retailers and food manufacturers. Inserts and coupons represent an important form of advertising for both groups. Agriculture-specific newspapers are another important medium for agribusinesses. They often have strong followings of agricultural producers and of other agribusiness professionals. Likewise, local agribusiness firms usually find advertising in local newspapers to be a cost-effective way to reach their clientele.

Direct mail remains an important media for agribusiness marketers. Agribusiness marketers can build huge databases containing detailed information on customers and prospects. Using these databases, marketers can tightly define targeted direct-mail promotions to very specific groups of individuals. For example, a feed company might desire to promote a new feed program only to Iowa pork producers with at least 1,000 sows, who use all-in/all-out production methods. Using the firm's database, contacting these groups with a letter or a promotional DVD is a relatively simple process. Such efforts are very cost effective and well received by the target audience as the information is targeted to their specific needs. Likewise, such databases can drive telemarketing efforts or email/e-letter campaigns with similar, positive responses.

Many of the direct mail tactics also apply to the email delivery of important information to key customers. Often, a targeted direct email is customized with the grower's name and specifics related to their operation. Links to videos or fact sheets are readily positioned within the direct email, making a customized approach directly targeted toward a specific customer. Agribusiness firms often find value in tracking who has read the email, followed through to the link or visited their website as a result of the communication.

Cell phones and text messaging can be an important means of connecting with customers. Another strategy taking advantage of communications technology is word of mouth marketing. Word of mouth teleconferences, where an expert leads a dialogue on a new product or service that is supported by a customer who relates personal experience with a product, can be a powerful way of providing information to potential buyers.

As alluded to earlier, the Internet is an important promotional tool for food and agribusiness firms. Company websites provide important product information, including the location of dealers who carry the product. Food companies have created highly educational and entertaining web sites to encourage frequent access to the sites. Password-protected areas are used to allow customers to access personal data, or to allow access to a higher level of information that the firm only wants to make available to qualified individuals. Banner ads can be used to promote goods and services on other sites. The ability to collect detailed information on customers allows the agribusiness marketer the ability for personalized email campaigns, and other more sophisticated website strategies. When the information management, communications capabilities, and convenience of the telephone/Internet are considered, it is clear that the Internet is part of a firm's product and place/distribution strategies, in addition to the promotion strategy role.

Determining how much to invest in advertising is a challenge for most agribusinesses, since it is difficult to determine the actual effect of advertising on sales. Large manufacturers of agribusiness products and their advertising agencies spend a great deal of money attempting to measure the effectiveness of different advertisements. As one executive put it, "I know half of my advertising is wasted—and if I could determine which half, we'd cut it out!" This is a big problem for smaller agribusinesses because they may not have the resources to effectively monitor the impact of advertising/promotion. Most local agribusinesses tend to do little media advertising, tending to focus on other promotion strategies. These firms argue that their best advertising in the local market is "satisfied customers," and choose to allocate their promotional dollars to customer meetings and personal contacts, or simply to sell at a lower cost. Advertising budgets for local farm-oriented businesses are generally limited to 1 to 2 percent of total sales or less. Larger organizations may spend 5 to 10 percent of total sales on advertising, especially if they are consumer goods companies looking to build national or international brands.

As with any economic equation, there may be a cost associated with choosing to limit or decline advertising opportunities. Companies large or small must consider the cost of not advertising, or of investing too little in an advertising effort. Competitors may take advantage of a firm's absence in advertising channels, thereby gaining an advantage in presence before the customers. Understanding the target market and where they get their news and information helps agribusinesses to determine where and how to invest their advertising budgets.

A standard marketing adage is that prospects must see or hear your marketing message an average of seven times before taking action to purchase a product or service from a company. An advertising strategy, combined with some or many of the tactics mentioned above can go long way in extending the value and repeating the message to reinforce customer awareness and their ultimate action toward purchasing products or services from your company.

Sales promotions

Sales promotions are programs and special offerings designed to encourage interested customers and prospects into making a positive buying decision. There is an almost infinite variety of such tools, and many are used extensively by agribusinesses to support personal selling and advertising activities. These tools range from the very expensive to the very inexpensive, but are felt by many to strongly influence customer decisions.

Some of these programs are aimed directly at the final consumer or the farmer. Giving prospects and customers hats, caps, jackets, belt buckles, pens, flash drives, and myriad other "freebies," all imprinted with the company logo, has become so common that farmers and ranchers have come to expect it. Often, larger producers are being "entertained" over a meal by marketing people as a means of getting their undivided attention. Food shoppers are the focus of a vast array of promotional activities including free samples, coupons, special offers (buy one, get one free), contests, games, incentive programs (accumulating "purchase points" to redeem for prizes, for example), and rebates. Loyalty programs, which encourage repeat buying by offering various rewards based on accumulated purchases, have become an important form of retail sales promotion.

Such sales promotion programs are an integral part of agribusiness marketing strategies. However, many of these sales promotions are easily copied which can reduce their effectiveness. As a result, some suppliers and retailers feel trapped by such promotions, but because of competitive pressures, are afraid to cut back on them. Thus expensive promotions and incentives should be entered into carefully with a clear objective in mind, and not simply as a quick reaction to a competitor's offering.

Other promotional programs include educational sales meetings sponsored by suppliers and retailers for farmers, ranchers, and growers. Evening meetings and day-long seminars, often including a complimentary meal, as well as webinars or teleconferences provide producers with a great deal of important technical information while subtly promoting the use of the manufacturer's products. Field days where farmers see products and services demonstrated in action are highly popular and effective. Regional trade shows where large numbers of suppliers attract thousands of farmers are also common. Farmer meetings and shows are an important communication and educational link between suppliers and producers. Similar activities are sometimes sponsored for food consumers. Cooking classes, wine tasting parties, and educational seminars on new foods can all encourage sales and build the firm's image.

The variety of sales promotions used in selling to dealers and distributors is even more elaborate. Sales contests and incentive vacation trips are common. Some especially productive agribusiness managers may "earn" trips to an exotic resort for themselves and their spouses in the slack season, at the expense of their supplier. Dealer and distributor meetings during the winter months are usually well planned, educational, and often elaborate and entertaining. Some suppliers develop educational and technical training programs for their customers' employees. Other incentives may link purchases with a key need of the dealer—buy a certain amount of product and receive an iPad, a laptop computer, or a cash rebate toward a particular type of crop protection chemical application equipment, for example.

Not all agribusinesses become extensively involved in well-developed promotional programs. Some choose instead to concentrate on service and price. However, sale promotions are an important part of the market communications strategy for most food and agricultural input firms.

Public relations

Public relations is another important form of market communications. Public relations is the management and maintenance of a favorable public image of the organization as it relates to its customers. These activities are somewhat unique as a form of market communications as they typically influence the target audience in an indirect way. Such influence may be through favorable news stories or a blog that creates a positive image for the firm. In many cases, such activities involve an outside, objective party in some way to carry the message. As such, public relations activities are likely to be viewed as more objective than other forms of market communications.

Public relations activities can range from very direct—food company expenditures on nutritional education programs for school children—to very indirect—a favorable news story that shows how a local agribusiness helped coordinate the fundraising effort for an injured farmer. Tools used for public relations by agribusiness firms include media relations, or placing news stories carrying the company's desired message in the news through television, radio, print, and digital media; company communications, or using company announcements (internal and external), speeches, and press releases to publicize the firm's desired message; and lobbying, or working with legislators to encourage laws and regulations favorable to the firm and its products.

In general, public relations activities help solidify the position or image the firm is creating in the market. For the nutritional campaign, the message may be that the food company is concerned about the nutritional needs of children. For the fundraising story, the message may be that the local firm really cares about the local community. Savvy agribusiness firms do not leave public relations activities to chance—they incorporate such activities into their promotional strategy. This may mean having the news media attend the roll-out of a new product, it may mean a column in the local newspaper on agronomic advice written by their field agronomist, or it may mean a well-publicized community service activity in which the firm's employees participate. Consumer or marketplace education activities are often highly effective promotional endeavors, and can be a positive tool toward building awareness and allow a unique opportunity for media coverage and propagation of company objectives. Such efforts may require little monetary investment, but may pay major dividends for the firm.

The explosion of social media can factor into public relations activities in favorable and unfavorable ways. Respected blogs or web postings that support a firm's products/services can provide exceptional visibility for an agribusiness. At the same time, critics or disgruntled customers using social media can create a major challenge for a firm who has to "set the story straight." Every major food and agribusiness has an aggressive and active digital media strategy to put this tool to work promoting products and services and monitoring critics and disgruntled customers.

Personal selling

In most agribusinesses, the salesperson plays an important part in the market communications process. Promoting a product through personal selling provides the most flexible and highest impact possible, since the salesperson can tailor the communication to meet the individual needs of the customer or prospect. This flexibility is especially important for complex products where usage and benefits may vary dramatically from customer to customer. For many agribusinesses, establishing a long-term relationship with priority customers is the focus of the marketing effort. And, personal selling plays a fundamentally important role in establishing such relationships. The agribusiness salesperson has the responsibility for not only taking the firm's product/service offering to the field, they also have the responsibility for keeping the firm informed about what customers and prospects want and need.

While personal selling can provide an important impact as a market communications tool, it is also an expensive form of communications. Individual sales calls are costly, and agribusinesses have invested considerable resources in technologies such as laptop computers, cell phones, and email, etc. to make salespeople as productive as possible. In addition, considerable effort is invested in targeting accounts that will be served via a salesperson, versus those that might be served via a less costly approach such as telemarketing.

Given the importance of this form of market communications, even the smallest local agribusinesses now have an individual with the title of salesperson on their staff. And, those that don't have a "salesperson" still rely heavily on personal contact and interpersonal communications to promote their product. Often the managers of such firms spend much of their time promoting products and services through personal contact. In larger agribusinesses, the personal selling process is far more formalized and highly structured. Management of the sales force and its organization take on great significance. Selecting, training, motivating, compensating, and territory allocation all become critically important decisions in the management of personal selling activities in the larger agribusiness.

Personal sales strategies are developed at all levels of the food and agribusiness markets. When a salesperson visits a farmer to discuss a new line of herbicides, the firm is using a personal sales strategy. Likewise, when a key account team from Kellogg's meets with the procurement group of Kroger, Kellogg's is using a personal sales strategy.

Personal selling clearly takes place throughout the many levels of the marketing channels for food and agribusiness products, not just at the final consumer or retail level. And, as customers, whether they are farmers, processors, or food companies, get larger and more sophisticated, the importance of personal selling increases. Likewise, as products and programs become more complex, personal selling becomes more important. Let's take a closer look at this important area of agribusiness management.

Marketing and sales

While sales and marketing are often talked about together, they are different activities. Reflecting on the description of the selling activity, we can begin to see how sales and marketing are related, and how these activities differ. As discussed earlier, a firm's marketing activities are generally longer term in nature. Agribusiness marketers focus on assessing the marketplace, considering what segments of the market to pursue, making decisions about all of the elements of the marketing mix. The focus of the marketing strategy is developing and supporting the firm's unique position in the market.

Selling is an important element of marketing—and a key dimension of the agribusiness firm's promotion strategy. In many companies, the sales force has the primary job for

Plate 7.3 Personal selling
Some customers like to make contact with their salesperson when taking a break from daily activities. Photo purchased from © istockphoto.com/msherida.

implementing the marketing plan. And, the sales force may be the most important part of the promotion strategy.

Selling is the process by which people in one company help match the value of the products, services, and information their company offers to the needs of targeted customers (Downey et al. 2011). It is the process of helping people buy and the process of creating a mutually beneficial relationship between the firm and the customer. An important part of sales is short term: generating results this week, this month, this quarter. But sales is also about building long-term relationships with targeted customers And, the sales force must act within the guidelines established by the company's marketing plan. In addition, the selling activity will be supported by other elements in the firm's marketing plan such as the product development effort, the pricing strategy, and other promotional activities.

Over time, agribusiness firms have increasingly put marketing tools in the hands of the agribusiness sales force. Here, the salesperson still has the basic responsibility to make sales happen. But, the salesperson is asked to treat his or her sales area as a mini-marketplace, and use the marketing tools developed in Chapters 6, 7, and 8 to assess opportunities, and to develop and implement a sales plan that is very focused on the needs of the specific territory served. This approach is called **field marketing**, and represents a move toward even closer integration of sales and marketing activities by agribusiness firms.

Functions of the salesperson

The food and agribusiness salesperson is directly responsible not only for generating revenue through sales, but also for providing the service that is the mainstay of a successful long-term relationship with customers, and for representing the company in the market area. Table 7.1

Table 7.1 Job description for feed salesperson

Job Title: Feed Salesperson

Purpose: Responsible for feed sales in southern half of state (35 county trade area).

Supervision: Works under direct supervision of general sales manager and is held responsible for sales results in feed department.

Major Areas of Responsibility
1. Responsible for profitable feed sales to livestock farmers in 35 county trade territory.
2. Helps producers increase their profits by advising them on state of the art nutritional programs and advances.
3. Promotes co-op products and co-op image to improve customer relations.
4. Manages customer and influencer relationships in trade territory.

Duties
1. Sells complete feeds, supplements, premixes, and animal health products to livestock producers in trade territory.
2. Sells co-op benefits, services, and nutritional programs to customers.
3. Follows-up on sales to make sure producers are satisfied.
4. Plans promotions to increase feed business.
5. Consults with customer on herd health/biosecurity, medication, waste management, and other special issues.
6. Utilizes electronic media as appropriate to connect with customers, prospects, and influencers.
7. Develops, promotes, and supervises all contacts.
8. Makes sales calls daily and reports results to sales manager on regular basis.
9. Prepares and maintains an up-to-date prospect list.
10. Handles any producer complaints promptly and professionally.
11. Monitors competition for prices and sales practices and reports results to sales manager.
12. Reviews monthly sales and tonnage figures with manager.
13. Helps develop annual sales budget.
14. Follows pricing and credit policy established by general manager.
15. Knows, interprets, and monitors any relevant regulatory issues.
16. Assists other departments by referring leads immediately.
17. Plans and schedules use of time.
18. Promotes and develops good customer relations.
19. Manages company truck and cell phone expense.
20. Attends sales and product meetings as directed by sales manager, participates in webinars as appropriate.
21. Studies and recommends ideas to improve internal operations and profits.
22. May perform other duties as directed by immediate sales supervisor.

Goals
1. Increase sales over last year by 10 percent.
2. Increase feed division profits by $250,000 over last year.
3. Average 3 sales calls per day.
4. Hold regular producer meetings during year.
5. Develop new sales and promotion plan by January 15.
6. Keep sales manager informed of results on a regular basis.
7. Pick up 5 new feed customers this year.

presents a job description for a typical entry-level feed salesperson position at a large farmer-owned cooperative.

Direct selling responsibility

Direct selling is the traditional and most basic function of the salesperson. The direct selling process involves prospecting for new customers, pre-call planning, getting the customer's attention and interest, making presentations, handling objections, closing the sale, and servicing the account. These steps may be carried out in formal or very informal ways. Many companies require sales personnel to document activities or time committed to each of these functions. The information collected provides the salesperson and the firm with important insights about the specific customer or prospect at the time of the call, and over time.

Indirect selling responsibility

Interestingly enough, **indirect selling** may take more of the agribusiness salesperson's time than direct selling. Indirect selling includes the service functions and follow-up provided by the salesperson. A long list of activities falls in this category, as shown in Table 7.1.

Market intelligence

Market intelligence is a common responsibility of the salesperson. It may be a formally stated responsibility or an informal expectation, but in either case the company recognizes that the salesperson is in a position to know what is going on in the field. The salesperson is expected to keep the company informed about competitors' actions, market prices, product performance, the "mood" of customers, weather and crop conditions, key customer trends, and product inventory levels. Many companies even require a weekly (or more frequent) marketing intelligence report to be prepared by their salesperson for the supervisor. This information is extremely valuable for supervisors and managers when they are making company-wide or division-wide decisions.

There are a variety of resources for a salesperson to tap in order to gain market intelligence. Many agribusinesses subscribe to market research reports that assess their market and benchmark activities of all competitors within a market segment. Monitoring competitor websites for promotional concepts or new products/services is yet another tactic for gathering market intelligence. Even monitoring a state-wide agricultural newspaper or magazine for articles or advertising can provide key clues to understanding what your competitors are engaging in as they compete for your customers' budgets. Combined, the information collected can help you and your company prepare to sell effectively.

Technical and product information

Being well versed on **technical and product information** is a fundamental part of a salesperson's job. Customers expect professional salespeople to be fully knowledgeable about the agribusiness's products and services. The salesperson must become an expert on the company's products, and understand how the products bring benefits to the customer, regardless of level in the marketing channel. Many companies provide intensive product information training for new salespeople during the first few months on the job and then regular ongoing training throughout their career. Typically, salespersons are given a wide array of resources in this area. And, many firms now provide such information via a company intranet so salespersons can access current product information and/or sales and decision-making tools using their computers.

Handling complaints

Handling complaints is often the salesperson's responsibility. Though this function is rarely a favorite part of the job, it is usually not a major problem. Most customers are quite reasonable, even when they have a complaint, and most companies have well-developed procedures for handling complaints. A well-handled complaint often turns into a real "plus" for the salesperson because it helps establish a deeper level of credibility and rapport with the customer.

Collections

Collecting accounts receivable may, infrequently, be part of the salesperson's responsibilities. An old agribusiness saying warns, "The sale is not complete until the money is collected." A salesperson that sells indiscriminately without concern for when and how payment will be made can create real problems for the company. One account that cannot be collected can wipe out all the profits for an entire region. Even when customers pay late, the cost to the company is usually significant. It is not uncommon for firms to counsel sales representatives on the importance of collecting payments from customers who are late paying their accounts. Others often handle this activity within the firm, but the salesperson that handles the particular account is often at least indirectly involved.

Public relations

Public relations is also an important part of the overall selling effort. How the general public and potential customers perceive the company is often very much a function of how the salesperson represents the company. The salesperson may work to build the company image through involvement in some community activities, and frequently takes part in trade shows, exhibits, field days, tests, and educational programs. Participation at county fairs through livestock auctions is one way for local agribusinesses to show community support. Other examples include supporting a local food bank or charitable organization. In food firms, trade shows may be an important part of the salesperson's responsibility. Someone other than the salesperson typically handles formal public relations in food firms. However, even here, a professional sales representative is always sensitive to this part of their position.

To most people, the salesperson is the company, because he or she is their only direct contact with the firm. Every action or lack thereof by the salesperson is part of this overall impression or image. The more local the company, the greater the significance of this impression. Even the salesperson's conduct in personal and community affairs has an important reflection on her or his effectiveness as a salesperson. Whether or not this is "fair," professional salespeople must realize the situation for what it is, and adapt to it.

Recordkeeping

Recordkeeping, budgeting, and administrative duties are a part of most professional salespeople's job responsibilities. Most salespeople submit weekly or more frequent reports on their activities, the number of calls they made, and market conditions. Usually, they must fill out order forms, take inventory, and collect special information for company surveys. Most salespeople are asked to prepare annual sales forecasts for their area and to develop their expense-budget requests. Salespeople must keep accurate expense records and fill out expense statements for reimbursement. All this is typically not as time consuming as it sounds, and when handled properly it can clear the way for more immediately productive duties.

Computers have greatly facilitated this planning and reporting process. Both sales representatives and the company benefit by having more information in a timely manner. In many agribusiness firms, the laptop computer is a fundamental tool for the sales representative and database software may support an intensive customer relationship management program. Reports and records may be kept on the computer, orders may be placed over the Internet, and customer records may be accessed to prepare for sales calls. Salespeople are expected to be "computer savvy"—using computers and the Internet to communicate with the company and with their customers.

As seen above, personal selling may well be the most important element of the firm's marketing strategy. We have only scratched the surface of the important role these individuals play and the strategies firms use to develop and implement an effective sales force management strategy.

Place decisions

Every agribusiness must decide how to move products to its customers. **Marketing channels** are systematic ways of transferring both the physical product and the ownership to the customer as efficiently as possible. In many ways, the channel is a communication system linking the manufacturer or producer to the customer. Consumer-demand signals flow through the distribution system to manufacturers, while supply and availability signals in the form of prices and costs flow to consumers. In many cases, independent agribusinesses such as wholesalers or distributors facilitate the transfer of ownership and physical product. In other cases, manufacturers find it more efficient to sell directly to the customer, handling these **distribution** functions inside the organization.

Physical distribution systems (PDS)

Decisions on **physical distribution systems (PDS)** are particularly important to much of agribusiness, since so many farm supplies and food items are bulky and highly seasonal in demand. Literally millions of tons of phosphate fertilizers must be moved from Florida mines, and millions of tons of potash fertilizers must be shipped from western Canada, to farms and ranches all over the United States and Canada. Likewise, highly perishable crops like lettuce, tomatoes, and peppers must find their way from California, Arizona, Texas, and Florida to food stores all over the United States. At the same time, millions of bushels of grain must be moved from local storage to the coasts for shipment to overseas markets.

The costs of physical distribution activities are high. And, in season, rail car and truck shortages can cause spot supply shortages, creating bottlenecks for agribusiness products in the distribution system. Consequently, a firm's marketing strategy incorporates plans for assuring a robust physical distribution system. Policies encouraging larger storage facilities at local levels, company ownership of rail cars, company-operated truck fleets, unit trains with 100-car shipments of the same commodity, transcontinental barges and pipelines, and partnering relationships with suppliers of logistics services are becoming common as a means of ensuring timeliness and reducing costs.

Even at the local level, agribusinesses are highly concerned about physical distribution. Bulky products must be broken down into prescription quantities to meet the needs of individual farmers quickly during intense high-use periods. Bulk feed delivery, on-farm storage, custom application of chemicals and fertilizer, on-farm breeding services, and myriad other products and services must be delivered effectively. For food retailers, Internet shopping and home delivery of purchases is increasing in frequency. Convenience is a major issue on the minds of many food shoppers, making store location decisions among the most fundamental a food retailer can make. Much of this physical distribution requires a great deal of highly specialized equipment and labor, as well as major investments in facilities. Indeed, physical distribution at all levels incurs a high marketing cost and is critical to the agribusiness.

Channel management

Channel management decisions are concerned with who owns and controls the product on its journey to the customer. These decisions have important implications for how the marketing functions will be carried out and who will carry them out. The market channel selected is closely tied to the physical distribution problem. But the question of who owns the product and who performs the various market functions required to transfer a product from the manufacturer to the consumer is much broader.

There are three basic systems used by most agribusinesses (see Figure 7.8). Each system differs in the extent and type of involvement of the middleman. In each system, all

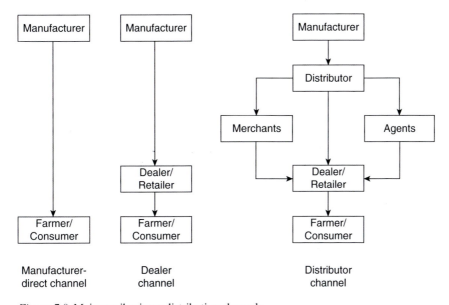

Figure 7.8 Major agribusiness distribution channels

marketing functions are performed. That is, products are owned, transported, financed, and stored. But in each system these functions are performed by different parties.

In a **manufacturer-direct distribution system**, the manufacturer sells directly to the farmer or food customer. The original manufacturer or producer, who owns and controls the product until the final user purchases it, performs all marketing functions. This system has the advantage of ensuring that the product will be priced, promoted, and sold in ways that are acceptable to the manufacturer. This method is used widely by smaller local or regional farm input manufacturers, who can develop their own sales force as they grow, and by catalog merchants, local market fruit and vegetable operations, and farmers' markets in the food market.

Some firms believe this strategy allows them to be more aggressive in the marketplace, because they can create and control their image with customers. This channel also works better where customers are concentrated. As the business grows and customers are distributed more widely, with increasingly different characteristics and needs, it becomes more difficult to manage the direct-selling system. Marketing to widely different customers often requires at least regionalized marketing policies, which become difficult to administer effectively. However, when organizations give their sales force considerable autonomy, the system can be effective even on a regional or national scale. Likewise, major developments in customer databases which allow manufacturers to "know" their end users have facilitated this channel. In addition, developments in e-commerce allow manufacturers to go directly to the end-user employing the Internet and the firm's web-site as their "virtual" sales force.

Note that many companies that sell directly do so by establishing their own wholesale and retail systems. The product must be physically transported and distributed as in any other system, but in the direct system company-owned warehouses and/or retail stores will be used, which allows manufacturers to ship and store products whenever and wherever they choose. This freedom provides some real economic advantages.

In a **dealer-distribution system**, manufacturers sell their products to dealers, who, in turn, sell products in their own local market. The big advantage is that the local dealer is more in touch with the needs of local customers and can maintain the flexibility to serve both manufacturers' and customers' needs quickly and efficiently. This eliminates the tendency for an executive 1,000 miles away to fill local storage space with a product simply to gain more room in a full warehouse, even though local farmers may not need the product in large quantities that season. In addition, some feel that independent dealers are more highly motivated to serve the local customer than are company employees.

Some manufacturers give their dealers (who may be called distributors, even though they sell directly to farmers or consumers) the right to sell their products. Local dealers often have a strong understanding of their local market and customers and find great success in selling a manufacturer's product as part of their business. This arrangement benefits both the local dealer, who makes a margin on the products sold, and benefits the manufacturer by having the local dealer's knowledge and presence in a given area. Although the manufacturer cannot control the sales areas of dealers, giving some dealers this right and refusing it to others can strategically limit the number of dealerships. To maintain the right to sell the manufacturer's products, dealers may agree to maintain certain levels of service to customers and promote the products in special ways. There may even be a contractual agreement, sometimes called a franchise, spelling out the responsibilities of both the dealer and the distributor.

Other manufacturers encourage distribution through as many dealers as possible. Products that are frequently purchased and less expensive generally tend to be mass-marketed in order to maximize convenience to the buyer and saturate the market. Many hard lines of farm supplies are marketed in this way. Products are sold to the dealer almost as they would be to a farmer-consumer. As farms and ranches grow bigger, many manufacturers are beginning to recognize them as "dealers," especially if the farmer resells at least some product to a neighbor. In effect, the traditional manufacturer–dealer–farmer system seems to be breaking down in some product areas.

In the food area, this channel has taken a different form with the emergence of major retail chains such as Wal-Mart, Kroger, and Costco that control much of the retail food market. Such retailers fill an important need by bringing the products of myriad manufacturers together under one roof for the convenience of the food consumer. While small independent food stores remain important in some areas, national and regional chains dominate the scene. These chains, by having access to food shoppers, are a very powerful force in the marketing channel. And, many of the larger chains are also integrated into manufacturing their own private-label food products that compete with the brands from manufacturers.

The **distributor system** uses both distributors, or **wholesalers**, and dealers to market products to farmers and consumers. This more complex marketing system usually evolves for economic reasons. Larger organizations can more easily afford to develop their own marketing system. Independent distributors may already have a well-developed network of transportation, salespeople, and customers, and their size allows them to operate quite efficiently. They can often add a new product line much more cheaply than the manufacturer can establish an entire distribution system. This allows manufacturers to concentrate on what they do best—manufacturing product—and allows distributors to do what they do best—support distribution activities.

Merchant-distributors, who actually take title to the manufacturer's product, are called distributors, jobbers, wholesalers, or cooperative buying groups. They physically order, receive, and distribute products. As totally independent businesses, they make their own decisions, relying on manufacturers only for technical assistance and information.

Agent-distributors perform the function of helping products move through the system, but they do not take title to the product and usually do not physically handle the product. Agent-distributors are known as brokers, sales agents, and manufacturer's representatives. They are independent businesses that simply locate customers, negotiate a deal, and receive a commission for the transaction. Agents and brokers often specialize in certain product lines and types of customers. Their primary tool is communication. In markets in which shortages are occurring, brokers are usually able to locate extra product for a special price. They perform the important function of bringing buyers and sellers together.

E-commerce firms represent a variety of manufacturers and have no physical "storefront," relying instead on sophisticated websites to assist consumers and producers in making purchase decisions. The customer or producer places the order over the Internet, financing is arranged over the Internet, and the merchandise is shipped to the home or place of business, or is made available for pick-up at a convenient location. These "e-dealers" will continue to search out the products and customers where they provide a more effective and efficient marketing channel than the traditional "bricks and mortar" channel.

The total distribution system can be far more complex than is described here. Many manufacturers may use several different systems simultaneously. For example, Agrium, a large fertilizer manufacturer based in Canada, markets fertilizer through its own retail outlets and through independent fertilizer dealers. Pepsi products are available virtually anywhere people get thirsty—from food and convenience stores, to sporting events, to study lounges, to restaurants and institutional food service outlets, to drink machines on almost every corner. Such distribution systems gradually evolved as a result of changing products, customers, and the competitive environment. And, this evolution can be expected to continue, especially in light of the rapid developments in the e-commerce arena.

Summary

Agribusiness marketers must translate the position they want to create for the target market into a product/service/information bundle that serves customer needs and communicates the desired image. The set of decisions to accomplish this task is called the marketing mix.

Product decisions determine what products, services, and/or information are offered by the agribusiness. The needs of the target market are at the center of any decision in this area. Agribusiness marketers create a value bundle that will satisfy customer needs. This bundle includes both the tangible attributes of the product or service as well as any intangible benefits the firm may offer the customer. As products are introduced they move through a systematic adoption and diffusion process. Each new product has a life cycle, passing through distinct phases from its introduction to its demise. Both the adoption-diffusion process and the product life cycle have important implications for market planning.

Pricing decisions are critical to marketing success. Pricing strategies are based on the perceived value of the firm's products and services, the firm's cost of doing business, the marketing goals of the firm, and competitive actions. A wide range of pricing strategies are available, from simple rules of thumb, to far more sophisticated approaches which involve carefully measuring the value delivered by the firm to the target market.

Promotional decisions determine how the agribusiness will communicate with the market. These decisions involve determining the proper mix of advertising, sales support, public relations, and personal selling needed to communicate the firm's desired image to the market. Developing a market communications strategy involves identifying the target audience, determining the communications objective, designing the message, selecting the communications channel, and managing the implementation. A coordinated set of activities which communicate the desired image to the target market is the goal of the agribusiness marketer in this area.

Finally, place decisions concentrate on the methods and channels of distribution that will optimize sales and profits. Logistics management plays an important role in place decisions as firms determine how products will physically move from manufacturer to customer. Issues of cost and efficiency, timeliness, freshness, customer service, customer access, and control all affect the choice of distribution channel by an agribusiness.

All elements of the marketing mix are critical decision areas for the marketing manager. In the end, the marketing mix must deliver a consistent message—the position—to the target market.

Discussion questions

1. Many retail food stores also sell flowers. Why do you suppose they do this? What marketing decision does this illustrate? Besides food products and flowers, what other products or services do retail food stores offer? Why?
2. Pick a food product or an agricultural input. Use the total product concept to break the product down into the generic product, the expected product, the value-added product, and the potential product. In what other ways could the food business or agribusiness add value to the product you have chosen?

3. Draw a product life-cycle curve for large, four-wheel-drive farm tractors. Where would you estimate this product's life cycle is currently? Why? What might manufacturers do to prolong its life?

4. If you were introducing a new electronic dairy feeding system that would reduce feeding costs by 20 to 25 percent, what pricing policy would you suggest? Why? Would you stay with this policy indefinitely? Why?

5. You are the marketing manager for a retail food company that has a new 16 ounce fruit juice product, packaged in a reusable squirt-type bottle. Your target market is the active 18–25 year-old consumer group. Develop a promotion plan for this new product. What market communication tools would you use?

6. You are the marketing manager for a large animal health company. Your firm has just developed a very effective anthelmetic (wormer) for cattle. Your target market is large feedlot operations in the western United States. Develop a promotion plan for this new product. What market communications tools would you use?

7. Based on your personal experiences and observations, how do salespeople vary from industry to industry? Why do we see these differences? Discuss some of these differences for:
   a) a salesperson at an electronics superstore
   b) a field salesperson at an agricultural cooperative
   c) a car salesperson
   d) a loan officer at a bank
   e) a salesperson for an advertising agency

8. Compare and contrast the role of a salesperson for a large food or agricultural input manufacturer with that of a local salesperson for a dealer or retail organization. If possible, interview these two types of salespersons. Where do they spend their time, i.e., what types of activities make up their week? Who do they report to? What type of records are they required to keep? Without getting specific, how are they paid?

9. What are the advantages of a manufacturer's selling directly to a farmer rather than to a distributor? Why can a dealer sometimes do a better job marketing to farmers than a manufacturer can?

10. Some retail food stores offer a service where they sell products via the Internet. Here, using communications software, the customer accesses the firm's inventory and price list through their website, chooses what they want, and the firm delivers the choices to the home at a time convenient to the customer. What do you see as the advantages of this system? What do you see as the disadvantages?

Case study: PecsBake

PecsBake is a medium-sized bakery company that supplies fresh baked breads and traditional Hungarian pastries to retail groceries in Southwestern Hungary. Pecs (say Paytch) is the fifth largest city in Hungary and a popular tourist destination near the Croatian border. On a recent management training and business development trip to the United States, the company's top management visited many American supermarkets. In the refrigerated goods sections they saw products not currently present in the Hungarian market—refrigerated breakfast pastry dough ready-made for microwave preparation, packaged in special cardboard/can containers. There were two common package sizes: two servings per container and six servings per container.

PecsBake's managers noted the increasing popularity of microwave ovens in Hungarian homes, and decided that they would like to introduce sweet Western-style pastry products (such as frosted cinnamon rolls) in Hungary. Their production experts were confident that PecsBake could also produce refrigerated, microwave-ready dough for traditional Hungarian pastries such as *turos taska* (a roll filled with sweetened cottage cheese), *lekvarosz batyu* (a roll filled with jam), and *kakaos csiga* (a roll filled with cocoa). On a per serving basis, the Hungarian pastries would require 1.5 times the volume of the American products.

In general, Hungarians don't like sweet breakfasts. Their morning pastries are only semi-sweet at most. If PecsBake decides to sell American-style cinnamon rolls, they may need to be positioned as dessert products unless the firm can educate consumers about this new breakfast taste.

Microwaves are just emerging in Hungary. At present they are in only three or four out of every ten homes in the capital city of Budapest, and with even fewer in the countryside. "Food-in-a-hurry" isn't a widely held concept in Hungary. However, this is changing quickly as many Hungarians are working longer hours and sometimes two or three jobs.

U.S. cardboard/can manufacturers are currently reluctant to produce containers sized for the proposed Hungarian products unless they are paid higher prices to cover the cost of manufacturing the special containers. At this time they are only offering prices which would be economical for the Hungarian bakery on the same cardboard/can containers that they are currently supplying to large American companies.

PecsBake's managers are not certain that the proposed products will be well received by Hungarian grocery stores that already have limited refrigeration space. Alternatively, one manager suggested that they provide stand-alone refrigerated displays and sell their products in appliance stores in areas near the microwave displays.

PecsBake has enough capital to begin producing and marketing refrigerated, ready-made microwaveable pastry dough on a limited scale. They would like your advice about what products to introduce, how to package their products, and how to reach their customers.

Questions

1. What target market should PecsBake pursue?
2. What position should they take with this target market?
3. Outline the marketing mix you would suggest for PecsBake as they attempt to communicate your suggested position with the target market. What product/service/information strategy would you employ? How should they price their products? What promotion or market communications strategy should they use? What place strategy or distribution channel would you use? You may want to consider both the short term and the long term in your strategy.

References and additional reading

Blakeman, Robyn. *Integrated Marketing Communication: Creative Strategy from Idea to Implementation.* Lanham, MD: Rowman & Littlefield, 2007.
Downey, W. Scott, W. David Downey, Michael A. Jackson, and Laura A. Downey. *ProSelling: A Professional Approach to Selling in Agriculture and Other Industries.* Henderson Communications, LLC, 2011.

Kotler, Philip and Kevin Lane Keller. *Marketing Management*. Upper Saddle River, NJ: Pearson/ Prentice Hall, 2011.

Manning, Gerald L. and Barry L. Reece. *Selling Today: An Extension of the Marketing Concept*. Needham Heights, MA: Allyn & Bacon, 1990.

Nagle, Thomas T. *The Strategy and Tactics of Pricing: A Guide to Profitable Decision Making*. Upper Saddle River, NJ: Prentice Hall, 1987.

Ries, Al and Laura Ries. *The 22 Immutable Laws of Branding: How to Build a Product or Service into a World-class Brand*. New York: HarperBusiness, 2002.

Rogers, Everett M. *Diffusion of Innovations*. 4th ed. New York: Free Press, 1995.

Stark, J. *Product Lifecycle Management: 21st Century Paradigm for Product Realisation*. Berlin: Springer, 2011.

Tybout, Alice M. and Tim Calkins. *Kellogg on Branding: The Marketing Faculty of the Kellogg School of Management*. Hoboken, NJ: Wiley, 2005.

Wanless, W. Brian. *The Product Manager's Guide to Pricing*. Charleston, SC: BookSurge, 2009.

8 Tools for marketing decisions in agribusiness

Objectives

- Outline the procedure for a marketing audit
- Analyze how sales forecasts are made and how they are used in the agribusiness firm
- Present methods for analyzing competitors
- Review techniques for studying customer attitudes and opinions

Introduction

Developing and managing a successful marketing program in an agribusiness can be a complex task, particularly in larger firms with many products. This chapter explores several analytical tools that are critical to agribusiness marketers' understanding. Whether you are selling a product, or managing programs, people or products, it is important to understand how each of these tools can work toward helping the agribusiness firm achieve goals and stay competitive.

The needs of customers are constantly evolving. Competitors are continually introducing new products, services, and programs. Nearly all agribusinesses face highly seasonal demand that creates the possibility of critical bottlenecks in servicing customers. Unpredictable weather patterns further complicate market planning, and volatile agricultural commodity prices often cause the demand for farm inputs and services to fluctuate. Because of such complexities, agribusiness marketing strategies require a great deal of planning. Successful managers spend much time analyzing their market, assessing their own strengths and weaknesses, and mapping their strategic marketing plan.

Agrimarketers use a wide assortment of analytical tools and concepts—market planning tools to assist them in the market planning process. These tools play an important role in conducting the SWOT analysis described in Chapter 6. In addition, these tools play an important role in the evaluation phase of the market planning process. Some of these tools are highly sophisticated and involve complex mathematical models and extensive marketing information systems. Other tools involve far simpler approaches to data collection, while still others are simply methods of capturing subjective "gut feelings" and intuition for the market.

One point is clear regardless of which tools are used—agribusinesses using an information-driven approach to market planning are more likely to be successful than those who don't put data to work in their planning efforts. This chapter will look at four broad sets of tools that agrimarketers can use in the market planning process—the marketing audit, sales forecasting, competitor analysis, and customer analysis.

The marketing audit

Nearly every agribusiness and certainly all publicly owned companies have financial audits performed regularly by outside auditors to ensure that there are no discrepancies or oversights that could cause serious problems for the business and/or investors in the business. Similarly, a **marketing audit** is an objective examination of a company's entire marketing program. The marketing audit examines the firm's marketing objectives and its plan for accomplishing these objectives in light of its resources, the market conditions, and its distinctive strengths and weaknesses (Figure 8.1). In the market planning process outlined in Chapter 6, the marketing audit plays a key role in the evaluation stage of the process. It is a tool that firms can use to better understand past marketing efforts in order that future efforts will be even more effective.

The first step in a marketing audit is to carefully analyze how the agribusiness is doing with each product or service it markets. This step involves estimating total market potential, determining the firm's share of the market, and attempting to identify what factors are responsible for the firm's market position with each product or service.

Here the firm will re-examine its marketing goals for each of its products or services and assess what progress they have made toward achieving the goal. Areas where the firm falls short of the goal should be carefully explored to better understand why performance was poor. Did the firm miss the mark when assessing the needs of the target market?

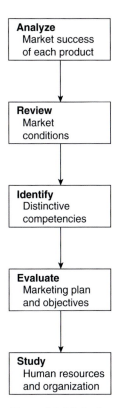

Figure 8.1 Marketing audit procedures

Did competitors introduce new products or programs that caused problems for the firm's marketing plan? Did the firm fail to execute the plan effectively? Or, was the marketing goal too ambitious? For example, a feed ingredients company that has an objective of a 10 percent annual increase in beef supplement sales at a time when the beef industry is under pressure from low prices might be better served by creating a new objective of holding beef supplement sales constant, while devoting more resources to expanding sales of supplements for another species where the economics are better.

Answers to these types of questions will be provided in part by the remaining steps of the marketing audit. But, before moving to step two of the marketing audit, it is important to note that while much focus is given to areas where performance was poor, there is another, equally important, perspective. An effective marketing audit also attempts to capture the insights provided by areas where performance was exceptionally good. If sales of a new granola snack bar are growing twice as fast as expected, the food firm should dig deeply into the situation to better understand why this is occurring, if it will continue, and how they can apply this success to other products.

The second step of the marketing audit reviews general market and competitive conditions. Marketing factors external to the firm are evaluated, and expected trends explored. Sometimes probabilities are attached to these expected trends or market scenarios. This information helps agribusiness managers to shape their marketing strategies. The focus here is re-visiting key assumptions about trends in technology, regulations and policies, general economic conditions, and the competitive environment. In today's dynamic market, a marketing plan based on dated forecasts of such areas is likely to fail. Marketers must challenge their previous assumptions, and generate new scenarios for the future they believe they will be moving into.

The third step of the marketing audit focuses on identifying the firm's distinctive competencies, that is, areas where the firm is particularly strong in relation to the competition. Distinctive competencies may include financial, human resource, marketing, and production advantages. As indicated earlier, these distinctive competencies often form the basis for the total marketing strategy. For example, consider a semen company that is fortunate enough to have an extremely good line of bulls with exceptionally strong performance records. This measurable product quality distinction can form the basis for a quality-oriented marketing strategy with a premium pricing approach, a relatively small field sales force, and considerable emphasis on progeny testing.

While firms must give careful consideration to the idea of distinctive competencies during the market planning process, the intent here in the marketing audit is to re-consider the issue to make sure the areas identified earlier remain strengths. This part of the marketing audit may involve data collected during a competitor analysis or during a customer needs analysis.

The fourth step of the marketing audit is to objectively evaluate the agribusiness's overall marketing strategy, given a review of past performance in the firm's target markets, a re-examination of the firm's market environment, and a re-assessment of the firm's distinctive competencies. In rapidly changing markets, strategies can become out of date and ineffective quite quickly.

This step of the marketing audit should also consider how the marketing plan is to be implemented. A good plan will be ineffective if it is poorly executed. Continuing to use the same channels of distribution because "that's the way we always do it" may be a poor choice. Do incentive travel packages offer the best type of sales promotion for dealers, or would it be best to return dollars in the form of a rebate—or perhaps just sell at lower prices in the first place? Did farmers find the weekly text message on pest pressure in their area helpful, or was it simply "one more message they had to delete"? Analysis of such implementation issues forces the marketer to think deeply about whether or not the current marketing strategy is still the correct one.

Given a thorough examination of where the firm has been and new forecasts for the future, the goal of this step is to make sure the firm's market strategy still fits. This is sometimes called **gap analysis** (Figure 8.2). The gap is the difference between desired performance at some point in the future and what performance will be if the firm does not change marketing strategies. Obviously, the larger the gap that exists, then the greater the need for the firm to revisit its marketing strategy. Through this analysis, the next marketing plan can be made more effective in terms of the current and expected market conditions.

Finally, the marketing audit objectively evaluates the firm's human resources and organizational structure. Given the critical role people and organizational structure play in the marketing process, this area deserves special attention. Consider the following questions:

Are salespeople adequately trained to advise growers on technical matters?

Should technical specialists in the field report to the area sales manager, or should they report to the home office?

Do field salespeople have the right level of price authority to meet the marketing objectives?

Does the organizational structure promote adequate cross-communications between salespeople, marketing staff, and the research and development department?

Is there adequate support and talent to drive the firm's digital media strategy?

The firm's revised marketing strategy becomes the focal point for this final step. The firm must determine if available human resources and the current organizational structure support what the firm wants to accomplish in the future. Evaluating human and organizational factors is one of the most critical facets of the marketing audit.

The marketing audit should be performed as objectively as possible. Sometimes it is difficult for managers to evaluate their own program objectively because they created it, so managers should consider hiring an outsider to periodically review the program. A qualified consultant can objectively evaluate a marketing program and raise important questions about the allocation of time, effort, and financial resources. In smaller firms with localized markets, a peer running a similar business in a different market may fill the role of the consultant nicely and offer important, objective insights into the firm's marketing efforts.

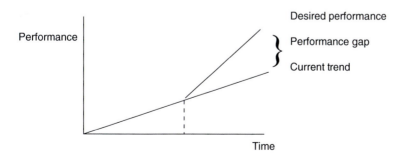

Figure 8.2 Gap analysis

Sales forecasting

Although agribusiness markets are well known for their volatility, agribusiness managers cannot escape the responsibility of forecasting sales. Nearly every management decision includes a critical assumption about the level and timing of sales volume. All production schedules are built around projected demand. Raw-material purchases are based on expected sales. The personnel function of hiring and firing is greatly influenced by anticipated sales. Cash needs are based on sales forecasts. Capital investments in new facilities are heavily influenced by sales projections. The allocation of resources to research and development is based heavily on the expected sales of the resulting products. The fact is that a great majority of management decisions and much of the entire planning process rests squarely on forecasted sales.

Sales forecasting involves predicting sales in dollars and physical units as accurately as possible for a specific period of time. Many times this means forecasting sales for the total market, and then determining what share of the market can be captured with a specific product or service (Figure 8.3).

Both short-term and long-term sales forecasts are useful for agribusiness. Short-term forecasts, usually one season or shorter for agribusiness firms, are useful in formulating current operating plans. In food firms, such forecasts may be weekly or daily. In a food service firm, forecasts may be hourly as the firm works to schedule food preparation to accommodate daily patterns. Longer-range sales forecasts are important for capacity and research and development decisions. In general, the longer the time period forecasted, the less accurate the forecast is likely to be. However, forecasting short-term volatility can be a major challenge as well.

Difficulty and complexity notwithstanding, agribusiness managers need relatively accurate sales forecasts. Such forecasts may be prepared in a formal manner using thorough economic and marketing analysis, or they may be more informal and based on assumptions from a variety of practical perspectives. Here, three types of **forecasts** will be considered—general economic forecasts, market forecasts, and sales forecasts.

General economic forecasts

General economic forecasts consider broad factors that affect the total economy. Government farm programs, inflation, the money supply, international policy and trade agreements, exchange rates, interest rates, population demographics, and a host of other factors are included in such forecasts. A great many government and private economists spend much time tracking economic trends and making such projections. Agribusiness managers watch these opinions carefully as they formulate market plans. Forecasts of such general economic indicators have a fundamental role in an assessment of the market environment as part of the SWOT analysis and in the marketing audit.

Typically, these types of forecasts are generated by sophisticated econometric models of the domestic and world economies. Using such models, forecasts for a variety of indicators

Figure 8.3 Sales forecasting model

at different points in the future can be generated. This information is very important to agribusiness marketers. A firm selling capital equipment to farmers and ranchers knows that purchases are heavily influenced by interest rates. Long-term prospects for stable to declining interest rates mean this factor in the farmer's capital equipment purchasing equation is positive. A regional retail food chain may find that economists are predicting a harsh recession in the area served by their stores. Such information will have important implications for the firm's sales as some customers reduce luxury purchases, and focus more on staple products.

Market forecasts

Market forecasts, or forecasts for specific industries or types of products, are based on general economic forecasts and a great deal of information about the specific industry involved. Agricultural economists continually monitor changing economic indicators that track or lead agricultural trends. Some use complex mathematical methods (econometric models) to predict demand for various products and commodities. In the food business, demographic data is carefully studied to forecast demand for specific products. Demographic factors such as family size, age, income level, and education tell market researchers much about what kind and how much of specific types of food products will be purchased in a region.

Factors determining farm market demand have been researched extensively. For example, agricultural economists have worked to understand various cycles or patterns in livestock production. Historically, pork production cycled every four years, while the cattle cycled about every nine years. During these cycles, prices fell as the number of animals on feed increased, and profits declined. As a result, some less efficient producers exited from the market, livestock numbers dropped, and prices gradually increased. The cattle cycle was longer because of the length of the gestation period for cattle, taking more time to increase production. Dramatic changes in the size and structure of pork and cattle operations over the past 20 years and the technologies used by pork and cattle producers have certainly affected these cycles. Still, information and forecasts on sow herd size, cattle on feed, dairy cow numbers, etc. is extremely important to nutrition companies, milling equipment companies, livestock marketing firms and meat processing companies because it directly impacts their prospects and customers and thereby their market.

The demand for most farm inputs such as animal health products and fertilizer is a **derived demand**. This means that the demand for a specific type of product or service depends greatly on the demand for another product or service for which it is used. The demand for fertilizer, for example, is a function of the demand for the crops it helps produce. When the manager of a fertilizer plant in the Midwest is projecting the demand for nitrogen, the corn market is carefully considered. The manager knows that the price farmers anticipate for corn in the next season will greatly affect the number of acres of corn they will plant and the amount of fertilizer they will want to buy. Consequently, agribusiness managers are careful students of the market for whatever products their supplies help to produce.

Not surprisingly, there is a great interest in current information on nearly every product produced by farmers. Summaries and analyses of market conditions for virtually every agricultural product are distributed widely each day—from both public and private sources. Important grain and livestock market information is instantly flashed to analysts and agribusinesses as transactions occur throughout the day via a variety of media—television, radio, satellite news services, and the Internet, to name a few. Government and private

Plate 8.1 Livestock production
Agribusiness marketers stay on track by using a variety of market planning tools. Photo courtesy of USDA Natural Resources Conservation Service.

reports estimating current and projected acreage and livestock numbers are released frequently throughout the year to help agribusinesses monitor trends and adjust their plans.

Like agricultural input firms, food firms are also very interested in market demand. Food marketers pay special attention to two key areas when forecasting sales—regionality and seasonality. Food consumption patterns can vary dramatically from one region of the country to another. For example, grits sell well in the Southeast U.S., but few consumers may even know about this product in other regions of the country. Consumption of food products will vary dramatically by season as well. Summer fruit, vegetable, and ice cream sales, and holiday sales of turkey and ham are excellent examples. Combined with good demographic data, bringing regional and seasonal factors into the equation helps food marketers fine-tune their market forecasts.

Note that despite all the sophisticated techniques, forecasting market demand is far from an exact science. Random events such as unexpected weather, consumer fads, a food safety scare, or an international crisis can play havoc with the most elaborate market demand forecast. Here, techniques such as contingency analysis or sensitivity analysis become important. The general idea here is to bound a forecast with an upper and lower range that helps the manager understand the uncertainty that comes with any forecast. For example, when forecasting market demand, a fertilizer firm may look at corn prices under strong export market, normal export market, and weak export market conditions. Such a range of corn price forecasts helps the manager better understand the market demand risk in the coming business environment and plan accordingly.

Specific product forecasts

The actual sales forecast for a specific product within the firm is driven in part by the general economic forecast and the market forecast. Sales of a particular firm's low-fat yogurt are clearly influenced by general trends in the overall economy and trends in the market for dairy products. However, forecasting sales of individual products or services is complicated by the actions of competitors. It is one thing to forecast how much insecticide cotton growers in Texas will use. It is quite another to forecast sales of the specific insecticides offered by the firms competing in the Texas market. Here, because of uncertainty in forecasting the impacts of competitive marketing programs, predicting sales of specific products is quite challenging.

One sales forecasting method that is widely used involves projecting sales objectively based on past trends and then adjusting these projections subjectively to take into account the expected economic, market, and competitive pressures. This **trend forecast**, while simple, is reasonably effective in stable market situations. For example, a feed firm might start with a trend forecast of 50,000 tons for its catfish feed. However, based on information gathered about competitive programs, the firm has learned that a new competitor will be aggressively entering the market with a penetration pricing strategy. The firm expects about 20 percent of its accounts to at least try the new feed on a trial basis, and estimates that these trial purchases will represent about 25 percent of this group's purchases. The firm then adjusts its trend sales estimate by 5 percent (20 percent trial times 25 percent use) to 47,500 tons to account for the expected impact of the new competitor.

Sales forecasts are sometimes built up from data collected by the sales force. A **build-up forecast** is constructed by asking salespeople to develop detailed sales forecasts for each of their major accounts. The accumulated sales estimates from all field salespeople then offer a grass-roots estimate of sales expectations. This method is particularly valuable where competition is intense, as in the case of many farm inputs. Of course, build-up forecasts may have some inherent biases and, depending on how the sales estimates are used, they can be under- or over-inflated. For instance, if available production is allocated to sales territories based on initial sales estimates, salespeople may inflate their estimates to make sure they will have an adequate supply if production happens to be short. The reverse may occur when salesperson performance is evaluated based on actual sales relative to forecast sales. Here, the salesperson may be inclined to offer a modest sales estimate in order to help insure that actual sales will be relatively higher and the resulting performance review positive.

Consumer surveys and test panels offer a great deal of information about buying intentions. Several regional and national organizations, such as Doane's, Inc., and *Farm Journal*, for example, as well as private firms, continually monitor farmers' attitudes and plans for the coming season through intention surveys. A panel of farmers may be paid a fee to give detailed reports about their intended farm plans on a regular basis, then report actual decisions made. Results of these private research studies are made available to subscribers on a fee basis. Farmers' planting intentions are also monitored by the USDA and released periodically throughout the year. Organizations like IRI (formerly Information Resources, Inc.) perform these same tasks for food firms. In many cases, these services utilize scanner data purchased or acquired from retail food stores to show food manufacturers and retailers key trends in food consumption at the product level. Electronic scanners make unparalleled amounts of information on consumer purchasing patterns available to food marketers. Such information can play an important role in their sales forecasting efforts.

The **Delphi approach** provides another useful tool for developing sales forecasts. Here, a panel of experts is asked to develop a forecast for the area of interest. These estimates are then pooled, reviewed, and any differences across the experts studied. The estimation process is repeated until a **consensus forecast** is achieved. This approach can be very useful when a forecast is needed quickly. The Delphi approach is also useful as a means to evaluate forecasts developed using other methods. Of course, experts can be wrong and the perspective of the panel members must be carefully considered when evaluating an expert opinion or Delphi forecast. This same method can also be used for forecasts of the general economic environment and the total market.

In some situations, especially with new products, a **test market** provides a useful way to collect data on potential sales. Here, an experiment is set up by selecting a test city or area with characteristics similar to the target market. The product is introduced, and the sales results are measured. These results are then generalized to the target market of interest. Such information is valuable as it reflects actual consumer purchase decisions and not just attitudes toward purchase decisions as might be gathered through a survey.

On the other hand, test markets can be expensive, and it can be difficult to control all the outside factors that might influence sales of the product. For example, a juice maker might run a test market for a new 16-ounce juice product in Des Moines, Iowa. While the experiment is running, the area is hit by an unprecedented heat wave and competitors have production trouble, leaving them unable to meet market demand. The firm with the new juice product now has to decide which sales were the result of the heat and the lack of competition, and which sales were the result of an appealing new product. Market researchers work hard to control for these kinds of events during the design of the test market experiment.

Competitor analysis

A thorough understanding of the competition is an important part of formulating any marketing strategy. Although it is usually unwise to simply react to competition, it is equally unwise to ignore competitors. Even the most dominant firms are often vulnerable to competitive encroachment from niche players, international competitors, or more traditional competitors with new technology or products. In fact, some marketing experts theorize that the larger and more successful a firm is, the more likely it is to fail. The argument is that large, successful firms often become complacent with their success, perpetuating the way of doing business that helped them become successful, and losing the edge that helped get them there. As markets and consumers change, old approaches become increasingly outdated, and smaller, more aggressive firms may begin to take over the market. Clearly, even successful firms must continually monitor competition.

One simple but effective method for analyzing competition is completing a formal strength and weakness analysis for each competitor. This tool simply involves listing the key strengths and weaknesses of a competitor in the same way firm strengths and weaknesses were analyzed earlier. With the list of strengths and weaknesses in hand, the marketer then focuses on the opportunities or threats each competitor presents. The final step in using this information is to develop a marketing strategy that capitalizes on the competitor's weaknesses and takes advantage of any opportunity that competitor vulnerabilities present.

In the example shown in Table 8.1, a small regional farm machinery dealer, Prairie View Equipment, has noted several key facts about Red River Tractor and Implement that can have important implications for Prairie View's marketing plan. Red River is owned by a national equipment manufacturer. Based in part on a careful assessment of Red River's

Table 8.1 Competitor strength and weakness analysis

COMPETITOR: Red River Tractor and Implement Company

DATE: January 15, 2012

COMPILED BY: Prairie Equipment Company

Strengths
1. New facility, large shop, impressive space for new and used equipment
2. Good location, conveniently located for area farmers
3. Large parts inventory
4. Quality "short lines," good relationships with short-line manufacturers
5. Favorable credit program
6. Manufacturer-owned facility has sound financial backing

Weaknesses
1. High overhead cost relative to Prairie View
2. No outside salespeople at this time, dependent on manufacturer reps for outside sales support
3. Poor on-farm repair service, not as responsive as growers demand
4. Major equipment line less popular locally than Prairie View offering
5. Manufacturer-owned store less flexible to meet local needs
6. New manager not well known in the area

Strategy for Competing Against Red River
—Upgrade emergency farm repair vehicle and promote this service
—Lever all relevant national support programs available to Prairie View
—Promote local owner's long-term interest in community and understanding of local needs
—Hold open house to familiarize customers with our location
—Emphasize importance of dealing with a local business, keeping money in community

business, Prairie View has developed a strategy that emphasizes its local ownership and flexibility in servicing farmers.

Information on competitors can come from a variety of sources. A search of the Internet will turn up a considerable amount of information on any major food or agricultural input firm. Annual reports, SEC filings, company press releases, and speeches by company executives can all offer useful information. Information supplied by salespersons or dealers can help keep tabs on what other firms are up to. Customers, industry experts, and other players in the marketing channel can all help provide a more complete picture of competitor activity.

The need for such information may seem so obvious to field marketing people that this exercise seems unnecessary. But formalizing it in this manner, discussing it thoroughly, and developing a competitive strategy often improves communication, even in small firms, and results in a more proactive approach to marketing decisions. When all significant competitors are analyzed periodically, there is a far greater likelihood that a logical marketing plan will be developed and executed.

Tool for analyzing customer needs

The case for understanding customer needs has been made in Chapters 6 and 7. How do agribusiness marketers learn what customers want from their firm? There are a variety of tools available to the marketer to help them better understand the needs of their customers and prospects. Some of the more important tools will be reviewed here.

Customer surveys

One of the best ways to learn what customers think about a product or service is to ask the customers directly. Agribusinesses can gain much valuable information, which can help in formulating market plans, by communicating directly with customers through surveys, interviews, and informal conversations. Although there may be reluctance among some customers who do not want to be bothered or who distrust any information-collecting activity, experience shows that food and agribusiness customers are willing to share their opinions with firms they do business with, especially when the data collection effort has been properly designed. When such information is used effectively, it is invaluable in making marketing decisions.

Market research relies heavily on surveys of various types to track customer attitudes. Extensive **personal interviews** lasting an hour or more may provide a great deal of information about customer purchasing decisions, attitudes, and how the product is used. Such in-depth interviews must be developed and performed by trained interviewers; they are therefore quite expensive, often averaging $100 or more per completed interview. In many cases today—especially if the interviewee is a large farmer or a professional such as a veterinarian—the person being interviewed also wants compensation for their time while being interviewed. This can easily add much more to the cost of the session.

Telephone interviews have gained in popularity because of their lower cost and the speed at which a telephone interview study can be completed. However, it is impossible to collect as much information by telephone as compared to a personal interview because telephone interviews seldom last more than 15 minutes. It is difficult to explore many issues very deeply in such a short period of time. Depending upon the length of the survey instrument, phone interviews by professional market researchers may cost from $15 to $70 (or more) per completed interview.

Written surveys remain a widely used method of studying customer opinions and attitudes. Written questionnaires can be short or long, but longer ones usually get a much lower response rate. A quick written survey delivered through the mail is considered successful when 15 to 25 percent of the questionnaires are completed and returned. It may be a very short survey response offered at a trade show, where customers and/or prospects are asked to respond to a few short questions. More formal mail surveys involving phone follow-up and multiple reminders will generate a substantially higher response rate—50 to 60 percent being very common. Many firms use online survey tools to distribute questionnaires. This medium can help execute a very quick, very focused survey of customers. While there are advantages to written surveys, it is difficult to collect much detail or in-depth reasoning behind responses from a written survey. Yet because they are relatively inexpensive, written surveys are considered a good way of collecting some kinds of **market information**.

For all types of surveys, careful **pretesting**, or evaluating the questions so that what is being asked is clear to the respondent, is important. Poorly worded questions can cause the results of a survey to be virtually meaningless. The meaning of a question may be clear to the author of the survey, but totally confusing to the respondent—or worse, it may be misunderstood, with the result that it elicits incorrect information.

Focus group techniques

Focus group interviews are another method of learning more about customer attitudes and one that is widely used by agribusiness marketers. The focus group allows companies to gain solid purchase decision information or other insights from a group of customers. Depending on the situation, focus groups can also be quite cost effective.

A focus group interview is simply a discussion among six to ten customers or other individuals of interest, guided by a skilled moderator. In many cases this discussion is recorded so careful analysis of the comments can be made. It is not a formal interview so much as it is an informal discussion where people get to know each other well enough to talk freely. As barriers to discussion break down, participants begin to react to each other and the conversation unfolds, hopefully yielding much valuable information about how the group feels about important marketing issues.

The key to success in a focus group interview is the synergistic effect of the informal discussion. The group chosen for the interview is extremely important. It must fairly represent the population of interest and it must be a group where free-flowing discussion is possible. The moderator plays a very important but extremely subtle role, making sure the right subjects are covered and that no one individual dominates the discussion. The moderator must also be careful not to bias responses in any way.

Focus group interviews can provide many new ideas and perceptions from the customer's viewpoint about advertising programs, packaging, quality of products, performance, and relative comparisons of competitors. Group interviews also add a great deal of support and help to clarify more quantitative surveys because they can suggest how strongly impressions are held.

However, focus group interviews can also be misused. They will likely generate very little factual or quantitative data. As such, results are very difficult to tabulate or quantify. Some group members may tend to dominate and to influence the thinking of others, perhaps creating a "bandwagon" effect. And any results must be interpreted with the nature of the group in mind. Thus it is critical not to extend the results of a focus group interview beyond their designed use. Still, focus group interviews offer a highly productive and relatively inexpensive method for gaining insights into customer attitudes and for generating marketing ideas.

Internal data analysis

Agribusiness marketers can often get so involved in developing and implementing a marketing plan that they have little time for detailed market analysis. This is particularly true in smaller or local agribusinesses, where marketing people may have a number of responsibilities and have limited time to devote to careful exploration of what is going on in the market. One typically underutilized resource for better understanding customer attitudes and preferences is internal customer and transactions data. By looking at the data a firm has on its own customers and their transactions with the firm, a marketer can learn much that will be helpful in developing or refining a successful marketing strategy.

Transactions data can provide a wealth of insights into a market. Sorting customers by their sales volumes can begin to help a firm understand the composition of its portfolio of customers. Looking at sales across product lines may point out important cross-selling opportunities. Exploring the timing of purchases may allow a firm to improve customer retention. If a firm knows that the Hendricks Vegetable Growers always place their seed orders by January 15, then any delay past that date becomes a warning sign that the customer may be looking elsewhere for seed. In many cases, firm transactions data are obtained and stored solely for accounting purposes. However, the investment it may take to make these available for market planning purposes is likely time and money well spent.

Plate 8.2 Focus group discussion
A good sales presentation requires thorough preparation. Photo courtesy of Purdue University Centre for Food and Agricultural Business.

Another tool for analyzing internal data is **market mapping**. It is common, for example, for much of the sales volume in a small agribusiness to be concentrated in limited geographical areas or among relatively few accounts. At the same time, other geographic areas have relatively little market penetration with many potential accounts left for someone else to serve.

In any given market, there may be physical reasons for an imbalance in market penetration. An interstate highway may make access to some areas difficult. Certain types of farms may be concentrated in some parts of the market area. More often, however, friends, relatives, or just well-established customers seem to predominate in one local area. Salespeople tend to spend less time in areas with which they are less familiar. In short, many agribusinesses have undiscovered market potential near them, if they were just able to discover and cultivate this potential.

One way of discovering these areas of untapped potential is through a market-mapping technique. This exercise can be done by hand in smaller firms. All current customers are pinpointed on a map of the market area (Figure 8.4). It is a good idea to color-code customers by volume of business, type of products purchased, or other informative characteristics when developing this map.

A market map can also be developed using any one of a number of computer software products designed specifically for this purpose. Recent developments in computer mapping software and geographic information systems (GIS) make it possible to download a variety of data on market characteristics such as number of pigs on feed, number of households with at

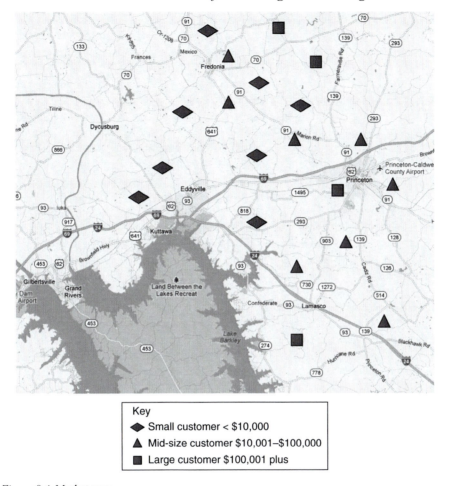

Key

◆ Small customer < $10,000

▲ Mid-size customer $10,001–$100,000

■ Large customer $100,001 plus

Figure 8.4 Market map

least two children and family income of $60,000, and so on. Then, these data can be overlaid with store locations or competitor locations to get a graphic picture of the market situation.

Once this mapping has been completed, visual observation provides a great deal of information about weak and strong areas. When this mapping technique is first used, it is often a real revelation for marketing and management people. The market map suggests areas in which sales efforts should be targeted. When effort is concentrated in a new area and new customers are obtained, it may be possible to expand the firm's presence in that area rapidly.

Summary

Planning a marketing strategy requires a variety of techniques and tools to analyze markets and make decisions. Some tools are simple applications of logic, while others are highly sophisticated analytical models.

A marketing audit is a thorough and objective examination of a firm's marketing program. In a marketing audit, the firm's market performance and potential for each product are analyzed; current and future market conditions are reviewed; distinctive competencies (i.e., areas of unique strength relative to competition) can be recognized; current marketing programs are evaluated and execution of the marketing program is considered; and finally, the human resources available and their organization are studied.

Sales forecasting is a highly useful marketing tool that is especially valuable in agribusiness because of the volatility of agricultural markets. It usually begins with general economic forecasts and becomes more and more specific as the forecaster moves toward forecasting sales for an individual product or service. A variety of tools is used for forecasting sales of individual products including trend forecasts, build-up forecasts, analysis of scanner data, the Delphi Approach, and test markets. Each of these techniques has advantages and disadvantages, so agribusiness marketers must understand each to know when each may be the appropriate tool to use.

Marketing managers must also analyze competition and monitor their marketing programs. Formal competitor strength and weakness analysis is a useful tool that suggests strategic marketing approaches for capitalizing on the vulnerabilities of a competitor, or addressing a competitive threat.

Various marketing research methods provide invaluable information for developing marketing plans. Customer surveys and personal and group interviews are popular methods. Focus group interviews are a commonly used technique for collecting information on customers. Internal transactions data can yield many insights into customer behavior. Simple tools, such as pinpointing customers by type or size on a map, can also provide much information.

In the end, marketing managers must synthesize information from a variety of sources to assist them in developing and executing a successful marketing program.

Discussion questions

1. What is the purpose of a marketing audit? Why is it important to have outsiders involved in marketing audits?
2. Why are sales forecasts particularly difficult to make in food and agribusiness firms?
3. What is meant by derived demand? Explain why the demand for animal health products is a derived demand.
4. Your cooperative is evaluating a new package of precision agricultural services they may offer to patron-members. This package includes an extensive field-mapping program, linking soil fertility information with yield monitor information, crop scouting in the summer months, and personal consultation in the winter. The package will require a significant investment of both financial and human resources. What data will the cooperative need to collect to make the go/no-go decision on this package? How should they collect this data?
5. What are the benefits of preparing a strengths and weaknesses analysis of competitors?
6. What are focus group interviews? Can a small firm use this tool? Why or why not? What are some important limitations of the focus group interview?
7. Give some of the reasons why customer maps often show customers clustered in particular areas. What can be done about this situation?

Case study: a big assignment

"Yes, I have had an agribusiness course," Leslie Turner said as she looked across the large desk. Her new boss was sitting on the other side of that desk, and, frankly, Leslie wondered what was coming next. She had just accepted a summer internship that would begin in a few weeks, but she had no idea of what her assignment would be at Valley Producers Co-op.

"Do you know anything about marketing, Leslie?" asked the manager.

"A little. I have studied marketing in some of my classes," answered Leslie nervously, still not sure what she was in for.

The manager continued, "Well, we'd like you to prepare an analysis of our petroleum marketing program this summer. As you know, we have three divisions: animal nutrition, crop inputs, and petroleum products—all managed out of our headquarters here. Although we want you to spend some time working in each division this summer, we'd like you to spend two days each week talking to people, looking at our records, or whatever else you feel would be helpful, to give us a good idea of where we stand in the petroleum market. Our petroleum sales have leveled off lately, and I think it's because our equipment is getting old and our service is poor.

"The board of directors is considering expanding our petroleum business with a new fuel depot/retail station and some expanded delivery routes, but we just aren't sure right now. There are a lot of cost factors that I'm working on, but I'd like you to take a look at the market side. Then we'd like you to make a report on what you find at our August board meeting. It's a big job, but we'd like to know what you can come up with."

Leslie swallowed hard. She wanted to make a good impression—and it did seem like a great opportunity to learn a lot about the business. Yet she wasn't sure she was up to it. She wasn't even sure how to begin. She began to think about some of the ideas they had discussed in her agribusiness management course…

Questions

1. What kinds of information do you think Leslie needs to find before she can complete this assignment successfully? How might she get this information?
2. What market analysis tools should Leslie consider using to collect the data she will need for her report?
3. Outline a procedure that Leslie might use to make her analysis and report.

References and additional reading

Kaplan, Robert S. and David P. Norton. *Strategy Maps: Converting Intangible Assets into Tangible Outcomes*. Boston, MA: Harvard Business School, 2004.

Liamputtong, Pranee. *Focus Group Methodology: Principle and Practice*. London: Sage, 2010.

Parmerlee, David. *Auditing Markets, Products, and Marketing Plans*. Lincolnwood, IL: NTC Business, 2000.

Safko, Lon and David K. Brake. *The Social Media Bible: Tactics, Tools, and Strategies for Business Success*. Hoboken, NJ: John Wiley & Sons, 2009.

Wilson, Aubrey. *The Marketing Audit Handbook: Tools, Techniques & Checklists to Exploit Your Marketing Resources*. London: Kogan Page, 2002.

Part IV
Financial management
for agribusiness

Part Plate IV Shot of money.
Cash is king. Money talks. Time is money. Put your money where your mouth is. All are clichés, but each expression holds an element of truth when it comes to effective management. This section explores the financial aspects of agribusiness management. Photo courtesy of USDA.

9 Understanding financial statements

Objectives

- Describe the importance of a financial information system in an agribusiness
- Develop a working knowledge of how financial statements aid the agribusiness manager's decision-making process
- Understand financial statement terminology as it is used by an agribusiness manager
- Describe the balance sheet and illustrate how the agribusiness manager uses it
- Describe the income statement and illustrate how the agribusiness manager uses it
- Understand the accrual basis of accounting
- Describe the statement of owner's equity and illustrate how agribusiness managers use it
- Describe the statement of cash flows and illustrate how the agribusiness manager uses it
- Understand how managers develop and use pro forma financial statements to make decisions affecting the future of the agribusiness

Introduction

Probably no term is used more often among managers than the word profit, or "the bottom line." For any business, the bottom line on the income statement is crucial. This figure represents a composite of how the firm, and its management, has performed over the past year. It is a guideline to measure the relative success or failure of the firm over this period of time. **Profit**, the amount remaining from a sale after cost of the product and operating expenses have been paid, is often used as a historical benchmark to provide evidence of the skill and ability demonstrated by decision-makers within the organization. The firm's CEO (chief executive officer), corporate board members, and management team are all enamored with this word "profit." The importance of this figure over time can be related to the ability of the firm to grow, enter new markets, and introduce new products.

Although the bottom line is of great importance in itself, other types of financial data are also needed to properly evaluate a firm's performance. The successful agribusiness manager must understand what the firm did (or did not do) that led to the resulting bottom line, and the successful manager uses this understanding to improve the bottom line in the future. This is what the study of financial management is all about. The successful manager understands the financial operations of the firm well enough to use this information as a tool for improving firm performance. Although the bottom line provides a benchmark for comparison, successful agribusiness managers must understand the interrelationships of other accounts on the balance sheet and the income statement to properly manage the business.

The importance of financial statements

Financial management requires a working knowledge of how to interpret financial informa-tion from a firm's records. Such information is used to satisfy two distinct needs of the agribusiness firm. First, and perhaps more importantly, is the need for information that can be used internally by managers in decision-making. Second, information is also needed for financial reporting, such as reporting financial performance to stockholders, entities outside the firm such as lenders, and others who have interests in the firm.

Without financial information, agribusiness managers at any level find it difficult to successfully pursue the goals and objectives of the organization. Each agribusiness enterprise therefore must accumulate historical records of financial information that are vital for its continued success. The importance of financial information and records is evidenced by the tons of paper, the billions of forms, the millions of computers, and the hundreds of thousands of people who are employed in recording business activities throughout the country.

Modern financial record keeping had its beginning some six centuries ago in Italy. The growth of commerce in Venice and Genoa, which were great commercial centers, created an accompanying need for business records. As a response to this need, a system of records and bookkeeping was developed that is still widely used throughout the world today. This system summarizes the records of a firm by dividing them into two basic documents. These documents are called the balance sheet and the income statement. Together, they make up the primary financial statements of the firm. The remainder of this chapter will be used to discuss the importance of these financial statements and illustrate how agribusiness managers may use these statements for decision-making.

Correct information at the proper time

Agribusinesses seek to generate the greatest possible returns from the resources they pos-sess. Associated with the profit objective are several other objectives, such as producing a quality product or service, rewarding the employees of the business, helping the business grow, striving for environmental stewardship, and promoting a positive public image for the firm as a "citizen" of the community. These types of objectives are common to all business organizations, from the huge food company to the rural, small-town feed dealer. Such objec-tives are usually not accomplished by means of a single, brilliant tactical maneuver, but rather through the consistent use of resources to their greatest potential over a long period of time. The consistent use of resources to meet the firm's objectives requires managers to have useful and timely financial information and records. Business records are tools to help managers guide the operation of the business intelligently and make good man-agement decisions that are consistent with the needs, objectives, and goals of the company. The collection and use of information reported for these purposes is often referred to as **managerial accounting**.

In addition, firms must also satisfy the reporting requirements that are established by various outside entities. For instance, every agribusiness must keep track of sales, purchases, expenses, and profit or loss. Records that document these areas are necessary to meet the reporting requirements of governmental units, lending institutions, investors, and suppliers to the business. The collection and use of information reported for these purposes is often referred to as **financial accounting**.

Although a records system must be designed to meet both the managerial and financial reporting needs of the firm, its design should be guided by the following criteria:

1. It should be simple and easy to understand.
2. It should be reliable, accurate, consistent, and timely.
3. It should be based on the uniqueness of the particular business.
4. It should be cost effective to implement and maintain.

When designing the records system for an agribusiness, it is usually advisable to secure the services of competent professional advisers or consultants who are not members of the firm. These professionals can help to determine objectively which system of records best fits the firm's needs. In addition, all but the smallest agribusinesses need trained and competent bookkeepers and/or accountants to maintain their managerial and financial reporting system.

Uses of a good accounting system

The accounting system also functions to prevent errors and to safeguard an agribusiness's resources. To do this, records must be maintained accurately and honestly by competent personnel. As the business grows larger, a system of checks and balances should be instituted to ensure that no one person has complete control over any transaction. For example, employees who are working as cashiers or collecting monies should not be engaged in

Plate 9.1 Recordkeeping using a computer
An effective accounting system is at the heart of good financial management. Photo courtesy of the USDA Natural Resources Conservation Service.

bookkeeping. The person who is performing purchasing duties should not be keeping the books or writing the checks.

Whenever and wherever possible, the responsibilities of records, reports, and controls should rest with at least two people. Outside auditors are typically used to verify the accuracy and integrity of the organization's financial records. All this is not to imply dishonesty so much as to confirm the credibility and integrity of all involved, and to verify that records are being kept properly. When proper checks are built into an accounting system, there is little reason to suspect impropriety.

Good financial records should provide the basis for:

1. Determining the success of the business in terms of profitability during specific time periods or cycles
2. Determining the general financial condition or health of the business at a given moment
3. Predicting the future ability of the business to meet the demands of creditors, of change, and of expansion
4. Analyzing the trends in performance as they relate to management's abilities and to the success or failure of the past decisions and achievements
5. Choosing among the various possible alternatives for future use of resources within the firm

Working with accountants

Some agribusiness managers, such as Chuck Altman, the owner and president of a sizable wholesale fertilizer company, confess to a fear of financial management and accounting simply because they are unfamiliar with the way the system works. Chuck's unfamiliarity stems from the fact that his company started small, and his financial knowledge and skills have not grown with the company. Many other managers have come up through the ranks in larger companies from the areas of sales, production, and operations. They also have not been exposed to the financial component of the business. It is not necessary for the manager to know how to do the accounting personally or to maintain the records of an organization. Instead, the agribusiness manager should concentrate on understanding how the system works and what information the record-keeping process produces that can be useful for decision-making and forecasting, and for financial reporting.

The agribusiness manager who works with controllers, accountants, and bookkeepers is likely to find many that view the world about them in a conceptual and abstract manner. The approach of such specialists can produce information, which, though accurate and interesting, may not be understandable or meaningful to those controlling and managing the organization. Determining what information is needed and what form it should take is the responsibility of the manager.

Each manager reviews the information supplied by the records of the organization, and determines if the information is to be used solely for managerial decision-making. If so, the information should be tested against the previously provided criterion. He or she must then ask such questions as: "Will this information or data allow management to make better decisions?", "Is the information prepared in such a way that managers can easily understand and interpret it?", and "Is it information that the particular agribusiness truly needs?" Records that do not meet these tests should be altered or dropped. However, information that will be used in financial reporting to governmental units, lenders, and others generally is much more standardized in terms of criteria (i.e., profitability, liquidity, and solvency) and measures (i.e., rates of return on assets and equity, solvency ratios, liquidity measures, etc.). The reporting of this information must be in accordance with generally accepted accounting principles and practices.

The accounting process

The record-keeping process derives largely from the original documents of the organization. These documents include such things as sales slips, receiving tickets, checks, invoices, employee time-cards, and bills. One could say that such original documents are the building blocks for the entire record-keeping system.

If we look closely at Chuck Altman's fertilizer business, we will see that each day the firm incurs more expenses and earns more revenue. These day-to-day transactions are recorded in a book or computer file called the journal. The journal is also referred to as the book of original entry for the business. Here, all the transactions of the business are recorded in chronological order. The journal, then, provides a running account of the day-to-day transactions or activities of the business. In a small business there may be only one book, computer file, or general journal in which all the transactions of the business are recorded. As a business such as Chuck Altman's grows larger in size, it is necessary to have several specialized journals or computer files for particular areas of the business to record such separate categories as sales, purchases, and available cash. While the journal records the transactions or activities of the business chronologically, it does not put them into any meaningful form by which the manager can interpret or use the information presented. This comes from financial statements that are prepared using the information recorded in the journal.

Business information must be organized

In looking at Chuck Altman's fertilizer business, it is apparent that he should have a record of its property or assets. Such a financial statement is called a **balance sheet**. The balance sheet shows the financial makeup and condition of a business at a specific time. It lists what the business owns, what it owes, and what the owners have invested in the business. It shows a balance between assets and claims against those assets. **Assets** are those things of value that are controlled by the business. Those who are interested in a particular agribusiness require such information as the amount of available cash, the amount of money that customers owe to the business, the amount of inventory or merchandise available, and the resources needed to carry on business activities, including buildings, land, office and sales space, and equipment.

Those who are interested in the business are also concerned with the **liabilities** of that business. Liabilities are the sums of money that have to be paid to creditors at specified dates in the future. To put it another way, liabilities represent the sums that are owed to people outside the business. Thus, liabilities represent claims by "outsiders" against business assets. In addition to information about assets and liabilities, the full financial picture requires information about the amount of money that the owners have invested in the business. This sum is called **owner equity** or **net worth**.

Then, too, there is the need for records that detail revenue and expenses in such a way that the manager may meaningfully measure the success of the business, in terms of profit or loss, for decision-making purposes and various public entities for tax purposes. These records are used to organize the information into ledger accounts for each source of revenue and for each expense category. These accounts are summarized in a financial statement called an income statement. Ledger accounts, then, provide for the separating, categorizing, and recording of related transactions or activities within the business, and they do so in an organized manner. Maintaining financial information in separate ledger accounts not only makes these data more usable, but provides information that is more easily understood by the agribusiness manager.

The accounts in the ledger are summarized on a predetermined regular basis called the **accounting period**. The accounting period typically represents a one-year time span in the operation of the business. This may be a calendar year (January–December) for some firms or a fiscal year for other firms (July–June). Many agribusinesses are seasonal in nature. A calendar year accounting period may not make sense for a seed corn firm since this really cuts across two different production and marketing seasons. Hence, firms tend to report financial information for one year that includes a single production period. Management in medium and large firms typically request updated monthly and/or quarterly financial statements. These updates represent summaries of the accounts in the ledger and help generate the key financial statements for the firm.

Financial statements

Financial statements are a summarized statement of the financial status of a business, usually prepared as a summary of **accounts** from the ledger. The primary financial statements usually consist of the balance sheet and income statement. As discussed previously, a balance sheet shows what a business owns, what it owes, and what investment the owners have in the business. It can be likened to a snapshot that shows the financial makeup and condition of the business at a specific point in time. The **income statement**, on the other hand, is a summary of business operations over a certain period, usually the period between the dates of two balance sheets. It could be compared to a video of the firm that details the financial activities as they occurred over a period of time. Generally, the balance sheet illustrates the current financial position of the business. The income statement, alternatively, demonstrates financial changes since the last time a balance sheet was prepared. The income statement is also known as the operating statement, the profit and loss statement, or simply the P&L statement.

The length of the accounting period and the dates for issuing financial statements are particularly important in agribusinesses that are highly seasonal in nature. In most parts of the country, fertilizer and chemical operations conduct a very large portion of their annual business in the three to four months before and during the planting season. For example, a balance sheet constructed just prior to the rush season is likely to show large amounts of fertilizer on hand and little money owed by customers. If this same statement is drawn up just after the busy season, it is likely to show less fertilizer on hand and larger amounts of money owed by customers. Such financial statements can be very misleading, if they are not interpreted in light of the seasonal characteristics of the business. Consequently, the agribusiness manager must understand why variations in financial statements are inescapable in highly seasonal agribusinesses. Previous years' financial statements often provide a more valid comparison than a simple month-by-month comparison.

Brookstone Feed and Grain company: an example

Brookstone Feed and Grain (BF&G) company typifies many smaller agribusiness firms. BF&G is a retail agribusiness firm located in the Midwest. It sells a wide range of fertilizers, chemicals, feed, seed, and farm supplies. BF&G also merchandises grain—primarily corn and soybeans. The firm provides a variety of services to its customers such as feed delivery, fertilizer application, drying grain, and grain storage. BF&G purchases fertilizer from national manufacturers and blends products to fit individual customer's needs. BF&G is located on a rail line and ships unit trains of corn to the Gulf and Southeast. The firm has a grain market area of about 25 miles. Table 9.1 and Table 9.2 summarize BF&G's operations during a recent year.

Table 9.1 Balance sheet for Brookstone Feed and Grain company, December 31, 2009

(a)	**Assets**			
(b)	**Current Assets:**			
(c)	Cash		175,000	
(d)	Accounts Receivable		1,600,000	
(e)	Inventory		2,500,000	
(f)	Prepaid Expenses		7,000	
(g)	Other		5,000	
(h)	Total Current Assets			$4,287,000
(i)	**Fixed Assets:**			
(j)	Land		1,150,000	
(k)	Building	600,000		
(l)	Less: Accumulated Depreciation	150,000	450,000	
(m)				
(n)	Equipment	1,300,000		
(o)	Less: Accumulated Depreciation	520,000	780,000	
(p)				
(q)	Total Fixed Assets			$2,380,000
(r)	**Other Assets**			10,000
(s)	**Total Assets**			**$6,677,000**
(aa)	**Liabilities**			
(bb)	**Current Liabilities:**			
(cc)	Accounts Payable		800,000	
(dd)	Notes Payable		1,000,000	
(ee)	Accrued Expenses		35,000	
(ff)	Advances		27,000	
(gg)	Total Current Liabilities			$1,862,000
(hh)	**Long-Term Liabilities:**			
(ii)	Mortgages		1,000,000	
(jj)	Other		150,000	
(kk)	Total Long-Term Liabilities			$1,150,000
(ll)	**Total Liabilities**			**$3,012,000**
(mm)	**Owner's Equity**			
(nn)	**Owner-invested Capital:**			
(oo)	Common Stock		1,885,000	
(pp)	Retained Earnings		1,780,000	
(qq)	**Total Owner Equity**			**$3,665,000**
(rr)	**Total Liabilities and Owner Equity**			**$6,677,000**

Table 9.2 Income statement for Brookstone Feed and Grain company, year ending December 31, 2009

	Sales:		
	Grain and Soybeans	$8,146,000	
	Seed	670,500	
	Fertilizer and Chemicals	2,213,000	
	Feed	1,810,000	
	Miscellaneous Supplies	402,300	
	Service Income	268,200	
	Gross Sales	$13,510,000	
	Less Returns, Allowances, and Discounts	100,000	
(a)	**Net Sales**	$13,410,000	100.00%
(b)	**Cost of Goods Sold:**		
	Grain and Soybeans	7,556,900	
	Seed	511,650	
	Fertilizer and Chemicals	1,791,420	
	Feed	1,534,380	
	Miscellaneous Supplies	330,650	
	Service Expense	0	
	Total Cost of Goods Sold	11,725,000	87.43%
(c)	**Gross Profit (Margin)**	$1,685,000	12.57%
(d)	**Operating Expenses:**		
(e)	Salaries and Benefits	210,000	1.57%
(f)	Full-time Wages	166,000	1.24%
(g)	Part-time Wages	10,400	0.08%
(h)	Commissions	42,740	0.32%
(i)	Depreciation	290,000	2.16%
(j)	Maintenance and Repairs	58,000	0.43%
(k)	Utilities	56,990	0.42%
(l)	Insurance	71,200	0.53%
(m)	Office Supplies/Expense	26,820	0.20%
(n)	Advertising/Promotion	6,400	0.05%
(o)	Gas and Oil	48,600	0.36%
(p)	Delivery and Freight	156,710	1.17%
(q)	Rent	6,300	0.05%
(r)	Taxes, Licenses, Fees	48,160	0.36%
(s)	Miscellaneous	3,300	0.02%
(t)	Payroll Tax	10,900	0.08%
(u)	Bad Debt	3,290	0.02%
(v)	**Total Operating Expenses**	$1,215,810	9.07%
(w)	**Net Operating Income**	$469,190	3.50%
(x)	Other Revenue	18,200	0.14%
(y)	Interest Expense	230,840	1.72%
(z)	**Net Income Before Taxes**	$256,550	1.91%
(aa)	Taxes	59,900	0.45%
(bb)	**Net Income After Taxes**	$196,650	1.47%

The balance sheet

As outlined above, the balance sheet represents a financial summary of what the business owns and owes and of the investment that the owners have made in the business (Table 9.1). Financial resources that have monetary value are called assets (a). Assets are usually listed at the top or the left-hand side of the balance sheet (Table 9.1, a to s).

The amount the business owes to creditors is called liabilities (aa). Liabilities are generally located in the middle section or on the right-hand side of the balance sheet (Table 9.1, aa to ll). Legally, the creditors of the business would have first claim against any of its assets. The value of the assets over and above the firm's liabilities is the owner's claim against the assets, or owner's equity. Owner's equity is also referred to as net worth (mm) and represents the summation of several specific accounts. The owner's equity section usually appears just below the liability section on the balance sheet (Table 9.1, mm to qq).

This brings us to the dual-aspect concept of the balance sheet. The balance sheet is set up to portray two aspects of each entry or transaction recorded. For each resource of value, or asset, there is an offsetting claim against that asset. The recognition of this concept leads to the accounting equation:

$$\text{Assets} = \text{Liabilities} + \text{Owner's Equity}$$

An examination of the following case will clarify this concept.

When Jody Snyder decided to start her landscaping business, she deposited $2,000 in cash in the bank. This sum represented an investment of $1,000 from her funds and $1,000 that she had borrowed from the bank. If Jody had prepared a balance sheet at that time, it would have shown assets of $2,000 cash balanced against a liability to the bank of $1,000 and an owner's claim of $1,000. Using the balance sheet formula:

$$\text{Assets} = \text{Liabilities} + \text{Owner's Equity}$$
$$\$2,000 = \$1,000 + \$1,000$$

As this formula indicates, there will always be a balance between assets and the claims against these financial resources (liabilities plus owner's equity). The balance sheet is so named because it always balances. The various components are presented in the following section.

Assets (a)

It was stated earlier that assets represent resources of value that are controlled by the business. Of course, the business does not legally own anything unless it is organized as a corporation (see Chapter 4). But regardless of whether the business is organized as a proprietorship, a partnership, or a corporation, all business bookkeeping should be tabulated as a separate entity and recorded separately from the personal funds and assets of its owner or owners. Small agribusinesses where personal and business assets are mixed have difficulty in sharply defining genuine business performance. Business assets are typically classified in three classes: current assets (b), fixed assets (i), and other assets (r).

Current assets (b)

For accounting purposes, the term **current assets** is used to designate cash or assets that will be converted to cash during one normal operating cycle of the business (usually one year). The distinction between current assets and fixed and other assets is important because lenders and others pay much attention to the total value of current assets. At a minimum, this figure gives an approximation of the cash generation potential of the firm.

The value of current assets bears a significant relationship to the stability of the business, because it represents the amount of cash that might be raised quickly to meet current obligations. For example, a nursery may discover that it is necessary to fumigate a large acreage prior to planting nursery stock. Owners might experience great difficulty raising the funds for this emergency because their current assets are limited.

The major current asset accounts may include the following:

Cash (c): **Cash** funds are those that are immediately available for use without restriction. These funds are usually in the form of checking account deposits in banks, cash register money, and petty cash. Cash amounts should be large enough to meet any obligations that fall due immediately. BF&G has cash balances of only $175,000 as of December 31 (see Table 9.1). As carloads of fertilizer or deliveries of seed arrive soon after the first of the year, BF&G may have to borrow additional short-term funds to meet its purchasing obligations.

Accounts receivable (d): **Accounts receivable** represents the total amount owed to the company by customers for past purchases. Essentially, these accounts result from the granting of credit to customers. They may take the form of charge accounts on which no interest or service charge is made or they may be of an interest-bearing nature. In either case, they are a drain on the cash position of the firm. The larger the outstanding amount in accounts receivable, the less money the company will have available to meet current needs. The amount of money in this account depends on the firm's credit policy, that is, how much credit is extended to customers and how efficient the business is at collecting these outstanding accounts.

Some agribusinesses depend heavily on credit as a selling tool. Agricultural production is a seasonal business, and many customers prefer to postpone payment until after harvest and/or selling of crops. BF&G is in an industry in which selling on credit is common. As Table 9.1 indicates, on December 31 Brookstone's customers still owed a total of $1,600,000 from sales made during the past year or earlier. This is a figure that BF&G's management and creditors will watch closely, since borrowing money to pay the firm's obligations is an added expense that reduces the profitably of the business. The challenge is for BF&G to offer enough credit so as not to hurt sales, while at the same time keeping its credit policy tight enough not to jeopardize its own cash-flow position. (This is described in more detail in Chapter 11.)

Inventory (e): **Inventory** is defined as those items that are held for sale in the ordinary course of business or that are to be consumed in the process of producing goods and services to be sold. Inventory items are usually valued at cost (actual funds expended) or market value (what they are worth), whichever is lower. BF&G has $2,500,000 worth of inventory (at cost) as of December 31. The firm may already be building some inventory for spring sales. The objective of its managers is to keep inventory as low as possible in order to minimize the cash investment while still maintaining an adequate supply of products to meet their customers' needs. Control of inventory and related inventory expenses is one of management's most important jobs, particularly for retailers. Good accounting records are particularly useful in controlling inventory. As BF&G becomes better at matching supplies of product with customers' demands, the firm will lower its inventory investment and increase its return to investment in inventory.

Prepaid expenses (f): **Prepaid expenses** represent assets that have been paid for in advance; usually, their usefulness is due to end after a short time. A good example would be prepaid insurance. A business often pays for insurance protection for as much as three to six months in advance. The right to this protection is a thing of value (an asset), and the prepaid or unused portion can be refunded or converted to cash. BF&G has $7,000 in prepaid expenses, insurance in this case. Other examples that fit this category would include prepaid rent and prepaid taxes.

Other current assets (g): A firm may have various other assets that can easily be converted into cash. For example, BF&G has $5,000 in "**marketable securities**." An example of **other current assets** could be an outside investment in another company's stocks or bonds, an investment that can be converted to cash during the accounting year if needed.

Fixed assets (i)

Fixed assets are those items that the business owns that have a relatively long life. Fixed assets are typically used to produce or sell other goods and services. If they were to be held for resale, they would have to be classified as inventory (current assets), even though the assets might be long-lived. Normally, fixed assets are categorized into the accounts: land, buildings, and equipment. However, some managers may list types of buildings and equipment separately on the balance sheet.

BF&G's balance sheet could be made more specific if its equipment (n) items were divided into three main categories: fertilizer equipment, grain storage and handling equipment, and rolling stock (trucks, spreaders, etc.). Some companies even list large, especially expensive equipment, such as self-propelled fertilizer applicators which may cost $250,000 or more, as separate entries on the balance sheet.

One other important aspect of tracking fixed assets for the balance sheet that should be considered is depreciation (l and o). Generally, all fixed assets, with the exception of land, depreciate (decrease in value) over time. For example, BF&G's largest applicator, which is three years old and showing wear, may be worth only $100,000, much less than its original $250,000 purchase cost. For a balance sheet to show the true value of the company's assets, it must reflect the asset's loss in value over this three-year period. This loss in value due to use, wear, and tear on the fixed asset is called depreciation. The net fixed asset value on the balance sheet reflects only the "accounting" value of the asset in its present state. The real value of fixed assets may be considerably different. The actual market value could be accurately established only by selling the asset, but an ongoing business cannot sell its assets.

Several methods may be used to determine the amount of depreciation. Annual depreciation is allowed as an expense item on the income statement (discussed later), and so it significantly affects total expenses, profits, and, consequently, taxes. Internal Revenue Service regulations typically determine the method used to calculate depreciation. But for both tax and accounting purposes the business can deduct the loss in the value of an asset each year during the useful life of the asset, until it reaches the point where the total purchase price (plus transportation and assembly costs) has been fully depreciated.

Land is usually entered at its purchase cost, even though its current value may be much greater. Accountants argue that because it is impossible to accurately determine its real market value without selling the land, the balance sheet should reflect its original purchase cost so as not to overstate the value and mislead the reader. Obviously, when agribusiness firms have significant land assets whose value has increased greatly, the balance sheet may vastly understate the real market value. For example, Jody Snyder's landscaping business is located on ten acres of land that her father purchased in 1941 for $10,000. A short time ago owners of a local retail store offered her $300,000 for the same ten acres. If Jody could revalue her land, her owner's equity would be much greater.

Accountants are working on new methods of reporting fixed assets whose value has been drastically changed by rapid inflation or devaluation, but most businesses still report the purchase cost, unless otherwise noted. If Jody were seeking additional bank funding for her business, she would be allowed to revalue the land account on her balance sheet to a more realistic level.

Other assets (r)

A miscellaneous category called other assets accounts for any investment of the firm in securities, such as stock in other private companies and bonds that are held for longer than one year. The category also includes intangible assets, such as patents, copyrights, franchise costs, and goodwill. Goodwill is the extent to which the price paid for an asset exceeds the asset's physical market value, usually because of the value of the reputation established in the market area by the previous owner. Items in the other assets category usually have a longer life than current asset items and are generally non-depreciable in nature. In many cases, they cannot easily be sold within the operating year or represent financial resources that the firm would not sell.

Plate 9.2 Farm land and farmstead
Most fixed assets depreciate over time, but land is unique because it does not depreciate. Photo courtesy of USDA Natural Resources Conservation Service.

Liabilities (aa)

Liabilities consist of money that the business owes to "outsiders" (other than capital invested by the owners). Liabilities are claims against the business's assets, but they may not be claims against any specific asset, except for some mortgages and equipment liens. This means that unless a creditor holds a lien or mortgage (legal claim) against a specific fertilizer truck, spreader, or parcel of land, that creditor has no claims against individual assets; his or her only claim is against a specific dollar portion of the total value of the company's assets. Essentially, liabilities are divided into two classes: current liabilities and long-term liabilities.

Current liabilities (bb)

Current liabilities describe those outsiders' claims against the business that will fall due within one normal operating cycle, usually one year. Some of the more important current liabilities entered on the balance sheet are the following:

Accounts payable (cc): **Accounts payable** represent the amount that BF&G owes to vendors, wholesalers, and other suppliers from whom the business has bought items on account. This category also includes any items of inventory, supplies, or capital equipment that have been purchased on credit and for which payment is expected in less than 1 year. For example, when BF&G purchases 100 tons of hog supplement from their supplier on short-term credit at $270 per ton, accounts payable immediately increases by $27,000. The total amount of accounts payable for BF&G on December 31 is $800,000.

Notes payable (dd): **Notes payable** is sometimes labeled as short-term loans or liabilities. This category represents those loans from individuals, banks, or other lending institutions that fall due within a year. Also included in this category is the specific portion of any long-term debt that will come due within a year.

In highly seasonal agribusinesses, short-term loans are a very important part of financial management (see Chapter 11). Cash needs intensify during the peak season, when the agribusiness must pay for increased inventory and for financing accounts receivable. This situation requires careful cash management. BF&G shows $1,000,000 in short-term credit as of December 31.

Accrued expenses (ee): The **accrued expenses** account represents the aggregation of several individual accounts such as wages payable and taxes payable. Each may be reported separately or one account may include all of these obligations. They include those obligations, **accruals**, that the business has incurred for which there has been no formal bill or invoice. An example of this would be accrued taxes. BF&G knows that the business has the obligation to pay $5,000 in taxes, an amount that is accruing or accumulating each day. The fact that the taxes do not have to be paid until a later date in the operating year does not diminish the daily obligation. Another example of accrued expenses would be BF&G's wages of $30,000. Although they are paid weekly or monthly, they are being earned daily or even hourly, and they constitute a valid claim against Brookstone's assets. An accurate balance sheet reflects these individual obligations.

Advances (ff): Sometimes firms receive payment for goods in advance. BF&G shows a $27,000 balance for this account. This means that the firm owes its customers $27,000 worth of product/services. A proper balance sheet will illustrate the payments from customers as advances or deferred income.

Long-term liabilities (hh)

Outsiders' claims against the business that do not come due within one year are called **long-term liabilities** or noncurrent liabilities. Included in this category are bonded indebtedness, mortgages, and long-term loans from individuals, banks, or others. Any part of the principal for a long-term debt that falls due within one year from the date of the balance sheet is recorded as part of the current liabilities of the business. BF&G has both a mortgage (ii) and other long-term debt (jj).

Owner's equity (mm)

The **owner's equity** or net worth section (mm) details the claims of the owners against the business's assets. It is a summation of the accounts that report owner equity (i.e., earnings retained in the business, contributions, paid-in capital, etc.). The balance sheet balances because of the inclusion of all applicable accounts and their respective amounts for all three sections of the balance sheet, including the owner equity section. Viewed a different way, the balance sheet formula becomes:

$$\text{Assets} - \text{Liabilities} = \text{Owner's Equity}$$

In an incorporated business, the owner's original or contributed investment to the business is listed as a separate entry called common stock (oo). This does not necessarily represent the current market value of the common stock, but rather its original value. (Market value of stock is a totally separate issue, determined solely by buyers' and sellers' perceptions of the value of the business.)

The category of retained earnings (pp) represents the net gain on the owners' original investment. If no profits were ever drawn from the business, the retained earnings figure would reflect the total amount of profit that the business has made since its inception. Of course, most owners expect to remove profits regularly from the business as a return on their investment. Thus, retained earnings represent whatever net profits the owners have chosen to leave in the business. BF&G owners have left $1,780,000 of earned profits in the business to combine with their original $1,885,000 investment. For most companies, retained earnings are an important source of capital for growth.

When the business is a sole proprietorship or partnership (see Chapter 4), the owner's equity is often reported as one entry and the owners' initial investment is not separated from the accumulated retained earnings of the business. However, in the case of the incorporated business, there are entries for stockholders' claims and also for earnings that have been accumulated and retained in the business. Of course, if the business has been consistently operating at a loss, the owners' claims may be less than the initial investment; and, in the case of a corporation, the balancing account could be an operating deficit rather than retained earnings.

The complete combination of all the entries outlined above creates a full balance sheet. This financial statement provides a great deal of information. It illustrates what the business owns and what claims exist against these resources. Managers need this information to help them decide what actions they should take in running their business. Outsiders seek this information to determine, among other things, the creditworthiness of the firm. Owners utilize this information to judge the performance of the management team.

Income statement

The **income statement** (Table 9.2) summarizes revenue and expenses during a specific period of time and reports the **accounting loss or profit** that results from the deduction of expenses from revenue. For these reasons, this financial statement is most commonly known as the income statement. Titles like the operating statement, profit and loss statement, or statement of earnings are also used for the income statement.

The income statement provides a primary measure of business profitability; therefore, it is a key financial statement for operating managers. Its very format emphasizes the basic profit formula, and, hence, holds the key to solving many operating management problems:

Net sales
– Cost of goods sold
Gross margin
– Operating expenses
Net operating income

Because this financial record summarizes the activities of the company over a specific period of time, it lists only those activities that can be expressed in terms of dollars relating to that specific period of operations for the firm. While comparing two balance sheets can indicate the changes in the position of the company for a particular accounting period, the income statement details how this change took place during that same period.

The accounting process helps in distinguishing between expenses and expenditures. An **expenditure** is incurred whenever the business acquires an asset, such as a truck, building, or fertilizer, whether it is used immediately or years later. **Expenses** are expenditures that are incurred by the business during the accounting period being reported. Expenses directly affect owner's equity—higher expenses mean lower profit, which, in turn, dictates a lower addition to the firm's owner's equity. Whenever an asset is acquired, the business must make arrangements to pay for it, either immediately or later. The date of cash payment is extremely important to the firm's cash flow, but it has little to do directly with profits or losses.

The income statement identifies the dollar volume of business during a specific period and then matches to it, as precisely as possible, the expenses incurred to perform these business operations. Not all the cash expenditures (dollars spent) during an accounting period can be attributed to business transacted during that period. For example, BF&G may purchase a truck in one year but use it for several years. It would be inappropriate to charge the entire cost of the truck (expenditure) to the business during the year in which it was purchased, since the truck will last for several years. Therefore, only that part that is used during the operating period is reported as an expense (previously referred to as depreciation). This loss in value is reported on the balance sheet (Table 9.1, l and o). Similarly, BF&G could have purchased seed (expenditure) and placed it in inventory near the end of an accounting period without selling it until the following period. This amount of inventory should not be charged as an expense for the period since it was not sold.

Therefore, only as an asset is used up or sold does it become an expense to the business. That is, as any asset becomes part of the operation and is directly or indirectly sold to a customer, it becomes an expense. As the BF&G truck is used, it wears out. For business purposes, one might even say that it is being sold to customers bit by bit as this wearing-out process occurs. These "bits" that are going to the customer are listed as depreciation expense for the current period.

The primary purpose of the income statement is to match precisely the expenses and the revenue from the business generated during that period so that management can accurately measure business profits and, thus, performance. This profit can then be compared to the asset base of the firm to begin to evaluate management performance and financial progress.

Accounting on a cash versus an accrual basis

The **cash-basis approach** to preparing an income statement implies that revenues and expenses occur when cash is received or paid. Many agricultural producers and some small agribusiness firms use this approach. The **accrual approach** says that revenues and expenses truly exist whenever they are earned or incurred regardless of when the cash transaction occurs. The accrual approach is a much more accurate approach for reporting net profit for a firm, because it more closely matches the expenses incurred during a period to the revenue earned.

If a cash-basis income statement is used, the net income reported can be misleading. Cash net profit can understate true accrual net income to the extent that:

- Revenue is earned but not converted to cash—such as an increase in accounts receivable or an increase in the amount of product stored or held in inventory.
- Expenses are incurred during prior or later years but cash is paid this year. Examples are a decrease in accounts payable, a decrease in accrued expenses, an increase in prepaid expenses, or an increase in purchased supplies.

Cash net income can overstate true accrual net profit to the extent that:

- Revenue generated in prior years is converted to cash this year—as in the opposite of that discussed above.
- Expenses are incurred this year but paid in cash in a prior or later year—as in the opposite of what was discussed above.

Cash record systems can be used to generate an "accrual adjusted" measure of net income by systematically adjusting the cash revenue for changes in certain inventory accounts, accounts receivable, etc., and by adjusting cash expenses for changes in accounts payable, accrued expenses, etc. These adjustments reflect the difference between the amounts shown in these accounts on the beginning and ending balance sheets for the year. The difference can be substantial. A study evaluating the difference in cash versus the accrual-adjusted net farm income for 1,045 farm operators in Illinois found that the average annual percentage difference for 2002–6 was 62 percent (Barnard et. al. 2010). Hence, the more accurate approach to reporting net income is to use the accrual approach. This approach will be used in the discussion that follows.

Income statement format

The format for the income statement varies somewhat from business to business, but such statements generally begin with sales and subtract the appropriate expenses, with profit showing as a remainder.

Net sales (a)

Sales represent the dollar value of all the products and services that have been sold during the period specified on the income statement. These may be either cash or credit sales. Sometimes customers return products after the products have been purchased. The dollar value of all returns is usually subtracted from the dollar value of all sales. In some cases, the returns are shown as a separate entry. Some customers may be given price discounts for the goods or services they buy. Either the discounted price or the full price may be shown on the income statement, with a special entry indicating how much discount has been given. The format to follow in such reporting might look like the following:

Gross sales

– Returns

– Discounts and allowances

Net sales

In Table 9.2, the income statement for BF&G illustrates five accounts for product sales revenues and one account for service income revenue. Formats for the sales figure vary, but more information is contained in this income statement versus one that might report total sales of $13,410,000 under one general account.

Cost of goods sold (b)

Cost of goods sold represents the total cost to the agribusiness of goods that were actually sold during the specified period. In the case of retail firms, whose purpose is to resell a previously purchased product, this category is a rather straightforward accounting of the actual purchases plus any additional freight charges. In BF&G's case, the grain that was purchased and resold during the year actually cost the firm $7,556,900, the seed cost $511,650, fertilizer and chemicals cost $1,791,420, etc.

Many types of agribusiness firms are involved in processing or manufacturing. In these cases, determining the cost of goods sold is considerably more complicated because it involves not only the costs for raw materials but also many internal, direct manufacturing costs. In such cases, the cost of goods sold section becomes more complex, and it is recommended that the cost of manufactured goods be detailed to show important cost breakdowns. A seed corn production firm would represent a good example of a manufacturing firm. They are assembling inputs to produce and market seed.

To provide an accurate cost of goods sold figure, current inventories of raw and finished products must be balanced against those of the previous accounting period. In a manufacturing or processing business, the cost of the raw materials, direct labor, and other resources that have been used during the accounting period are usually included in the cost of goods sold, and are subtracted from net sales to calculate the gross margin or gross profit. Decreases or increases in inventories from one accounting period to another reflect consumption of or additions to inventories, so that the balancing of changes in inventory is intended to reflect the actual costs incurred during the current accounting period.

For example, if a firm consumed a large amount of raw materials, which naturally would decrease inventories from the previous accounting period, the net change in inventory would be reflected in the cost of goods sold. BF&G had an inventory of $2,800,000 in the previous period; now it shows an inventory of $2,500,000. The decrease in inventory of $300,000 would have to be added to new purchases of $11,425,000 to equal the total cost of goods sold of $11,725,000 (b). The formula is:

Beginning inventory	$2,800,000
− Ending inventory	− 2,500,000
Net inventory change	300,000
+ Purchases	+11,425,000
= Costs of goods sold	$11,725,000

In addition, if BF&G paid any freight or transportation expense in receiving inventory at their facility, this expense would also be included as part of cost of goods sold.

Gross margin (gross profit) (c)

Gross margin or **gross profit** represents the difference between net sales and total cost of goods sold. The gross margin is the money that is available to cover the operating expenses and the interest expense and still leave a profit. If the gross margin is not large enough to cover operating expenses and the interest expense of the business, losses, and not profits, will be the result. Note in the example that this account is actually labeled as "gross profit." Since service income revenue has been included under the net sales figure, BF&G utilizes gross profit to reflect gross margin from the five product lines plus all service income revenue.

Gross margins are particularly important to retail agribusinesses because such businesses have relatively little control over cost of goods sold. The prices of goods an agribusiness purchase are critical factors that affect its gross margin. Different products usually have different individual gross margins, so the total gross margin for the business will also depend on the particular combination or mix of products and their sources. Often management can affect the cost of goods sold through careful purchasing. BF&G has a gross margin of $1,685,000, which is enough to cover its expenses and still leave a profit.

To demonstrate the importance of pricing decisions on gross margin and bottom line profit, let us assume that BF&G was able to raise its price by 1 percent on current net sales of $13,410,000. This would have increased net sales to $13,544,100. With the cost of goods sold remaining constant, gross profit would have increased to $1,819,100; but after operating expenses have been subtracted, net operating income would have increased by 28.6 percent to $603,290, and net income before tax would have increased by over 52 percent. The same kind of effect on the bottom line would be seen if the cost of purchased fertilizer or seed (cost of goods sold) were reduced slightly. This effect illustrates the fact that business success is largely centered on relatively small but important changes, and illustrates the tremendous importance of using relevant financial data to explore such changes. (These kinds of changes and their analysis are explored further in Chapter 12.)

Operating expenses (d)

Operating expenses represent the costs that are associated with the specific sales transacted during the time period designated on the income statement. It is easier to interpret these expenses if they have been divided into major divisions such as:

Marketing expenses, including:
  Sales, wages, salaries, and commissions

Transportation
Advertising and promotion
Administrative expenses, including:
Auditing fees
Directors' fees
Management salary
Office expenses
Travel expenses
General expenses (overhead), including:
Depreciation
Insurance
Taxes
Rent
Repairs
Utilities
(Manufacturing costs, where incurred, are included in cost of goods sold.)

In BF&G's income statement, the various expense categories are simply listed (e through u). The returns and allowances have already been excluded. Net sales for the year ending December 31 were $13,410,000. This detailed listing of operating expenses in the above categories will make the analysis and interpretation of this valuable financial information much easier for BF&G management.

Net operating income (w)

Also called the net operating margin, the **net operating income** is the amount left over when total operating expenses (v) are subtracted from the gross margin or gross profit (c). The net operating income is affected by the same factors that influence gross margins, plus the factors associated with business operating expenses.

Net income before taxes (z)

Net income (profit) before taxes is the amount that remains after taking into account any non-operating revenue or expenses. Non-operating revenue would include any revenue derived from other sources, such as interest or dividends earned on outside investments (x). Local cooperatives may include patronage refunds from their regional cooperative in other revenue. BF&G generated $18,200 in other non-operating revenue from interest on investments and the sale of some very old equipment. On the other hand, BF&G incurred interest expenses of $230,840 (y). This $230,840 is interest on money that BF&G had borrowed from various sources (as they appeared on the balance sheet), and so is not directly a part of the operation.

Net income after taxes (bb)

Net income (profit) after taxes, or net profit as it is sometimes called, simply takes into account the federal business profits tax (aa). The rate of tax depends on many factors, including the size of the profits, profit levels in previous years, type of business organization, and several complicated tax regulations. In larger corporate organizations, tax rates often reach nearly 40 percent of the profits. In the case of proprietorships and partnerships, federal profit taxes are not levied against the businesses themselves, but are assessed against the individual owners. Profits are taxed as personal income (see Chapter 4). Cooperative businesses often have lower entries either for taxes or for after-tax profits due to the nature of their organization and its respective operating objectives (see Chapter 4).

Statement of owner's equity

The **statement of owner's equity** is usually the shortest and least complicated of the financial statements. It details the changes that affect the owner's equity accounts. The primary change is usually a change in retained earnings resulting from a net income or loss. Other changes could occur due to contributions made or distributions withdrawn from the owner's invested capital. Also, stock could be issued by the agribusiness.

The statement of owner's equity for Brookstone Feed and Grain company for the year ending December 31, 2009 is provided in Table 9.3. As can be seen, the common stock equity account did not change from beginning to end of year. However, BF&G made a net profit after taxes of $196,650, as reported on its income statement for 2009. Of that amount, the owner withdrew $96,650 from the business and retained the remainder of the profit in the business. So the retained earnings account increased from $1,680,000 on December 31, 2008 to $1,780,000 on December 31, 2009. Consequently, owner's equity increased by $100,000, from $3,565,000 on December 31, 2008 to $3,665,000 on December 31, 2009.

Statement of cash flows

This statement is basically a way to show the cash inflows and outflows of the firm for a period of time. It can be tabulated at the end of a period, like the balance sheet and income statement, to help interested parties see what happened. Or, more importantly, it can be constructed at the beginning of a period in an attempt to budget appropriate changes over the period.

The statement of cash flows, like the balance sheet, always balances, i.e., sources of cash (dollars flowing into the business) always equals uses of cash (dollars flowing out of the business) over the period. The primary categories for this statement are: (1) cash flows from operations, (2) cash flows from investments (disinvestments) made by the firm, and (3) cash

Table 9.3 Statement of owner's equity for Brookstone Feed and Grain, year ending December 31, 2009

Owner's Equity, December 31, 2008				$3,565,000
Retained Earnings, December 31, 2008		$1,680,000		
Net Income After Taxes, 2009	$196,650			
– Dividends	$0			
– Withdrawals	$96,650			
Increase (Decrease) in Retained Earnings		$100,000		
Retained Earnings, December 31, 2009			$1,780,000	
Common Stock, December 31, 2008		$1,885,000		
+ Increases	$0			
– Decreases	$0			
Increase (Decrease) in Common Stock		$0		
Common Stock, December 31, 2009			$1,885,000	
Owner's Equity, December 31, 2009				$3,665,000

Plate 9.3 Grain elevator
Pro forma statements, such as a statement of cash flows, are used to manage cash. The management of cash is essential for all firms, but is particularly true for firms that sell seasonal products. Photo courtesy of USDA Natural Resources Conservation Service.

flows from financing transactions, such as contributions from owners, borrowing, and repaying debt. The statement of cash flows for BF&G at the end of the accounting period is shown in Table 9.4.

Pro forma statements: a case study

Each of the four financial statements discussed in this chapter provides a way to report historical accounting information. Historical information provides information needed to analyze past financial performance, but it does not provide the information needed to assess future plans. To provide such information, financial statements can be prepared for a future period. Such statements are called **pro forma statements**. The sample case study presented below is used to illustrate two pro forma statements—a balance sheet and a statement of cash flows.

The Aggieland Landscaping company provides landscaping services to a wide region of east central Texas. This company has done reasonably well since its inception five years ago. However, the owner, Ted Henderson, has a problem. He needs to replace $50,000 of depreciated equipment, but he does not have the cash to pay for the new equipment. He thinks he can sell the depreciated equipment for $5,000, but it will cost $55,000 to replace it.

Table 9.4 Statement of cash flows for Brookstone Feed and Grain company, year ending December 31, 2009

Cash Flow from Operating Activities		
Net Income after Taxes	$196,650	
+ Depreciation	290,000	
− Increase in Accounts Receivable	20,000	
− Decrease in Accounts Payable	15,000	
− Decrease in Accrued Expenses	15,000	
Net Cash from Operating Activities		$436,650
Cash Flow from Investing Activities		
Cash Proceeds from Sale of Equipment	$10,000	
− Cash Purchase of Equipment	336,650	
Net Cash from Investing Activities		$(326,650)
Cash Flow from Financing Activities		
+ Increase in Notes Payable	$45,000	
− Decrease in Mortgages	75,000	
Net Cash from Financing Activities		$(30,000)
Net Change in Cash		$80,000
Beginning Cash Balance		$95,000
Ending Cash Balance		$175,000

Thus, Ted visited his banker and discussed the possibility of a loan. Ted constructed the balance sheet shown in Table 9.5 for the visit to his banker.

Ted, after a discussion with his banker, decided he would purchase the $55,000 of equipment in order to be able to replace the worn-out equipment and be in a position to handle more business. Ted wants to estimate the impact this will have on his firm in the short run, so he wants to develop a pro forma statement of cash flows. He believes that the inventory, accounts receivable, accounts payable, and accrued expense accounts will stay the same.

Table 9.5 Balance sheet for Aggieland landscaping company, year ending December 31, 2011

Assets			Liabilities:	
Current Assets:			Current Liabilities:	
Cash		$0	Accounts Payable	$5,000
Accounts Receivable		14,000	Accrued Expenses	2,000
Inventory		21,000	Current Portion of	10,000
Fixed Assets:			Long-Term Debt	
Equipment	$100,000		Long-Term Liabilities:	
Buildings	50,000		Long-Term Debt	40,000
− Accumulated Depreciation	80,000			
Net Buildings & Equip.		70,000	Total liabilities:	$57,000
Land		80,000		
			Owner's equity	$128,000
Total assets		$185,000	Total liabilities and owner's equity	$185,000

Depreciation for the next year will be $25,000. In addition, during the next year Ted has payments of $10,000 to make on his existing long-term debt and he will need to make a principal payment of $10,000 on his new debt. He estimates next year's net income after taxes will be $55,000, including the $5,000 gain on the sale of the depreciated equipment. He plans to withdraw $50,000 for family living, so he will retain $5,000 in the business. With this information and these forecasts, Ted can now develop a pro forma statement of cash flows (Table 9.6). In addition, he can construct a pro forma balance sheet (Table 9.7).

The accounts reported on the pro forma balance sheet as of 12/31/2012 for Aggieland Landscaping company are determined as follows. First, the accounts receivable, inventory,

Table 9.6 Pro forma statement of cash flows for Aggieland landscaping company, year ending December 31, 2012

Cash Flow from Operating Activities		
Net Income after Taxes	$50,000	
+ Depreciation	+ 25,000	
± Change in Accounts Receivable	0	
± Change in Accounts Payable	0	
± Change in Accrued Expenses	0	
− Withdrawal for Family Living	−50,000	
Net Cash from Operating Activities		$25,000
Cash Flow from Investing Activities		
Cash Proceeds from Sale of Equipment	$5,000	
− Cash Purchases of Equipment	−55,000	
Net Cash from Investing Activities		$(50,000)
Cash Flow from Financing Activities		
+ Increase in Equipment Notes	$50,000	
− Principal Payments on Long-term and Equipment Notes	−20,000	
Net Cash from Financing Activities		+ $30,000
Net Change in Cash		+ $5,000
Beginning Cash Balance		0
Ending Cash Balance		$5,000

Table 9.7 Pro forma balance sheet for Aggieland landscaping company, year ending December 31, 2012

Assets			Liabilities	
Current Assets:			Current Liabilities:	
Cash		$5,000	Accounts Payable	$5,000
Accounts Receivable		14,000	Accrued Expenses	2,000
Inventory		21,000	Current Portion of	
Fixed Assets:			Long-Term Debt	20,000
Equipment	$105,000		Long-Term Liabilities:	
Buildings	50,000		Long-Term Debt	60,000
− Accumulated Depreciation	55,000		Total liabilities	$87,000
Net Buildings and Equipment		100,000	Owner equity	$133,000
Land		80,000	Total liabilities and owner equity	$220,000
Total assets		$220,000		

land, accounts payable, and accrued expenses are assumed to remain the same as reported on the balance sheet prepared as of 12/31/2011. Second, the cash balance increases from $0 on the 12/31/2011 balance sheet to $5,000 on the 12/31/2012 balance sheet as reported on the statement of cash flows. Third, the original amount reported for equipment of $100,000 was reduced by $50,000 from the sale of the depreciated piece of equipment, and then increased by $55,000 from the purchase of the new piece of equipment. So, the amount reported on the pro forma balance sheet is $105,000. Also, the accumulated depreciation reported on the 12/31/2011 balance sheet of $80,000 (includes the depreciation taken on the depreciated piece of equipment) is reduced by $50,000 due to the sale of that piece of equipment, and then is increased by the depreciation taken during 2012 ($25,000), resulting in $55,000 of accumulated depreciation reported on 12/31/2012. Fourth, the total long-term liabilities reported on 12/31/2011 were $50,000 ($10,000 reported as current and $40,000 reported as long-term). The equipment loan would be increased by the $50,000 borrowed for the new piece of equipment, but then $20,000 would be paid by the end of 2012 ($10,000 on the original loan and $10,000 on the new equipment loan) leaving a total long-term loan balance of $80,000 ($40,000 on the original loan and $40,000 on the new loan). Of that amount, $20,000 would be owed during 2013 and the remainder would be reported as long-term liabilities. Finally, the withdrawal for family living amount equals net income after taxes that will arise from the operation of the firm, so owner's equity would increase by only the $5,000 gain on the sale of equipment.

Ted's estimated statement of cash flows balances if he requests a loan of $50,000, of which $10,000 plus interest is due by the end of 2012. This is an absolute minimum for the loan request, however. As can be seen by examining the pro forma statement of cash flows, Ted will need all of the profits for personal living expenses, and he has made no allowance for contingencies. In addition, at the end of the period the first payment on the new loan will be due. In reality, Ted's request to the bank must be a figure that both he and the banker can live with. A conservative approach to estimating profits and other relevant changes in the firm's financial statements is probably the best approach.

Some important accounting principles

It is important that agribusiness managers understand the following principles and ideas about financial accounting:

1. Only facts that can be recorded in monetary terms should be reported on the balance sheet and income statement.
2. Records or accounts are kept for business entities. Personal and business transactions must be carefully separated.
3. Accounting methods assume the business will continue to operate indefinitely.
4. Resources (called assets) owned by the business are ordinarily recorded at their cost or market value—whichever is lower. This practice is called the cost basis of valuation. The amounts listed on the financial statement do not necessarily reflect the true market value of the asset.
5. Every accounting event is composed of two transactions: changes in assets and changes in liabilities and/or owner's equity. All assets are claimed by someone; therefore, claims against assets must always equal the assets listed for the firm. These claims can be found among banks, suppliers, owners, stockholders, etc.

6. Most accounting is handled on the accrual basis of accounting. The objective of the accrual method is to report revenue in the income statement for the period during which it is earned (regardless of when the cash payment is received), and to report an expense in the period when it is incurred (regardless of when the cash disbursement is made). This procedure more clearly reflects the profits of the business.
7. The format for the income statement must reflect the unique needs of the organization. To do this requires the continued help of competent financial professionals.
8. Once a format is developed, it is not sacred and should be changed as necessary to meet changing conditions. However, a degree of consistency should also be maintained to allow comparison on a historical basis to previous financial statements.
9. Finally, one of the major purposes of records and financial information is to provide the necessary information for informed decision-making on the part of agribusiness managers.

Summary

Profit is the focal point of any business, but it is the net result of many factors, many of which are reflected on the two primary financial statements. Agribusiness managers rely on financial statements to evaluate how the business is doing, to suggest the direction it should take, and to report its financial condition and performance to outside entities. It is important that this financial data be current, complete, and accurate to facilitate financial decision-making within the firm.

All financial statements rely on a systematic record-keeping system. Accountants have developed highly refined sets of rules for handling every conceivable financial transaction. The daily transactions are summarized in balance sheets, income statements, and other financial reports for owners, managers, and other concerned parties.

A balance sheet shows assets, or what the business owns, at a certain point in time. It also shows liabilities, or claims of creditors against those assets, and the value of owners' claims against the assets. Assets always equal liabilities plus owners' equity as all of the assets must be claimed by someone. Both assets and liabilities are broken down into several classes to provide a useful financial picture of the business.

The income statement summarizes the revenue over a period of time and then carefully matches the appropriate expenses incurred in generating that revenue. Any excess of revenue over expenses is profit. The format of the income statement emphasizes gross margin, or revenue left after the cost of goods sold has been covered. The gross margin represents dollars left to pay operating expenses and the interest expense, which are generally itemized on this report, and the remaining amount is net income or profit.

The statement of owners' equity and the statement of cash flows are useful in helping understand changes in these two key areas. The two statements help managers understand why changes occurred in those two areas on the two corresponding balance sheets.

Pro forma statements are projections, based on careful forecasts of key variables. Such statements help managers use financial data to make decisions that will impact the future of the organization. Agribusiness managers must be familiar with the intricacies of all of these statements, both actual and pro forma, since they become the core of many management decisions.

Discussion questions

1. Why is financial data important to the agribusiness firm and the agribusiness manager?

2. List and discuss three uses for the balance sheet and three uses for the income statement for agribusiness managers.
3. What are the major sections of a balance sheet? Why does the balance sheet equation always balance?
4. What are current assets? Why is the management of current assets so important to food and agribusiness firms?
5. Why do accountants usually value assets at their cost or market value, whichever is lower?
6. Define the difference between current and long-term liabilities. Why is this distinction important?
7. What are the major sections of the income statement?
8. Discuss the meaning of depreciation and describe how it is treated on the balance sheet and income statement. How is the amount of depreciation determined?
9. Define the difference between expenditure and an expense from an accounting point of view.
10. What is the difference between gross margin and net income, and how are those two measures related?
11. Managers may have other business objectives besides making a profit. What are three examples of these objectives? Discuss how these objectives compete with the profit objective.
12. For the case study on Aggieland Landscaping company, assume two new landscape firms have opened in Ted's trade territory. Ted now believes that instead of a net income after tax of $55,000 in the coming year, his business will only generate a profit of $30,000, excluding the gain on the equipment sold. If none of his other assumptions change, how much will he need to borrow to buy the new equipment? Is this a good idea, given his new profit forecast? Why or why not?

Case study: Julie Rowe

Julie Rowe graduated from high school five years ago with a background in agronomy. Julie had worked for a lawn care service until a year ago, when she decided to start her own business selling soil testing kits to homeowners. Julie saved $10,000 during the past five years. She decided to invest the $10,000 in a proprietorship to sell the soil testing kits in her local community.

Julie purchased the following capital items to start the business. First, she purchased a service truck that cost her $40,000, which she estimates will last for another five years. Second, she purchased her own storage tank for gasoline to be used for the truck, and this cost another $1,000. Third, she purchased a computer and some other office equipment for a total of $4,000.

She spent $4,750 for gas and other supplies. Julie calculated she needed at least $1,000 to make ends meet before she received the first check. Julie also spent $19,250 to purchase kits that will be placed in inventory. Julie's sister agreed to keep the books. Julie's father let her use the family garage for an office and agreed not to charge rent the first year. Julie's father was willing to lend her $10,000. The principal is to be repaid in 18 months. The interest rate is 6 percent per year. At the end of 12 months Julie will repay her father the interest for 12 months, but no principal. At the end of 18 months Julie will pay her father interest for six months, plus all principal owed on the loan.

Julie borrowed the balance of what she needed from First National Bank. The loan was to be repaid in five equal, annual principal payments, with interest at an annual rate of 7 percent.

At the end of the first year Julie's expenses were as follows: gas, oil, repairs, and tires $7,900 and telephone $600. During her first year she purchased 1,000 kits at $35.00/kit that were in addition to the $19,250 spent on kits to start the business. The freight on the kits was $2,000. At the end of the first year of the business she had $19,250 in inventory.

Her gross revenue from the business was $87,000. Kits sold that had been returned for a refund had been sold for $200. She had been making $45,500 per year when working at her previous job, and she calculated that she should make at least that much to justify the time spent in the business. Her sister spent about one day per week doing the office work, and Julie felt that she should be reimbursed at a rate of $50 per day for her efforts. Her sister worked 50 weeks and went on vacation for two weeks.

Questions

1. Prepare a balance sheet as of the first day of business for Julie. The balance sheet is to be prepared after she purchased the assets needed to start the business and borrowed the money from her father and the bank. The date for the balance sheet is 12/31/2010. How much did she have to borrow from the bank?
2. Prepare an income statement for Julie's first year of business, 1/1/2011–12/31/2011. Make the following assumptions:
   - Depreciate all fixed assets over five years and assume a salvage value of $0.
   - Julie makes her payment to the bank. She also pays her father interest only on the loan from him. She makes both payments on 12/30/2011.
   - Assume Julie does not pay Social Security tax on her sister's salary and that she does not have to pay any state and Federal income taxes.
3. Prepare a balance sheet as of the end of the first year for Julie's business. Use the information provided on Julie Rowe's beginning balance sheet and income statement to complete an ending balance sheet for Julie Rowe. The ending balance sheet date is as of 12/31/2011. Note: You will need to calculate Julie's cash balance on 12/31/2011, because it is not $ 1,000. Make the following assumptions:
   - The ending inventory for Julie's supplies is the same amount as her beginning inventory, $ 4,750.
   - The ending inventory is the same amount as her beginning inventory, $19,250.00
   - Julie lives with her parents, which reduces her living expenses. She decided to withdraw $25,000 for family living expenses.
4. Prepare a statement of owner's equity for Julie's business for her first year.
5. Julie's principal payment on her long-term debt and her withdrawal for family living expenses exceeded her net income after taxes, but she did make the principal payment on the loan. How did she make the payment? Discuss Julie's situation as she assesses her ability to make her payments in 2012.

Additional references and reading

Barnard, Freddie L., Paul N. Ellinger, and Christine Wilson. "Measurement Issues in Assessing Farm Profitability through Cash Tax Returns." *Journal of the American Society of Farm Managers and Rural Appraisers* (2010): pp. 207–17.

Financial Guidelines for Agricultural Producers. "Farm Financial Standards Council." 2010. www.ffsc.org.

10 Analyzing financial statements

Objectives

- Discuss how different viewpoints are possible depending on who evaluates agribusiness financial statements
- Explain the importance of establishing benchmarks for financial relationships in the firm
- Calculate and interpret financial ratios in the four major areas of analysis
- Illustrate how financial ratios can aid the decision-making process for an agribusiness manager
- Outline and discuss the limitations of financial ratio analysis
- Describe the profitability analysis system and understand its role in decision-making in the agribusiness firm

Introduction

The financial statements of any agribusiness provide a wealth of information for managers, owners, lending institutions, and the government. Some of this information requires little interpretation, but much of it is meaningless unless it is put into proper perspective. Many managers who look at a financial statement are like the explorer who sees an iceberg for the first time and fails to realize that what is seen is only the tip and that 90 percent of the iceberg is hidden under water. Highly useful information can be found in financial statements, but this is not always apparent to the casual observer. Without proper analysis, financial statements can be meaningless scraps of paper.

Financial analysis might be compared to a person's medical checkup, where much more is expected than a superficial glance from the physician. For physicians to understand if or where a problem may exist, a series of tests must be performed and many questions must be asked. Those who are interested in the financial well being and progress of the business must follow the same procedure. Agribusiness firms that survive and prosper must have managers who use the tools of financial analysis to check the vital financial functions and health of the firm and then prescribe the changes needed to keep the business on course to meet its goals and remain viable and competitive in the future. Tools which allow those who are interested in the business to use financial analysis in determining how successful the business performance has been, what problems or opportunities exist, and what alternative or remedial courses of action might improve performance in the future are discussed in this chapter.

Plate 10.1 Tools
Like any professional, the agribusiness manager has a set of tools that can be used to assess the financial health of the firm. Photo courtesy of USDA.

Financial statements: their use in evaluating performance

Because they can be interpreted from differing points of view, a company's financial statements should provide enough perspectives to satisfy all interested parties. The community looks at what the agribusiness is spending on being a good citizen. Members of a cooperative are interested in the efficiency and savings that result from patronage. Suppliers are interested in the firm's ability to market and pay for products. Customers are interested in the long-term viability of the firm and its ability to provide products at a reasonable price and in a timely manner. Employees are interested in reaching firm goals which, in turn, should increase their compensation, while the board of directors is interested in the effectiveness of the management team in using the firm's financial resources in the most profitable manner.

A manager such as Barry Meade, president of Meade Food Brokerage, is inclined to approach the business financial statements primarily from two points of view. First, to evaluate how the business has performed, and to determine ways financial information can be used to improve decision-making in the future. Profit is the primary gauge for success or failure. Some firms will organize the firm into separate "profit centers" to facilitate this analysis. Second, the manager must also keep in mind that the financial statements and their analysis should provide complete, accurate, and timely information for lenders, investors, and the government, since success requires the satisfaction of these interested parties.

When Pilar Fernandez invested in ConAgra, she had a high degree of interest in this firm's profits and general health. However, her primary interest was centered on the rate of return generated on the funds she had invested in the stock of this company. She expected her investment to equal or surpass alternative investment opportunities with similar risks. Members of cooperatives, on the other hand, concentrate their interest on the efficiency of the firm and the savings accruing to them through their patronage. These represent the implicit returns for patron members as discussed in Chapter 4.

Meanwhile, Mary Hartman, who heads the commercial loan department of Farmers' Bank and Trust, is interested in not only a firm's profits, but also its cash flow, because it is an important barometer of the firm's ability to repay loans. Because she is interested in protecting the loan against loss, the firm's assets versus liabilities are an additional focus for her, as for all lenders.

Governmental units are interested in financial statements from several points of view, depending on their particular needs. For example, the Internal Revenue Service is interested in profits, the tax assessor is interested in asset valuation, and the Labor Department is interested in wages and employee information. Each of the many governmental units will require certain kinds of information, and supplying it in proper form is mandatory for the business.

The agribusiness manager must be aware of each of the perspectives in designing and analyzing the financial statements of the business. Construction of these statements in a format useful to the agribusiness firm is the first important step. This chapter outlines how these statements may be used to evaluate agribusiness performance—the second important step in effective financial management.

Timely analysis

A successful agribusiness operation depends greatly on managerial planning. However, since planning involves the consideration of an uncertain future, even the best management plans can go astray. Therefore, the management team must monitor the firm's progress, or lack of it, toward previously established goals. Many agribusinesses fail because management discovered too late that goals were not being realized. Through continual evaluation of financial records, management might have recognized the problem as it was developing, which would have allowed sufficient time for corrective action. This assumes the records were complete and accurate. Proper and timely evaluation allows management to begin to implement contingency plans, when necessary.

Use of financial data in firm evaluation is analogous to an automobile's oil level. There is a pressure gauge to indicate when the oil level is dangerously low. However, the sensible motorist will check the oil periodically to prevent potential problems. It is the same with business records. These records should be timely enough to prevent serious problems from developing. A spot-check of the business's health should be taken at regular intervals. In most businesses, the financial statements should be prepared and analyzed on a monthly basis, or at the least on a quarterly basis, so that problems or opportunities can be determined before they develop or pass by. The cost of the process is small compared to the risk of discovering too late that problems or opportunities have been missed.

What areas require analysis?

The collection of data can become an unending process with increasing costs and diminishing returns. Generally, data should be relevant to the decision-making process to be useful for management.

Agribusiness managers can use ratios to help monitor financial position and performance. Four areas are normally explored when financial ratios are used to analyze a firm. These areas are profitability, liquidity, solvency, and efficiency. The information provided on the firm in each of these areas is presented below.

Profitability ratios:

Trends in revenues and expenses, such as sales, operating expenses, overhead costs, and wages

The firm's success in terms of actual profitability, trends in profitability, and how the firm's profitability compares to other firms

The firm's use of resources to generate a return on equity sufficient to satisfy current and future investors

The firm's ability to repay long-term debts

Liquidity ratios:

The firm's cash position; that is, its ability to meet current commitments, such as payrolls and supply purchases

The ability of the firm to react to uncertainty in the marketplace

Solvency ratios:

The firm's capital structure and its ability to meet future plans to change and expand

The ability of the firm to deal with risk and absorb future losses

Efficiency ratios:

Trends in production and performance, measured in accordance with previously established standards of efficiency

The competency of the management team in terms of the proper financial and operating use of the resources of the firm

The firm's ability to be globally competitive in a constantly changing marketplace

Begin by establishing benchmarks

The interpretation of financial information need not be a complex process. It is centered largely on developing benchmarks or points of reference. Much information can be secured by very simple procedures. One of the easiest ways to determine trends and identify problems or opportunities is simply to compare the current period with similar periods from the past. Comparisons between last year's numbers and the current period or with an average figure, or comparisons between the current month and the same month last year, or to trends, may be useful.

At this point, an important concept should be noted. Financial analysis and records do not solve problems or create opportunities—people do. All the analysis of records can do is to help the manager ask the relevant questions in order to identify problems and opportunities. Alternative courses of action or constraints to action may be suggested and identified, but these records alone do not have a cognitive value. The manager must take specific actions based upon his or her financial analysis for this process to be useful.

Suppose that Neil Gray, controller of the Dixie Manufacturing Company, notes that accounts receivable for December stands at $349,000. That figure in and of itself may have little significance. However, if he notes that last year's December accounts receivable was $270,000, he can be alerted to a potential problem or opportunity (see Table 10.1).

There are many possible reasons for this change. More questions (and answers) may well be needed to provide sufficient information for the manager. Product prices could simply have gone up 29 percent, thereby raising the value of accounts receivable, or the total sales for the year could have been 29 percent higher. On the other hand, Neil may need to more carefully monitor the payments of the accounts receivable and then consider changes in the credit policy of the firm.

The critical issue is that a simple comparison with a past period gave the figure added significance. This simple and easily prepared comparison is one of the best methods for identifying points where the manager should raise questions. To evaluate this properly, Neil needs the answers to several questions. Has the firm changed its credit policy? Have sales increased significantly over this time period? Which of Dixie's accounts represent the bulk of the $349,000 in receivables due their firm? Has this changed in the past year? Answers to these and similar questions will help Neil determine if any action is necessary. So Neil would find the answers to the questions posed, identify the cause of the deviation, and then, if needed, take corrective action(s).

Performance measures can also be compared to industry averages. Various trade organizations, universities, governmental agencies, consulting firms, etc., collect, compile and analyze industry data. Such reports can also be used for comparative purposes.

The financial statements and the budgeted forecasts provide another excellent comparison. This is particularly true if the former is an income statement. Table 10.2 presents income statement information in a useful manner for comparative purposes. The first column contains the previous year's actual figures for sales, cost of goods, gross margin, and expense data. The second set of columns contains this year's budgeted figures. In other words, these data represent Pacey's financial goals for the current period. The third set of columns of financial information illustrates the actual amounts for the current year. The final two sets of columns present similar information—budgeted and actual—for the most recent quarter.

Management of Pacey farm store can compare actual operating results to the budget and previous year's figures to indicate relative performance in cost control (expenses), buying (cost of goods), and pricing (sales). Cursory analysis indicates Pacey has a significant gross margin problem. Currently, gross margin is about $4,600 under the budgeted goal for this point during the period ($42,810, year-to-date, actual, versus $47,439, year-to-date, budget). Both the pricing decisions and buying practices must be reviewed to determine what specific problems exist.

Table 10.1 Dixie manufacturing company comparative balance sheets

Current Assets	December 31, 2010 ($)	December 31, 2009 ($)
Cash	272,000	210,000
Marketable Securities	380,000	395,000
Accounts Receivable	349,000	270,000
Inventory	550,000	610,000
Total Current Assets	1,551,000	1,485,000

Table 10.2 Pacey farm store expense budget and control report

	Last year to date (Actual)		This year to date (Budget)		This year to date (Actual)		90-day (Budget)		90-day (Actual)	
	Dollars	*Percent of Sales*	*Dollars*	*Percent of Sales*	*Dollars*	*Percent of Sales*	*Dollars*	*Percent of Sales*	*Dollars*	*Percent of Sales*
Net sales	175,502	100.0	180,000	100.0	185,310	100.0	81,889	100.0	85,305	100.0
Cost of goods sold	131,566	75.0	132,561	73.6	142,500	76.9	62,185	75.9	66,847	78.4
Gross margin	43,936	25.0	47,439	26.4	42,810	23.1	19,704	24.1	18,458	21.6
Full-time labor	19,764	11.3	20,500	11.4	19,764	10.7	9,882	12.1	9,527	11.2
Part-time labor	4,392	2.5	5,000	2.8	4,392	2.4	2,196	2.7	1,929	2.3
Overtime labor	0	0	0	0	0	0	0	0	0	0
Management fee	4,500	2.6	4,500	2.5	4,569	2.5	2,000	2.4	2,031	2.4
Total property expenses	1,800	1.0	1,800	1.0	1,800	.9	900	1.1	900	1.0
Warehouse expenses	550	.3	500	.3	580	.3	250	.3	290	.3
Advance and sales promotion	4,725	2.7	4,500	2.5	5,374	2.9	2,000	2.4	1,388	1.6
Interest	3,750	2.1	3,750	2.1	3,583	1.9	1,875	2.3	1,592	1.9
Other general expenses	365	.2	500	.3	1,244	.7	165	.2	411	.5
Total expenses*	39,846	22.7	41,050	22.9	41,306	22.3	19,268	23.5	18,068	21.2
Net operating margin	4,090	2.3	6,389	3.5	1,504	.8	436	.6	390	.4

Note: * Some totals for percents may not equal sums of categories due to rounding.

Common-size analysis

Common-size analysis is another useful method in effectively evaluating a business's financial situation. The greatest benefit of this tool is to put things in perspective. Common-size analysis simply expresses the balance sheet and income statement figures as percentages of some key base figure, which could be derived from similar businesses or from the firm's own total sales, total assets, budgets, or forecasts. They provide the manager with benchmarks that give figures an added dimension.

For example, the Pacey farm store (Table 10.2) may show a figure of $5,374 for sales promotion in the "This year to date" column. When one realizes that this accounts for 2.9 percent of net sales, the magnitude of the sales promotion figure has some meaning. A comparison to similar figures from previous periods yields even more insight. Realization that last year's promotion expense was only $4,725 might elicit a hazy reaction, but comparison with a promotion expense last year that constituted only 2.7 percent of net sales will trigger an immediate response. When Heidi McClain, the sales manager, looks at this comparison, she can see that promotion expenses are 19 percent above the budgeted figure, [($5,374 − $4,500) ÷ $4,500] × 100. A similar analysis relative to other expenses indicates that "Other general expenses" are more than triple year-ago levels. Action, or at least an investigation, is called for at this point.

Common-size analysis should include raw data from the original statements to prevent distortion or masking. This is particularly true when comparing an individual firm's percentages with those of similar firms. One firm may be very large and have sales in the hundreds of millions, while a smaller firm's sales might be in the millions or even thousands. The actual dollar figures and not just percentages would help amplify and clarify differences.

Ratio analysis

One of the most important tools for financial analysis is **ratio analysis**. The strength of financial ratio analysis lies in the fact that the relationships used between data on financial statements eliminate the weaknesses of dollar comparisons, which are sometimes not only confusing but may be misleading. Ratio analysis permits relative comparisons of important financial data and relationships, and such relative comparisons can be very insightful.

For example, we may consider the following relationships for two firms:

	Firm A	*Firm B*
Current Assets	$200,000	$1,000,000
Current Liabilities	100,000	900,000
Net Working Capital	$100,000	$100,000

Note that the difference between current assets and current liabilities is called net working capital. Both firms have the same net working capital, $100,000. However, Firm A, all things being equal, is in a healthier financial condition than Firm B because the current ratio, an indicator of liquidity (current assets ÷ current liabilities), for Firm A is 2:1; whereas, the current ratio of Firm B is only 1.1:1. The current ratio is the number of dollars of current assets available to meet obligations due during the upcoming year. In this case, it is the ratio of current assets to current liabilities that provides the more accurate reading of the situation, rather than the straight dollar comparison.

Why use financial ratio analysis?

Financial ratio analysis is often used to measure the performance of the many facets of the business mentioned in the introduction to this chapter. When properly used (with its limitations understood), this financial management tool can be a very useful management aid. Many agribusiness managers use ratio analysis extensively because it not only provides better indicators for managerial decisions but also is useful in the following ways:

1. *Easy to calculate*: Most ratios compare two accounts that are normally provided by the income statement or the balance sheet. Because these data are readily available, not much time or expense is required to compute a financial ratio.
2. *Easy to make comparisons*: Ratios facilitate comparison of past with present performance, as well as comparisons with firms of a similar nature. Ratios are of particular value to corporate boards of directors.
3. *Easily understood*: Not all members of the management team are financial sophisticates, and ratios provide overview information simply and clearly for all management personnel.
4. *Able to communicate a firm's financial position and performance to outside interested parties:* For example, financial authorities and stockholders, cooperative patrons, or investors may rely on ratios to determine a firm's credit-worthiness and success in the use of its resources.

Agribusiness managers and analysts are likely to develop their own favorite set of financial indicators. Also, lenders may use certain ratios to evaluate a firm's credit-worthiness, so those ratios would need to be monitored by management. It would not be productive to present an exhaustive set of ratios nor pretend that we can produce a selective set of ratios that is of use to *every* agribusiness firm since these firms vary so greatly in size and type.

We present below some of the more commonly used and popular financial ratios that cover the four criteria used for evaluation. In many instances, the ratios discussed can be calculated either before or after taxes, interest and other adjustments. The ratios discussed in the following sections are calculated after interest and taxes. However, a key point to remember when comparing and evaluating ratios is to be consistent with the approach used to calculate the comparative benchmarks.

Selecting the proper ratios

Agribusiness managers should exercise care in selecting those ratios that provide useful information for decision-making in their own unique businesses. Professional advice from outside the business can often be of great help. The first consideration to be made in selecting key ratios is whether the ratios cover those areas of the business where knowledge is critical to good business decisions.

For example, Brookstone Feed and Grain (BF&G) (Chapter 9) would have a high degree of interest in ratios that relate to accounts receivable and inventory because its fertilizer and grain business is so seasonal. Loss of control over either of these important accounts could be fatal to maintaining the firm's liquidity. Large variations in different periods are therefore an important criterion for determining which accounts to analyze. Another factor is the sheer size of an account. A corn processor like National Starch would be extremely aware of changes in costs for direct labor and raw materials, because those costs account for the major portion of production costs. Agribusiness managers must study their own operations and use those financial ratios that are best suited for the unique business involved.

Just a few of the more commonly used and most helpful ratios are discussed below. These ratios will be related to the balance sheet and the income statement for BF&G (review Tables 9.1 and 9.2 in Chapter 9). From a manager's point of view, there are four key criteria to monitor, and hence four types of ratios to explore:

1. Profitability ratios
2. Liquidity ratios
3. Solvency ratios
4. Operating or efficiency ratios

Profitability ratios

Profitability ratios include several different indicators that help assess a firm's profitability and record of performance. The net sales figure is used in three of the five ratios rather than the gross sales figure because sales, after returns, allowances, and discounts provides a more accurate measure of the true sales for a firm. The net sales figure is not inflated by amounts that were ultimately returned to customers in the form of discounts and allowances, or refunds for returned merchandise.

Earnings on sales ratio: *net operating income divided by net sales*. The relationship between net operating income that BF&G generated and net sales (the *earnings on sales* ratio) are shown here:

$$\text{Net Operating Income} \ / \ \text{Net Sales} = \text{EOS}(\text{Earnings on Sales}) \tag{1}$$

$$\$469,190 \ / \ \$13,410,000 = 0.035 \text{ or } 3.5\%$$

$$(\text{From Income Statement, w and a})$$

The earnings on sales ratio (Equation 1) focuses on management decisions that reflect operating efficiency and pricing policy. Earnings may be increased by changes in pricing policy. Low prices may generate increased sales, but could produce zero profits, while higher prices might reduce sales significantly. The pricing strategy must be developed after careful consideration of the competitive environment. Sales forecasts can be helpful in this area, and ratios may be used to improve sales projections. Likewise, a low EOS ratio may indicate costs are out of line. BF&G can attempt, through management decisions, to reduce such things as labor, administrative expenses, and selling costs.

Return on sales ratio: *net income after taxes divided by net sales*. Managers often find it helpful to look at income after all business expenses, including interest and taxes. The *return on sales ratio* is:

$$\text{Net Income After Taxes} \ / \ \text{Net Sales} = \text{ROS} \ (\text{Return on Sales}) \tag{2}$$

$$\$196,650 \ / \ \$13,410,000 = 0.0147 \text{ or } 1.5\%$$

$$(\text{From Income Statement, bb and a})$$

Equation 2 indicates how profitable BF&G was when all costs and other income of the business have been included and compared to overall sales. This ratio is one on which all those interested in BF&G will place a priority, and any deviations will be monitored carefully. ROS is a key ratio for management as it addresses virtually every aspect of their job: marketing and setting prices, purchasing, and cost management.

Return on equity ratio: *net income after taxes divided by owner's equity*. This ratio is probably the most widely used profitability ratio and takes the investor's point of view of the firm. The *return on equity ratio*, which determines the return on investor ownership, is particularly valued by owners when comparing investment opportunities.

$$\text{Net Income After Taxes / Owner's Equity} = \text{ROE}\left(\text{Return on Equity}\right) \qquad (3)$$

$$\$196,650 / \$3,665,000 = 0.0537 \text{ or } 5.4\%$$

$$\left(\text{From Income Statement, bb, and Balance Sheet, qq}\right)$$

This ratio is useful in determining the wisdom of investment in BF&G. It can be invaluable in encouraging additional investment of equity capital if greater cash flow is needed in the business. Stockholders also use this ratio as an indicator of the relative value of their stock.

Return on assets ratio: *net income after taxes plus interest expense divided by total assets*. A slightly different profitability ratio is called the return on assets ratio. This ratio measures the net profit generated on the total investment in the business. The return to the total investment would include not only the return to owners, but also the return to creditors' investment in the business. So interest costs must be added to the net profit. Thus, this ratio is more inclusive than the ROE ratio discussed above. It measures net returns relative to both outsider and insider investment in the business.

$$\left(\text{Net Income After Taxes} + \text{Interest}\right) / \text{Total Assets} = \text{ROA}\left(\text{Return on Assets}\right) \qquad (4)$$

$$\left(\$196,650 + \$230,840\right) / \$6,677,000 = 0.064 \text{ or } 6.4\ \%$$

$$\left(\text{From Income Statement, bb and y, and Balance Sheet, s}\right)$$

Gross margin ratio: *gross margin divided by net sales*. Depending on how the firm's income statement is set up, this may also be called the gross profit ratio. The gross margin ratio shows how much BF&G has left from each dollar of net sales to pay operational and other business expenses plus make a profit.

$$\text{Gross Margin / Net Sales} = \text{GM}\left(\text{Gross Margin Ratio}\right) \qquad (5)$$

$$\left(\$1,685,000\right) / \$13,410,000 = 0.1257 \text{ or } 12.57\%$$

$$\left(\text{From Income Statement, c and a}\right)$$

Here BF&G has 12.57 cents of each sales dollar left to cover expenses and go to profit. As prices and BF&G's product mix (combination of products sold) change, gross margin will also change. More detailed analysis may be needed here if the gross margin is too low. Costs of goods or raw product and shrinkage may be pinpointed for further study. This ratio is crucial. Any drop in gross margin is a signal for immediate managerial action. Small changes here have a great impact on the bottom line.

Liquidity ratios

Liquidity refers to the ability of the firm to meet financial obligations as those obligations come due. Hence the focus of **liquidity ratios** is on assets that can be easily converted to cash, and liabilities that must be paid in the short term, which is often defined as one year but could be a month or quarter. Liquidity ratios are another comparison tool in financial ratio analysis that can be used to help agribusiness professionals more clearly determine short-term cash flow problems. Let's consider some of the most common liquidity ratios that are useful in determining BF&G's ability to meet its short-run obligations. Often firms refer to the amount of working capital needed in their businesses.

Net working capital: *total current assets minus total current liabilities.*

$$\text{Total Current Assets} - \text{Total Current Liabilities} = \text{NWC}(\text{Net Working Capital}) \qquad (6)$$

$$\$4,287,000 - \$1,862,000 = \$2,425,000$$

$$(\text{From Balance Sheet, h and gg})$$

However, this is a dollar figure and, for reasons discussed earlier in this chapter, a ratio of two numbers may provide a better measure of liquidity.

Current ratio: *total current assets divided by total current liabilities.* The current ratio is probably the most popular liquidity ratio. It is calculated as shown below:

$$\text{Total Current Assets} / \text{Total Current Liabilities} = \text{CR}(\text{Current Ratio}) \qquad (7)$$

$$\$4,287,000 / \$1,862,000 = 2.3$$

$$(\text{From Balance Sheet, h and gg})$$

This ratio indicates BF&G's ability to meet its current obligations. In this case, there is $2.30 of current assets for every $1.00 of current debt. In most cases, a current ratio somewhere around 2.0 signifies ample liquidity for the firm.

There is concern among many financial analysts that the current ratio may have some limitations as an indicator of a firm's ability to meet current obligations. The need to quickly liquidate inventories, accounts receivable, marketable securities, etc., to raise cash may cause a sharp decrease in their value. Therefore, managers often use a second ratio that more clearly delineates a firm's ability to meet immediate cash needs.

Quick ratio: *total current assets minus inventory divided by total current liabilities.*

$$(\text{Total Current Assets} - \text{Inventory}) / \text{Total Current Liabilities} = \text{QR}(\text{Quick Ratio}) \qquad (8)$$

$$(\$4,287,000 - \$2,500,000) / \$1,862,000 = 0.96$$

$$(\text{From Balance Sheet, h, e, and gg})$$

For most firms a quick ratio between 0.8 and 1.0 signifies sufficient strength in liquidity. Consequently, at first glance BF&G would appear to have adequate liquidity. However, the ratio would need to be monitored because any difficulty in collecting accounts receivable could cause problems. This ratio is of great interest to lenders of short-term funds. These funds may be needed because any change in value for marketable securities and for accounts receivable could result in their immediate cash values being lower than the ratio indicates.

A new or rapidly growing firm with immediate cash needs for labor, supplies, and goods must be more aware of this ratio than older, more established businesses. The ease of converting inventory to cash must also be considered. It is possible for a firm to be making a profit, and have a strong owner's equity position in relation to total assets, and still be so starved for available cash that it is unable to take advantage of discounts or quantity buying, meet emergencies, or even pay current bills. Bankruptcy results when a firm is unable to pay its bills as they come due, so the liquidity area is one of fundamental concern for agribusiness managers.

Solvency ratios

A third challenge to management is keeping the firm solvent. Solvency is related primarily to a firm's ability to meet all of its claims over the long-run or total liabilities. **Solvency ratios** pinpoint the portions of a business's capital requirements that are being furnished by owners and by lenders. Evaluation of solvency ratios gives an indication of the likelihood that lenders will incur problems in recovering their money. These ratios can have a real effect on the amount of long-term money a firm can borrow and affect alternative sources of outside capital. If creditors supply a greater portion of the total business capital, and, thus, assume a greater share of the risk, they normally would demand more financial documentation and would more closely monitor management's decisions. These ratios can also indicate when a firm should consider borrowing more of its capital needs, with consequent opportunity for increasing return on its own investment.

Debt-to-equity ratio: *total liabilities divided by owner's equity.* This ratio (Equation 9) indicates the relationship of BF&G's owner's equity to the total liabilities of the firm:

Total Liabilities / Owner's Equity = Debt-to-Equity Ratio　　　　　　　　(9)

$3,012,000 / $3,665,000 = 0.82

(From Balance Sheet, ll and qq)

In the case of BF&G, we find a ratio of 0.82 to 1, or total liabilities that are equal to 82.0 percent of owner equity. Interpreted another way, this ratio suggests that for every $1.00 of owner investment in BF&G, there is 82 cents of outsider investment. Lenders tend to get nervous when their investment is greater than that of owners, which would result in a debt-to-equity ratio greater than 1.0.

Here we can see the ownership interest in contrast to the creditor interest in the firm. Some lenders require the 1:1 ratio mentioned above as the absolute upper limit. Changes in this ratio over a period of time can be of great significance in planning long-range financial programs for BF&G. As BF&G is able to continue generating healthy solvency figures, lenders may begin viewing the firm as a good credit risk and offer "preferred customer" status and, potentially lower interest rates.

Solvency ratio: *owner's equity divided by total net assets*. This solvency ratio (Equation 10) shows the relationship between what the owners are contributing toward supporting the firm and the total net assets of the firm.

Owner's Equity / Total Net Assets = Solvency   (10)

$3,665,000 / $3,655,000 = 1.00

(From Balance Sheet, qq, h, gg, q, and kk)

Note that in the equation above, Total Net Assets = Net Working Capital + Net Fixed Assets: that is, Total Net Assets = (h – gg) + (q – kk). Net working capital is calculated by subtracting current liabilities from current assets, and net fixed assets are calculated by subtracting long-term liabilities from fixed assets.

There is no exact standard for every business, but usually if owners contribute less than 50 percent of the total net assets of a firm, one is more likely to find solvency problems developing and to experience difficulty in securing more long- and short-term credit. So this ratio typically needs to be greater than 0.5.

Debt-to-asset ratio: *total liabilities divided by total assets*. The third solvency ratio is used to determine the proportion that lenders are contributing to the total capital of the firm:

Total Liabilities / Total Assets = Debt-to-Asset Ratio   (11)

$3,012,000 / $6,677,000 = 0.45

(From Balance Sheet, ll and s)

Note that the debt-to-asset ratio (Equation 11) conveys the same information as the debt-to-equity ratio (Equation 9). Both ratios are used to report the solvency position of a firm.

Changes in this ratio can signal danger if the lenders' portion becomes excessively high. By the same token, a low percentage invested by lenders could signal the opportunity for expansion or additional borrowing potential. It would appear from this ratio that BF&G could expand its use of debt or liabilities. Expansion plans and current interest rates would be important factors to consider in making this decision. The upper limit lenders assign to this ratio is usually 0.50 or less, which corresponds to a 1:1 upper limit to the debt-to-equity ratio. At 50 percent both outsiders and insiders have equal investments in the firm.

Efficiency ratios

The final area to be discussed in relation to the use of financial ratios is in the area of firm efficiency. This area, in particular, offers the greatest opportunity for BF&G's management to develop unique, meaningful ratios that will be of greatest value to its business in the efficiency or operations area. Here, ratios tend to be highly tailored to fit the specific type of business being evaluated, and the efficiency ratios needed to monitor a retail farm equipment dealership are very different than those used by a soybean processor.

Asset turnover ratio: *net sales divided by total assets*. The asset turnover ratio can be used to determine the intensity with which BF&G's assets are used, as measured by the number of times assets "turn over" in a period:

Net Sales / Total Assets = Asset Turnover (12)

$13,410,000 / $6,677,000 = 2.01

(From Income Statement, a; Balance Sheet, s)

This figure shows that BF&G turned its assets about two times during the year. For this ratio to take on meaning, BF&G managers would have to compare it with the situation in previous years and to the turnover ratio in similar businesses. If last year's turnover ratio had been only 1.8, BF&G would know that it has improved asset utilization. A retail grocer would be very unhappy with this ratio because of the necessity for rapid turnover in that kind of business, while an agricultural producer would be extremely happy with this ratio, since production agriculture tends to use a huge amount of assets relative to sales.

The asset turnover ratio (Equation 12) suggests that the more BF&G can sell with a given set of assets, the higher its return on investment. Many large agribusiness firms use this as a primary measure of effectiveness or efficiency of the management team. Management strategies that affect this ratio are primarily focused on increasing sales volume, using assets more effectively, increasing prices, reducing ineffectively used assets, reducing accounts receivable or inventory, or choosing better alternatives for use of available cash.

Inventory turnover ratio: *cost of goods sold divided by ending inventory*. Another similar, yet more specific measure of efficiency is focused on inventory. In most firms, the inventory turnover ratio is of great concern. A significant portion of a firm's assets may be tied up in inventory:

Cost of Goods Sold / Ending Inventory = Inventory Turnover Ratio (13)

$11,725,000 / $2,500,000 = 4.69

(From Income Statement, b; Balance Sheet, e)

An inventory turnover ratio of 4.7 means BF&G was able to sell its inventory 4.7 times during the course of the previous year. In a different view, BF&G was able to generate $ 4.69 in sales for every $1 invested in inventory.

Here, caution must be used, since the measure of inventory must be meaningful. This is a static reading that is taken. In BF&G, with an extremely seasonal business, the ending inventory is not representative, and could provide a meaningless figure. The manager may need to average beginning and ending inventory; he or she may also take monthly or estimated average inventories to arrive at an acceptable figure. In a firm like BF&G, the typical monthly average would probably be a more valid figure to use in an analysis of inventory efficiency. When comparing the firm's sales level and inventory level, the correct figures must be used. In most cases, firms value inventory on an "at cost" basis. Thus, the cost of goods sold figure must be used as an indicator of sales activity.

The rate of inventory turnover indicates how successfully working capital has been managed. If capital is being tied up in inventory, a higher margin will be required on sales, because too much stock is on hand. Poor inventory management can also add a severe burden, interest expense, if short-term financing at a high rate of interest is being used to finance the investment in inventory. Alternatively, a high rate of inventory turnover could indicate a lost opportunity for sales because of out-of-stock conditions or inability to meet delivery requirements. Agribusiness managers must also consider discounts for early delivery and match these against current interest rates. If BF&G has storage facilities for fertilizer and the discount received from a supplier is greater than its interest cost, profit can be enhanced by adding to inventory levels.

Days sales in accounts receivable ratio: *accounts receivable divided by net sales, and the result multiplied by 360 days*. Another measure of efficiency is found in the average collection period of accounts receivable. An extended period for collection of accounts receivable could indicate that profits might be reduced because of added collection costs, interest on funds needed to support the accounts, and bad-debt losses. On the other hand, too low a figure could indicate that an overly strict credit policy was causing lost sales. Two important criteria should be used; generally, the calculated collection period (1) should match that of others in the industry, and (2) should be at least equal to the time extended by suppliers or vendors of the firm. This important area can be monitored by means of the *days sales in accounts receivable ratio*:

$$\left(\text{Accounts Receivable / Net Sales}\right) \times 360 \text{ days} = \text{Days Sales in Accounts Receivable} \quad (14)$$

$$\left(\$1,600,000 / \$13,410,000\right) \times 360 = 42.95 \text{ days}$$

$$\left(\text{From Balance Sheet, d; Income Statement, a}\right)$$

A firm's credit policy and standing with creditors, as well as changes or trends, should be indicators of efficiency in managing working capital. One of the best rules of thumb in relation to accounts receivable is that the collection period should not exceed the regular payment period by more than one-third. If, for example, the credit policy states that accounts are due in 30 days, the calculated collection period (days sales in accounts receivables) should not exceed 40 days. In the case of BF&G, they are slightly over the 40-day guideline and should evaluate the collection of their accounts receivable.

Caution must be used in evaluating the receivables ratio, because accounts receivable may vary from time to time or due to seasonally in a firm because of the nature of its business or general economic conditions, and these factors should always be taken into consideration when interpreting the ratio.

To aid the manager in monitoring accounts receivable the following measures can also be used.

Aging accounts receivable: *reporting accounts receivable on a monthly basis in accordance with the number of days since the accounts receivable was charged to the customer*. The most important tool in monitoring a credit program and accounts receivable is the monthly aging of accounts receivable. Each account from the ledger is summarized in a report similar to the one shown in Table 10.3. An increase in the

Plate 10.2 Grocery inventory
Monitoring inventory levels and the collection of accounts receivable are critical when managing an agribusiness. Photo courtesy of USDA.

Table 10.3 Account aging schedule

Period Outstanding	Accounts Receivable	Percentage of Total This Period	Percentage of Total Last Period	Percentage Change
Less than 30 days	$672,000	42	41	2.4
30–60 days	560,000	35	34	2.9
61–90 days	256,000	16	17	(5.9)
Over 90 days	112,000	7	8	(12.5)
Total	$1,600,000	100	100	

percentage of accounts that are slow paying, or increasing amounts of receivables, calls for additional emphasis on the collection of accounts receivable and a review of the credit program and credit policies before the situation becomes dangerous to the firm's financial health.

Percentage change in credit sales: *credit sales for the current period divided by the credit sales for a previous period.* This ratio can also be used to assist in monitoring changes in accounts receivable. In order to put the accounts receivable situation for the firm into a historical context, the percentage change ratio can be used to assess changes in credit sales volume from one period to another:

$$(\text{Credit Sales for Current Period} / \text{Credit Sales for Previous Period}) \times 100 \qquad (15)$$
$$= \text{Percentage Change in Credit Sales}$$

This simple ratio provides a quick indication as to how the proportion of credit sales is changing over time.

Bad debts as a percentage of credit sales: *amount of bad debts divided by total accounts receivable multiplied by 100.* Bad debts are an agribusiness manager's nightmare. When the agribusiness sells products and then fails to collect the amount of those sales, it is far worse than not making the sale at all. Not only does the business suffer from the loss in gross margin, but it also has to chalk up the loss from the cost of the goods or service sold, plus the aggravation and cost of trying (usually unsuccessfully) to collect the debt. One simple way to monitor bad debts is the formula:

$$(\text{Bad Debts} / \text{Total Credit Sales}) \times 100 = \text{Bad Debts as a \% of Credit Sales} \qquad (16)$$

This figure can be tracked over time and checked regularly to insure it is within predetermined bounds.

The cost of bad debts is very serious for many agribusinesses. Table 10.4 provides a better understanding of just how seriously this cost affects business profits. The tremendous amount of sales increase necessary to offset bad debt loss is vividly demonstrated in this table. For example, a $5,000 bad debt requires an increase in sales of at least $50,000 at a 10 percent contribution margin on sales just to bring profits back to what they were without the bad debt. The contribution margin for BF&G is 10.36 percent. (The contribution margin is gross margin less variable costs. This figure is discussed further in Chapter 12.) Credit sales have to be monitored very carefully or they can quickly consume all the profits a business is generating. Because the stakes are so high, a carefully conceived and executed credit program is necessary for any agribusiness and its management team.

Wage efficiency ratio: *labor cost divided by net sales.* A number of efficiency ratios can be developed by exploring relationships between costs and sales. These should be unique and meaningful to the individual business and to the type of industry. In this area,

Table 10.4 Sales increases required to offset bad debt losses

Bad Debt Loss($)	Contribution Margin ($)		
	5%	10%	20%
	(You must increase sales by the amount.)		
1,000	20,000	10,000	5,000
5,000	100,000	50,000	25,000
20,000	400,000	200,000	100,000

management should be operating on predetermined control standards of efficiency. Only one specialized efficiency ratio will be examined here, the wage efficiency ratio (Equation 17). However, numerous other ratios can be used. Two other popular ratios are sales per square foot and administrative costs per dollar of sales:

Labor Cost / Net Sales = Wage Efficiency Ratio $\qquad$ (17)

$\$440,040 / \$13,410,000 = 0.033$ or 3.3%

(From Income Statement, e, f, g, h, t, and a)

The wage efficiency ratio is calculated by summing all of the operating expenses related to labor (i.e., salaries and benefits, full-time wages, part-time wages, commissions and payroll tax) and then dividing that amount by net sales to determine the wage cost as a percentage of net sales, which can then be compared to previous periods or comparative data.

It is particularly important for management to monitor labor costs, especially if the business is expanding through new product lines or if new equipment is being added to the business.

Summary of ratio analysis

1. Many ratios can be expressed in reverse order; that is, "sales to receivables" to one person may be "receivables to sales" to another. Either is correct, but the interpretation should also be reversed.
2. All ratio comparisons should be based on similar data from similar businesses; to compare the "sales to fixed assets" ratio of a breakfast cereal manufacturing firm to the same ratio for a small veterinary clinic would be meaningless.
3. In addition to comparisons of ratios between companies, comparisons of ratios from period to period for the same agribusiness are often useful. Seasonality, for example, in many agribusinesses dictates that a variety of ratios must be evaluated monthly or quarterly with different goals for each period.
4. Monitoring trends is an important aspect of financial ratio analysis. For example, gradually improving ratios are more impressive than static, declining or highly variable ratios.
5. The development and use of a large number of financial ratios may be confusing. Hence, ratios should be specifically selected with regard to the nature of the problems for which solutions are desired within the firm.
6. In addition to ratios from balance sheet and/or income statement accounts, ratios related to the physical nature of the business are often used as measures of efficiency. For example, inventory throughput ratios, i.e., tons spread per day or per truck might be used by a firm like BF&G. These may be called management ratios, physical efficiency ratios, or general efficiency ratios.
7. At their best, ratios are aids to better decision-making within the agribusiness, not substitutes for it. They should be used in tandem with other financial tools to properly assess performance.

Limitations of financial ratio analysis

Because financial ratio analysis is being used extensively today, there is a potential for misuse of the technique. In spite of their advantages, financial ratios are merely indicators of performance. If a particular facet of the business is headed for trouble, a change in a ratio can only sound a warning. Even a drastic change in a given ratio may not isolate and identify the actual cause of the problem. More often than not, additional analysis is required before the appropriate corrective action can be taken. Care must be taken to ensure that all comparisons are between genuinely similar elements. Some of the more general limitations of financial ratios are discussed below. In addition, each specific ratio may have limitations that are unique to its use, and many of these were highlighted above.

Changes in the accounting methods of the agribusiness itself, or differences between the firm's accounting methods and those of similar firms, may limit the use of ratios. If BF&G were to change the way it values inventory, assets, and/or change its depreciation method, comparisons of its ratios with ratios of previous periods would lose validity.

Time factors also pose a significant constraint on ratio analysis. Financial statements are indicative of one period of time. Comparing one monthly period to a different monthly period or to a yearly statement can present a distorted view of the business, because of the seasonality aspects of some businesses. Comparing BF&G's January accounts receivable as a percentage of current assets to its July accounts receivable percentage would provide a comparison that would be virtually useless, because of the seasonality aspects of the business. Bad information or analysis can be worse than no information at all.

Also, extraordinary items can distort the financial ratios for a firm. A one-time revenue or expense is an example of such a distortion. The gain or loss resulting from the extraordinary sale of a capital item can distort financial ratios, since this sale is not part of the routine business for the firm.

As mentioned in Chapter 9, the use of income statement data using the cash basis of accounting can result in tremendous variation and distortion in profitability and efficiency ratios. Data from income statements prepared using the accrual basis of accounting should be used whenever possible for calculating financial ratios.

The profitability analysis model

Three fundamental measures of how well the business is being managed are (1) return on sales, (2) return on assets, and (3) leverage. The combination of these very important financial relationships into a single ratio, return on equity or ROE, provides one of the most useful financial tools available to measure the performance of the agribusiness and to assess the skill and ability of the management team. Many sophisticated managers, bankers, investors, and boards of directors depend on this conceptual measure as the primary gauge of a business's success.

ROE in perspective

Figure 10.1 shows the step-by-step process of developing an ROE analysis model. This model is called the profitability model or profitability analysis system. Sometimes, this type of analysis is also referred to as the DuPont model. ROE is measured here in terms of return on equity. The diagram illustrates the three key component ratios which individually and together affect ROE. Management can use this chart as a tracking system or early warning system to determine when action is needed if the firm is to continue to move toward its ROE goals.

Figure 10.1 indicates that ROE is directly affected by (1) the earnings from sales (net income after taxes divided by net sales), (2) the intensity assets are used, measured by asset turnover (net sales divided by total assets), and (3) the use of outsiders' funds to expand the

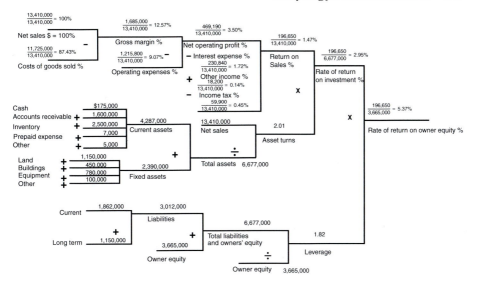

Figure 10.1 Profitability analysis model for Brookstone Feed and Grain company

business, measured by the leverage ratio (total assets divided by owner's equity). These three areas can be considered "paths to profit" and anything that impacts one of the three paths will impact ROE. One path, measured by the return on sales ratio, is the operating path. Here managers worry about sales and expenses. The second path is the asset efficiency path, measured by the asset turnover ratio. On this path, managers worry about making efficient use of the assets invested in the firm. The final path is the debt path. This path is measured by the leverage ratio. Here, managers focus on using debt in a profitable way. So, for a manager who wants to improve ROE, there are three possible paths to pursue—operations, asset efficiency, and debt. The step-by-step process for constructing the profitability analysis model is illustrated using the financial statements for BF&G (Tables 9.1 and 9.2).

Each of these paths to profit is important to reaching the firm's profit goal, and should be carefully considered. The top part of Figure 10.1 relates to the earnings picture and helps the manager focus on operating problems related to personnel, pricing, product mix, etc. Careful control of expenses is essential, and monitoring systems must be implemented to deal with internal as well as external changes over time, i.e., internal personnel and management decisions versus decisions driven by external factors such as competition. As can be seen in Figure 10.1 cost of goods sold (87.43 percent), operating expenses (9.07 percent), interest expense (1.72 percent), other income (0.14 percent), and the tax expense (0.45 percent) are all divided by net sales to calculate each as a percentage of net sales.

The asset turnover concept, the second part of the profitability analysis model, suggests that the higher the sales volume produced with a given set of assets, the higher the firm's ROE. For example, as more feed and grain are sold for BF&G, the associated assets are being utilized more effectively, up to a point. A firm may attempt to push volume to a level at which physical processing or handling capacity is reached. However, the cost of squeezing out the marginal volume may be prohibitive as these capacity limits are approached.

In the asset utilization area, managers must frequently evaluate their investment in assets; when should equipment be replaced, what fixed facilities are needed and what should be rented, whether inventories can be reduced without reducing sales, how extra cash should be invested, etc. All of these decisions relate directly to asset efficiency and indirectly back to the ROE ratio.

When return on sales (1.47 percent) is multiplied by the asset turnover ratio (2.01), the result is the return on investment (2.95 percent). Note that the **return on investment (ROI)** used in this model differs slightly from ROA. ROI has the interest expense subtracted from net operating income, whereas ROA includes the interest expense as a return to assets.

The third critical area of the profitability analysis system relates to solvency via financial leverage, or use of debt. Should the firm expand, given an acceptable solvency ratio? What implications does expansion have for the firm's future earnings? Can a larger firm be managed as efficiently? Obviously these are all tough questions faced by management, stockholders, bankers, etc. However, careful evaluation of the solvency relationship helps managers better understand how use of debt will impact the profitability of the business. For BF&G, total liabilities and owner's equity ($6,677,000) is divided by owner's equity ($3,665,000) for a leverage ratio of 1.82.

Improvements in any of the three individual ratios, or paths, will improve profitability as measured by ROE. It is important for the manager to understand that these ratios are inter-related; changes in one may affect performance in the others. Thus, the final impact of a given change in the firm's ROE must be viewed as a dynamic relationship among these three separate ratios. For example, using more debt will raise the leverage ratio, which would tend to increase ROE. However, more debt also means more interest expense, which will reduce ROE. Both the leverage affect and the ROS effect must be considered to determine the final impact on ROE.

Price is an important consideration

When a price increases, some customers will shift to other firms and some will remain. If it were foreseen that most customers would stay despite the price increase, the earning power would rise because any reduction in asset turnover would be offset by an increase in the firm's gross margin.

If the firm lowered prices, hopefully an increase in the asset turnover would offset the decline in gross margin. But the question is: how much will sales be increased, or what is the "elasticity" of demand (see Chapter 3)?

Successful use of a low margin and high asset turnover strategy is evident in the rapid increase in the number and patronage of discount firms and warehouse stores. Generally, businesses with a low turnover will have a high margin, and firms with a high turnover will have a low margin, which is the case with the discount firms.

ROE, or the earning power of the business, offers the advantage of bringing together in a single figure the complex relationship of asset turnover and return on sales, and allows managers additional insights into how decisions and changes made in either area affect the other. Decision-making in any agribusiness does not occur in a vacuum. An attempt to control inventory or reduce assets is likely to affect sales. Certain items may be out of stock, for instance, and some sales will be lost. The use of ROE and the profitability analysis model will help the agribusiness manager gauge the effects of such decisions on overall earning power.

While ROE is certainly not a ratio that can be compared from agribusiness to agribusiness on an unqualified basis, it does offer a more easily compared measure of different firms' resources than almost any other ratio. For this reason, ROE is considered the most accurate measure of effective resource use by managers, boards of directors, lending institutions, investors, and others interested in the business. The ROE is sensitive enough so that even small changes in trends should cause the manager to be pleased (if it is improving) and try more of the same, or to be concerned (if it is declining) and begin searching for methods of improvement.

Changes in figures on the asset turnover, return on sales, or leverage ratios, can also point to or help identify places where problems or opportunities arise. For example, BF&G might note a drop in its ROE figure and see that the asset turnover figure was up slightly, but the ROS ratio was down somewhat. In this instance, the firm could concentrate its management efforts on such areas as sales expenses or administrative costs or the selling price. Careful use of ROE through the profitability analysis model can be the single most helpful indicator of complete firm performance available to the agribusiness manager. By classifying expenses into categories on the income statement (sales, administration, etc.), and by combining income statement and balance sheet data into an easily understood format, problems and opportunities can be more easily located to take corrective action.

Graphing to increase understanding

Simple graphs of financial ratios often enhance the ability of managers to interpret financial data and information. Graphing of important ratios, for example, allows additional periods and time spans to be compared and the more time, or periods, or ways in which something can be compared, the more meaningful the data become (Figure 10.2).

The graph illustrates the impact of a period when BF&G lowered prices from period 5 to period 11. Asset turnover increased (the solid line in Figure 10.12), but at the same time,

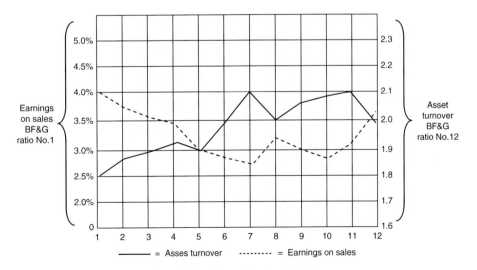

Figure 10.2 Graph of key ratios for Brookstone Feed and Grain company

Plate 10.3 Nursery
Graphing financial information can help a manager determine underlying trends and patterns. This approach can enhance the evaluation of performance across time periods. Photo courtesy of USDA.

earnings on sales (the dashed line in Figure 10.2) decreased as a percentage. If another factor, ROE, was compared, BF&G could measure visually the net effect of price changes, and plan its sales strategy accordingly. Monthly reassessment by means of these ratios would allow BF&G to see whether its plans were still on target.

Graphing increases comprehension by presenting a visual picture and it allows for comparison of separate aspects of financial information in a very clear manner. A graph also can be widely distributed to less sophisticated members of the management team for use in decision-making, since it is easier to conceptualize than a set of numbers.

Summary

Financial statements provide a wealth of information for a variety of persons and organizations interested in evaluating the agribusiness. Owners, managers, lenders, and government agencies all look at financial statements from a different perspective.

Analysis of financial statements is often comparative: over time, against budget, or relative to similar firms. Ratios show important financial relationships in the business. These ratios must be understood and used carefully or they will be misleading. If ratios are used properly, they are indicators of strengths and weaknesses in the business.

Ratios generally measure the important criteria of profitability, liquidity, solvency, and efficiency. There are important ratios for each area that provide useful indicators of performance. Return on the owner's investment (return on equity or ROE) is the most fundamental measure of profitability. The profitability analysis model shows the relationship of profit, sales, assets, and owner's equity. Sometimes graphing financial ratios over time is a highly valuable management tool.

One of the areas in which development of a strong control system is most important is credit, where upward spiraling costs often cause serious financial problems for agribusinesses. Two possible solutions are to make the extension of credit a profit center or to offer a discount for cash sales. In any event, credit programs should be planned and monitored carefully in order to develop systems for determining a customer's credit-worthiness and for minimizing accounts receivable or outright bad debts.

Financial analysis is a fundamental tool for the agribusiness manager. Although it is not a substitute for good judgment, financial analysis gives the manager important insights for improved decision-making.

Discussion questions

1. Discuss the major value to agribusiness managers of evaluating the financial condition and performance of the firm.
2. Discuss the value of common-size analysis to the agribusiness manager. What insights do these statements provide?
3. Describe what financial ratios a general manager, the president of the firm's bank, a prospective investor, and a government official might track in an agribusiness. Explain your reasoning.
4. What are the major categories of financial ratios? Do all the categories need to be evaluated for every firm? Why?
5. What are two reasons why an agribusiness firm might need to evaluate ratios monthly? Under what circumstances would a less frequent financial evaluation be sufficient?
6. List the limitations of ratio analysis for the agribusiness manager. What key issues must the agribusiness manager be aware of if he or she is going to use financial ratios effectively?
7. What criteria should the agribusiness manager use to select the financial ratios the firm will monitor?
8. What are the advantages of using the profitability analysis model as an analysis tool for agribusiness managers? What specific ratios are used in the profitability analysis model to calculate ROE?
9. What specific actions might agribusiness managers take if the earnings side (ROS) of the profitability analysis model was below the desired level? And if the asset turnover side was below the desired level?
10. How is the leverage ratio (debt path) related to the ROS (operating path) and asset turnover (asset efficiency path)? If the amount of debt used in the firm increases, how will ROE be impacted?
11. Discuss the merits of graphing ratios. What insights does graphing provide to an agribusiness manager?

Case study: ABC farm supply store

Use the following condensed financial statements (Tables 10.5 and 10.6) from the ABC farm supply store to develop a profitability analysis model for the company.

Table 10.5 ABC farm supply store condensed balance sheet (in dollars)

Assets	
Current Assets:	
—Cash	171,000
—Accounts receivable	698,000
—Inventory	897,000
Total current assets	1,766,000
Total fixed assets	2,482,000
Total assets	4,248,000
Liabilities and Owner's Equity	
Current Liabilities:	
Accounts payable	483,000
Notes payable	565,000
Total current liabilities	1,048,000
Long-term liabilities	2,000,000
Total liabilities	3,048,000
Owner's contribution	1,000,000
Retained earnings	200,000
Total Owner's Equity	1,200,000
Total liabilities and owner's equity	4,248,000

Table 10.6 ABC farm supply store condensed income statement (in dollars)

Net Sales	5,215,000
Cost of goods sold	3,285,450
Gross margin	1,929,550
Operating expenses	1,202,423
Administrative expenses	320,646
Other expenses	80,161
Total operating expenses	1,603,230
Net operating income	326,320
Interest expense	152,400
Net income before taxes	173,920
Income tax	42,480
Net income after taxes	131,440

Questions

1. Follow the step-by-step formula shown in Figure 10.1 and develop a profitability analysis model for ABC Farm Supply Store. What is the firm's ROE?
2. When the profitability analysis model has been completed, calculate and interpret at least one profitability, liquidity, solvency, and efficiency ratio, using the information in Tables 10.5 and 10.6.
3. What are some strengths and weaknesses of the ABC Farm Supply Store identified by your ratio analysis? What other information would be helpful to you in answering this question?

Reference

Truth in Lending, Regulation Z, Supervision Manual, Board of Governors of the Federal Reserve System. Washington, DC, 2011.

11 Financing the agribusiness

Objectives

- Discuss the reasons an agribusiness may choose to increase its financial resources
- Describe the alternative types of capital available to the agribusiness
- Outline the various types of loans available to the agribusiness and the situation that would cause the agribusiness to select each specific type
- Explain how specific variables impact the annual percentage rate (APR) paid on a loan
- Discuss the relationship between the agribusiness firm's tax rate and APR
- Show the usefulness of the cash budget in making loan requests
- Learn and apply the steps for developing budgets
- Understand qualitative and quantitative techniques for developing forecasts and budgets
- Understand the usefulness of pro forma financial statements in financial planning
- List some of the important external sources of financing
- Discuss leasing alternatives used in agriculture, including land, operating, custom hire, and capital leases
- Describe the means of generating capital funds internally and the importance of this financing alternative

Introduction

Cash is king. Proper cash management is the lifeblood of any agribusiness. Although money itself is not capital, it represents the amount of capital a firm could control. Cash is needed for financing such assets as machinery and equipment, accounts receivable, materials, and supplies. This is why the managers of an agribusiness are expected to be experts in cash management.

Managers must make sure sales on credit (accounts receivable) turn into cash for the firm, that inventories are maintained and sold to generate cash, and that cash is available to meet short-term financial commitments—both planned and those unforeseen. Whenever and wherever financial resources are secured, money is used in the enterprise with the full expectation that it will be returned with a profit. This profit-making ability is essential for the viability of the firm, and the manager who lacks this expertise will find the agribusiness hard pressed for funds.

There are three sources from which the manager may raise the funds needed to operate an agribusiness: (1) investment by owners, (2) borrowing, or (3) funds generated by profits and retained in the business. In most medium-to-large businesses, the major source of funds (over 50 percent) is the owner's equity in the firm (also called "owned capital"). The larger the company, the more it depends on owner's equity as a source of funds. One major reason for this is that larger companies usually enjoy access to public offerings for their stock or equity, and possess the ability to attract investors, a situation that is not shared by smaller companies. Whatever the kind or size of a business, its ability to generate profits will ultimately determine the amount of funds that are made available for its use.

Reasons for increasing financial resources

The ultimate reason for increasing the financial resources of an agribusiness is to increase its revenues, and ultimately its profits, by generating additional business. Extra funds are used for general purposes, to increase liquidity or the cash position, or for expansion and growth. An agribusiness may find that its funds are tied up in current or fixed assets and that it is unable to meet its day-to-day obligations. Bills cannot be paid with such non-liquid assets as accounts receivable, inventory, new orders, or a piece of equipment. Consequently, an agribusiness requires working capital in the form of cash. The principal source of cash must be the revenue generated by the business itself, but in short-term situations additional cash may be required to meet the day-to-day obligations of the business. This is particularly true of the many agribusinesses that are highly seasonal in nature. In this case, cash funds can become tied up in inventory and in accounts receivable, which will not be turned into cash until some later date. As a rule, many agribusinesses find it advisable to keep on hand enough cash to equal 20 to 25 percent of the amount of their current liabilities. This helps ensure the firm's ability to make short-term payments as well as any unexpected obligations.

The most important use for additional financial resources is for expansion. Expansion can require either a short- or long-term commitment of funds. Short-term expansion involves such factors as increased labor, inventories, and accounts receivable. Long-run expansion encourages more ambitious projects, such as the purchase of new equipment, buildings, and land. The objective of increasing the **capital** of an agribusiness is to increase its sales volume and revenues, and consequently its profit, through the shrewd application of increased assets. Capital, or the financial resources of a business, comprises in its broadest sense all the assets of that business, and represents funds provided by the owners of the firm and the contributions by outsiders.

Determining when financial resources should be increased

As an agribusiness manager considers the possibility of acquiring additional financial resources, several questions should be asked and carefully answered:

1. Why are additional funds needed?
2. How does the use of additional funds fit with the overall mission of the business?
3. What increases in revenue, profit, and/or net cash flow will be generated by the additional funds?
4. What sources are available to provide additional funds?
5. How much will these additional funds cost the agribusiness?
6. How much is needed in the way of additional financial resources?
7. When is this increase in revenue flow expected?
8. When will these additional funds be needed?
9. For what time period will these additional funds be needed?

10. If the funds are borrowed, how will the indebtedness be repaid?
11. How will this indebtedness affect profit?
12. How will this indebtedness affect liquidity and solvency?
13. What risk is involved that may delay the time period when funds may be repaid?

The manager who is seeking additional financial resources for the agribusiness should use the foregoing as a checklist to select the one alternative that is likely to be the most beneficial to the firm.

Davies Farm Structures, Inc.

Doug Davies started his farm-building company some 20 years ago with $1,000 in cash he had saved plus $1,000 he had borrowed from the bank. Today, Doug's company is a corporation that is owned primarily by members of the family. Doug is currently investigating an expansion opportunity, and his opportunity will be used to illustrate some of the decisions involved in financing an agribusiness.

Doug's current annual sales exceed $2 million, and although he now erects some commercial and public buildings, his major source of revenue remains farm buildings of various kinds. His workforce often exceeds 50 people. Recently, Doug was offered the opportunity to purchase a small lumberyard in Roland, a town of 6,500 people. The lumberyard had a yearly gross of over $750,000 and was earning 15 percent on owner equity and 5 percent on sales in net income after taxes. Doug had used the financial tools discussed in previous chapters to analyze the business, and felt the lumberyard would be a great opportunity to expand and integrate into his own business. He knew that he had two expansion alternatives: either to expand his current operation or to diversify his business. He saw the lumberyard as an opportunity to do both.

Doug analyzed a number of advantages. His analysis of the lumberyard revealed that it could benefit from an increase in inventory turnover. By combining his building company's needs for lumber with the lumberyard's need for increased sales, he could increase the sales volume of the lumberyard by about 70 percent. The added purchasing volume for the construction company would allow him to buy lumber more cheaply because he could buy it in greater quantities and in full carloads. He could also consolidate his storage and handling operations and operate more efficiently because he would be located on a rail siding. His offices and entire operation could be moved to one location, and he determined that combining the operation would result in lower administrative costs.

With savings in cost of goods sold and administrative expenses, along with more operational efficiency, he foresaw the potential of lowering the prices for both businesses and being more competitive in both marketplaces. His projections showed that even if he lowered prices by 5 percent and assumed existing sales volumes for the two operations, he could maintain existing gross margins. But he hoped that the lowered price would help sales eventually climb as much as 50 to 75 percent because of his strongly competitive price position and his positive image in the farm structure business. At this point, the future looked very bright for Doug and his family. They felt they had successfully addressed questions 1, 2, and 3: "Why are additional funds needed?", "How does the use of additional funds fit with the overall mission of the business?" and "What increases in revenue, profit, and/or cash flow will be generated by the additional funds?" While Doug's own company was in a very comfortable position financially, he knew that he would have to secure added financial resources to purchase and operate the lumberyard. The balance of this chapter will relate to the major tools and alternatives that Doug Davies should consider in making this expansion decision.

Debt or equity financing

The next question that Doug had to ask himself was, "What sources are available to provide the additional funds?" Basically, there are four types of capital:

1. Short-term loans: one year or less
2. Intermediate-term loans: one to five years
3. Long-term loans: more than five years
4. Equity capital: no due date

Short-term loans

Short-term loans are generally defined as loans for one year or less, and they are used whenever the requirement for additional funds is temporary. Doug recognized the need for funds to increase inventory for the spring and summer, when the building business is at its seasonal peak. Some of these funds would also be needed to support accounts receivable as inventory is sold to customers. An important characteristic of short-term loans is that they are usually self-liquidating, that is, they often start a chain reaction process that results in their repayment:

Loan = > inventories = > receivables = > cash = > repay loan

While short-term loans may be made on an unsecured basis to firms that are well established, there is often a requirement for collateral, or for the loan to be secured by some of the firm's assets. Collateral can take many forms, but for short-term loans it most often takes the form of current assets. Some of the most common kinds of collateral are inventory, accounts receivable, warehouse receipts, and marketable securities. Also, a personal guarantee of the loan is often required by the owners of smaller agribusinesses. In other words, the owner or owners endorse the obligation to repay the debt, and become personally liable if the firm is unable to meet the payment.

Short-term loans may be regular-term loans, with a specific amount due at a specified time, or they may be revolving or line of credit loans. Managers who anticipate a need for short-term funds often apply for a line of credit in advance of their needs. A **line of credit** is a commitment by the lender to make available a certain sum of money to the firm, usually for a one-year period and at a specified rate of interest, at whatever time the firm needs the loan. Usually, the loan must be repaid during the operating year of the firm.

With a line of credit, a manager is assured of protection in the form of cash that is available as it is needed; there is also the added advantage of not incurring interest on the borrowed funds until they are actually used. Lenders who make a line of credit available to an agribusiness often require that a monthly copy of the firm's financial statements be furnished to them so that they can monitor the financial health of the firm. Doug Davies wanted to avail himself of a line of credit for his short-term cash needs for seasonal purposes. He did not feel that he would have a problem securing these funds because he could pledge his inventory and accounts receivable as collateral against any outstanding loans.

It is important for the agribusiness manager to recognize that short-term borrowing is only appropriate for temporary uses. When, for example, funds are borrowed to increase inventories in order to accommodate increased sales volumes, and the loan is expected to remain in force for some time, a more permanent form of funds is needed. Such a permanent loan will increase the total working capital of the firm. Likewise, short-term loans should not be used to acquire fixed assets whose repayment term will likely be much longer than one year.

Intermediate-term loans

Intermediate-term loans are typically used to provide capital for one to five years. Such a loan is almost always amortized; that is, the process in which the amount of a loan is reduced by equal, periodic (i.e., monthly, quarterly, annual, etc.) loan payments. These payments include both interest and principal. A simple illustration is provided in Table 11.1.

The purpose of the intermediate-term loan is to provide the agribusiness with a source of capital that will allow growth or modernization without forcing the owners to surrender control of the business. These loans allow for additional working capital, which can be used to increase revenues and sales; the funds generated by the increased revenues will, in turn, help to retire the loan.

In many respects the intermediate-term loan is similar to the short-term loan. Most require some sort of collateral and/or security against fixed assets, if that is the purpose of the loan. Intermediate-term loans provide permanent increases in capital for the agribusiness whenever larger inventories, larger accounts receivable, new equipment, and/or modernization are essential to the growth and profitability of the firm. Doug Davies foresaw a need for an intermediate-term loan. He wanted to increase both his accounts receivable and his inventory as he acquired the lumberyard. He also needed funds to pay for moving and consolidating his operation at the new central site.

Long-term loans

In general, **long-term loans** have a duration of more than five years. The time distinctions among these loans are somewhat arbitrary, and there is some overlap in the functions of intermediate- and long-term loans, depending on the philosophies and policies of lender and borrower. But the real difference between intermediate- and long-term loans usually rests

Table 11.1 Example of the repayment schedule for a $5000 loan[a]

End of Year	(1) Payment ($)	(2) Interest[b] ($)	(3) Principal (1–2) ($)	(4) Balance ($)[c]
0				5,000.00
1	2,010.54	500.00	1,510.54	3,489.46
2	2,010.54	348.95	1,661.59	1,827.87
3	2,010.66[d]	182.79	1,827.87	0

Notes: [a] Amortized with three equal annual payments and a 10 percent interest rate.
[b] Calculate by multiplying the balance at the start of the year by the contractual rate of interest (10 percent).
[c] Balance at the start of the year minus the principal payments [column (3)] for the year.
[d] Sometimes the last payment must be adjusted slightly to completely repay the loan due to rounding.

with the planned use for the funds, as well as with the long-term prospects for the existence of the firm and its solvency. The purpose of the long-term loan is most often for real estate, that is, for land and buildings. As the lender examines requests for long-term loans, he or she becomes deeply concerned with evaluating the past track record of the firm, the skill and ability of the management team, and the stability of the business enterprise. The collateral for long-term loans is usually a mortgage or claim on the fixed assets of the firm, and the longer the period of the loan, the riskier it becomes for the lender. There is always the chance that an unstable enterprise will be forced to dispose of fixed assets in a forced sale, where these assets may bring only a fraction of their value at the time the loan was closed.

Long-term loans are nearly always amortized over the loan period and secured by a mortgage or claim on a specific fixed asset. Sometimes bonds are used to secure long-term capital, but a small firm seldom has the size or financial strength to sell a bond issue. Because Doug Davies plans to build new storage facilities at his new site as well as enlarge the office building to accommodate the consolidated business, he will also need a long-term loan.

Equity capital

If the agribusiness is not in a strong financial position (solvency is discussed in Chapter 10) or cannot meet the stiff collateral requirements set by lenders, it may have to turn to equity capital to meet its long-term needs. **Equity capital** can be used for the same purpose as borrowed funds, but there is an important difference: equity capital does not have to be repaid. It becomes a permanent part of the capital of the business. Equity capital is secured either by reinvesting profits from the business or by finding investors who are willing to invest additional funding in the business.

Lenders pay particular attention to equity when they are making long-term loan commitments, and they may insist that a larger percentage of the owner's money be invested in the capital of the agribusiness than the lenders'. This is particularly true of new businesses, where risks are more difficult to calculate. Some owners do not wish to increase their equity for various reasons, but it may be the only prudent way of securing long-term capital funds. Doug Davies will strongly consider expanding his equity base. Inasmuch as his business is already organized as a corporation, it will be easier for him to make the move should he so desire. (A more detailed analysis will appear later in the chapter.)

The cost of capital

When a business borrows money, it incurs special costs that are paid to the lender. One of these is **interest**, but interest is not the only cost of borrowing money. Several other factors affect the net cost of borrowed capital:

1. Repayment terms and conditions
2. Compensatory balances, points, and stock investments
3. The income tax bracket of the firm

Repayment terms

The repayment terms and conditions directly affect the rate of interest that is actually paid. If Doug Davies borrowed $100,000 for one year at the stated interest rate of 8 percent, the amount of interest paid would be $8,000. At the end of the year Doug would pay the lender

$108,000, and his interest rate would have been the same as the stated rate of 8 percent because he used the entire $100,000 for the entire year. This type of interest is called **simple interest**. The formula for simple interest is:

$$(\text{Amount of Interest Paid} / \text{Amount of Available Capital}) \times 100$$
$$= \text{Annual Interest Rate}$$
$$(\$8,000 / \$100,000) \times 100 = 8\%$$

Sometimes, however, loans are **discounted**, which means that the amount of interest to be paid is deducted from the amount the lender makes available to the borrower. If this method had been used in Doug's case, the $8,000 interest to be paid, or $0.08 \times \$100,000$, would have been deducted from the loan amount, and Doug would have had the use of only $92,000 in capital. The discounted loan formula is as follows:

$$\text{Amount of Loan} - \text{Amount of Interest Paid} = \text{Amount of Available Capital}$$

At the end of the year, $100,000 would have been repaid to the lender; but because Doug had the use of only $92,000, the "effective" interest rate was not the stated rate. The "effective" interest rate for a discounted loan is calculated as follows:

$$(\text{Amount of Interest Paid} / \text{Amount of Available Capital}) \times 100$$
$$= \text{Annual Effective Interest Rate}$$
$$(\$8,000 / \$92,000) \times 100 = 8.7\%$$

The cost of interest on this discounted loan was then 8.7 percent and not the stated rate of 8 percent, because Doug did not get to use the entire amount borrowed even though he paid interest on the entire amount for the entire time the money was borrowed.

Banks often require that borrowers have a **compensating balance** in their accounts at the lending bank. To obtain a $100,000 loan, Doug might be required to maintain a minimum balance of $20,000 in his company bank account while the loan is outstanding. This means that he would have the use of only $80,000 in additional capital from the loan, while paying interest on the entire amount borrowed for the entire time the money was borrowed. The formula for calculating the effective rate of interest in this case is:

$$(\text{Amount of Interest Paid} / \text{Amount of Available Capital}) \times 100$$
$$= \text{Annual Effective Interest Rate}$$
$$(\$8,000 / \$80,000) \times 100 = 10\%$$

If Doug normally carries a cash balance, this amount could be deducted from the compensating balance to lessen the increase of the effective interest cost.

Sometimes lending institutions also require that a certain number of **points** (service charges based on the face value of the loan) be paid to obtain the loan. These charges for risk and loan servicing are made in advance, and the amounts charged are usually deducted from the total amount borrowed at the time the loan is made. If Doug borrowed $100,000 at 8 percent with two points, his total loan cost would be:

$$\$100,000 \times 0.08 \rightarrow \$8,000 \rightarrow \text{interest}$$
$$+100,000 \times 0.02 \rightarrow \$2,000 \rightarrow \text{points}$$
$$\text{Total cost} \rightarrow \$100,000$$

Thus, a point amounts to 1 percent of the value of the loan.

Another demand that lenders sometimes make is that the borrower purchase a certain amount of stock in the lending institution, an amount that is determined by the value of the loan. The lender might require the purchase of one share of stock, valued at $10, for each $1,000 that is borrowed. In reality, this is a form of discounting that can be used to determine the effective cost of the loan. Actual or effective interest rates must be revealed to individual borrowers by commercial lenders under federal truth-in-lending laws, but this law applies to consumer loans and time purchases. It does not apply to most commercial or business transactions.

If the loan was repaid in monthly installments, the effective rate of interest would increase substantially. This rate of interest is called the **annual percentage rate** of interest, or **APR**. The formula for calculating the APR on an installment loan is as follows:

$$\text{APR} = \left(\frac{2 \times P \times F}{B \times (T+1)} \right) \times 100$$

Where:

APR = annual percentage rate of interest
P = payments per year
F = dollars paid in interest
B = amount of capital borrowed
T = total number of payments

If the terms on Doug's loan included an 8 percent interest rate and monthly installment payments, the APR calculation would be:

$$\text{APR} = \left(\frac{2 \times 12 \times \$8,000}{\$100,00(12+1)} \right) \times 100$$

$$\text{APR} = \left(\frac{\$192,000}{\$1,300,000} \right) \times 100 = 14.8\%$$

The simple interest loan gives the borrower the use of the greatest amount of borrowed funds for the longest period of time. The discounted and compensating balance loans result in a slight decrease in the amount of borrowed funds while paying interest on the total amount for the entire time of the loan, so the borrower pays a higher annual percentage rate.

The installment loan results in the highest APR since the full amount of the loan is available for only one month. At the end of the first month, part of the principal is repaid to the lender.

Other restrictions

Lenders often place restrictions on the management prerogatives of an agribusiness during the loan period. These restrictions vary from requiring monthly and annual financial statements or other financial information regarding inventories, accounts receivable, and accounts payable to actual restrictions on expending capital funds without the approval of the lender. Often banks require that firms maintain certain ratios during the loan period, such as a current ratio not below 2.0. Agribusiness managers must be sure that they can live comfortably with these restrictions before they agree to them. Otherwise, they may find themselves severely handicapped in decision-making and in their flexibility to meet changing conditions and capitalize on new opportunities.

Interest rates and taxes

One of the things that agribusiness managers often overlook is that they can deduct from the business's taxable income every dollar of interest paid, because the interest is a business expense. To know the effective cost of borrowing funds, the manager must know the after-tax cost of interest. This effect can best be seen by looking at net income after taxes, before and after borrowing.

For example, assume Doug Davies's company (a corporation) borrowed the $100,000 at 8 percent interest; the following tabular information is used to illustrate the impact of interest paid on the after-tax cost of borrowing:

	Before loan	After loan
Net operating income	$50,000	$50,000
Interest charges	– 0	–$8,000
Net income before taxes	$50,000	$42,000
Income tax (assume 25% rate)	–$12,500	–$10,500
Net income after taxes	$37,500	$31,500

The difference between the two situations is $6,000. The effective interest rate for decision-making purposes is then only 6 percent. The formula is:

$$\text{After-tax Cost} = \text{Before-Tax cost} \times (1.0 - \text{Marginal Tax Rate})$$
$$\text{After-tax Cost} = 8\% \times (1.0 - 0.25) = 6\%$$

In this example, the firm paid $8,000 in interest on the original $100,000 loan. However, since these interest payments are tax deductible business expenses, the IRS really subsidizes the interest payments. The amount of the subsidy is equal to the firm's marginal tax rate, in this case 25 percent. So the firm paid "out of pocket interest costs" of $6,000.

The marginal income tax rate mentioned is the rate of income tax paid on the last increment of taxable income. Proprietorships and partnerships (see Chapter 4) must also be aware of this cost as they decide between investing their own funds and borrowing capital funds for their businesses.

The leverage principle

Leverage is the concept of financing through long-term debt instead of equity capital. Many managers like to use debt as a lever against equity as much as possible so that they can maximize the amount of assets or capital at their disposal. Several factors affect the leverage principle. First, it must be remembered that as the proportion of debt to equity increases, lenders are likely to increase the cost of supplying borrowed funds because of the deterioration in the solvency measures and the resulting increase in risk. It must be understood that risks for equity holders also increase as debt increases, because they hold a last-place claim on the firm's assets in the event that the assets of the firm must be liquidated to satisfy the firm's debt obligations. In general, equity capital is risk capital—in the event of financial problems, all other creditors are paid before equity owners are paid. Leverage, or increasing the proportion of debt to equity, can be either a profitable or an unprofitable decision.

As a rule of thumb, the after-tax rate of return on the capital of the agribusiness must exceed the after-tax cost of the debt undertaken to increase profits. For example, if the firm's overall ability is to return 10 percent on the borrowed capital and the after-tax cost of borrowing that capital, or money, is 6 percent, borrowing more money should increase profits.

Determining how much agribusinesses should borrow

The question of how much an agribusiness should borrow is one that agribusiness managers frequently ask. Some answer by saying, "All I can get," while others say, "Let's pay off the mortgage and eliminate our long-term debt." These philosophical generalizations are not adequate for determining how much an agribusiness should borrow. The good manager always establishes criteria and a frame of reference for such decisions. This section will deal primarily with intermediate- and long-term debt, since it is assumed that short-term debt will be paid off from conversion of current assets to cash. The amount of debt that is most desirable depends on several factors, some of which have already been discussed. Many of these factors are easy to measure, but others are more difficult.

The first factor to consider is the amount that the agribusiness will be able to generate for debt servicing (repayment of the loan). While available funds can be calculated from all sources of cash flow, generally two factors are considered the primary inputs for debt servicing: (1) net operating income for the year and (2) depreciation. Net operating income must be further reduced by any interest that is due, income tax to be paid, dividends owed on owner equity, or patronage refunds in the case of a cooperative (see Chapter 4).

For example, if Doug Davies has a net operating income of $50,000 and depreciation of $25,000, he has a preliminary total of $75,000 in cash. Depreciation is added to net operating income, because it is a noncash operating expense that is subtracted from gross margin (profit) to calculate net operating income. However, the depreciation expense is not paid to an entity outside the firm, so those dollars are available to pay debt obligations. For debt servicing purposes, he would have to deduct $8,000 in interest expense, $25,000 in taxes,

Plate 11.1 Dairy barn expansion
Careful analysis is required to determine the right type and level of financing for an agribusiness. This is true for all agribusinesses, but takes on added importance when undergoing an expansion using borrowed funds. Photo courtesy of the USDA Natural Resources Conservation Service.

and $5,000 for stock dividends, which would leave the firm with only $37,000 for debt servicing:

Net Operating Income	$50,000
Depreciation	25,000
Total Cash Available	$75,000
Interest	8,000
Income Tax	25,000
Dividend	5,000
Total Cash Required	$38,000
Amount Available for Debt Servicing:	$37,000

Doug would also have to consider other possible needs for these funds, such as boosting working capital, returning capital equities, and increasing stockholder dividends. When lending institutions look at these debt servicing figures, many use the rule that no more than 50 to 60 percent of the total should actually be counted on as available for debt servicing, because of the possibility of missing budgeted figures or emergency situations.

　　If the additional capital that is to be borrowed will increase revenues and profits, thereby increasing debt servicing potential, then the amount borrowed can be increased accordingly. Forecasting such new earnings accurately is crucial. Many managers tend to be overly optimistic, especially in the short run. Remember Murphy's Law in this regard: "If anything can possibly go wrong, it will." The risk can be lessened considerably if the manager's profit forecast is understated. For example, if Doug feels that he will add $10,000 to his debt servicing capability through the loan, for the first year, at least, he would be advised to actually figure on only half this amount, or $5,000, as available for debt servicing.

Several other factors must be considered as Doug analyzes his **borrowing capacity**. Debt servicing costs can be extended above the accepted upper limits if:

1. Investors agree not to withdraw funds if the firm faces adverse market or competitive conditions
2. The firm has a favorable debt-to-equity ratio (solvency), or large amounts of working capital
3. The firm has fixed assets that can readily be converted to cash without incurring large losses
4. There are redundant fixed assets that can be sold
5. There is a low risk on the asset purchased, as, for example, with a new piece of equipment that will save labor

If accelerated depreciation or special depreciation measures are used to increase the amount of depreciation that is taken each accounting period, then the amount available for debt servicing must be considered in that context, and the manager may want to increase the amount of this particular contribution to debt servicing. However, if the long-term plans of the firm will not result in those levels of depreciation continuing during the remainder of the term of the loan, the debt servicing ability in the future may be more limited than in the short term. Finally, the manager will want to take a long, hard look at the overall stability and success of the firm and of its management team. Such factors as profits, control of inventories, accounts receivable, asset turnover, and efficiency will be the final elements in determining the amount of capital that the firm should borrow.

Other tools for financing decisions

Two other techniques, or tools, play an important part in financing the agribusiness firm. These are the cash budget, or cash flow statement, and pro forma financial statements, both of which can help the agribusiness manager to look ahead intelligently and can aid the decision-making process immeasurably. Both of these tools were introduced in Chapter 9, but will be explored in more detail here.

Cash flow statement

A **cash flow statement** is really a projection of the firm's cash inflows and outflows for a future time period (Table 11.2). It allows the manager to estimate the amount of cash needed to take advantage of cash discounts, to finance seasonal demands, to develop sound borrowing programs, to expand, and to make plans for debt servicing.

The length of time covered by a cash flow statement depends on the unique nature of the agribusiness. The primary considerations are the current supply of cash, the distributions of transactions throughout the period and the seasonality of cash inflows and outflows for the business. Highly seasonal agribusinesses will need to prepare their cash flow statements over longer periods of time than those whose business activity is fairly constant.

Table 11.2 Cash flow statement for three months ending March 2012

	January		February		March	
	Budget	Actual	Budget	Actual	Budget	Actual
Expected cash receipts:						
1. Cash sales						
2. Collections on accounts receivable						
3. Other income, investments called						
4. Total cash receipts						
Expected cash payments:						
5. Raw materials						
6. Payroll						
7. Other factory expenses (including maintenance)						
8. Advertising						
9. Selling expense						
10. Administrative expense (including salary of owner-manager)						
11. New plant and equipment						
12. Other payments (taxes, including estimated income tax; repayment of loans; interest)						
13. Total cash payments						
14. Expected cash balance at beginning of the month						
15. Cash increase or decrease (item 4 minus item 13)						
16. Expected cash balance at end of month (item 14 plus item 15)						
17. Desired working cash balance						
18. Short-term loans needed (item 17 minus item 16, if item 17 is larger)						
19. Cash available for dividends, capital cash expenditures, and/ or short-term investments (item 16 minus item 17, if item 16 is larger than item 17)						
Capital cash:						
20. Cash available (item 19 after deducting dividends, etc.)						
21. Desired capital cash (item 11, new plant equipment)						
22. Long-term loans needed (item 21 less item 20, if item 21 is larger than item 20)						

When Doug Davies prepares his cash flow statement, he will follow the steps outlined in the following section on budgeting. With the help of his planning committee, he will estimate from both his existing business and the one he hopes to acquire his cash receipts and cash payments. These estimates in reality become goals or budgeted figures, so careful and honest input is needed. Both cash receipts and expenditures are recorded on a month-to-month basis during the period, the end result being the cash balance at the end of the period. A goal must be set to determine whether the amount is sufficient (Chapter 10). For example, Doug might decide that the cash equivalent of a certain number of days' sales, or a certain percentage of current liabilities, would be the benchmark or goal.

If the cash balance is inadequate, then short-term borrowing or other adjustments might be needed. If the cash balance is larger than needed, the excess can be invested temporarily in marketable securities, other income-producing assets, or used to reduce current or long-term debt. The cash flow statement can help the manager to decide whether there is a need for short-, intermediate-, or long-term loans or equity capital. If the cash amounts are sufficient at certain times and inadequate at others, short-term capital is needed. If there is a persistent trend on the inadequate side, intermediate- or long-term capital is needed.

Budgeting: a tool used to determine future borrowing needs

A **budget** is a specific forecast of financial performance that is used as a tool for not only control of a business, but also for determining future borrowing needs and repayment schedules. An organization may have a cash budget, a capital budget, an advertising budget, and a research and development budget. The size and complexity of the organization will determine the kinds of budgets that are needed for success. A small business may need only an overall budget with different sections, such as sales, production, and finance. A large business may have budgets for departments, divisions, regions, products, etc. Budgets may be either short term or long range. A **short-term budget** is generally one that will be implemented within a year, and it usually requires shorter reporting periods. A **long-range budget** is two or more years in implementation and is usually reported on a semiannual or annual basis. The short-term budget, therefore, becomes a component in reaching the long-range budget objectives. Budgets may also be prepared for specific projects. Examples here might include constructing a new building, launching a new program, or introducing a new product.

It is important to recognize that budgets help determine organizational direction. Investing in or reducing the financial and human resources devoted to the different areas of the agribusiness determines the long-run direction of the firm in terms of growth, new products, and size. With the allocation of resources, managers bring the company's vision and mission to life. Budgets should reflect the priorities and directions or goals of the business.

For example, as Doug Davies considers the purchase of the lumberyard, the management team may decide to actively seek a larger share of the commercial building market. In turn, the capital, marketing, and cash budgets would need to reflect this objective. Doug's capital budget might be revised to provide more resources for production facilities to serve the commercial building market. The marketing budget might well show expanded investment in advertising and promotion, as well as additional sales personnel who would focus on the commercial building market. The cash budget would then reflect the impact on cash inflows and outflows that would result from this change.

Budgets and forecasts

What is the difference between a budget and a forecast? Though it is true that some budgets are forecasts and some forecasts are budgets, in management a **forecast** generally refers to some prediction of the future. We may have a forecast for the general economic situation, or a sales forecast for a specific territory. (Sales forecasts were discussed in Chapter 8.) As indicated above, the **budget** is typically a specific forecast of financial performance that is used as a tool for control and to project cash inflows and outflows. For example, Doug Davies' business would have a sales forecast or a prediction of the amount of business the organization expects to conduct during a certain period. To accompany this, Doug would also develop a budget that is related to the advertising and promotional expenditures needed to secure the projected sales. Because the survival of the organization depends on the capacity of revenues to exceed expenses, the budget and the sales forecast are inseparable.

Pro forma financial statements

Because the cash flow statement deals with only one account, cash, it is wise to go one step further and prepare a pro forma balance sheet and income statement, which were discussed in Chapter 9. These statements really just project the best estimates of what the business will look like in the future (Tables 11.3 and 11.4). However, that information is not only useful for Doug Davies, but it is also useful to his lender. The pro forma financial statements are typically prepared on a quarterly basis for an operating year. Again, the more seasonal an agribusiness, the more frequently pro forma statements should be prepared.

The **pro forma financial statements** will provide a look into the future of the business and will help the manager determine what the financial needs of the business will be during and at the end of the operating period. If Doug fails to use this tool, he may not recognize problems until they actually arise, and then it may be too late to take corrective action. The most important figure in the preparation of these pro forma statements is estimated sales (Chapter 9). This is a situation in which as many well-informed people as possible should

Table 11.3 Pro forma monthly income statement

PRO FORMA MONTHLY INCOME STATEMENT For the Month Ending—	
	Figures Based On:
Sales Revenue	Sales forecast for the month
Cost of goods sold	Sales forecast, historical data
Gross margin	
Operating expenses:	
Selling expenses	Budget for the month
General expenses	Sales forecast, historical data
Total operating expenses	
Net operating income	
Other expense:	
Interest expense	Outstanding debt, expected additional debt
Net income before taxes	
Income taxes	Tax rate
Net income after taxes	
Earnings withdrawn	Owner's intentions
Retained earnings	

Table 11.4 Pro forma balance sheet

PRO FORMA BALANCE SHEET As of—	
	Figures Based On:
Assets	
Current assets:	
Cash	Desired cash balance
Accounts receivable	Average collection period
Inventory	Monthly inventory turnover for the season
Total current assets	
Fixed assets	Present figure adjusted for period's depreciation and any planned investments
Total assets	
Liabilities	
Current liabilities:	
Notes payable	Amount of borrowed funds needed to balance assets with equities
Accounts payable	Expectation of number of days' purchases on the books
Accrued liabilities	Same as preceding period
Total current liabilities	
Long-term debt	Expected and additional borrowings
Total liabilities	
Owner's Equity	
Paid-in capital	
Retained earnings	Present amount plus period earnings to be retained
Total owner's equity	
Total liabilities and owner's equity	

become involved. Doug might well involve his family, the bookkeeper for the lumberyard, salespeople from both firms, supplier representatives, and his lender, to name a few. Past experience and future price trends are key ingredients, along with expected competition from other firms in the area, and general economic conditions.

It is vital that these two tools be based on solid goals in the areas of cash balances, inventory turnover, accounts receivable collection periods, revenues, and expenses. These goals help the manager in the budgeting and forecasting process. Specific goals also imply there is a management plan that can be objectively evaluated at the end of the period.

With documented goals, management can use the interim cash flow statement and financial statements to check their progress against their estimates and assumptions. If actual and planned performances vary widely at any point, the reason can be explored and the weaknesses corrected. As a professional manager, Doug Davies will avail himself of all these financial tools as he progresses in his new venture, prepared and as ready as anyone can be for the future.

External sources of financing

There are a multitude of sources of capital available to any agribusiness. Some of these sources are used only in specific situations, while others are used more routinely. The most important sources of financing for an agribusiness will be discussed in the following sections.

Trade credit

Trade credit is one of the most neglected sources of capital available to agribusinesses managers. It is the credit advanced by suppliers and vendors of the agribusiness firm. If the agribusiness is creditworthy, most suppliers and vendors will allow credit terms. The manager can often negotiate for longer credit terms than are usually offered. For example, Doug Davies was such a steady purchaser of treated lumber that he was able to get his supplier to extend his normal 30-day credit terms to 90 days from invoicing. In Doug's case, he had often collected for the farm building prior to the 90-day credit period, so in a very real sense the lumber supplier also became a supplier of Doug's business capital, but without any cost to Doug. In other cases, a supplier may be willing to sell to an agribusiness on consignment. This means that the business does not have to pay for supplies until it is able to actually sell them. The agribusiness manager should make sure that suppliers and vendors are extending maximum terms, and that the procedure for paying accounts payable takes every advantage of all credit terms extended.

Commercial banks

Commercial banks are the major source of borrowed funds for most agribusinesses, with the exception of trade credit. Commercial banks usually offer a full line of banking services, including checking accounts, savings accounts, and loans. Banks make many kinds of loans, such as short-, intermediate-, and long-term loans, lines of credit, and special loans.

Banks also make personal unsecured loans to owners, and many other kinds of secured loans, such as mortgages against real property; chattel mortgages against tools and equipment; and loans against the owner's life insurance policies, stocks and bonds, etc.

Often a bank will offer to help sell a product by buying sales installment contracts from the seller. Sales installment contracts are contracts made by the buyer to pay for the product in a specified manner over a period of time. When a financial institution buys the contract, payments are made directly to that institution. The business gets its money immediately. This procedure makes it easier for the customer to finance the purchase and help the cash flow of the business. This is particularly helpful to retailers who are selling relatively expensive items, such as farm implements, tractors, and combines.

Insurance companies

Insurance companies are always looking for places to invest funds they have collected from policyholders. Most insurance companies are interested in intermediate- and long-term loans on fixed assets, such as equipment or real estate. They prefer large loans and mortgages for collateral. If the owners or the agribusiness itself have insurance policies with a particular company, that company will usually lend the agribusiness amounts that are equal to the cash value of the policy at very favorable interest rates.

Commercial finance companies

Commercial finance companies are those finance companies that specialize in business and commercial loans. They are not to be confused with personal finance companies, which make loans to individuals. Commercial finance companies often grant loans that are riskier than those that banks will accept, so commercial finance companies normally charge higher interest rates than banks. Commercial finance companies may also demand a considerable amount of control over management decisions. This is particularly true if the loan involved is high risk. Sometimes commercial finance companies will pay off all firm debts in order to consolidate the firm's indebtedness into one loan held by the finance company. This can be of particular value if cash flow presents a problem, because payment schedules can be reconstructed within the constraints of the agribusiness's cash flow.

Cooperative borrowing

Cooperatives, of course, have all the conventional borrowing sources, but in addition, agribusiness cooperatives can borrow from CoBank, which is part of the Farm Credit System. In **cooperative borrowing**, the cooperative patrons, who are also its borrowers, own these special banks. The bank makes short-, intermediate-, and long-term loans to its members. To receive a loan, a cooperative must purchase an amount of membership stock that is equivalent to the amount of money being borrowed. This stock is revolved or repurchased whenever the debt is repaid and the firm has funds available for that purpose. Often CoBank can offer better interest rates than some commercial banks because it is a nonprofit organization operated exclusively for the benefit of its members. Because they specialize in loans to cooperatives, the bank's personnel are often able to offer management help and guidance to member-borrowers.

Types of loans

Several types of loans are available to agribusinesses, depending on the terms and the collateral the manager desires. For example, the manager may want to pledge his accounts receivable as collateral to obtain short-term credit during the time it takes to collect those accounts receivable. Or the manager may want to pledge the inventory that is being carried for collateral and pay the loan amount as the inventory is sold. A third alternative is to sign a promissory note and pledge assets such as equipment, buildings, and real estate as collateral and spread the payments over several years. A few of the more common loan types are discussed in the paragraphs that follow.

Accounts Receivable Loans are loans in which the bank lists a business's accounts receivable as collateral. This may be done on either a notification or non-notification basis. Notification means that the bank informs the debtors (customers of the agribusiness) that it wishes to collect the money that is owed. The bank receives the payment from the customer and then deducts a service charge and interest. The bank then credits the balance against the loan to the agribusiness. Under non-notification, the agribusiness (borrower from the bank) collects the receivables and then forwards the payments to the bank. Record keeping and interest costs are usually high, and managerial flexibility is lost when using non-notification, so non-notification loans should typically be avoided.

Many bankers are reluctant to provide accounts receivable loans and charge higher interest rates on such loans to discourage their use by agribusinesses. Also, since there is no guarantee that all of a firm's accounts receivable will be collected, the bank will limit the amount of accounts receivable that may be used as collateral against any loan. This limit will be a function of the firm's credit policy, record of collections, and current as well as forecasted future economic conditions. It is common for this limit to approach 50 percent of a firm's accounts receivable.

Warehouse receipts represent a means of using inventory as security for a loan. As inventory is stored in the warehouse, the borrower sells the inventory to the bank, and then buys back the receipts from the bank as the product is sold. This type of loan is feasible only on nonperishable items, and allows the borrower to manage with limited working capital.

Warehouse facilities may represent a large storage building, a grain bin or shed, for example, or simply be a fence around a large site of coal to be used by a major processing organization to generate electricity. A major reason for a bank to use a warehouse receipt is that the bank is aware when the product is sold and can immediately collect the payment from the agribusiness. The key requirement when using warehouse receipts, from a lender's point of view, is to know reliably what is in the warehouse facility. Thus, if a borrower has financed $2 million worth of grain through a warehouse receipt, it is critical the representative of the bank makes sure the grain is in the storage facility and has the ability to measure quantity and assess quality. This comes at a cost that is borne by the borrower. Hence, these loans are used less frequently by most agribusiness firms compared to other financing alternatives.

A **promissory note** is a promise by the borrower to pay to the lender a particular amount of money and a particular amount of interest after a specified period of time. Promissory notes are common to agribusiness firms and are used by banks, private individuals, and other creditors. Agribusiness firms may also accept promissory notes from their customers. Such notes may be negotiable, that is, the holder can sell them and the new owner will have the same claim against the borrower as the original lender. When an agribusiness firm holding negotiable notes from customers needs cash, negotiable promissory notes can be sold to a bank or other person, usually at a discount. For example, Doug Davies might sell a farmer some materials to help build a new dairy barn, say $50,000 worth, and accept in return a negotiable note that is due in 6 months and bears a 10 percent interest rate. In the meantime, Doug might need cash, in which case he could sell the note to a bank or other financial intermediary. If the farmer's credit is good, and the banker feels the interest rate is good, the note might be purchased by the bank for face value or at a very small discount that reflects a service charge. The farmer would then pay the bank when the note was due.

Leasing and renting

An alternative to owning a durable asset is to lease that asset. A **lease** is a contract by which the control over the right to use an asset is transferred from the **lessor** (owner) to the **lessee** (person acquiring control) for a specified time in return for a rental payment. There are several types of leases, which are discussed below.

Leasing land is a common method of acquiring control of a durable asset in agriculture, land. A **land lease** is a contract that conveys control over the use rights in real property from the lessor to the lessee without transferring title. The contract usually specifies the property's intended use and the conditions of payment for that use.

An **operating lease** is usually a short-term rental arrangement (i.e., hourly, daily, weekly, monthly, etc.) in which the rental charge is calculated on a time-of-use basis. The lessor owns the assets and performs almost all the functions of ownership, including maintenance. The lessee pays the direct costs, such as fuel and labor. However, the terms may vary and may even be negotiated between the two parties.

Examples of operating leases are rental cars, trailers, moving trucks, etc. Agricultural equipment can also be leased. This is particularly true for part-time producers who operate small acreages and cannot afford to own general-purpose pieces of equipment, and for producers who farm larger acreages and have equipment breakdowns or have been delayed in planting, harvesting, etc. Also, specific-purpose types of equipment, whose demand varies by region or by type of service, are popular items for operating lease arrangements.

A **capital lease** is a long-term contractual arrangement in which the lessee acquires control of an asset in return for rental payments to the lessor. The contract usually runs for several years and cannot be cancelled. So the lessee acquires all the benefits, risks, and costs of ownership, except price variations of the asset, but does not have to make the usual investment of equity capital. It is comparable to a credit purchase that is financed by a loan with 100 percent financing. However, it should be recognized that lease prepayments have the same cash flow effects as down payments for credit purchases.

Leasing provides an opportunity for many agribusiness firms to extend their capital assets without having to borrow. However, leasing is the equivalent of borrowing, because it takes its place as a means of acquiring capital. Much of the money used in leasing comes from financial institutions and insurance companies. Special organizations have been set up to lease a business almost anything. Doug Davies is seriously considering leasing trucks for his business in order to conserve cash.

The typical lease, as would be expected, will cost more than the interest on a loan. The lessor (person granting the lease) must charge an amount to return an adequate amount of profit for arranging the lease, a charge to cover an element of risk, interest on the capital involved, and the depreciation on the item leased. The longer the lease period, the lower the lease charges will be per period, which means that if Doug Davies leases a truck for four years, he will pay a lower yearly rate than he would if he leases it for two years. In many cases, the lessee (person renting the property) can arrange to purchase the property at the end of the leasing period for a predetermined amount. The popularity of leasing has grown significantly in recent years. Only ten years ago, this financing arrangement was relegated to business use only. Today, however, leasing is one of the most popular ways for individuals to acquire the use of new and used automobiles.

Advantages and disadvantages of leasing

A business leases to avoid using its cash resources for purchasing assets. It will not have to resort to borrowing or selling equity. Many agribusinesses take the position that their funds should be used for expanding their operations rather than buying assets that can just as easily be leased. Leasing is also a deductible expense, and, in some cases, may be cheaper than borrowing, buying, and incurring the cost of depreciation. Another advantage is that leased assets can be turned back to the lessor and newer or better assets procured. This is of special value when change or new technology is pertinent to the asset. Today, for example, many firms lease computer and copying equipment for a specific period of time, say three years, and then turn the hardware in for new equipment. This allows firms to utilize up-to-date technology at a reasonable cost. Also, leasing can be used to acquire access to very specialized equipment that would have a very low resale value if the agribusiness owned the equipment and then decides to sell it and purchase new equipment.

But leasing is not without its drawbacks. For most businesses, leasing will cost more than borrowing. Leasing also commits the business to certain payments, whereas if the asset were

Plate 11.2 Harvesting equipment
Leasing, a form of financing, is commonly used to finance large and/or specialized equipment. Photo courtesy of USDA Natural Resources Conservation Service.

owned it could be sold to, at least, minimize the amount of the financial commitment. Finally, leased property may increase in value, and such increases in value are only of benefit to the lessor or owner.

Internal financing for the agribusiness

One of the most important sources of capital is the money obtained from retained earnings. Some managers fail to fully understand the importance and role of retained earnings. It is not that a manager lacks awareness of these funds, but because he or she simply has not used the financial tools and techniques previously described, he or she has no idea how to use retained earnings to the fullest extent.

Equity capital

Equity capital represents funds that are obtained by the firm through retaining the profits it has made, through the investment of more money by the owners, or through taking into the business additional people who are willing to risk their funds. In some small or new businesses, this may be the only alternative for securing capital funds. A specialized type of financing organization, the **venture capitalist**, focuses on providing equity capital to new and high-potential businesses. These venture capital firms typically take an equity position in a firm that may be very risky, but be deemed to have major long-term potential. Many of the Internet start-up companies in the food and agricultural markets have venture capital backing.

Some owners are not anxious to sell equity to other people. These owners feel that the loss of complete control over the business is not worth the additional capital. Such owners should be aware that the borrowing of funds may place far more restraints on their control than the sharing of ownership. And if an owner defaults, or is slow in paying a term loan, he or she can completely lose control of the management of the business. Remember, equity capital does not have to be repaid at any certain time, and often there is no absolute need to generate funds for distribution to the owners. Equity capital should always be considered as an alternative, and weighed against other capital sources.

Common stock

The most prevalent form of equity capital is the kind that is secured through the sale of **common stock**. For the small company, this may mean selling shares of stock primarily to people who are known to the present owners. There are always people in any community who have funds to invest in a promising business venture. The firm's banker can often be helpful in suggesting interested people. Employees of the firm are also a potential source of stock purchasers, especially if the firm offers a special purchase plan that grants employees preferential prices. Common stock is usually voting stock; that is, owners of common stock have a voice in the management of the firm. Sometimes common stock is divided into classes, of which only one kind carries the voting privilege.

Doug Davies has carefully studied the financial needs of his firm. He has decided on what he views as an optimum mix of borrowed and equity funds. His intentions are to offer the lumberyard's owner, as part of the purchase price, a certain amount of stock. He also intends to offer stock to his employees and to members of the community on a limited basis. He determined this ratio of equity to borrowing by using the tools in Chapter 10 that relate to solvency.

Care must be exercised that laws relating to the sale of securities are observed when stock is offered to the public. All states have blue-sky laws, which regulate the sale of securities and stocks. In some cases, federal laws regulating the sale of stocks also apply. It is essential that a team of advisors be assembled before a public offering of stock is made. The business's banker, legal counsel, and auditor should be among those involved. If a firm wants to make a larger public offering, it will usually secure the services of an investment banker. These bankers perform a very special service by offering for sale the new stock offerings presented by companies. When an investment banker underwrites a stock issue, that banker makes an agreement with the corporation to market its securities by buying them and reselling them to the public. Investment bankers typically charge a commission for underwriting a stock issue.

Present owners of the business do not necessarily have to lose control of a business by sale of its common stock. They can retain control by keeping a sufficient amount of the stocks issued themselves. Often bonds or debentures are sold as convertible issues. This means that they can be converted at some future time to a certain quantity of common stock. Companies offer this conversion feature as an inducement to secure buyers for their bonds and debentures, because if a company is successful, its stock may appreciate considerably in value.

Preferred stock

Preferred stock is the stock to which a corporation shows preference. In the event of the liquidation of the corporation, the owners of preferred stock would be repaid before holders of common stock. Most preferred stock also has a definite annual dividend rate, which means that it would pay a percentage (say 6 percent) of the face or issue value on an annual basis. Sometimes corporations will reserve the right to defer this dividend until a later date should the corporation have financial difficulties. In exchange for its preferred nature in the event of liquidation, most preferred stock does not carry with it any voting rights or control in the management affairs of the corporation.

Other internal financing

Partnerships may secure more capital by selling portions of their business to others who are willing to risk their money in the business. These others may be either general or silent partners. A general partner assumes the same rights and liabilities as other partners, while a silent partner has restricted rights and liabilities (see Chapter 4). Or an owner may simply lend money to the business just as any outside creditor would, if that owner does not wish to commit any additional funds on an equity basis.

Summary

As the agribusiness manager strives to turn everything that he or she touches into gold, it is important to remember that not all sources of financial help are equally useful or equally applicable to all situations. The securing and managing of the financial resources of any agribusiness firm is a complex function, but careful attention to the tools, techniques, and principles discussed in this chapter will increase the agribusiness manager's chances of success.

The agribusiness manager needs to know the various kinds of loans, the cost of borrowing, and whether short-, intermediate-, or long-term capital is needed. The manager must explore all sources of capital to discover whether borrowing, equity financing, or some combination thereof is best for the particular agribusiness involved. But even more importantly, the manager's ability to assess the optimum amount to be borrowed, and to formulate a realistic plan for repayment, will make the agribusiness's financial strategy a firm and steady foundation for the future.

Financing the agribusiness is a necessary and important management responsibility. Money must be available to finance capital purchases and operate the business on a day-in, day-out basis. There are three primary sources of capital: borrowing, funds generated from business operations, and additional investments from owners.

Borrowing can take many forms. Short-term loans of a year or less are normally used to finance seasonal business needs. Intermediate-term loans of one to five years are generally used to purchase equipment or finance increases in the volume of business. Long-term loans are usually for major business expansion, such as buying land and erecting buildings. Interest rates and repayment schedules vary according to a great many factors, including time, risk, amount of money borrowed, past experience, and the soundness of the firm's financial base.

Some agribusiness firms gain the control and use of assets by leasing those assets. Leases can be for a short period of time, such as days or months, or for longer periods of time that could contain an option for the agribusiness to purchase the asset at the end of the lease period. Leasing has become more and more popular for not only business assets, but also for such personal assets as automobiles.

Some agribusinesses, particularly newer ones, rely heavily on equity financing. Equity capital results from retaining profits in the business rather than distributing them to owners. Other agribusinesses sell additional stock to attract additional dollars for the business. Each financing method has pros and cons and must be considered carefully by management.

Discussion questions

1. Suppose an agribusiness firm has decided it must increase capital. What are three ways to accomplish this? Would the method selected be different for: (a) a corporation, (b) a partnership, or (c) a proprietorship? Why? Defend the "best" selection for each business form.
2. What are the three general classes of loans? Give two examples of a firm needing each type of loan, and list the specific asset or type of capital acquisition you have in mind.
3. Why would a firm usually not finance a new truck with short-term debt? What problems could this cause?
4. What are the advantages of a line of credit as compared to a short-term loan?
5. Is there ever a situation when a borrower would prefer a loan that requires a compensating balance to a simple interest loan? Explain your answer.
6. You purchase a house for $200,000. The bank is willing to loan 90 percent of the value of your home plus two points. How much money do you need at the "closing" (i.e., when you take possession of your home)?
7. What financial information should you make available to the lender when you seek a loan? Be specific.
8. Explain how the IRS helps pay some of the interest on your business loan from the bank.
9. What are the major sections of the projected cash flow statement? For each section, outline the sources of information or the tools of finance you can use to forecast the section.
10. What is the value of pro forma statements?
11. Why is trade credit important to consider as a way to finance an agribusiness?
12. If you own an agribusiness in a rural area, under what conditions would you prefer not to work through your local town bank? Be specific.

Case study: Woods Landscaping Service

James Woods, CEO of Woods Landscaping Service, needs to increase the firm's operating loan, because the firm was a successful bidder for landscaping a new subdivision. Using a projected cash flow statement, Mr. Woods knows the amount of capital needed, when it can be repaid, and, after consultation with the board of directors, that these funds would need to come from external sources.

Mr. Woods determined the firm's additional capital requirements will total $500,000. The money will be borrowed for one year, which is the amount of time needed to complete the landscaping project. Mr. Woods is evaluating various loan terms as he considers his borrowing options. Assume the tax rate for Woods Landscaping is 30 percent and the simple rate of interest is 6 percent.

Questions

Given this information, please answer the following questions. Show the formula used to arrive at your answer. Note: the first four questions ask for two answers, one in dollars and the other in percent.

1. Calculate the amount of interest paid and the effective interest rate for a simple interest loan.
2. Calculate the amount of interest paid and the effective interest rate if this loan also requires a compensating balance of $20,000.
3. Calculate the amount of interest paid and the effective interest rate if this loan is a discounted loan.
4. If this was a one-year installment loan with 12 equal, monthly payments, show the APR and the amount of interest paid on the loan.
5. What is the after-tax cost of borrowing for Woods Landscaping? How would this change if the firm was in the 25 percent tax bracket rather than the 30 percent tax bracket? What does this say about debt versus equity financing?

12 Tools for evaluating operating decisions

Objectives

- Understanding the decision-making process and how it may be used to solve management problems
- Explain variable and fixed costs and their relationship with business volume and profit
- Learn to calculate the breakeven point for a firm
- Apply volume–cost analysis techniques to important agribusiness operating decisions
- Discuss alternative strategies to reduce a firm's breakeven point
- Evaluate pricing decisions within the agribusiness firm and estimate the impact of a price reduction on the breakeven point

Introduction

Effective decision-making is a critical talent of the successful food and agribusiness manager. Regardless of which commodities, services, products, and activities an agribusiness focuses on, the manager of that organization is faced daily with myriad decisions to be made at many different levels. Those decisions can range from where to order lunch for the staff meeting, to determining where the next production facility should be built. And it is the manager's responsibility to make effective, timely and sound decisions for the ultimate good of the business.

Professional managers approach this decision-making activity systematically. The process of decision-making involves identifying the problem, summarizing facts, identifying and analyzing alternatives, making a decision, taking action and evaluating results. This chapter examines some of those critical decision-making steps and the tools used to facilitate the process. Our focus in this chapter is on operating or shorter-term decisions. In the next chapter, we turn our attention to longer-term investment decisions.

Perfect Pallet

The Perfect Pallet company has grown steadily over the past decade and management has been pleased with its record of performance. Recently, however, the business had been sold to an international food company. As the new owners assumed control, they have begun to apply pressure for better performance and a higher return on their investment. Sandy Johnson, the newly appointed general manager at Perfect Pallet, is struggling with all kinds of questions, alternatives, and ideas for improving profits. Although she has some good accounting information, she is not sure how to best use this information to answer tough management questions including:

- How much must Perfect Pallet sell to cover all costs?
- What volume of business is necessary to generate a 10 percent ROE?
- If prices are lowered by 5 percent to improve sales volume, will this be profitable?
- Can we afford to hire a new salesperson?
- Can Perfect Pallet afford new computer-controlled, electronic sawing equipment?
- How should the board of directors be advised about which of several alternative expansion investments is best for the business?

Some of these questions frame operating decisions, or decisions that have a shorter (usually one year or less) time frame. Some of these questions frame investment decisions with impacts that will last much longer than a single year. Regardless of focus, operating, or investment, professional agribusiness managers view decision-making as a process and use analytical tools to help make decisions whenever feasible. Then they complement formal analyses and decision-making with their personal experience, judgment, and intuitive feel for the situation. With greater access to many sources of information—both financial and marketing—managers today rely much more heavily on computer-generated spreadsheets and database analysis systems to help them make more informed management decisions.

Plate 12.1 Ripple rings of water
Like ripples on a pond, many decisions made by agribusiness managers have consequences that expand over time. Photo courtesy of USDA Natural Resources Conservation Service.

Decision-making

An overview

Decision-making is the process of choosing between different alternatives for the purpose of achieving desired goals. In the following sections, we will look more closely at this definition.

Process

The first important idea here is the recognition that decision-making involves some type of process. The word *process* implies activity, or doing something. It is important to recognize that good decision-making is an active process in which the manager is aggressively and personally involved. Of course, decisions can be made by default; that is, one can do nothing for so long that there is no longer a decision to be made. Putting off decisions until it is too late is a problem most people know something about. But effective decision-making includes an active participant whose actions are timely.

It is important to note that deciding to do nothing is *not* always a default decision. Deciding to "wait and see" may be a logical and correct choice. A default decision represents a failure to decide. The end result may be quite acceptable, but any positive result of a default decision is purely accidental. Any success is in spite of management, not because of it; therefore, most professional managers do not make default decisions.

Choosing

The second key idea in the definition of decision-making is *choosing*. Choosing implies there are alternatives from which one must select. When one has no alternatives, then there is no decision to make. The alternatives must also be feasible. They must be realistic and reachable. For example, quitting or exiting is always an alternative, but it is seldom a realistic one. Choosing also involves selection—picking from among the available options. Such selection, picking the "right" alternative, is at the heart of decision-making.

Goals

Finally, decision-making is purposeful. Effective decision-making requires that a clear goal be firmly in mind. If management refuses to set clear-cut *goals* at the beginning of the year, it is impossible to evaluate performance at the end of the year. Firm performance should be evaluated as one would evaluate employees of the firm. Goals or anticipated results should be clearly outlined as quantitatively as possible to allow assessment of performance at year's end. Likewise, effective choice requires that some criteria, such as goals, be used to guide the selection process.

Goals, like alternatives, must be feasible and specific. To say "My goal is to make as much profit as possible" is not much help in operating a large California vegetable grower-shipper operation. This is far too general a goal to be of much use. But a specific goal, such as "To generate a 15 percent after-tax return on investment, maintain an annual growth rate of 5 percent, and provide an opportunity for meaningful employment for family members," will be exceedingly helpful in guiding and evaluating day-to-day decisions.

The decision-making process

The decision-making process is simply a logical procedure for identifying a problem, analyzing it, and arriving at a solution. This can be carried out in a formal manner, where many people are involved in its various aspects, work for many weeks or months on analysis, spend a great deal of money, and publish lengthy reports which outline proposed solutions. Or the process can occur informally over coffee in just a few minutes with no written report at all. The more important the issue, the more likely the process will be formalized. In any case, effective decision-making is a systematic process that involves some key elements and several rather specific steps.

Three necessary elements are part of the decision-making process. First, decision-making is built around facts. The less relevant, factual information there is available, the more difficult the decision-making process. Second, decision-making involves analysis of this factual information. Analysis may be a highly rigorous statistical treatment using large computer spreadsheets, or it can be simply a logical thinking process. In either case, decision-making requires the careful examination of facts. Finally, the decision-making process requires an element of judgment, a subjective evaluation of the situation based on experience and common sense. Although it is theoretically possible to be completely mechanical in the decision-making process, seldom, if ever, are there enough facts available or sufficient resources or time to completely analyze the situation. Human judgment is a necessary part of professional decision-making.

With these three elements in mind, let's look at the steps involved in the decision-making process:

1. *Problem Identification*: This is often the toughest part of decision-making. It is easy to confuse symptoms with the real problem. The problem may seem to be low profits, when low profits are simply the result of an inefficient, high-cost distribution system. Once the problem is clearly defined, it can usually be more easily addressed.
2. *Summary of facts*: This step brings to the surface and highlights information pertinent to the problem and its solution. It may be critical to note overall company goals, the impact of the problem on the business, environmental factors limiting possible solutions, or technical facts that affect the outcome.
3. *Identifying alternatives*: This step identifies and lists feasible alternative solutions, exploring various possibilities. Only feasible solutions should be considered.
4. *Analysis*: This step may require rigorous examination, weighing the costs and benefits of each alternative. Analysis considers both short- and long-term company goals. Although analysis should be objective, the final selection process should include some subjective evaluation of alternatives.
5. *Action*: One of the most critical steps in the decision-making process involves implementing the chosen alternative. Often this requires careful planning prior to the execution, but it is a critical step. Management responsibility goes much further than just deciding; it requires execution and results.
6. *Evaluation*: The final step in this process occurs some period of time after action has been taken. Management must evaluate whether or not the firm is better off by the action taken. If the situation has improved, no further action is necessary. However, if the action taken has not caused the desired results, management must go through this process again and seek new action alternatives.

Decision tools

There are numerous tools for analyzing alternatives and making management decisions, and the number is growing rapidly. Some of these tools are complex, while others are simple.

The decision-making process just described is, in itself, a decision tool. But among the more important decision tools used by agribusiness managers is volume–cost or breakeven analysis. This is because most food and agricultural businesses are relatively capital intensive, requiring large investments in land, plants, and equipment. The food and agricultural industries are so seasonal that such large investments in many firms can be used only for very short periods of time, for example during planting or harvesting. The capital-intensive nature of the industry emphasizes the importance of investment decisions and the efficient use of fixed assets.

The remainder of this chapter is devoted to a discussion of this important management tool. Volume–cost analysis techniques are discussed and a format for utilizing this tool is presented. Numerical examples from the firm presented in Chapter 9—Brookstone Feed and Grain (BF&G)—will be used to illustrate the use of breakeven analysis and the many questions this decision tool can help management address.

Volume–cost analysis

Volume–cost analaysis, or **breakeven analysis** as it is sometimes called, is a tool for examining the relationship between costs and the volume of business generated by the firm. This tool analyzes differences in the kinds of costs encountered by every agribusiness and how the volume of business affects them. Volume–cost analysis shows the level of business necessary to breakeven and/or to earn a specific amount of profit under various cost and price assumptions.

Volume–cost analysis can show the impact of changes in selling price on the volume of business necessary to reach a certain profit level. It can reveal specifically how anticipated cost changes will affect profit levels. It can be useful in evaluating various marketing strategies, such as advertising and promotion expenditures, individual product pricing decisions, and the amount of sales a new salesperson must generate to cover her salary and other costs.

The basis for volume–cost analysis is the separation of costs into two categories: fixed and variable. **Fixed costs** are those costs that do not fluctuate with the volume of business. Examples of fixed costs would be depreciation, interest, and insurance. **Variable costs** are those costs that change directly with the volume of sales. Examples would include the cost of goods sold, overtime, and commissions. The key question in classifying costs into these two classes is whether the cost is *directly* affected by how much is sold. Said another way, fixed costs are present regardless of the amount sales. As soon as a business gears up for a particular level of sales, it incurs a certain amount of expense whether or not it makes any sales at all. These are fixed or sunk costs.

On the other hand, some additional expenses are incurred as product is sold. These incremental expenses are not charged to the income statement if the sale is not completed. These are variable costs. Note that the emphasis is on the sale. The actual sale of a product or service is the point of determination for this cost. Even in a manufacturing or processing plant, where costs are incurred throughout the production process, the crucial point is the actual sale. Until the sales transaction is completed, no costs are counted as expenses and are therefore not included on the income statement. Instead, they remain in inventory and show only on the balance sheet. If there are no sales during a period, by definition, there are no variable costs. Selling something actually causes the variable costs to be incurred.

Some people tend to confuse variable costs with controllable costs, but they are not the same things. While some variable costs are controllable by management, others are not.

For example, fuel cost associated with delivering products is variable because it is incurred automatically when and only when product is actually sold and delivered. But management usually can do little to control it. On the other hand, advertising costs are generally controllable, but they do not vary directly with sales. Theoretically at least, advertising causes sales, which is the opposite situation from a variable cost. Once the advertising expenditure is committed, whether sales result or not has nothing to do with paying the advertising bill. Thus, advertising is a fixed cost, even though it is controllable.

Perhaps a graphical illustration can further clarify these important fixed and variable cost concepts. Assume the LCM Nursery, Inc. has total fixed costs or overhead, as it is sometimes called, of $200,000 per year.

Fixed costs

Fixed costs are constant regardless of the volume sold during the period. If LCM, Inc. opens for business but has no sales at all, then its total fixed costs are $200,000. If its sales volume is $200,000, its fixed costs remain at $200,000. If its sales volume is $500,000, its fixed costs are still $200,000. The horizontal line in Figure 12.1 shows that regardless of sales volume, fixed costs will remain at $200,000.

Now, look at fixed costs as a percentage of sales. If LCM, Inc. sells only $200,000 worth of nursery products during the year, its fixed cost per dollar of sales is 100 percent ($200,000 fixed costs / $200,000 sales × 100). If sales are $400,000, fixed costs drop to 50 percent of sales. If sales are $500,000, the fixed cost percentage drops to 40 percent of sales.

Plate 12.2 Nursery
Some costs of doing business for LCM Nursery are fixed, and other costs are variable. Photo courtesy of USDA.

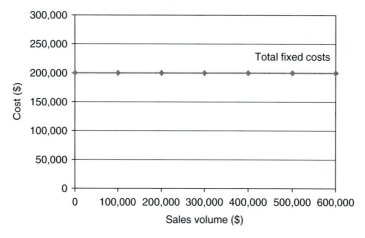

Figure 12.1 Total fixed costs, LCM Nursery, Inc.

At $1 million of sales, fixed costs drop to 20 percent of sales. This fixed cost percentage continues to drop as long as volume is increased in the same physical plant (Figure 12.2). The fact that fixed costs as a percentage of sales falls rapidly as sales increase is extremely important to operating efficiency in any agribusiness. Firms often make expansion decisions based upon this economy of scale efficiency. As long as no additional assets are required to farm an additional 80 acres, the farmer expands and is able to lower average fixed cost. Of course, this can't go on forever—at some point limits to resources force additional increments of capacity to be added, and total fixed costs increase.

Variable costs

Variable costs, on the other hand, behave quite differently. Assume that the variable cost per unit of sales for LCM, Inc., averages 60 percent of each dollar of sales; that is, every time a

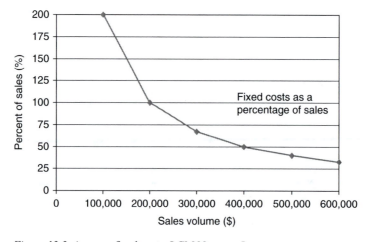

Figure 12.2 Average fixed costs, LCM Nursery, Inc.

dollar's worth of product is sold, a 60-cent cost is incurred (including the cost of goods). At zero sales, LCM, Inc. incurs no variable cost, so the initial total variable cost is zero. If sales are $200,000 and each dollar of sales incurs 60 cents in variable costs, total variable costs would be $120,000 for the period (0.60 × $200,000). At $400,000 sales, total variable cost is $240,000 (0.60 × $400,000) (Figure 12.3).

Now, looking at variable costs per dollar of sales, if LCM, Inc. sells $200,000, its variable cost per dollar is 60 percent. If its sales are $400,000, its variable cost per dollar is 60 percent. In fact, no matter what the volume of sales, the variable cost per dollar sales remains essentially at 60 percent, or, in other words, constant (Figure 12.4) when calculated as a percentage of sales.

The key ideas presented in these graphs can be summarized as follows: (1) as sales increase, **total fixed costs** remain constant but fixed cost as a percentage of sales falls; and

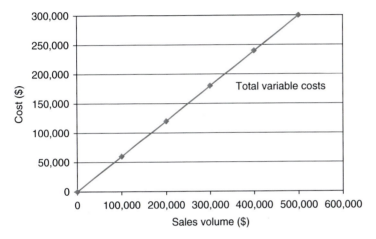

Figure 12.3 Total variable costs, LCM Nursery, Inc.

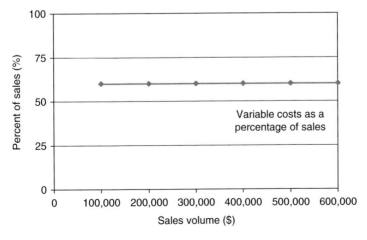

Figure 12.4 Average variable costs, LCM Nursery, Inc.

(2) as sales increase, **total variable costs** increase but variable cost as a percentage of sales remains constant.

Semi-variable costs

Semi-variable costs are a third type of cost. This is a cost that is partly fixed and partly variable, such as the electricity costs. There is a fixed, or minimum, charge per month, and then the usage charges increase with business activity and most likely with sales. These types of cost behavior can and should be considered in volume–cost relationships. A simple way of handling semi-variable costs is to carefully estimate the fixed portion; the amount that is part of the cost of just being open for business, and then estimates the portion that is incremental with each additional sale. With this allocation of semi-variable costs, volume–cost analysis can proceed.

Special problems in cost classification

There are certain situations that create special problems in classifying costs as fixed or variable. These are examined in the discussion below.

Incremental costs not constant

One difficulty can be variable costs that increase incrementally with sales, but not along a straight line. That is, as sales increase to higher levels, the additional cost for each unit becomes increasingly smaller, or greater. This situation can be handled nicely, so long as the exact relationships are known. The graphical or mathematical analysis becomes more complicated, but the analysis can be performed and used in the same way. For example, consider what a firm can do to reduce per unit variable costs. One way to do this is for the agribusiness to secure volume discounts from suppliers. For LCM, Inc. this may mean their cost per 1,000 plant containers is reduced by 1 cent per container if the firm purchases over 5,000 containers from their supplier. As additional containers are used, variable costs go up, but not as much as before the volume discount. This would result in the curvilinear relationship between volume and variable cost depicted in Figure 12.5.

Lumpiness

Some costs are lumpy, that is, they are fixed within certain sales volume ranges, but then once a certain point is reached, a whole new set of fixed costs are incurred. For example, when a delivery truck reaches its maximum capacity, sales cannot be increased further unless another truck is purchased. Purchasing an additional truck suddenly increases fixed costs, such as depreciation, insurance, and licenses for the new truck (Figure 12.6). This lumpiness can also be included in graphical or mathematical volume–cost analysis. Again, it just becomes more complicated, the principles do not change.

Allocating costs

With the calculation of breakeven for the entire firm completed, many agribusiness managers desire to take this analysis one step further. If they run a diversified firm selling many products, they may want information about breakeven for each of these product lines

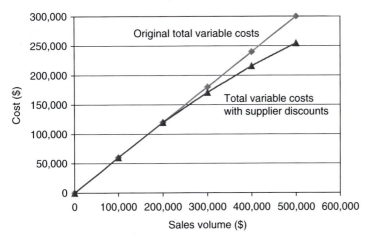

Figure 12.5 Total variable costs with supplier discounts, LCM Nursery, Inc.

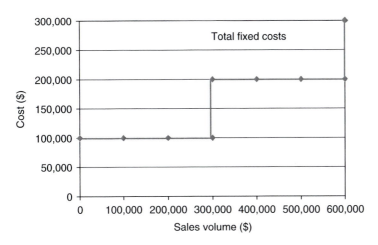

Figure 12.6 Changes in total fixed cost, LCM Nursery, Inc.

or divisions of the company. Although it is clear where many costs will fit, i.e., what division will be responsible for a particular cost, there are several expenses that must be allocated among several divisions.

As one can imagine, it may at times be quite difficult to allocate these costs. For example, in a diversified agribusiness operation like BF&G, some of the manager's salary should be allocated to the grain division, some to the feed division, seed, etc. The question is, "How much?" Some managers simply allocate costs based upon sales of the different divisions. Thus, if grain represented 61 percent of firm sales, the grain division would be "billed" for 61 percent of the manager's salary. This allocation scheme is often the worst method of dividing costs among divisions of the firm. The grain volume for the firm may be great, but upon further investigation we may find that the manager only spends about 25 percent of his/her time in this area. Thus, in deciding upon a proper cost allocation system, it is often important to ask many questions and make sure the scheme selected is the fairest allocation method.

Length of time period

The length of the time period under consideration has a great deal to do with whether a cost is classified as fixed or variable. In the very long run, all costs become variable with sales volume. Even depreciation, often considered the classic fixed cost, can vary with the volume of business if the time period is sufficiently long that new facilities can be built and equipment purchased. For example, over a five-year period, if the business grows, an entire new set of facilities may be constructed as a direct result of the increased volume of business. But in the very short run, say one day, all but the most direct costs associated with the cost of the product and the actual cost of the sale are fixed and cannot be changed within that period.

Therefore, it is important to define the time period that is under consideration. The time period selected depends entirely on the problems that are of concern and the decisions to be made. In attempting to utilize volume–cost analysis, time periods considered are usually reasonably short, such as a season or a quarter or, most commonly, a year.

In practice, the fine points of separating fixed and variable costs are not that critical to making rough approximations of the volume–cost relationships. The analysis, of course, can be no better than the information used in making the analysis. But experience shows that so long as reasonable care is taken in classifying costs as fixed and variable, and a realistic time period is assumed, close approximations of fixed and variable costs may be made without regard to semi-variable costs allocations, non-linear variable costs, or lumpiness. Volume–cost analysis can then proceed, providing highly useful insights into important management questions. Of course, if major violations of the simple assumptions are known to exist, caution should be used, and one should attempt to take these special situations into account in the analysis.

Volume–cost analysis procedure

Let's take a typical operating statement from BF&G (Chapter 9) and analyze the volume–cost relationships. There are four distinct steps in determining the breakeven point from the firm's income statement:

Step 1: classify fixed and variable costs

The actual classification of expense items from a firm's income statement depends on the makeup of each. Thus, it is necessary to be familiar with the operation and its accounting system in order to be accurate with the classifications. For example, rent for one firm may be strictly a fixed monthly amount, while another firm may have a rental contract that ties rent to the level of sales, making it a variable cost.

Take a look at BF&G (Table 12.1) and classify its fixed and variable costs for the year. BF&G is an actual agribusiness firm operating in the Midwest; the determination of its fixed and variable costs is based on the actual situation as interpreted by its manager. Note that in most cases fixed costs are tracked in total dollars, and variable costs are calculated as a percentage of sales.

Plate 12.3 Grain elevator
The breakeven point for Brookstone Feed and Grain, Inc. is that point where sales revenue just
covers total cost. Photo courtesy of USDA Natural Resources Conservation Service.

Cost of goods sold—variable. For most production-oriented agribusinesses this is the largest
single variable cost. It, in fact, is a perfect example of what was depicted in the graphs
shown earlier in this chapter for variable cost. No charge is made under cost of goods
sold until the product is actually sold. If product is purchased from a supplier but not
sold by period's end, there is no charge against cost of goods sold, thus no variable
cost.

Salaries and benefits—fixed. BF&G pays its manager a set salary. This represents a fixed
cost to the firm. Some weeks the manager may only put in 40 hours, but during the busy
season BF&G's manager works in excess of 60 hours. The manager is paid a fixed
amount monthly.

Full-time wages—fixed. Although these people are paid by the hour, this is still considered
a fixed cost. If BF&G had paid any overtime, this part of wages should be considered a
variable cost. Since it is hard to attract and retain good employees, BF&G pays workers
a minimum of 40 hours per week, even though in slow times the manager must "find
work" for them to do.

Part-time wages—semi-variable, half fixed, half variable. BF&G employs some "permanent" part-time people. They are paid a lower wage than their full-time counterparts and
receive fewer benefits. They also do not work a 40-hour week. As sales increase, part-
time hours tend to increase, thus the equal split between fixed and variable costs.

Table 12.1 Income statement for Brookstone Feed and Grain, year ending December 31, 2009

	Income/Expenses	Dollars	Percent
	Gross Sales:		
	Grain and Soybeans	8,146,000	
	Fertilizer and Chemicals	2,213,000	
	Feed	1,810,000	
	Seed	670,500	
	Miscellaneous Supplies	402,300	
	Service Income	268,200	
	Gross Sales	13,510,000	
	Less Returns, Allowances, and Discounts	100,000	
(a)	Net Sales	13,410,000	100.00
(b)	Cost of Goods Sold:		
	Grain and Soybeans	7,556,900	
	Fertilizer and Chemicals	1,791,420	
	Feed	1,534,380	
	Seed	511,650	
	Miscellaneous Supplies	330,650	
	Service Expense	0	
	Total Cost of Goods Sold	11,725,000	87.43
(c)	Gross Profit (Margin)	1,685,000	12.57
(d)	Operating Expenses:		
(e)	Salaries and Benefits	210,000	1.57
(f)	Full-time Wages	166,000	1.24
(g)	Part-time Wages	10,400	0.08
(h)	Commissions	42,740	0.32
(i)	Depreciation	290,000	2.16
(j)	Maintenance and Repairs	58,000	0.43
(k)	Utilities	56,990	0.42
(l)	Insurance	71,200	0.53
(m)	Office Supplies/Expense	26,820	0.20
(n)	Advertising/Promotion	6,400	0.05
(o)	Gas and Oil	48,600	0.36
(p)	Delivery and Freight	156,710	1.17
(q)	Rent	6,300	0.05
(r)	Taxes, Licenses, Fees	48,160	0.36
(s)	Miscellaneous	3,300	0.02
(t)	Payroll Tax	10,900	0.08
(u)	Bad Debt	3,290	0.02
(v)	Total Operating Expenses	1,215,810	9.07
(w)	Net Operating Income	469,190	3.50
(x)	Other Revenue	18,200	0.14
(y)	Interest Expense	230,840	1.72
(z)	Net Income Before Taxes	256,550	1.91
(aa)	Taxes	59,900	0.45
(bb)	Net Income After Taxes	196,650	1.47

Commissions—variable. BF&G pays a commission to its salespeople as part of their compensation. Since commissions aren't paid until a sale is made, this represents a variable cost.

Depreciation—fixed. These costs are not a function of sales. Even with depreciation schedules that do not have the same depreciation charge each year, this amount is not tied to sales.

Maintenance and repair—semi-variable, half fixed, half variable. Since equipment is on a scheduled maintenance program regardless of use, the manager has split this cost equally between fixed and variable. The fixed portion captures the regularly scheduled maintenance, and the variable portion captures those repair costs that are related to volume, or use of the facility and equipment.

Utilities—semi-variable, two-thirds fixed, one-third variable. Since extra utility costs in the fall are caused by higher grain sales, the manager felt some of this expense should be classified as variable.

Insurance—fixed. This cost is not dependent upon sales.

Office supplies/expense—semi-variable, half fixed, half variable. Since more sales result in higher supply costs, some of these costs are variable. Yet, some office expenses are borne by the firm regardless of sales. Hence, this cost is split between variable and fixed.

Advertising/promotion—fixed. These are expenses intended to create sales, they are not caused by sales. Only promotional programs like trading stamps, incentive gifts, and double coupons would be a variable cost.

Gas and oil—semi-variable, half fixed, half variable. Since more sales result in higher gas and oil expenses, part of this cost is variable. But, some gas and oil expenses are borne by the firm regardless of sales.

Delivery and freight—variable. Here, there is no expense unless there is a sale.

Rent—fixed. BF&G makes a flat monthly payment to the owners for rent. Thus, this expense is not related to sales.

Taxes, licenses, fees—fixed. These are typically a flat fee and not related to sales.

Miscellaneous—variable. The manager of BF&G estimated that the majority of these costs did, in fact, vary with sales. This expense category represents the aggregation of several small expenses that do not need to be listed separately on the income statement.

Payroll tax—fixed. This cost is tied primarily to salaries and benefits and is not a function of sales.

Bad debt—variable. This expense tends to increase as sales increase. Firms often develop guidelines for bad debt costs. These benchmarks tend to be expressed as a percent of sales.

Interest—fixed. This expense varies with the amount of money borrowed, not sales volume. Interest on long-term loans is clearly a fixed cost. The status of interest on short-term, in-season loans is less clear. However, borrowing to finance inventory is not caused by the sale. It is to enable an anticipated sale. Only in circumstances where borrowing is caused by a sale would this part of total interest be classified as variable.

Step 2: summarize fixed and variable costs

The next step in the procedure to calculate breakeven is to summarize fixed and variable costs. Total dollar fixed costs are summed first. Then variable costs as a percent of sales are added together. Variable costs may be tracked in dollars/unit, i.e., dollars per ton or dollars per bushel or as a percent of sales. The physical unit measure is acceptable for a firm that sells product in one physical size—a fertilizer firm sells only fertilizer and prices it by the ton. However, most agribusinesses sell a variety of products in several different physical units. Thus, tracking variable cost as a percent of sales is usually the best option. Totals for BF&G example are included in Table 12.2.

The fixed-variable cost summary shows that BF&G committed itself to a cost of $1,149,722 the day it opened its doors for business. Additionally, every time it sold a dollar's worth of product, it incurred, on average, an incremental or additional cost of 89.64 cents.

Step 3: calculate the contribution to overhead

CTO (contribution to overhead) is the heart of volume–cost analysis and an important figure for many management decisions. It shows the portion of each unit of sales that remains after variable costs are covered and that can be applied toward paying or covering fixed or overhead costs. Each time a unit of product is sold, the variable costs must be covered first. Anything that remains makes a contribution to overhead.

In this example, $1 of sales, of course, generates $1 of revenue. Of this $1 of revenue, 89.64 cents must go to cover variable costs. This leaves $1.00 – $0.8964 = $0.1036 as a contribution to overhead for each $1 of sales.

Revenue (Sales) $1.000
Less: Variable Cost   – 0.8964
Contribution to Overhead $0.1036

Table 12.2 Classification of fixed and variable costs for Brookstone Feed and Grain company

Expense	Fixed Cost (dollars)	Variable Cost (percent of sales)
Cost of Goods Sold		87.43
Salaries and Benefits	210,000	
Full-time Wages	166,000	
Part-time Wages	5,200	0.04
Commissions		0.32
Depreciation	290,000	
Maintenance and Repairs	29,000	0.22
Utilities	38,012	0.14
Insurance	71,200	
Office Supplies/Expense	13,410	0.10
Advertising/Promotion	6,400	
Gas and Oil	24,300	0.18
Delivery and Freight		1.17
Rent	6,300	
Taxes, Licenses, Fees	48,160	
Miscellaneous		0.02
Payroll Tax	10,900	
Bad Debt		0.02
Interest	230,840	
TOTAL	1,149,722	89.64

Thus, for every dollar generated in sales, BF&G has 10.36 cents left to contribute to the firm's overhead after variable costs have been paid. Thus, BF&G's contribution to overhead or CTO is 10.36 cents or 10.36 percent.

The breakeven relationships essentially answer the question of how many unit contributions at 10.36 cents per unit BF&G has to make before its overhead is paid. One can think of overhead as a tank that must be filled over the operating period before any profits are made. In our example, this fixed cost tank has a constant capacity of $1,149,722.

Step 4: calculate the breakeven point

The question is: How many units (dollars) of sales must there be, with each unit contributing 10.36 cents toward the $1,149,722 overhead, to completely cover all costs?

If BF&G opens its doors but sells nothing during the period, it incurs its fixed costs of $1,149,722, but has no revenue, so the entire $1,149,722 is a net loss. If they manage to sell one unit ($100 per unit) of product, they incur the fixed cost of $1,149,722 and the variable cost of $89.64 for that unit. The total cost is $1,149,811.64 against an income of $100.00. The loss is $1,149,711.64—pretty bad, but this loss is not as great as if they sold nothing. The loss is reduced by $10.36 or 10.36 cents per dollar of sales. This represents BF&G's **contribution margin.**

Conversely, if the selling price does not cover the variable cost of $89.64 per unit (i.e., the selling price is $79.00), the loss per unit of sales would be $10.64 and the total loss from the sale of one unit would be $1,149,732.64, which is greater than if they sold nothing. Hence, the firm wants to produce as long as the selling price per unit is greater than the variable cost per unit, which results in a positive contribution to overhead. If the selling price per unit does not exceed the variable cost per unit, then the least-cost level of production for the firm is zero units, and the amount of the loss is limited to the amount of the fixed costs, $1,149,722.

The obvious and critical question then is: How many times does this process need to be repeated before the firm reaches the zero-loss point? Or, stated differently: What is the firm's breakeven point? Each time another $100 unit is sold, its revenue is used first to cover the variable cost of $89.64. The remaining $10.36 is used to cover the fixed cost or "overhead" burden.

The CTO in any breakeven example may also be calculated as a percent of sales or in dollars (cents) per unit. In these examples, CTO is assumed to be SP – VC (selling price minus variable costs), in percent or dollars/unit. CTO may also be calculated as GM – VC (gross margin minus variable costs), again, as a percent or in dollars per unit. Either approach produces the same result since sales minus cost of goods sold equals gross margin. If variable costs are measured as a percent of sales, the breakeven amount is in sales dollars and is calculated as shown below:

$$\text{Breakeven in Sales Dollars} = \frac{\text{Fixed Costs}}{1.0 - \text{Variable Costs as a proportion of Net Sales}}$$

If variable costs are measured in dollars (cents) per unit, then breakeven volume is in units and is calculated as shown below:

$$\text{Breakeven in Units} = \frac{\text{Fixed Costs}}{\text{Selling Price Per Unit} - \text{Variable Costs Per Unit}}$$

In our example, BF&G tracked variable costs as a percent of sales, so CTO is:

$$\text{CTO} = \text{SP} - \text{VC} = 100\% - 89.64\% = 10.36\%$$

Since we are using percentages, in this format SP or selling price is always 100 percent of selling price or it equals 1.0. So, CTO can be calculated as shown below:

$$\text{CTO} = \text{SP} - \text{VC} = 1.0 - 0.8964 = 0.1036$$

For BF&G, the breakeven sales volume in dollars is:

$$\frac{\$1,149,722}{0.1036} = \$11,097,702.70$$

For BF&G, breakeven has been calculated to be sales of $11,097,703. If BF&G generates sales greater than this amount over the operating period, the firm will make a profit. With sales above the breakeven level, the contribution margin continues to be generated, but the fixed costs have already been covered. Thus, CTO now becomes **CTP (contribution to profit)**. The number is the same—10.36 cents—but now this "margin" contributes to profit for BF&G.

BF&G's actual sales were $13,410,000. Since actual sales are higher than the calculated level of breakeven sales, BF&G made a profit. Given our calculation of CTO, we should be able to estimate the net operating profit (including the interest expense as an operating expense) for BF&G that is illustrated in Table 12.1.

Actual Sales	$13,410,000
− Breakeven sales	$11,097,703
Sales above Breakeven	$2,312,297
×CTP	0.1036
	$239,554

The estimate of net income before taxes can be calculated by adding other revenue, $18,200 (Table 12.1), to $239,554, which yields $257,754. The estimated amount is close to the amount reported on the income statement for the year ending December 31, 2009, $256,550. Rounding some of the variable cost percent figures calculated in Table 12.2 causes the difference of $1,204. The important concept here is to understand that as the firm generates sales above the breakeven level, variable costs continue to be paid—these go on forever. Regardless of the level of sales, BF&G pays 89.64 percent of each sales dollar to variable cost.

Assumptions of volume–cost analysis

As the manager begins to utilize the breakeven calculation, it is important to understand the assumptions made for the breakeven procedure. These assumptions are:

1. Fixed costs are constant
2. Efficiency is unchanged
3. Input prices are fixed
4. Product mix is constant
5. Selling price is unchanged

The first assumption listed above relates to Figure 12.1. By definition, fixed costs are constant over the operating period. Any decision made, such as the purchase of a new piece of equipment, will change fixed costs and, thus, the breakeven level. The second assumption relates both to fixed and variable costs. The manager assumes the firm is at a specific point on the average fixed-cost curve, Figure 12.2, and the firm cannot reduce per unit variable costs, for example, by taking advantage of volume discounts from suppliers. If efficiency can be increased in some way, a new breakeven level must be calculated.

The third assumption relates to Figure 12.4 where the variable costs of inputs are shown to be a constant percentage of sales. If suppliers or the firm does anything to alter input costs, breakeven changes. The fourth assumption is one that is often overlooked. In a diversified firm there are revenues and costs from several different product categories. Some of these product divisions may have significantly higher percentages of variable costs. Thus, as the firm sells relatively more of this product, the total variable costs for the firm shift. Hence, one makes the assumption of a constant product mix, which means the percentage of sales from each division or department is fixed. The final breakeven assumption is straightforward. Basically, anytime a firm changes selling price, it also changes the contribution margin. Thus, if prices change, breakeven must be recalculated.

Uses of volume–cost analysis

Profit planning

Volume–cost relationships are useful for much more than just calculating the breakeven point. They can also be used to determine the volume of business necessary to generate certain levels of profit, which is an essential part of profit planning.

Since revenue above variable costs is profit once the overhead has been covered, a similar calculation can be used to determine the additional sales necessary to reach a given profit level. If BF&G has a net operating income (after interest) goal of $250,000, it will take an additional $2,413,127 sales above their breakeven volume of $11,097,703 to achieve the profit goal. The additional sales needed to accomplish that goal is calculated as shown below:

$$\text{Additional Sales to Reach Profit Goal} = \frac{\text{Profit Goal}}{\text{CTP}}$$

$$\frac{\$250,000}{0.1036} = \$2,413,127$$

Thus, to reach this profit goal BF&G must generate sales of:

Breakeven Sales	$11,097,703
Additional Sales to Reach Profit Goal	$2,413,127
New Total Sales Goal	$13,510,830

Management now must follow through with a marketing and sales program that will allow BF&G to reach its profit goal.

Changes in costs

Volume–cost analysis also helps answer questions about how changes in the cost structure will affect profit levels. Suppose, for example, that BF&G is considering the purchase of an additional truck that costs $50,000. The truck would be depreciated over a five-year period. The annual fixed costs for this additional truck, including depreciation, are projected to be $10,000. Variable operating costs for the new truck should be about the same as the current truck. With this information, BF&G management can examine the impact that purchasing this new truck will have on breakeven and profit.

The breakeven calculation with this new cost information shows that BF&G must generate additional sales of $96,525 before it is in any better financial position. The truck purchase, with depreciation over five years, would obligate the firm to increase sales by $96,525 each of the next five years before profits improve. The calculation to determine the additional sales volume needed is:

$$\text{Additional Sales to Cover New Fixed Costs} = \frac{\text{Additional Fixed Cost}}{\text{CTO}}$$

$$\frac{\$10,000}{0.1036} = \$96,525$$

It is important to note that breakeven does not tell management "what to do." The breakeven relationship simply begins to identify how changes (in this case, the addition of a new truck) have an impact upon the firm. To insure good management decision-making when using this tool, it is imperative that the manager is able to identify the cost changes caused by the new action, in this case, buying a truck. (We will take a closer look at investment decisions in Chapter 13.)

Another use of breakeven analysis is to determine the effect of changes in variable costs. For example, suppose that BF&G's supplier increased the prices paid by BF&G for products, so that the cost of goods sold increased by 1 percentage point, but competition in the area was so keen that BF&G's management felt it could not increase the selling price of its products. The result is the CTO is lowered.

$$FC = \$1,149,722$$
$$VC = 89.64\% \text{ of Sales or } 0.8964$$
$$\text{Old CTO} = 1.0 - 0.8964 = 0.1036$$
$$\text{Old Breakeven} = \$11,097,703$$
$$\text{New CTO} = 1.0 - (0.8964 + 0.01) = 0.0936$$
$$\text{New Breakeven} = \$12,283,355$$

This increase in variable costs causes breakeven sales to increase:

New Breakeven $12,283,355
Old Breakeven $11,097,703
Additional Sales $1,185,652

This result shows that if BF&G absorbs the cost increase rather than increasing the selling prices of their products, the breakeven point will increase by $1,185,652.

Similarly, shrewd purchasing of products or a reduction in manufacturing costs reduces the cost of goods sold and variable costs. In BF&G's case, an improvement in purchasing practices which lowered the cost of goods sold by 1 percent would increase the CTO to 11.36 cents, and reduce the breakeven point by $976,911.

$FC = \$1,149,722$

$VC = 89.64\%$ of Sales or 0.8964

Old CTO $= 1.0 - 0.8964 = 0.1036$

Old Breakeven $= \$11,097,703$

New CTO $= 1.0 - (0.8964 - 0.01) = 0.1136$

New Breakeven $= \$10,120,792$

As variable costs fall, the breakeven sales also fall:

Old Breakeven $11,097,703
New Breakeven $10,120,792
Decreased Sales $976,911

The impact of any cost change can be anticipated using these techniques. Managers who are skillful in the application of volume–cost analysis find it very useful in projecting the probable results of various alternatives before making final decisions. Also, the level of CTO magnifies the cost changes dramatically. With a great deal of grain business, BF&G has a relatively high variable cost and, thus, a small CTO. A little change in costs will make a dramatic difference in BF&G's breakeven level. For example, when BF&G's variable cost increased one percent, the breakeven sales level increased about 10.7 percent.

Changes in price

Volume–cost analysis is also very useful in analyzing the impact of changing prices. Since CTO is selling price per unit less variable cost per unit, then any change in selling price directly impacts the CTO. Let's assume management of BF&G wants to evaluate a 2 percent price reduction in an attempt to increase sales. The new breakeven is:

Old CTO $= 1.0 - 0.8964 = 0.1036$

New CTO $= 0.98 - 0.8964 = 0.0836$

As prices fall, CTO falls and breakeven sales increase:

New Breakeven $13,752,656

Old Breakeven $11,097,703

Additional Sales $2,654,953

In this scenario, if BF&G decided to reduce selling price by 2 percentage points, its breakeven would increase by $2,654,953 or roughly 24 percent. Again, volume–cost analysis does not answer the question of what should be done—this is still the manager's decision. What volume–cost analysis does, in this case, is to show the manager that if BF&G cuts price by two percentage points, BF&G must increase sales by $2,654,953 to be in the same financial position as they were before the price cut. It is the manager's job to decide whether or not this move makes sense in the BF&G market area.

One word of caution about price changes: lowering the price may increase sales only temporarily. For many food and agribusiness firms, total demand may well be reasonably constant in a market area and/or during a season. Competitors may react to a firm's price reduction with a similar price cut. The net effect may be to lower price and CTO for all firms in the market without any appreciable increase in sales. The obvious result is much lower profits (or higher losses).

In only the most unusual circumstances can a firm afford to sell any product at a price lower than its variable cost. The variable cost for a product represents, for all practical purposes, the lowest possible price for that product. To sell when variable cost is not being covered, means that some of the variable costs are not covered, and none of the overhead can be covered. Losses will be less if the sale is not made at all, because in this case only fixed costs are lost at zero sales volume.

So, when would a firm sell product below its variable cost? Two possibilities exist where this decision may make economic sense. First, recall the pricing strategies outlined in Chapter 7. One of these strategies was identified as "loss leader" pricing. In this case, the product is priced below its total cost, and sometimes even below its variable cost. For example, in order to gain additional customers, a supermarket may price milk below the supplier cost. The low price would be advertised in the store's weekly flyer for customers to see. The strategy used by the store, in this case, is to get customers into the store by advertising a product at a very attractive price. The store makes money on the other items customers purchase on their trip to the store. This strategy may backfire, however, if the store has a lot of customers who come in only to shop for specials.

The second scenario, where selling below variable cost makes sense, is related to the demand factor of tastes and preferences. Suppose a firm has an inventory of a specific type of farm equipment. The firm is notified that the manufacturer is planning to introduce a new model that has many new features and will sell at the same price. As potential customers become aware of this new model, they have little use for the firm's inventory of the old model. Hence, if the firm is to generate any revenue from this inventory, it will most likely have to cut the selling price—probably significantly. This strategy may make more sense than having to write-off obsolete inventory, or sell the equipment later at an even higher level of discount.

Graphical analysis

Graphical illustration of volume–cost relationships is quite useful for many managers as a means of visualizing how changes in price, various costs, or volume impacts profit. Figure 12.7 illustrates BF&G's breakeven point and graphically shows its profit at the current $13.410 million sales volume. (Note that profit is the difference between total revenue

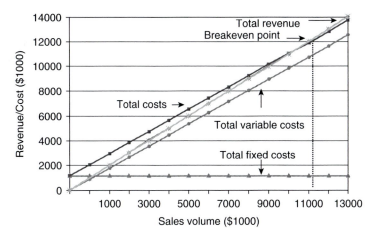

Figure 12.7 Volume–cost relationships for Brookstone Feed and Grain company

and total costs at a specific volume level.) The impact of almost any cost or price change can be shown by simply including the change and observing the resulting effect on profits.

One of the best features of volume–cost analysis is its simplicity and its applicability to real-world situations. Any manager with an income statement and an understanding of fixed and variable cost concepts can estimate the impact of various decision alternatives on profit levels. Although the categorizing of fixed and variable costs may not be perfect, experience has shown that a good approximation can be made and will be useful. And the conclusions are fairly accurate, so long as the proper definitions of fixed and variable costs are used.

Summary

Decision-making is one of the primary responsibilities of agribusiness managers. Professional managers approach this activity in a systematic way—identifying the problem, summarizing facts, identifying and analyzing alternatives, taking action, and evaluating results. Their analysis often uses a wide variety of analytic tools to facilitate this entire process.

Volume–cost analysis is one of the more powerful tools used by agribusiness managers. By separating fixed costs (those not related to volume of business) from variable costs (those directly related to volume), managers can study the impact of a variety of cost and price changes on their profit and determine the amount of business necessary to break even. They can even project the amount of business necessary to reach a certain profit level.

Volume–cost analysis helps managers and owners of agribusiness firms determine the impact of a variety of important decisions to the firm. Should a salesperson be added, can we afford to cut selling price, and what happens if we can reduce our input costs? Those interested in applying volume–cost analysis to a particular firm should note that variable costs for agribusinesses can vary dramatically—from less than 50 percent to 90 percent or more. The BF&G example provides an example with a relatively low contribution to overhead (CTO). There is a good reason for this. About 61 percent of BF&G's volume is from grain sales.

This is a business that operates with very thin margins and makes money on turnover. Alternatively, if our example firm had been a seed business, CTO would have been higher. It is important to know the nature of the business you evaluate.

Finally, volume–cost analysis is an important planning tool for making operating decisions. This financial management tool is used to help make and/or evaluate decisions for the next operating period. Other financial tools, specifically those related to capital investment analysis, take a longer-term planning horizon. These tools will be discussed in the next chapter.

Discussion questions

1. What are the major steps in the decision-making process? What are some of the problems decision-makers encounter when trying to use this process?
2. Is volume–cost analysis better used as a short-term or long-term planning tool? Why?
3. Explain the difference between variable costs and controllable costs. Give an example of each of these types of costs.
4. A particular cost can be variable under some circumstances but fixed in others. Given the following expense items, what conditions might make each fixed and what might make each variable? Into which category do you think each generally is assigned, fixed or variable? Why?
    a   Part-time labor expense
    b   Sales compensation
    c   Truck maintenance expense
    d   Truck rental expense
    e   Cost of goods sold
5. What are the major assumptions made in determining the breakeven point? Which of these assumptions do you feel is likely the most restrictive in practice? Why?
6. The manager of a firm wants his assistant to "take action to lower our breakeven." Describe at least two ways to accomplish this goal. Are these choices good ones for a typical firm? Why or why not?
7. Consider the actions below. How would you examine the impact these changes would have on the firm's breakeven level? Be specific. How would each of these actions affect the firm's breakeven point?
    a   Hire a new salesperson
    b   Pay additional overtime help
    c   Increase advertising expense
    d   Fire one of three assistant managers

Case study: True Red Greenhouse

Bob Collins works as an engineer and his wife, Julie, teaches middle school. About five years ago they built a 30′ × 120′ greenhouse to grow tomatoes to sell at a farmers' market and to local grocery stores. The project started as a hobby, but business has grown and now Bob and Julie want to evaluate several changes in the business to improve their return on equity, because Bob is considering retiring and working full-time in the greenhouse. They have decided to use volume–cost analysis to evaluate the changes.

Bob, with the help of his accountant, has determined that True Red's fixed costs or overhead for the coming year will be $5,032. They produce about 17,600 pounds of tomatoes per year and their average selling price is about $1.50/lb. Their cost of goods sold equals about $0.73/lb and their additional costs that seem to vary with sales amount to about $0.23/lb.

Questions

1. Calculate the breakeven point for True Red Greenhouse in dollars and in pounds.
2. The owners, Bob and Julie Collins, have about $100,000 invested in the business. Their desired rate of return on this investment is 10 percent. What volume of business (again, in dollars and in pounds) must be generated to reach this ROE goal?
3. Bob expects to eliminate his part-time labor, because he will work in the greenhouse full time, which amounts to a reduction in variable costs of $0.17/lb. With no other changes to the base situation, what impact would this have on the business? Show your answer in dollars and in pounds.
4. Bob and Julie are considering an upgrade to some of their watering equipment and they expect the capital investment to cost about $10,000, including installation. Bob assumes this new equipment can be depreciated over a five-year period. If the depreciation for the equipment is equal each year and there is no salvage value, what additional sales will True Red need for this to be a profitable decision? Assume no other changes will be made to the base situation. Answer this question in both pounds and in dollars.
5. Bob and Julie are interested in ways for True Red to increase sales. One change they are considering is to reduce the selling price for their tomatoes. They hope this change will increase sales in the near term and help them maintain sales later if a competitor should enter the market. What would the impact of a 10 percent price reduction have on the business? Assume no other changes are made to the base situation in Question 1. Answer this question in dollars and pounds.

13 Tools for evaluating capital investment decisions

Objectives

- Describe the role of capital investment decisions in an agribusiness
- Examine and learn to apply basic tools for analyzing capital investment decisions in agribusiness
- Discuss the payback, simple rate of return, net present value, and internal rate of return methods for evaluating capital investment decisions
- Examine the data needs when using the net present value and internal rate of return methods for evaluating capital investments
- Describe the decision criteria for making and rejecting capital investments when using the net present value and internal rate of return methods

Introduction

An area of major consequence for agribusiness managers is making capital investment decisions. **Capital investment** refers to the addition of durable assets to an agribusiness, which usually require relatively large financial outlays and will last over a long period of time. Typical capital investments might include trucks, manufacturing equipment, or storage facilities. Even relatively small firms can spend millions each year on capital investments. These investments tie up funds for long periods and release them slowly as the investment produces revenue. The impact of these investment decisions may affect the business for years to come. In addition to deciding whether or not to make a specific investment, the agribusiness manager must also decide how to finance the investment. Capital investments can be financed through cash purchase, borrowing, or leasing.

This chapter will explore tools for evaluating capital investment decisions. Both relatively simple tools and more sophisticated tools will be covered. Given the very large amounts of funds involved, and the long-term nature of the investments, careful analysis of capital investment decisions is another important skill of the effective manager.

Capital budgeting

There are many investment decisions that Brookstone Feed and Grain (BF&G) might face in the normal course of business activity. Some of these include:

1. *Expansion projects*: Would it be profitable to expand the grain storage and handling facility now?

2. *Replacement projects*: Should the custom application fertilizer applicator be replaced now, or should it be kept for another year?
3. *Alternative investment projects*: Which would be more profitable, stainless steel or mild steel storage tanks?

The procedure for evaluating the effects of an agribusiness manager's investment choices on the profitability, risk, and liquidity of a business is called **capital budgeting** or investment analysis. Capital budgeting is an orderly sequence of steps that produces information relevant to an investment choice. These steps are:

1. Identification of investment alternatives
2. Selection of an appropriate capital budgeting evaluation method
3. Collection of relevant data
4. Analysis of the data
5. Interpretation of the results

These five steps are developed and explained in the following sections.

Plate 13.1 Irrigation equipment
Capital budgeting focuses on the longer-term decisions of an agribusiness. Photo courtesy of USDA Natural Resources Conservation Service.

Identification of investment alternatives

An important function of management is to identify profitable investment alternatives. This is an essential function because even though an investment may be of high value and be profitable today, capital obsolescence and even price declines may reduce the value of the investment in the not too distant future. Consequently, management must continuously search for investment alternatives.

When money is tied up in a capital investment, management expects to get more back than was invested in the project. The excess of revenue over cost is referred to as the return. The return should be higher than that which could be earned by putting the same money in a "safe" place, such as savings accounts or government bonds. In addition to making a return for the use of the capital that is comparable to other investment alternatives, the return should also compensate owners of capital for any additional risk associated with the investment.

The idea here is a relatively straightforward one. If a person could earn 2 percent per year on an investment in a bank certificate of deposit (CD), how much more than a 2 percent return would that person require to invest in a food or agribusiness firm? The return for the CD is relatively low, but so is the risk. The person will get their principal back plus the 2 percent interest at the end of the year. The investment in the agribusiness is more risky. The general market, the competition, the management, and a host of other factors will influence the investor's return from the agribusiness. This added risk means that investors will want a lot more than 2 percent return to put their money into a food or agribusiness firm.

Some people think that if their business borrows the money to purchase a new piece of equipment, they have transferred the risk to the lender. In reality, this is not true because the bank is almost sure to be repaid, except in the extreme case of bankruptcy. If the manager makes a bad decision, the total business will suffer the loss because the loan will be repaid from other, more successful ventures. So managers must have a systematic approach for identifying investment alternatives. They must also understand that using financial leverage or debt to acquire investments can change the firm's risk and liquidity positions. (Financing the agribusiness was discussed in Chapter 11.)

The identification of investment opportunities falls into one of the four categories listed below:

1. Maintenance and replacement of depreciable capital items
2. Cost-reducing investments
3. Income-increasing investments
4. A combination of the preceding categories

For example, consider a swine finishing operation that is very labor-intensive. The manager is evaluating the changes needed to replace worn out facilities. One investment alternative to consider is a mechanized feeding system. However, the size of the operation needs to increase to fully use the mechanized system. This investment should cut labor costs, but the manager needs to better understand the cost of operating the mechanized system. In addition, the system may allow for better control of the nutrition program, which may allow the producer to do a better job of managing carcass quality. This could potentially increase returns if the producer sells the hogs on a carcass-merit (quality) basis. Given the complexity of the decision, the manager in this situation needs a systematic procedure to evaluate the investment alternative.

Concepts of the time value of money

Two of the four methods used to evaluate capital investments, net present value and internal rate of return, are based on the time value of money. So an introduction to the concepts of time value of money is needed prior to discussing the evaluation methods. This section develops the basic ideas underlying the time value of money. The first of those ideas is that an interest rate serves as the pricing mechanism for the time value of money. The **interest rate** reflects investors' time preferences for money and serves as the exchange price between money received today versus money received at some point in the future. In essence, a dollar received today can be exchanged for a dollar plus an amount of interest $(1 + i)$ received one period in the future. The value for the dollar invested for multiple periods, with the interest added to the principal to earn interest, would be calculated by multiplying the amount of the investment by $(1 + i)^n$, in which n is the number of periods. So, the formula used to calculate the future value is:

$$\text{Future Value of the Investment} = (\text{Present Value of the Investment}) \times (1+i)^n$$

Where : i = Interest Rate

n = Number of Periods

Alternatively, one dollar received one period in the future exchanges for $1 \div (1 + i)$, or the amount of the investment multiplied by $(1 + i)^{-n}$. The amount in today's dollars is normally referred to as the present value. The formula used to calculate present value is:

$$\text{Present Value of Investment} = (\text{Future Value of Investment}) / (1+i)^n \text{ or}$$

$$= (\text{Future Value of Investment}) \times (1+i)^{-n}$$

Where : i = Interest Rate

n = Number of Periods

For example, $1,000 invested today for one year at 10 percent will be worth $1,100 at the end of the year. So, the present value of $1,100 received in one year, at a 10 percent discount rate would equal $1,000. The $1,100 investment has been "discounted" to its present value of $1,000.

So for our example:

$$\text{Future Value} = \$1,000(1+0.10)^1 = \$1,100$$

and

$$\text{Present Value} = \$1,100 / (1+0.10)^1 = \$1,100 / 1.10 = \$1,000$$

or

$$\text{Present Value} = \$1,100 \times (1+0.10)^{-1}$$

Hence, there are two aspects of the time value of money. One is to take a present amount and determine what that amount would equal at some point in the future, if invested at a given interest rate, or compounding. The second is to take an amount in the future and determine what that amount would equal in present dollars at a given interest or discount rate, or discounting. Both aspects are discussed in the following sections.

Compounding

Compounding is a method of calculating interest earned periodically, when that interest is added to the principal and becomes part of the principal base on which future interest is earned. A simple example is used to illustrate this method. Suppose the relative of a high school graduate invests $1,000 at the time of graduation and plans to leave that money invested during the next four years, while the graduate attends college. The relative plans to give the college graduate the $1,000, plus the interest earned after four years, as a graduation present. How much will the $1,000 be worth at the end of four years, if interest is 5 percent and it is compounded annually?

Compounded annually means that interest earned during the first year of our example ($1,000.00 × 0.05 = $50.00) will be added to the original investment (**principal**) ($1,000.00 + $50.00 = $1,050.00), so that in year two, the entire principal investment ($1,050.00) will earn interest at the 5 percent rate. Each year additional interest earned is added to the investment, and it too earns interest. When the formula discussed above is used the result would be as follows:

$$\$1,000(1+0.05)^4 = \$1,215.50$$

To make calculations simpler, managers often use tables of future values (Table 13.1) or use financial calculators or spreadsheets to quickly calculate the future value of an investment. The factors presented in the tables are simply the factor calculations using the respective interest rates and number of periods.

For our example, the factor from Table 13.1 for 5 percent interest and 4 periods would be 1.2155. So, the calculation would be:

$$\$1,000(1.2155) = \$1,215.50$$

Discounting

Discounting is a method of converting a future value to a **present value** by adjusting the future value by its discount rate. Suppose in this example, a relative gives a new high school graduate a note promising him or her $1,000 upon graduation from college four years later. Assuming that the time value of money is 5 percent (interest rate), what is the present value of that gift? Although the formula is the same as before, this is more difficult to calculate.

$$\text{Present Value} = \$1,000/(1+0.05)^4$$
$$= \$1,000/(1.05 \times 1.05 \times 1.05 \times 1.05)$$
$$= \$1,000/1.2155 = \$822.70$$

Table 13.1 Future value of $1 (compounded annually)

Year (N)	$(1 + i)^n$ 1%	3%	5%	6%	7%
1	1.0100	1.0300	1.0500	1.0600	1.0700
2	1.0201	1.0609	1.1025	1.1236	1.1449
3	1.0303	1.0927	1.1576	1.1910	1.2250
4	1.0406	1.1255	1.2155	1.2625	1.3108
5	1.0510	1.1593	1.2763	1.3382	1.4026
6	1.0615	1.1941	1.3401	1.4185	1.5007
7	1.0721	1.2299	1.4071	1.5036	1.6058
8	1.0829	1.2668	1.4775	1.5938	1.7182
9	1.0937	1.3048	1.5513	1.6895	1.8385
10	1.1046	1.3439	1.5259	1.7908	1.9672
15	1.1610	1.5580	2.0789	2.3966	2.7590
20	1.2202	1.8061	2.6533	3.2071	3.8697
25	1.2824	2.0938	3.3864	4.2919	5.4274

Year (N)	$(1 + i)^n$ 8%	9%	10%	12%	14%
1	1.0800	1.0900	1.1000	1.1200	1.1400
2	1.1664	1.1881	1.2100	1.2544	1.2996
3	1.2597	1.2950	1.3310	1.4049	1.4815
4	1.3605	1.4116	1.4641	1.5735	1.6890
5	1.4693	1.5386	1.6105	1.7623	1.9254
6	1.5869	1.6771	1.7716	1.9738	2.1950
7	1.7138	1.8280	1.9487	2.2107	2.5023
8	1.8509	1.9926	2.1436	2.4760	2.8526
9	1.9990	2.1719	2.3579	2.7731	3.2519
10	2.1589	2.3674	2.5937	3.1058	3.7072
15	3.1722	3.6425	4.1772	5.4736	7.1379
20	4.6610	5.6044	6.7275	9.6463	13.7430
25	6.8485	8.6231	10.8340	17.0000	26.4610

Again, to make things simpler, tables of present values (Table 13.2) can be used or one can use a financial calculator or spreadsheet to quickly calculate the present value of the investment. In this example, the present value of $1 four years from now at 5 percent is given in the present value table as 0.8227, so the present value of $1,000 would be:

Present Value = $1,000 \times 0.8227 = $822.70

Table 13.2 Present value of $1 (compounded annually)

Year (N)	1%	$(1 + i)^{-n}$ 3%	5%	6%	7%
1	0.9901	0.9709	0.9524	0.9434	0.9346
2	0.9803	0.9426	0.9070	0.8900	0.8734
3	0.9706	0.9152	0.8638	0.8396	0.8163
4	0.9610	0.8885	0.8227	0.7921	0.7629
5	0.9515	0.8626	0.7835	0.7473	0.7130
6	0.9420	0.8375	0.7462	0.7050	0.6663
7	0.9327	0.8131	0.7107	0.6651	0.6228
8	0.9235	0.7894	0.6768	0.6274	0.5820
9	0.9143	0.7664	0.6446	0.5919	0.5439
10	0.9053	0.7441	0.6139	0.5584	0.5083
15	0.8613	0.6419	0.4810	0.4173	0.3624
20	0.8195	0.5537	0.3769	0.3118	0.2584
25	0.7798	0.4776	0.2953	0.2330	0.1842

Year (N)	8%	$(1 + i)^{-n}$ 9%	10%	12%	14%
1	0.9259	0.9174	0.9091	0.8929	0.8772
2	0.8573	0.8417	0.8264	0.7972	0.7695
3	0.7938	0.7722	0.7513	0.7118	0.6750
4	0.7350	0.7084	0.6830	0.6355	0.5921
5	0.6806	0.6499	0.6209	0.5674	0.5194
6	0.6302	0.5963	0.5645	0.5066	0.4556
7	0.5835	0.5470	0.5132	0.4523	0.3996
8	0.5403	0.5019	0.4665	0.4039	0.3506
9	0.5002	0.4604	0.4241	0.3606	0.3075
10	0.4632	0.4224	0.3855	0.3223	0.2697
15	0.3152	0.2745	0.2394	0.1827	0.1401
20	0.2145	0.1784	0.1486	0.1037	0.0728
25	0.1460	0.1160	0.0923	0.0588	0.0378

In other words, if the relative invests $822.70 today at 5 percent interest, compounded annually, that investment will be worth $1,000 in four years.

Annuities

Annuities are a stream of incomes and/or costs that are equal amounts for each of the number of periods evaluated. The time value of money concept can then be used to determine the amount of the stream at some point in the future or to calculate the present value of a future stream.

There are numerous examples in which the future value of a stream of income is useful; including the amount needed to save in order to accumulate a sufficient amount to retire, the amount needed to save each period to fund a child's education, and the amount needed to save in order to save enough for a down payment to purchase a house or a business. The factors for compounding a series of payments for selected interest rates are provided in Table 13.3.

Table 13.3 Future value of $1 at compounded interest for an equal series of payments

Year(N)	1%	3%	5%	6%	7%
1	1.0000	1.0000	1.0000	1.0000	1.0000
2	2.0100	2.0300	2.0500	2.0600	2.0700
3	3.0301	3.0909	3.1525	3.1836	3.2149
4	4.0604	4.1836	4.3101	4.3746	4.4399
5	5.1010	5.3091	5.5256	5.6371	5.7507
6	6.1520	6.4684	6.8019	6.9753	7.1533
7	7.2135	7.6625	8.1420	8.3938	8.6540
8	8.2857	8.8923	9.5491	9.8975	10.260
9	9.3685	10.159	11.027	11.491	11.978
10	10.462	11.464	12.578	13.181	13.816
15	16.097	18.599	21.578	23.276	25.129
20	22.019	26.870	33.066	36.785	40.995
25	28.243	36.459	47.726	54.864	63.248

Year(N)	8%	9%	10%	12%	14%
1	1.0000	1.0000	1.0000	1.0000	1.0000
2	2.0800	2.0900	2.1000	2.1200	2.1400
3	3.2464	3.2781	3.3100	3.3744	3.4396
4	4.5061	4.5731	4.6410	4.7793	4.9211
5	5.8666	5.9847	6.1051	6.3528	6.6101
6	7.3359	7.5233	7.7156	8.1152	8.5355
7	8.9229	9.2004	9.4872	10.089	10.730
8	10.637	11.028	11.436	12.300	13.233
9	12.488	13.021	13.579	14.776	16.085
10	14.487	15.193	15.937	17.549	19.337
15	27.152	29.361	31.772	37.280	43.842
20	45.762	51.159	57.274	72.052	91.024
25	73.105	84.699	98.346	133.333	181.867

For example, if someone saved $1,000 each year for the next 25 years and invested that amount at 6 percent and the interest earned each year remained invested the amount at the end of 25 years would be:

$$\text{Future Value} = \$1,000\ (54.864)$$
$$= \$54,864.$$

The factor, 54.864, is the factor for 25 years and 6 percent. Also, if an individual wanted to accumulate $1,000,000 over a 25-year career in order to retire and the interest rate was assumed to be 5 percent, the amount could be calculated as shown below:

$$\$1,000,000 = \text{Amount Needed to Invest Each Year}\ (47.726)$$
$$\$20,953 = \text{Amount Needed to Invest Each Year.}$$

The factor, 47.726 was taken form Table 13.3 and is the factor for 25 years and 5 percent.

Of course, one approach to determine the present value of the entire stream is to find the present value of the income or cost each year and then sum the present values for each of the years. Alternatively, in situations in which there are equal periodic amounts with a constant discount factor the computational procedure can be simplified by using discount factors for an annuity. Again, there are situations in which a future series of cash payments would need to be discounted to the present value. This includes a series of equal loan payments over a repayment schedule or to determine the value of a series of payments that will be paid from an annuity that is being considered for retirement. Discount factors for selected interest rates and periods are provided in Table 13.4.

For example, if an individual borrowed $100,000 to purchase a house and the repayment period was 25 years and the interest was 5 percent, the amount of the annual payment could be calculated as follows:

$$\$100,000 = \text{Annual Payment}\ (14.0939)$$
$$\$7,095.27 = \text{Annual Payment}$$

Again, the factor, 14.0939, was taken from Table 13.4 and is the discount factor for a uniform series of 25 years and for 5 percent.

Non-annual periods

Non-annual periods can also occur when compounding and discounting and should also be discussed. Up until now, all of the compounding and discounting examples have involved annual periods. However, institutions can compound quarterly, monthly, and even daily. Likewise, many payments are scheduled to be due monthly rather than annually. Fortunately, the compounding for a period shorter than a year can be handled the same as for annual compounding and discounting, except the period and the interest rate must match. For example, if a person invests money for five years with quarterly compounding at a 4 percent annual rate, the number of periods increases from five years to 20 quarters. Likewise, the rate is no longer 4 percent per

Table 13.4 Present value of $1 at compounded interest for an equal series of payments

Year(N)	1%	3%	5%	6%	7%
1	0.9901	0.9709	0.9524	0.9434	0.9346
2	1.9704	1.9135	1.8594	1.8334	1.8080
3	2.9410	2.8286	2.7232	2.6730	2.6243
4	3.9020	3.7171	3.5460	3.4651	3.3872
5	4.8534	4.5797	4.3295	4.2124	4.1002
6	5.7955	5.4172	5.0757	4.9173	4.7665
7	6.7282	6.2303	5.7864	5.5824	5.3893
8	7.5517	7.0197	6.4632	6.2098	5.9713
9	8.5660	7.7851	7.1078	6.8017	6.5152
10	9.4713	8.5302	7.7217	7.3601	7.0236
15	13.8651	11.9379	10.3797	9.7122	9.1079
20	18.0456	14.8775	12.4662	11.4699	10.5940
25	22.0232	17.4131	14.0939	12.7834	11.6536

Year(N)	8%	9%	10%	12%	14%
1	0.9259	0.9174	0.9091	0.8929	0.8772
2	1.7833	1.7591	1.7355	1.6901	1.6467
3	2.5771	2.5313	2.4869	2.4018	2.3216
4	3.3121	3.2397	3.1699	3.0373	2.9137
5	3.9927	3.8897	3.7908	3.5048	3.4331
6	4.6229	4.4859	4.3553	4.1114	3.8887
7	5.2064	5.0330	4.8684	4.5638	4.2883
8	5.7466	5.5348	5.3349	4.9676	4.6389
9	6.2469	5.9952	5.7590	5.3292	4.9464
10	6.7101	6.4177	6.1446	5.6502	5.2161
15	8.5595	8.0607	7.6061	6.8109	6.1422
20	9.8181	9.1285	8.5136	7.4694	6.6231
25	10.6748	9.8226	9.0770	7.8431	6.8729

year but 1 percent per quarter. This adjustment process can be generalized using the following formula:

Future Value = Present Value $(1+i/m)^{mn}$

Where : n = Number of Years Compounding Occurs

i = Annual Interest (Discount) Rate

m = Number of Times Compounding Occurs during the Year

Hence, the number of periods and the interest rate per period must be adjusted to match as determined by the problem being solved.

With this background on the time value of money, compounding and discounting, and non-annual periods, some of the tools for evaluating capital investments can now be discussed.

Capital budgeting evaluation methods

The next step is to choose an evaluation method that can be used to rank, accept, or reject investment alternatives. There are several methods for evaluating capital investment decisions. Some of them are simple, while others are quite complex, requiring sophisticated mathematical analysis. Four methods will be discussed here. Listed in order of complexity they are: payback period, simple rate of return, net present value, and internal rate of return.

Two investment alternatives for BF&G are used to illustrate the capital budgeting evaluation methods discussed in the following sections. The two alternatives are to purchase a self-propelled fertilizer applicator and to expand the grain storage and handling facility by 250,000 bushels. The applicator costs $300,000 and the grain facility expansion costs $312,500. Both alternatives would be income-increasing investments and have initial cost outlays that are about equal. However, the net cash flows for the two alternatives are very different and are used to illustrate differences in the four capital budgeting methods.

Payback period

The length of time it will take an investment to generate sufficient additional cash flows to pay for it is called the **payback period**. This simple tool allows the agribusiness manager to compare investment alternatives and determine which will recoup its initial investment in the shortest period of time. Consequently, that alternative would be the most desirable. The formula to calculate payback period is simple:

$$\text{Payback Period} = (\text{Investment})/(\text{Average Annual Net Cash Flow})$$

The accept–reject criterion centers on whether the project's payback period is less than or equal to a firm's maximum desired payback period. If two projects have payback periods that are less than the maximum desired period, then the one with the shorter period is accepted.

For example, the new self-propelled fertilizer applicator BF&G is considering, which costs $300,000, has floatation tires, a GPS system, would reduce soil compaction, allow for site-specific application, and upgrade the services provided to producers. The firm plans to charge customers for the full cost of these applications plus a profit margin. Estimated average annual net cash flows to the business before depreciation is estimated to be $149,200. (Note that since depreciation is a method of offsetting initial cost, it must be omitted in the calculation of the payback period.) A second investment alternative being considered is 250,000 bushels of additional grain storage and grain handling equipment at a cost of $312,500. Estimated annual net cash flow before depreciation is $70,000.

$$\text{Applicator Payback Period} = (\text{Investment})/(\text{Avg. Annual Net Cash Flow})$$
$$= \$300,000/(\$149,200/\text{year}) = 2.0 \text{ years}$$
$$\text{Grain Storage Payback Period} = (\text{Investment})/(\text{Avg. Annual Net Cash Flow})$$
$$= \$312,500/(\$70,000/\text{year}) = 4.5 \text{ years}$$

Plate 13.2 Extended hands
The payback period is the length of time it takes an investment to pay for itself. Photo courtesy of USDA Natural Resources Conservation Service.

Generally, the shorter the payback period, the better the investment is rated. So it would appear from this simple method that the fertilizer applicator is the better alternative because it will pay for itself in two years, compared to 4.5 years for the additional grain storage.

The payback method only indirectly considers risk in the decision process. The payback principle suggests that by accepting the project with the lowest payback, that project has the lowest risk. This is based on the investor desiring the cash flow as soon as possible due to the uncertainty involved in receiving the cash and the opportunity to reinvest that cash sooner with a shorter payback period. Here, the manager is assumed to be comparing similar investment options and time is the primary risk factor under consideration. Thus, an investment that is repaid by cash flows in two years involves less risk than a project that pays back its original investment in 4.5 years.

The payback period method is widely used, partly because of its simplicity. But it ignores the length of life of the investment. In this example, the additional grain storage lasts for 20 years, while the applicator lasts only five years with regular cash flows. Now, the decision is more complicated and the payback period does not capture the difference in the life expectancy of the two investments. In such a case, a more sophisticated investment evaluation method is needed. Although this limitation is a serious drawback, when cash flow is critical, the payback method is useful.

In a somewhat similar limitation, the payback method ignores cash flows generated after the payback period. Hence, payback gives more weight to those investment alternatives that have the majority of cash flows generated early in the life of the project or investment alternative. Some investments may generate small cash flows early due to various startup costs, but the cash flow may increase over certain periods of the lives of alternative investments. These cash flows would be ignored when compared to an investment that generates the majority of its cash flow in the first few years.

Another weakness of the payback method is a failure to account for the time value of money. Thus, $1 of cash flow received three years from today is given the same "weight" in payback analysis as $1 received today. As discussed in the section on time value of money, cash flows received after one period need to be discounted. So if all the cash flows have equal value regardless of when they are received, the cash flows received in three years are overvalued relative to those received in one year. Other methods for evaluating investments have been developed to help address these limitations of the payback period.

Simple rate of return

The **simple rate of return** method refers to the profit generated by the investment as a percentage of the investment. The most common variation of this method uses the average return and the average investment to give a more accurate analysis. The simple rate of return calculation is:

$$\text{Simple Rate of Return} = \left(\text{Average Annual Return} / \text{Average Investment}\right)$$

Simple rate of return is perhaps the most commonly used method of capital budgeting. This method considers net earnings over the entire expected life of the investment. It is easy to understand and is consistent with ROE goals imposed by management. In fact, many firms have estimated ROE standards that serve as a cutoff point for investment projects. Unless an investment proposal exceeds these minimal standards, it will not be seriously considered. A standard of 15 to 25 percent is common for many food and agribusiness firms.

To illustrate the calculations of the simple rate of return, the two investment alternatives BF&G is considering will be used. The net returns expected from this $300,000 applicator investment decline over its life because of increasing maintenance and repair costs. BF&G estimates that average net profit after depreciation for the new applicator equals $89,200 and the calculations are shown in Table 13.5. The average rate of return would be:

$$\text{Simple Rate of Return} = \left(\text{Average Annual Return} / \text{Average Investment}\right)$$
$$= \left(\$89,200 / \$150,000\right) = 59\%$$

BF&G would rank this investment alternative higher than those with returns under 59 percent.

Next, the cash flows from the additional grain storage and handling equipment are presented and the simple rate of return is calculated.

So, the simple rate of return for the fertilizer applicator is higher (59 percent) than the rate of return for the additional grain storage (35 percent). Consequently, if the simple rate of return is used to analyze the two investment alternatives, then the fertilizer applicator would be selected over the additional grain storage. However, the simple rate of return has limitations much like the payback period method.

The chief limitation of the simple rate of return method is that it fails to consider the timing of cash flows. When the initial net cash flow is high, but falls off quickly, the situation is far different than when the initial net cash flow is low, but increases over time. A consequence of this problem is that incorrect conclusions may be drawn because the method fails to consider that a dollar returned now is significantly more valuable than a dollar of cash flow received several years later. Also, the simple rate of return is a rate and is influenced by the size of the investment. So, an investment project may be very small, but have a very high

Plate 13.3 Applicator
Capital equipment, like this applicator, generates profit for the agribusiness over time. Photo
courtesy of USDA Natural Resources Conservation Service.

Table 13.5 Self-propelled fertilizer applicator simple rate of return
calculations

Year	Net Cash Flow Before Depreciation (dollars)	Depreciation (dollars)
1	150,000	60,000
2	148,000	60,000
3	146,000	60,000
4	144,000	60,000
5	158,000	60,000
Total	746,000	300,000
Average	149,200	60,000

Average Investment = $300,000 / 2 = $150,000

$$\text{Simple Rate of Return} = \frac{\text{Average Net Cash Flow} - \text{Average Depreciation}}{\text{Average Investment}}$$

$$= \frac{\$149,200 - \$60,000}{\$150,000} = 59\%$$

Table 13.6 Expansion of the grain storage simple rate of return calculations

Year	Net Cash Flow Before Depreciation (dollars)	Depreciation (dollars)
1	70,000	15,625
2	70,000	15,625
3	70,000	15,625
4	70,000	15,625
5	70,000	15,625
.	.	.
.	.	.
.	.	.
20	70,000	15,625
Total	1,400,000	312,500
Average	70,000	15,625

Average Investment $= \$312,500 \div 2 = \$156,250$

$$\text{Simple Rate of Return} = \frac{\text{Average Net Cash Flow} - \text{Average Depreciation}}{\text{Average Investment}}$$

$$= \frac{\$70,000 - \$15,625}{\$156,250} = 35\%$$

simple rate of return. At the same time, a much larger project may have a lower simple rate of return, but generate far more dollars for the agribusiness.

Net present value

Net present value (NPV) is the current, net value of an investment, taking the time value of money into consideration when evaluating costs and returns. As discussed earlier, the time value of money captures the fact that a dollar received now is worth more than a dollar received at some future date. In essence, net present value provides a measurement of the net value of a multi-year investment in today's dollars. The net present value method uses the discounting formula discussed previously to value the projected cash flows for each investment alternative. The net present value model is set up as presented below:

$$\text{NPV} = -\text{INV} + \frac{P_1}{1+i} + \frac{P_2}{(1+i)^2} + \dots + \frac{P_N}{(1+i)^N} + \frac{V_N}{(1+i)^N}$$

Where:

NPV = net present value of the investment alternative

INV = intial investment

Pi = net cash flows attributed to the investment

VN = terminal or salvage value of the investment

N = length of the planning horizon

i = interest rate or required rate of return, also called the cost of captial or discount rate

Initial investment

The **initial investment** refers to the initial amount the investor commits to the investment. It is important to ensure all the costs necessary to make the investment operational are included (i.e., freight, installation, sales taxes, modifications to buildings, etc.) as well as the cost of the asset. All of these costs may not occur in the initial period, so outlays that occur later must be reflected in the periods in which they occur. Also, the trade-in or salvage value of a replaced asset should be subtracted from the purchase price of the new asset.

Net cash flows

For the net present value method, net cash flow from the business rather than accounting profits is used as the measure of returns. **Net cash flows** include all the cash inflows and all the cash outflows for operating expenses and any other capital expenditures. In essence, net cash flow is the stream of cash the owner can withdraw from the investment.

Note that net cash flows are not the same as net income as reported on an income statement, because the accrual accounting method differs from the cash basis of accounting. And, a difference between net income reported on the income statement using the accrual accounting method and the net cash flow will very likely occur. This difference occurs because revenues and expenses reported on the income statement are assigned to the fiscal year in which they are earned or are incurred rather than when they are received or paid in cash. Annual depreciation and inventory changes are examples of income statement items that do not directly impact the cash flow. Only future net cash flows are relevant for inclusion in the net present value calculation. (Note that income taxes complicate the analysis a bit. While we will not address this topic here, the normal rule is to use after-tax cash flow figures and an after-tax discount rate.)

Terminal value

The **terminal value** for the investment is the residual value the investment is expected to have at the end of the planning horizon. For depreciable assets such as machinery, this value is often called the salvage value. There could also be some appreciation in the value of the investment, which would result in capital gains at the end of the planning period.

Discount rate

The **discount rate** or cost of capital is the interest rate used in capital budgeting, which is the firm's required rate of return on its equity capital. This was referred to earlier in this text as the opportunity cost (Chapter 3). The discount rate (i) used in capital budgeting consists of three components:

- A risk-free interest rate
- A risk premium
- An inflation premium

The risk premium reflects the riskiness associated with the expected net cash flow. The inflation premium reflects the anticipated rate of inflation. This rate should reflect the rate of return that the firm expects to earn on its equity capital.

Planning horizon

A multi-year planning horizon is used for the investment in capital assets, because the assets generate cash flows for the firm for more than one year. A major factor that influences the length of the planning horizon is the productive life of the asset that is being purchased.

The acceptability of an investment depends on whether the net present value is positive or negative. The criteria used for decision-making are:

- If the net present value exceeds zero, accept the investment
- If the net present value equals zero, be indifferent
- If the net present value is less than zero, reject the investment

Keep in mind that when the net present value exceeds zero the method implies that the investment is profitable; however, it is profitable relative to the required rate of return implied by the discount rate. Rejection of an investment, which is based on a negative net present value, implies that an alternative investment with the rate of return (discount) used in the analysis is more profitable than the investment being evaluated.

When several investments are being considered, all are income generating, and all have positive net present values, the size of the net present value is used as part of the decision criteria. In this situation, the investment with the largest net present value is most favored, with the next largest net present value second, etc. If the investment under consideration is cost reducing, then the projected cash flows would reflect cash outlays (i.e., expenses). When cost-reducing investments are compared, the decision criteria are based on the minimum net present value of cash outlays.

Again, assume BF&G is considering two investment alternatives: the addition of the self-propelled fertilizer applicator costing $300,000 and the expansion of the grain storage and handling facility costing $312,500. However, this time the net present value method will be used to perform the analysis. BF&G's owners insist that additional investment alternatives return a minimum of 14 percent. Based on internal records from operating costs of current application equipment and the best estimates of customer response to additional service equipment, the net cash inflows shown in Table 13.7 are expected from the new custom applicator.

The net cash inflow generally declines each year because of increased maintenance and repair costs as the equipment gets older. Taking this pattern of cash flows and the time value of money into consideration, there is a different present value associated with each year. The net present value of the investment is shown in Table 13.8.

The present value of the cash flows for this investment using a 14 percent discount rate is $305,351.60, which is considerably more than the $300,000 cost of the investment, so the NPV is positive. This means that the investment will meet the owners' 14 percent cost of capital criterion, since the NPV is $5,351.60.

The present value of the cash flows for the additional grain storage ($54,375) using a 14 percent discount rate is $360,131. This amount is calculated by multiplying the annual net cash flow series of $54,375 by the discount factor from Table 13.4 for 14 percent and 20 years, which equals 6.6231. Since the net present value of the annual series of net cash flows

Table 13.7 Net cash inflows for the self-propelled applicator investment

Year	Net Cash Inflow (dollars)*
1	90,000
2	88,000
3	86,000
4	84,000
5	98,000**

Notes: * The net cash inflow is the excess of cash revenue over cash expenses attributed directly to the investment. Depreciation and other noncash expenses are excluded.
** Includes $16,000 from sale of the applicator when scrapped.

Table 13.8 Net present value for applicator investment with 14 per cent discount factor

Year	Net Cash Inflow (dollars)	14 Percent Discount Factor (dollars) *	Present Value
1	90,000	0.8772	= $78,948.00
2	88,000	0.7695	= 67,716.00
3	86,000	0.6750	= 58,050.00
4	84,000	0.5921	= 49,736.40
5	98,000	0.5194	= 50,901.20
	Total Present Value		$305,351.60
	Initial Investment in Applicator		$300,000.00
	Net Present Value		$5,351.60

Note: * see Table 13.2.

is more than the investment cost ($312,500), the NPV is positive for the grain storage invest-ment alternative as well. This means the grain storage expansion investment also meets the owners' 14 percent criterion, since the NPV is $47,631.

The net present value method of investment analysis has several advantages. First, it deals with cash flows rather than accounting profits. Second, the method is sensitive to the actual timing of the cash flows resulting from the investment. Third, the time value of money enables the user to compare benefits and costs in today's dollars. Finally, because invest-ments are accepted if a positive net present value is calculated, the acceptance of an invest-ment will increase the value of the firm. That is consistent with the goal of managers to maximize shareholders' wealth.

One disadvantage of the net present value method results from the need for detailed, long-term forecasts of cash flows. These forecasts over long time periods are just that, forecasts. So, there is considerable pressure on the manager to forecast cash inflows and outflows as accurately as possible.

Internal rate of return

The same equation used to calculate the net present value of an investment can be used to determine the **internal rate of return (IRR)** for the investment. The internal rate of return is called by various names: discounted rate of return, marginal efficiency of capital, yield, etc. However, it is essentially the discount rate that equates the net present value of the projected net cash flows to zero.

To calculate the internal rate of return for an investment, set up the net present value model as outlined above. Determine the projected cash flows and set the net present value to zero, then solve for i as shown below:

$$NPV(\$0) = -INV + \frac{P_1}{1+i} + \frac{P_2}{(1+i)^2} + \ldots + \frac{P_N}{(1+i)^N} + \frac{V_N}{(1+i)^N}$$

The discount rate that satisfies this equation is the internal rate of return.

To illustrate this method, let's find the internal rate of return for an investment that requires a \$1,000 initial investment and yields a \$1,200 cash payment one year in the future. The IRR model is set up as shown below:

$$0 = -1,000 + \frac{1,200}{1+i}$$

Solving the equation for i results in the following:

$$1+i = \frac{1,200}{1,000} = 1.2$$
$$i = 0.2$$

So, the IRR for this investment is 20 percent.

When the planning horizon exceeds one year, the procedure is essentially a trial-and-error approach to determine the discount rate that will yield a zero net present value. Today, spreadsheets are used to determine the IRR given the complexity of the calculation.

Investments can be ranked and accepted or rejected on the basis of their internal rates of return. The ranking is based on the relative sizes of the internal rates of returns, with the largest being the most favored. The acceptance of each investment depends upon the comparison of its internal rate of return with the investor's required rate of return. Acceptability is based on the following decision rules:

- If the internal rate of return exceeds the required rate of return, accept the investment.
- If the internal rate of return equals the required rate of return, be indifferent.
- If the internal rate of return is less than the required rate of return, reject the investment.

Since the net present value of the applicator is positive using the 14 percent rate of return, the project is acceptable. However, in order to compare the project to other projects being considered, the internal rate of return is needed. The trial-and-error approach is used to calculate the net present value for the self-propelled fertilizer applicator for BF&G. A discount factor of 15 percent is used and the net present value is calculated to be – $1,897.40 (Table 13.9), which is negative, but closer to 0 than the net present value for 14 percent. Hence, the internal rate of return is slightly below 15 percent. In fact, the exact IRR for the fertilizer applicator is calculated using a financial calculator and is determined to be 14.7336 percent.

So, the applicator project is an acceptable project, but to determine if the applicator project should be selected by management, the IRRs for other projects being considered by BF&G would need to be calculated and compared to that of the applicator. The project that satisfies the required rate of return criterion and has the highest IRR should be selected.

Using a financial calculator, the calculated IRR for the grain storage expansion alternative is 16.5925 percent. So, the additional grain storage would be selected over the self-propelled fertilizer applicator investment alternative when the IRR method is used. However, recall the opposite was the case when the payback and simple rate of return methods were used to analyze the investment alternatives.

Comparing net present value and internal rate of return

The net present value and internal rate of return methods are closely linked because each uses the same discounting procedure. However, the net present value method requires a specified discount rate, while the internal rate of return method solves for the discount rate that yields a zero net present value.

The IRR method gives the same ranking of investments as the NPV method under most circumstances. Although both methods account for differences in the time pattern of cash flows, occasional differences in ranking can arise because of different assumptions about the rate of return on reinvested net cash flows. The IRR method implicitly assumes that net cash inflows from an investment are reinvested at the same rate as the internal rate of return of the investment under consideration. The NPV method, on the other hand, assumes that these funds can be reinvested to earn a rate of return that is the same as the firm's discount rate.

Which reinvestment is more realistic? The NPV rate has the advantage of being consistently applied to all investment proposals. Also, the NPV rate may be more realistic if the

Table 13.9 Net present value for applicator investment with 15 per cent discount factor

Year	Net Cash Inflow (dollars)	15 Percent Discount Factor	Present Value (dollars)
1	90,000	0.8696	= 78,264.00
2	88,000	0.7561	= 66,536.80
3	86,000	0.6575	= 56,545.00
4	84,000	0.5718	= 48,031.20
5	98,000	0.4972	= 48,725.60
	Total Present Value		298,102.60
	Initial Investment in Applicator		300,000.00
	Net Present Value		–1,897.40

discount rate is determined by the opportunity cost of capital. On the other hand, the internal rate of return from each investment alternative can be compared against a common required rate of return. The internal rate of return also represents profitability in percentage terms, which is often preferred by business managers, even though the increases in wealth measured by the net present values more directly reflect the objectives sought by the firm. In the end, both approaches provide useful insights into the evaluation of capital investment decisions.

Summary

Capital investment decisions are among the most important decisions made by management. Their impact is long range and greatly impacts the flexibility of the business. Professional managers approach these decisions in a systematic way by first identifying the problem, then summarizing the facts, analyzing the alternatives, taking action, and evaluating results. The procedure for evaluating investment choices is called capital budgeting.

Four methods for evaluating capital investment decisions are discussed in this chapter. Listed in order of complexity, the four methods are the payback period, simple rate of return, net present value, and internal rate of return.

Simplistic approaches such as the payback period and simple rate of return are widely used methods for making investment decisions. However, the methods may lead to incomplete or even inconsistent conclusions. By recognizing the time value of money and using the net present value method or the internal rate of return method, managers can get a more realistic assessment of investment alternatives.

Discussion questions

1. Why are capital investment choices so important to the agribusiness manager? Why are these decisions more complex than most operating decisions?
2. What are the advantages and the disadvantages of the payback period method of evaluating capital investments?
3. What information is needed to calculate the simple rate of return? What are the advantages and disadvantages of this method of evaluating capital investments?
4. Why is net cash flow used in the net present value method rather than net income from a pro forma income statement prepared using accrual accounting?
5. Which type of business would likely have a higher cost of capital, a small biotechnology company, or a large food retailer? Why?
6. What are the advantages and disadvantages of NPV and IRR for evaluating capital investments? Why are these approaches superior to the payback period and simple rate of return approaches?
7. What are the similarities and the differences between the net present value method and the internal rate of return method?

Case study: Perfect Choice packing plant

Perfect Choice packing plant packs and ships apples and stores fruit for area growers. John Bradley, Perfect Choice's new manager, was being pressured by the owners to evaluate several possible changes in the business, including a major upgradng of the packing line.

Table 13.10 Estimated net profit and depreciation expense for new sizing equipment

	Net Profit	
Year	Before Depreciation (dollars)*	Depreciation (dollars)
1	250,000	80,000
2	225,000	80,000
3	200,000	80,000
4	150,000	80,000
5	135,000	80,000

* Net Profit here includes only cash inflows and outflows.

Perhaps you can help John by applying some of the decision tools discussed in this chapter to the decisions he faces.

Perfect Choice has the option of significantly upgrading their plant by adding electronic sizing and sorting equipment. The cost of this equipment is $400,000, with an expected life of five years. Equipment of this nature is not expected to have an appreciable salvage. There will be significant labor savings involved. Initially, the new equipment will require little maintenance and repair, but as it gets older, the cost of maintenance will go up sharply. Generally, Perfect Choice's owners and management feel that a 12 percent return should be expected from any new investment project before it can be undertaken. Expected net returns before depreciation resulting from the investment and estimated depreciation expenses are shown in Table 13.10.

Questions

1. Initially, before any calculations, what is your general reaction? Should Perfect Choice invest in the new equipment?
2. What is the payback period for this investment?
3. What is the simple rate of return for this investment?
4. What is the net present value of this investment, using the 12 percent minimum return required by the owners?
5. What are the limitations of each of these approaches?
6. In the final analysis, do you believe this investment project would be good for Perfect Choice? Why or why not?
7. Using a financial calculator or spreadsheet, determine the internal rate of return for the investment.

Part V

Operations management for agribusiness

Plate Part V Production Process
Operations and logistics: this section explores plans and processes for getting products and services developed, produced, and delivered. Photo courtesy of USDA Natural Resources Conservation Service.

14 Production planning and management

Objectives

- Develop an understanding of operations management, including the definition, background, and current issues in the area
- Discuss some of the unique characteristics of agricultural commodities and products as they impact operations management and production planning
- Summarize the key elements involved in plant and facility location decisions
- Identify some of the factors to consider in determining the capacity of a plant or facility
- Differentiate between process, product, hybrid, and fixed-position facility layouts
- Understand the key elements of job design

Introduction

Operations management refers to the direction and control of the processes used by food and agribusiness firms to produce goods and services. In the past, operations management was concerned primarily with manufacturing in factories. Today we recognize that service managers in supermarkets, financial institutions, web-based industries, and agribusiness consulting firms have the same questions and considerations of job design, location choice, facility design, purchasing, transportation, and scheduling as does the manufacturing sector. Operations management for food and agribusiness firms can be broken into two distinct areas: (1) **production planning** and (2) **supply chain management**. Chapter 14 is devoted to production planning as it pertains to both agribusiness service and manufacturing firms, while in Chapter 15 we look at the related area of supply chain management in the food and agribusiness industries.

Modern operations management begins with the work of Frederick W. Taylor, who introduced the concept of **scientific management** in the early 1900s. Taylor observed and studied production focusing on workers, the methods of work, and the wages paid for increased output. From these observations, Taylor developed a basic set of tenets for scientific management, using his scientific or analytical approach. Taylor believed in the following:

1. A standardized set of procedures that were to be used for a job each time it was performed
2. Determination of the most efficient procedures for each job through scientific comparison tests

3. Careful screening, hiring, and training of workers to match them with the most appropriate job
4. A functional division of labor that would allow each person to perform the most suitable task in the production process, with management and workers jointly devising the best system for the division of labor

A period of extensive research on operations management followed Taylor's early work. The development of modern computers in the 1940s further advanced operations management. Although the first machines were both expensive and difficult to use, they greatly magnified the scope of numerical computations and quantitative models. George Dantzig introduced linear programming in the 1940s, a mathematical technique that determines the most profitable allocation of resources in situations such as transportation, least cost feed rations, and crop acreage allocations. Production scheduling models and critical path methods were developed in the 1950s. During the 1960s, computer simulations were developed, and the 1970s saw the introduction of a powerful materials management system called **materials requirement planning (MRP)**. The 1980s and 1990s saw the incorporation of robotics, flexible-manufacturing systems, and computer integrated manufacturing systems into the operations management arena. More recently, information technology has further advanced in operations management, and is now known as **enterprise requirement planning (ERP)**. ERP systems connect a firm's manufacturing systems with other areas such as finance, customer relationship management, human resources, and supply chain management, integrating internal and external information across the entire organization.

The **production planning** aspect of operations management includes a wide range of decisions and activities including:

*   Devising a quality program
*   Locating a plant
*   Choosing the appropriate level of capacity
*   Designing the layout of the operation
*   Deciding on the process design
*   Specifying job tasks and responsibilities

The **supply chain management** function of operations management is discussed at length in the next chapter. Since both production planning and supply chain management are integral parts of operations management, they must be considered in tandem. Supply chain management in operations management consists of an equally wide range of decisions and activities including:

*   Aggregate production planning
*   Production scheduling
*   Purchasing of materials for production
*   Management of the various types of inventories
*   Transportation management
*   Distributing the finished goods or services

Operations management involves a system of interrelated activities and players as shown in Figure 14.1. **Suppliers** provide the inputs to the system. Timely delivery of high-quality inputs influences all activities in the system. **Inputs** consist of the human resources (skilled

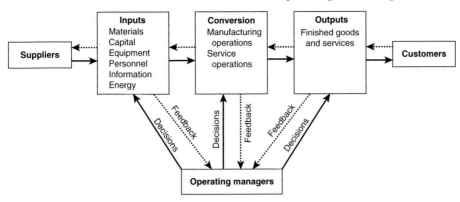

Figure 14.1 Operations management system

workers and managers), capital (equipment), materials, information, and energy required to produce the desired **outputs**. The conversion or **transformation** of inputs into outputs involves the system of facilities, processes, and procedures by which goods and services are produced. **Customers** purchase the outputs from the system, and their feedback to the rest of the system is essential in generating and designing new products and services. Finally, managers make decisions and obtain feedback on those decisions to make the total production system flow smoothly. One key distinction is that production management focuses on optimizing the management of the firm's conversion process, while supply chain management seeks to optimize activities among the value chain, from the suppliers to the customers.

For example, a dairy begins with raw milk and can produce a variety of milk, cheeses, ice cream, and other products. The technology in a dairy is quite different from the technology used to sell crop protection chemicals and provide agronomic services, yet the problems of scheduling, controlling, storing, shipping, and general management of the two processes are quite similar. Other examples are shown in Table 14.1.

Table 14.1 Examples of production systems and components

Manager	Suppliers	Inputs	Conversion	Outputs	Customers
Restaurant Manager	Food Distributors Meat Suppliers Equipment Mfrs Packaging	Meats Vegetables Food Servers Utensils Equipment	Cooking Meal Preparation Serving	Prepared Foods Satisfied Customers	Hungry Diners
Crop Farm Producer	Equipment Dealer Seed Firms Chemical Mfrs	Land Labor Equipment Seed Chemicals Fertilizer	Tilling Planting Spraying Harvesting	Fruits Vegetables Grains	Food Processors Ethanol Plants Livestock Farms Exporters

Issues in operations management

Whereas cost and efficiency were once the main issues of operations managers, five issues concern operations management for the food and agribusiness sectors:

1. The growing service sector
2. Time-based competition
3. Productivity improvement
4. Global competition
5. Quality

The growing service sector

Operations management was once simply known as production management because of its focus on the manufacturing sector. However, the service sector is now the fastest growing sector of the U.S. economy, comprising roughly 62 percent of U.S. GDP (U.S. Department of Commerce 2011). There are, of course, differences between manufacturing and service organizations, but the differences are shrinking as techniques for managing manufacturing firms find their way to service firms and vice versa. Some characteristics that distinguish the two sectors are shown in Table 14.2.

Goods producers are distinguished from service producers because their products are physical, durable, and can be inventoried. Service firms produce intangibles—ideas, information, performances, etc. Some service organizations like restaurants typically produce a good and a service—food and service. Many farm supply retailers not only provide quality products, but also services such as product information, delivery, product assembly, and credit. Service providers, unlike manufacturers, tend to have high levels of customer contact, and response time to customers is often measured in minutes, rather than days and weeks for goods producers.

Goods producers tend to serve regional or even international markets whereas services tend not to be able to be shipped. Rather, service producers tend to locate near the customer (although this is changing with web services like Amazon). Quality is more easily measured

Table 14.2 Characteristics of goods producers and service providers

More Like a Goods Producer	More Like a Service Provider
Physical, durable product	Intangible, perishable product
Output can be inventoried	Output cannot be inventoried
Low customer contact	High customer contact
Long response time	Short response time
Large facilities	Small facilities
Capital intensive	Labor intensive
Quality easily measured	Quality not easily measured

with goods producers as it can be measured and tested. Quality in service producers is difficult to measure because it is measured on intangibles such as customer perceptions, communications, and time, each subjective in nature.

Time-based competition

Time-based competition is competing for customers and market share using the dimension of time as a source of competitive advantage. Quicker response to changing customer needs is one example of time-based competition. Technological innovations, especially with the Internet, have enabled firms to compete on the basis of time. Global competition and higher expectations by consumers are other reasons. Agribusinesses are reducing the time it takes to develop and introduce new products or services. As well, they are responding faster to customer orders, deliveries, service needs, and problems.

Productivity

Productivity can be defined as the dollars (or quantity) of output (goods and services) produced divided by the dollars (or quantity) of resources (materials, wages, equipment cost) used. Productivity is the prime determinant of a nation's standard of living because employee wages are generally determined by the productivity of human resources. Part of the concern over productivity has arisen because of the shift to a service-oriented economy. Many economists believe that it is more difficult to achieve the same improvements in productivity for the service sector as can be achieved in the manufacturing sector.

From 1948 to 2008, agricultural productivity has been about half of the productivity of the non-farm sector (Ball 2010). Between 1948 and 2008, U.S. agricultural output grew at the average annual rate of 1.6 percent compared to 3.6 percent for the non-farm sector. Moreover, the growth rate of productivity in agriculture has varied tremendously. Some speculate that U.S. agriculture is losing its competitive advantage. Reasons cited include the increasing use of marginal land, real increases in prices for water and energy, increased regulations for pesticide and chemical use, increased regulations for confined animal feeding operations, and the lagged effects of decreasing real investment in agricultural research as a public good.

Labor productivity in the retail food industry has increased moderately, but erratically, because of extensive mechanization and technological improvements. Technological improvements in supermarkets include computer-assisted checkouts and data processing. New store concepts (i.e., food warehouses) that provide fewer services (and less labor inputs) have also increased productivity. But productivity has also declined with some food retailers because they have implemented expanded services, such as salad bars, delicatessens, and in-store bakeries that require more labor. Some eating and drinking establishments have also experienced declining productivity rates because of enhanced customer service and longer store hours (generating revenues that are marginally higher than input rates).

Global competition

Globalization is affecting the operations management of agribusiness. As noted in Chapter 5, trade is critical to this nation's agricultural economy. About 34 percent of U.S. agricultural production is exported and imports account for a varied, but growing share of U.S. consumption of agricultural products (World Agricultural Outlook Board 2011). Exports of

U.S. agricultural products (including foods, feeds, and beverages) were roughly $108 billion in fiscal 2010. Operations managers must factor the effects of globalization into their decision-making. Decisions such as determining where to place a new production plant are more complex as countries with promising markets and/or low cost inputs should be considered. As well, decisions on the size or capacity of a plant must factor in the potential rapid growth of exports. Exported products may require modification to fit the needs of a different consumer; therefore, plant layouts and equipment must be flexible. Also, domestic markets no longer imply domestic competitors. For example, seven of the top 30 food retailers in the U.S. are affiliates of foreign-owned retailers. Operations managers in retail food operations must determine how to positively respond to these new competitors from abroad.

Quality

High-quality products and services at reasonable prices have been the source of success for many food and agribusiness firms, but the importance of **quality** has escalated with increased competition. The results of poor quality are often increased costs of production and lost market share. Furthermore with food products, quality is also associated with expectations of food safety. Concerns over an e-coli breakout can affect sales for entire industries as the UDSA and FDA try to identify the source.

For today's operations managers, a key challenge is to provide top-quality products or services efficiently. But "quality" without reference is a nebulous term. Like "comfort" and

Plate 14.1 Fresh produce
Timeliness in the delivery of seasonal products requires efficient production, foreman processing, and delivery. Photo courtesy of USDA Natural Resources. Conservation Service.

"beauty," everyone has his or her own idea of what "quality" is. It becomes the manager's job to understand what type or level of quality their customers expect, want, and need. Quality is a factor that must be present to market any product, but the issues include what kind of quality and how much quality. From a planning perspective, managing that quality is a critical element in any successful food and agribusiness operation.

These types of issues, including a new definition of convenience, the number of choices available, and an overriding demand for value in purchases has placed unprecedented demands on operations managers. The challenge for the operations manager is to ensure that quality is effectively delivered consistently, at a price buyers are willing to pay.

The definition of quality may differ depending upon to whom one is talking. Consumers typically define quality as **fitness for use**. Currently, many companies have come to interpret fitness for use as "meeting or exceeding customer expectations." Consumers also tend to talk about **value**, or how well the product or service meets its intended purpose at the price the consumer is willing to pay. On the other hand, manufacturing managers offer a different quality definition: **conformance to specifications**.

Fitness for use and conformance to specifications provides the fundamental basis for managing operations to produce quality products. Marketing and design's role is to understand customer needs and then to translate those needs into appropriate specifications for goods and services. With these specifications, it is up to the manufacturing or service operation to ensure that the specifications are met or exceeded. Poor communication between marketing, design, or operations can result in inferior quality.

What are the implications of good-quality products and services? From a marketing standpoint, higher quality can increase profits and/or market share. One important aspect of market share is attracting and retaining customers. A recent study revealed that of the customers who make complaints, more than half will give the firm a second chance if the complaint is resolved. The figure jumps to 95 percent if the complaint is resolved in a timely manner. Higher profits are realized because high-quality products and services can typically be priced higher than comparable, but lower-quality products.

From a cost standpoint, defective products or services can increase the costs of production. Production costs related to quality include the following:

1. Prevention costs
2. Appraisal costs
3. Internal failure costs
4. External failure costs

Prevention costs are the costs associated with stopping defects before they happen. **Appraisal costs** are incurred in monitoring the quality level of products and services during the course of production. **Internal failure costs** are the costs that are generated during the production and/or rework of defective parts and services. Finally, **external failure costs** are incurred when the product or service fails once it is in the consumer hands.

Since the 1980s, food and agribusiness firms have made significant improvements in their product and service quality, which have enabled many to gain a significant advantage over competitors. Today's emphasis on Six Sigma programs to identify defects can be traced to the total quality management movement of the 1980s.

In the food industry, **hazard analysis critical control point (HACCP)** has become an important, recognized food safety program. It has gained rapid acceptance as the result of the public and legislative demands for increased food safety protection. Also, the increased global sourcing of raw materials and distribution of food products has also driven the need for a standard food safety program that is acceptable by the international community.

HACCP's basic premise is focused on the prevention of food safety problems rather than controlling them. Although HACCP is primarily helpful in the processing of safe food, it is also applicable to raw materials suppliers. The benefits of HACCP include reducing the risk of manufacturing and selling unsafe products, an increased awareness of hazards in the workplace, and better product quality. The HACCP system consists of seven principles, which describe how to establish, implement, and maintain the system in an operation. The principles are outlined below:

1. Conduct a hazard analysis. Prepare a list of steps in the process where significant hazards occur and describe the preventative measures.
2. Identify the Critical Control Points in the process.
3. Establish Critical Limits for preventative measures associated with each identified Critical Control Point.
4. Establish Critical Control Point monitoring requirements. Establish procedures from the results of monitoring to adjust the process and maintain control.
5. Establish corrective actions to be taken when monitoring indicates a deviation from an established critical limit.

Plate 14.2 Strawberries
Seasonality and perishability of agricultural products present real challenges for operations and logistics managers in the food and agribusiness markets. Photo courtesy of USDA Natural Resources Conservation Service.

6. Establish effective record-keeping procedures that document the HACCP system.
7. Establish procedures for verification that the HACCP System is working correctly.

Unique issues with agricultural products

Special problems inherent in the production of agricultural products influence many of the decisions involved in operations management including the choice of plant location, method of transportation, and scheduling. Two such problems are **seasonality** and **perishability**. (A more complete list of these factors was presented in Chapter 1.)

Agribusiness supply firms are engaged in highly seasonal production processes. During the peak planting and harvesting seasons, facilities are often strained to the utmost to produce the services and products producers need to utilize in a very short period of time. While the manufacture and processing of farm supplies is scheduled as evenly as possible throughout the year to maximize efficiency, lack of sufficient storage to accommodate peak season needs places tremendous pressure on production facilities as they struggle to keep up.

Perishability is in some ways related to the problem of seasonality. Of course, fruits and vegetables are highly perishable and must be processed quickly to prevent spoilage. At the same time, some of these products are so highly seasonal that processors, canners, freezers, and packers are left with virtually idle facilities after a peak season. Some industries have evolved successful ways of counteracting this dual problem and the tomato industry is one. Storing tomatoes in aseptic, non-refrigerated, stainless steel vats effectively eliminates problems of deterioration. Operations that produce tomato products are now able to run consistently for 12 months of the year without fear of spoilage, thus reducing costs during the peak season and increasing productivity in the off-season. Fresh tomatoes can be shipped across the country in aseptic railroad cars, which produces significant savings in transportation costs.

Yet another typical problem of agricultural products is **bulk**; the costs for shipping bulky loads of oranges from Florida to the Pacific Northwest can be extremely high. Handlers must also wrestle with the physical problems of storing bulky products as they await processing or shipping. As with most such problems, this difficulty is also reflected in costs.

Variability in quality and quantity must still be managed in the agricultural industry although consumer demand for consistency has had significant impacts in this area. Processors, canners, and freezers of lobster and shrimp, for example, must weigh and differentiate among fish of unequal quality. Apples and other fruits are sorted using near infrared technology on the basis of size, shape, and color. Eggs and milk must be graded, as are many other products. In some cases, product weights must be standardized to fit certain-size packages or selling weights; this can sometimes produce waste.

A final difficulty experienced in the production of agricultural products is *variation in value*. Price efficiency demands that production managers manufacture outputs with the highest possible value consistent with the costs of production. A dairy processor may find that cheese has a higher market value than milk for table consumption; but if its value is only one-third more than that of milk, and it requires twice the production cost, then price efficiency tends to favor producing the milk. Because there is such a wide variety of value in agricultural products (in different cuts of beef, for example) this is an important area for agribusinesses to explore. This influences decisions related to product mix, which were discussed earlier in Chapter 7.

Location

Manufacturing firms in the U.S. typically build more than 3,000 new plants each year and expand 7,500 others. The decision to locate a plant is a strategic decision that will have a lasting impact on issues such as operating costs, the price at which goods and services can be offered, and a company's ability to compete in the marketplace. A classic example is the beef meat packing industry. In the 1960s, meat packers were located in major railway cities where live cattle were shipped and high wages were paid. As well, the packing plants were old, multi-story buildings that did not operate at full capacity because of inconsistent supply. Meat packers new to the industry saw the opportunity to reduce costs and increase productivity by locating processing plants near cattle production feedlots and employing low-skilled operators in highly mechanized plants.

Another example—have you ever wondered why White Castle locates its eating establishments near manufacturing plants? White Castle's strategy is to segment the market and cater specifically to a target population of blue-collar workers and away from other competitors such as McDonald's. These two examples illustrate how important inputs (cattle and labor) and customers are to the success of a firm. Thus, location of the plant is a strategic choice, and many factors that influence choice of location should be considered when making these decisions. The following sections outline current location trends in the U.S. followed by factors that affect location decisions.

Significant U.S. trends

Geographic diversity, locating plants in nonunion states, and the competition among states to develop industries are three of the more important trends currently affecting plant location. Industries were once concentrated in certain geographic regions. For example, most automobile manufacturing was once in Michigan. Today, geography and distance are becoming less relevant for many location decisions. Why? Both transportation and communication technologies have improved dramatically. Telecommunications (voice and data) are enabling business firms to conduct business across the globe. Also, wage differentials between regions of the United States are gradually disappearing; e.g., in 2010, production workers in the south earned around 80 percent of what workers in the northeast.

A second trend is that more service and manufacturing firms are relocating to the nonunion states, many of which are in the south. Many firms are moving operations to the south, because of lower relative labor costs, less unionism, and a perceived stronger work ethic. Of course, a milder climate is also a factor, as is a population shift towards the south (as baby boomers are retiring); e.g., dairy farming has shifted to the Sunbelt states of Texas, New Mexico, Idaho, and California. Today, more milk is produced in California than in Wisconsin.

The third U.S. trend is that state and local governments are enticing firms to locate in their areas by offering generous **tax and incentive packages**. These economic development packages may include items such as special loans for machinery and equipment, state matching funds, state-sponsored employee hiring and training programs, and tax exemptions on corporate property, or excise taxes. Governments offer these incentives since bringing business to the town, county or state may help boost the economy in the long run. However, there is a concern that the state incentives promote wasteful competition among units of government, as they later struggle to provide for infrastructure, schools, etc. to support the new plants and their employees.

Factors affecting location decisions

When food and agribusiness managers choose a site for their facilities, they consider many factors. Of course, the relative importance of any factor is dependent on the type of product or service produced, plant size, plant type, environmental restrictions, and geographic location. Six of the more important factors in firm location include:

1. Proximity to raw materials and suppliers
2. Location of markets
3. Labor climate
4. Agglomeration
5. Taxes and incentives
6. Proximity to other company facilities

Proximity to raw materials and suppliers

Agribusinesses may wish to have *proximity to raw materials and suppliers*—especially if one major raw material input is needed and that input is costly to ship in its raw state. Examples of food and agribusinesses very dependent on sources of supplies include canning industries, corn processors, and meat packers. In the beef meat packing industry for example, cattle would be bulky and costly to ship from Nebraska to New York, so they are slaughtered near finishing feedlots and shipped long-distance in the more manageable form of boxed beef. By locating near cattle feedlots and lower-wage markets, meat packers have seen industry cattle kill-costs cut by 50 percent and plant utilization rates increased to about 90 percent compared to the 60 percent industry average of that time.

Agricultural industries that transport large volumes of material, often perishable, must also consider locating where bulk transportation resources are available. Most of the large grain elevators are located on either large water or rail systems. Thus, firm location attempts to minimize both the costs of production and transportation of raw materials and suppliers.

Location of markets

There is an old real estate adage that states the three most important factors in real estate are location, location, and location. *Location of markets* is especially important to retailers because customers will often not travel long distances to buy from a retailer. Agricultural goods that are bulky, perishable, or heavy can receive higher prices if they are located near markets because of higher quality, better service, and lower transportation costs. Agribusinesses that produce inputs for other firms often locate facilities near these buyers to minimize distribution costs and to provide better service.

Locating near markets is very important for service firms. Equipment manufacturers have found that aftermarket (replacement) parts sales and service requires relatively close locations to markets because producers will only drive limited distances for parts and services. Rather than maintaining full dealerships, manufacturers are locating satellite service facilities near these markets to provide for aftermarket parts, sales, and service.

Labor climate

In a survey and interview of firms on factors considered in locating a new manufacturing plant in the United States, 76 percent of the respondents indicated that a favorable labor climate was a dominant factor (Schmenner 1993). Labor factors such as wage rates, worker productivity, training requirements, attitudes toward work, and union strength are also important considerations. One other such factor is the availability of qualified labor. Food and agricultural companies that require a great deal of research may find it advantageous to locate near a large land-grant university where highly skilled, technical resources are concentrated. In the meat packing industry example, meat packers located in unfavorable labor climates and agreements were at a competitive disadvantage because wages and benefits could be as much as 40 percent higher than a competitor's.

Agglomeration

Agglomeration, another factor in facility location decisions, is the accumulation of business activity around a specific location. Firms often locate in close proximity to one another because they can increase the efficiency of services both at the business, household, and social level. For example, a firm may locate near a group of existing firms because they can share in the existing infrastructure such as transportation, water, or sewage systems. The amenities of the agglomeration of restaurants, theaters, and/or professional sports teams can also produce social benefits for the employees and management of agribusinesses.

Taxes and incentives

As mentioned, states are using tax and incentive packages as part of an economic development package to attract industries. The fast and vast expansion in the North Carolina hog industry provides an example of just how a thriving business sector can help give back to the economy. In 1986, North Carolina hog farmers raised 2.4 million hogs and pigs on about 15,000 hog operations. Of those, only about 800 farms had more than 500 head of hogs. By 2009, the number of hog farmers in North Carolina had shrunk to about 2,800 while the state's total hog production climbed to 9.6 million head. Ninety-nine percent of those hogs were raised on about 1,600 farms, each handling 1,000 head or more. Overall North Carolina pork production including growing, packing, and processing, and their associated industries were responsible for an estimated 46,660 full-time jobs in 2007, with $7.2 billion in sales.

Proximity to other company facilities

Food and agribusinesses may also locate new facilities considering their *proximity to other company facilities*. For example, agribusinesses may opt to open a new service facility in a region that is not adequately serving its customers currently with existing company facilities. Agribusinesses affected by climatic conditions may pursue a risk management strategy of having facilities spread out across a variety of geographic, temperature, and soil conditions. Seed firms locate production facilities in different areas (even countries) to assure themselves of seed production and to minimize the uncertainty of poor weather. Some agribusinesses may locate new facilities in relative proximity to other company facilities because they supply parts to one another or share management and staff. Also, proximity to providers of packaging, software, etc. can lead firms to choose a location.

Location decisions for service businesses

Location decisions in service businesses can be even more important than in manufacturing businesses. Factors such as convenience to customers, traffic volumes, income levels, and residential density are important sales indicators and thus influence location decisions. For example, most people shop at the supermarkets located on the way home from work or at grocery stores within two miles of their homes.

Location of competitor stores can also be an important consideration for service firms—a new supermarket located near a new housing development and away from competitors may provide a distinct competitive advantage for that firm. In contrast, it is interesting to note that locating near competitors can sometimes be advantageous as well. A greater number of total customers (or a *critical mass*) may be attracted to a group of stores clustered in one location versus the total number of customers who would stop at the same stores at scattered locations. A cluster of fast food restaurants off an interstate exit typically produces a critical mass.

A restaurant chain with operations in North America and Japan considers six primary factors when determining the location of a quick service (fast food) restaurant:

1. Area employment
2. Retail activity
3. Proximity to successful competitors
4. Traffic flow
5. Residential density
6. Accessibility and visibility

Area employment is important because the chain is targeting 20- to 45-year-old workers on lunch breaks. The chain also confirms that area firms allow workers to take lunch breaks off premises. *Retail activity*, the second factor, is important because a lot of quick service eating is done on impulse by shoppers. Being near successful competitors is seen as an advantage because they signal that the area is a good market. *Traffic flows* are also important because most business is from people in cars. In fact, traffic flow of 16,000 cars every 24 hours is considered good. A *residential population* of about 20,000 upper-middle-class residents within a two-mile radius is considered to be adequate to ensure weekend and evening business. Finally, *accessibility and visibility* are also important factors in considering location. Specifically, traffic direction, intersections, traffic backups during rush hour, and surrounding buildings and signs are important accessibility and visibility factors that are considered.

Capacity planning

Capacity planning includes the activities that are undertaken to determine what the appropriate size of a manufacturing plant or service location should be, so that a certain quantity can be produced over a specific time-period. A food or agribusiness firm must balance the cost of having excess capacity against the potential of lost sales due to too little capacity. If not anticipated correctly, lost sales and disappointed customers may have serious effects on a firm's short-term and long-term profitability. Accurate forecasts of present and future demand are critical in capacity planning. Thus, an understanding of the product life cycle can assist in forecasting overall demand product (Chapter 7). Many factors should be considered in determining the appropriate capacity, five of which are detailed here:

1. Economies of scale
2. Flexibility

3.   Seasonality and other patterns of production
4.   Fluctuating demand
5.   Multiple versus single shifts

Economies of scale

According to the **economies of scale** principle, larger plants usually result in lower per unit costs because fixed costs may be spread out over a larger quantity of output. Volume–cost analysis can be used to determine how much volume is needed to cover fixed costs (Chapter 12). Economies of scale are often associated with firms utilizing large quantities of expensive processing equipment (such as large breweries) where large, bulk quantities are produced. Construction costs are also reduced when a facility producing 10,000 units is built versus two separate facilities producing 5,000 units each. In addition, larger plants enjoy specialization of labor, management, and byproduct utilization.

Flexibility

An alternative view to economies-of-scale is flexibility. One concept of bringing flexibility to production processes is the **focused factory,** first proposed by Skinner in the early 1970s. Several factors brought about this alternative view to plant size and capacity; including shorter product life cycles, the importance of quality, and needed flexibility. The focused factory concept holds that several smaller factories will improve individual plant performance because the operations manager can concentrate on fewer tasks and can more easily motivate a smaller workforce toward one goal. There are also fewer layers of management, the plants are more flexible in introducing new products, and a team approach can be taken to problem solving. Furthermore, smaller firms may offer flexibility in terms of proximity to sources of raw materials and proximity to market destinations, which in turn could result in lower transportation costs.

Seasonality

Highly seasonal agricultural products can produce special headaches for an operations manager. Manufacturers of farm inputs such as seed, fertilizers, and chemicals see heavy demand for their products in the spring. Grain elevators experience peak demand in the fall. On the food side, holiday items such as whole turkeys and cranberries see their demand peak in the weeks preceding Thanksgiving.

   In some cases, peripheral operations can be done or other products can be produced in the off-season to balance the resource needs of the food or agribusiness. Where this is not possible, a plant large enough to handle peak productivity levels becomes a costly operation when output is significantly reduced in the off-season. In such cases, it may actually be more economical to run several smaller plants and to close down plants that are not needed during the off-season. This does not reduce the overhead costs associated with an unused facility, but it does limit the day-to-day expenditures of running an unnecessary part of a larger operation.

Fluctuating demand

Fluctuating demand in manufacturing can be solved by building up inventory during slow demand periods. However, the perishability and bulkiness associated with agricultural products may prevent this option. A distinct difference between manufacturing and service is that services are typically produced and consumed simultaneously. Thus, service firms must build enough capacity into their facilities to meet peak periods of demand. For example, a supermarket must have enough checkout counters to meet not only average demand but also for peak demand periods (such as the week before Thanksgiving). Of course, service firms can shift or smooth out demand by altering consumer behavior. Offering discounts or other incentives during off-peak hours are some ways that are used to shift consumer demand.

Multiple shifts vs. single shifts

Multiple shifts may be an alternative to operating a facility at maximum capacity—if the labor is available. Theoretically, it is possible to produce twice as much in a plant with double shifts, while limiting the need for space by spreading out the working hours. Agricultural-chemical companies require multiple shifts because of the chemical nature of their products and large investments in equipment. Likewise, corn and soybean processing facilities typically run 24 hours a day, seven days a week—stopping only for emergencies or routine maintenance. In plants where this is not the case, managers must carefully evaluate the costs of a larger facility versus the increased costs of sometimes less productive and possibly more accident-prone labor.

Layout planning

Layout planning refers to the specific design of the physical arrangement within a facility. When planning the physical layout of a plant, consideration must be given to utilize space and labor effectively, minimize material handling, and maintain flexibility for future changes in product or demand. The goal of layout planning is to allow both the workers and equipment to run the operation in the most efficient and effective manner. There are four basic categories of facility layout:

1. Process
2. Product
3. Hybrid
4. Fixed position

Process layout

A **process layout** arranges activities by function. Thus in a process layout, regardless of the product being created or assembled, all like functions are grouped in the same place—that is, canning equipment with canning equipment, inspectors with inspectors, etc. The process layout is common where different goods or services are produced intermittently to serve different customers (Figure 14.2). As a result, general resources and equipment are utilized to make the process layout more flexible to changes in product mix or marketing strategies. Disadvantages of the process layout include slower overall processing rates (because of the switching between products), higher levels of inventory, increased time lags between specific operations, and higher costs for material handling.

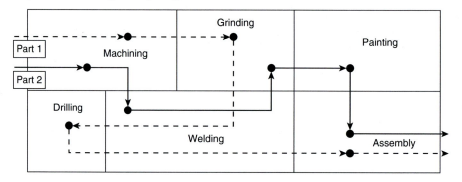

Figure 14.2 Process layout—farm implement manufacturing facility

Product layout

A **product layout** is geared specifically to the continuous production process because it produces one product at a time, step by step, with one function following another in sequence as the product is assembled, and with much fewer variations in product (Figure 14.3). Workers grading and packing peaches on a conveyor belt, for example, are operating in a product layout framework. One person may remove debris, the next may be responsible for sorting, while another oversees packing into crates, and so forth.

Advantages of product layouts include faster processing rates, lower inventories, less skilled labor required, less time lost to product changeovers, and less materials handling. One significant disadvantage is that less flexible and more capital-intensive resources are

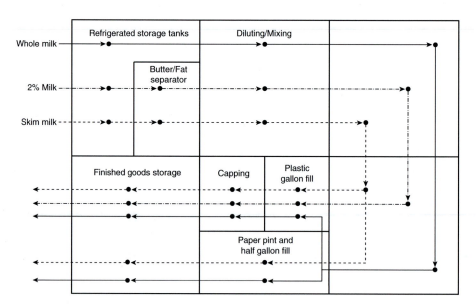

Figure 14.3 Product layout—fluid milk facility

dedicated to specific products that may have uncertain life cycles. In addition, a line can work only as fast as its slowest operation and downtime can be expensive when one machine on the production line breaks down.

Hybrid layout

A **hybrid layout** combines the process and product layouts to balance the advantages of each (Figure 14.4). Managers may choose this form of layout when introducing flexible manufacturing systems. In group technology applications, different machines are brought together to produce a group (or family) of similar parts in an assembly-like fashion. Some manufacturing firms have decreased work-in-process inventories by up to 90 percent using such systems. The hybrid layout form is very popular in operations such as plastics molding and even supermarkets. In a supermarket for example, the manager may place similar merchandise in the same location to aid customers in finding the desired items (a process layout). However, the supermarket layout is designed to *lead* customers through the entire store (up and down aisles) maximizing their exposure to the full line of goods (a product layout).

Fixed position layout

A **fixed position layout** is used in the construction of large items such as farm buildings and silos (Figure 14.5). This layout is used in situations where the item being constructed is too

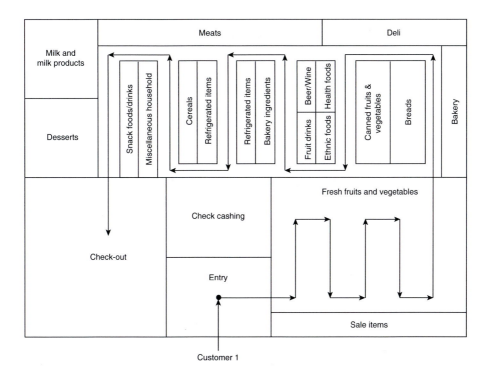

Figure 14.4 Hybrid layout—supermarket

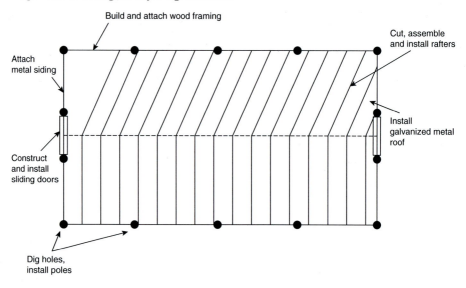

Figure 14.5 Fixed position layout—farm building

large or bulky to move easily or where the item is to be built fixed in place. Construction is accomplished in one place, and tools and materials are brought to the assembly location. A fixed-position layout eliminates or minimizes the number of times that a product must be moved, and it is often the only feasible layout solution.

Process design

Process design is selecting the specific inputs, operations, and methods that are to be used to produce the good or service. Decisions concerning process design are very important because of their implications for cost of production, level of personalized customer service, convenience, and flexibility. The first step in process design is outlining a step-by-step description of each operation that is to be completed. Four general aspects are considered in process design:

1. Capital intensity
2. Resource flexibility
3. Vertical integration
4. Customer involvement

Capital intensity

The determination of **capital intensity** is simply choosing which tasks humans will perform and which tasks machines will perform. Many levels of capital intensity are available today with the advent of new technology and computer-assisted equipment. Hazardous or difficult operations in meat packing companies have been automated reducing the risk of injury to employees. The level of capital intensity significantly impacts production costs. Customer interaction is also impacted. For example, Wal-Mart and other retailers are shifting to self-checkout by customers. These systems allow one employee to oversee as many as eight cash registers at once. Although increased computer sophistication, labor shortages, and costs drove the change, customer acceptance and ease of use were critical success factors.

Resource flexibility

Resource flexibility can be defined as the ease with which employees and equipment can operate a wide variety of products, functions, and levels of output. Shorter product life cycles require more general equipment and a broader range of employee skills. Thus, more job training may be required for employees. However, the benefits of a flexible workforce are real: improved productivity, higher morale, and a wider product offering to customers.

Vertical integration

Vertical integration is associated with owning some or all of the various steps that are taken to produce a product from start to finish (i.e., from raw materials to the delivery of the finished product). The more processes a firm in the chain owns, the more vertically integrated the firm is said to be. Vertical integration can be advantageous to a firm if the firm has the relevant skills for each step it controls and if the company views the industry into which it is integrating as being important to its future success. One challenge with vertical integration is matching the capacity of your manufacturers with your retailers. If manufacturing plant size compared to retail demand is too large, you end up with excess capacity. This means that you either run your plant at less than full capacity or you sell the extra production to competitors.

For example, Kroger company, the largest food retail chain in the United States, has pursued vertical integration aggressively. Kroger's operations include 2,468 supermarkets, 777 convenience stores, and 40 manufacturing plants producing store branded products from water to spaghetti sauce, dairy products to peanut butter.

Customer involvement

Customer involvement is the degree with which the customer is allowed to interact with the process. Particularly in service industries, customer contact is critical to customer satisfaction. Customer involvement can take the form of interaction with self-service options, product selection, product design, time, and location of service. High levels of customer involvement tend to be found in processes that are less capital intensive and more flexible.

Customer involvement in business management decisions has increased as more information is provided on the Web. A good example of customer involvement is a farm equipment manufacturer's web page that allows a farm producer to search and access parts inventory. When used in the evening, the producer can check stock, order the part, and pick it up the next morning. The system also allows the producer to cross-reference over 400,000 competitive equipment parts that correspond to the manufacturer's parts. This allows the producer to consolidate parts runs into one stop.

The self-service level of customer involvement extends from the fuel pump (pay at the pump), to grocery store self-checkout. Automated teller machines (ATMs) involve the customer interaction through the selection of menu items. Through technology advancements, the customer has changed—and what they expect and what they are willing to do for the sake of convenience has continued to drive changes in this area.

Job design

Detailed job design follows process design and is distinguished by the focus on the individual operator. **Job design** can be defined as the broad set of activities that determine the tasks and responsibilities of each employee's job, the employee's surrounding work environment, and the detailed order of operations that will be used to complete the tasks required to meet production requirements. The objectives of job design are two-fold: (1) meet the production and quality goals of the organization; and (2) make jobs safe, satisfying, and motivating for the employees.

Traditional job design began with Frederick Taylor and his scientific management approach. Operations were divided into their individual components and studied to determine the most efficient manner to perform an operation. Today, job design can be thought of as comprising two major categories: (1) the social or psychological environment; and (2) the physical environment.

The social environment

The non-physical or behavioral issues in the workplace are included in the *social* or *psychological environment*. Items such as training, the proper level of supervision, job expectations and responsibilities, and performance feedback are all subsets of an employee's social environment. In particular, employee motivation to consistently perform at high levels is the result of a positive social environment. Many theories of work motivation have been developed over the past century.

Psychologists contend that highly repetitive jobs lead to boredom, injuries, and poor job performance. Declining job performance is often associated with absenteeism, high turnover, grievances, and poor quality. New approaches to job design are an attempt to counter poor job performance. These approaches include job rotation, job enlargement, job enrichment, and work teams.

Job rotation allows operators to perform different jobs during their shifts. Rotation increases the overall skills of the employees and minimizes work-related injuries (as long as the jobs differ in the motions used). **Job enlargement** is simply increasing the number of tasks that each operator performs. Here, **job repetition** is reduced because the cycle time of each job has increased. **Job enrichment** expands the duties and responsibilities of the operator. For example, a technician at a brewery might be responsible for monitoring the filtering process. Job enrichment increases those responsibilities to include taking and analyzing quality measurements, inspecting the filters, and deciding when the filtering equipment needs maintenance.

Work teams are another method of giving employees more responsibility and decision-making authority. Quality circles, used extensively in Japan, are teams that meet to work out solutions to quality issues. Other teams are often formed for special purposes. Issues such as new work policies, the details of an employee bonus plan, or a labor-management issue are examples of issues that these teams have attacked. Self-managing work teams are also common. Teams of three to 15 employees meet to organize and run a definable work area. Team members learn all job tasks, rotate among jobs, schedule vacations and overtime, order supplies, and make hiring decisions.

The physical environment

The *physical environment* for employees can have substantial effects on employee morale, productivity, health, and safety. The physical environment in job design consists of items such as safe working conditions, lighting, noise, temperature, and ergonomics. Ergonomics, or human factors, is the study of the interaction between the person and their workstation, tools, and equipment. The objectives of ergonomics are to improve human performance by increasing speed and accuracy, reduce fatigue, reduce accidents due to human error, and improve user comfort and acceptance.

Examples of ergonomics in the food and agribusiness markets abound. Farm producers using tractors see the effects of ergonomics in their tractor cabs. Cabs are placed in a location where they can best view the operations of the tractor with comfortable but supportive seats, grips on the steering wheel, levers positioned for easy access, and dials that are easy to read.

Summary

Operations management involves a complex network of decisions that affects agribusinesses in the production of goods and services. In considering the production planning aspects of operations management, agribusiness managers must consider the uniqueness of agricultural production: seasonality, perishability, bulkiness, and variations in quantity, quality, or value. Operations management involves production planning and supply chain management, and must be viewed as a total system.

Production planning decisions entail quality management, location, capacity, layout, and process design of the plant or facility, and job design. Supply chain management decisions include purchasing, production scheduling, inventory control, and distribution. Many factors affect each of these sets of decisions, and food and agribusiness managers must consider all factors and their effect on the total system before making a decision.

Discussion questions

1. List and describe some of the activities that an operations manager may be engaged in. How would you describe the agribusiness operations manager's role? How does this role relate to the systems approach outlined in Figure 14.1?
2. In your view, what are the most difficult operations management problems for the following types of firms: (a) a veterinary practice that serves both the farm and companion animal markets; (b) a large California dairy operation; and (c) a retail food store located in Minnesota?
3. Why is Frederick Taylor called "the father of scientific management?"
4. Differentiate between the four types of plant or facility layouts and give an example of a specific agribusiness that might employ each layout. Visit a food or agribusiness firm of your choice. Map the layout of the facility and identify the type of facility layout used by the food or agribusiness firm.
5. What factors are involved in the choice of plant or facility location? Name some food and agribusiness companies whose locations reflect consideration of these factors.
6. What are some of the factors that may be considered in determining the optimal capacity for a food or agribusiness firm?

7. For either a job you have held, or for a job held by someone you know, carefully explore the design of the job. Evaluate both the social environment and the physical environment of the job you have selected.

Case study: BioAg—part I[1]

BioAg's company history

BioAg is a small Midwestern firm manufacturing agricultural chemicals that are environmentally sensitive. Important patents help protect BioAg's 60 percent market share in its market segment. Although still small, the niche market for environmentally sensitive agricultural chemicals has been growing about 50 percent per year since 2004.

BioAg has experienced rapid growth in sales because of an increasing societal concern about environmental issues (see Table 14.3 for a summary of BioAg's sales and marketing activities). In 2004, the company started with two products. By 2011, the BioAg product line included 36 different chemicals for use on wheat, barley, corn, soybeans, and specialty crops. BioAg has no retail outlets, but rather sells their products through farm input supply firms. As the number of products has grown, BioAg has sold its products through more and more supply firms. The company now sells their products through 420 supply firms in 24 states, up from only eight supply firms in one state in 2004. They anticipate selling in international markets within three years.

Questions

1. What are some of the production planning and management issues that BioAg has had to face as their product line has expanded and the firm has grown?
2. Why would quality management be an important area for BioAg given the type of product it produces? What are some of the characteristics of the firm's products that would make quality management important?
3. BioAg is considering an addition to its production capacity to support additional growth. The firm is considering adding to the current site, and building a new plant in West Texas. What are some of the issues the firm will need to consider as it explores these two options?

Table 14.3 Sales and marketing statistics for BioAg

Item	Year							
	2004	2005	2006	2007	2008	2009	2010	2011
Sales (million $)	.50	.75	1.25	2.50	3.75	7.50	12.50	18.00
Number of Products	2	4	5	7	8	12	20	36
Number of Farm Supply Sellers	8	12	22	40	70	140	280	420
Number of States Where Product Sold	1	2	3	6	8	12	16	24

4. BioAg management is also working to decide just how large the addition to capacity should be. What suggestions do you have for the firm's management? What issues will they need to consider as they determine how much to expand?

Note

1 This case originally published as Frank Dooley and Jay Akridge, "Supply Chain Management: A Case Study of Issues for BioAg," *International Food and Agribusiness Management Review*, 1(3): 435–441, 1998.

References and additional reading

Alvarez, Valente B., Winston Bash, Bill Cornelius, Polly Courtney, and Lynn Knipe. "Ensuring Safe Food—A HACCP-Based Plan for Ensuring Food Safety in Retail Establishments." Ohio State University, Food Science and Technology. Bulletin 901, 2010. http://ohioline.osu.edu/b901/index.html

Ball, Eldon. "Agricultural Productivity in the United States." U.S. Department of Agriculture. Economic Research Service, 2010. www.ers.usda.gov/Data/AgProductivity/

Dooley, Frank and Jay T. Akridge. "Supply Chain Management: A Case Study of Issues for BioAg." *International Food and Agribusiness Management Review*, 1(3): 435–41, 1998.

Krajewski, Lee J., Larry P. Ritzman, and Manoj K. Halhotra. *Operations Management*. 9th ed. Upper Saddle River, NJ: Prentice Hall, 2009.

Schmenner, Roger W. *Operations Management from the Inside Out,* 5th ed. MacMillan College Division, 1993.

U.S. Department of Commerce. "Gross-Domestic-Product-(GDP)-by-Industry Accounts." Bureau of Economic Analysis, Washington, DC, 2011. www.bea.gov/industry/gpotables/default.cfm

World Agricultural Outlook Board. "USDA Agricultural Projections to 2020." U.S. Department of Agriculture, OCE-2011-1, 2011. www.usda.gov/oce/commodity/archive_projections/USDAAgriculturalProjections2020.pdf

15 Supply chain management for agribusiness

Objectives

- Outline the various objectives and functions of supply chain management
- Understand the steps involved in the supply chain management process
- Describe the role of, and activities involved in, purchasing/procurement in food and agribusiness firms
- Distinguish between material requirements planning (MRP) and just-in-time (JIT) production operations systems
- Identify the role of inventory in the agribusiness and the different types of inventory firms hold
- Describe the different types of inventory tracking systems used in agribusiness
- Explore the role of physical distribution in the agribusiness
- Consider how information technology, especially the Internet, impacts the supply chain management process

Introduction

The previous chapter provided an overview of the production planning aspects of operations management in the agribusiness. Production planning functions include determining the location, layout, capacity, and specific processes to be used by the agribusiness in producing goods and services. A related critical aspect in running the agribusiness is managing the flow of materials, products, and information into and out of the firm—or **supply chain management**.

Supply chain management considers the range of activities related to how inputs for the agribusiness are scheduled and procured, as well as how finished products are stored and distributed to customers. More specifically, supply chain management is defined by the Council of Supply Chain Management Professionals as "the planning and management of all activities involved in sourcing and procurement, conversion, and all logistics management activities." Logistics management activities include "inbound and outbound transportation management, fleet management, warehousing, materials handling, order fulfillment, logistics network design, inventory management, supply/demand planning, and management of third party logistics service providers." Many see logistics management as the activities occurring within the firm, while supply chain management involves the coordination among firms. The essence of supply chain management is focused around shipping and storing inputs, finished products, and information.

Importance of supply chain management

Some companies such as Wal-Mart have made supply chain management the cornerstone of their total business strategy. Its increasing importance has also motivated agribusiness firms to restructure their organizations creating supply chain management departments whose manager reports directly to the company CEO. But why is supply chain management so important?

Three examples show its importance to a company's total profitability and success. First, take the critical function of inventory control—just one part of supply chain management. Inventory typically represents 35 to 50 percent of the current assets in a company. With such a significant share of assets, decisions about how to best manage inventory play a critical role in the total profitability of the agribusiness. Other supply chain functions involve purchasing inputs for use in production, coordinating the smooth production of goods and services, determining the appropriate levels of inventory, and probably most importantly, serving as the linkage between the agribusiness, its suppliers, and its customers. This last set of functions involves distribution of the agribusiness firm's products and services.

Second, increasingly industry sectors have come to understand the importance of collaboration. One important food industry concept of supply chain management is a business strategy called **Efficient Consumer Response (ECR)** (Food Marketing Institute). ECR is a responsive, accurate, information-based system that links food manufacturers and distributors with retail supermarkets. The four aspects of ECR include:

- Replenishment of products as they are used
- Providing the right assortment of products
- Introducing new products
- Developing effective promotion strategies

The benefits of ECR are increased sales, fresher products, less damage, reduced cycle time, more accurate invoicing, increased cash flow, and fewer instances of out-of-stock products.

For the production agriculture sector, AgGateway has similar aspirations.

A third reason logistics has become important is a concept called **cycle-time-to-market**. Also called "quick response," cycle-time-to-market has become a central strategic focus for many agribusinesses. The goal is to reduce the time it takes for a product to go from an idea to a finished product in the customer's hands. To reduce cycle-time-to-market, a team of sales, logistics, marketing, design, and manufacturing employees work closely together to plan, design, produce, and market new products. Supply chain management plays a critical role in reducing cycle-time-to-market by integrating suppliers into new product development, thereby minimizing time and supplier production issues. Supply chain management provides the equipment and information infrastructure beginning with suppliers and purchasing, through production, and finally to the physical distribution systems. Many firms have developed integrated information systems to reduce cycle-time-to-market.

Supply chain management objectives

Supply chain management, as it is defined today, is a relatively new field of study which has evolved dramatically in the past 40 years. In the past, agribusinesses narrowly focused their efforts on the physical distribution of their finished products, attempting to optimize inventory levels and reduce transportation costs.

In the past 20 years, firms have integrated their materials and distribution functions to operate and control the agribusiness. The result has been a joined system of purchasing, scheduling, production control, inventory, and distribution activities. Several of the more current, expanded supply chain management objectives include:

- Improved information technology
- Better customer service
- Reduction of risk
- Globalization of operations

Information technology

Fundamental to the increased attention of supply chain management are the improvements in **information technology**. These improvements let the agribusiness link suppliers, distributors, and end customers. New information technology developments continue to transform logistics capabilities. For example, RFID chips (radio frequency identification) have begun to replace UPC codes on packages. Suppliers to large retailers can obtain daily downloads of product sales by retail store. In some cases, inventory systems have automated ordering, with electronic orders being sent to a supplier when the inventory in a store drops to a predetermined level.

Customer service

Customer service has become another important objective for supply chain managers in agribusinesses. Customer service can be one tactical method of differentiating the goods or services of an agribusiness. For example, timely information about the status of a delivery or a speedy inventory replenishment system for efficient and effective customer service is one way of differentiating a firm's product or service. Increasingly, retailers monitor the performance of suppliers in factors such as on-time delivery or damaged items.

Risk reduction

Agribusinesses are also collaborating more with other firms to achieve **risk reduction**. Supply chain managers may establish contracts with suppliers or customers allowing for shared information and shared investments in transportation, facilities, new technologies, inventories, and product distribution. Agribusinesses can leverage their strengths and the strengths of partner firms to reduce risk as well. For example, one agribusiness may have expertise in distribution, while a supplier may have expertise in producing and servicing a certain component for that agribusiness. Sharing expertise allows agribusinesses to focus on their core competencies, while also benefiting from the strengths of key partners.

Globalization

Globalization is certainly on the minds of most agribusiness firms today as we saw in Chapter 5. Markets continue to expand abroad while competitors with foreign affiliation enter domestic markets. However, a global enterprise can be managed only if an effective logistics system is in place. On the input side, agribusinesses are increasingly going outside the United States to source raw materials. Information, and methods of shipment, must be developed to guarantee timely arrival of inputs. On the output side, agribusinesses seeking to export their products or to expand their operations globally must develop their own market channels or form partnerships with foreign firms. To do so, agribusinesses must understand the special needs and wants of the foreign consumer. Relationships must be developed with new suppliers, distributors, and retailers that often operate under different regulatory and cultural environments.

Supply chain management functions

This chapter provides the framework for understanding the role of supply chain management in the agribusiness and its interrelationship with the other functions of an agribusiness. Figure 15.1 shows the different activities of the supply chain management process. As you view this figure, keep in mind that the unique features of agricultural products such as per-ishability, seasonality, and bulkiness drive the way these functions are performed.

The supply chain management function begins where the marketing function of forecast-ing demand ended. **Aggregate production planning** transforms the long-term demand fore-casts into general production plans for the next quarter and year. **Master production scheduling** follows with a final production schedule detailing the exact timing and specific quantities to be produced. Purchasing uses the master production schedule to perform the

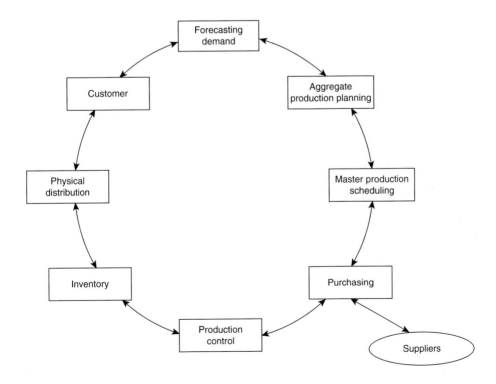

Figure 15.1 Supply chain management process

primary function of procuring the necessary inputs for the production of the finished goods. With the right quantity of inputs available, production control directs the internal logistics function creating detailed internal scheduling of sub-assemblies, machines, and coordinating the overall production process. Production control is focused on any last minute changes in the quantities of products produced, and accounts for production lost through scrap or downtime.

Once the products have been produced, they are then shipped for distribution or put into inventory. Many factors determine inventory levels as will be seen later. Distribution can take on many facets in terms of how goods are channeled to the end customer. This brings us full circle to complete the supply chain management functions. Customers purchase the finished goods and they drive forecasted demand for additional products. This quick overview of the activities of supply chain management is followed now by more detailed descriptions of the various functions.

Forecasting demand

Forecasting demand, a marketing function, was described in Chapter 7 and is briefly summarized now to put its role into perspective with the supply chain functions that follow. Highly seasonal demand, unpredictable weather, volatile market prices, and an evolving market characterize the agricultural industry. These market characteristics require extensive planning on the part of firm management. As described earlier, the general economic, market, and sales forecasts provide the foundation for many management planning decisions including supply chain management decisions.

General economic and market forecasts (i.e., long-range forecasts) drive decisions concerning distribution facilities, warehouse size, transportation equipment, and long-term supplier contracts. Market and sales forecasts (i.e., short-range forecasts) drive the short-term purchasing of raw materials for conversion into finished goods, inventory control decisions, and aggregate production planning.

Aggregate production planning

Aggregate production planning is the process of developing the specific production quantities and rates, and workforce sizes and rates, while balancing customer requirements and capacity limitations of plant and equipment. Monthly, quarterly, and annual aggregate production plans are developed using the longer-term general economic and market forecasts. Besides maximizing customer service, aggregate production plans strive to minimize inventories, minimize changes in workforce levels and production rates, and to maximize utilization of the plant and equipment.

For example, a food company may be forecasting future demand of its packaged cereals and cereal bars. Examining the past quarter's consumption of food products in the United States, the production planner notes the increased consumption of high-energy cereal bars. In addition, upcoming promotions and increasing interest by stores in stocking cereal bars provides valuable customer demand information. In aggregate production planning, these demand forecasts are combined with current production capacity limitations, inventories, and other information to plan how much ingredients, labor, and equipment are required for the next three to 12 months. Where aggregate planning shows a bottleneck in an item, such as a piece of equipment or a specific labor skill, plans can be put into place to alleviate the shortage temporarily or permanently.

The aggregate production plan does not specify the exact quantities of specific flavors or types of cereal bars that are going to be required. Rather, it estimates the rough quantities of total product types that are going to be needed, so that approximate quantities of raw materials, labor, and equipment can be determined. The exact quantities of individual **stocking keeping units (SKUs)** demanded are determined from sales forecasts (provided by sales representatives) and actual orders. These two items form the basis for the next step, the detailed master production schedule.

Master production scheduling

The master production schedule (MPS) is created once specific orders for products have been received and/or short-range sales forecasts have been determined. The MPS details the final quantities of SKUs that are to be made in specific blocks of time. The MPS typically provides weekly product requirements for a six-to-12-month time horizon. In the average production plant, the next six weeks of production are not changed to allow purchasing and production control time to finalize their purchases and plans (note this can vary dramatically with the product being produced). Beyond the approximate six-week time frame, the quantities of specific products have not been determined, but will firm up as the time span to production shortens. The **master scheduler** must consider the total demand on the resources and capacities of the agribusiness as well as the supplier's capacities. Figure 15.2 displays a simplified MPS process.

There are three basic MPS strategies. A **make-to-stock strategy** means the firm is producing for inventory, and the production occurs before the actual sale is made. Examples here would be the production of agricultural chemicals, seed, and many food products.

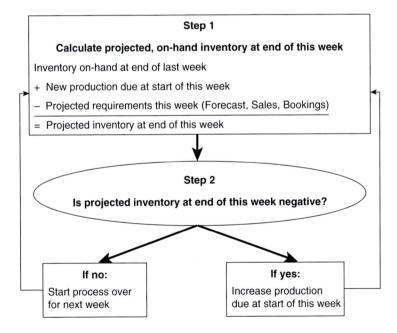

Figure 15.2 Simplified master production schedule process

Under an **assemble-to-order** strategy, a firm assembles available components when an order is placed. Farm tractors and machinery would be a good example of this strategy. When employing a make-to-stock strategy, the firm actually builds to order. A good example here would be firms in the dairy equipment business who build sophisticated milking systems precisely to a producer's specifications. Clearly, each of these strategies would employ the master production schedule idea in different ways.

Purchasing

With a realistic master production schedule completed, **purchasing** begins its tasks of procuring the inputs necessary to meet the requirements of the production schedule. Purchasing is a common function for every organization. Although it varies by industry, the typical firm spends about 40 to 60 percent of its total sales on purchased materials and services. As a result, even a small percentage reduction in such a huge portion of the overall costs for an agribusiness firm can have a significant effect on the firm's bottom line. For example, if net profits in the agribusiness are 5 percent of sales, then a 1 percent reduction in purchasing costs will fall through to the bottom line, thus increasing profits by 20 percent over their previous level. This example illustrates the relationship between costs of production (purchasing) and the firm's profits.

Some agribusinesses have centralized buying where materials are purchased in large quantities, often at substantial discounts. Other firms have decentralized purchasing where each location purchases just the goods that are needed, when they are needed. Both have their advantages and most agribusinesses use a combination of both. An agribusiness typically purchases four kinds of products.

- Products used for further processing
- Products that are resold
- Products used directly in the firm's final products
- Products used to make the product but not used in the product itself

The purchasing function performs many activities, which include the following:

- *Receive a purchase requisition*: purchasing examines these documents to determine if a less costly item can be substituted or eliminated entirely.
- *Select a qualified supplier*: purchasing selects suppliers based primarily on four factors—price, quality, timeliness, and customer service.
- *Place the order*: ordering procedures range from routine computer-based systems to very time-consuming manual systems, depending on the nature of the purchase and the buyer–supplier relationship.
- *Track the order*: purchasing monitors deliveries and production schedules and expedites orders as necessary; follow-up is particularly important when a delay could disrupt production, cause a loss of customer goodwill, and/or a potential loss of future sales.
- *Receive the order and approve payment*: purchasing works with receiving and accounting at this point to ensure all goods are received satisfactorily before authorizing payment.

The purchasing activity of selecting suppliers is critical because of the impact of input prices on the agribusiness's bottom line. As mentioned earlier, the four primary factors used in selecting suppliers are quality, price, timeliness, and customer service. **Quality** is a very important consideration. An agribusiness that uses a purchased part only to find out later that it is defective incurs numerous costs, including costs internal to the firm as well as potential loss of goodwill and future sales.

The price of purchased inputs is fundamentally important in selecting a supplier because the typical firm spends nearly half of its total sales on purchased items. **Timely delivery** of purchased inputs from suppliers is also very important. Parts priced at just pennies can cost the firm thousands of dollars for every minute that a production line is not running. The opportunity costs of such a problem can be enormous, as an agribusiness does not want to miss sales because they lack inventory of finished goods. On the other hand, having too many goods in inventory can be very costly. Carrying costs, physical storage space, record-keeping expenses, taxes, insurance, and interest lost on capital tied up in inventory can eat up as much as 35 percent of the inventory's purchase value. Consequently, **customer service** is another critical, but often overlooked, item. Shorter lead times and on-time delivery of purchased items help the agribusiness to provide higher levels of customer service with fewer inventories.

Production control

With the materials for production ordered, the supply chain responsibility now shifts to **production control**. Control of production flow is one of the most important daily functions of the operations manager. The responsibilities of production control include:

- Controlling raw materials inventory
- Providing detailed production scheduling information
- Controlling work-in-process inventory
- Communicating changes to master production scheduling and purchasing
- Controlling finished goods inventory

The tasks of production control are essential for a smooth, continuous flow of work through the agribusiness. Two production operations systems that can facilitate the smooth flow of production are material requirements planning (MRP) and just-in-time (JIT) systems. MRP is often referred to as a "push" system whereas JIT is a "pull" system. We will explore MRP and JIT to better understand why push and pull are very descriptive of these two types of production operations systems.

MRP production operations systems

Material requirements planning (MRP) is a computerized information system for managing production operations. Its purpose is to ensure that the right materials, components, and sub-assemblies are available in the right quantities at the right time so that finished products can be produced according to the master production schedule.

MRP operates in the following manner. First, the finished product requirements from the master production schedule are broken down into the requirements for individual parts or subassemblies. These requirements are compared with on-hand inventory to determine the quantities of units that still need to be produced. Schedules are created, inputs are purchased and received, and production begins. Parts produced in-house are combined with purchased component parts to form the most basic sub-assemblies. These are then "pushed" to the next level of sub-assemblies. These sub-assemblies receive further operations and are "pushed" to the next step of the manufacturing sequence to form larger sub-assemblies. The process of completing operations and pushing to the next operation continues until the finished product is completed. The entire production system is based on producing components and pushing them to their next stage of production.

JIT production operation systems

Another type of production operations systems is **just-in-time (JIT)**. The goal of a JIT system is to produce or deliver goods just as they are needed, in effect, attempting to completely eliminate inventories. JIT is more of a philosophy than a production operations system. The goals here are to eliminate waste, inefficiencies, and unproductive time. In fact, JIT almost always requires changes in process design, scheduling, and inventory. When used effectively, JIT reduces inventory levels, reduces costs, improves quality, reduces setup times, and smoothes the flow of production. Suppliers also play a critical role in JIT systems. In JIT systems, suppliers make smaller deliveries on a frequent basis (sometimes several times each day), which has encouraged some suppliers to locate close to the agribusiness.

Inventory

Beginning with suppliers and moving through the production process to the end customer, some form and level of inventories are maintained. Furthermore, the activities of purchasing and inventory control are closely related. Operations managers keep their inventory counts current and accurate, so that they can alert the purchasing department when more product is needed and so that they can track inventory turnover.

Inventory is important to an agribusiness firm from a financial and operations standpoint. Recall that inventory is an asset and for the average company, it represents 35 to 50 percent of the current assets. Although inventories are an asset from an accounting perspective, they are really a cost of doing business. The dollar value of goods held in inventories could be invested in a bank note generating interest or in a productive piece of equipment. Thus, the interest or **opportunity costs** of inventory can be high. Storage and handling costs for holding inventory can also be high. Large physical storage spaces are often required to store inventory, preventing such space from being used for more productive purposes.

So why have inventories? One principal reason for maintaining inventories is to provide **customer service** because products are available immediately for consumption. Another reason is to minimize the effects of varying demand for finished goods—especially in agricultural products. For example, it may be forecasted that 10,000 units of a short-season popcorn variety will be demanded for the spring planting season in Indiana. A late spring that delays planting forces producers to switch to this short-season variety, doubling demand to over 20,000 units. A shortage of the popcorn seed may force customers to wait for shipment from another location or to purchase seed from a competitor. Lost sales opportunities now or in the future may be the result (i.e., customers may switch to a more reliable supplier).

Inventories are maintained sometimes for other reasons (Table 15.1). Ordering costs can be minimized because larger quantities can be purchased less often. Costs to set up equipment and run a second batch of product can sometimes make holding extra inventory advantageous. Transportation costs per unit can be reduced if a truck is filled with product and delivered full versus a partial shipment. Finally, inventories are sometimes held to maximize equipment utilization.

Table 15.1 Reasons for different inventory levels

Reasons for Smaller Inventories	Reasons for Larger Inventories
Interest or opportunity costs	Customer service and varying demand
Storage and handling costs	Ordering or set-up costs
Improved quality	Labor and facility utilization
Property taxes and insurance premiums	Transportation costs
Shrinkage costs—obsolescence, pilferage	Quantity discounts

In recent years, many agribusiness firms have found that inventory levels can be reduced significantly without reducing customer service because better information systems have reduced the time between placing an order and inventory replenishment. Smaller inventories can improve quality levels because the feedback loop between production and use is shorter. Not surprisingly, better quality and the flexibility to produce smaller quantities of products have increased labor and equipment utilization. As a result, the savings combined from all of these improvements have offset higher ordering costs and loss of quantity discounts. In addition, obsolescence costs and pilferage have been minimized with smaller levels of inventory.

Inventory can be broken down into three general categories used for accounting purposes. Inventory in the procurement or **raw material** phase comprises about 30 percent of total inventory. For example, various grains, vitamin supplements, by-products, and preventive health ingredients are all raw materials used to make hog feed. A second accounting category of inventory is **work-in-process (WIP)** or inventories that are in the conversion phase. These inventories make up an additional 30 percent of total inventory on average. Examples of WIP are engine sub-assemblies awaiting final assembly into a farm implement. The third category of inventory is **finished goods** inventory, the remaining 40 percent of inventory. Finished goods are the outputs from the conversion process, which are now ready for usage. Breaded veal cutlets in cold storage would be an example of finished goods inventory.

Types of inventory

Now, let's give an example of different types of inventories. Rita Tyner is vice president in charge of production for a power equipment manufacturing company located in Indiana. Though the firm manufactures several products, one of its most profitable items is a garden tiller. Rita's company sells garden tillers at an average rate of 25 per week. When the warehouse stock of garden tillers reaches a certain, agreed-upon level of depletion, called the **reorder point**, Mike Torres, the warehouse manager, sends Rita an order for more tillers. The total time for the order cycle takes two weeks (i.e., paperwork, receipt and filling of the order, transportation, and receipt at the warehouse). The amount of stock that Mike has on hand when he reaches that critical reorder point depends on the kind of inventory being used.

Pipeline inventories are the minimum amount of inventory needed to cover the period of time between the warehouse's reordering and its receipt of the additional stock, or lead-time.

Since the average demand for garden tillers is 25 per week, and it takes Mike two weeks to receive the order, he will need at least 50 garden tillers in stock to avoid running out during lead time.

Despite the fact that Mike and Rita's lead-time is two weeks, it is not necessary for Mike to issue an order every two weeks. For example, suppose that each truck were capable of loading and delivering 100 garden tillers. In the pipeline inventory system, this would mean that a truck delivering every two weeks would go from factory to warehouse half-empty. Rather than use this costly method of operation and fill out double the paperwork, Mike would probably order 100 garden tillers every four weeks. Since **cycle** or **lot-size inventories** may be considerably larger than pipeline inventories, it goes without saying that use of this method is subject to constraints of available storage space and transportation savings, and dependent on projected future sales.

We have been assuming that Mike and Rita are dealing with rock-steady weekly demands, constant lead times, and standard truck capacities. In the real world of agribusiness enterprise, this is never the case. Demand varies from week to week, as does the length of time it takes to get an order filled. These differences are taken into account by **safety stock** or **buffer inventories**, which provide additional stock to offset potential variations.

As explained in Chapter 14, agribusiness products are often highly seasonal. Mike and Rita might sell as many as 200 garden tillers a week during peak season, or as few as two during the off-season. Rita has the choice of planning for much higher labor costs at peak season or for costly storage of extra garden tillers in off-season. Both these risks can be avoided by **anticipation** or **seasonal inventories**. Under this system, storage space is provided for products whose demand is not constant so that more are available during peak seasons.

Inventory management systems

Supply chain management systems typically look at demand in two different ways—independent demand and dependent demand. Retail merchandise, services, and finished goods are types of goods driven by independent demand. The demand for a combine is an example of independent demand—individual farmers demand combines. Dependent demand, on the other hand, is derived from the demand for another item or from production decisions. For example, the demand for tires for new combines is derived from production schedule decisions and ultimately from the farmer demand for the combine. There are two basic inventory tracking systems for products with independent demand: periodic or continuous. Although most agribusinesses use a combination of both systems, firms are increasingly relying on continuous tracking systems that are automated.

Periodic inventory is an actual physical count of stock on hand, conducted at regular intervals, perhaps each month (Figure 15.3). This kind of inventory has the disadvantage that, taken by itself, it leaves the day-to-day status of the inventory in doubt. However, record keeping is minimized and the periodic inventory is very reliable at that time. A good example of this system is the direct store-door delivery of soft drinks and salted snacks to supermarkets by suppliers. On a regular basis, weekly or more frequently, the inventory of these products is reviewed and orders placed.

Continuous inventory is exactly what its name indicates, a constant monitoring of stock on hand (Figure 15.4). Whenever sales are made or inventories are replenished, the total amount is subtracted from or added to the previous inventory total. Usually, a count of

Plate 15.1 Two men inspecting a watermelon
Because of the investment and cost of inventory, effective inventory management is a key factor driving profitability for many agribusiness firms. Photo courtesy of USDA Natural Resources Conservation Service.

inventories to be received is also kept, to eliminate the dangers of ordering too much. Several forms of automated continuous inventory tracking systems exist. Bar-code scanners at supermarkets, for example, are a technology that enables inventories to be tracked continuously and product to be replenished as it is purchased.

One advantage of continuous systems is that the inventory count is always current. The disadvantage is that even with a sophisticated, computerized inventory system, the reliability of the inventory quantity on-hand is only as good as the people who update it. The integrity of the system will be lost if employees forget or by-pass the system. Theft and shrinkage also will affect the accuracy of the continuous inventory system.

Distribution

Customers, markets, and competitors are always changing. Manufacturers have numerous options and resources available to them to distribute their products to the ultimate end consumer. Therein lies the challenge of managing the distribution element of supply chain management. **Physical distribution systems (PDS)** are the series of marketing channels through which parts, products, and finished inventory are stored and moved from suppliers, among outlets, and ultimately, to consumers. PDS encompasses transportation, storage/warehousing, and delivery of the finished product to the ultimate consumer. PDS must be carefully managed and coordinated to meet delivery requirements of business

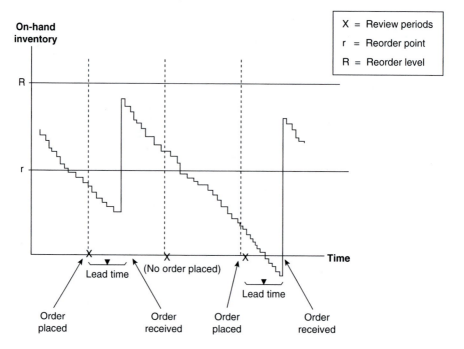

Figure 15.3 Periodic review inventory system

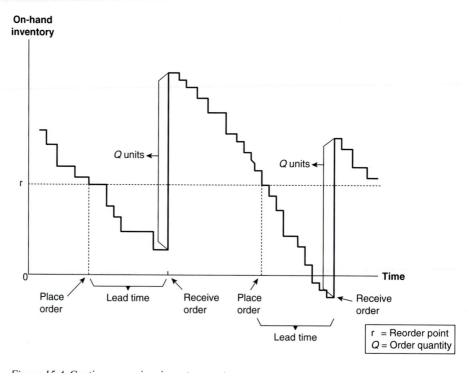

Figure 15.4 Continuous review inventory system

customers successfully. Manufacturers, wholesalers, distributors, retailers, as well as the consumer are all affected by the adequate and accurate execution of successful distribution.

Physical distribution systems comprise a costly component of the overall business plan. In many U.S. industries, assets required by distribution can account for more than 30 percent of corporate assets. Physical distribution costs are often estimated to be as much as 30 to 40 percent of total costs. "Doing the math" shows that PDS can exceed 25 percent of each sales dollar at the manufacturing level.

Today's agribusiness manager will benefit from an understanding of supply chain management of physical distribution systems even if they are not directly involved in the management of those resources. Effective PDS can mean opportunities for improving customer services and for reducing costs. For many businesses, making the product available to the customer is the road to customer satisfaction. While those opportunities for improvement and growth are true, so are the opportunities for failure or inefficiency. A repair part delivered a few hours late may cost a customer thousands of dollars in lost production time. The PDS will vary dramatically by product. The role of PDS for Hormel salami will differ from the role of PDS for Monsanto's Roundup® herbicide due to the nature of the product, the types of warehousing, transportation, and storage that can be used in delivering the product to the customers.

Distribution and marketing

Place, or **distribution**, was one of the four critical marketing decisions (four Ps) examined in Chapter 7. We will briefly summarize that chapter's discussion in the context of the overall supply chain function. The choice of a marketing channel is very important to an agribusiness because a tradeoff must be made between providing the dual and competing objectives of customer service (product available wherever and whenever) and minimizing distribution costs. Distribution adds a time and place dimension to marketing that can provide an agribusiness with a competitive advantage. In addition, the special problems of bulkiness, seasonality, and perishability in agribusinesses can make the choices of where to store finished goods and how to transport them a difficult one. The choice of distribution system depends on the geographical distribution of customers, the amount of personal and specialized customer service that is required, and the need to control or influence the image or relationship with the customer.

Chapter 7 detailed the three basis distribution systems:

- Manufacturer-direct distribution system
- Dealer-distribution system
- Distributor system

In supply chain management, physical distribution systems can be broken down into three basic categories. Each of these categories involves choices and decisions for the supply chain manager in making the optimum decisions for the operation. Three basic components of distribution are:

- Warehousing—where finished goods will be stored
- Transportation—how goods will be moved
- Carrier—the scheduling, routing, and selection of the carrier

Warehousing

Manufacturing plants, warehouses, distribution centers, and retail outlets all fall into this category of where goods are "warehoused" or stored before delivery. **Warehousing** can represent a huge cost in terms of the operating costs and capital investment in buildings and facilities required to properly store a company's products. Consideration must be given to the location, size, service levels, proposed new or additional facilities, etc.

Efficient and effective handling and storing of inventory can also provide huge savings to a firm. Product movement may be affected by packaging. A change in either product movement or in the packaging can impact the type of warehousing necessary—and again, the bottom line. A new type of package for a meat product may mean easier shipment as well as easier warehousing. The container which can be moved by rail, highway, or by sea may provide managers with a delivery-ready, cost-effective means for warehousing products.

In considering warehousing, there are two basic choices in determining where finished goods are stored. Forward placement locates finished goods near customers at a warehouse, wholesaler, or retailer. The advantages of forward placement are faster delivery times after receipt of order and increased sales (demand is stimulated by product availability). For example, a farm equipment manufacturer may allow inventories of selected parts to be stocked directly on the farm in anticipation of a producer's future needs. Periodically, the inventory will be checked and the producer will be invoiced for parts he/she has used.

Backward placement of finished goods holds goods at the production facility. The primary advantage of holding goods at the manufacturer location is that a centralized warehousing system can reduce the total number of goods held in inventory. However, a key disadvantage is a lower level of overall customer service.

Transportation

The mode of **transportation** must also be chosen. The five basic modes of transporting goods are highway, rail, water, pipeline, and air. The advantages and disadvantages of each can be evaluated by considering their length of transit time, geographic and product flexibility, cost, damages in transit, and the number of times goods are re-handled. For example, Monsanto initially chose to deliver BST to dairy farmers via an overnight delivery system because it allowed for fast delivery and a centralized warehousing system. On the other hand, a bulk commodity like oil is transported via pipeline. Barge and rail are the transport methods of choice for bulk commodities such as grain, where cost is a major factor.

Developing cost-effective transportation is essential for the physical distribution system to be complete and successful. Managers must carefully weigh the issues surrounding physical distribution of products in terms of getting the product delivered successfully and in a timely manner to the customer. Take, for example, a food processing equipment company, which made changes in the shipping method of some components from air transport to sea transport. This move saved over $15 million dollars in a single year in shipping costs. However, the slower delivery meant product parts were not available when needed, which meant dealers didn't have parts they needed when or where they needed them, which eventually cost the company lost sales. The bottom line is the change in shipping was ineffective because it adversely affected sales.

Plate 15.2 Grain loaded onto a ship
Whether by highway, water, or air, decisions about the transportation of products is an important area for logistics managers. Photo courtesy of USDA.

Carrier scheduling, routing, and selection

Finally, the **scheduling**, **routing**, and selection of the finished goods carrier can be a rather complex decision because of varying rate differentials, destinations, routing methods, and the mixing of shipments. As a result, sophisticated transportation models have been developed to enable firms to provide finished goods sooner, consolidate freight, take advantage of vendor discounts, and minimize administrative and warehouse labor costs.

Effective scheduling, routing, and selection require a network of information that transcends the physical distribution system. Order processing, transportation, delivery status, inventory turnover, and system performance are each itemized and carefully calculated in the efficiently run distribution system. Today's information systems in the distribution network often involve computerized tracking methods unimagined just 20 years ago. Compare how your grandparents ordered goods from the (no longer existent) Sears catalog with a pencil and a stamp, mailing in the order form. Today, the order can be placed online at Sears. com at the customer's convenience, and the appropriate distributor can get the product to the customer from the location nearest them for the most cost-effective distribution.

The scheduling, routing, and shipping of products must be coordinated with the inventory supply management of goods to meet demand. Needless to say, the information processing technology available today helps to effectively communicate timely and accurate information about inventory levels, location, delivery status, etc. to the appropriate channels. Knowledge of delivery efficacy can help with overall customer satisfaction. It can also help measure customer service outcomes. Information back-flow is an often overlooked, yet critical component of the physical distribution system. Accurate tracking of distribution and inventory information can help the company accomplish distribution objectives, and measure customer service quality, as well as examine, identify, and/or choose management alternatives.

Technology and operations

Technology is simply any manual, automated, or mental process used to transform inputs into products and services. Each operation within a food or agribusiness employs some technology, even if it is manual. Agribusiness managers invest in technologies to improve productivity and quality. They also must consider how technology relates to their operations strategy. For example, if a firm wants to be the low-cost producer, it may possibly want to invest in automation and a product layout that can produce high volumes of parts at low costs.

Technology factors may also influence plant locations by altering the manufacturing process. For example, genetic technologies and new processing technologies that have extended the shelf life of food products without freezing or refrigeration have allowed some industries to move away from end-use markets. Tomatoes imported from Mexico are extended shelf life (ESL) tomato varieties. ESL varieties contain a gene that has been manipulated to allow the tomato stay on the vine until 90 percent of the fruit is pink or red. ESL tomato varieties last longer—they can stay on the supermarket shelf a week longer than other varieties.

Technology is important for several reasons. New technological innovations and intense competition have necessitated continued improvements in productivity and higher levels of technology, especially information technology (IT). Shorter product life cycles and increased marketing pressure are requiring more flexibility on the part of service and manufacturing operations—again, requiring better technology. Products and materials are also becoming increasingly complex to build, so new technologies for more challenging production processes are needed. Information technology advancements including speed of processing, data storage, data transmission, and improved software are changing how business is conducted.

Access and availability dramatically change the way business can be done thanks to the 24/7 availability of information through the Internet. In many regards, the farmer located in an isolated rural location in central Kansas may no longer be limited to shopping at the single equipment store in the county. Agriculture's seasonal nature means farmers (customers) are often not available to make purchases during daylight hours, when the rest of the business world is working. Availability of information on the Web means that issue will no longer prevent farmers from researching, shopping, and purchasing products and services. Classifieds, bulletin boards, and chat rooms posted on the Web connect farmers who have never been exposed to one another before. These rapid changes in how business is done will no doubt impact agribusiness managers in the years to come, primarily because issues of access and availability will and do impact logistics strategies. For some companies or suppliers, these changes will create opportunity. For others, such developments will bring intense challenges.

Despite all of these changes, it is important to remember that supply chain management is still important. UPS may now ship a particular animal health product directly from a centralized warehouse to the farm, or groceries ordered online might be picked up at the supermarket by a consumer trying to save time. In both cases, supply chain management systems are involved throughout the process of moving the product from the manufacturer to the buyer.

Many other examples of advanced technologies impacting production and logistics can be found in the food industry. Electronic data interchange (EDI) is an old information technology that allows business interactions between firms to take place electronically using a standard language format. The standardization enables EDI to be used by any company and has improved accuracy, shortened response time, and has even cut inventory.

Summary

Understanding the functions of supply chain management is imperative to the agribusiness manager's success. Supply chain management has become a key business function over the last few years, growing in both relevance and importance. More agribusinesses now find greater efficiencies through going outside their own operations and linking their materials and physical distribution systems directly with supplier and customer systems.

Inventory control, transportation management, and cycle-time-to-market illustrate how a company's profitability can be impacted through effective supply chain management. Other supply chain functions include purchasing the inputs for production, coordinating the production of goals, determining the levels of inventory, and probably most importantly, serving as the linkage between the agribusiness, suppliers, and customers.

Agribusiness production managers who wish to maintain control of their operations will have to forecast trends, purchase in line with these trends, control the amount of inventory on hand, and employ sophisticated scheduling methods and quality controls. Purchasing is an activity that requires skill, knowledge, and honesty in dealing with bids and negotiations from suppliers. Such factors as quantity, quality, price, time, and customer service are elements of efficient purchasing.

The amount of inventory and kind of inventory systems used depend upon an agribusiness's size, complexity, and management sophistication. Physical distribution systems (PDS) include warehousing, transporting and scheduling, routing, and selecting product delivery. The right technology applied at the right time and in the right place can help supply chain managers increase overall efficiency while expediting the accurate and timely delivery of top quality products to the customer. The manager who is able to exercise control over these facets of supply chain management will have a tightly run operation that stands a good chance of maximizing profits.

Discussion questions

1. Why is supply chain management important in an agribusiness firm? Describe the various functions and responsibilities of supply chain management.
2. What are some of the objectives of an efficient supply chain management system? How have these objectives changed over time?
3. What are the principle activities of purchasing? Explain some of the factors to consider in selecting a supplier.
4. Why might inventory levels be minimized and why might some level of inventory be acceptable?

5. What are the advantages and disadvantages of a MRP system? A JIT system? In your opinion, which would be better for a fast-food restaurant?
6. Pick a food or agribusiness of your choice. Describe its physical distribution system. Try to describe each of the components of a physical distribution system outlined in the chapter for the business you choose.

Case study: BioAg—part II[1]

Supply chain management

The top management of BioAg consists of a microbiologist (Abe) and a cereal scientist (Ben). They are excellent research scientists and have shared leadership of the company. Abe and Ben recently attended the American Crop Protection Association (ACPA) annual meeting, which featured several sessions about supply chain management.

During one session, Farmco, a large regional input supply firm and BioAg's major reseller, announced their intentions to move aggressively with supply chain management initiatives. In a pilot project with a seed company, Farmco lowered inventory stocks by 10 percent and increased customer service (as measured by on-time deliveries) by 5 percent. Farmco feels there are three keys to building a successful supply chain relationship. First, the buyer and seller must move from an adversarial to a partnership-type relationship. Second, to manage inventory levels, the two firms must coordinate and streamline their logistics. Finally, information systems must allow them to share key information, thereby improving communication, allowing quicker action, and better decision-making.

Upon their return, Abe and Ben convene in a meeting with four key BioAg managers, Cindy, Dee, Ernie, and Fred. Cindy is the sales manager, Dee runs information technology (IT), Ernie heads research and development (R&D), and Fred leads logistics. Abe and Ben show the other four a graphic from the ACPA meeting and ask how BioAg should proceed to adopt this type of change with Farmco and other customers (Figure 15.5).

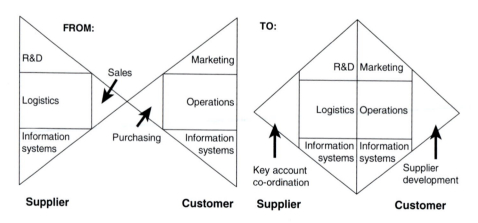

Figure 15.5 Changes in procurement with shift to supply chain management

"I think this would be a huge mistake," starts Cindy, the sales manager. "We have been aggressively expanding our supplier base. Look at how I've expanded the number of farm input supply firms we sell through in the past four years. It is the competition among the dealers that is leading to our growth. Besides, my job is to sell. Others are supposed to service accounts."

Ben replies, "I understand that, but Farmco has $500 million in sales. They account for 35 percent of our sales and 20 percent of our 420 dealers. They are among our most important customers."

"I'm also skeptical", adds Ernie. "We are a company living with proprietary technology. Your idea seems to imply that we share our R&D with our customers. How do I know that our ideas won't end up in the hands of our competitors?"

Abe says, "That is an important question, Ernie. But we're looking at our relationship with Farmco as a partner. Don't we have to trust our partners?"

Dee from IT then offers, "I'm sure that we could eventually get there. However, most of our efforts are focusing on upgrading existing computer systems. I'm sure that Farmco and our competition won't move for at least two years."

Abe responds, "I think you may be wrong. According to Farmco people, they have made upgrading their information technology a priority for the next fiscal year."

Abe and Ben then turn to Fred who has remained silent throughout the meeting. Fred frowns and says, "I don't know how I can improve service while cutting inventory levels. Our forecasting ability has already diminished because of the number of products we now offer and markets we serve. Remember that we just built two new distribution centers. And don't forget that we plan to expand to 1,000 dealers in the next two years. I guess I'm with the others. This is not a good fit for BioAg."

Ben answers, "Fred, are you suggesting that our distribution capabilities drive the future direction of the firm? I'd also like your appraisal of Farmco's pilot study. They said they would share the results with us. How did they do it?"

After the meeting Abe and Ben are silent for a few moments. Ben says, "This seemed like such a good idea at the ACPA meeting." Abe replies, "Yeah, and I overheard that Farmco plans to move forward with our competitors if we aren't interested. Can we wait?" They decide to reconvene their team and consider the following questions.

Questions

1. What are the potential risk and benefits to BioAg in pursuing the supply chain management initiative with Farmco?
2. Farmco cites three main factors in moving toward supply chain management. Which factor will be easiest to achieve in this case? Which factor will be the greatest obstacle? Does a successful supply chain relationship require all three factors?
3. Assume that BioAg and Farmco move forward with their supply chain initiative. How might this effect BioAg's relationship with its other farm input supply firms?

Note

1 This case originally published as Frank Dooley and Jay Akridge, "Supply Chain Management: A Case Study of Issues for BioAg," *International Food and Agribusiness Management Review*, 1(3): 435–441, 1998. It may be useful to review BioAg—part I in Chapter 14 before working on this case.

References and additional reading

AgGateway. "About AgGateway," 2011. www.aggateway.org/AboutUs.aspx

Council of Supply Chain Management Professionals. "CSCMP Supply Chain Management Definitions," 2011. http://cscmp.org/aboutcscmp/definitions.asp

Dooley, Frank and Jay T. Akridge. "Supply Chain Management: A Case Study of Issues for BioAg." *International Food and Agribusiness Management Review.* 1(3): pp. 435–41, 1998.

Food Marketing Institute. "Backgrounder: Efficient Consumer Response." 2011. www.fmi.org/media/bg/?fuseaction=ecr1

Krajewski, Lee J., Larry P. Ritzman, and Manoj K. Halhotra. "Operations Management", 9th ed. Upper Saddle River, NJ: Prentice Hall, 2009.

Part VI

Human resource management for agribusiness

Plate Part VI Man working in a lab
Human resources: this section develops some of the concepts behind the human element of management, and the management of the potential value and contributions individuals can make to an
organization. Photo courtesy of USDA Natural Resources Conservation Service.

16 Managing organizational structure

Objectives

- Differentiate between responsibility, authority, and accountability relationships in agribusiness
- Describe formal organizational structures used in agribusiness
- Understand organizational principles as they apply to the development of agribusiness organizational structures
- Discuss the impact of informal organizational relationships on the success of the agribusiness
- Identify various leadership styles employed by agribusiness managers
- Review current theories of managing and motivating employees
- Discuss the types of recognition and their role in motivating employees

Introduction

Food and agribusiness firms are made up of people working together toward a common purpose. As soon as an agribusiness involves more than one person, a variety of organizational, personnel, leadership, and motivational issues inevitably arise. The larger the organization, the more complex and critical these issues become. One of the fundamental responsibilities of management is to acquire, organize, motivate, lead, and manage its human resources to accomplish its business objectives as effectively as possible. Given this charge, management must address whatever complex issues may challenge or potentially disrupt that responsibility.

Managing the human resources in an agribusiness involves many dimensions. First, management must develop an organizational structure where the responsibilities, authority, and accountability of individuals are clearly defined. By **organizational structure**, we mean the formal way that employee responsibilities are assigned in a firm—who reports to whom, who has responsibility for what, etc. Basically, we are talking about the firm's organizational chart. Management must also concentrate on directing and supervising the day-to-day activities of employees. This involves the total personnel function—recruiting, hiring, training, evaluating, promoting, administering compensation and benefits, firing, and, in some agribusinesses, working with organized labor (see Chapter 17).

This chapter will focus on issues of organization and leadership. The organizational structure may well determine whether or not an agribusiness succeeds or fails. There are many important decisions to make when developing the organization's formal reporting relationships. Creating a structure that is flexible, responsive to the marketplace, affords employees growth opportunities, and manages accountability and responsibility, is a major challenge. Leadership is critical to business success as managers seek to motivate and manage human resources to maximize productivity. Managing people successfully requires more than a charismatic personality; it requires an understanding of the basic concepts of supervision and leadership. We will explore these issues in this chapter, and then turn our attention to the more focused area of personnel management in Chapter 17.

GreenThumb, Inc.: managing people in a growing business

Marie and Bob Jordan founded GreenThumb, Inc. six years ago. Capitalizing on Marie's experience in managing a retail lawn and garden center, Bob's experiences in a commercial greenhouse, and some funds from their extended family, Marie and Bob set out to make their dream a reality. Beginning modestly with a small greenhouse and an attached lawn and garden shop, they quickly established their business in the community. Marie's creative ads in the local newspaper, her flair for creative in-store displays and landscape ideas, and her outgoing personality really drove the sales and marketing side of the business. Bob's natural talent with growing plants and his previous experience as a field supervisor for a large corporate greenhouse provided a steady supply of quality bedding plants and flowers for sale in the store.

At first, business was simple. During the first two years, Marie and Bob did just about everything themselves, filling in labor needs with the part-time help of a retired hobby gardener and several high school students. Things were going so well that in the third year they decided to purchase six adjoining acres and begin growing some of their own nursery stock. By the end of their third year, the business was growing so rapidly that Marie and Bob had to begin adding full-time help—they just could not take the long hours required to handle all the work that the expanded business required. First, GreenThumb hired three managers: one each for the nursery, the greenhouse, and the retail store. Several workers reported to each of these managers, the exact number depending on the season. Bob acted as General Manager and Marie assumed the role of Assistant General Manager. Marie handled everything when Bob was away on buying trips and kept the books and records. In addition, she kept her role as chief salesperson and marketer for the growing company.

Adjusting to this expanded operation was a genuine struggle for both Marie and Bob. It became harder and harder to stay in touch with the customers, and it had been so much fun in the business initially. They seemed to spend their time doing more administrative things—hiring people, meeting with the managers, working on the firm's finances. Less and less time was spent in the greenhouses, or with customers. Yet the business was successful and profits were good, so they continued to expand and grow.

In their fifth year, things began to go wrong. By this time GreenThumb employed about 50 people during the peak season. Recently, a number of troubling problems had required a lot of attention from Bob and Marie. Some of these problems included: inventory damage in the cramped warehouse, high turnover among part-time help, and unexplained escalating costs. Most serious of all was an increase in insect and disease problems in the nursery and greenhouse. While none of these problems were huge, together they were most disturbing—especially since they were leading to some dissatisfied customers, and lagging sales.

Both Marie and Bob felt they had lost touch with the business. Bob simply could not be on top of the technical problems because he was tied up with management problems. In fact, many of the disease problems they were encountering were beyond his experience and expertise. Similarly, Marie had no formal training in accounting, but she did realize that GreenThumb needed better financial information to make good management decisions. She had spent a lot of time learning the computerized records program they used, but this was just not her area. This became extremely clear when financial statements illustrated that higher costs and lower sales had significantly reduced profits—and neither Bob nor Marie knew exactly why. To make matters worse, all the time with the books kept Marie from putting her marketing and sales skills to work.

After a careful deliberation of the problems faced by GreenThumb, Bob and Marie interviewed and hired an aggressive young woman who had a degree in horticulture and had completed an internship with a larger grower. They also hired an accountant who had graduated from a business college five years before and had worked as an office manager in a local electronics store. Both Marie and Bob felt that these two new staff members, although relatively costly additions to the payroll, would pay off in improved productivity and financial control within GreenThumb.

This plan worked well for GreenThumb for about a year. But then, early in March of her second year, the horticulturalist walked into Bob's office and quit. She said she was fed up with the way things were done at GreenThumb. After a rather emotional discussion, it became clear that her frustrations resulted from a series of incidents where she had strongly recommended several cultural practices to the nursery manager, only to be ignored. Finally, after she discovered that some new stock had been planted too deep and was likely to die, she had taken matters into her own hands. The nursery manager had been away for the morning, and she felt it necessary to handle the problem immediately, so she told two part-timers to spend the morning resetting the stock. When the nursery manager returned and found that the horticulturalist had pulled the workers off the job he had assigned, he was livid and confronted her. There had been quite a scene in the field, and several workers seemed to enjoy the very heated argument.

GreenThumb has reached a point where it is truly riddled with people problems. The business has been profitable and has potential for considerably more growth. But, Bob and Marie are almost overwhelmed—how did the people side of their thriving business get so out of control? How should they structure the business to address these problems? GreenThumb provides a good example of issues which organizational structure and people can give agribusiness managers. These situations can often give managers their best successes and some of their biggest challenges.

The formal organization

Organizations depend on two kinds of structure to operate efficiently. We first look at the **formal structure** that serves as the foundation for all activities. Then, in the next section, we will look at the **informal interpersonal relationships** that also affect how work gets done.

In the U.S. business economy, the owners of a firm provide the firm with the financial resources with which to operate. They also set the general direction for the organization either directly or through duly elected representatives (the board of directors). The owners in turn delegate authority to managers to make decisions, and management is held accountable for the success of the business. Management then develops an organizational structure specifying the various responsibilities, authority, and accountability of employees. Employees help develop and execute plans for accomplishing business objectives. It all sounds simple—but in practice things are rarely so.

Responsibility, authority, and accountability

Responsibility is the obligation to see a task through to completion. It may be a contractual obligation or it may be voluntarily assumed, but it cannot be given away. Responsibility can be shared with another person or group, but it can never be passed downward with no further obligation. The obligation remains undiluted with its originator.

Authority is the right to command or force an action by another. Authority allows instructions to be given to another individual with the expectation that they will be carried out explicitly. Authority is a derivative of responsibility, since it must come from the ultimate source of responsibility.

Accountability involves being answerable to another person for performance. Associated with accountability is the notion of a reward for acceptable behavior or penalty for unacceptable results. Accountability too is derived from responsibility.

The formal organizational structure of an agribusiness defines areas of responsibility and authority, and delineates who is accountable to whom and for what. Historically, the larger the agribusiness, the more formalized and structured its organization is likely to be. In fact, in very large businesses it is not uncommon for specialists in organizational development to constantly review the organizational structure, with an eye toward changes that may facilitate the total management process and improve productivity. Today's trend, even among large agribusiness firms, is to flatten this organizational chart in an attempt to facilitate communication and responsibility from top to bottom, and to keep the costs of administration as low as possible.

Principles of organization

There is no shortage of books, articles, magazines, and websites on "how to be successful" in business management. Many factors can be cited, but perhaps the most far-reaching is the human element: culture, value systems, structures, communications, and personalities. Although organizations are always in a fluid state because they are continually changing, there are several key *principles* that are useful in developing an effective organizational structure.

The **span-of-control principle** states that the number of people who can be supervised effectively by one individual is limited. The maximum number depends on many factors, including the frequency of contacts that must be made, the type of work, the level of subordinates, and the skill of the supervisor. In military organizations, the number of individuals directly supervised is seldom more than four to seven, while on assembly lines where work is routine, a supervisor may oversee 30 to 40 people. Information technologies such as e-mail, cell phones, and the Internet have in general expanded the span of control, with managers supervising more people than they did previously.

The **minimal layer principle** states the number of levels of management should be kept as low as possible, which is consistent with the goal of maintaining an effective span of control. As organizations grow, there is a tendency for the levels of management to proliferate, but each additional level increases the complexity of communications and the opportunities for breakdowns. More recent trends, consistent with a growing span of control, are for organizations to "flatten," taking out layers of management, and giving each layer more responsibility and authority.

The **delegation downward principle** states that authority should be delegated downward to the lowest level at which the decision can be made competently. This allows upper management to concentrate on more important decisions. At the same time, delegation of authority never relieves the delegator of the original responsibility. The supervisor always remains responsible for everything that happens under their supervision. This principle has become extremely important as firms have grown, and markets have demanded local responsiveness.

The **parity of responsibility and authority principle** states that a person should have enough authority to carry out assigned responsibilities. It would be totally unfair to hold employees accountable for areas in which they have not been granted enough authority to make the decisions that affect an outcome. While this principle makes good common sense, it is not unusual to see it violated in practice.

The **flexibility principle** states that an organization should maintain its structural flexibility so that it can adjust to its changing internal and external environments. Organizations are always changing. Since the organizational structure involves people, changing the power structure can be a very delicate issue as people often feel threatened by change and tend to resist it. Periodic reviews and a mechanism for changing structure are necessary for healthy organizations. At the same time, changing the organizational structure is highly disruptive and takes people's focus off day-to-day operations—just ask any food and agribusiness employee who has been through a major merger or acquisition.

Types of organizational structures

The foregoing organizational principles give rise to three primary types of organizational structure: **line, line and staff, and functional**. There are actually many, many variations on these basic types, and a pure organizational type seldom occurs. Generally, the larger a business becomes, the more complex its structure. But, most are designed around these three basic types.

Line organization

A **line organization** is a structure in which there is one simple, clear line of authority extending downward from top management to each person in the organization. Each subordinate reports to only one person, and everyone in the organization is directly involved in performing functions that are primary to the existence of the business. Figure 16.1 shows an early organizational chart for GreenThumb, an example of a line organization.

The line organization is ideal for smaller agribusinesses, such as GreenThumb, in their first few years of doing business. In such cases, lines of authority and accountability are simple and cannot be easily confused, communication channels are clear and rapid with few people involved. Top management are often the owners of the business, who find it easy to stay informed and make effective business decisions with good information. Marie and Bob Jordan, as the managers of GreenThumb, Inc., could react quickly and personally to a shoplifting problem in their retail store or a disease problem in the nursery, because of their relative proximity to the problem area.

But as a business grows, it becomes more complex. The more people there are and the more levels of management that are added, the less effective the pure line organization becomes. Lengthening the chain of command reduces the speed of important decisions and increases the probability of communication breakdowns. If an assistant nursery manager is hired and nursery workers are specialized into field hands, delivery person, and mechanics, the owner/manager may not learn of a feud between two delivery people until one of them quits, unless the lines of communication are working exceptionally well.

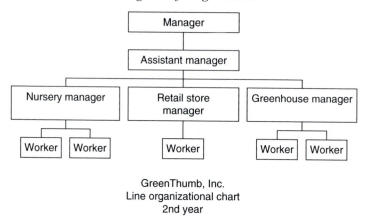

GreenThumb, Inc.
Line organizational chart
2nd year

Figure 16.1 Line organization

Furthermore, there is really no place in a line organization for specialists. As a business grows, it requires a more diversified structure. As GreenThumb grew, it became obvious that an office manager/accountant would be needed, as well as a professional horticulturist to advise on matters of disease control, plant propagation, and field practices. In a line organization, such specialists should be in a position to offer advice, but typically are not directly involved in the line of authority over activities in the nursery or greenhouses.

Line and staff organization

The **line and staff organization** is a variation of the line organization. The difference is that it includes a place for specialists, sometimes known as staff (Figure 16.2). In this type of organization, staff personnel have direct accountability to key line managers and are responsible for offering advice on problems or providing services in their area of specialization. Typically, these specialists or staffs have no authority except over assistants who may be assigned to them. Their advice can be accepted or rejected by line managers, who retain responsibility for all decisions.

GreenThumb management is likely to find the advice of a staff horticulturalist and accountant invaluable in making technical decisions and analyzing operating costs. The highly trained horticulturalist can work with the nursery manager and the greenhouse manager, advising them on disease problems in the nursery or propagation problems in the greenhouse, or assisting them with customer problems in the retail store. Under this structure, no one is required to accept all the specialists' suggestions, but professional advice and services can be extremely beneficial to the business. Staff specialists can be advisory, they can handle service problems, and/or they can provide control functions, as do quality inspectors in a processing plant. In any case, they typically do not have line authority over others in their organization, and this is one major drawback of the line and staff organization.

Staff specialists must be positioned to avoid undermining the authority of line management. This is difficult, since their position and special knowledge often give them considerable status and prestige that can easily be misused. Line managers or workers may not welcome changes or policies that these staff specialists may legitimately suggest. Specialists

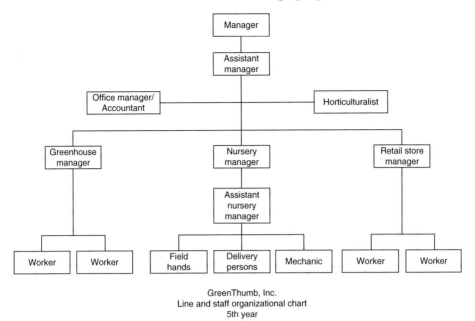

GreenThumb, Inc.
Line and staff organizational chart
5th year

Figure 16.2 Line and staff organization

may feel so strongly about a particular issue that they may apply pressure or go around the normal chain of command. If GreenThumbs's horticulturalist tells nursery workers to begin treating growing beds with insecticide, such a request may be in direct conflict with the nursery manager's established work schedule, creating much confusion among employees and ill feelings with management.

Functional organization

A **functional organizational structure** meets the problems of staff specialists' authority head-on by granting them authority in the areas of their specialty (Figure 16.3). The horticulturalist that sees the need for an immediate insecticide treatment of bedding plants has the responsibility and the authority to command workers to make the application.

Of course, a functional organization offers an almost unlimited potential for conflict and confusion. Who has the highest authority? From whom do workers really take orders? The key to making the functional structure work is coordination of staff and line management efforts. A cooperative attitude and good communication are absolutely essential for this organizational structure to work. While complex, this organizational structure, or a variant, is very common in agribusinesses, especially larger ones. Such businesses have found that the advantages of functional organization outweigh the disadvantages.

Communication: the key to success

No matter how well thought-out the organizational structure, there will be times when it breaks down. Agribusinesses, large and small, are complex operations that do not always

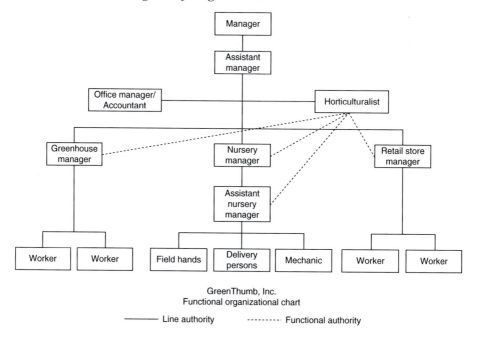

GreenThumb, Inc.
Functional organizational chart

————— Line authority   -------- Functional authority

Figure 16.3 Functional organization

work the way management intends. No organizational structure is better than the people in it. Their understanding of the structure and the employee's willingness to work within it are essential. Yet, even when people are trying to make it work, problems arise. People have emotions, misunderstandings, ego needs and family issues that sometimes get in the way. Effective organizations recognize the need for interpreting the formal structure in terms of the human element, by adjusting and working through misunderstandings when they occur. No organizational structure can be successful without a constant focus on honest but tactful communication at all levels. Some of the basic keys to communication are that it should be timely, consistent, and thorough. Management should attempt to make communications "transparent," i.e., seek input and share some reasoning for decisions. Transparency tends to be a bit of a slippery slope—as it is often difficult to ascertain how much information to share with employees—they like to be "kept in the loop." However, some issues and decisions need to be left to management and managers need to realize that they will be held responsible for their decisions—both good and bad, and may often be blamed for decisions that seem to be capricious, but are actually well thought out.

The informal organization

The formal organization is concerned primarily with the activities of people as they perform their job functions. But the formal organizational structure cannot possibly control all of the personal relationships that exist in any agribusiness. Whenever people come together, informal relationships develop that may have significant impact upon the effectiveness of the formal organization. The **informal organization** is primarily concerned with interpersonal relationships among people; that is, their emotions, feelings, communications, and values. The informal organization is an important part of an organization's culture.

The informal organization is crucial to the success of any firm, since it contributes greatly to the fulfillment of individuals' personal needs. A great many (if not most) professional people and workers spend as many or more hours on the job as they do at home or with their families. And for some, the hours spent on the job may be a primary source of ego fulfillment and social relationships. Their role on the job, their status among peers, and their personal feelings about their job are critical to their well-being; therefore, all these factors directly affect how well the formal organization works. Personal lives of employees can affect an organization's efficiency positively or negatively.

Managers who cultivate a positive informal organization will discover a desirable fringe benefit: the formal organization will be much more productive. Any gaps caused by unexpected situations can be handled far more easily. Communication will be facilitated through informal channels. The span of control can be lengthened because people will work together more effectively. The end result is that more and better quality work is completed as people feel a commitment to the common goal.

On the other hand, where the informal organization is ignored or when personal relationships interfere, results are less predictable, people are less flexible, and they may spend considerably more time on activities that are counterproductive to company goals. Managers who ignore the power of the informal organization, who dictate without regard to sensitive

Plate 16.1 Hands
A positive and vibrant informal organization helps insure that the formal organization is effective and profitable. Photo courtesy of USDA Natural Resources Conservation Service.

interpersonal factors, may even experience "malicious obedience" among employees, that is, a situation where an employee spitefully carries out a superior's command to the nth degree, even when the employee knows that such literalism is not called for in the situation and may produce a negative result.

Informal organization begins with the primary group, or the people with whom an employee works most closely. Within this group, as in the larger organization, relationships develop as the result of status, power, and politics. **Status** is the social rank or position of a person in a group. Status and symbols of status exist in every group. **Symbols** include title, age, experience, physical characteristics, knowledge, physical possessions, authority, location, privileges, acquaintances, and a host of other factors, depending on the situation.

At GreenThumb, Inc., who gets to drive the newest pickup truck and who has the first locker in the clean-up room have become status symbols among workers. Insensitivity in assigning trucks to work crews could create problems in the organization. However, status is not necessarily bad, because it helps people fulfill ego needs and can serve as a method by which managers can motivate subordinates.

Power is the ability to control another person's behavior. Power may come from the formal authority issued through the chain of command, or its source may be less formal, arising out of respect, knowledge, status, proximity to a source of power, or control of a resource. Effective agribusiness managers recognize the importance of power—both their own power and that of others in the organization. They can use power productively to accomplish corporate objectives, or they can abuse their power to emphasize their own importance. Managers must recognize that by withholding full cooperation, employees can exert a great deal of unofficial power themselves.

Marie and Bob Jordan must recognize the power plays currently operating between the nursery manager and their staff horticulturalist. Both are struggling for power they believe is rightfully theirs. The nursery manager may feel threatened by the horticulturalist's higher position and knowledge, or he may undervalue her because of her gender. The Jordans must deal with the informal aspects of the power struggle as well as the structure of the formal organization. And, they may well find, as many agribusiness managers do, that managing the informal organization is much harder than structuring the formal organization.

Politics is the manner in which power and status are used. Politics involves the manipulation of people and situations to accomplish a particular goal. Everyone is at least superficially familiar with the formal political process of give-and-take, individual and group coalitions, and negotiating. The formal political process in the state or national sense is a complex but systematic application of power and persuasion. Within the agribusiness, however, politics is an intricate part of the informal organization. Although it is likely to be more obvious in larger organizations, politics is necessary for getting things done when one lacks total authority to dictate an action, and can be useful even when authority is present.

The greenhouse manager at GreenThumb understands the role of politics, so he will plan his request for an automatic overhead sprinkler system very carefully. He knows that investment funds are limited and that he will be in direct competition for these funds with the retail store manager and the nursery manager. If the office political situation is such that the accountant can and does influence the Jordan's investment decisions, the greenhouse manager may well cultivate a relationship with the accountant and subtly look for ways of gaining this individual's support.

Politics has positive value: it encourages compromise and offers a way of solving problems without direct explosive confrontation. In larger organizations, politics offers a method for accomplishing things that would be cumbersome to handle through purely formal channels. While politics may seem manipulative or even unethical to some, it is a fact of life and influential to some degree in all organizations. Effective managers recognize its existence and deal with it realistically.

Leadership

Managers are designated leaders, formally appointed by the chain of command that originates with ownership. But leadership is much more than issuing authoritarian commands. It requires working with personnel and motivating them to accomplish the firm's objectives. **Leadership** is in part the ability to combine personal style and organizational goals in correct proportions.

Styles of leadership

Leadership and leadership styles are heavily studied areas. Obviously, business could profit greatly from a consistent way of identifying good leaders, or of teaching selected individuals how to be effective leaders. Although a great deal is known about leadership, there are no consistent or simple answers to the question, "What makes a good leader?" What makes a good leader in one situation does not necessarily work in another. Some research suggests that a strong will, extroversion, power need, and achievement are key variables in a leader. Other work identifies intelligence, social maturity, breadth of development, inner motivation, and a positive human relations attitude as necessary ingredients to leadership.

All of these factors are subjective and difficult to measure. The conclusion is that leadership is not static but dynamic, and must adapt to the specific circumstances of the situation. However, there are a number of leadership styles that have been identified, and understanding these styles can help in assessing what type of leadership may be most appropriate in a given situation. One popular classification scheme describes managers as authoritarian, democratic, free reign, and transformational.

Authoritarian

Authoritarian, also called **autocratic**, is a leader-centered style, in which the thoughts, ideas, and wishes of the leader are expected to be obeyed completely, without question. Authoritarian leaders seldom consult subordinates before making decisions. Also, decisions may be changed suddenly for no apparent reason. The hard-nosed autocrat is coercive in relationships with subordinates, and often threatens them if they do not perform to the autocrat's level of expectation.

Yet there are also other styles of authoritarian leadership. **Benevolent autocrats** convince followers to do what they want by being so well liked that no one would consider being disloyal or of "letting the chief down." The benevolent autocrat gives so much praise that employees are shamed into obedience. Another form of autocratic style is that of the **manipulative autocrat**, who creates the illusion that employees are participating in the decision-making process. This leader's motto is "make them think they thought of it."

Note that in each autocrat style outlined above, all decisions originate with the autocrat, and the autocrat maintains firm control. The only difference among the three is the manner in which the control is exercised. Some argue that the autocratic style of leadership is always bad and leads to poor performance and ill feelings, but this is not so. Although the authoritarian style would seldom be the only method of operation for any given leader, those who are primarily autocratic can show excellent results, particularly when the leader has a good feel for the situation. Over a period of time, autocratic leaders tend to surround themselves with subordinates who enjoy not having responsibility; they just like to "follow orders." This combination of leadership and following is often quite productive, at least temporarily. However, it is limited completely by the individual autocrat's ability and can result in utter chaos if that leader becomes incapacitated, or if the situation changes in a way that does not play to the strengths of the autocrat. The autocratic style is common and is most likely seen in smaller, owner-managed businesses.

Democratic

The **democratic** or participative leadership style favors a shared decision-making process, with the leader maintaining the ultimate responsibility for decisions while actively seeking significant input from followers. Research shows that while this style may require a considerable amount of skill, it stimulates employees' involvement, and enhances favorable employee attitudes toward their jobs. The only real disadvantage is that a democratic leadership style requires management skills and time that may not always be available—so this leadership style may not be appropriate for all situations.

Free rein

Free rein or **laissez-faire** leadership literally relinquishes all decision making to followers. The leader essentially abdicates his or her responsibility to the group and simply joins the group as an equal; thus, the group decides what to do. Although free rein leadership may work with some decisions, it seldom leads to consistently good decisions, and often results in poor outcome and frustration among employees. This leadership style is highly dependent on the quality of the employee team, and it takes a very capable group of individuals to make this work. Figure 16.4 shows the increasing participation of a member of a group (the employee) on the continuum from autocratic leadership to laissez-faire. The horizontal axis describes the type of action taken by the manager in dealing with their employees.

Transformational

As discussed in Chapter 2, managers' jobs include planning, organizing, directing, and controlling. And, as agribusiness markets have evolved over time, it has become increasingly

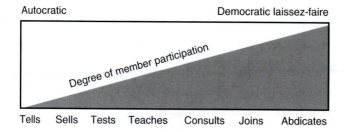

Figure 16.4 The leadership continuum
Note: horizontal axis outlines the action taken by the manager (leader) in dealing with group members (employees).

clear that a new type of leader is required to accomplish these tasks in an environment of rapid change and intense competition. One newer style of leadership, **transformational leadership**, has been identified as particularly helpful in guiding organizations and employees through such changes. Transformational leadership, as defined by Bernard Bass in his book *Leadership Performance Beyond Expectation*, is a form of leadership that motivates followers to work for transcendental goals and for aroused higher-level needs of self-actualization rather than for immediate self-interest. Essentially, transformational leaders (TLs) motivate individuals in an organization to proactively work for a "transformation" in how the company does some aspect or aspects of its business.

Transformational leadership involves three steps:

1. Recognizing the changes in the market
2. Creating a vision of the firm in this new market
3. Institutionalizing the change

Transformational leaders are usually found in a chaotic marketplace. At a time of upheaval, it is transformational leaders who, in the midst of struggle, can identify those issues that are most critical. They create a vision for dealing with the situation, usually by "thinking outside of the box," that is, thinking beyond the normal ways in which such situations are handled. But it doesn't stop there. TLs follow through by making the change a reality. They foster a company culture that understands the need for change and embraces the vision.

TLs have the ability to influence major changes in organizations by influencing changes in followers' attitudes and assumptions. They typically exhibit some combination of two or more of the following four characteristics: idealized influence, inspirational motivation, intellectual stimulation, and individualized consideration.

Idealized influence. TLs often act as role models. They have a high degree of self-confidence and strong conviction regarding their own ideas and beliefs. They consider others' needs, share risk, and are consistent and responsible, and demonstrate accountability.

Inspirational motivation. TLs inspire followers to exert themselves beyond what is expected. They are good at generating enthusiasm, team spirit, and optimism by demonstrating self-determination and commitment.

Intellectual stimulation. TLs encourage creativity by acting as teachers. They offer a breath of fresh air by analyzing old problems in new ways and by using intelligence and reasoning instead of unsupported opinions. They encourage followers to think about actions before taking action.

Individualized consideration. TLs give each follower individual attention. They find a follower's individual talent, offer criticism, and provide opportunities for learning. This one-on-one coach or mentor notion makes followers feel accepted, valued, secure, and may help them become more loyal followers.

Agribusinesses continue to face changes and challenges in an ever-more competitive business climate. As a result, today's agribusiness managers may have even more opportunities in the future to apply the principles of transformational leadership—or some of its components—in their organizations.

Beyond these four basic styles of leadership, there are a host of refinements and behavioral patterns that can, when studied in detail, contribute greatly to leadership effectiveness. Some of these theories provide classic insights into human behavior and managerial effectiveness. We will review two here: Theory X and Theory Y, and management by objectives (MBO).

Theory X, Theory Y

Douglas McGregor suggested a dual theory about human behavior in business that has important implications for management style and methods of motivation. McGregor based his theory on what has come to be known as the "dual nature of humankind." For centuries, philosophers have noted that people have the capacity for love, warmth, kindness, and sympathy, but at the same time can exhibit hate, harshness, and cruelty. This dichotomy led McGregor to an explanation of management style that is based on assumptions managers make about the people they supervise. McGregor referred to his dual theories as **Theory X** and **Theory Y**.

Theory X

McGregor believed that traditional management practices and methods are based on the following set of assumptions about employees:

1. Most employees have an inherent dislike for work, and will avoid it if at all possible.
2. People will work only when they are coerced, threatened, or at least controlled in all their activities.
3. Most people actually prefer to be closely controlled because they dislike responsibility and have little ambition.
4. Most people are basically self-centered and selfish.
5. Security is very important to most employees, and they are threatened by change.
6. Most employees are gullible, will believe anything, and are not very intelligent.

McGregor believed that for centuries these assumptions had served as the basis for most management and leadership styles: strong control with little concern for employee needs. Most of the supervisory practices resulting from Theory X assumptions have failed to tap the human resource potential in the employees being supervised.

Theory Y

At the other end of the continuum is another set of assumptions derived from a belief in the natural goodness and creativity of human beings. Theory Y assumptions include the following:

1. Work, both physical and mental, is as natural as play or rest.
2. People can and will exercise self-control and evidence motivation to achieve goals to which they are personally committed.
3. The level of commitment is dependent on the rewards received for reaching the goals.
4. People basically like responsibility and will seek it.
5. People are naturally creative and have far more capability than is generally utilized.

Theory Y assumptions lead to a very different management and leadership style. Theory Y managers focus attention on employees themselves, attempt to draw out their creativity, and appeal to their willingness to accept responsibility. These managers do not abdicate their responsibility and authority to their employees. They are quick to enter into a dialogue that will help both the manager and employee arrive at mutually acceptable goals, and to establish a reward system that is fulfilling to the employee. Theory Y management is not an easy style. It requires patience and a great deal of people skills on the part of managers.

Obviously, there is much appeal to the Theory Y management approach, and McGregor was a strong proponent of it, especially early in his career. If one fully accepted these appealing assumptions, there would be little need for time clocks, fixed working schedules, production quotas, and the like. Many organizations have made strong attempts over the past several decades to move closer to a Theory Y style of management, though there are still holdovers.

However, it should not be assumed automatically that Theory X management is bad and Theory Y management is good. It is said that McGregor used the Theory X, Theory Y terminology on purpose, so as not to imply superiority of one style, even though he preferred the Theory Y approach. In fact, McGregor himself softened his strong support of the Theory Y position later in his career when he became a university administrator and personally experienced some of the frustrations associated with applying strong Theory Y management assumptions. Some employees hold Theory X type assumptions about themselves and so perhaps prefer to be treated in a manner consistent with this belief. But clearly there is great merit in the Theory Y approach, and agribusinesses have generally moved in this direction.

Management by objectives

Management by objectives (MBO) concentrates on results rather than on the process by which they are achieved. It is a system of management whereby the supervisor and the subordinate jointly:

1. Set objectives that both agree are reasonable and in line with corporate goals.
2. Determine how performance will be measured in each area of major responsibility.

First introduced by Peter Drucker in 1954, but continued to be used broadly, the MBO process usually begins with a very broad set of objectives and sense of direction as established by the board of directors. Top management develops its own objectives, consistent with the board's framework, and submits them to the board for reaction. Top management then asks middle management to develop and submit goals that are consistent with overall corporate goals as interpreted and applied to the middle managers' respective departments. Then, top management and middle management coordinate these goals through a negotiating process until an acceptable set of goals and yardstick to measure progress have been established. Next, middle management works with lower management, and so on down the line until the process has been repeated throughout the organization.

There are obvious advantages to such a system. First, since it accords individuals a certain amount of input into their own goals, employees tend to become emotionally committed to accomplishing whatever they have targeted for themselves. Second, with MBO, the criteria for evaluation become crystal clear and are agreed on by all concerned, which eliminates many problems later. It is important that objectives be clearly established and clearly measurable in the MBO process. As manager and subordinate meet for evaluation, judging whether or not objectives have been met should not be subjective.

The process is also quite time-consuming, however. Often, proposed objectives are submitted, negotiated, and resubmitted repeatedly before agreement is reached. Although the MBO system is intended to enhance communication, its success is built on assumptions of preexisting communication and mutual trust. If subordinates intentionally establish goals that are unrealistically low, so that they can exceed their goals easily and look good, the entire system breaks down. Additionally, there must be commitment to the system from the top down. Whenever top management resorts to dictating all the objectives, others assess how feasible those objectives are to achieve and react based on that assessment. Yet the appeal of an effective MBO system is strong and if done properly, it can be highly successful.

Motivation

Motivation is a stimulus that produces action, and directed action is a primary function of management. This is why managers are so concerned with the concept of motivation. There have been many arguments about whether it is possible for a manager to actually motivate employees. Some say that a good manager is skillful in stimulating others to accomplish targeted objectives. But others argue that all motivation is really self-motivation, which comes from within each individual. Those holding this view say that managers affect the environment and provide the stimulus, but it is ultimately up to the employee to decide to act. No matter which point of view seems more logical, management is responsible for results and must somehow stimulate, encourage, or coerce the employee behavior necessary to accomplish organizational goals and objectives, or else it must create an environment that will produce the same effect.

Motivation has many dimensions. It can be negative, as when an employee's attitude results in activity that undermines company goals, or it can be so positive that the employee becomes emotionally and personally involved in completing assignments at the highest level of their capabilities. Employees can be stimulated by positive rewards or by fear of undesirable treatment or lost privileges.

Like leadership, motivation has been studied extensively. As a result, there are a number of theories that have been suggested to explain how motivation works within individuals and organizations. Most researchers agree that in some way motivation comes down to a matter of rewards and punishments. By controlling rewards and punishments, management can significantly affect employee performance.

The basic problem comes in trying to determine what rewards and punishments work in which circumstances. The situation is further complicated by the wide variation in people. A simple "thank you" may be motivating to one person, while a new title may be of paramount importance to another. Some employees place high priority on monetary rewards, others on getting challenging assignments, while still others value perks like company cars and expense accounts. This very, very wide range in what employees value demonstrates the scope of the problem in developing a successful motivation system within the agribusiness.

Psychologists suggest that there are two types of motivation: intrinsic and extrinsic. Intrinsic motivation refers to motivation that is driven by an interest or enjoyment in the task itself, and exists within the individual rather than relying on external pressure. Examples here would be learning to broaden one's scope of knowledge, or being motivated to reach a goal such as climbing Mt. Rainier in the state of Washington. This contrasts with extrinsic motivation, which is motivation that comes from outside of the individual. In a job, extrinsic motivation is a reward like money; in school a grade would be an extrinsic motivator.

The threat of punishment is another example of extrinsic motivation; in general competition is extrinsic because it encourages the competitor to win and beat others, not to enjoy the intrinsic rewards of the activity. Below, we give a brief overview of some widely used theories of motivation, which provide useful ideas for managing and motivating people in agribusinesses.

Maslow's needs hierarchy

Motivation focuses attention on the personal needs of human beings, so some understanding of human needs is necessary for effective supervision. Psychologist Abraham H. Maslow developed one widely used model of human needs. **Maslow's needs hierarchy** is based on the idea that different kinds of needs have different levels of importance to individuals, according to the individual's current level of satisfaction (Figure 16.5). Usually the needs of one level must be met before the next level becomes a motivating force. Needs basic to human survival take priority over other needs, but only until survival has been assured. After that point, other needs form the basis for the individual's behavior.

Survival. Maslow suggested that every human's most basic concern is physical survival: food, water, air, warmth, shelter, and so forth. Obviously, humans cannot live unless these needs are at least minimally fulfilled. These most basic needs are immediate and current. It takes only moments for a person gasping for breath to be more concerned about survival than about anything else in the world. Survival here and now is even more critical than survival over the days or weeks ahead. For example, the call of "fire" prompts immediate action—notions such as financial concerns or etiquette are quickly forgotten.

Safety. Once immediate survival has been assured, humans become concerned about the security of their future physical survival. Today, this concern often takes the form of income guarantees, insurance, retirement programs, and the like. In a depressed agricul-tural economy, farmers will be more conservative spenders than they would be in more

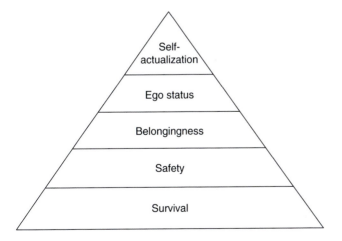

Figure 16.5 Maslow's needs hierarchy
Source: Maslow 2010.

prosperous times. They're less likely to be innovators and will be more concerned about getting a "tried-and-true" product at the lowest cost. In such an environment, safety is a much more important motivator than the prospect for larger financial rewards.

Belongingness. After they have achieved a reasonable degree of confidence in their safety, people become concerned with their social acceptance and belonging. Social approval and peer acceptance can cause a great deal of self-applied pressure and can be a strong source of motivation. If others are shifting to a new product or practice, farmers may be motivated to try the idea to "keep up" with their neighboring producers. Likewise, food consumers may be interested in trying out the latest energy drink as they "keep up" with other members of the health club where they work out.

Ego status. With a comfortable degree of social acceptance, most individuals become concerned with their self-esteem or status relative to their group. Group respect and the need to feel important depend heavily on the responses of other group members. Recognition from superiors and peers is a compelling drive for many people and may be responsible for the upward movement of a great many successful people. When salespeople help customers excel, they're appealing to the customer's self-esteem or egos. For example, a livestock or poultry producer may be motivated to have the top rate of gain, highest milk production, or fewest days to market. An incentive/recognition program such as "Salesperson of the Year" may work well for salespersons in a food manufacturing firm who are highly motivated to be the very best in the region.

Self-actualization. The highest level of need, and the one that becomes important only when lower-level needs have been relatively well satisfied, is self-actualization, the feeling of self-worth or personal accomplishment. This category of needs is highly abstract and takes a multitude of forms among different individuals. Self-actualization may be achieved through creative activities such as art, music, helping others in community activities, or building a business. The results of self-actualization embrace an attitude of "I feel I've made an important and worthwhile contribution."

In our society, most people's survival and safety needs are relatively well taken care of, so these are seldom strong motivators. Only when these needs are threatened do they become much of an issue. Although employees may feel good about a retirement plan, retirement benefits are seldom a factor in motivating them to higher levels of productivity. Even when job security becomes the focal point of labor negotiations, few would argue that such factors motivate employees to a very large degree, since they are becoming expected as normal and reasonable.

Belongingness or group acceptance can exert somewhat more pressure on people. New line workers may seek out belongingness as they try to fit in with other workers on their shift. The dynamics of the group will determine whether or not this attempt to fit in results in positive or negative outcomes from the firm's standpoint. Supervisors must recognize and encourage peer group acceptance and manager acceptance as important to employee performance.

Ego status or recognition is one of the most common and most productive needs through which agribusiness managers supervise and motivate employees. A great many people seem to be responsive to ego need fulfillment. Nearly everyone feels they want to be important and recognized. Managers who give employees recognition frequently, honestly, and positively are often rewarded with highly motivated personnel. Such recognition can take many forms. The simplest kind may be verbal: compliments are very effective when they are honest. They can also be nonverbal: simply a smile or a nod of approval. Listening is also very powerful.

Caring enough to listen to subordinates and to consider their opinions and feelings is one of the most powerful ways to recognize employees. Every successful manager has his or her own way of recognizing people effectively, but no matter what the technique, it is not accidental. It is an important management activity that relates directly to firm productivity.

Self-actualization is not quite as easy to deal within a management context because it comes from within the individual. However, this need can be a very important one for individuals who have "done it all." Examples here might be the department manager who has demonstrated exceptional performance year after year, and is now looking for the next challenge; or, the veteran salesperson who has received every major sales award and is looking for what's next. Management can best address self-actualization by:

1. Recognizing that some employees will be motivated by their own sense of self-accomplishment
2. Allowing this to happen
3. Encouraging the proper environment for it, whenever possible

Herzberg's two-factor theory

A popular but somewhat controversial theory of employee motivation is one developed by Frederick Herzberg. He argued that there are certain "satisfiers" and "dissatisfiers" for employees at work.

Hygienic factors (so called because like hygiene, the presence will not make you healthier, but absence can cause deterioration of health) are conditions necessary to maintain an employee's social, mental, and physical health. Research suggests that there are several such factors—including company benefits and policies, working conditions, job security, supervision, and pay. Herzberg argued that the presence of these factors does not make a worker happy, but if they are lacking, the employee is likely to become unhappy.

Motivators are reward producers, or conditions that encourage employees to apply themselves, mentally and physically, more productively to their jobs. Motivators bring about commitment to the task. Most motivators are predominantly psychological, such as recognition, advancement, responsibility, challenging work, and the opportunity for further growth.

Figure 16.6 shows the continuum where absence of hygiene factors causes dissatisfaction, but their presence provides no motivation. Likewise, the absence of motivators does not cause dissatisfaction, but their presence does cause motivation.

One of the controversies surrounding Herzberg's theory is whether compensation is a hygiene factor or motivator. Many agribusinesses use compensation as an incentive to motivate employees to higher levels of performance. Proponents of such plans feel strongly that both salespeople on commission and field or line workers on wages tied to productivity are highly motivated to maximize their performance.

Yet Herzberg argues that these payment techniques are hygienic because they do not have the effect of increasing commitment to the job. He says that pay incentives work well temporarily, but once a particular pay and performance level has been reached, and the employee adapts to it, the pay itself is no longer a motivator. In fact, if something happens to cut the

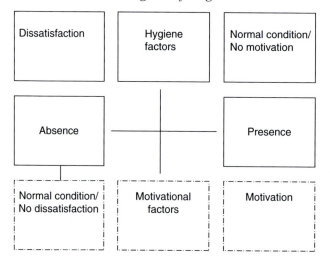

Figure 16.6 Herzberg's two-factor theory
Note: hygiene factors—presence causes no motivation, absence causes dissatisfaction; motivational factors—presence causes motivation, absence causes no dissatisfaction.

pay level, the employee is likely to become frustrated and dissatisfied. Salaried employees seem particularly susceptible to this phenomenon. Although they may work harder to achieve a pay raise, soon after it has been accomplished, their standard of living and expectations move up to form a new base point of normalcy: at the same time, their performance often regresses to a more comfortable level.

Although there is controversy surrounding Herzberg's idea that money is not truly a motivator, there is much to be gained from his theory. The message is that agribusiness managers should work to enrich their employees' jobs. He suggests doing this by providing constant feedback, variety in tasks, and a means of making the job more important. This, he feels, will help the employee to become more enthusiastic about their work.

Vroom's expectancy theory

Victor Vroom, a Yale psychology professor, proposed an Expectancy Theory which states that, in the workplace, individuals have a variety of goals and that they can be motivated if they believe that:

1. There is a positive correlation between efforts and performance.
2. Favorable performance will result in a reward.
3. The reward's value to the employee can be determined,
4. The desire to satisfy the need is strong enough to make the effort worthwhile.

The actual equation is: Motivation = E (I x V), where:

1. *E = Expectancy.* Employees have different expectations and levels of confidence about what they are capable of doing. Managers must discover what resources, training, or supervision employees need. Expectancy is measured as a probability insofar as the

employee asks, "What are the chances that, given my knowledge, skills, and the resources available to me, I am able to complete the assigned task?"

2. *I = Instrumentality*. The perception of employees—expressed as a probability—that there will actually be a reward associated with completing the assigned task. Management must ensure that promises of rewards are fulfilled and that employees are aware of that.

3. *V = Valence*. Valence refers to the emotional orientations people hold with respect to rewards, i.e., the depth of the want of an employee for extrinsic (money, praise, promotion, time-off, benefits) or intrinsic satisfaction (rewards). Not all outcomes possess a positive valence; getting a promotion, coupled with a transfer to an undesirable location, may well result in a negative valence. Effective managers thus seek to discover what employees value.

Vroom suggests that an employee's beliefs about expectancy, instrumentality, and valence interact psychologically to create a motivational force such that employees act in ways that bring pleasure and avoid pain. This force can be "calculated" via the following formula: Motivation = Expectancy × (Instrumentality × Valence). In the example in Figure 16.7, both employee A and B's task is to achieve some target (sales goal or piecework productivity) and the desired outcome of achieving their target is a pay raise. In this example, Employee B would have the greater motivation.

Employee recognition and motivation

Everyone needs to be noticed. Agribusiness managers will find that effective communication with employees regarding their particular situation, a current project, or their state of being can be a powerful management tool. In fact, some experts argue that a manager cannot communicate "too much," due to the fact that most managers do not communicate enough. Effectively addressing individuals as individuals can greatly enhance motivation and performance.

	Valence (V)	Expectancy (E)	Instrumentality (I)	M = E (I x V)	M
	i.e. Desired outcome	i.e. Employee's assessment of how likely it is that the task will be achieved	i.e. Employee's perception that there will actually be a reward	i.e. Expectancy multiplied by product of instrumentality and valence	i.e. Employees's motivation
Employee A	The employee believes that the outcome is very attractive. = 0.8	As past performance is poor, employee assessed the task as difficult to achieve = 0.2	Employee definitely believes that there will be a reward = 1.0	M = 0.2 (1 x 0.8)	M = 0.16
Employee B	The employee believes that the outcome is relatively attractive. =0.6	As past performance is reasonable, employee assessed the task as reasonably achievable = 0.6	Employee definitely believes that there will be a reward = 1.0	M = 0.6 (1 x 0.6)	M = 0.36

Figure 16.7 Example of Vroom's expectancy theory
Note: each variable is assigned a perceived value, and then the calculation is performed.

Communication

Effective communication is critical to good supervision. It is the manager's responsibility, not the subordinate's, to ensure good communication. Although one would hope that the subordinate would try to communicate objectively, the superior has no assurance of that, and so must assume that responsibility personally. Approaching communication from the adult perspective (i.e., taking a "step back," and not getting sucked into a "cat fight," or "he said, she said") can help the supervisor avoid getting "hooked" and losing control of the situation. Professionals need to maintain control.

Strokes

Every person has the need to feel valued and recognized by others. Any recognition of another person's presence is known as a stroke. It could be a word, simply "hello." It could be a gesture—a smile or nod. It could be a touch—a handshake or an actual pat on the back. A stroke is anything that says, "I know you're there." We have all experienced them, and we know the "warm fuzzy feeling" they give us. This is what an agribusiness manager should strive for. They should be appropriate and not overused, but can be effective motivators.

Strokes are necessary for growth and survival. Some people need many strokes in order to feel socially secure. For a great number of people, a primary source of strokes is their job.

Plate 16.2 Producer and consultant
Serving as a consultant or advisor to customers can help fulfill the need for self-actualization.
Photo courtesy of USDA Natural Resources Conservation Service.

They work hard and do a good job to receive strokes—both from their peers and their supervisor. In fact, hunger for strokes probably affects everyone's behavior on the job to some extent. Employee awards are an example of a stroke which can be very effective. A well designed employee award program can be a positive motivator by recognizing employees in front of their peers.

Positive strokes

Positive strokes are any form of recognition that leaves another person feeling good, alive, and significant. Friendships and close relationships are often built around positive strokes. People like those who stroke them, who give them attention and care enough to listen. Positive strokes give real meaning to life for most people, and there are many kinds of positive strokes.

Positive unconditional strokes

Positive unconditional strokes convey the spoken or implied message, "I like you… you're OK with me." There are no conditions to the acceptance. These are thought to be the most meaningful kind of strokes; they are common among family members and close friends, but are frequently found in the business world as well. They are reflected in all kinds of behavior and conversation. Unconditional strokes may be affectionate or complimentary:

> "Good morning!"
> "I like that shirt!"
> "I just don't know how we'd get along without you."
> "You really know how to close a sale."
> "Come join me for coffee."
> "Your decision was very well thought-out."

Note that unconditional strokes enhance people's feelings about themselves. If the strokes are honest, genuine, and not overdone, they are of great benefit to a person's ego. Unconditional strokes cannot really be considered a management tool, since there cannot be any attempt to manipulate another's behavior with them. These are given freely, without strings. Yet managers who easily give recognition and show genuine approval fulfill important needs of subordinates, and the result is often positive motivation.

Positive conditional strokes

Positive conditional strokes are recognitions given to intentionally modify another's behavior. Since it is management's job to motivate and guide the behavior of employees, positive conditional strokes are widely and appropriately used as a management tool. Conditional strokes essentially say, "You're OK, if…" Acceptance of the other person is conditional on some expected behavior.

> "If you keep that up, you'll get the bonus we discussed."
> "I'm impressed when you work overtime."

"You look good today, for a change."

"If you make $1 million in sales, you'll receive a trip to Aruba."

Though they qualify acceptance with an "if," positive conditional strokes are not unethical—quite the contrary. They are a very popular and effective management and motivational tool—positive conditional strokes can help a person feel good about themselves.

Negative strokes

Negative forms of recognition also give attention and status to people. Negative strokes do not make people feel as good as positive strokes, but at least the person is getting some attention, and that is sometimes preferable to being ignored. Negative strokes most often come in the form of verbal criticism and reprimands. They are meant to squelch and usually to hurt another person:

"What's the matter with you?"

"That's the trouble with this next generation."

"Can't you do anything right?"

"OK, I'll do it just for you!"

Negative strokes are an effective way of getting attention. People who are ignored sometimes learn that inappropriate behavior can get them attention much faster and more predictably than any other type of action.

It is difficult to manipulate others into giving positive strokes, but it is easy to get negative strokes. As strange as it may sound, some workers may be so accustomed to negative strokes, that negative strokes are the only thing they know how to get or how to handle. They may subconsciously create circumstances in which they get much-needed attention. It is possible that a person who is habitually late for work is looking for strokes. Positive strokes are usually considered a more effective management technique than negative strokes. Clearly, however, recognition of employees in general is an extremely powerful form of motivating and supervising.

Summary

Managing human resources is a fundamental responsibility of agribusiness managers. Managers must develop an organizational structure in which the responsibilities, authority, and accountability of individuals are clearly defined. Management must then direct and supervise daily activities, leading and motivating employees to maximize productivity.

Many agribusinesses use a formal organizational chart to clarify the responsibilities, authority, and accountability of employees. Line organizations are structures in which everyone is in the chain of command and has direct responsibility for the primary functions of the business. In the line and staff organizational structure, specialists without authority are added to advise line managers. Finally, in the functional organizational structure, specialists and advisors are given the authority to implement ideas in their area of special responsibilities.

Leadership is a challenging task for most agribusiness managers. There are many different styles of leadership, ranging from authoritarian to democratic to free rein to transformational. Management theorists have developed many models and theories to explain effective leadership. McGregor's Theory X and Theory Y and Drucker's management by objectives are examples of such models that have helped agribusiness managers become more effective.

Motivating means stimulating employees to act in a specific way. Maslow explained people's basic needs as a hierarchy, and suggested that fulfillment of these basic needs is what motivates people. Herzberg pointed out that while some factors motivate people, other factors, such as money, become part of people's expectations. Such factors, if not maintained at expected levels, can lead to dissatisfaction. Vroom postulated that individuals have a variety of goals and they can be motivated if they believe that there is a positive correlation between efforts and performance; that favorable performance will result in a reward; that the reward's value to them can be determined; and that the desire to satisfy the need is strong enough to make the effort worthwhile.

In the end, there are no fixed formulas or precise answers on the best way to manage people. Management is a complex process based on the individual characteristics of the leader, subordinates, and the situation. But there are many approaches and theories that can help the agribusiness manager develop a leadership style that results in improved firm performance, content employees, and a satisfied management team.

Discussion questions

1. Explain the differences between the formal and informal organizational structure of an agribusiness.
2. Discuss the span of control principle and what factors influence it.
3. Some businesses have a "flat" organizational structure. What principle is at work in these firms and what advantages does it have?
4. The line organization is one type of organizational structure. Discuss the advantages and disadvantages of this type of business set up.
5. Discuss how status in an organization is defined and how it affects individuals in the agribusiness.
6. Authoritarian leadership is one style of leadership—outline the pros and cons of this style.
7. How does the democratic style of leadership work?
8. Outline the differences in employees as postulated by McGregor's Theory X and Theory Y, and implications for employee management.
9. Discuss Maslow's needs hierarchy and how an agribusiness manager can utilize this theory in managing workers.
10. Outline the underlying thoughts behind Vroom's expectancy theory and work through an example of how a manager might utilize it to motivate employees.

References and additional reading

Bass, Bernard. *Leadership Performance Beyond Expectation.* New York: Free Press. 1985.

Drucker, Peter. *The Practice of Management.* New York: Harper Paperbacks. 2006.

Maslow, Abraham. *Toward a Psychology of Being* (Reprint of 1962 edition). Eastford, CT: Martino Fine Books. 2010.

McGregor, Douglas. *The Human Side of Enterprise*, Annotated Edition. New York: McGraw-Hill. 2005.

Herzberg, Frederick. "One More Time, How Do You Motivate Employees?" *Harvard Business Review*, reprinted September–October, 65(5): 5–16, 1987. www.facilitif.eu/user_files/file/herzburg_article.pdf

Vroom, Victor H. *Work and Motivation*. New York: John Wiley & Sons, 1964.

17 Managing human resources in agribusiness

Objectives

- Explain how human resource management and managing employee motivation in agri-businesses are related
- Discuss the functions of human resource management in agribusiness
- Understand the difference between job specifications and a job description
- Describe recruitment methods and the process of employee selection in agribusiness
- Explain the major steps of job orientation in an agribusiness
- Identify the important criteria that determine employee compensation and benefits
- Discuss the performance evaluation process in an agribusiness
- Describe the purpose and types of training programs in agribusiness
- Outline valid criteria for promotion and employee advancement in agribusiness
- Explain the purpose, format, and importance of an exit interview
- Describe the role and impact that labor unions have on the agribusiness sector

Introduction

An agribusiness firm's people are among its most valuable and important assets. Unfortunately, they are sometimes the "forgotten" asset, as owners and managers often think of physical assets such as trucks, land, cash, or equipment when they list their company's assets (and perhaps because it is these types of assets which are listed on the agribusiness firm's balance sheet—and its people are not).

The basics of human resource management are pretty straightforward—determine what jobs and tasks the agribusiness needs performed, find and hire good people, evaluate them periodically, and then compensate them appropriately. However, implementing this function in the firm is the challenge, and each step is important to the success of the company. **Human resource (HR) management** is much like production agriculture—part art and part science, requiring the right balance of a variety of resources, and the right conditions, to yield a bumper crop.

The scope of human resource management

Human resource management can be divided into two separate but closely related areas:

1. Managing human resource functions
2. Managing employee motivation

In other words, the mechanics of managing people and the finer points of motivating people are highly interdependent. If the person and the job are not carefully matched, no amount of motivation is likely to make much difference. In Chapter 16 we explored the important areas of organizational design, leadership, and motivation. The emphasis in this chapter will be on the functions of human resource management.

Key issues

Three major issues affect the management of human resources in most organizations: the size of the firm, knowledge of the human resource functions, and top management's philosophy toward human resources.

Sometimes, particularly in small firms, the human resource (or personnel, as it may be called in smaller firms) function is carried out more by accident than by design. Regardless of the size of the agribusiness, jobs must be defined, people hired, legal requirements met, employees trained, wages set, and customers served. Because a small agribusiness usually cannot afford to hire qualified full-time people to handle HR management, this task is often left to the general manager. In these cases, people may only get attention when a crisis occurs. Examples of such crises include a key employee leaving the company, a lawsuit filed by an employee, or customer service slipping dramatically. Unfortunately, in some agribusiness firms, human resource management is almost completely ignored until such problems reach crisis stage.

There is no absolute size of firm, in terms of number of employees or sales volume, which dictates when a full-time person (or persons) should be designated to handle human resource management. The kind of agribusiness, its complexity, the diversity of its jobs, and its degree of seasonality are all factors. A rough rule of thumb is that once an agribusiness has reached 75 to 100 full-time employees, management should examine its need for a full-time human resource manager. Another helpful guide is that a full-time HR department can be profitable when 1 to 2 percent or less of total wages will support that department's budget.

The size of an HR department also varies greatly by what they may outsource. For example, if a firm does payroll, benefits administration, and recruiting in-house, they may need additional staff to manage these functions. Many smaller companies will either have the accounting department help with payroll, or it may be worthwhile to outsource this function to specialized payroll firms such as ADP™ (Automatic Data Processing, which calls themselves "The Business Behind the Business") or Paychex™.

Examining a growing midsize cooperative, the Culpen County Farmers' Co-op, illustrates some of the key issues involved in managing human resources. The general manager, Kevin Staton, has been with the firm about five years. The firm primarily focuses on crop inputs and fuel and has annual sales averaging approximately $7.5 million. The cooperative sells and services a complete line of agronomic inputs including fertilizer, crop protection chemicals, and seed. In addition, Culpen sells gasoline, diesel fuel, and LP gas to farmers, small businesses, and homeowners in their four-county area. The cooperative has 35 full-time employees, plus another eight to ten part-time employees during the busy season. While the business has grown somewhat, the number of employees has remained relatively constant over the last couple of years because new equipment and technology has allowed the firm to increase productivity.

Until recently, the labor force had been stable, and Kevin felt that the organization really had no personnel problems. Yet in the last year, a number of events have occurred that have radically changed his perspective: the co-op's workers' compensation rate had increased substantially; the firm was cited for six violations of safety laws; a new plant which manufactured auto parts for Toyota had just opened in an adjacent county; and several of his departmental managers had been forced to spend time driving trucks, running the plant and the like. Because of a work-related accident in which an employee lost an arm, Kevin had to cancel a trip to Europe that he and his family had been planning for two years. While ten of the 35 full-time employees have been with the organization for over ten years, records show that last year 18 new people were hired. The plant employees have no benefits other than those required by law. The firm obviously has an employee turnover problem, and Kevin expects this situation to only get worse given the benefit package offered by the new auto parts plant. He also knows that Culpen is not hiring employees that have the experience and work attributes that they need to keep the cooperative competitive.

Culpen County Farmers' Co-op has no formal or written human resource policies. Just a few short years ago, the firm had only one location and a dozen employees, and such a policy seemed like a lot of red tape. A rudimentary form is used as a job application. Applicants are interviewed and hired by whatever manager has the time to talk to the individual applying for the job. There are no well-defined job qualifications, and job functions have not been described formally. Training and orientation consists of, "You go out and help in the plant— whoever is there will show you the ropes." Because total employee costs are high, the wage policy consists of "pay as little as you can." Except for a token raise each year for everybody, raises are generally given only when a person wants to resign, as an inducement to stay. At that point, it is often too late to change the employee's decision.

Larger firms can also be guilty of having human resource programs almost as haphazard as those of the Culpen County Farmers' Co-op. Sheer size often forces a much more fully developed, formal human resource program in larger companies, but such a program can be almost as ineffective as Culpen's if poorly organized and managed. A relatively large agri-business with over 2,000 employees provides a good example. The current personnel direc-tor was promoted to his job some 15 years ago, primarily because he was available at the time. He had been in the training department (which was not well run) and had no formal HR management training. More importantly, since taking the position, he has never tried to learn more about the job in any organized way. His appointment clearly mirrors the attitude of top management—who believe the HR function is relatively unimportant. "Find the bodies" and "pay them as little as possible" are the two implicit, but primary, personnel objectives. In this firm, the HR director is not regarded as top management, and is not included in important planning and policy-making processes. In fact, the warehouse superintendent and mainte-nance supervisor have far more influence than the HR manager does. Labor productivity is down, turnover and absenteeism are high, grievances continue to increase, strikes are antici-pated, and top management wonders why!

Clearly, things must change in both firms. Without major changes in their human resource management approaches, both firms will continue to lose business to competitors or fail to survive. People problems affect productivity, costs, and profits. Both of these firms provide examples of the major issues (size, skill, and knowledge of the HR staff, and managerial philosophy and attitude) that must be addressed in successfully managing the human resource area. Let's dig a bit deeper into the human resource management function and explore ways to help the agribusiness manager maximize their returns from investment in people.

The functions of human resource management

There are a number of steps in an effective human resource management program. These steps focus on finding the right people for the right jobs, and then providing for their continued productivity and development. Jim Collins in his book *Good to Great* outlines this concept as the approach of good managers to "first get the right people on the bus (and the wrong people off the bus) and then figure out where to drive it," with the metaphor of the bus being the agribusiness. The steps (or functions of a HR department) include:

1. Determine the firm's human resource needs
2. Find and recruit people
3. Select and hire employees
4. Orient new employees to their jobs
5. Set terms of compensation and benefits
6. Evaluate performance
7. Oversee training and development
8. Provide for promotions and advancement
9. Manage terminations or transfers

Literally thousands of people enter the job market each month. Some of them have never worked before; others have many years of experience and training. Each of these prospective employees has the potential for performing a lifetime of service as a productive and satisfied employee. Unfortunately, each employee has the same potential for being dissatisfied, unhappy, and unproductive. The agribusiness manager's challenge is to tap the hidden resources of each new employee and guide these resources to benefit both the firm and the employee. This process begins with an evaluation of the firm's human resource needs.

Defining the jobs to be performed

The first step in human resource management is often the one missed by those new to formal people management. The reason this step is neglected is simple—practically speaking, it does not seem absolutely necessary. One can hire people without knowing specifically what job they are supposed to do, or why or how they are supposed to do it. It is easy to go into a hiring situation with only a vague idea of what the new hire should do. It is also easy to hire a person to fill a vacant position with no real thought about whether or not the job responsibilities should be changed. The challenge of defining the job rests on a sound, well-developed organizational plan (Chapter 16). Every position should have job goals that contribute to the firm's success. The job should be defined two ways: (1) job specifications and (2) a job description.

Job specifications

Job specifications spell out the qualifications needed to perform a job satisfactorily. A set of job specifications should be developed for each job, regardless of the size or kind of agribusiness. In the Culpen County Farmers' Co-op, one of the department managers, perhaps the office manager, should be put in charge of the HR function. Delegation of this responsibility to one person will help free top management from crises that occur because of inadequate personnel programs. The person to whom the HR responsibility is delegated can develop a set of job specifications that use the following format:

1. The purpose of the job. What are the job goals? What activities are necessary to accomplish those goals?

2. The type of job. How is the employee supervised? What are the responsibilities and training opportunities? Is this a single level job or one that offers growth and promotion opportunities?
3. The requirements of the job. What educational level is required? What experience, special skills, physical strength or condition, emotional or personality factors would be helpful for this position?
4. Other factors. What testing would provide useful information? What work experience or other factors might determine the applicant's ability to do the job?

Every manager wants someone who is as creative as Thomas Edison, as intelligent as Albert Einstein, and as motivated as Olympic swimmer Michael Phelps, but such perfect people just do not exist. Qualifications that are set too high can be just as bad as those that are set too low. For this reason, job specifications should reflect the actual needs of the job. Generally speaking, a series of concise statements will suffice for a job specification. The person who supervises the job in question can often provide the information the HR manager needs. If the agribusiness manager cannot inventory the requirements of a job, it may be wiser to leave it unfilled, since the manager will never know whether or not it is being done well. Table 17.1 provides an example set of job specifications for a specific position with Culpen County Farmers' Co-op.

Job description

At the same time that job specifications are being developed, a **job description** should also be formulated. A job description stresses a job's activities and duties. Like the job specification, the immediate supervisor of the job in question is the best source of information about

Table 17.1 Example of job specifications

Culpen County Farmers' Co-op: Job Specifications

Job: Millhand

1. Purpose of job: To service customers' needs in unloading and loading grain, mixing and loading feed, and filling customers' orders.

2. Responsibilities: To direct and assist farmers in unloading grain rapidly and efficiently; to operate feed-mixing equipment; to load mixed and bagged feed; to maintain clean and safe conditions in the mill and elevator at all times; and to provide prompt and courteous service to customers.

3. Requirements: Education—High school diploma (minimum)

        Experience—Farm background or 1 year grain elevator experience

        Physical—Good health and free from dust allergies

        Personality—Must be friendly and outgoing, and work well with others.

4. Opportunities: This position provides the necessary experience to move into management as mill supervisor and eventually into sales or general management.

5. Special Considerations: Any applicant must be willing to work in dusty and noisy conditions and to work as many as 4 to 6 hours overtime per day during the harvest season.

what activities are important to the job. The format of a job description is relatively simple (Table 17.2):

1. A brief summary paragraph of the job and the goals it is intended to accomplish
2. A list of the duties, responsibilities, and attendant authority
3. A statement defining lines of authority
4. An indication of how and when job performance and standards will be evaluated

While the outline of the job description should be exact enough to provide guidance for the employee and the supervisor, they should also be flexible enough to allow for special situations, emergencies, or minor changes. It seems obvious that finding the right person for the job requires a careful appraisal of the qualities needed by the person filling the job, and of the duties to be performed and responsibilities to be assumed. These steps are clearly the starting points toward effective HR management.

Table 17.2 Example of a job description

Culpen County Farmers' Co-op: Job Description

Job: Millhand

Brief Description: The primary responsibility of the millhand is to assist customers in unloading and loading grain, grinding and mixing feed to customer specifications, bagging or loading feed onto trucks, and filling customer orders for premixed feed and animal health products. The job will require significant overtime hours during harvest season. The millhand has a great deal of customer contact and is responsible for providing friendly, efficient service to farmers.

Duties and Responsibilities:

1. Unload and load grain.
2. Grind and mix feed to customer specifications as per work order.
3. Load feed.
4. Fill customer orders as per work order.
5. Maintain clean and orderly conditions in stock room feed grinding, and elevator areas at all times.
6. Sweep and clean all work areas daily.
7. Maintain and enforce all safety regulations at all times.
8. Take inventory of products weekly.
9. Perform routine maintenance of unloading and mixing equipment as scheduled.
10. Maintain helpful, friendly attitude toward customers at all times.

Supervision: Millhands report to and receive instruction from the mill supervisor. The supervisor will have authority and responsibility for all activities in the elevator and the mill. Suggestions or complaints should be made through the supervisor.

Evaluation: Performance of millhands will be evaluated semiannually. This evaluation will be completed by the immediate supervisor, initialed by the general manager, and discussed with the millhand. This evaluation will establish the millhand's strengths and areas of needed improvement. It will serve as the basis for wage increases and promotions.

Finding or recruiting employees

Prospective employees can be secured from many sources. The qualifications for the job, its wage or salary, the kind and size of organization and the location of the agribusiness will all play an important role in locating new employees. Just as with customers, there may be no better recommendation for the HR program of a firm than to have current employees tell their friends, "This is a good place to work." Many well-managed firms have long lists of people who want to work for them because of present employees' satisfaction with their jobs.

If some present employees see the available position as a promotion, those employees may be good prospects for the job, assuming that they are qualified. If the job requires special training or education, school or university placement services or counselors can provide help in finding recruits. Private employment agencies and government employment services can often help locate the applicant needed. The wise manager is always alert to the existence of top-notch people in competitors' firms or others who may be interested in a change of jobs. In today's economy, many positions are posted online and some firms purchase access to online resume databases. Advertising in newspapers is effective for hourly jobs and trade journal postings can be useful for niche-type careers (commodity buyers, livestock nutritionists, plant breeders, etc.).

Selecting the right person

Each of the available applicants should be screened against both the job specifications and the job description for that particular job (Tables 17.1 and 17.2). First, the job applicant should be compared to the job specifications. A good job application should elicit information on personal history, education and special skills, experience, personal references, and previous employment—all consistent with the background and skill set required for the position (Table 17.3).

Human resource managers also have to be very careful not to seek information that the applicant does not legally have to provide. Care must be taken in designing the application so that it does not violate the Civil Rights Acts, which make it illegal to discriminate against any person on the basis of race, color, religion, gender, age, or national origin. Seeking information like marital status, financial position, number of children, and age can get a firm into a lot of trouble if the firm uses the information in some discriminatory way. And a firm that is audited for civil rights violations will be glad it has designed a set of job specifications for each job. If these are carefully designed to represent those factors needed to perform the job successfully, and if the person interviewing the applicants has filled them out honestly, the firm will be in a stronger position to defend its hiring practices.

The job application can be simple, but it should provide the applicant with a chance to present qualifications in an organized and fair manner. The task of managing the process for finding and screening applicants should fall to the person(s) responsible for the HR function. There are several reasons for this: (1) the person doing the screening interview develops skills through experience; hence that person is the most qualified for the task; (2) there is consistency in interviewing when one person handles all screening interviews; and (3) when a HR specialist handles this function, others are not interrupted in their tasks. Note that for many positions, the HR specialist may well involve a number of others in the full hiring process—the supervisor, coworkers, staff specialists, etc. But even here, the HR specialist will likely manage or lead the process to insure that the best possible person is hired and that all legal requirements are met.

Table 17.3 Example of a job application

Culpen County Farmers' Co-op: Job Application

Name: _____

Address: _____

_____

Phone: Home: _____

        Cell: _____

E-mail: _____

Education:

Name and Address of School	Degree	Graduation Date

Experience and Special Skills not included in previous employment below:

Previous Employment (please list with most recent employer first)

Employer	Supervisor	Phone	E-mail	Years employed	Reason for leaving

May we contact your present employer? ____ Yes ____ No

References:

Name/Title Address and Phone

_____

_____

_____

_____

The ability to learn whatever needs to be known depends on the skills of the interviewer. Matching the job specifications and job description against the application form can provide solid facts, but the interviewer's subjective judgment must be trusted to determine the applicant's attitude, personality, and ability to fulfill the responsibilities of this position. In addition, it is common for larger organizations to use a variety of personality/problem-solving/leadership tests to more objectively evaluate individuals in these more subjective areas.

For best results, the interview should be planned in advance. The interview should be held in a private, quiet place where the applicant recognizes that the manager's interest is real and that the job is important to the organization. When the interview begins, the manager should help the applicant relax. It is critical to establish rapport with the interviewee to give the applicant every opportunity to demonstrate his or her potential. Good icebreaker topics include the last job or the applicant's aspirations. Then the manager should ask leading questions and be a good listener. A good interviewer does not monopolize the conversation. The applicant should be given an accurate description of the background of the firm and the job in question. The position should not be either undersold or oversold. When interviewing, it is useful for the manager to give applicants a copy of the job specifications and the job description, so that they can refer to this information.

With today's abundance of information (much via the internet), there are many tools for job seekers, so that interviewers may need to "evolve" their skills when interviewing. One way to do this is to use probing questions. For example, the interviewer may have ten structured questions, but also have an additional ten probing questions based on the job applicant's responses. For example: "What was your most frustrating day at work?" Applicant: "The day I went out and my pickup truck would not start and I had the wrong chemicals." Some interviewers might take this response and just move on. But the better prepared interviewer will use probing questions to dig deeper. Probing questions might be: "Why did the truck not start? Why were the chemicals wrong?" Did the applicant make a mistake and learn from it, were they defiant about something, were they careless, and was it someone else's truck? Thus, probing further may help the interviewer truly see the applicant's behavior, and the best predictor of future performance is past performance or behavior.

References can be helpful and should be checked out—after securing permission from the applicant to do so. The manager should check to see whether the information given by the applicant is correct as well as whether the reference is a positive one. Checking by phone has an advantage over checking by letter. People may talk more over the telephone than they will write on paper, and the tone of voice, along with the things that are not said, can be significant. Judgment must be used in interpreting references, and good references from former employers are the manager's best criteria. In today's business environment, references may be very cautious to do anything except for validating employment. It may take some persistent effort to learn more about a job candidate in these situations, but again, getting some feedback from references is a very important step in the hiring process.

As mentioned, testing can also be helpful in screening applicants for some jobs, but the manager must make sure that the test really measures the factors important to the job. In any event, tests should not be the only criteria for hiring. Testing is most often done in five general areas: intelligence, aptitude, personality, manual dexterity, and physical condition. Some testing programs are more accurate than others. For example, manual dexterity and physical fitness tests are usually quite accurate in predicting a person's physical performance capabilities, while attitude or personality tests have less accuracy. If the test provides useful insights into areas that are required by the job, the manager's success in matching jobs with people can be improved significantly.

Once the HR manager has reduced the list of candidates to two or three qualified individuals, the immediate supervisor for the vacant position (and perhaps other employees interacting with the candidate) should interview them and make the final selection. This important step builds the relationship between the position supervisor and the new employee in two ways:

1. A new employee tends to have a positive feeling toward the supervisor who personally selected them.
2. The supervisor who has taken part in the selection process tends to have a special feeling of responsibility for helping the new person succeed on the job.

Job orientation

When the best potential employee has been found, the successful applicant must be introduced to the job. Every time someone is hired, the organization is betting heavily on that person's success. The right start, quick adjustment, and future productivity depend on effective **job orientation**. At the start, the new employee is more receptive than at any other time to developing the attitudes necessary to produce a long-lasting and successful career. Texas Instruments determined that employees who completed their orientation reached full productivity two months faster than those who did not do so. Corning Glass determined that employees were 69 percent more likely to remain with them after three years if they completed their orientation program. Job orientation involves four major steps:

1. Introducing the company to the employee
2. Establishing job relationships and encouraging familiarity with the facilities
3. Helping the employee to begin the job
4. Following up and evaluating the employee's adjustment

The first step in orientation is helping the new employee better understand the company and the job. This is a very important step and the amount of time devoted to it will depend on the position and the company. A part-time employee in a retail farm supply business may get a very brief orientation. A new sales hire in a large, complex agribusiness may well have an orientation program that lasts a full year.

At this point, the history, nature, and scope of the organization, and information relative to hours of work, pay, benefits, rules or restriction, company policies, regulations, overtime, special programs, and facilities should be reviewed. Of course, the new employee will not be able to remember all this information, so it is helpful for it to be written down for future reference. In a small organization, this may involve a couple of copied sheets in a folder; in a large organization, it may take the form of an employee handbook. A tour of the entire facility will help to foster an overview of the organization and an understanding of where the employee fits in. Again, in a larger company, this process may involve an extended period of job shadowing.

The second step is establishing **job relationships**. Here supervisory responsibility should be outlined. The new employee should be introduced to their new supervisor, if this person is different than the one who interviewed candidates, fellow workers, and to the union steward if there is one. The physical layout, parking, washrooms, lunchroom, etc., should be pointed out. The immediate supervisor should review work-related matters, such as safety regulations, and job expectations. It is often helpful to assign a new employee a "buddy" or "mentor" who will help that person get acquainted and feel at home in the new job.

The next step is helping the employee to actually begin the job. Supplies, safety devices, equipment operation, work accessories, and the like should be discussed, even if the new employee has previous experience. After these explanations, the supervisor should allow the new employee to try the job. The speed of this phase will vary according to the level and complexity of the job and the employee's skills. The supervisor should not try to push too much information on the new employee at once, but should let learning occur step by step.

The supervisor should be sure to stress the required work habits and the norms and expectations of job performance. Again, a fellow worker assigned as a buddy can be helpful in giving the new person proper orientation. Managers must recognize that, like it or not, much of what the new employee learns about how to do the job and about work habits and attitudes will come from fellow workers. So, if rules are specified on paper but never enforced, the new employee will learn this very quickly. When a new person comes on board, problems often surface in firms that do not abide by the rules and regulations they outline in the employee handbook.

The final step in orientation is follow-up. Good HR managers do not assume that things are going well: they make sure that they are. This routine follow-up is usually best handled in an informal, on-the-job situation. The manager should determine how the new employee is getting along on the job and with fellow workers and supervisors. The manager should learn what problems exist, if any, and help solve them. Follow-up is not only useful in making sure that things are going as they should be, and allowing for corrective action, but it also gives management an opportunity to encourage new employees and assure them of the firm's continuing interest in their careers. In many firms, a 30-, or 60-, and/or 90-day review is simply specified up front, and is therefore expected by the new employee.

In large companies, several people may handle orientation, while in a smaller firm the manager may perform this important step. Some larger firms have orientation schools or sessions. These may be several days (or weeks) in length, particularly for management or administrative jobs. The more that fellow employees and immediate supervisors are involved, the more they will feel responsible for the new employee's success as a team member. Fellow employees and immediate supervisors should be trained to perform orientation functions.

Even the smallest firm should have a planned job orientation program to ensure that new employees get off to a good start. Again, this cannot be overemphasized—this is the time to help the new employee understand the organization and expectations, and to help them to quickly become a part of the team—it will definitely pay off.

Compensation and benefits

Attitudes toward **compensation** vary across agribusiness firms. In addition, the labor market facing a food or agribusiness has a tremendous amount of influence on the level of compensation an agribusiness offers. Firms located near rapidly growing suburban areas may find their wage structure substantially higher than a firm located in a more rural, slow-growing market. The agribusiness firm must consider both its ability to pay and competing compensation rates for similar jobs in the area or industry. Often the local Chambers of Commerce or trade associations can provide guidelines for wage and salary levels. Some agribusiness trade associations may sponsor compensation surveys conducted by a university in the region or by consulting firms.

Please note that the base wage is only the starting point for many agribusiness compensation programs. **Commissions** tied to productivity, bonuses if certain levels of performance are reached, stock options for more senior positions, may all be a part of the compensation package. While exploring all of these areas is beyond the scope of this book, it is important to understand that the compensation of an employee will likely involve more than just the base salary.

Benefits are also important factors in securing motivated employees and keeping them satisfied. And, benefits are growing in importance. They range from those required by law to health benefits, vacations, sick pay, life insurance, wellness programs (benefits that encourage healthy living habits like nutritious diets and exercise), and retirement benefits. Management of larger firms will devote considerable time to the development of benefit policies and programs. Their counterparts in smaller agribusiness firms can consult insurance companies and other firms in the area for guidance in determining the kinds and costs of benefits for their employees. Today with the concern about rising health care costs, many prospective employees are as concerned about this area as they are about wages or salary. Leading edge

Plate 17.1 Man training employees
Managing human resources is all about helping people reach their maximum potential. Photo courtesy of USDA Natural Resources Conservation Service.

agribusinesses attempt to offer their employees a benefit program that fits their particular needs. Hence, many benefit programs offer employees choices of the benefits that they desire.

Compensation satisfies employees' need for security and provides concrete feedback on the value of their contribution to the organization. Competitive factors, employees' need for recognition and self-esteem, and the skills and knowledge required all play a part in determining the level and composition of the total compensation package. The compensation program of the agribusiness firm must consider the true cost of compensation in terms of the jobs that need doing. The firm's ability to pay must be measured against the person's productivity. Putting together a "package" of wages, incentives, and benefits requires careful study by management.

Evaluating performance

Performance evaluation is critical to successful human resource management programs. Managers and employees both benefit from a carefully conceived and implemented performance evaluation program. The goals of an employee performance evaluation program are to:

1. Improve future performance
2. Identify employees with untapped potential, in order to help them realize that potential

3. Provide employees with a benchmark of their achievements
4. Provide information relating to decisions about promotion, advancement, and pay
5. Give the manager guidelines for helping employees in the future

Performance appraisals should not only evaluate the employee and make them aware of their contributions, but should also focus on results of the workers' efforts and their goals for the next evaluation period. Good evaluation programs concentrate not only on past performance but also on future opportunities. In addition, employee goals should be linked to the goals of the organization. For example, how can the receptionist help the business with its goal of increasing feed sales and production by 30 percent this year? Do they understand what the goal means? Management should work to integrate all employee goals with company goals.

Both the manager and the subordinate often view evaluations with apprehension. The manager should remember that evaluation is a tool and not a weapon, crutch, or cure-all. The major purpose of evaluation is to improve performance, not to punish employees. The successes as well as the failures of both the manager and those managed are recorded during an effective evaluation.

As with any tool, the effective use of performance appraisal depends on the skill of the operator as well as the quality of the tool. The evaluation instrument itself should be as objective and clear as possible. Letting the subordinate use the document for self-evaluation prior to the session is helpful. A comparison of the manager and employee ratings opens the way for good communication flow. Managers must understand that they are not in a position of judgment, but rather are seeking to create an honest two-way discussion aimed at positive reinforcement of morale and improved productivity.

The evaluation should be conducted in a private, quiet place without interruption. The manager should make the process relatively informal and be willing to listen. As in the job interview, the manager should put the employee at ease as quickly as possible. Discussion of personality factors should be avoided, if possible. However, if the subordinate is in the mood for such a discussion and this discussion could improve job performance, then the manager may make the most of the opportunity.

Follow-up discussions after the evaluation give the manager a chance to encourage improvement if and when it occurs. Such discussions or "checkups" also keep the manager current on changes in performance. Follow-up (particularly when a subordinate's evaluation was substandard) allows the manager the opportunity to offer recommendations and suggestions, and, if necessary, to exercise disciplinary practices to improve performance.

Another evaluation/feedback concept that works well is for a manager or supervisor to utilize a monthly 1 x 1 (one-on-one meeting) with employees. Such meetings can be helpful in eliminating surprises during formal evaluations. A simple 1 x 1 format may include:

1. Current open items (things being worked on)/what's going on in "their world"?
2. What can the manager do to help, what additional things does the employee need to do their job?
3. Encourage feedback, as this sets the tone that feedback is encouraged and welcome.

New employees should be evaluated formally with great frequency. Established employees should be evaluated at least semiannually to ensure that work performance is progressing satisfactorily. An annual checkup usually is not sufficient to catch problems and change work habits or productivity factors that need improvement. Of course, formal evaluation does not replace the need for day-to-day evaluation and coaching that is a constant part of the manager's job. Employees want and need on-the-spot feedback if they are to enjoy satisfaction from their jobs (Chapter 16).

Evaluation must measure work habits and personal traits, as well as success at reaching job goals. Many agribusiness firms use a management concept called management by objectives (Chapter 16). Table 17.4 provides an example of a simple, traditional employer appraisal form.

Training and development

The benefits of training are high quality, efficient, and safe work—all of which are vital to the agribusiness and to the employee. Employees also want to feel that they are growing personally and professionally in a job, and training plays an important role here. Training needs vary according to the circumstances faced by the firm and the specific job position. The kind of agribusiness, the level of complexity of the job, and the experience and educational level of the employee all determine the kind of training needed. **Training programs** are devised to meet one or more of the following objectives: reduce mistakes and accidents; increase motivation and productivity; and prepare the employee for promotion, growth, and development. Managers can increase each employee's value to the firm through training.

All training programs should be based upon specific objectives and meet the test of the following formula:

What should be known – what is known = what must be learned

The employee's present abilities and future capabilities should be analyzed by the person responsible for this function, with the help of the employee. Today there is a real emphasis on lifelong learning—a longer-term plan for developing the employee through targeted, ongoing education and training. Regardless of type, training and development programs generally fall into the following major categories:

1. On-the-job
2. Formal in-house
3. Outside formal

On-the-job training

Most training in small agribusiness firms, or at lower job-levels in large firms, is handled on-the-job. Here the objective is very simple: to teach the skills or procedures for accomplishing a specific task or job. **On-the-job training** begins by determining what needs to be taught. Next, the manager must decide who is to do the training, and be sure the trainer understands the job operations, safety rules, etc.

Regardless of the job, the actual process will be one of show, do, and judge. The supervisor should show employees step-by-step how to do the job, let them do it, then evaluate and offer suggestions and encouragement until a sufficient level of skill has been developed. The training period will vary with the complexity of the job, the experience level of the employee, the skill of the "instructor," and the ability of the employee to learn. The benefits of such training are high quality, efficient and safe work, all of which are vital to the business and to the employee.

Table 17.4 Culpen County Farmers' Co-op: employee evaluation

Employee _____   Date _____

Job _____

Work Habits:

Areas of Strength:

    1. _____

    2. _____

    3. _____

Areas of Improvement:

    1. _____

    2. _____

    3. _____

Personal Characteristics:

Areas of Strength:

    1. _____

    2. _____

    3. _____

Areas of Improvement:

    1. _____

    2. _____

    3. _____

Employee Growth Plan/Goals for Next Period:

    1. _____

    2. _____

    3. _____

Evaluation of Performance	Score (1–5: 1 high, 5 low)	Comments
Team Player		
Meets Deadlines		
Organizational Skills		
Communication Skills		
Leadership Ability		
Interaction with co-workers		
Attendance		
Quality of work		

Signatures:

Employee: _____

Supervisor: _____

Manager: _____

A specific type of on-the-job training is the apprenticeship. An **apprenticeship** is when a new employee works with a more experienced person, and learns under that person's direction over a period of time. This can be of great help in jobs requiring greater skills. Many agribusiness firms train salespeople, skilled operators, and managers by means of this system.

Formal in-house training

In larger firms, there is often a full-time training staff. Managers of smaller agribusiness firms may think they have fewer options for **formal internal training and development**. However, many more training opportunities are available to all sizes of firms today, if managers will just take the time to seek them out. For example, such training programs are provided by suppliers, trade associations, consultants, manufacturers, and schools or universities. Online courses, DVDs, videotapes, films, slide programs, audiotapes, correspondence courses, and programmed learning kits are but a few of the options available to all agribusiness managers for enriching their training programs.

Training on every conceivable topic, from financial management to trimming a head of lettuce, is available in some form. Suppliers, trade associations, and extension service personnel at the nearest land-grant university can help the trainer locate the latest and best training aides. Committee or staff meetings can provide a convenient and fertile ground for

Plate 17.2 Man and son in a hog barn
Guiding new employees through on-the-job training that enables them to experience the nuances of a new job can be both productive and rewarding. Photo courtesy of USDA Natural Resources Conservation Service.

training and development if the agendas are carefully controlled and directed toward this end. Sharing information in this setting can satisfy the need for employee recognition and participation and can help make employees feel more a part of the organization.

Formal external training and development

Agribusiness abounds with conventions, conferences, lectures, workshops, seminars, and the like, on every known subject. In addition, there are trade schools, extension courses, high school and university courses, and business and trade courses that can provide enhancement and/or enrichment to employees and employers simultaneously. Almost every community has most of these alternatives available. Most agribusinesses will be affiliated with a trade association or group that sponsors educational experiences. The trick is to use sufficient self-discipline to determine what specifically must be learned. Many managers are not discriminating enough in choosing educational experiences to improve their employees' productivity. Employee participation in selecting the best training options is often beneficial.

In today's fiercely competitive marketplace, learning should challenge a firm's people from top to bottom. This is recommended not only to improve basic skills (the best way of doing anything has not yet been discovered!), but also to encourage the positive psychological effect on people of working for a progressive, aggressive firm interested in developing its employees. Training and development involves some cost, but the returns in the form of a more dynamic, effective human resource far offset this expenditure. Training of employees should be regarded as an investment in the future of the firm.

Promotion and advancement

An agribusiness firm's promotion program and policies are related to the factors previously discussed in this chapter. Finding and hiring promotable people, determining their compensation, and overseeing training and development programs, all lead to the question of promotion, since promotion may be viewed as another form of compensation. To many employees, a **promotion** says, "You've done a good job—the firm appreciates you!"

At any time a position is open anywhere but the lowest level in the organization, a fundamental question is raised: should the firm promote someone from within, or hire someone from outside of the business? The answer to this question should be whoever has the best qualifications, skills, knowledge, and communication ability for the job. However, a strong case can be made for promoting from within, provided that the right people are available. Such a program of advancement encourages employees to grow in their current jobs—as they have a potentially higher-level position to aspire toward. In other words, the potential for promotion can be a strong motivational factor. At the same time, management must be careful that the firm does not become too inbred—new ideas, approaches, and methods need to be introduced from time to time, and hiring from the outside can help make this happen.

The criteria for promotion, then, becomes the critical factor. Several criteria must be considered. In a union operation, this may be the primary consideration. Other factors to evaluate are the merit or contribution of the employee in the past, and the employee's attitude and personality (in particular, the ability to function with the new team). A careful performance evaluation program will prove its value here. The employee's potential for growth must also be considered. Finally, the individual employee must want the promotion and be able to handle the new assignment.

Plate 17.3 Man and young man using equipment
Formal training can be very effective for new employees or employees changing jobs. Photo courtesy of USDA Natural Resources Conservation Service.

Too often managers assume that everyone wants to be promoted, when, in fact, some employees may lack the confidence or desire needed to handle this step, at least at this point in their career. In these situations, perhaps there are other ways of recognizing and rewarding a particular employee besides promotion. Offering added responsibility and pay, without increased stature in the organizational hierarchy, may be a better option in some cases. Other employees may be quite comfortable in their current job, and will make their greatest contribution to the company if they are simply left alone.

Agribusiness managers must continually guard against the greatest error made in promotions. Simply because a person excels at one job is no guarantee that the same person will excel at a job involving more responsibility and decision making. For example, a good plant employee may not be a good truck driver, nor will a good salesperson necessarily make a good sales manager. To reiterate: the job and the person must be matched carefully!

Termination and dismissal

It is inevitable that each employee will eventually leave the firm for some reason. Some will quit, some will be fired, and some will retire. In every case, the agribusiness manager should attempt to hold to a minimum the loss to the firm and the possible pain for the employee. The loss of any employee can be seen as a learning experience, if the manager takes the time to conduct an exit interview.

An **exit interview** simply gives the person who is responsible for the HR function the opportunity to do two things: make sure the employee leaves as a friend (if possible), and find out what caused the employee to leave, so that any problem areas influencing this decision can be addressed in the future. Retirees should go through the exit interview as well. Often they can offer valuable information in terms of job function and the company's HR management practices. Retirees may serve as an unbiased judge of firm strengths and weaknesses. The manager should take every opportunity to collect and evaluate their comments. Even if the employee has been fired or has quit in anger, a well-conducted exit interview that allows the person to express dissatisfaction will often allow the employee to vent this frustration. A friend or even a neutral party is better than an enemy.

The following exit interview questions would likely work best with processing line, retail sales floor, production plant, or other lower-level job positions within the firm. These questions would need to be altered to fit higher-level, management employees. Some possible questions for the exit interview include:

1. What did you enjoy most about working for our firm? (Starting with open ended questions puts the person at ease and also gets the person talking.)
2. What, if anything, did you dislike about working for our firm?
3. If you had a "magic wand," what are two or three things you would change about our firm, or your experience at our firm?
4. Was the selection process adequate? Did you understand the job, the compensation, and working conditions?
5. Were the job description and job specifications useful? Were you and the job matched carefully during placement?
6. Was orientation to the job adequate? Did you feel at home and a part of the team? Did you thoroughly understand the firm's expectations?
7. Were wages, benefits, and working conditions reasonable, fair and competitive? Were employee evaluations fair? Was there adequate feedback and reinforcement from the supervisor?
8. Were there any personality conflicts with your supervisor or fellow workers? Were discipline and work rules fair? Was there any favoritism or erratic or unusual discipline?
9. Were you given a chance to grow and develop? Was training given in a meaningful way? Were promotion policies understood and fair?

Turnover is one of the most expensive of all business costs. The cost of filling high-level positions often runs into tens of thousands of dollars (or more, depending on the size of the firm, and the responsibility of the position). There is the direct cost of finding, hiring, orienting, and training a new employee. There is also the indirect cost of the job not being performed at its highest level during the "lame duck period" before the old employee leaves. Finally, there's the downtime, from the time of the vacancy until the new employee develops the skill level to do the job. Often, there is poor morale among employees if turnover is high. And, customer service and sales efforts can suffer if high levels of turnover make it difficult to establish and support customer relationships.

There is a real loss to all concerned when termination and turnover occur. And, the answers to the exit interview questions are quite likely to be biased, especially if the person is quitting or being fired. In today's agribusiness labor market, frequent job changes are a fact of life. Despite the very best efforts of firms to create a supportive work climate, to pay competitive salaries, and to offer opportunities for growth—employees will leave. Still, an exit interview can assist the firm in improving in all of these areas.

Labor unions

Many larger agribusiness firms deal with unions, or organized labor. **Labor unions** are organized essentially to protect and promote the interests of their members. In the United States economy, both managers and workers believe that productivity and profits are essential to firm success. The question upon which management and labor are divided is what share of these profits and productivity each should receive. Workers need strong, profitable enterprises to compensate them well, and management needs productive workers to make reasonable profits for firm owners.

Unions have become a potent force only since the 1930s, when the Norris–LaGuardia Act (1932) and the Wagner–Connery Act (1935) gave workers the right to organize and bargain collectively with their employers. Many states also passed legislation called closed shop laws, which, in essence, required everyone working for a company that has voted to have a union to belong to that union. Some labor unions are small or local in nature, usually referred to as shop unions. They may encompass as few as one firm or just certain workers within a firm. However, in 2009, most of the more than 15.3 million union workers in the United States belonged to the more than 200 national or international unions, such as the Teamsters (the largest), United Auto Workers, and United Steelworkers. These workers represented 12.3 percent of all wage and salary workers in the United States (Bureau of Labor Standards, Union Members Survey).

A union is organized within a firm when employees petition the National Labor Relations Board (a governmental agency) to conduct an election. Laws and regulations require that certain conditions be met, and if everything is in order, the vote is conducted. If over 50 percent of the firm's designated workers vote for a specific union to represent them, the firm must deal with that union and develop a labor contract. These labor contracts can and usually do deal with wages, benefits, other forms of compensation, seniority, promotion, hours of work, layoffs, grievance procedures, and mediation. Most of the areas discussed previously in HR management are referred to in the contract. It is essential that the agribusiness firm consult competent legal advice if it is confronted by an attempt to organize workers or if a union already exists and management is forced into collective bargaining and contractual relations with its workers.

When an agribusiness has a union, it is not a case of management dealing with labor; rather, it is a case of business managers dealing and negotiating with labor union managers. Labor union managers are usually highly skilled and well-paid representatives of the unionized workers. The process called **collective bargaining** is, broadly speaking, one in which employers and representatives of employees attempt to arrive at agreements governing the conditions under which the employees are willing to work for the employer. If the collective bargaining process fails and no contractual agreement is reached, workers then have the right to withhold their services, or strike. A **strike** is used by both parties to apply economic pressures to the other until an agreement is reached.

The labor union and organized labor are a well-established part of the American business economy. Their continued success and growth seems likely, since managers' and workers' ideas of the ideal split of power and profits from business activities will always be different. Collective bargaining offers a process whereby these divisions are determined while the free enterprise system is maintained.

Summary

People are the most important asset of any agribusiness. The human resource function of management is concerned with administering the mechanics of employment, and creating a working environment that helps employees feel valued, growing both personally and professionally. The larger the agribusiness, the more formal and complex the process, but the HR function must be accomplished in any agribusiness.

HR management begins with determining employment needs. This usually requires defining the job and developing job specifications and a job description so that the right person can be recruited. Recruiting involves searching for qualified candidates, interviewing, and assisting in the selection of the best person. And, once a new person is on the job, it is an HR function to see that he or she gets off to a good start with proper orientation, training, and follow-up.

Another HR function is the development and administration of employee benefit programs. Insurance, retirement, health care, safety, continuing education, and related programs are all designed to increase the welfare and productivity of employees. And a well-designed benefits program represents a significant investment of both time and money by management. The HR manager is also responsible for ensuring that the firm meets complex government and labor union regulations concerning employees and working conditions.

In most agribusinesses, the human resource function also includes regular evaluation of employee performance and ensuring continued professional growth through ongoing training or formal seminars, but regardless of source, the goal is greater productivity, and more satisfied employees. The HR manager must also become involved in the termination of some employees. In this case, the manager must ensure that employees' rights are not violated and that there is just cause for dismissal.

HR managers are often designated to coordinate the agribusiness's relationship with labor unions. Negotiating union contracts and carrying out contract specifications are difficult but important human resource management functions.

Discussion questions

1. Discuss the functions of human resource management.
2. At what point should an agribusiness hire a full-time HR manager? What are the specific reasons a firm should invest resources in a full-time HR manager?
3. Draw up a set of job specifications and a job description for a food or agribusiness job with which you are familiar. (This could be a job you have recently held.) Contrast and compare them. What are the main differences? Are there any similarities? How are these two HR tools related?
4. What are the key elements of a good job application?
5. Explain the steps involved in job orientation. Think about the most recent job you have held. Were these steps followed when you were introduced to the job? Which ones were

followed and which ones were not? How could the organization you worked for have improved their job orientation process? (If you have not had the opportunity to have a job that had some type of orientation process, do this question as an interview with a friend who has.)

6. Explain why delegation is important in managing a business. Give an example of a task or project that was delegated to you by a manager or supervisor and how you carried out the task. Give a further example of a task or project you have delegated to someone else, how you assured that the task was done and what the final outcome was.

7. Discuss the objectives of evaluating employee performance and how such an evaluation should be conducted.

8. What are some examples of "formal in-house" training, and why is training important?

9. What are the pros and cons of promoting employees from within the agribusiness firm?

10. What is the purpose and format of an exit interview?

Glossary

account A specific category of financial information such as sales, labor expense, or cash; also can refer to a specific customer who owes the business money for credit purchases.

accountability In organizational structure, being answerable to another for performance.

accounting period A predetermined regular interval for which financial transactions are summarized.

accounting profit The net income that remains after all actual, measurable costs are subtracted from total revenue.

accounts payable The amount of money owed by a firm to outside businesses for any items purchased on credit and for which payment is expected to be made in less than one year.

accounts receivable The total amount customers owe to a business for purchases made on credit.

accounts receivable loan A loan where a firm's accounts receivable are used as collateral.

accrual-basis approach An accounting method of reporting revenue when it is earned (regardless of when the cash is collected), and reporting expenses when they are incurred (regardless of when the cash disbursement is made).

accruals Those financial obligations that have been incurred, but not invoiced or paid, such as taxes payable and wages payable.

accrued expense An account summarizing the firm's accruals.

acid test ratio See **quick ratio**.

acquisition The process of buying another firm or business unit; a method of direct investment that allows a firm to gain country- and market-specific knowledge without incurring a long and costly learning process.

advertising Mass communication with customers or prospects, usually through public media.

aging accounts receivable Reporting accounts receivable on a monthly basis in accordance with the number of days since the accounts receivable was charged to the customer.

agglomeration The accumulation of business activity around a specific location; firms often locate in close proximity to one another because they can increase the efficiency of services at the business, household, and social level.

aggregate production planning The process of developing time-phased specific production quantities and rates, and workforce sizes and rates, while balancing customer requirements and the capacity limitations of plant and equipment.

agribusiness   Any business organization that supplies farm inputs or services, or that processes, distributes, or wholesales agricultural products, or retails them to consumers.

agribusiness management   The management of any firm involved in the food and fiber production and marketing system.

agricultural services and financing   A segment of the input supply sector that focuses on providing services, information, and financing to production agriculture; includes farm management services, veterinary clinics, consulting businesses, and farm lenders.

analyzing facts   A step in the planning process requiring answers to such questions as "Where are we?" and "How did we get here?"; helps pinpoint existing problems and opportunities, and provides insights upon which to base successful decisions.

annual percentage rate of interest (APR)   The true annual rate of interest which is charged on a loan:

$$APR = \left(\frac{2 \times P \times F}{B \times (T+1)} \right) \times 100$$

where P = payments per year, F = dollars paid in interest, B = amount of capital borrowed, and T = total number of payments.

annuities   A stream of incomes and / or costs that are equal amounts for each of the number of periods evaluated.

anticipation inventories   Inventories held for products where demand is not constant so that adequate supplies are available during peak seasons.

appraisal costs   Costs incurred in monitoring the quality level of products and services during the course of production.

apprenticeship   A form of training where a new employee works with a more experienced person, and learns under that person's direction.

articles of incorporation   Legal documents filed with the state government where the organization is incorporated and which set forth the basic purpose of the corporation and the means of financing it.

assemble to order   A process for producing products that have many options after the customer's order has been placed.

asset turnover ratio A financial ratio measuring efficiency; net sales / total assets.

assets   Items of value, including physical and financial property, that are owned by the business.

authoritarian leadership   A leader-centered style of leadership (also called autocratic), in which the thoughts, ideas, and wishes of the leader are expected to be obeyed completely, without question.

authority   In organizational structure, the right to command or force an action by another.

autocratic leadership   See **authoritarian leadership**.

bad debts as a percentage of credit sales   A financial measure used to monitor the effectiveness of a firm's credit policy; amount of bad debts divided by total accounts receivable multiplied by 100.

balance sheet   A financial statement that shows the financial makeup and condition of a business at a specific point in time by listing what the business owns, what it owes, and what the owners have invested in the business.

behavioral segmentation   In marketing, a means of classifying or categorizing customers or potential customers by their behavioral tendencies.

belongingness   A component of Maslow's needs hierarchy; suggests that after people have achieved a reasonable degree of confidence in their safety, they become concerned with their social acceptance and belonging.

benchmarking A technique for internal assessment that involves identifying a non-competitive firm known for excellence in a particular area, carefully studying that firm to see how they deliver this excellence, and then comparing the findings of this study against the firm's current practices.

benefits   Policies and programs offered to employees as a part of their compensation package. Examples range from health insurance, vacation, sick pay, life insurance, wellness programs (benefits that encourage healthy living habits like nutritious diets and exercise), and retirement savings.

benevolent autocrat   A leadership style in which leaders convince followers to do what they want by being so well liked that no one would consider being disloyal and giving so much praise that employees are shamed into obedience.

blue-sky laws   State laws which regulate the way in which corporation stock may be sold and which protect the rights of investors.

board of directors   The governing body of a corporation; elected by the stockholders to supervise the affairs of the corporation; the number on the board may vary according to the bylaws of the organization.

borrowing capacity   The total amount of loan repayment ability possessed by a firm or customer.

brand recognition   The ability of customers and prospects to readily identify a firm's brands in the market.

breakeven analysis   See **volume–cost analysis**.

breakeven point (BE)   The point at which income generated from sales just equals the total costs incurred from those sales.

budget   A forecast of sales, expenses, cash and / or other financial information for a future operating period; primarily used for control purposes.

buffer inventory   Inventory (usually relatively small amounts) held in reserve to accommodate uncertainty in production and / or sales; also known as safety stock.

build-up forecast   A sales forecast developed from data collected by the sales force or other employees with considerable customer interaction.

bulk   The size and weight conditions or circumstances associated with products; a challenge associated with packing and shipping agricultural products.

bureaucracy   A highly specialized organizational structure in which work is divided into specific categories, is carried out by special departments, and a strict set of guidelines determines the course of activities to ensure predictability and eliminate risk.

bylaws   In a corporation, the legal documents which set forth such rules of operation as election of directors, duties of officers and directors, voting procedures, and dissolution.

capacity   In credit analysis, refers to the earnings and cash flow available to meet financial obligations; in production management, refers to the maximum amount of activity possible for a facility, piece of equipment, or process. See **borrowing capacity**.

capacity planning   All activities that are undertaken to determine what the appropriate size of a manufacturing plant or service location should be, so that a certain quantity can be produced over a specific time period.

capital   The financial resources of a business, comprising in the broadest sense all the assets of the business and representing both owned and borrowed funds.

capital budgeting   A procedure for evaluating long-term investment decisions which takes into account the timing of the cash flows associated with the investment, and the time value of money.

capital intensity   The proportion of tasks in a production or service process performed by machines, relative to the tasks performed by humans.

capital investment   The addition of long-lived assets, typically used in the production of products or services, to an agribusiness.

capital lease   A long-term contractual arrangement in which the lessee acquires control of an asset in return for rental payments to the lessor.

capitalism   An economic system based on private ownership of the means of production and distribution of goods; characterized by a free, competitive market and an incentive structure motivated by profit.

Capper–Volstead Act of 1922   Important cooperative legislation ensuring the right of farmers to organize and market their products collectively so long as the association conducts at least half its business with members of the association and no member of the association has more than one vote, or the association limits dividends on stock to 8 percent.

cash   Funds that are immediately available for use without restriction, such as checking account deposits in banks and petty cash.

cash-basis approach   An accounting system of recognizing income when it is actually received and expenses when they are actually paid.

cash budget   A projection of a firm's cash receipts and cash requirements made on a periodic basis to enable management to plan for and control cash.

cash flow statement   An accounting statement reconciling the firm's cash balance between two points in time; typically shows cash receipts and cash disbursements for a prior accounting period but can also be used to project cash receipts and disbursements for a future period of time.

chain of command   In organizational structure, the authority–responsibility relationships or links between managers and those they supervise.

chain store   A set of 11 or more retail store locations operating under one management.

change in demand   A situation where the demand curve shifts to the right or left signaling a change in the quantity demanded at every specific price.

change in supply   A situation where the supply curve shifts to the right or left signaling a change in the quantity supplied at every specific price.

change in the quantity demanded   A movement along a given demand curve.

change in the quantity supplied   A movement along a given supply curve.

channel management   A set of decisions concerned with who owns and controls the product on its journey from manufacturer or producer to the customer, and the roles the different entities will play on this journey.

character   In evaluating creditworthiness, the personal habits, conduct, honesty, and attitude of the credit customer.

collateral   Assets pledged to guarantee payment of a loan.

collective bargaining   A process in which an employer and representatives of employees (generally a union) attempt to arrive at an agreement governing the conditions under which the employees are willing to work for the employer.

commercial banks   An investor-owned institution that accepts deposits and then allows checks to be written against those deposits as a means of making payments; the primary source of borrowed funds for most agribusinesses.

commercial farms   A category of farms that are family farms with income over $250,000 or nonfamily farms.

commercial finance companies   Those finance companies or specialized lenders that focus on business and commercial loans.

commission   The fee paid to a salesperson or other individual for providing a service; typically a percentage of the total amount of business transacted.

common-size analysis   A financial analysis technique where the firm's financial statements are expressed as percentages of some key base figure such as total sales or total assets, and then the resulting common size statements are used to make comparisons over time, or against peer firm data.

common stock   A specific form of equity investment in a corporation that carries with it the right (and obligation) to share in any profits or losses incurred by the business.

communication   The successful exchange of information or ideas between two or more individuals.

compensating balance   A specified amount of money that must be retained in a bank account while a loan is outstanding.

compensation   The total amount of salary, commissions, bonuses, benefits, and perquisites that are given to an employee in exchange for work done.

competitive advantage   The set of firm competencies that are important to customers where the firm has a clear and distinct advantage over the competition.

competitive pricing   A simple pricing method, based primarily on competitors' prices where prices are set at the "going rate."

compounding   A method of calculating interest in which interest earned periodically is added to the principal and becomes part of the base on which future interest is earned.

conformance to specification   A term used in quality management to confirm the adherence to specification of a produce or service.

consensus forecast   A forecast (usually generated by the Delphi method) where agreement is reached by a group on a set of future outcomes, scenarios, or indicators.

contingency planning   The development of alternative plans in case the assumptions made in the planning process do not materialize.

continuous inventory   In inventory management, the constant monitoring of stock on hand.

continuous production   A total production process that involves the flow of inputs in an uninterrupted way through a standardized system to produce outputs that are basically identical.

contribution margin   Gross margin less variable costs.

contribution to overhead (CTO)   The portion of each unit (dollar) of sales that remains after variable costs are covered and that can be applied toward covering fixed costs.

contribution to profit (CTP)   The portion of each unit (dollar) of sales that remains after variable costs and all fixed costs are covered; CTO at sales volumes greater than the firm's breakeven point.

control   The process of monitoring performance, as compared with pre-established standards, for the purpose of making adjustments to ensure that goals will be accomplished.

controlling   One of four tasks of management; represents the monitoring and evaluation of activities, and assessment of whether the goals and performance objectives developed within the planning function are achieved.

cooperative   A distinctive form of corporation that is organized to serve the needs of its member-patrons rather than to make a profit for investors.

cooperative advertising   A common advertising practice in agribusiness in which local advertising is sponsored, and usually funded, jointly by the manufacturer and the local dealer or distributor.

cooperative borrowing   A type of loan made to agribusiness cooperatives from CoBank, which is part of the Farm Credit System.

corporation   A form of legal organization with the powers, rights, and obligations of an individual; a corporation's assets and liabilities are controlled by the legal entity, not by the owners (stockholders).

cost-based pricing   A pricing method based on adding a constant margin to the basic cost of the individual product or service.

cost basis of valuation   A valuation practice by which assets are recorded on accounting records at their acquisition price, not their current market value.

cost leadership One of two generic business strategies; involves meeting competitors' product offerings with an offering of comparable quality and features, but beating the competitor on price.

cost of capital   The rate of return a firm requires of its investments.

cost of goods sold   The total cost to the business of goods that were actually sold during a specified time period; includes such items as raw material costs, in-coming freight costs, and the cost of any damaged or lost goods that must be absorbed.

cost-plus pricing   See **cost-based pricing**.

critical path method (CPM)   A method of scheduling that involves a diagrammatic representation of the network of activities which comprise a production operation.

cross price elasticity of demand   A measure of the relative responsiveness of quantity demanded of a given commodity to changes in the price of a related commodity.

CTO (contribution-to-overhead) pricing   A pricing strategy for encouraging extra sales by selling additional product above and beyond some base sales projection, at a price slightly greater than the additional out-of-pocket costs of handling the product.

culture   The set of socially transmitted behaviors, arts, beliefs, speech, and all other products of human work and thought that characterize a particular population.

current assets   An accounting term designating actual cash or assets that are expected to be converted to cash during one normal operating cycle of the business, typically one year.

current liabilities   An accounting term designating those outsiders' claims to a business that must be paid within one normal operating cycle, usually one year.

current ratio   A financial ratio measuring liquidity; total current assets divided by total current liabilities.

custom hiring   A form of leasing that combines labor services with the use of the asset being leased.

customer service   Activities between the buyer and seller that enhance or facilitate the sale of the seller's products or services.

customers   Those who purchase outputs (products, services, and or information) from a firm.

cycle inventory   An inventory quantity that is tied to truck capacity, pallet size, manufacturer promotion, or some other factor that increases inventory levels relative to a normal pipeline inventory; also called lot-size inventory.

cycle-time-to-market   The time required for a supplier to complete a single cycle, beginning with receipt of an order and ending with the fulfillment of the order; reducing cycle-time-to-market (also called quick response) has become a central strategic goal for many agribusinesses.

days sales in accounts receivables ratio   A financial ratio measuring efficiency; the average collection period of accounts receivables; (accounts receivable / net sales) × 360.

dealer-distribution system   A marketing channel in which manufacturers sell their products to dealers or retailers, who, in turn, sell products in their own local market.

debt-to-asset ratio   A financial ratio measuring solvency; shows the proportion that lenders are contributing to the total capital of the firm (total liabilities / total assets).

debt-to-equity ratio   A financial ratio measuring the use of debt; total liabilities divided by owner's equity.

decision-making process   A logical procedure for identifying a problem, discovering alternative solutions, analyzing them, and choosing a course of action.

decline stage   A period in the product life cycle in which sales decline, sometimes rapidly.

delegation downward principle   In organizational structure, the idea that authority should be delegated downward to the lowest level at which the decision can be made competently.

Delphi approach   A tool for developing forecasts in which a panel of experts is asked to develop a forecast for an area of interest; the estimates are pooled, reviewed and any differences noted; and the process is repeated until a consensus forecast is achieved.

demand   The quantity of a product or service that consumers are willing to buy at different prices; the relationship between price and the quantity demanded.

demand curve   A graphic or algebraic representation of a product's demand.

demand elasticity   A measure showing the relative change in quantity demanded as price changes; reflects the responsiveness of quantity demanded to a given change in price.

democratic leadership   A leadership style, also called participative leadership, which favors a shared decision-making process, with the leader maintaining the ultimate responsibility for decisions while actively seeking significant input from followers.

demographic segmentation   A market segmentation approach which groups customers based on demographics such as age, income, size of household, education, number of children, type of employment, etc.

derived demand   A situation where demand for one product or service (usually an input) is based on the demand for another product or service (usually the final product).

developing alternatives   A step in the planning process; after performance objectives have been set, the process of generating different ways of achieving the objectives.

development stage   The stage early in the product life cycle in which the market is analyzed, and both the product and the broader marketing strategy are developed.

differential advantage   One of two generic business strategies; involves offering buyers unique products and services which add value for the buyer but are unavailable from other firms.

differentiation value   In pricing, the perceived value of the product's unique attributes.

diminishing marginal utility   A law of economics that states that as more and more of a product is consumed, the extra satisfaction of consuming an additional unit actually declines; translates directly into the inverse relationship between price and the quantity demanded.

direct exporting   Mode of entry in international business in which the agribusiness itself handles the details of exporting their products.

direct selling   A process that involves prospecting for new customers, pre-call planning, getting the customer's attention and interest, making presentations, handling objections, closing the sale, and servicing the account in direct, on-on-one contact with customers.

directing   One of the four tasks of management; involves guiding the efforts of others toward achieving a common goal and leading, supervising, motivating, delegating, and evaluating human resources.

directors   See **board of directors**.

discount pricing   A method of pricing that offers customers a reduction from the published or list price for specified reasons, such as volume purchases or preseason ordering.

discount rate   The interest rate used to determine the present value of a stream of cash flows to be received in the future.

discounted loan   A loan where the amount of interest to be paid is deducted from the amount the lender provides the borrower; amount of loan – amount of interest paid = amount of available capital.

discounting   A method of converting a future value to a present value by adjusting the future value by its discount rate.

distribution   In marketing, one of the four elements of the marketing mix (also known as place); involves all decisions related to how the product moves from the manufacturer to consumer.

distributor system   A system of channel management that uses both middleman-distributors, or wholesalers, and dealers to move products to customers.

diversification   The process of entering alternative lines of business that pose different risks and opportunities so that the likelihood of a loss in one area will be offset by the possibility of gain in another.

division of labor   The process by which jobs are broken into components and then are assigned to members or groups.

dormant partner   A partner not active in managing the partnership and not known by the general public; retains limited liability.

early adopters   The second group of buyers (next 13.5 percent after innovators) to try a new idea, product, or service; tend to be progressive and well-respected individuals.

early majority   The third group of buyers (next 34 percent after the early adopters) to try a new idea, product, or service; tend to be deliberate people who see themselves as fairly progressive, but not generally as leaders.

earnings on sales ratio   A financial ratio measuring profitability; (net operating profit / net sales).

economic profit   A measure of profit that takes into consideration alternative uses for the resources; accounting profit less opportunity cost.

economic value analysis   A method of pricing that is based on the economic value of a product.

economics   The study of how scarce resources (land, labor, capital and management) are allocated to meet the needs of a society with unlimited wants.

economies of scale   A production situation where the larger the scale of the operation, the lower the per-unit cost.

efficiency ratios   A class of financial ratios that measures the output or production of a system or process per unit of input.

efficient consumer response (ECR)   An information-based system that links distributors and suppliers together with retail supermarkets; the food industry's concept of supply chain management.

ego status A component of Maslow's need hierarchy that suggests that once a comfortable degree of social acceptance has been attained, most individuals become concerned with their self-esteem or status relative to their group.

elastic In supply and demand analysis, a condition where a change in price brings a proportionately larger change in quantity supplied (demanded).

elasticity In economics, a measure of the responsiveness of one variable to changes in another.

electronic data interchange (EDI) systems An information technology that allows business interactions between firms to take place electronically using a standard format.

enterprise requirement planning (ERP) A system used to connect a firm's manufacturing systems with other areas of the firm such as finance, customer relationship management, human resources, and supply chain management, integrating internal and external information across the entire organization.

equilibrium In economics, a state or situation in which opposing forces balance each other and stability is attained.

equity capital Funds provided by the owners of a business either directly or by reinvesting profits back into the business; the risk capital of a firm.

evaluating results A step in the planning process; involves a careful review and assessment that helps determine whether or not the plan is on course.

exchange rates The relative value of one country's currency compared to that of another country.

exit interview An interview with a departing employee that is designed to better understand the employee's attitudes and reasons for leaving and to provide suggestions for improving the workplace.

expected product A part of the total product concept; surrounds the generic product with the minimum set of features / services that the customer expects when they make a purchase.

expenditure An outlay of cash for operating or investment purposes.

expenses The value of resources consumed by the business in acquiring, producing, and selling goods and services; includes only those resources consumed by actual sales during the accounting period.

external failure costs Costs incurred when the product or service fails once it is in the consumer hands.

factors of production In economics, land, labor, capital and management; scarce resources used in the production process.

farm As defined by USDA, any rural unit grossing $1,000 or more per year in agricultural sales.

farm-food marketing bill A breakdown of the consumer's food dollar into the proportion the farmer gets for producing the raw material and the proportion the food industry gets for marketing (in a broad sense) the final product.

fast food / quick service restaurants Limited menu and limited service restaurants focused on providing convenience and speed of service.

field marketing A sales strategy that puts marketing tools in the hands of the agribusiness sales force; the salesperson is asked to treat his or her sales area as a mini-marketplace, and use marketing tools to assess opportunities, and to develop and implement a sales plan that is very focused on the needs of the specific territory served.

financial accounting Financial record keeping conducted in a manner that meets the reporting requirements of governmental units, lending institutions, investors, and suppliers.

financial management   One of the four functions of management; managing the assets, liabilities, and owner's investment in the firm; generating the financial data required to make decisions, and using the tools of finance to make effective decisions.

financial statement   A summary statement of the financial status of a business such as a balance sheet or an income statement; usually prepared by summarizing accounts from the general ledger.

financing   The process of raising or acquiring the funds required to operate a business.

finished goods   Products that are ready for sale.

fitness for use   A definition used by some customers for quality, which can be summarized as "meeting or exceeding customer expectations."

fixed assets   Those items the business owns that have a relatively long productive life, such as land, buildings, and equipment.

fixed costs   Costs that do not fluctuate with the volume of business; considered the costs of being in business.

fixed position layout   A production process layout used in situations where the item being constructed is too large or bulky to move easily or where the item is to be built fixed in place; construction is accomplished in one place, and tools and materials are brought to the assembly location.

flexibility principle   In organizational structure, the concept that an organization should maintain its structural flexibility so that it can adjust to its changing internal and external environments.

fluctuating demand   Demand in the industrial sector which rises and falls sharply in response to changing economic conditions and consumer spending patterns.

focus group interview   In market research, a guided discussion among users or potential users of a product or service that is designed to discover attitudes and opinions toward those products or services.

focused factory   A production concept intended to operationalize the notion of flexibility; holds that several smaller factories will improve individual plant performance because the operations manager can concentrate on fewer tasks and can more easily motivate a smaller workforce toward one goal.

food processing and manufacturing   Part of the food sector; includes a broad range of firms that take raw agricultural commodities and turn those commodities into ingredients for further processing, or into final consumer products; examples include meat packers, bakers, wet corn processors, and brewers.

food production and marketing system   The system of firms and organizations that encompass all economic activity supporting production agriculture, producing raw farm commodities, converting raw farm products to consumable food and fiber products, and distributing these final products to end consumers.

food retailers   Firms involved in the retail distribution of food; includes supermarkets, warehouse stores, and combo stores.

food sector   The sector of the food production and marketing system in which food processing, marketing, and distribution occur.

food security   The state of affairs in a society where all people at all times have access to safe and nutritious food to maintain a healthy and active life.

food service   Firms providing prepared food, typically ready to eat, including traditional restaurants, fast food / quick service restaurants, and institutional food services.

forecast   An estimate of some future business activity or indicator.

forecasting change   The third element of the planning process, after analyzing the facts. It is interrelated with the other five steps of the planning process and it is the logical extension of analysis into a future time setting.

forecasting demand   An estimate of future customer demand. Forecasts are typically made using scientific techniques based on historical usage and adjusted to accommodate various factors such as life cycle, cyclical usage patterns, promotions, and pricing actions.

formal internal training and development   A type of employee training; typical in larger firms, this is job, or task specific instruction conducted by a full-time training staff.

formal structure   In organizational structure, the formal reporting relationships between employees in an organization; one of two kinds of organizational structure required to operate effectively.

forward contracting   A formal, binding agreement to buy or sell products at some established terms for delivery at some specified future date.

free market system   A type of economic system in which consumer wants are expressed directly in the marketplace using a market-determined pricing mechanism as the basis for allocation of scarce resources.

free-reign leadership   A leadership style (also called laissez faire leadership) in which the leader literally relinquishes all decision-making to followers.

fringe benefits   A nonsalary benefit offered to all employees; ranges from those required by law to health benefits, vacations, sick pay, life insurance, and retirement benefits.

functional organization structure   An organizational structure that grants staff specialists authority in the areas of their specialty.

futures market   A specialized type of market where promises to deliver or accept delivery of a standardized unit of product at some specified future date are traded; reflects anticipated future supply and demand situations.

gap analysis   An evaluation of the difference between a firm's desired performance at some point in the future and what performance will be if the firm does not change strategies or approaches.

gathering facts   A step in the planning process; involves gathering sufficient information to identify the need for a plan, and systematic gathering of the information needed to make the plan work once it has been developed.

General Agreement on Tariffs and Trade   (GATT)   An international organization established in 1947 to reduce global trade barriers through multilateral trade negotiations; evolved into the **World Trade Organization (WTO)** in 1995.

general economic forecast   A forecast of conditions in the general economy for a specific future time period.

general partner   A partner who is active in the management of the partnership, typically has an investment in the business, and is subject to unlimited liability; unless specified differently in writing, all partners are assumed to be general partners.

general partnership   The association of two or more people as owners of a business in which each individual partner, regardless of the percentage of capital contributed, has equal rights and liabilities, unless stated differently in the partnership agreement.

generic advertising   A form of advertising aimed at promoting a class of products or an industry, not a specific company or brand; also called institutional advertising.

generic product   One component of the total product concept; the standard product as offered to the customer with no special services or features attached.

genetically modified organisms (GMO)   An organism that has been modified by the application of recombinant DNA technology (a set of techniques enabling the manipulation of DNA).

geographic segmentation   In marketing, a means of classifying or categorizing customers or potential customers by their geographic location.

globalization   The process of incorporating a worldwide perspective into the processes of a firm and into the attitudes and practices of a firm's employees.

goals   The specific quantitative or qualitative aims of the organization that provide direction and standards one can use to measure performance.

greenfield investment   A method of direct investment by a firm into a particular country or new business where the firm handles all elements of the entry, including building plants, developing distribution, locating markets, etc.

gross margin   The difference between net sales and the cost of goods sold; income remaining after paying for raw materials or merchandise to cover operating expenses and generate a profit; gross margin plus service income is sometimes called gross profit.

gross margin ratio   A financial ratio measuring profitability; gross margin expressed as a percentage of net sales; (net sales {-} cost of goods sold) / net sales.

growth stage   A period in the product life cycle of rapid expansion, during which sales gain momentum and firms tend to hold prices steady or increase them slightly as they try to develop customer loyalty.

hazard analysis critical control point (HACCP)   An important, widely recognized food safety program; basic premise is the prevention of food safety problems rather than attempting to control them.

Herzberg's two-factor theory   A popular but somewhat controversial theory of employee motivation developed by Frederick Herzberg which argues that two separate factors explain employees' level of motivation: hygienic factors and motivators.

high value products (HVPs)   Agricultural products that have received additional processing or require special handling or shipping; also known as value-added products.

human resources (HR)   The talents and assets offered to a company by the people it employs.

human resource management   One of the four functions of management; acquiring, organizing, motivating, leading, and managing the firm's people resources to accomplish its business objectives as effectively as possible.

hybrid layout   A production process layout that combines the process and product layouts to balance the advantages of each; used extensively when introducing flexible manufacturing systems

hygienic factors   One component of Herzberg's two-factor theory; also called pain relievers, these are conditions necessary to maintain an employee's social, mental, and physical health.

income elasticity of demand   The relative responsiveness of quantity demanded to changes in income.

income statement   Financial statement summarizing the firm's revenue, expenses, and profit during a specific period of time.

indirect exporting   Mode of product movement in international business in which a firm uses a trading company or an export management company to handle the logistics of exporting.

indirect selling   Activities outside the sales call interview process; involves providing service and follow-up to customers.

individual proprietorship See **sole proprietorship**.

inelastic In supply and demand analysis, a condition where a change in price brings a proportionately smaller change in quantity supplied (demanded).

inferior good An inferior good for income elasticity is one in which the quantity demanded varies inversely with real income; increases in real income reduce the quantity demanded and decreases in real income increase the quantity demanded of inferior goods.

informal organization The firm's organization outside the organizational chart; primarily concerned with interpersonal relationships among people, their emotions, feelings, communications, and values; an important part of the organization's culture.

informal personal relationships The relationships that are within an agribusiness which are not part of the structured system—see **informal organization**.

information technology Any electronic technology focused on processing, storing, transmitting, and reporting data and information.

initial investment The initial equity an investor commits to an investment.

innovators The first group of buyers (initial 2.5 percent) to try a new idea, product, or service; tend to be venturesome people who like to try new ideas.

input distributors Organizations engaged in moving products from the input manufacturer to the farm and providing services that insure productive use of the inputs.

input manufacturers Organizations engaged in the manufacture and production of inputs for use in production agriculture.

input supply sector The sector of the food and fiber production and marketing system that manufacturers and distributes supplies and services to farmers for use in the production of agricultural products.

inputs Resources used to create outputs in a production process; includes human resources (skilled workers and managers), capital (equipment), materials, information, and energy, among other such resources.

institutional advertising See **generic advertising**.

institutional food services Firms and organizations providing reliable, convenient meals and / or the components necessary to make the meals for outlets such as schools, hospitals, and government facilities.

insurance companies A source of financing for agribusiness; typically provide longer-term financing as these firms look for opportunities to invest funds they have collected from policyholders.

interest The charges made by a lender for the use of money.

interest rate Interest expressed in percentage form; reflects investors' time and risk preferences and serves as the exchange price between borrower and lender.

intermediate farms A category of farms that includes operators reporting farming as the major occupation and gross sales of under $250,000.

intermediate-term loan A temporary grant of money to be paid back to the lender, usually in one to five years.

internal failure costs In total quality management, costs that are generated during the production and / or rework of defective parts and services.

internal rate of return (IRR) A method of ranking and accepting or rejecting capital investments; the discount rate that yields a zero net present value.

introductory stage The stage in the product life cycle in which the new product first appears on the market.

inventory Items that are held for sale in the ordinary course of business, that have been purchased for use in producing goods and services to be sold, and work in progress.

inventory turnover ratio   A financial ratio measuring efficiency; shows the relationship between inventory and sales volume; cost of goods sold / ending inventory.

inverse price ratio   The ratio of two prices; used extensively in economic analysis as it reflects the relative prices of two items.

ISO 9000   A series of international standards and guidelines on quality management and quality assurance; standardized definition of quality focuses on conformance to customer requirements.

ISO 14000   A worldwide standard for quality applied to the environment; provides the framework and systems for managing legislative and regulatory orders for environmental compliance.

job description   A list and description of a job's activities and duties.

job orientation   Process used to introduce a new employee to a job; involves four major steps: introducing the company to the employee, establishing job relationships and encouraging familiarity with the facilities, helping the employee to begin the job, and following up and evaluating the employee's adjustment.

job relationships   The network of individuals an employee interacts with on the job; includes the supervisor, fellow workers, the union steward, payroll, and benefits personnel, among others.

job specifications   A written set of qualifications of an employee that are needed to perform a specific job satisfactorily.

joint venture   A type of collaboration between two or more firms; involves sharing resources in research, production, marketing, and / or financing, as well as costs and risks.

junior partner   A partner who is typically younger and not involved in the business as long as a senior partner; receives a smaller portion of the business profits; rarely takes an active role in managing the business affairs of the partnership.

just-in-time (JIT)   An operating philosophy and production system with the goal of producing and / or delivering goods just as they are needed, in effect, eliminating inventories.

key indicators (KI)   See **key performance areas**.

key influencers   Individuals or organizations that have some influence on the purchase decision, but don't actually make the decision.

key performance areas (KPA)   Important points of focus in management control systems; also called key indicators.

labor unions   Groups organized to protect and promote the interests of their worker / members.

laggards   The final group of buyers (last 16 percent) to try a new idea, product, or service; tend to be tradition-bound people who take so long to adopt new ideas that by the time the ideas are adopted, they no longer are new.

laissez faire leadership   See **free-reign leadership**.

land lease   A contract that conveys control over the use rights of real property from the lessor to the lessee without transferring title.

late majority   The fourth group of buyers (next 34 percent after the early majority) to try a new idea, product, or service; tend to be skeptical people who adopt new ideas only after considerable evidence has been accumulated.

layout planning   The specific design of the physical arrangement within a facility

leadership   The process of helping individuals or groups to accomplish organizational goals by unleashing each person's individual potential as a contribution to organizational success.

lead-time In logistics management, the amount of time necessary to cover the period between the warehouse's reordering and its receipt of the additional stock.

lease A contract by which the control over the right to use an asset is transferred from the lessor (owner) to the lessee (person acquiring control) for a specified period of time in return for a lease payment.

leasing A form of renting, usually involving a contractual agreement that specifies the terms of the arrangement; normally for a longer period of time than a rental agreement.

lessee A person or organization that pays for the privilege of using the property of another for a specified period of time.

lessor A person or organization that leases property to another person or organization but maintains ownership of the property for the period of the lease.

leverage In finance, the concept of using borrowed funds to expand the total capital of the firm beyond the amount of owner equity.

liabilities Anything a business owes to those outside the business, such as accounts payable, loans, bonds, and mortgages; the total debt of the business.

licensing A business arrangement where a firm (licensee) in the target market produces and distributes another firm's (licensor) product; in return the licensor receives a fee or royalty for the right to license the product.

limited liability company (LLC) A form of business organization that closely resembles a partnership, but provides its members limited liability; creditors or others who have a claim against an LLC can pursue the assets of the LLC to satisfy debt and other obligations, but they cannot pursue personal or business assets owned by the individual members of the LLC.

limited partner A partner who has taken steps to limit his/her liability in a partnership; the agreement must be in writing and limited partners may not take an active role in managing the partnership.

limited partnership An association of two or more people as owners of a business in which some partners contribute money or ownership capital to the partnership without incurring the full legal liability of a general partner.

limited returns In cooperatives, the requirement that returns on member equity be limited to a nominal amount, not greater than the going interest rate, or 8 percent (whichever is higher); done to ensure that members of the cooperative do not view the cooperative as an investment in and of itself.

line organization An organizational structure in which there is one simple, clear line of authority extending downward from top management to each person in the organization.

line and staff organization An organizational structure that is a variation of the line organization in that a place for specialists is included.

line of credit A commitment by the lender to make available to the firm a certain sum of money, usually for a one-year period, at a specified rate of interest at whatever time the firm needs the loan; also known as a revolving loan.

linear projection A quantitative procedure for projecting past trends into to a future time setting for developing forecasts.

liquidity ratios A class of financial ratios that measure the firm's ability to pay short-term obligations as they come due.

logic A qualitative technique involving the combination of fact, induction, and deduction to solve a problem.

logistics management   One of the four functions of management (along with operations management); involves the set of activities around storing and transporting goods and services from manufacturer to buyer.

long-range budget   A budget that is generally more than one year in scope.

long-term liabilities   Liabilities that are scheduled to be repaid over one year or longer, such as bonds, mortgages, and long-term loans.

long-term loans   A temporary grant of money from a lender to be repaid over a period of more than five years.

loss-leader pricing   A pricing method that involves offering one or more products at a significantly reduced price for the purpose of attracting additional customers who will purchase other regularly priced items.

lot-size inventory   See **cycle inventory**.

macroeconomics   The study of how consumers, businesses, and governments in the aggregate interact to allocate scarce resources; includes topics such as inflation, interest rates, gross domestic product, and fiscal and monetary policy.

make-to-order strategy   A production approach where the firm actually builds to order.

make-to-stock strategy   A production approach where the firm is producing for inventory, and the production occurs before the actual sale is made.

management   The art and science of successfully pursuing the organization's desired results with the resources available to the organization.

management by exception   A management philosophy with the basic premise that management should not spend time on areas that are progressing according to plan, but should identify and concentrate on areas that are not generating acceptable performance.

management by objectives (MBO)   A management philosophy introduced by Peter Drucker in 1954 whereby the supervisor and the subordinate jointly set objectives that both agree are reasonable and in line with corporate goals, and then determine how performance will be measured in each area of major responsibility.

manager   The person charged with the responsibility of planning, organizing, directing and controlling the activities of a business organization to accomplish the objectives established by the owners.

managerial accounting   Financial record keeping for the purpose of helping managers guide the operation of the business and make more effective management decisions that are consistent with the needs, objectives and goals of a firm.

manipulative autocrat   A leadership style in which the manager creates the illusion that employees are participating in the decision-making process; another form of autocratic leadership.

manufacturer-direct distribution system   A marketing channel in which the manufacturer sells directly to the farmer or food customer.

manufacturers   Organizations that develop through research and development the inputs needed by agricultural producers to produce food and fiber.

manufacturers' sales offices and sales branches   Wholesale divisions or subsidiaries typically run by large manufacturing or processing firms to market their own products.

marginal cost   In economics, the additional cost incurred in producing one more unit; the change in total cost divided by the change in output.

marginal rate of substitution   In economics, the relationship between two inputs in the production process.

marginal revenue   In economics, the additional revenue generated by selling one more unit of output.

marginality   In economics, a concept important in maximizing (profit) or minimizing (cost) a particular objective; focuses attention the incremental change in the objective caused by an incremental change in a variable or variables.

market efficiency   A measure of productivity of the marketing process in terms of the resources used and output generated during the process; involves operating efficiency and pricing efficiency.

market forecast   A forecast for a specific industry or type of products.

market information   Any pertinent details and data such as news and industry specific research which is used by buyers, sellers, inventory holders, wholesalers and others in the industry to make decisions.

market mapping   A tool for visually presenting information about a firm's customers and markets by plotting relevant data on a map either manually or using a computer-based geographic information system (GIS).

market penetration   The proportion of a specific market that a firm controls..

market research   The study of customers, competition, and trends in the marketplace, with the goal of providing objective information on which to base marketing decisions.

market risks   Any number of uncertain outcomes involving the market for goods and services; includes the possibility of price declines or increases, changes in consumer preferences, and / or changes in the nature of competition.

market segmentation   In marketing, the process of classifying customers into categories that have members who will react in a common way to a firm's marketing offer.

marketable securities   Stocks, bonds, and other investments that can be easily turned into cash during an operating period (usually one year).

market-driven philosophy   A marketing approach based on a true understanding of customer needs; the focus on customer needs drives all decisions and activities in the organization.

marketing   In the macro sense, the process by which products flow through the U.S. food production and marketing system from producer to final consumer; involves the physical and economic activities performed in moving products from the initial producer through intermediaries to the final consumer; from a managerial perspective, the process of identifying customer needs, and creating, pricing, promoting, and distributing products and services to meet those needs profitably.

marketing audit   An objective examination and review of a company's entire marketing strategy.

marketing channel   The network of firms that manage the flow of products, services, information, and money between producers and consumers.

marketing management   One of the four functions of management; involves managing the total process of identifying customer needs, developing products and services to meet those needs, establishing promotional programs and pricing policies, and designing a system of distributing products and services to customers.

marketing mix   In marketing management, the combination of product, price, promotion, and place strategies developed and implemented by a firm to support a specific position in the market.

Maslow's needs hierarchy   A theory of human behavior based on the idea that different kinds of needs have different levels of importance to individuals, and depend on the needs that are currently being satisfied.

master production schedule (MPS)   In operations management, details the final quantities stocking keeping units that are to be made in specific blocks of time; created once specific orders for products have been received and / or short-range sales forecasts have been determined.

master scheduler   In operations management, the individual(s) that must consider the total demand on the resources and capacities of the agribusiness as well as the supplier's capacities in developing production plans.

material requirement planning (MRP)   A computerized information system for managing production operations; purpose is to ensure that the right materials, components, and sub-assemblies are available in the right quantities at the right time so that finished products can be produced according to the master production schedule.

maturity stage   A period in the product life cycle characterized by slow growth or even some decline of sales as the market becomes saturated.

merchant wholesalers   Firms in the market channel that buy products from processors or manufacturers, and then resell those products to retailers, institutions or other businesses.

microeconomics   The study of how scarce resources are allocated, primarily focused on consumer choice and firm production decisions, and how these are related to markets and prices.

minimal layer principle   In organizational structure, the idea that the number of levels of management should be kept at a minimum, while at the same time maintaining an effective span of control.

mission statement   A firm's declaration of the business they are in, the customers they serve, and the basic concepts or beliefs they hold.

model   An abstract representation of a system or situation, usually in mathematical terms, that exhibits the factors believed to be most pertinent to the system or situation.

motivation   A stimulus that produces action.

motivators   An element of Herzberg's two-factor theory of motivation; reward producers, or conditions that encourage employees to apply themselves, mentally and physically, more productively to their jobs.

negative strokes   In interpersonal communications, an interaction which often takes the form of verbal criticism and reprimands; do not make individuals feel as good as positive strokes, but gives the person attention which may be preferred to being ignored.

net cash flow   The difference between total cash inflows and total cash outflows for an operating period.

net farm income   At the aggregate level, the portion of the net value added by agriculture to the national economy that is earned by farm operators. At the firm level, net operating income or profit, plus other income and minus the interest expense. Net farm income can be reported as either before or after taxes.

net income (profit) after taxes   Net profit before taxes and after adjusting for the federal business profits tax; sometimes called net income.

net income (profit) before taxes   The amount remaining after net operating profit is adjusted for any non-operating revenue or expenses.

net operating income or profit The amount remaining after operating expenses are subtracted from gross margin; represents profit from the primary operations of the firm.

net present value (NPV) A method for evaluating capital investment decisions; involves calculating the current value of a stream of net cash flows to be received over some specified future period of time using the firm's cost of capital as the discount rate.

net working capital Total current assets less total current liabilities.

net worth See **owner equity**.

nominal partner A partner in name only; is not active in the partnership and has no investment.

nonprofit corporation A corporation that is exempt from certain forms of taxation, and that generally cannot directly enrich its owners financially.

normal goods A normal good for income elasticity is one for which the quantity demanded varies directly with real income.

notes payable Short-term loans or liabilities from individuals, banks or other lending institutions that must be repaid within a year.

objectives See **performance objectives**.

on time delivery A metric which measures the performance of a supplier / vendor on their delivery commitment and to what extent he / she is matching with the lead times expressed in percentage terms.

on-the-job training Training conducted while the employee is actually performing the job they were hired to do.

operating characteristics segmentation A market segmentation approach based on characteristics such as type of operation (for example, crop versus livestock), size of operation, production technology used (for example, no-till versus conventional till), and form of ownership (owner / operator versus cash rent versus crop share).

operating expenses Those expenses associated with the actual operation of the business; does not include expenses not directly associated with operations, such as interest expense, and non-related legal expenses.

operating lease A leasing method that is usually a short-term rental arrangement (i.e., hourly, daily, weekly, monthly, etc.) in which the lease charge is calculated on a time-of-use basis.

operations management One of the four functions of management (along with logistics management); involves direction and control of the processes used by food and agribusiness firms to produce goods and services.

opinion leaders Well-respected individuals or firms who tend to adopt products and services more quickly than others; and shape the attitudes of others in a market.

opportunity cost The income given up by not choosing the next best alternative for the use of resources; represents the amount that the business forfeits by not choosing a specific alternative course of action.

order point The inventory method that places an order for a lot whenever the quantity on hand is reduced to a predetermined level known as the order point.

organizational chart A graphic representation of a firm's formal organizational structure which shows reporting relationships and areas of responsibility.

organizational structure The formal assignment of employee responsibilities in a firm— who reports to whom, who has responsibility for what, etc.

organizing   One of the four tasks of management; the systematic classification and grouping of human and other resources in a manner that effectively accomplishes the firm's goals.

other current assets   Any of a variety of assets that are likely to be converted to cash, or can be converted into cash, within a year; normally does not include cash, accounts receivable, inventory, or marketable securities.

output–input ratio   An efficiency ratio that relates the output of a process to the inputs employed in the process.

outputs   Any product that is the result of a production process.

owner equity   The value of the owners' investment in the business; the total assets of the business less all obligations to non-owners; also called net worth.

parity of responsibility and authority principle   In organizational structure, the idea that a person should have enough authority to carry out their assigned responsibilities.

participative leadership   See democratic leadership.

partnership   A form of business organization in which two or more people jointly own the assets and / or manage the business.

patronage refunds   A return of net margin to members or patrons of a cooperative.

payback period   The length of time it will take an investment to generate sufficient additional cash flows to pay for itself.

penetration pricing   A pricing strategy that consists of offering a product at a low price, perhaps even at a loss, in order to gain wide market acceptance quickly.

percentage change in credit sales   A financial measure used to assist in monitoring changes in accounts receivable; credit sales for the current period divided by the credit sales for a previous period.

performance evaluation   An appraisal of an employee's performance; makes the employee aware of their contributions and their strengths and weaknesses; normally includes goals for the next evaluation period.

performance objectives   Measurable, definable goals that are set for specific units and / or individuals; provide shorter-term performance targets at the unit and / or individual level that are consistent with broader, longer-range strategic goals.

periodic inventory   An actual physical count of inventory on hand conducted at regular intervals.

perishability   The characteristic of rapid deterioration in the quality of some agricultural or food products after harvest or processing.

perpetual inventory   See **continuous inventory**.

personal interviews   A market research technique that involves direct dialogue with a customer, prospect, influencer, or other individual of interest.

personnel   The people employed in an organization; also can be a department of a firm that deals with employee issues such as hiring, benefits, and records.

physical distribution systems (PDS)   The series of channels through which parts, products, and finished inventory are stored and moved from suppliers, between outlets and, ultimately, to consumers.

physical risks   The uncertainty and potential damage or losses that can result from such phenomena as wind, fire, hail, flood, theft, and spoilage.

pipeline inventory   The minimum amount of inventory needed to cover the period of time between the warehouse's reordering and its receipt of the additional stock.

planning   Forward thinking directed at specific objectives about courses of action based upon a full understanding of all factors involved.

points   Service charges, based on the face value of the loan, that are paid to the lending institution to secure the loan.

policy   A rule or guideline that sets the boundaries for handling specific situations that occur frequently.

politics   The manner in which power and status are used in an organization; involves the manipulation of people and situations to accomplish a particular goal.

position   The specific market space, image, set of activities, and / or products and services that a firm wants to be known for among its target customers.

positioning   The process of creating the desired image or position in the customer's or prospect's mind.

positive conditional strokes   In interpersonal communication,   any form of interaction that while positive, the acceptance of the other person is conditional on some expected behavior.

positive unconditional strokes   In interpersonal communication,   any form of interaction that conveys the spoken or implied message, "I like you...you're OK with me," with no conditions on the acceptance.

potential product   One component of the total product concept; the product as it can become; the next benefit that customers will seek from the firm; and how the product-service-information bundle will be managed to add even more value for customers.

power   The ability to control another person's behavior.

practices   Activities and processes as they are actually performed in the agribusiness; may conflict with policies and procedures.

preferred stock   A type of ownership position in a corporation that does not carry the privileges of voting for directors, but has a preferred position in receiving dividends and in redemption in the case of liquidation.

prepaid expenses   Current assets that represent prepayment of an item or service that will be consumed or used during a future accounting period at which point it will become an expense.

present value   The current value of a stream of payments to be to be made or received over some specified period of time in the future.

presentation   In selling, the heart of the sales call in which the primary objective is to present the product or service so effectively that the customer will see it as satisfying a particular need.

prestige pricing   A pricing strategy that appeals to an elite image and plays to the attitude that price and quality go together: "You get what you pay for."

pretesting   In market research, evaluating research questions before actually using them with a group of respondents to insure that the questions are effective at gathering the desired information.

prevention costs   In total quality management, the costs associated with stopping defects and errors before they happen.

price   The value of an item or service in monetary terms.

price discovery   The process in which producers and consumers meet in the marketplace, and the equilibrium quantity and price is determined.

price elastic   One of the three levels of price elasticity of demand; price elasticity of demand in absolute terms is greater than 1.0; or a small change in price will result in a relatively large change in the quantity demanded.

price inelastic   One of the three levels of price elasticity of demand; price elasticity of demand in absolute terms is less than 1.0; or a change in price has a relatively small impact on quantity demanded.

principal   The initial sum of money invested or borrowed; the portion of the original loan that has yet to be repaid.

principles   Ideas, values, philosophies, and beliefs regarding an issue or issues.

pro forma financial statements   Projected financial statements for some specified time period in the future.

procedure   A step-by-step guide to performing a specific activity or function.

process design   Selecting the specific inputs, operations, and methods that are to be used to produce the good or service.

process layout   In production planning, an arrangement in which all like functions are grouped in the same place.

product advertising   Advertising designed to promote a specific product, service, or idea.

product layout   In production planning, an arrangement that involves a step-by-step sequence of functions as the product is assembled.

product life cycles   The predictable way in which sales and profits of a product unfold as a product is introduced, sales grow rapidly, the market matures, and the product ultimately declines in the market place.

product mix   The breadth, depth, and combination of products, services, and information offered to the market.

product-driven philosophy   A marketing approach based on offering a unique product that satisfies a specific customer need; creating a product that is so good customers will seek it out.

production agriculture   The farms and ranches that produce the crop and livestock products that provide inputs to the food and fiber sector.

production agriculture sector   The sector of the food production and marketing system in which purchased inputs, natural resources, and managerial talent come together to produce crop and livestock products.

production control   All activities related to controlling raw materials inventory, providing detailed production scheduling information, controlling work-in-process inventory, communicating changes to master production scheduling and purchasing, and controlling finished goods inventory.

production planning   An important aspect of operations management; includes a wide range of decisions and activities including devising a quality program; locating a plant; choosing the appropriate level of capacity; designing the layout of the operation; deciding on the process design; and specifying job tasks and responsibilities.

productivity   See **output–input ratio**.

profit   A general term for the difference between total revenue and total cost.

profit and loss statement   See **income statement**.

profitability ratios   A class of financial ratios that measure a firm's profitability.

program evaluation review technique (PERT)   An approach to project management developed by the U.S. Navy; involves a diagrammatic representation of a network of activities and a search for the most sensitive or restrictive steps in the network.

promissory note   A promise by a borrower to repay a lender a specific sum of money, loaned at a specific rate of interest for a specified period of time.

promotion In marketing, an element of the marketing mix; all activities related to communicating the firm's offering to the market; in human resource management, advancement in job responsibilities or position.

proprietorship See **sole proprietorship**.

prospecting In selling, the process of identifying and locating potential customers.

psychographic segmentation A market segmentation approach based on classifying or categorizing customers or potential customers by a combination of their psychological profiles and demographic data.

psychological pricing A pricing method that involves establishing prices that are emotionally satisfying because they carry the perception of good value, e.g., two for 99 cents instead of 50 cents each.

public relations An element of a firm's promotion (market communications) strategy; the management and maintenance of a favorable public image of the organization as it relates to its customers; somewhat unique as a form of market communications as the target audience is influenced in an indirect way.

purchasing All tasks involved in procuring the raw materials and inputs necessary to meet the requirements of the production schedule.

quality The degree to which a set of defined characteristics of a product or service fulfills known requirements. The common element of the business definitions is that the quality of a product or service refers to the perception of the degree to which the product or service meets the customer's expectations.

quick ratio A financial ratio measuring liquidity; reflects a firm's ability to meet cash needs with funds that are quickly available; (cash + marketable securities + accounts receivable) / total current liabilities.

ratio analysis A method of financial statement analysis that uses relationships between key accounting data to better understand the relative position of an organization.

raw materials Basic goods from which other products are made.

reference value In pricing, the price of a competing product or the closest substitute; forms the starting point for an economic value pricing strategy.

reorder point When the warehouse inventory of a product reaches a certain, agreed-upon level of depletion

responsibility The obligation to see a task through to its completion.

resumé A written summary of the personal, educational, and professional qualifications of a person seeking employment.

return on assets (ROA) ratio A financial ratio measuring profitability; measures the return to the total investment in the business; (net income after taxes + interest expense) / total assets.

return on equity (ROE) ratio A financial ratio measuring profitability; measures the return to the owner's investment in the business; (net income after taxes / owner's equity).

return on investment (ROI) pricing A pricing method where a mark-up sufficient to earn a specified return on investment is added to the basic cost of an individual product or service.

return on investment (ROI) ratio In the profitability analysis model, a measure of return to assets where interest expense has been subtracted from net profit (net profit after taxes) / total assets; more broadly, a general term referring to any of a class of financial ratios measuring profitability or the return on some type of investment: (profit / investment).

return on net worth (RONW)   See **return on equity**.

return on sales ratio (ROS)   A financial ratio measuring profitability; reflects the return on each sales dollar the organization generates; (net income after taxes / net sales).

revolving fund financing   A unique feature of cooperatives that gives them the option of issuing patronage refunds in the form of stock; periodically, the cooperative revolves the stock by allowing older stock to be cashed in.

risk   A situation where outcomes are unknown, but where probabilities of occurrence can be assigned to each possible outcome.

Rochdale Principles   Formal business and organizational principles adopted by the Rochdale Society in 1844 which have served as a model for the development of modern cooperatives.

routing   Process of determining how shipment will move between origin and destination. Routing information includes designation of carrier(s) involved, actual route of carrier and estimated time in route.

rural residence farms   A category of farms that include limited resource, retirement, and residential / lifestyle farms.

safety   A component of Maslow's needs hierarchy that suggests that once immediate survival has been assured, humans become concerned about the security of their future physical survival.

safety stock   See **buffer inventory**.

sales   The total dollar value of all the products and services that have been sold for cash or on credit during the period specified on the profit and loss statement.

sales forecast   An estimate of sales in dollars and / or physical units for a specific future period of time.

sales promotions   A form of promotion (market communications) strategy; programs and special offers designed to motivate interested customers to purchase a product or service.

sales-driven philosophy   A marketing approach based on intensifying the sales effort and / or reducing prices in order to improve sales.

sanitary and phytosanitary (SPS) regulations   Rules and guidelines that are intended to protect human, animal, or plant life or health; instituted in many countries as consumers in developed countries are increasingly demanding a higher level of food safety.

scenario analysis   A qualitative forecasting technique in which a series of future business possibilities or environments are developed based on a careful understanding of what is known, and systematically varying the possibilities for what is not known.

scheduling   The systems that enable the creation of detailed optimized plans and schedules taking into account the resource, material, and dependency constraints to meet the deadlines.

scientific management   A management concept introduced by Frederick W. Taylor in the early 1900s; focused on standardized procedures, determination of the most efficient procedures through scientific testing, matching worker skills with job requirements, and management and workers jointly devising the best system for division of labor.

S-corporation   A closely held corporation where it is possible for the owners of the corporation to elect to be taxed as individuals rather than as a corporation.

seasonal inventories   See **anticipation inventories**.

seasonality   The characteristic of many agricultural goods which can only be produced one time per year, during that product's growing season; also a characteristic of consumption of some goods where use ebbs and flows in a regular pattern across a year.

secret partner   A partner that takes an active role in managing the partnership but is not known to be a partner by the general public.

self-actualization   A component of Maslow's need hierarchy; the highest level of need, and one that becomes important only when all lower-level needs have been relatively well satisfied; the feeling of self-worth or personal accomplishment.

selling   The process by which people in one company help match the value of the products, services and information their company offers to the needs of targeted customers; the process of helping people buy and the process of creating a mutually beneficial relationship between the firm and the customer.

semi variable cost   A cost that is partly fixed and partly variable.

senior partner   A partner which has an investment in the firm, has major responsibilities for management of the organization, and receives the major portion of partnership profits; typically an individual that helped form the partnership or one who has seniority in the business.

short-term budget   A budget that generally covers a time period of one year or less.

short-term loan   A temporary grant of money to be paid back in one year or less; may be a note with regular terms, or a revolving or line-of-credit loan.

silent partner   A partner who has restricted management rights and responsibilities and limited liability for the organization's actions.

simple interest rate   The type of interest charge used on many personal loans; involves a rate of interest applied to an amount available for the entire period of the loan; the amount of interest paid divided by the amount of available capital.

simple rate of return   A commonly used ratio for capital investment analysis; the profit generated by an investment expressed as a percentage of the investment.

simulation   A systematic approach to problem solving that usually involves evaluation of several possibilities (sometimes thousands) derived from a model based on past operating experience and records; used to project the probability of different outcomes.

skimming the market   A pricing method where a product is introduced at a high price that affluent or highly interested customers can afford, then the price is gradually lowered over time to bring less affluent and less interested customers into the market.

sole proprietorship   A form of business owned and controlled by one person.

solvency   The firm's ability to meet long-term financial obligations.

solvency ratio   A solvency ratio that shows the relationship between what the owners are contributing toward supporting the firm and the total assets of the firm; calculated by dividing total assets into owner's equity.

solvency ratios   A class of financial ratios that measure a firm's ability to meet long-term financial obligations.

span-of-control principle   In organizational structure, the concept that there is a limit to the number of people who can be supervised effectively by one individual.

statement of owner's equity   A financial statement that details the changes in the owner's equity accounts from one operating period to the next.

status   The social rank or position of a person in a group.

stock   Units of ownership in a corporation.

stock certificate   A legal document detailing the amount of an owners' investment in a corporation.

stock keeping unit (SKU)   A specific item of goods for sale for which individual records are kept and that is tracked throughout a firm's logistics system.

stockholders   Individuals who own the stock of a corporation.

strategic alliances   Agreements to collaborate between firms that go beyond normal firm-to-firm dealings, but fall short of merger or full partnership and ownership.

strategic marketing plan   A set of activities intended to help a firm anticipate the needs of targeted customers and find ways to meet those needs profitably.

strategic planning   The process of developing a long-range plan for an organization; tackles the broadest elements of an agribusiness firm's strategy: what countries will we operate in, what businesses will we be in, what plants will we build, etc.?

strength, weakness, opportunity, and threat (SWOT) analysis   An assessment tool used to evaluate the competitive environment facing a business and the firm's relative position in that environment; requires careful study of general trends in the market, strengths and weaknesses of key competitors, current and anticipated customer needs, and the firm's strengths and weaknesses.

strike   An organized work stoppage by employees of an organization.

stroke   Any recognition of another's presence by word, gesture, or touch.

supermarket   Any retail food store that carries about 15,000 items in a 10,000 to 25,000 square foot store.

suppliers   Firms providing raw materials, supplies or other inputs to a business.

supply   The quantities that producers are willing and able to put on the market at various prices; the relationship between price and quantity supplied.

supply chain management   The process of managing the complete input acquisition and output distribution channels for a firm; involves linking the materials and physical distribution systems of a firm directly with supplier and customer systems resulting in greater efficiencies.

supply elasticity   A measure showing the relative change in quantity supplied as price changes; reflects the responsiveness of quantity supplied to a given change in price.

survival   A component of Maslow's needs hierarchy; suggests that every human's most basic concern is physical survival: food, water, air, warmth, shelter, etc.

symbols   A variety of factors that help establish the relative position of individuals in the informal organization; may include title, age, experience, physical characteristics, knowledge, physical possessions, authority, location, privileges, acquaintances, and a host of other factors, depending on the situation.

tactical planning   Smaller scale, more immediate plans developed to implement the strategic plan; typically addresses a time period of one year or less, and may be developed by virtually every employee in an organization.

target market   A market segment prioritized by a firm and the focus of a marketing effort involving a set of decisions tailored to meet the unique needs of the segment.

tax and incentive package   Economic development incentives offered by governments to encourage businesses to locate in a city, county, state or other location. These may include such incentives as special loans, hiring and training programs, tax exemptions, etc.

telephone interviews   A market research technique that involves asking questions of individuals over the telephone.

terminal value   The residual value an investment is expected to have at the end of the planning horizon.

test market A market research technique which involves an experiment designed to test consumer behavior under actual buying condition; a test city or area with characteristics similar to the target market is selected, a product (typically a new product) is introduced into the test city or area, sales results are measured and evaluated, and these results are then generalized to the target market of interest.

Theory X, Theory Y   Douglas McGregor's theory about human behavior in business; based on the notion of the "dual nature of humankind" or people's capacity for love, warmth, kindness, and sympathy, and at the same time the capacity for hate, harshness, and cruelty.

time-based competition   Competing for customer and market share using the dimension of time as a source of competitive advantage; includes ideas such as cycle-time-to-market, customer responsiveness, and flexibility in operations.

total asset turnover ratio   A financial ratio measuring efficiency; show the sales dollars the firm is able to generate for every dollar invested in assets; total sales / total assets. See **asset turnover ratio**.

total cost   The sum of total variable cost and total fixed cost.

total fixed cost   The total of all fixed costs incurred during an operating period; the total of all costs that are constant during the operating period, regardless of the level of production.

total product concept   A means to relate the customer's definition of value to the agribusiness firm's product-service-information strategy by visualizing the four parts of the firm's product / service offering: the generic product, the expected product, the value-added product, and the potential product.

total quality management (TQM) An integrated management concept directed toward continuous quality improvement; involves ideas such as business success can only be achieved by understanding and satisfying the customer's needs, statistics and factual data are the basis for problem solving and continuous improvement, and multi-function work teams best perform problem solving and process improvements.

total revenue   The total income from operations received during an accounting or operating period.

total variable cost   The total of all variable costs incurred during an operating period; the total of all costs that vary directly with the level of production during the operating period.

trade credit   Credit advanced by suppliers and vendors to an agribusiness firm in the process of providing goods and services to the firm.

traditional restaurants   Restaurants that offers menu, sit down and dine service.

training programs Learning opportunities for employees devised to meet one or more of the following objectives: reduce mistakes and accidents; increase motivation and productivity; and prepare the employee for promotion, growth, and development.

training programs   Educational programs offered by the agribusiness to: reduce mistakes and accidents; increase motivation and productivity; and prepare employees for promotion, growth and development.

transactions data   Internal firm data derived from business relationships with customers and suppliers.

transformational leadership   A form of leadership that motivates followers to work for transcendental (higher) goals and for aroused higher-level needs of self-actualization rather than for immediate self-interest.

transportation   The means of getting products from one point to another; five basic modes include highway, rail, water, pipeline, and air.

transportation and storage firms   Firms that acquire or assemble commodities from agricultural producers, and store and transport these products for food manufacturing and processing firms.

trend forecast   A forecasting method which involves projecting sales objectively based on past trends, and then adjusting these projections subjectively to take into account the expected economic, market, and competitive pressures.

turnover   A measure of a firm's ability to retain employees once hired; measures the proportion of employees who leave an organization in a period (usually a year) relative to the total employee base.

uncertainty   A situation where outcomes are unknown and where probabilities of occurrence cannot be assigned to each possible outcome.

unit train   An entire, uninterrupted locomotive, car and caboose movement routed between a single origin and destination.

value The ratio of what the customer receives (perceived benefits) relative to what they give up (perceived costs).

value added product   One component of the total product concept; the first opportunity for the agribusiness firm to truly exceed the customer's expectations by going beyond the tangible, physical properties of the product and the minimum services that are typically provided with the product.

value-based pricing   A pricing method based on pricing a product or service at a level at or slightly lower than the estimated perceived value of the value bundle.

value bundle   The set of tangible and intangible benefits customers receive from the products, services, and information an agribusiness provides.

variable cost   Those costs that increase directly with the volume of sales; the costs of doing business.

venture capital   Money used for investment in projects (normally new) that involve a high risk but offer the possibility of large profits.

vertical integration   The process of extending a firm's presence in the marketing channel either forward toward the consumer, or backward toward suppliers, usually through ownership of new stages in the channel.

visibility   The ability to visualize the status of inventory in the supply chain throughout the distribution and retail channels.

volume–cost analysis   An analytic tool for examining the relationship between costs and the volume of business; also called breakeven analysis.

wage efficiency ratio   A financial ratio measuring efficiency; shows the relationship between labor cost and sales volume (labor cost / net sales).

warehouse receipts   A means of using inventory as security for a loan.

warehousing   The process of storing goods for resale.

wholesale agents and brokers   Firms who buy and / or sell as representatives of others for a commission; typically do not physically handle products, nor do they actually take over title to the products.

wholesalers   A firm which buys from one firm and sells to another, in many cases buying from a processor or manufacturer and selling to a retailer.

World Trade Organization (WTO)   Created in 1995, a body to regulate, monitor, and encourage world trade; with more than 150 member countries, its rules apply to over 97 percent of international trade.

written surveys   A market research technique in which individuals respond to written questionnaires.

Index